Goode on Payment Obligations in Commercial and Financial Transactions

Fourth Edition

Goode on Payment Obligations in Commercial and Financial Transactions

Fourth Edition

Edited by

Victoria Dixon

SWEET & MAXWELL

First Edition	1983
Second Edition	2009
Third Edition	2016
Fourth Edition	2020

Published in 2021 by Thomson Reuters, trading as Sweet & Maxwell. Thomson Reuters is registered in England & Wales, Company No.1679046. Registered Office and address for service: 5 Canada Square, Canary Wharf, London, E14 5AQ.

For further information on our products and services, visit *http://www.sweetandmaxwell.co.uk*.

Typeset by Letterpart Limited, Caterham on the Hill, Surrey, CR3 5XL.

Printed and bound in Great Britain by CPI Group (UK) Ltd, Croydon, CR0 4YY.

A CIP catalogue record of this book is available from the British Library.

Whilst Sir Roy Goode is no longer responsible for this or future editions of this work, the right of Sir Roy Goode to be identified as the author of the 1st, 2nd and 3rd Editions of this work has been asserted in accordance with the Copyright, Designs and Patents Act 1988.

ISBN (print): 978-0-414-06797-4

ISBN (e-book): 978-0-414-08431-5

ISBN (print and e-book): 978-0-414-08430-8

Thomson Reuters, the Thomson Reuters Logo and Sweet & Maxwell ® are trademarks of Thomson Reuters.

Crown copyright material is reproduced with the permission of the Controller of HMSO and the Queen's Printer for Scotland.

All rights reserved. No part of this publication may be reproduced, or transmitted in any form, or by any means, or stored in any retrieval system of any nature, without prior written permission, except for permitted fair dealing under the Copyright, Designs and Patents Act 1988, or in accordance with the terms of a licence issued by the Copyright Licensing Agency in respect of photocopying and/or reprographic reproduction. Application for permission for other use of copyright material, including permission to reproduce extracts in other published works should be made to the publishers. Full acknowledgement of the author, publisher and source must be given.

© 2021 Thomson Reuters (Professional) UK Limited

Preface to the Fourth Edition

Money is one of those things we take for granted. What could be simpler than to pay someone money? However, delve deeper and the concepts of "money", "payment" and "payment obligations" which are the subject of this book raise surprisingly complex issues which are not only interesting from a theoretical perspective but also of considerable practical importance. I am very grateful to Professor Sir Roy Goode and to Charles Proctor, editor of the Second Edition and my co-editor for the Third Edition, for giving me the opportunity to take the lead in preparing this edition.

There are three things in particular which add to the challenge of mastering this particular area of law. The first is that the law relating to payment obligations is not a discrete area of law. Instead, it spans areas of law including contract, tort, trusts, banking, regulation and often conflicts of law. Although this work does not deal with these subjects in depth, it attempts to pull from them the legal rules and doctrines which are most relevant to payment obligations. The second is that the commercial background against which the law operates is constantly evolving. The story of this edition, continued from previous editions, is in some respects one of the law struggling to keep up with the pace of change. At the most basic level, we continue to grapple with the challenges posed to our traditional notions of "money" and "payment" by the increasing popularity of virtual currencies or "cryptocurrencies" and the rise in the use of payment services and systems provided by entities other than banks and financial institutions. Finally, and related to the second point, we can note the increasing importance of legislation and regulation in an area of law traditionally dominated by case-law. One of the challenges for regulators has been to encompass within existing regulatory structures the alternative forms and methods of payment which have developed over the past two decades. Although this work is not intended to be one on payments regulation, I have attempted to summarise the main regulatory measures and developments which may interest readers and to describe in outline their effect on payment obligations. It is worth noting, however, the potential impact of "Brexit" in this regard. At the time of finalising this preface, the transition period for the UK's exit from the EU, formally effected on 31 January 2020, will end on 31 December 2020. Since a large part of the UK's regulatory structure for payments derives from EU law, an uncertain period lies ahead as the UK attempts to forge its own path outside the EU.

The focus throughout this work is on English law, although comparative references have been made where appropriate to aid and add interest to the analysis.

I would also like to express my gratitude to Sweet & Maxwell for the practical assistance and ongoing support they have given in producing this edition.

I have attempted to state the law based on materials available to me as at 31 June 2020.

Victoria Dixon
Merton College, Oxford
11 November 2020

Materials referred to by abbreviation

Chitty:	*Chitty on Contracts*, 33rd edn (London: Sweet & Maxwell, 2018).
Dicey, Morris & Collins:	*Dicey, Morris & Collins on the Conflict of Laws*, edited by Lord Collins of Mapesbury et al, 15th edn (London: Sweet & Maxwell, 2012).
Law of Bank Payments:	M. Brindle and R. Cox, *Law of Bank Payments*, 5th edn (London: Sweet & Maxwell, 2018).
Mann:	Dr F.A. Mann, *Mann on the Legal Aspect of Money*, 7th edn (Oxford: Oxford University Press, 2012).
Legal Problems of Credit and Security:	L. Gullifer (ed.), *Goode and Gullifer on Legal Problems of Credit and Security*, 6th edn (London: Sweet & Maxwell, 2018).
Rome I:	Regulation 593/2008 on the law applicable to contractual obligations [2008] OJ L177/6.

Preface to the First Edition

The most difficult problems confronting the practising commercial lawyer and his client are often to be found not in the sophisticated technical point or the latest gloss on a statute or a case but in fundamental legal conceptions. To apply a rule mechanically without reference to its history and without knowledge of the underlying principle and policy is to court serious error, sometimes with commercially disastrous consequences. But the busy practitioner, faced with an ever-increasing case load and the intricacies of new legislation, is hard pressed to find time for research into fundamentals. It was with this in mind that I ventured to offer a series of public lectures in 1982 on the legal problem of credit and security, later published by Sweet & Maxwell and the Centre for Commercial Law Studies, Queen Mary College.

The warm response both to the lectures and to the resulting publication emboldened me to deliver a second series of lectures at the Centre in 1983, taking as my theme the concepts of money, payment and payment obligations, with particular reference to commercial and financial transactions. This new little book reproduces in revised form the text of these lectures. The subject is one of cardinal importance in business life, yet in many respects the law remains both complex and obscure. I have endeavoured to shed light on some of the darker areas and to offer some new insights into familiar problems.

In gathering information about the London Clearing System and about the operation of BACS and SWIFT I have been greatly helped by Mr. Martin Karmel and Mr. John Buxton (respectively Senior Deputy Secretary and Deputy Secretary of the Committee of London Clearing Bankers), the officials of the Clearing Houses, Clearing Services and Mr. Jonathan Lass and his colleagues at Citibank. To all of these I should like to express my warm thanks. They, however, are in no way responsible for any errors I may have perpetrated in describing in simplified form what can be quite complex banking operations.

Finally, I am indebted to Sweet & Maxwell for the care taken in producing this book and for the preparation of the tables and index.

The law is believed to be correctly stated as at September 18, 1983.

R. M. Goode
Centre for Commercial Law Studies
Queen Mary College
London
1983

Preface to the Second Edition

I have been an enthusiastic user of Payment Obligations for some 25 years, both on account of its clarity of exposition and its refreshing style, which sets it apart from so many legal text books. I was therefore delighted to receive Professor Sir Roy Goode's invitation to prepare a second edition.

It is an unfailing rule that each successive edition of a legal text will be longer than its predecessor. The present work is no exception and the period since 1983 has obviously seen a number of developments; money laundering regulations, the increasing use of sanctions and measures such as the US PATRIOT Act, to name but a few. I have tried to take account of these developments without overloading the text with long lists of cases, which may often serve to obscure, rather than to clarify, the issues at hand. I have instead tried to focus on more detailed explanations of individual cases which seem to me to highlight fundamental monetary issues. Cases such as *Tayeb v HSBC Bank plc* and the Australian decision in *European Bank Ltd v Citibank Ltd* fall into this category.

I would like to record my gratitude to the many others who have contributed to the appearance of this work.

First of all, Professor Goode was kind enough both to extend the original invitation and to assist the process throughout; he also diverted me away from the paths of error with unfailing courtesy! It is right to observe that Payment Obligations is only a part of his massive contribution to commercial law over several decades, and to pay tribute to the universally acclaimed quality of his work.

Secondly, I would like to thank those associated with the production of the text, including James Douse, Melanie Purdie and Lesley Davis at Sweet & Maxwell. Andrew Prideaux and Jane Belford respectively prepared the index and the tables.

Finally, and most importantly of all, my wife Martina not only supported this project but undertook much of the initial research required to fill the gap between 1983 and 2008. My debt to her is beyond calculation.

I should add that, of course, I remain wholly responsible for any errors, omissions or other infelicities.

I have endeavoured to state the law based on the materials available to me as at December 31, 2008.

Charles Proctor
London EC3
11 March 2009

Preface to the Third Edition

It has been my pleasure to be involved in the production of the third edition of Professor Goode's distinguished and well-known work on payment obligations.

Only a few years have elapsed since the appearance of the second edition but, inevitably, the current edition appears against the backdrop of an increasing pace of change.

The definition of "money" itself remains under challenge, with the appearance of virtual or digital currencies threatening the traditional nexus between money, a central bank and an issuing state. In addition, and whilst the UK has an uncertain future within the European Union, EU legislation within the financial services arena continues to exert a significant influence on our domestic law. For example, the Payment Services Directive has encouraged the use of non-bank service providers within the payments system. New decisions in the spheres of sale of goods, contractual penalties and many related areas have also appeared since the second edition. These cases and many other developments have been addressed in the pages that follow. Of course, every legal text expands with each successive edition, but the attraction of *Payment Obligations* has always been its treatment of a complex range of subjects within a reasonable compass. We have attempted to preserve this notable feature of the work whilst, at the same time, ensuring that all relevant developments have been addressed.

I would like to note that Professor Goode retains a close interest in this work and has provided valuable comments and insight on the new material. However, as I am sure he would agree, the greatest burden of research and reorganisation of the text has fallen on Victoria Dixon, a Lecturer in Law attached to Merton College, Oxford. The credit for the progress made in this new edition belongs entirely to her.

Charles Proctor
London
24 August 2016

TABLE OF CONTENTS

	PAGE
Preface to the Fourth Edition	v
Materials referred to by abbreviation	vii
Preface to the First Edition	ix
Preface to the Second Edition	xi
Preface to the Third Edition	xiii
Table of Cases	xvii
Table of Statutes	xlix
Table of Statutory Instruments	li
Table of EC and EU Legislation	liii
Table of International Treaties and Conventions	lv

PARA

1. THE CONCEPT OF MONEY
1. The Concept of Money 1–01
2. Developments in Money 1–09

2. THE CONCEPT OF PAYMENT
1. The Concept of Payment 2–01
2. Categories of Payment Obligation 2–36

3. THE RIGHT TO PAYMENT AND THE DEFENCES TO A PAYMENT CLAIM
1. The Right to Payment 3–02
2. Defences to a Liquidated Claim 3–23
3. Remedies for Non-Payment 3–52
4. The Recovery of Payments Made 3–79

4. STIPULATIONS AS TO TIME: INTEREST
1. The Significance of Stipulations as to Time 4–01
2. Express Stipulations as to Time 4–02

3. Implied Terms as to Time 4–21

4. Termination of Contract for Delay in Payment 4–24

5. Acceleration of Liability 4–36

6. Interest on Contract Debts 4–37

5. THE LEGAL IMPLICATIONS OF PAYMENTS THROUGH BANKING AND NON-BANK SYSTEMS

1. The Changing Payments Landscape 5–01

2. Legislative and Regulatory Background 5–05

3. Payments Through the Banking System 5–13

4. Non-Bank Payment Systems and Services 5–62

5. Brexit 5–77

6. FOREIGN MONEY OBLIGATIONS

1. The Problems Outlined 6–02

2. Performance of the Payment Obligation 6–08

3. Foreign Currency Claims and Judgments 6–29

4. The Applicable Law Under English Conflict of Laws Rules 6–45

PAGE

Index 291

TABLE OF CASES

216 Jamaica Avenue, LLC v S & R Playhouse Realty Co 540 F.3d 433 (12 June 2008, US Court of Appeals, 6th Cir.3–05
A Ltd v B Bank [1997] 6 Bank. L.R. 85; [1997] I.L.Pr. 586; [1997] F.S.R. 165; (1997) 20(2) I.P.D. 20015 CA (Civ Div) 1–07
A/S Tankexpress v Compagnie Financière Belge des Petroles SA [1949] A.C. 76; [1948] 2 All E.R. 939; (1948–49) 82 Ll. L. Rep. 43; [1949] L.J.R. 170; (1949) 93 S.J. 26 HL 2–01, 4–13, 4–27
AB Kemp Ltd v Tolland (t/a James Tolland & Co) [1956] 2 Lloyd's Rep. 681 4–60
ABB Australia Pty Ltd v Commissioner of Taxation [2007] FCA 1063 2–17
Aberdeen Asset Management Plc v Revenue and Customs Commissioners [2013] CSIH 84; [2014] S.T.C. 438; 2014 S.C. 271; 2014 S.L.T. 54; [2013] B.T.C. 726; 2013 G.W.D. 40-773 2–16
Accuba Ltd v Allied Shoe Repairs Ltd [1975] 1 W.L.R. 1559; [1975] 3 All E.R. 782; (1975) 30 P. & C.R. 403; (1975) 119 S.J. 775 4–31
Adam v Newbigging; sub nom. Newbigging v Adam (1888) L.R. 13 App. Cas. 308 HL; 57 LJ Ch 1066 3–81
ADC Orange, Inc v Coyote Acres, Inc., 2000 NY Slip Op 07699 . . . . 4–26, 4–28
Addax Bank BSC v Wellesley Partners LLP [2010] EWHC 1904 (QB) 6–08
Adelaide Electric Supply Co Ltd v Prudential Assurance Co Ltd [1934] A.C. 122 HL 6–19
AES-3C Maritza East 1 EOOD v Credit Agricole Corporate and Investment Bank [2011] EWHC 123 (TCC); [2011] B.L.R. 249; [2011] C.I.L.L. 2985 3–44
Afovos Shipping Co SA v R Pagnan & Fratelli (The Afovos) [1983] 1 W.L.R. 195; [1983] 1 All E.R. 449; [1983] 1 Lloyd's Rep. 335; [1983] Com. L.R. 83; (1983) 127 S.J. 98 HL 4–03
Afovos, The. *See* Afovos Shipping Co SA v R Pagnan & Fratelli
Ageas (UK) Ltd v Kwik-Fit (GB) Ltd [2014] EWHC 2178 (QB); [2014] Bus. L.R. 1338; [2015] Lloyd's Rep. I.R. 1 . . . . 6–39, 6–44
Agip (Africa) Ltd v Jackson [1991] Ch. 547; [1991] 3 W.L.R. 116; [1992] 4 All E.R. 451; (1991) 135 S.J. 117 CA (Civ Div) 3–82
Agroexport State Enterprise for Foreign Trade v Compagnie Européene de Céreales [1974] 1 Lloyd's Rep. 499 6–24
Ahmed v Wingrove [2007] EWHC 1777 (Ch); [2007] 31 E.G. 81 (C.S.); [2007] 2 P. & C.R. DG24 4–30
Aktor, The. *See* PT Berlian Laju Tanker TBK v Nuse Shipping Ltd
Al Wahab, The. *See* Amin Rasheed Shipping Corp v Kuwait Insurance Co
Alan Auld Associates Ltd v Rick Pollard Associates [2008] EWCA Civ 655; [2008] B.L.R. 419; (2008) 152(21) S.J.L.B. 28 CA (Civ Div) 4–33, 4–35
Alaskan Trader, The. *See* Clea Shipping Corp v Bulk Oil International
Alchemy Estates Limited v Astor [2008] EWHC 2675 4–29
Alcoa Minerals of Jamaica Inc v Broderick [2002] 1 A.C. 371; [2000] 3 W.L.R. 23; [2000] B.L.R. 279; (2000) 2 T.C.L.R. 850; [2000] Env. L.R. 734; (2000) 144 S.J.L.B. 182 PC (Jam) 6–39
Alec Lobb Garages Ltd v Total Oil Great Britain Ltd [1985] 1 W.L.R. 173; [1985] 1 All E.R. 303; [1985] 1 E.G.L.R. 33; (1985) 273 E.G. 659; (1985) 82 L.S.G. 45; (1985) 129 S.J. 83 CA (Civ Div) 3–36
Alex Lawrie Factors Ltd v Modern Injection Moulds Ltd [1981] 3 All E.R. 658 . . . . 4–58, 4–60
Allgemeine Gold und Silberscheideanstalt v Customs and Excise Commissioners (1987) 9 E.H.R.R. 1 ECtHR 1–04
Alternative Power Solution Ltd v Central Electricity Board [2014] UKPC 31; [2015] 1 W.L.R. 697; [2014] 4 All E.R. 882; [2014] 2 All E.R. (Comm) 1096; [2014] 2 C.L.C. 371 PC (Mauritius) 2–45, 3–44, 3–45

Amalgamated Investment and Property Co Ltd, Re [1985] Ch. 349; [1984] 3 W.L.R. 1101; [1984] 3 All E.R. 272; (1984) 1 B.C.C. 99104; [1985] F.L.R. 11; (1985) 82 L.S.G. 276; (1984) 128 S.J. 798 Ch D 6–33
American Accord, The. *See* United City Merchants (Investments) Ltd v Royal Bank of Canada
AMEV-UDC Finance Ltd v Austin (1986) 162 C.L.R. 170; (1987) 68 A.L.R. 185 3–33
Amin Rasheed Shipping Corp v Kuwait Insurance Co (The Al Wahab) [1984] A.C. 50; [1983] 3 W.L.R. 241; [1983] 2 All E.R. 884; [1983] 2 Lloyd's Rep. 365; (1983) 127 S.J. 492 HL 4–26
Amman Aviation Pty Ltd v Commonwealth of Australia [1990] FCA 55 4–03
Ampurius NU Homes Holdings Ltd v Telford Homes (Creekside) Ltd [2013] EWCA Civ 577; [2013] 4 All E.R. 377; [2013] B.L.R. 400; 148 Con. L.R. 1; [2013] 23 E.G. 76 (C.S.) 4–31, 4–35
Anderson v Equitable Life Assurance Society (1929) 134 L.T. 557 6–12
Andrews v Australia and New Zealand Banking Group Ltd (2012) 247 C.L.R. 205 3–34
Angelic Star, The. *See* Oresundsvarvet AB v Lemos
Antares III, The. *See* Transpacific Eternity SA v Kanematsu Corp
Aodhcon LLP v Bridgeco Ltd [2014] EWHC 535 (Ch); [2014] 2 All E.R. (Comm) 928; [2014] 2 B.C.L.C. 237 3–31
Aquafaith, The. *See* Isabella Shipowner SA v Shagang Shipping Co Ltd (The Aquafaith)
Arab Bank Ltd v Barclays Bank (Dominion, Colonial and Overseas) [1954] A.C. 495; [1954] 2 W.L.R. 1022; [1954] 2 All E.R. 226; (1954) 98 S.J. 350 HL 2–33, 5–46, 6–26
Arcos Ltd v EA Ronaasen & Son; sub nom. Ronaasen & Son v Arcos Ltd [1933] A.C. 470; (1933) 45 Ll. L. Rep. 33, HL 3–15
Aries Tanker Corp v Total Transport Ltd (The Aries) [1977] 1 W.L.R. 185; [1977] 1 All E.R. 398; [1977] 1 Lloyd's Rep. 334; (1977) 121 S.J. 117 HL 2–07
Arnold v Britton [2015] UKSC 36; [2015] A.C. 1619; [2015] 2 W.L.R. 1593; [2016] 1 All E.R. 1; [2015] H.L.R. 31; [2015] 2 P. & C.R. 14; [2015] L. & T.R. 25; [2015] C.I.L.L. 3689 .... 3–08, 6–16
Aruna Mills Ltd v Dhanrajmal Gobindram [1968] 1 Q.B. 655; [1968] 2 W.L.R. 101; [1968] 1 All E.R. 113; [1968] 1 Lloyd's Rep. 304; (1967) 111 S.J. 924 6–11
Associated British Ports v Ferryways NV [2009] EWCA Civ 189; [2009] 1 Lloyd's Rep. 595; [2009] 1 C.L.C. 350 2–43
Astea (UK) Ltd v Time Group Ltd [2003] EWHC 725 (TCC) 4–15
Astley v Weldon (1801) 2 B. & P. 346 4–51
Attica Sea Carriers Corp v Ferrostaal Poseidon Bulk Reederei GmbH (The Puerto Buitrago) [1976] 1 Lloyd's Rep. 250 CA (Civ Div) 3–20, 3–21
Attorney General of Ghana v Texaco Overseas Tankships Ltd (The Texaco Melbourne) [1994] 1 Lloyd's Rep. 473; [1994] C.L.C. 155 HL 6–39
Attorney General v Barker Bros [1976] 2 N.Z.L.R. 495 3–08
Australian Workers Union v Commonwealth Railway Commission (1933) 49 C.L.R. 589 3–07
AV Pound & Co v MW Hardy & Co Inc [1956] A.C. 588; [1956] 2 W.L.R. 683; [1956] 1 All E.R. 639; [1956] 1 Lloyd's Rep. 255; (1956) 100 S.J. 208 HL 6–25
Avocet Industrial Estates LLP v Merol Ltd [2011] EWHC 3422 (Ch); [2012] L. & T.R. 13; [2012] 1 E.G.L.R. 65; [2012] 14 E.G. 64 .... 2–01, 2–25, 4–03, 5–27
Avon CC v Howlett [1983] 1 W.L.R. 605; [1983] 1 All E.R. 1073; [1983] I.R.L.R. 171; 81 L.G.R. 555; (1983) 133 N.L.J. 377; (1983) 127 S.J. 173 CA (Civ Div) 3–82
Awilco of Oslo A/S v Fulvia SpA di Navigazione of Cagliari (The Chikuma) [1981] 1 W.L.R. 314; [1981] 1 All E.R. 652; [1981] 1 Lloyd's Rep. 371; [1981] Com. L.R. 64; (1981) 125 S.J. 184 HL 1–08, 1–23, 2–23, 5–51, 5–52, 5–55, 6–19
Aziz v Caixa d'Estalvis de Catalunya, Tarragona i Manresa (Catalunyacaixa) (C-415/11) [2013] 3 C.M.L.R. 5; [2013] All E.R. (EC) 770 ECJ 4–53
Aztec Properties Inc v Union Planters National Bank of Memphis, 530 S.W. 2d 756 (1975) 3–08
B Liggett (Liverpool) Ltd v Barclays Bank Ltd [1928] 1 K.B. 48 KBD 5–29

Babacomp Ltd v Rightside Properties Ltd [1974] 1 All E.R. 142; (1973) 26 P. & C.R. 526
  CA (Civ Div) 4–31
Ballantyne Butchery (Pvt) Ltd v Chisvinga & Others (Civil Appeal No. SC 243/12) [2015]
  ZWSC 06 6–013
Banco de Portugal v Waterlow & Sons Ltd; Waterlow & Sons Ltd v Banco de Portugal
  [1932] A.C. 452; [1932] All E.R. Rep. 181 HL 1–04
Bank of Credit and Commerce International SA (In Liquidation) (No.8), Re; sub nom.
  Morris v Rayners Enterprises Inc, Morris v Agrichemicals Ltd, Bank of Credit and
  Commerce International SA (No.3), Re [1998] A.C. 214; [1997] 3 W.L.R. 909; [1997] 4
  All E.R. 568; [1998] Lloyd's Rep. Bank. 48; [1997] B.C.C. 965; [1998] 1 B.C.L.C. 68;
  [1998] B.P.I.R. 211; (1997) 94(44) L.S.G. 35; (1997) 147 N.L.J. 1653; (1997) 141
  S.J.L.B. 229 HL 3–57
Bank of America Canada v Mutual Trust Co [2002] S.C.R. 601 4–56
Bank of Baroda v Panessar [1987] Ch. 335; [1987] 2 W.L.R. 208; [1986] 3 All E.R. 751;
  (1986) 2 B.C.C. 99288; [1987] P.C.C. 165; (1987) 84 L.S.G. 339; (1986) 136 N.L.J.
  963; (1987) 131 S.J. 21 4–11
Bank of Baroda v Patel [1996] 1 Lloyd's Rep. 391 4–12
Bank of Credit and Commerce International SA (In Liquidation) (No.8), Re [1998] A.C.
  214; [1997] 3 W.L.R. 909; [1997] 4 All E.R. 568; [1998] Lloyd's Rep. Bank. 48; [1997]
  B.C.C. 965; [1998] 1 B.C.L.C. 68; [1998] B.P.I.R. 211; (1997) 94(44) L.S.G. 35; (1997)
  147 N.L.J. 1653; (1997) 141 S.J.L.B. 229 HL 3–51
Bank of Ireland v AMCD (Property Holdings) Ltd [2001] 2 All E.R. (Comm) 894; [2001]
  N.P.C. 61 ....4–11, 4–21
Bank of Montreal v Carnival National Leasing Ltd. [2011] O.J. No. 671 Ontario Superior
  Court 4–11
Bank of New South Wales v Brown (1983) 151 C.L.R. 514 2–03
Banque Belge pour l'Etranger v Hambrouck [1921] 1 K.B. 321 CA 1–08
Banque de l'Indochine et de Suez SA v JH Rayner (Mincing Lane) Ltd [1983] Q.B. 711;
  [1983] 2 W.L.R. 841; [1983] 1 All E.R. 1137; [1983] 1 Lloyd's Rep. 228; (1983) 127
  S.J. 361 CA (Civ Div) 3–80, 5–52, 5–55
Banque Saudi Fransi v Lear Siegler Services Inc [2006] EWCA Civ 1130; [2007] 1 All E.R.
  (Comm) 67; [2007] 2 Lloyd's Rep. 47 CA (Civ Div) 3–38
Barboraft Pty Ltd v Geobel Pty Ltd [2003] VCAT 1700 3–08
Barclays Bank International Ltd v Levin Bros (Bradford) Ltd [1977] Q.B. 270; [1976] 3
  W.L.R. 852; [1976] 3 All E.R. 900; [1977] 1 Lloyd's Rep. 51; (1976) 120 S.J.
  801 ....6–19, 6–32
Barclays Bank Ltd v Quistclose Investments Ltd; sub nom. Quistclose Investments Ltd v
  Rolls Razor Ltd (In Voluntary Liquidation) [1970] A.C. 567; [1968] 3 W.L.R. 1097;
  [1968] 3 All E.R. 651; (1968) 112 S.J. 903 HL 2–23
Barclays Bank Ltd v WJ Simms Son & Cooke (Southern) Ltd [1980] Q.B. 677; [1980] 2
  W.L.R. 218; [1979] 3 All E.R. 522; [1980] 1 Lloyd's Rep. 225; (1979) 123 S.J. 785
  QBD 1–08, 2–29, 3–82,
                                                                   5–29
Barings Plc (In Liquidation) v Coopers & Lybrand (No.8); Barings Futures (Singapore) Pte
  Ltd (In Liquidation) v Mattar (No.8) [2003] EWHC 2371 (Ch) 6–41
Barnes Will Trusts, Re [1972] 1 W.L.R. 587; [1972] 2 All E.R. 639; (1972) 116 S.J.
  336 1–02
Barton v Gwyn-Jones [2019] EWCA Civ 1999; [2020] 2 All E.R. (Comm)
  652 ....3–17, 3–18
Bayoil SA v Seawind Tankers Corp (The Leonidas) [2001] 1 All E.R. (Comm) 392; [2001]
  1 Lloyd's Rep. 533; [2001] C.L.C. 1800 QBD 4–21
Beevers v Mason (1979) 37 P. & C.R. 452; (1978) 248 E.G. 781; (1978) 122 S.J.
  610 2–01
Behzadi v Shaftesbury Hotels Ltd [1992] Ch. 1; [1991] 2 W.L.R. 1251; [1991] 2 All E.R.
  477; (1991) 62 P. & C.R. 163; [1990] E.G. 111 (C.S.); (1990) 140 N.L.J. 1385 CA (Civ
  Div) 4–24, 4–31
Beijing Jianlong Heavy Industry Group v Golden Ocean Group Ltd [2013] EWHC 1063
  (Comm); [2013] 2 All E.R. (Comm) 436; [2013] 2 Lloyd's Rep. 61; [2013] 1 C.L.C.
  906; [2013] Bus. L.R. D58 ....3–25, 6–25
Bellami, The. See George Veflings Rederi A/S v President of India

Belmont Park Investments Pty Ltd v BNY Corporate Trustee Services Ltd [2011] UKSC 38; [2012] 1 A.C. 383; [2011] 3 W.L.R. 521; [2012] 1 All E.R. 505; [2011] Bus. L.R. 1266; [2011] B.C.C. 734; [2012] 1 B.C.L.C. 163; [2011] B.P.I.R. 1223 3–55
Benedetti v Sawiris [2013] UKSC 50; [2014] A.C. 938; [2013] 3 W.L.R. 351; [2013] 4 All E.R. 253; [2013] 2 All E.R. (Comm) 801; 149 Con. L.R. 1 3–18
Bennett-Cohen v The State, 1985 (2) SA 465 1–04
Bitumen Invest AS v Richmond Mercantile Ltd FZC [2016] EWHC 2957 (Comm); [2017] 1 Lloyd's Rep. 219; [2017] B.L.R. 74 3–43
Blackett v Clutterbuck Bros (Adelaide) Ltd [1923] S.A.S.R. 301 4–12
Blackstar (Isle of Man) Ltd v Imperium Trust Co Ltd [2016] EWHC 3216 (Ch) 3–17
Blue Sky One Ltd v Mahan Air [2009] EWHC 3314 (Comm) 6–26
Blumberg v Life Interests and Reversionary Securities Corp [1898] 1 Ch. 27 CA 2–28
BNP Paribas SA v Yukos Oil Co [2005] EWHC 1321 (Ch); [2005] All E.R. (D) 281 3–64
BNP Paribas v Wockhardt EU Operations (Swiss) AG [2009] EWHC 3116 (Comm); 132 Con. L.R. 177 .... 2–14, 3–33, 3–35
Board Solutions Australia Pty Ltd v Westpac Banking Corp [2009] VSC 474 SC (Victoria) 3–50
Bocotra Construction Pte Ltd v Attorney General (No.2) [1995] 2 S.L.R. 733 .... 3–45, 3–50
Boissevain v Weil [1950] A.C. 327; [1950] 1 All E.R. 728; 66 T.L.R. (Pt 1) 771; (1950) 94 S.J. 319 HL 6–27
Bolivinter Oil SA v Chase Manhattan Bank NA [1984] 1 W.L.R. 392; [1984] 1 Lloyd's Rep. 251; (1984) 128 S.J. 153 CA (Civ Div) 3–45
Bolt & Nut Co (Tipton) Ltd v Rowlands Nicholls & Co Ltd [1964] 2 Q.B. 10; [1964] 2 W.L.R. 98; [1964] 1 All E.R. 137; (1963) 107 S.J. 909 CA 5–248
Bolton v Mahadeva [1972] 1 W.L.R. 1009; [1972] 2 All E.R. 1322; (1972) 116 S.J. 564 CA (Civ Div) 3–15
Bonython v Australia [1951] A.C. 201; 66 T.L.R. (Pt 2) 969; [1948] 2 D.L.R. 672; (1950) 94 S.J. 821 PC (Aus) 6–08, 6–46
Booker Industries Pty Ltd v Wilson Parking (Qld) Pty Ltd (1982) 56 A.L.J.R. 825 3–08
Booth Steamship Co Ltd v Cargo Fleet Iron Co Ltd [1916] 2 K.B. 570, CA; 85 LJKB 1577; 13 Asp MLC 451; [1916–1917] All E.R. Rep. 938; 115 LT 199; 32 TLR 535 3–78
Boral Framework v Action Makers [2003] NSWSC 713 3–50
Botham v Ministry of Defence. *See* Edwards v Chesterfield Royal Hospital NHS Foundation Trust
Bovill v Endle [1896] 1 Ch. 648 Ch D 4–18
Bowes v Shand; sub nom. Shand v Bowes (1876–77) L.R. 2 App. Cas. 455 HL 4–27
Boyd v Emerson, 111 E.R. 71; (1834) 2 Ad. & El. 184 KB 5–59
BP Exploration Co (Libya) Ltd v Hunt (No.2) [1983] 2 A.C. 352; [1982] 2 W.L.R. 253; [1982] 1 All E.R. 925 HL 3–39, 6–41
Brabant, The. *See* Gesellschaft bürgerlichen Rechts v Stockholms Rederi AB Svea
Branston & Gothard Ltd, Re; sub nom. Hill v Phillips [1999] 1 All E.R. (Comm) 289; [1999] Lloyd's Rep. Bank. 251; [1999] B.P.I.R. 466; [2007] W.T.L.R. 85 Ch D 2–23
Brazzill v Willoughby [2010] EWCA Civ 561; [2010] 2 B.C.L.C. 259; [2011] W.T.L.R. 79 .... 5–36, 6–33
Brett Ronald Larsen v Rick Dees Ltd [2007] NZSC 39 5–22
Bridge v Campbell Discount Co Ltd; sub nom. Campbell Discount Co Ltd v Bridge [1962] A.C. 600; [1962] 2 W.L.R. 439; [1962] 1 All E.R. 385; (1962) 106 S.J. 94 HL 3–29
Brightlife Ltd, Re [1987] Ch. 200; [1987] 2 W.L.R. 197; [1986] 3 All E.R. 673; (1986) 2 B.C.C. 99359; [1986] P.C.C. 435; (1987) 84 L.S.G. 653; (1987) 131 S.J. 132 3–61
Brighton and Hove City Council v Audus [2009] EWHC 340 (Ch); [2010] 1 All E.R. (Comm) 343; [2009] 2 E.G.L.R. 131; [2009] 9 E.G. 192 (C.S.); [2009] N.P.C. 31 4–19

Brimnes, The. *See* Tenax Steamship Co v Owners of the Motor Vessel Brimnes
Britannia Bulk Plc (In Liquidation) v Bulk Trading SA. *See* Lomas v JFB Firth Rixson Inc
British Anzani (Felixstowe) Ltd v International Marine Management (UK) Ltd [1980] Q.B.
 137; [1979] 3 W.L.R. 451; [1979] 2 All E.R. 1063; (1980) 39 P. & C.R. 189; (1978) 250
 E.G. 1183; (1979) 123 S.J. 64 QBD 3–48
British & Commonwealth Holdings Plc v Quadrex Holdings Inc (No.1) [1989] Q.B. 842;
 [1989] 3 W.L.R. 723; [1989] 3 All E.R. 492; (1989) 86(23) L.S.G. 42; (1989) 133 S.J.
 694 CA (Civ Div) 4–25, 4–31
British American Continental Bank Ltd, Re; sub nom. Goldzieher and Penso's Claim, Re
 [1922] 2 Ch. 575; (1922) 12 Ll. L. Rep. 113 CA 6–33
British Bank of the Middle East v Sun Life Assurance Co of Canada (UK) [1983] 2 Lloyd's
 Rep. 9; [1983] Com. L.R. 187; (1983) 133 N.L.J. 575 HL 2–27, 5–26, 5–51
British Eagle International Airlines Ltd v Compagnie Nationale Air France [1975] 1 W.L.R.
 758; [1975] 2 All E.R. 390; [1975] 2 Lloyd's Rep. 43; (1975) 119 S.J. 368
 HL 5–55
Broadwick Financial Services Ltd v Spencer [2002] EWCA Civ 35; [2002] 1 All E.R.
 (Comm) 446; (2002) 99(11) L.S.G. 36; (2002) 146 S.J.L.B. 53 CA (Civ
 Div) 4–43
Brown Boveri (Australia) Pty v Baltic Shipping Co (The Nadezhda Krupskaya) (1989) 93
 A.L.R. 171; [1989] 1 Lloyd's Rep. 518 CA (NSW) 3–04
Brown v Cole, 60 E.R. 424; (1845) 14 Sim. 427 Ch 4–18
Brown v West Midlands Patio Doors Ltd [1997] C.L.Y. 933 3–15
Brown's Bay Resort Ltd v Pozzoni [2016] UKPC 10 PC (Antigua and
 Barbuda) 2–29
Buchan Biogas Ltd v BSG Civil Engineering Ltd [2020] CSOH 42; 2020 G.W.D.
 17-244 3–42
Buckland v Farmar & Moody [1979] 1 W.L.R. 221; [1978] 3 All E.R. 929; (1978) 36 P. &
 C.R. 330; (1978) 122 S.J. 211 CA (Civ Div) 4–31
Budana v Leeds Teaching Hospitals NHS Trust [2017] EWCA Civ 1980; [2018] 1 W.L.R.
 1965; [2017] 6 Costs L.R. 1135; (2018) 159 B.M.L.R. 50; Times, January 19,
 2018 3–13
Bunge Corp v Tradax Export SA [1981] 1 W.L.R. 711; [1981] 2 All E.R. 540; [1981] 2
 Lloyd's Rep. 1; (1981) 125 S.J. 373 HL 4–26, 4–27
Bunge SA v Nidera BV (formerly Nidera Handelscompagnie BV) [2015] UKSC 43; [2015]
 3 All E.R. 1082; [2015] 2 All E.R. (Comm) 789; [2015] Bus. L.R. 987; [2015] 2 Lloyd's
 Rep. 469 4–03
C21 London Estates Ltd v Maurice Macneill Iona Ltd [2017] EWHC 998
 (Ch) 4–35
Callander v Howard (1850) 10 C.B. 290; 138 E.R. 117; 1 LM & P 562 2–03
Calvan Consolidated Oil and Gas Co Ltd v Manning [1959] S.C.R. 253 Sup Ct
 (Can) 3–08
Camdex International Ltd v Bank of Zambia (No.3) [1997] 6 Bank. L.R. 44; [1997] C.L.C.
 714 CA (Civ Div) 1–07
Camillo Tank Steamship Co Ltd v Alexandria Engineering Works (1921) 38 T.L.R.
 134 2–03
Campbell Discount Co Ltd v Bridge. *See* Bridge v Campbell Discount Co Ltd
Campbell v French and Hobson, 101 E.R. 510; (1795) 6 Term. Rep. 200 KB 4–14
Canmer International Inc v UK Mutual Steamship Assurance Association (Bermuda) Ltd
 (The Rays) [2005] EWHC 1694 (Comm); [2005] 2 Lloyd's Rep. 479 .... 2–02, 2–17
Capital Finance Co Ltd v Donati (1977) 121 S.J. 270 CA (Civ Div) 3–33
Car & Universal Finance Co Ltd v Caldwell [1965] 1 Q.B. 525; [1964] 2 W.L.R. 600;
 [1964] 1 All E.R. 290; (1964) 108 S.J. 15 CA 3–78
Carapanayoti & Co v Comptoir Commercial & Cie SA [1972] 1 Lloyd's Rep. 139; (1972)
 116 S.J. 96 CA (Civ Div) 4–10
Carey Group PLC v AIB Group (UK) Plc [2011] EWHC 567 (Ch); [2012] Ch. 304; [2012]
 2 W.L.R. 564; [2011] 2 All E.R. (Comm) 461 4–21
Carey v HSBC Bank Plc [2009] EWHC 3417 (QB); [2010] Bus. L.R. 1142; [2009] C.T.L.C.
 103; (2010) 154(2) S.J.L.B. 28 3–37
Carey Value Added SL (formerly Losan Hotels World Value Added I SL) v Grupo Urvasco
 SA [2010] EWHC 1905 (Comm); [2011] 2 All E.R. (Comm) 140; [2011] 1 B.C.L.C.
 352; 132 Con. L.R. 15 3–42

Cargill International Trading Pte Ltd v Uttam Galva Steels Ltd [2019] EWHC 476
(Comm) 3–30, 3–31, 4–52,
6–25
Carnegie v Giessen [2005] EWCA Civ 191; [2005] 1 W.L.R. 2510; [2005] C.P. Rep. 24;
[2005] 1 C.L.C. 259; (2005) 102(18) L.S.G. 23 6–43
Cartwright v MacCormack [1963] 1 W.L.R. 18; [1963] 1 All E.R. 11; [1962] 2 Lloyd's Rep.
328; (1962) 106 S.J. 957 CA 4–07, 4–09
Carney v NM Rothschild & Sons Ltd [2018] EWHC 959 (Comm) 3–37
Caterpillar Ltd (formerly FG Wilson (Engineering) Ltd) v John Holt & Co (Liverpool) Ltd.
See FG Wilson (Engineering) Ltd v John Holt & Co (Liverpool) Ltd
Caterpillar Motoren GmbH & Co KG v Mutual Benefits Assurance Co [2015] EWHC 2304
(Comm); [2016] 2 All E.R. (Comm) 322; [2015] 2 Lloyd's Rep. 261; [2016] 1 B.C.L.C.
419. . . . . 3–43, 3–45
Cathay Pacific Airlines Ltd v Lufthansa Technik AG [2019] EWHC 715 (Ch); [2019] 1
W.L.R. 5057; [2019] Costs L.R. 479 6–32
Cavacich v Riordan [1994] N.Z.L.R. 502 3–61
Cavendish Square Holding BV v Talal El Makdessi [2015] UKSC 67; [2015] 3 W.L.R.
1373; [2016] 2 All E.R. 519; [2016] 2 All E.R. (Comm) 1; [2016] 1 Lloyd's Rep. 55;
[2016] B.L.R. 1; 162 Con. L.R. 1; [2016] R.T.R. 8; [2016] C.I.L.L. 3769 . . . 2–42, 3–28, 3–29,
3–30, 3–31, 3–33, 3–34, 3–58, 4–51,
4–52, 4–54
Cawdery Kaye Fireman & Taylor v Minkin. *See* Minkin v Cawdery Kaye Fireman & Taylor
(t/a CKFT)
Celestial Aviation Trading 71 Ltd v Paramount Airways Private Ltd [2010] EWHC 185
(Comm); [2011] 1 All E.R. (Comm) 259; [2011] 1 Lloyd's Rep. 9; [2010] 1 C.L.C.
165 4–04
Central Estates (Belgravia) Ltd v Woolgar (No.2) [1972] 1 W.L.R. 1048; [1972] 3 All E.R.
610; (1972) 24 P. & C.R. 103; (1972) 116 S.J. 566 CA (Civ Div) 2–28
Chaitlal v Ramlal PC (Trin) 4–31
Challinor v Juliet Bellis & Co [2015] EWCA Civ 59; [2016] W.T.L.R. 43; [2015] 2 P. &
C.R. DG3 2–23
Charge Card Services Ltd (No.2), Re [1989] Ch. 497; [1988] 3 W.L.R. 764; [1988] 3 All
E.R. 702; (1988) 4 B.C.C. 524; [1988] B.C.L.C. 711; [1988] P.C.C. 390; [1988] Fin.
L.R. 308; (1989) 8 Tr. L.R. 86; (1988) 85(42) L.S.G. 46; (1988) 138 N.L.J. Rep. 201;
(1988) 132 S.J. 1458 CA (Civ Div) 2–30, 3–57, 5–30,
5–31, 5–38, 5–40, 5–66
Charles Rickards Ltd v Oppenheim; sub nom. Rickards (Charles) v Oppenhaim [1950] 1
K.B. 616; [1950] 1 All E.R. 420; 66 T.L.R. (Pt 1) 435; (1950) 94 S.J. 161
CA 4–33
Chase Manhattan Bank NA v Israel-British Bank (London) Ltd [1981] Ch. 105; [1980] 2
W.L.R. 202; [1979] 3 All E.R. 1025; (1980) 124 S.J. 99 . . . . 2–29, 3–82
Cherry v Boultbee (1839) 4 My. & C. 442; 41 E.R. 171 2–09
Chesterman's Trusts, Re; Mott v Browning [1923] 2 Ch. 466, CA; 93 LJ CH 263; [1923] All
E.R. Rep. 705; 130 LT 109. 6–47
Chikuma, The. *See* Awilco of Oslo A/S v Fulvia SpA di Navigazione of Cagliari
Child Maintenance and Enforcement Commission v Wilson [2013] CSIH 95; 2014 S.L.T.
46; 2013 G.W.D. 39-744 2–22
Cie Commerciale Sucres et Denrées v C Czarnikow Ltd (The Naxos) [1990] 1 W.L.R. 1337;
[1990] 3 All E.R. 641; [1991] 1 Lloyd's Rep. 29; (1990) 134 S.J. 1301
HL 4–27
Citibank NA v Nyland and the Republic of the Philippines, 878 F. 2d 620 (2d Cir.,
1989) 4–51
Citibank NA v Wells Fargo Asia Ltd (1990) 495 US 660 1–10
City Motors v Southern Aerial Super Service Pty Ltd (1961) 106 C.L.R. 477 2–17
Cityland & Property (Holdings) Ltd v Dabrah [1968] Ch. 166; [1968] Ch. 166; [1967] 3
W.L.R. 605; [1967] 2 All E.R. 639; (1967) 111 S.J. 518 Ch D 4–58
Ciudad de Neiva, The. *See* Mitsui & Co Ltd v Flota Mercante Grancolombiana SA
Ciudad de Pasto, The. *See* Mitsui & Co Ltd v Flota Mercante Grancolombiana SA
CKR Contract Services Pte v Asplenium Land Pte Ltd [2015] 3 SLR 1041 CA
(Singapore). 3–45, 3–50

Claim by Helbert Wagg & Co Ltd, Re; sub nom. Prudential Assurance Co Ltd, Re [1956]
  Ch. 323; [1956] 2 W.L.R. 183; [1956] 1 All E.R. 129; (1956) 100 S.J. 53 5–46
Clayton's Case. *See* Devaynes v Noble
Clea Shipping Corp v Bulk Oil International Ltd (The Alaskan Trader) (No.2) [1984] 1 All
  E.R. 129; [1983] 2 Lloyd's Rep. 645 3–21
Cleadon Trust Ltd, Re [1939] Ch. 286, CA; [1938] 4 All E.R. 518; 108 LJ Ch 81; 82 S.J.
  1030; 160 LT 45; 55 TLR 154 . . . . 5–29, 5–25
Cleveland Bridge UK Ltd v Multiplex Constructions (UK) Ltd [2010] EWCA Civ
  139 3–16
Cleveland Manufacturing Co Ltd v Muslim Commercial Bank Ltd [1981] 2 Lloyd's Rep.
  646; [1981] Com. L.R. 247 2–27
Clifford Maersk, The [1982] 1 W.L.R. 1292; [1982] 3 All E.R. 905; [1982] 2 Lloyd's Rep.
  251; (1982) 79 L.S.G. 988; (1982) 126 S.J. 446 4–055
Clough Engineering Ltd v Oil and Natural Gas Corp Ltd (2008) 249 ALR
  458 3–50
Clough Engineering Ltd v Oil and Natural Gas Corporation Ltd (No. 2) (2008) FCAFC
  136 3–50
Cochrane (Decorators) v Sarabandi (1983) 133 N.L.J. 588 QBD 4–24
Cohen v Hale (1877) 3 Q.B.D. 371 5–28
Cohen v Roche [1927] 1 K.B. 169; 95 LJKB 945; 136 LT 219; 42 TLR 674; 70 S.J.
  942 2–32
Colley v Overseas Exporters (1919) Ltd [1921] 3 K.B. 302; (1921) 8 Ll. L. Rep. 127; 90
  LJKB 1301; 26 Com Cas 325; [1921] All E.R. Rep. 596; 126 LT 58; 37 TLR
  797 . . . . 2–175, 4–22
Collier v P & MJ Wright (Holdings) Ltd [2007] EWCA Civ 1329; [2008] 1 W.L.R. 643;
  [2007] B.P.I.R. 1452; [2007] N.P.C. 136 CA (Civ Div) 3–17
Colonial Trusts Corp Ex p. Bradshaw, Re (1880) L.R. 15 Ch. D. 465 3–74
Colt Technologies Services v SG Global Group SRL [2020] EWHC 1417
  (Ch) 6–25
Coltrane v Day; sub nom. Day v Coltrane [2003] EWCA Civ 342; [2003] 1 W.L.R. 1379;
  [2003] H.L.R. 56; [2003] L. & T.R. 23; [2003] 2 E.G.L.R. 21; [2003] 30 E.G. 146;
  [2003] 17 E.G. 146 (C.S.); (2003) 100(19) L.S.G. 30; (2003) 147 S.J.L.B. 355; [2003]
  N.P.C. 36 CA (Civ Div) 2–01, 5–28
Commissioner of Taxation v Desalination Technology Pty Ltd [2014] FCA
  1120 2–03
Continental Illinois National Bank & Trust Co of Chicago v Papanicolaou (The Fedora, The
  Tatiana and The Eretrea II)
Fedora, The, Tatiana, The, Eretrea II, The [1986] 2 Lloyd's Rep. 441; [1986] Fin. L.R. 373;
  (1986) 83 L.S.G. 2569 CA (Civ Div) 3–48
Cook v Fowler; Cook v Wood; Cook v Roberts (1874–75) L.R. 7 H.L. 27 HL 4–51, 4–58
Corbett v Gaskin Unreported, April 21, 2008 4–56
Cornelius v Banque Franco-Serbe [1942] 1 K.B. 29 6–24
County Leasing Ltd v East [2007] EWHC 2907 (QB); [2007] All E.R.(D) 371 . . . . 3–32, 4–51
Crantrave Ltd (In Liquidation) v Lloyds Bank Plc [2000] Q.B. 917; [2000] 3 W.L.R. 877;
  [2000] 4 All E.R. 473; [2000] 2 All E.R. (Comm) 89; [2000] Lloyd's Rep. Bank. 181;
  [2000] C.L.C. 1194; [2001] B.P.I.R. 57; (2000) 97(20) L.S.G. 42; (2000) 144 S.J.L.B.
  219 CA (Civ Div) 3–82, 5–29
Credit & Mercantile Plc v Marks [2004] EWCA Civ 568; [2005] Ch. 81; [2004] 3 W.L.R.
  489; (2004) 101(22) L.S.G. 32; (2004) 148 S.J.L.B. 632; [2004] N.P.C. 74; [2004] 2 P.
  & C.R. DG12 CA (Civ Div) 3–73
Crocs Europe BV v Anderson (t/a Spectrum Agencies (A Partnership)) [2012] EWCA Civ
  1400; [2013] 1 Lloyd's Rep. 1; [2013] E.C.C. 1 4–29
Cubitt Building & Interiors Ltd v Richardson Roofing (Industrial) Ltd [2008] EWHC 1020
  (TCC); [2008] B.L.R. 354; 119 Con. L.R. 137; [2008] C.I.L.L. 2588 4–21
Cukurova Finance International Ltd v Alfa Telecom Turkey Ltd [2013] UKPC 20; [2015] 2
  W.L.R. 875; [2013] 4 All E.R. 936 PC (British Virgin Islands) 2–17, 3–84, 4–04
Cumberland Court (Brighton) Ltd v Taylor [1964] Ch. 29; [1963] 3 W.L.R. 313; [1963] 2
  All E.R. 536; (1963) 107 S.J. 594 4–31
Customs and Excise Commissioners v National Westminster Bank Plc (Authorisation:
  Mistake) [2002] EWHC 2204 (Ch); [2003] 1 All E.R. (Comm) 327; (2002) 99(48)
  L.S.G. 27 5–36

Cutter v Powell (1795) 6 Term Rep. 320; 101 E.R. 573; [1775–1802] All E.R. Rep.
159 3–13
D&D Wines International Ltd (In Liquidation), Re; sub nom. Angove Pty Ltd v Bailey,
Bailey v Angove's Pty Ltd [2016] UKSC 47; [2016] 1 W.L.R. 3179; [2017] 1 All E.R.
773; [2017] 1 All E.R. (Comm) 583; [2016] 2 Lloyd's Rep. 409; [2016] B.C.C. 594;
[2017] 1 B.C.L.C. 1; [2016] 2 C.L.C. 228; [2016] E.C.C. 28; [2016] B.P.I.R. 1361;
[2016] W.T.L.R. 1309; [2017] 1 P. & C.R. DG2 5–36
Dairy Containers Ltd v Tasman Orient Line CV (The Tasman Discoverer) [2004] UKPC 22;
[2005] 1 W.L.R. 215; [2004] 2 All E.R. (Comm) 667; [2004] 2 Lloyd's Rep. 647; [2004]
2 C.L.C. 794 PC (NZ) 3–05
Dalkia Utilities Services Plc v Celtech International Ltd [2006] EWHC 63 (Comm); [2006]
All E.R. (D) 203; [2006] 1 Lloyd's Rep. 599; [2006] 2 P. & C.R. 9 .... 4–31, 4–34
Damayanti Kantilal Doshi v Indian Bank [1999] 4 S.L.R. 1, 11 CA (Sing) 2–33
Dana Gas PJSC v Dana Gas Sukuk Ltd [2017] EWHC 2928; [2018] 1 Lloyd's Rep. 177;
[2017] 2 C.L.C. 735 .... 6–24, 6–25
Dauphin Offshore Engineering & Trading Pte Ltd v The Private Office of HRH Sheikh
Sultan bin Khalifa bin Zayed Al Nahyan [2000] 1 S.L.R. 117; affirmed in JBE Properties
Pte Ltd v Gammon Pte Ltd [2011] 2 S.L.R. 47 3–50
Davies v Revelan Estates (Wigston) Ltd [2019] B.P.I.R. 1102 4–11
Davys v Richardson (1888) L.R. 21 Q.B.D. 202 CA 2–42
Day & Dent Constructions Pty Ltd v North Australian Properties Pty Ltd (1982) 150 C.L.R.
85; (1982) 40 A.C.R. 399 2–40
Debtor, Ex p. Richie Bros Auctioneers (No.51/SD/1991), Re [1992] 1 W.L.R. 1294; [1993] 2
All E.R. 40 6–33
Decro-Wall International SA v Practitioners in Marketing [1971] 1 W.L.R. 361; [1971] 2 All
E.R. 216; (1970) 115 S.J. 171 CA (Civ Div) 4–26, 4–33, 4–35
Decura IM Investments LLP v UBS AG London Branch [2015] EWHC 171
(Comm) 3–64
Delbrueck & Co v Manufacturers Hanover Trust Co, 609 F. 2d 1047 (1979); affirming 464
F. Supp. 989 (1979) 5–34, 5–46, 5–53,
5–55, 5–60
Deputy Commissioner of Taxation v Horsburgh [1984] V.R. 773 3–61
Despina R, The. See Owners of the Eleftherotria v Owners of the Despina R
Deutsche Bank AG v Unitech Global Ltd, Deutsche Bank AG v Unitech Ltd, Graiseley
Properties Ltd v Barclays Bank Plc [2013] EWCA Civ 1372 4–46
Deutsche Bank AG v Unitech Global Ltd [2016] EWCA Civ 119; [2016] 1 W.L.R. 3598;
[2017] 1 All E.R. 570; [2016] 2 All E.R. (Comm) 689; [2016] 1 C.L.C.
453 .... 3–24, 3–25, 6–24,
6–25
Deutsche Bank (Suisse) SA v Khan [2013] EWHC 482 (Comm) 3–37
Deutsche Bank und Disconto Gesellschaft v Banque des Marchands de Moscou (1931–32)
107 L.J. K.B. 386; (1931) 158 L.T. 364; (1931) 4 Legal Decisions Affecting Bankers
293 CA 4–42
Devaynes v Noble, Clayton's Case (1816) 1 Mer. 529; (1816) 8 LJ Ch 256; 35 ER 767;
[1814–1823] All E.R. Rep. 1 2–03
DFC Financial Services Ltd v Coffey [1991] 2 N.Z.L.R. 513 3–61
Di Luca v Juraise (Springs) Ltd (2000) 79 P. & C.R. 193; [1998] 2 E.G.L.R. 125; [1998] 18
E.G. 131; (1998) 75 P. & C.R. D15 CA (Civ Div) 4–30
Diamandis v Wills [2015] EWHC 312 (Ch) 3–15
Dimskal Shipping Co SA v International Transport Workers Federation (The Evia Luck)
(No.2) [1992] 2 A.C. 152; [1991] 3 W.L.R. 875; [1991] 4 All E.R. 871; [1992] 1 Lloyd's
Rep. 115; [1992] I.C.R. 37; [1992] I.R.L.R. 78 HL 3–83
Director General of Fair Trading v First National Bank Plc [2001] UKHL 52; [2002] 1 A.C.
481; [2001] 3 W.L.R. 1297; [2002] 1 All E.R. 97; [2001] 2 All E.R. (Comm) 1000;
[2002] 1 Lloyd's Rep. 489; [2002] E.C.C. 22; (2001) 151 N.L.J. 1610 HL 4–54
Discount Records Ltd v Barclays Bank Ltd [1975] 1 W.L.R. 315; [1975] 1 All E.R. 1071;
[1975] 1 Lloyd's Rep. 444; (1974) 119 S.J. 133 .... 2–45, 3–44, 3–45
Dodds v Walker [1981] 1 W.L.R. 1027; [1981] 2 All E.R. 609; (1981) 42 P. & C.R. 131;
(1981) 125 S.J. 463 HL 4–06, 4–14
Doherty v Fannigan Holdings Ltd [2018] EWCA Civ 1615; [2018] 2 B.C.L.C. 623; [2018]
B.P.I.R. 1266 4–11

Donegal International Ltd v Zambia [2007] EWHC 197 (Comm); [2007] 1 Lloyd's Rep.
397 4–51
Donovan v Grainmarket Asset Management LLP [2020] EWHC 17 (Comm) 3–13
Doosan Babcock Ltd v Comercializadora de Equipos y Materiales Mabe Lda (formerly
Mabe Chile Lda) [2013] EWHC 3010 (TCC); [2014] 1 Lloyd's Rep. 464 3–49
Dovey v Bank of New Zealand [2003] 3 N.Z.L.R. 650 CA (NZ) 2–258
Dowman Imports Ltd v 2 Toobz Ltd [2020] EWHC 291 (Comm); [2020] B.L.R.
465 3–18
Dunbar Assets Plc v Fowler; sub nom. Fowler, Re [2013] B.P.I.R. 46 Ch D (Bankruptcy
Court) 4–11
Dunlop Pneumatic Tyre Co Ltd v New Garage & Motor Co Ltd [1915] A.C. 79
HL 3–28, 4–51
Dynamics Corp of America (In Liquidation) (No.2), Re [1976] 1 W.L.R. 757; [1976] 2 All
E.R. 669; (1976) 120 S.J. 450 6–33
East Ayrshire Council v Zurich Insurance Plc [2014] CSOH 102; 2014 G.W.D.
23-432 3–41
Eastgate Ex p. Ward, Re [1905] 1 K.B. 465; 74 LJKB 324; 12 Mans 11; 53 WR 432; [1904]
7 All E.R. 890; 49 S.J. 205; 92 LT 207; 21 T.L.R. 597 3–78
ED&F Man Ltd v Nigerian Sweets & Confectionery Co [1977] 2 Lloyd's Rep.
50 . . . . 2–25, 5–28
Edelstein v Schuler & Co [1902] 2 K.B. 144; 71 LJKB 572; 7 Com Cas 172; 50 WR 493;
[1900–1903] All E.R. Rep. 884; 46 S.J. 500; 87 LT 204; 18 T.L.R. 597 4–48
Edgeworth Capital (Luxembourg) Sarl v Ramblas Investments BV [2016] EWCA Civ 412;
[2017] 1 All E.R. (Comm) 3–29, 3–59
Edmondson v Copland [1911] 2 Ch. 301 2–17
Edward Owen Engineering Ltd v Barclays Bank International Ltd [1978] Q.B. 159; [1977] 3
W.L.R. 764; [1978] 1 All E.R. 976; [1978] 1 Lloyd's Rep. 166; 6 B.L.R. 1; (1977) 121
S.J. 617 CA (Civ Div) 2–45, 3–45
Edwards v Chesterfield Royal Hospital NHS Foundation Trust, Botham v Ministry of
Defence [2011] UKSC 58; [2012] 2 A.C. 22; [2012] 2 W.L.R. 55; [2012] 2 All E.R. 278;
[2012] I.C.R. 201; [2012] I.R.L.R. 129; [2012] Med. L.R. 93; (2012) 124 B.M.L.R. 51;
(2012) 162 N.L.J. 30; (2011) 155(48) S.J.L.B. 31 3–22
Edwards v Stock [2008] TASSC 12 4–12
Edwinton Commercial Corp v Tsavliris Russ (Worldwide Salvage & Towage) Ltd (The Sea
Angel) [2007] EWCA Civ 547; [2007] 2 All E.R. (Comm) 634; [2007] 2 Lloyd's Rep.
517; [2007] 1 C.L.C. 876 6–26
Effy, The. See Zim Israel Navigation Co Ltd v Effy Shipping Corp
EFT Commercial Ltd v Security Change Ltd (No.1), 1992 S.C. 414; 1993 S.L.T. 128; 1992
S.C.L.R. 706 IH (1 Div) 3–29
Eider, The [1893] P. 119 CA 6–03
EJ Riley Investments Ltd v Eurostile Holdings Ltd [1985] 1 W.L.R. 1139; [1985] 3 All E.R.
181; (1986) 51 P. & C.R. 36; [1985] 2 E.G.L.R. 124; (1985) 82 L.S.G. 2500; (1985) 135
N.L.J. 887; (1985) 129 S.J. 523 CA (Civ Div) 4–10
Electricity Supply Nominees Ltd v Thorn EMI Retail Ltd (1992) 63 P. & C.R. 143; [1991] 2
E.G.L.R. 46; [1991] 35 E.G. 114; [1991] E.G. 48 (C.S.) 2–29
Elena d'Amico, The. See Koch Marine Inc v d'Amica Societa di Navigazione arl
Elenin's Estate, Re [2015] EWHC 2962 (Ch); [2016] 1 W.L.R. 2091; [2016] B.P.I.R.
94 6–33
Elmdene Estates Ltd v White [1960] 1 Q.B. 1; [1959] 3 W.L.R. 185; [1959] 2 All E.R. 605;
(1959) 103 S.J. 656 CA 2–16
Elsey v JG Collins Insurance Agencies Ltd (1978) 83 D.L.R. (3d) 1 3–33
Elsinora Global Ltd v Healthscope Ltd (No.2) [2006] F.L.A. 18 1–03
Emerald Meats (London) Ltd v AIB Group (UK) Plc [2002] EWCA Civ 460 . . . . 4–39, 4–41, 5–28
Emeraldian LP v Wellmix Shipping Ltd (The Vine) [2010] EWHC 1411 (Comm); [2011] 1
Lloyd's Rep. 301; [2010] 1 C.L.C. 993 3–25
Eminence Property Developments Ltd v Heaney [2010] EWCA Civ 1168; [2011] 2 All E.R.
(Comm) 223; [2010] 3 E.G.L.R. 165; [2010] 43 E.G. 99 (C.S.) 4–35
Empresa Cubana de Fletes v Lagonisi Shipping Co Ltd (The Georgios C) [1971] 1 Q.B.
488; [1971] 2 W.L.R. 221; [1971] 1 All E.R. 193; [1971] 1 Lloyd's Rep. 7; (1970) 114
S.J. 862 CA (Civ Div) 2–28, 4–28

ENE 1 Kos Ltd v Petroleo Brasileiro SA Petrobras (The Kos) [2012] UKSC 17; [2012] 2
  A.C. 164; [2012] 2 W.L.R. 976; [2012] 4 All E.R. 1; [2013] 1 All E.R. (Comm) 32;
  [2012] 2 Lloyd's Rep. 292; [2013] 1 C.L.C. 1; 149 Con. L.R. 76; (2012) 162 N.L.J.
  680 4–35
Enka Insaat Ve Sanayi AS v Banca Popolare dell'Alto Adige SpA [2009] EWHC 2410
  (Comm); [2009] C.I.L.L. 2777 .... 3–44, 3–45
Enron Australia Finance Pty Ltd v TXU Electricity Ltd [2003] NSWSC 1169 3–54
Equitable Trust Co of New York v Dawson Partners Ltd (1927) 27 Ll. L. Rep. 49
  HL 3–15
Equuscorp Pty Ltd v Glengallan Investments Pty Ltd [2004] HCA 55 HC
  (Australia) 2–01
Erven Warnink BV v J Townend & Sons (Hull) Ltd (No.2) [1982] 3 All E.R. 312; [1982]
  Com. L.R. 184; [1982] R.P.C. 511; (1982) 79 L.S.G. 987; (1982) 126 S.J. 465 CA (Civ
  Div) 4–61
Esal (Commodities) Ltd and Reltor Ltd v Oriental Credit Ltd and Wells Fargo Bank NA;
  Banque du Caire SAE v Wells Fargo Bank NA [1985] 2 Lloyd's Rep. 546; [1986] Fin.
  L.R. 70 CA (Civ Div) 3–41
Esso Exploration & Production UK Ltd v Electricity Supply Board [2004] EWHC 723;
  [2004] 1 All E.R. (Comm) 926 .... 3–06, 3–08
Esso Petroleum Co Ltd v Alstonbridge Properties Ltd [1975] 1 W.L.R. 1474; [1975] 3 All
  E.R. 358; (1975) 30 P. & C.R. 170; (1975) 237 E.G. 881; (1975) 119 S.J.
  727 4–12
Esso Petroleum Co Ltd v Milton [1997] 1 W.L.R. 1060; [1997] 1 W.L.R. 938; [1997] 2 All
  E.R. 593; [1997] C.L.C. 634; (1997) 16 Tr. L.R. 250 CA (Civ Div) 2–25, 5–34
Eurobank Ergasias SA v Kalliroi Navigation Co Ltd [2015] EWHC 2377
  (Comm) 6–25
European Bank Ltd v Citibank Ltd [2004] NSWCA 76 .... 5–23, 5–48
Evans & Associates v Citibank Ltd [2003] NSWC 204 5–48
Evans & Associates v Citibank Ltd [2007] NSWSC 1004 6–45
Evans v Rival Granite Quarries Ltd [1910] 2 K.B. 979, CA; 79 LJKB 970; 18 Mans 64; 54
  S.J. 580; 26 T.L.R. 509 3–74
Evia Luck, The. See Dimskal Shipping Co SA v International Transport Workers Federation
Export Credits Guarantee Department v Universal Oil Products Co [1983] 1 W.L.R. 399;
  [1983] 2 All E.R. 205; [1983] 2 Lloyd's Rep. 152; 23 B.L.R. 106; (1983) 133 N.L.J.
  662; (1983) 127 S.J. 408 HL 3–29
F&C Alternative Investments (Holdings) Ltd v Barthelemy [2011] EWHC 1731 (Ch); [2012]
  Ch. 613; [2012] 3 W.L.R. 10; [2012] Bus. L.R. 891 2–17
Fairfield Sentry Ltd (In Liquidation) v Migani [2014] UKPC 9; [2014] 1 C.L.C. 611 PC
  (British Virgin Islands) 3–82
Falco Finance Ltd v Gough (1999) 17 Tr. L.R. 526; [1999] C.C.L.R. 16; (1999) 149 N.L.J.
  7 4–51
Fanfield Ltd v Revenue and Customs Commissioners, Thexton Training Ltd v Revenue and
  Customs Commissioners [2011] UKFTT 42 (TC); [2011] S.F.T.D 324; [2011] S.T.I.
  674 1–03
Farrant v Oliver (1922) 91 L.J. Ch. 758; [1922] All E.R. Rep. 783 4–31
Farrell v Burden [2019] EWHC 3671 (QB) 2–20
FBC Construction Co Ltd v Ben Lee [2014] 2 HKLRD 1054 (Hong Kong Court of
  Appeal) 2–20
Fearns (t/a Autopaint International) v Anglo-Dutch Paint & Chemical Co Ltd [2010] EWHC
  2366 (Ch); [2011] 1 W.L.R. 366; [2011] Bus. L.R. 579; (2010) 154(37) S.J.L.B.
  29 .... 2–11, 4–36
Federal Commerce & Navigation Co Ltd v Molena Alpha Inc (The Nanfri) [1979] A.C. 757;
  [1978] 3 W.L.R. 991; [1979] 1 All E.R. 307; [1979] 1 Lloyd's Rep. 201; (1978) 122 S.J.
  843 HL 4–35
Federal Commerce & Navigation Co Ltd v Tradax Export SA (The Maratha Envoy) [1978]
  A.C. 1; [1977] 3 W.L.R. 126; [1977] 2 All E.R. 849; [1977] 2 Lloyd's Rep. 301; (1977)
  121 S.J. 459 .... 6–32, 6–36
Federal Huron, The. See Société Franµaise Bunge SA v Belcan NV
Federal-Mogul Asbestos Personal Injury Trust v Federal-Mogul Ltd (formerly T&N Plc)
  [2014] EWHC 2002 (Comm); [2014] Lloyd's Rep. I.R. 671 .... 1–02, 1–08, 2–05
Feltham Management Ltd v Feltham [2017] 12 WLUK 641 EAT 3–22

Fergusson v Fyffe, 8 E.R. 49; (1841) 8 Cl. & Fin. 121 HL 4–42
FG Wilson (Engineering) Ltd v John Holt & Co (Liverpool) Ltd; sub nom. Caterpillar (NI) Ltd (formerly FG Wilson (Engineering) Ltd) v John Holt & Co (Liverpool) Ltd [2013] EWCA Civ 1232; [2014] 1 W.L.R. 2365; [2014] 1 All E.R. 785; [2014] 1 All E.R. (Comm) 393; [2014] 1 Lloyd's Rep. 180; [2013] 2 C.L.C. 501; [2014] B.L.R. 103; [2014] B.P.I.R. 1104 .... 3–48, 4–22
Fibrosa Spolka Akcyjna v Fairbairn Lawson Combe Barbour Ltd; sub nom. Fibrosa Société Anonyme v Fairbairn Lawson Combe Barbour Ltd [1943] A.C. 32; [1942] 2 All E.R. 122; (1942) 73 Ll. L. Rep. 45; 144 A.L.R. 1298 HL 6–28
Figgis, Re; sub nom. Roberts v MacLaren [1969] 1 Ch. 123; [1968] 2 W.L.R. 1173; [1968] 1 All E.R. 999; (1968) 112 S.J. 156 4–09
Financings Ltd v Baldock [1963] 2 Q.B. 104; [1963] 2 W.L.R. 359; [1963] 1 All E.R. 443; (1963) 107 S.J. 15 CA 3–33
Fire Nymph Products Ltd v Heating Centre Pty Ltd (1992) 7 A.C.S.R. 365 3–61
First Mutual Life Assurance v Muzivi (HH 4-20, HC 10027/19) [2020] ZWHHC 4 6–13
First National Bank of Chicago v Customs and Excise Commissioners (C–172/96); sub nom. Customs and Excise Commissioners v First National Bank of Chicago (C–172/96) [1999] Q.B. 570; [1999] 2 W.L.R. 230; [1998] All E.R. (EC) 744; [1998] S.T.C. 850; [1998] E.C.R. I–4387; [1998] 3 C.M.L.R. 353; [1998] C.E.C. 896; [1998] B.T.C. 5332; [1998] B.V.C. 389 ECJ 1–03, 1–04
First Personnel Services Ltd v Halfords Ltd [2016] EWHC 3220 (Ch) [2016] EWHC 3220 (Ch) 3–31
First Sport Ltd v Barclays Bank Plc [1993] 1 W.L.R. 1229; [1993] 3 All E.R. 789; (1993) 12 Tr. L.R. 69 CA (Civ Div) 5–30
Fitzpatrick v Sarcon (No 177) Ltd [2012] NICA 58; 2014] N.I. 35 4–24
FJ Chalke Ltd v Revenue and Customs Commissioners [2009] EWHC 952 (Ch) 4–56
Foakes v Beer; sub nom. Beer v Foakes (1883–84) L.R. 9 App. Cas. 605 HL 3–17
Foley v Hill (1848) 2 H.L. Cas. 28 9 E.R. 1002; [1843–1860] All E.R. Rep. 16 HL 1–03, 5–36, 5–48
Folias, The. *See* Owners of the Eleftherotria v Owners of the Despina R
Forney v Bushe [1954] C.L.Y. 3183 3–13
Fortis Bank SA/NV v Indian Overseas Bank [2011] EWCA Civ 58; [2011] 2 All E.R. (Comm) 288; [2012] Bus. L.R. 141; [2011] 2 Lloyd's Rep. 33; [2011] 1 C.L.C. 276 3–15
Fortman Holdings Ltd v Modem Holdings Ltd [2001] EWCA Civ 1235 4–34
Foster v Driscoll [1929] 1 K.B. 470 CA 3–25
Four-maids Ltd v Dudley Marshall (Properties) Ltd [1957] Ch. 317; [1957] 2 W.L.R. 931; [1957] 2 All E.R. 35; (1957) 101 S.J. 408 3–73
Foxholes Nursing Home Ltd v Accora Ltd [2013] EWHC 3712 (Ch) 3–11, 3–15
Francis v Vista del Mar Development Ltd [2019] UKPC 14 4–15
G & T Earle Ltd v Hemsworth RDC (1928) 140 L.T. 69 2–38
GA Investments Pty Ltd v Standard Insurance Co Ltd [1964] W.A.R. 264 4–18
Gallacher v Emerald Law Unreported, 15 January 2019 QBD 3–13
Gamerco SA v ICM/Fair Warning (Agency) Ltd [1995] 1 W.L.R. 1226; [1995] C.L.C. 536; [1995] E.M.L.R. 263 6–28
Garden City, The. *See* Polish Steamship Co v Atlantic Maritime Co
Gardener Steel v Sheffield Brothers (Profiles) [1978] 1 W.L.R. 916; [1978] 3 All E.R. 399; (1978) 122 S.J. 488, 4–60
Garfitt v Allen; Allen v Longstaffe (1887) L.R. 37 Ch. D. 48; 57 LJ Ch 420; 36 WR 413; 57 LT 848 3–73
Gator Shipping Corp v Trans-Asiatic Oil SA (The Odenfeld) [1978] 2 Lloyd's Rep. 357 3–21
General Trading Co (Holdings) Ltd v Richmond Corp Ltd [2008] EWHC 1479 (Comm); [2008] 2 Lloyd's Rep. 475 2–17
George Veflings Rederi A/S v President of India (The Bellami); Monrovia Tramp Shipping Co v President of India (The Pearl Merchant); Marperfecta Compania Naviera SA v President of India (The Doric Chariot) [1979] 1 W.L.R. 59; [1979] 1 All E.R. 380; [1979] 1 Lloyd's Rep. 123; (1978) 122 S.J. 843 CA (Civ Div) 6–37
Georgios C, The. *See* Empresa Cubana de Fletes v Lagonisi Shipping Co Ltd

Gesellschaft bürgerlichen Rechts v Stockholms Rederi AB Svea (The Brabant); sub nom.
Gesellschaft bürgerlichen Rechts v Stockholms Rederiaktiebolag Svea, (SS Brabant)
[1967] 1 Q.B. 588; [1966] 2 W.L.R. 909; [1966] 1 All E.R. 961; [1965] 2 Lloyd's Rep.
546; (1966) 110 S.J. 265 QBD 4–21
Get Nominees Ltd v Trinity Welsh Homes Ltd [2015] EWHC 4737; [2009] 1 W.L.R. 940;
[2009] 2 P. & C.R. 5; [2008] 3 E.G.L.R. 143 4–29
Geys v Societe Generale [2012] UKSC 63; [2013] 1 A.C. 523; [2013] 2 W.L.R. 50; [2013] 1
All E.R. 1061; [2013] I.C.R. 117; [2013] I.R.L.R. 122 .... 3–19, 3–22
GHL Pte Ltd v Unitrack Building Construction Pte Ltd [1999] 3 S.L.R. 44 3–50
Gift Bob David Samanyau v Fleximail (Pvt) Ltd 2011 HH 108-11 6–13
Gilbert Ash (Northern) Ltd v Modern Engineering (Bristol) Ltd [1974] A.C. 689; [1973] 3
W.L.R. 421; [1973] 3 All E.R. 195; 1 B.L.R. 73; 72 L.G.R. 1; (1973) 117 S.J. 745
HL 2–07
Gill v Heer Manak Solicitors [2018] EWHC 2881 (QB); [2018] 5 Costs L.R. 1165; [2019]
P.N.L.R. 10 3–13
GKN Contractors Ltd v Lloyds Bank Plc, 30 B.L.R. 48 CA (Civ Div) 3–44
Global Trader Europe Ltd (In Liquidation), Re [2009] EWHC 602 (Ch); [2009] 2 B.C.L.C.
18; [2009] B.P.I.R. 446 5–36
Glory Wealth Shipping Pte Ltd v North China Shipping Ltd (The North Prince) [2010]
EWHC 1692 4–03
Golden Strait Corp v Nippon Yusen Kubishika Kaisha (The Golden Victory) [2007] UKHL
12; [2007] 2 A.C. 353; [2007] Bus. L.R. 997; [2007] 2 W.L.R. 691; [2007] 3 All E.R. 1;
[2007] 2 All E.R. (Comm) 97; [2007] 2 Lloyd's Rep. 164; [2007] 1 C.L.C. 352; (2007)
157 N.L.J. 518; (2007) 151 S.J.L.B. 468 HL 6–08, 6–39, 6–44
Golden Victory, The. See Golden Strait Corp v Nippon Yusen Kubishika Kaisha
Goulston Discount Co v Harman (1962) 106 S.J. 369 CA 3–29
Grace v Black Horse Ltd [2014] EWCA Civ 1413; [2015] 3 All E.R. 223; [2015] 2 All E.R.
(Comm) 465; [2015] Bus. L.R. 1; [2015] E.C.C. 23; [2014] C.T.L.C. 312 3–37
Graham v Pitkin [1992] 1 W.L.R. 403; [1992] 2 All E.R. 235; (1992) 64 P. & C.R. 522;
(1992) 136 S.J.L.B. 97; [1992] N.P.C. 37 PC 4–31
Graiseley Properties Ltd v Barclays Bank Plc. See Deutsche Bank AG v Unitech Global Ltd
Granor Finance v Liquidator of Eastore, 1974 S.L.T. 296 OH 3–29
Granton Advertising BV v Inspecteur van de Belastingdienst Haaglanden/kantoor Den Haag
(C-461/12) [2014] S.T.C. 2375; [2014] B.V.C. 31; [2014] S.T.I. 2113 1–05
Green v Sevin (1879–80) L.R. 13 Ch. D. 589 .... 4–24, 4–31
Green Deal Marketing Southern Ltd v Economy Energy Trading Ltd [2019] EWHC 507
(Ch); [2019] 2 All E.R. (Comm) 191; [2019] 1 C.L.C. 522 4–35
Griffith v Ystradyfodwg School Board (1890) L.R. 24 Q.B.D. 307 2–17
Griffiths, Re [2004] FCAFC 102 6–33
Group Josi Re Co SA v Walbrook Insurance Co Ltd, Deutsche Ruckversicherung AG v
Walbrook Insurance Co Ltd; sub nom. Group Josi Re (formerly Group Josi Reassurance
SA) v Walbrook Insurance Co Ltd [1995] 1 W.L.R. 1017; [1994] 4 All E.R. 181; [1995]
1 Lloyd's Rep. 153; [1994] C.L.C. 415; (1994) 91(25) L.S.G. 30; (1994) 138 S.J.L.B.
111 QBD 3–45
Grupo Hotelero Urvasco v Carey Value Added SL [2013] EWHC 1039 (Comm); [2013]
Bus. L.R. D45 3–64
Guinness Mahon & Co Ltd v Kensington and Chelsea RLBC [1999] Q.B. 215; [1998] 3
W.L.R. 829; [1998] 2 All E.R. 272; [1998] Lloyd's Rep. Bank. 109; [1998] C.L.C. 662;
(1998) 95(13) L.S.G. 28; (1998) 148 N.L.J. 366; (1998) 142 S.J.L.B. 92 CA (Civ
Div) 3–81
Gwyn v Godby, 128 E.R. 363; (1812) 4 Taunt. 346 CCP 4–40
H Dakin & Co v Lee; sub nom. Dakin & Co v Lee [1916] 1 K.B. 566 CA 3–15
Habib Bank Ltd v Tailor [1982] 1 W.L.R. 1218; [1982] 3 All E.R. 561; (1982) 44 P. & C.R.
365; (1982) 126 S.J. 448 CA (Civ Div) 4–11
Hadley v Baxendale, 156 E.R. 145; (1854) 9 Ex. 341 .... 4–55, 4–56, 6–34,
6–38, 6–44
Hall v Royal Bank of Scotland Plc [2009] EWHC 3163 4–21
Hamzeh Malas & Sons v British Imex Industries Ltd [1958] 2 Q.B. 127; [1958] 2 W.L.R.
100; [1958] 1 All E.R. 262; [1957] 2 Lloyd's Rep. 549; (1958) 102 S.J. 68
CA 2–45, 3–44

Hanoman v Southwark LBC [2009] UKHL 29; [2009] 1 W.L.R. 1367; [2009] 4 All E.R.
  585; [2009] P.T.S.R. 1059; [2010] H.L.R. 5; [2009] 24 E.G. 84 (C.S.); [2009] N.P.C. 74;
  [2009] 2 P. & C.R. DG14 2–16
Hardy v Griffiths [2014] EWHC 3947 (Ch); [2015] Ch. 417; [2015] 2 W.L.R. 1239; [2015]
  1 P. & C.R. 16 4–29
Hare v Nicoll; sub nom. Hare v Nichol [1966] 2 Q.B. 130; [1966] 2 W.L.R. 441; [1966] 1
  All E.R. 285; (1966) 110 S.J. 11 CA 4–29, 4–30
Harlequin Property (SVG) Ltd v Wilkins Kennedy [2016] EWHC 3188 (TCC); [2017] 4
  W.L.R. 30; 170 Con. L.R. 86 . . . . 6–32, 6–38
Harlequin Property (SVG) Ltd v Wilkins Kennedy [2016] EWHC 3233 (TCC); [2016] 6
  Costs L.R. 1201 . . . . 6–32, 6–38
Harmony & Montague Tin and Copper Mining Co, Re; sub nom. Spargo's Case (1872–73)
  L.R. 8 Ch. App. 407; [1861–73] All E.R. Rep. 261 . . . . 2–03, 2–05
Harrison v Black Horse Ltd [2011] EWCA Civ 1128; [2012] E.C.C. 7; [2012] Lloyd's Rep.
  I.R. 521; [2011] C.T.L.C. 105; (2011) 155(39) S.J.L.B. 31 3–37
Hartley v Hymans [1920] 3 K.B. 475; 90 LJKB 14; Com Cas 365; [1920] All E.R. Rep.
  328; 124 LT 31; v 36 T.L.R. 805 4–27
Hartley v King Edward VI College [2017] UKSC 39; [2017] 4 All E.R. 637; [2017] I.C.R.
  774; [2017] I.R.L.R. 763; [2017] E.L.R. 39 3–13
Haugland Tankers AS v RMK Marine Gemi Yapim Sanayii ve Deniz Tasimaciligi Isletmesi
  AS [2005] EWHC 321 (Comm); [2005] 1 All E.R. (Comm) 679; [2005] 1 Lloyd's Rep.
  573; [2005] 1 C.L.C. 271 4–30
Hausler v J P Morgan Chase NA 12-1264(L) 5–46
Hawkes v Salter, 130 E.R. 944; (1828) 4 Bing. 715 4–07
Hayfin Opal Luxco 3 SARL v Windermere VII CMBS Plc [2016] EWHC 782 (Ch); [2018]
  1 B.C.L.C. 118 . . . . 3–31, 4–52
Hazell v Hammersmith and Fulham LBC [1992] 2 A.C. 1; [1991] 2 W.L.R. 372; [1991] 1
  All E.R. 545; 89 L.G.R. 271; (1991) 3 Admin. L.R. 549; [1991] R.V.R. 28; (1991) 155
  J.P.N. 527; (1991) 155 L.G. Rev. 527; (1991) 88(8) L.S.G. 36; (1991) 141 N.L.J. 127
  HL 3–82
Hazlewood Grocery Ltd v Lion Foods Ltd [2007] EWHC 1887 (QB); [2007] All E.R. (D)
  433 3–15
HB Haina Associates Inc, Re (1978) D.L.R. (2d) 262 2–23
HDK Ltd (t/a Unique Home) v Sunshine Ventures Ltd [2009] EWHC 2866
  (QB) 4–31
Helbert Wagg's Claim. *See* Claim by Helbert Wagg & Co Ltd, Re
Helmsing Schiffahrts GmbH v Malta Drydocks Corp [1977] 2 Lloyd's Rep.
  444 6–49
Henderson & Keay Ltd v AM Carmichael Ltd, 1956 S.L.T. (Notes) 58 OH 4–22
Hepworth v Owners of the Medina Princess (The Medina Princess) [1962] 2 Lloyd's Rep.
  17; (1962) 106 S.J. 573 4–60
HJ Symons & Co v Barclays Bank Plc [2003] EWHC 1249 (Comm) 5–29
Hobson Street v Honey Bees Preschool [2019] NZCA 122 3–34
Hoenig v Isaacs [1952] 2 All E.R. 176; [1952] 1 T.L.R. 1360 CA 3–15
Hoffman v Sofaer [1982] 1 W.L.R. 1350; (1982) 79 L.S.G. 1291 QBD 6–32
Holyoake v Candy [2017] EWHC 3397 (Ch) 3–29, 3–32, 3–37
Homes v Smith [2000] Lloyd's Rep. Bank. 139 CA (Civ Div) 2–25, 5–27, 5–28
Honam Jade, The. *See* Phibro Energy AG v Nissho Iwai Corp
Hone (A Bankrupt), Re; sub nom. Trustee Ex p. v Kensington BC [1951] Ch. 85; [1950] 2
  All E.R. 716; 66 T.L.R. (Pt 2) 350; (1950) 114 J.P. 495; 43 R. & I.T. 608 . . . . 2–25, 5–27
Hong Kong and Shanghai Banking Corp v Kloeckner & Co AG [1990] 2 Q.B. 514; [1990] 3
  W.L.R. 634; [1989] 3 All E.R. 513; [1989] 2 Lloyd's Rep 323 3–48
Hong Kong Society for Rehabilitation v Cadia Ho [2003] HKCFI 752 4–29
Hongkong Fir Shipping Co Ltd v Kawasaki Kisen Kaisha Ltd (The Hongkong Fir) [1962] 2
  Q.B. 26; [1962] 2 W.L.R. 474; [1962] 1 All E.R. 474; [1961] 2 Lloyd's Rep. 478; (1961)
  106 S.J. 35 4–35
Horsham Properties Group Ltd v Clark [2008] EWHC 2327 (Ch); [2009] 1 W.L.R. 1255;
  [2009] 1 All E.R. (Comm) 745; [2009] 1 P. & C.R. 8; [2008] 3 E.G.L.R. 75; [2008] 47
  E.G. 114; [2008] 41 E.G. 156 (C.S.); (2008) 158 N.L.J. 1458; [2008] N.P.C.
  107 3–73

Howard-Jones v Tate [2011] EWCA Civ 1330; [2012] 2 All E.R. 369; [2012] 1 All E.R.
  (Comm) 1136; [2012] 1 P. & C.R. 11; [2011] N.P.C. 121; [2012] Bus. L.R.
  D89 4–24
Howe Richardson Scale Co v Polimex-Cekop [1978] 1 Lloyd's Rep. 161 CA (Civ
  Div) 2–45
Hudson Bay Apparel Brands LLC v Umbro International Ltd [2009] EWHC 2861 (Ch);
  [2010] E.T.M.R. 15 2–17
Hughes v Lenny, 151 E.R. 79; (1839) 5 M. & W. 183 Exchr 4–23
Hughes v Pump House Hotel Co Ltd (No.1) [1902] 2 K.B. 190 CA 2–38
Hungerfords v Walker (1989) 171 C.L.R. 125 4–56
Hunt v RM Douglas (Roofing) Ltd [1990] 1 A.C. 398; [1988] 3 W.L.R. 975; [1988] 3 All
  E.R. 823; [1997] Costs L.R. (Core Vol.) 136; (1989) 86(1) L.S.G. 40; (1988) 138 N.L.J.
  Rep. 324; (1988) 132 S.J. 1592 HL 4–61
Huntington v Attrill; sub nom. Huntingdon v Attrill [1893] A.C. 150 PC
  (Can)...5–48
Hyundai Heavy Industries Co Ltd v Papadopoulos [1980] 1 W.L.R. 1129; [1980] 2 All E.R.
  29; [1980] 2 Lloyd's Rep. 1; (1980) 124 S.J. 592 HL......................2–43
Ibrahim v Barclays Bank Plc [2012] EWCA Civ 640; [2013] Ch. 400; [2013] 2 W.L.R. 768;
  [2012] 4 All E.R. 160; [2012] 2 All E.R. (Comm) 1167; [2012] 2 Lloyd's Rep. 13;
  [2012] 2 B.C.L.C. 1; [2012] 2 C.L.C. 240 2–29
ICICI Bank UK Plc v Assam Oil Co Ltd [2019] EWHC 750 (Comm) 4–52
IE Contractors Ltd v Lloyds Bank Plc; IE Contractors Ltd v Rafidain Bank [1990] 2 Lloyd's
  Rep. 496; (1990) 51 B.L.R. 5 CA (Civ Div)................................3–41
IIG Capital LLC v Van der Merwe [2008] EWCA Civ 542; [2008] 2 All E.R. (Comm) 1173;
  [2008] 2 Lloyd's Rep. 187 ....3–42, 4–48
IM Properties Plc v Cape & Dalgleish [1999] Q.B. 297; [1998] 3 W.L.R. 457; [1998] 3 All
  E.R. 203; (1998) 95(24) L.S.G. 34; (1998) 95(31) L.S.G. 34; (1998) 148 N.L.J. 906;
  (1998) 142 S.J.L.B. 174 CA (Civ Div) 4–60
Independent Trustee Services Ltd v GP Noble Trustees Ltd [2012] EWCA Civ 195; [2013]
  Ch. 91; [2012] 3 W.L.R. 597; [2012] 3 All E.R. 210; [2012] 3 F.C.R. 1; [2012] W.T.L.R.
  1171 1–08
India v Taylor; sub nom. Delhi Electric Supply & Traction Co Ltd, Re [1955] A.C. 491;
  [1955] 2 W.L.R. 303; [1955] 1 All E.R. 292; 48 R. & I.T. 98; (1955) 34 A.T.C. 10;
  [1955] T.R. 9; (1955) 99 S.J. 94 HL 5–48
Indrisie v General Credit [1985] V.R. 251 SC (Victoria) 3–48
Industries Perron Inc v R [2013] FCA 176 Federal Court of Appeal (Canada) ..2–37
International Minerals & Chemical Corp v Karl O Helm AG [1986] 1 Lloyd's Rep.
  81 6–444
Investment Trust Companies (In Liquidation) v Revenue and Customs Commissioners
  [2012] EWHC 458 (Ch); [2012] S.T.C. 1150; [2012] Eu. L.R. 470; [2012] B.V.C. 109;
  [2012] S.T.I. 1373; [2013] S.T.I. 1488 2–03
Ipsos SA v Dentsu Aegis Network Ltd (formerly Aegis Group Plc) [2015] EWHC 1726
  (Comm) 3–64
Isaac Naylor & Sons Ltd v New Zealand Co-operative Wool Marketing Association Ltd
  [1981] 1 N.Z.L.R. 361 6–44
Isaacs v Royal Insurance Co (1869-70) L.R. 5 Ex. 296 Exchr 4–166
Isabella Shipowner SA v Shagang Shipping Co Ltd (The Aquafaith) [2012] EWHC 1077
  (Comm) 3–20, 3–21
Ispahani v Bank Melli Iran [1998] Lloyd's Rep. Bank. 133, CA (Civ Div); (1997) Times,
  December 29 ....3–25, 6–25
Jacobs Marcus & Co v Credit Lyonnais (1883–84) L.R. 12 Q.B.D. 589 CA 6–27
JD Brian Ltd (In Liquidation), Re [2015] IESC 62 3–61
Jeancharm Ltd (t/a Beaver International) v Barnet Football Club Ltd [2003] EWCA Civ 58;
  92 Con. L.R. 26 CA (Civ Div) 3–31
John Wilkins (Motor Engineers) Ltd v Revenue and Customs Commissioners [2010] EWCA
  Civ 923 4–56
Johnson v Agnew [1980] A.C. 367; [1979] 2 W.L.R. 487; [1979] 1 All E.R. 883; (1979) 38
  P. & C.R. 424; (1979) 251 E.G. 1167; (1979) 123 S.J. 217 HL 4–24, 6–39, 6–44
Johnson v King, The [1904] A.C. 817 PC (Sierra Leone) 4–55

Johnson v Unisys Ltd [2001] UKHL 13; [2003] 1 A.C. 518; [2001] 2 W.L.R. 1076; [2001] 2
  All E.R. 801; [2001] I.C.R. 480; [2001] I.R.L.R. 279; [2001] Emp. L.R.
  469 3–22
Jones v Arthur (1840) 8 Dowl. 442; 4 Jur 859 2–32
Jones v Churcher [2009] EWHC 722 (QB); [2009] 2 Lloyd's Rep. 94 ....2–29, 3–82
Jotunheim, The. *See* More OG Romsdal Fylkesbatar AS v Demise Charterers of the
  Jotunheim
JSC BTA Bank v Ablyazov (Granton Action) [2013] EWHC 867 (Comm) 4–56
K v A [2019] EWHC 1118 (Comm); [2020] 1 Lloyd's Rep. 28 ....1–08, 2–23, 2–32,
  5–37, 5–51, 5–53
Kaupthing Singer & Friedlander v UBS AG [2016] EWCA Civ 319 ....2–30, 5–26
Kaur (Pritam) v S Russell & Sons Ltd [1973] Q.B. 336; [1973] 2 W.L.R. 147; [1973] 1 All
  E.R. 617; (1972) 117 S.J. 91 CA (Civ Div) 4–05
Kayford Ltd (In Liquidation), Re [1975] 1 W.L.R. 279; [1975] 1 All E.R. 604; (1974) 118
  S.J. 752 2–23
Keighley Maxsted & Co v Durant (t/a Bryan Durant & Co); sub nom. Durant & Co v
  Roberts [1901] A.C. 240; 70 LJKB 662 HL 5–51
Kelly v Sovereign Leasing [1995] C.L.Y. 720 3–33
Kerr's Policy, Re (1869) L.R. 8 Eq. 331 4–58
Ketley v Scott [1981] I.C.R. 241 3–38
Kiely & Sons v Medcraft (1965) 109 S.J. 829 CA 3–15
Kinetics Technology International SpA v Cross Seas Shipping Corp (The Mosconici) [2001]
  2 Lloyd's Rep. 313 6–40
Kitchen v HSBC Bank Plc [2000] 1 All E.R. (Comm) 787; [2000] Lloyd's Rep. Bank. 173
  CA (Civ Div) 4–42
Kleinwort Benson Ltd v Lincoln City Council; Kleinwort Benson Ltd v Birmingham City
  Council; Kleinwort Benson Ltd v Southwark LBC; Kleinwort Benson Ltd v Kensington
  and Chelsea RLBC [1999] 2 A.C. 349; [1998] 3 W.L.R. 1095; [1998] 4 All E.R. 513;
  [1998] Lloyd's Rep. Bank. 387; [1999] C.L.C. 332; (1999) 1 L.G.L.R. 148; (1999) 11
  Admin. L.R. 130; [1998] R.V.R. 315; (1998) 148 N.L.J. 1674; (1998) 142 S.J.L.B. 279;
  [1998] N.P.C. 145, HL 3–82
Kleinwort Sons & Co v Ungarische Baumwolle Industrie AG [1939] 2 K.B. 678; [1939] 3
  All E.R. 38 CA 3–25
Knightsbridge Estates Trust Ltd v Byrne [1940] A.C. 613; [1940] 2 All E.R. 401
  HL 4–19, 4–20
Knox v Lee; Parker v Davies (1970) 12 Wall (79) U.S. 457 SC (US) 3–02
Koch Marine Inc v d'Amica Societa di Navigazione arl (The Elena d'Amico) [1980] 1
  Lloyd's Rep. 75 4–03
Kornatzki v Oppenheimer [1937] 4 All E.R. 133 6–12
Kuwait Rocks Co v AMN Bulkcarriers Inc (The Astra) [2013] EWHC 865; [2013] 2 All
  E.R. (Comm) 689; [2013] 2 Lloyd's Rep. 69; [2013] 1 C.L.C. 819 ....4–13, 4–24, 4–26,
  4–27, 4–28, 4–35
Kvaerner Singapore Pte Ltd v UDL Shipbuilding (Singapore) Pte Ltd [1993] 3 S.L.R.
  350 3–45
L Schuler AG v Wickman Machine Tool Sales Ltd; sub nom. Wickman Machine Tool Sales
  Ltd v L Schuler AG [1974] A.C. 235; [1973] 2 W.L.R. 683; [1973] 2 All E.R. 39; [1973]
  2 Lloyd's Rep. 53; (1973) 117 S.J. 340 HL 4–35
La Pintada, The. *See* President of India v La Pintada Compania Navigacion SA
Laconia, The. *See* Mardorf Peach & Co Ltd v Attica Sea Carriers Corp of Liberia
Lady Navigation Inc v LauritzenCool AB. *See* LauritzenCool AB v Lady Navigation Inc
Lamesa Investments Ltd v Cynergy Bank Ltd [2020] EWCA Civ 821 5–46
Lampert v Lloyds Bank Plc [1998] All E.R. (D) 627 CA (Civ Div) 4–21
Lancashire Waggon Co Ltd v Nuttall (1879) 42 L.T. 465; 44 J.P. 536 CA 4–18
Lancore Services Ltd v Barclays Bank Plc [2008] EWHC 1264 (Ch); [2008] 1 C.L.C.
  1039 4–04
LauritzenCool AB v Lady Navigation Inc; sub nom. Lady Navigation Inc v LauritzenCool
  AB [2005] EWCA Civ 579; [2005] 1 W.L.R. 3686; [2006] 1 All E.R. 866; [2005] 2 All
  E.R. (Comm) 183; [2005] 2 Lloyd's Rep. 63; [2005] 1 C.L.C. 758 CA (Civ
  Div) 3–84
Law Debenture Trust Corporation plc v Ukraine. *See* Ukraine v Law Debenture Trust Corp
  Plc

Law Society v Blavo; sub nom. Blavo v Law Society [2018] EWCA Civ 2250; [2019] 1
W.L.R. 1977; [2018] B.P.I.R. 1704 4–11
Laycock v Pickles (1863) 4 B. & S. 497 2–03
Le Puy Ltd v Potter [2015] EWHC 193 (QB); [2015] I.R.L.R. 554 3–19
Leeds City Council v Waco UK Ltd [2015] EWHC 1400 (TCC); [2015] T.C.L.R. 5; 160
Con. L.R. 58; [2015] C.I.L.L. 3682 4–32
Lehman Bros Holdings Inc v Metavante Case No.08-13555 (JMP), Bankr SDNY, September
15, 2009 3–55
Lehman Brothers International (Europe) (In Administration), Re, Lehman Brothers Ltd (In
Administration), Re, LB Holdings Intermediate 2 Ltd (In Administration), Re; sub nom.
Joint Administrators of LB Holdings Intermediate 2 Ltd (In Administration) v Lomas
[2017] UKSC 38; [2018] A.C. 465; [2017] 2 W.L.R. 1497; [2018] 1 All E.R. 205; [2018]
1 All E.R. (Comm) 629; [2017] B.C.C. 235; [2017] 2 B.C.L.C. 149 .... 4–62, 6–33
Lennon v Napper (1802) 2 Sch. & Lef. 682 4–26
Leonidas, The. *See* Bayoil SA v Seawind Tankers Corp
Les Labaratoires Servier v Apotex Inc [2008] EWHC 3289 (Pat); (2009) 32(3) I.P.D.
3202 6–49
Lesotho Highlands Development Authority v Impregilo SpA [2005] UKHL 43; [2006] 1
A.C. 221; [2005] 3 W.L.R. 129; [2005] 3 All E.R. 789; [2005] 2 All E.R. (Comm) 265;
[2005] 2 Lloyd's Rep. 310; [2005] 2 C.L.C. 1; [2005] B.L.R. 351; 101 Con. L.R. 1;
[2005] 27 E.G. 220 (C.S.); (2005) 155 N.L.J. 1046 6–39
Libyan Arab Foreign Bank v Bankers Trust Co [1989] Q.B. 728; [1989] 3 W.L.R. 314;
[1989] 3 All E.R. 252; [1988] 1 Lloyd's Rep. 259; [1987] 2 F.T.L.R. 509; (1989) 133
S.J. 568 .... 1–02, 1–10, 2–01,
2–32, 5–27, 5–45, 5–46, 5–48, 5–49,
5–53, 6–19, 6–20, 6–26
Libyan Arab Foreign Bank v Manufacturers Hanover Trust (No.2) [1989] 1 Lloyd's Rep.
608 QBD 5–46
Libyan Investment Authority v Goldman Sachs International [2016] EWHC 2530
(Ch) 3–36
Liddle v Cree [2011] EWHC 3294 (Ch) 3–36
Lilly Icos LLC v 8PM Chemists Ltd [2009] EWHC 1905 (Ch) 6–25
Lines Bros (In Liquidation), Re [1983] Ch. 1; [1982] 2 W.L.R. 1010; [1982] 2 All E.R. 183;
[1982] Com. L.R. 81; (1982) 126 S.J. 197 CA (Civ Div) 6–33
Lipkin Gorman v Karpnale Ltd [1991] 2 A.C. 548; [1991] 3 W.L.R. 10; [1992] 4 All E.R.
512; (1991) 88(26) L.S.G. 31; (1991) 141 N.L.J. 815; (1991) 135 S.J.L.B. 36
HL 3–82
Lips, The. *See* President of India v Lips Maritime Corp
Littlewoods Retail Ltd v Revenue and Customs Commissioners [2017] UKSC 70; [2018]
A.C. 869; [2017] 3 W.L.R. 1401; [2018] 1 All E.R. 83; [2017] S.T.C. 2413; [2017]
B.V.C. 54; [2017] S.T.I. 2238 .... 4–56, 4–59
Lloyds Bank Ltd v Margolis [1954] 1 W.L.R. 644; [1954] 1 All E.R. 734; (1954) 98 S.J.
250 4–11
Lloyds Bank Plc v Independent Insurance Co Ltd [2000] Q.B. 110; [1999] 2 W.L.R. 986;
[1999] 1 All E.R. (Comm.) 8; [1999] Lloyd's Rep. Bank. 1; [1999] C.L.C. 510; (1999)
96(3) L.S.G. 31 CA (Civ Div) 1–08, 3–82
Lloyds Bank Plc v Lampert [1999] 1 All E.R. (Comm.) 161; [1999] Lloyd's Rep. Bank.
138; [1999] B.C.C. 507 CA (Civ Div) 4–21
Lloyds Bank Plc v Voller; sub nom. Voller v Lloyds Bank Plc [2000] 2 All E.R. (Comm)
978; [2001] Lloyd's Rep. Bank. 67 CA (Civ Div) 4–39
Lomas v JFB Firth Rixson Inc, Britannia Bulk Plc (In Liquidation) v Bulk Trading SA,
Lehman Brothers Special Financing Inc v Carlton Communications Ltd, Pioneer Freight
Futures Co Ltd (In Liquidation) v Cosco Bulk Carrier Co Ltd [2012] EWCA Civ 419;
[2012] 2 All E.R. (Comm) 1076; [2012] 2 Lloyd's Rep. 548; [2013] 1 B.C.L.C. 27;
[2012] 1 C.L.C. 713 .... 2–15, 3–54, 3–55,
3–56, 3–57
Lombard North Central Plc v Blower [2014] EWHC 2267 (Ch); [2014] I.L.Pr. 46; [2014]
B.P.I.R. 1501 4–11
Lombard North Central Plc v Brooks [1999] B.P.I.R. 701 Ch D 3–29

Lombard North Central Plc v Butterworth [1987] Q.B. 527; [1987] 2 W.L.R. 7; [1987] 1 All
  E.R. 267; (1987) 6 Tr. L.R. 65; (1986) 83 L.S.G. 2750 CA (Civ Div) 3–33, 4–25, 4–27,
  4–28, 4–35
Lombard Tricity Finance v Paton [1989] 1 All E.R. 918; (1989) 8 Tr. L.R. 129; (1988) 138
  N.L.J. Rep. 333 CA (Civ Div). 4–43
London Chatham & Dover Railway Co v South Eastern Railway Co [1893] A.C. 429
  HL 4–39, 4–55, 4–56,
  5–59, 6–44
London Scottish Finance Ltd (In Administration), Re; sub no. Jack v Craig [2014] Bus. L.R.
  424; [2013] C.T.L.C. 231 3–37
Lonsdale v National Westminster Bank Plc [2018] EWHC 1843 (QB); [2019] Lloyd's Rep.
  F.C. 94 5–42
Lordsvale Finance Plc v Bank of Zambia [1996] Q.B. 752; [1996] 3 W.L.R. 688; [1996] 3
  All E.R. 156; [1996] C.L.C. 1849 . . . . 3–30, 3–31, 4–51,
  4–52
Louinder v Leis (1982) 149 C.L.R. 509; (1982) 56 A.L.J.R. 433 4–31
Luck v White (1973) 26 P. & C.R. 89; (1973) 117 S.J. 486 4–32
Ludgater Holdings Ltd v Gerling Australia Co Pty Ltd [2010] NZSC 49 SC (New
  Zealand) 5–48
Lumley v Simmons (1887) L.R. 34 Ch. D. 698, CA; 56 LJ Ch 329; 35 WR 422; 56 LT
  134 3–59
Lutetian, The. *See* Tradax Export SA v Dorada Compania Naviera SA of Panama
Luttenberger v North Thoresby Farms Ltd [1993] 1 E.G.L.R. 3; [1993] 17 E.G.
  102 2–01
Mackay v Dick (1880–81) L.R. 6 App. Cas. 251, HL; 29 WR 541; 18 S.L.R. 387
  HL 2–17
Mackenzie v Kentcade Properties Pty Ltd [2012] QSC 299 SC (Queensland) 4–12
Maclaine v Gatty; sub nom. Gatty v Maclaine [1921] 1 A. C. 376; 1921 S.C. (H.L.) 1;
  (1921) 1 S.L.T.51 HL 4–13
Madhatter Mining Co ltd v Tapfuma [2014] ZWSC 51 6–13
Magdeev v Tsvetkov [2020] EWHC 887 (Comm) 2–17
Magellan Spirit ApS v Vital SA, Magellan Spirit, The [2016] EWHC 454 (Comm) [2017] 1
  All E.R. (Comm) 241; [2016] 2 Lloyd's Rep. 1; [2016] 1 C.L.C. 480 5–51
Mahoney v Furches 468 A.2d 458 4–18
Mahonia Ltd v JP Morgan Chase Bank (No.1) [2003] EWHC 1927 (Comm); [2003] 2
  Lloyd's Rep. 911 . . . . 3–45, 3–47
Mahonia Ltd v JP Morgan Chase Bank (No.2); Mahonia Ltd v West LB AG [2004] EWHC
  1938 (Comm) 3–25
Mahonia Ltd v West LB AG. *See* Mahonia Ltd v JP Morgan Chase Bank (No.2)
Makdessi v Cavendish Square Holding BV. *See* Cavendish Square Holding BV v Makdessi
Makoni v Sea Harvest (Ref SC 19/08) [2015] ZWHHC 197 6–13
Manchester Ship Canal Co Ltd v Vauxhall Motors UK Ltd (formerly General Motors UK
  Ltd); sub nom. Vauxhall Motors Ltd (formerly General Motors UK Ltd) v Manchester
  Ship Canal Co Ltd [2019] UKSC 46; [2019] 3 W.L.R. 852; [2020] 2 All E.R.
  81 . . . . 3–84, 4–04
Mandarin Container Re [2004] HKLRD 554; [2004] HKEC 1355; 2004 WL
  2371009. . . . . 3–31, 4–52
Manners v Pearson & Son [1898] 1 Ch. 581, CA; 67 LJ Ch. 304, 46 WR 498; [1895–1899]
  All E.R. Rep. 415; 42 S.J. 413; 78 LT 432; 14 T.L.R. 312 6–30
Manorlike Ltd v Le Vitas Travel Agency and Consultative Services [1986] 1 All E.R. 573;
  [1986] 1 E.G.L.R. 79; (1986) 278 E.G. 412 CA (Civ Div). 4–14
Manurewa Transport Ltd, Re [1971] N.Z.L.R. 909 3–61
Maratha Envoy, The. *See* Federal Commerce & Navigation Co Ltd v Tradax Export SA
Mardorf Peach & Co Ltd v Attica Sea Carriers Corp of Liberia (The Laconia), Laconia, The
  [1977] A.C. 850; [1977] 2 W.L.R. 286; [1977] 1 All E.R. 545; [1977] 1 Lloyd's Rep.
  315; (1977) 121 S.J. 134 HL 2–28, 4–05, 4–13,
  4–28, 5–26, 5–44, 6–19
Marine Trade SA v Pioneer Freight Futures Co Ltd BVI [2009] EWHC 2656 (Comm);
  [2010] 1 Lloyd's Rep. 631; [2009] 2 C.L.C. 657 . . . . 3–54, 3–56
Marme Inversiones 2007 SL v NatWest Markets plc [2019] EWHC 366
  (Comm) 4–46

Marquess of Anglesey, Re Wilmott v Gardner [1901] 2 Ch. 548 4–41
Marrache v Ashton [1943] A.C. 311; [1943] 1 All E.R. 276 PC (Gibraltar) 6–19
Martindale v Smith (1841) 1 Q.B. 389; 10 LJQB 155 1 Gal 6 Jur 932 4–26
Marubeni Hong Kong & South China Ltd v Mongolia [2005] EWCA Civ 395; [2005] 1
  W.L.R. 2497; [2005] 2 All E.R. (Comm) 289 (CA); [2005] 2 Lloyd's Rep. 231; [2005] 1
  C.L.C. 540 CA (Civ Div) 3–40, 3–42
Matthew v Sedman [2019] EWCA Civ 475; [2020] Ch. 85; [2019] 3 W.L.R.
  417 4–06
Mauri Garments Trading and Marketing Ltd v Mauritius Commercial Bank Ltd [2015]
  UKPC 14 PC (Mauritius) 3–49
McGuffick v Royal Bank of Scotland Plc [2009] EWHC 2386 (Comm); [2010] 1 All E.R.
  634; [2010] 1 All E.R. (Comm) 48; [2010] Bus. L.R. 1108; [2010] E.C.C.
  11 3–37
McGuinness v Norwich and Peterborough Building Society [2011] EWCA Civ 1286; [2012]
  2 All E.R. (Comm) 265; [2012] 2 B.C.L.C. 233; [2012] B.P.I.R. 145; [2011] N.P.C.
  117 . . . . 2–43, 4–11
McLarty v R [2008] 2 SCR 79 2–37
McLeod v Prestige Finance Ltd; sub nom. McLeod v Prestige Credit Ltd [2016] CSIH 87;
  2016 G.W.D. 39-690 2–22
McMullon v Secure the Bridge Ltd [2015] EWCA Civ 884 3–37
Mears Ltd v Shoreline Housing Partnership Ltd [2015] EWHC 1396 (TCC); 160 Con. L.R.
  157 3–82
Medina Princess, The. See Hepworth v Owners of the Medina Princess
Mellowes Archital Ltd v Bell Projects Ltd 87 B.L.R. 26; 58 Con. L.R. 22; (1998) 14 Const.
  L.J. 444 CA (Civ Div) 2–077
Mercedes–Benz Finance Ltd v Clydesdale Bank Plc 1997 S.L.T. 905; 1996 S.C.L.R. 1005;
  [1998] Lloyd's Rep. Bank. 249; [1997] C.L.C. 81 OH 5–34
Mercuria Energy Trading PTE Ltd v Citibank NA [2015] EWHC 1481
  (Comm) 2–15, 3–54
Meritz Fire & Marine Insurance Co Ltd v Jan de Nul NV [2010] EWHC 3362 (Comm);
  [2011] 1 All E.R. (Comm) 1049; [2011] 1 C.L.C. 48; [2011] B.L.R. 320; [2011] T.C.L.R.
  2; 134 Con. L.R. 252 . . . . 2–45, 3–42
Mersey Steel & Iron Co Ltd v Naylor Benzon & Co (1883–84) L.R. 9 App. Cas. 434
  HL 3–11, 4–26
Metaalhandel JA Magnus BV v Ardfields Transport [1988] 1 Lloyd's Rep. 197; [1987] 2
  F.T.L.R. 319 6–39
Metal Box Ltd v Currys Ltd [1988] 1 W.L.R. 175; [1988] 1 All E.R. 341; (1987) 84 L.S.G.
  3657; (1988) 132 S.J. 52 4–60
MetLife Seguros De Retiro SA v JP Morgan Chase Bank, National Association [2016]
  EWCA Civ 1248 6–16
Metropolitan Water Board v Dick Kerr & Co Ltd [1918] A.C. 119 HL 3–39
MHB-Bank AG v Shanpark Ltd [2015] EWHC 408 (Comm); [2016] 1 B.C.L.C.
  527 2–14
Michael Aronis & Aronis Nominees Pty Ltd (trading as Welland Tyrepower) v Hallett Brick
  Industries Ltd [1999] S.A.S.C. 92 2–25
Milan Nigeria Ltd v Angeliki B Maritime Co (The Angeliki B) [2011] EWHC 892 (Comm);
  [2011] Arb. L.R. 24 6–39
Miliangos v George Frank (Textiles) Ltd [1976] A.C. 443; [1975] 3 W.L.R. 758; [1975] 3
  All E.R. 801; [1976] 1 Lloyd's Rep. 201; [1975] 2 C.M.L.R. 585; (1975) 119 S.J. 774
  HL 1–07, 6–01, 6–06,
            6–31, 6–32, 6–33, 6–34, 6–35, 6–36,
                   6–42, 6–43, 6–46, 6–49
Minder Music Ltd v Sharples [2015] EWHC 1454 (IPEC); [2016] F.S.R. 2 3–36
Ministry of Sound (Ireland) Ltd v World Online Ltd [2003] EWHC 2178 (Ch); [2003] 2 All
  E.R. (Comm) 823 3–21
Minkin v Cawdery Kaye Fireman & Taylor (t/a CKFT); sub nom. Cawdery Kaye Fireman &
  Taylor (A Firm) v Minkin [2012] EWCA Civ 546; [2012] 3 All E.R. 1117; [2012] 4
  Costs L.R. 650; [2013] 2 F.C.R. 125; [2012] P.N.L.R. 26; [2012] 19 E.G. 94 (C.S.);
  (2012) 162 N.L.J. 681; (2012) 156(18) S.J.L.B. 31 3–13
Mirabita v Imperial Ottoman Bank (1877–78) L.R. 3 Ex. D. 164 CA 2–17
Mitchell v King, 172 E.R. 1223; (1833) 6 Car. & P. 237 Assizes 2–17

Mitsui & Co Ltd v Flota Mercante Grancolombiana SA (The Ciudad de Pasto and The
  Ciudad de Neiva) [1988] 1 W.L.R. 1145; [1989] 1 All E.R. 951; [1988] 2 Lloyd's Rep.
  208 CA (Civ Div) 4–34
Mitsui Osk Lines Ltd v Salgaocar Mining Industries Private Ltd (The Unta) [2015] EWHC
  565 (Comm); [2015] 2 Lloyd's Rep. 518 4–03
MJP Media Services Ltd v Revenue and Customs Commissioners [2011] UKUT 100 (TCC);
  [2011] S.T.C. 2290; [2011] B.T.C. 1857; [2011] S.T.I. 2602 2–03
Modern Trading Co Ltd v Swale Building and Construction Ltd (1990) 24 Con LR
  59 2–11
Momm v Barclays Bank International Ltd; sub nom. Delbrueck & Co v Barclays Bank
  International Ltd; Delbrueck & Co v Barclays Bank International Ltd [1977] Q.B. 790;
  [1977] 2 W.L.R. 407; [1976] 3 All E.R. 588; [1976] 2 Lloyd's Rep. 341; (1976) 120 S.J.
  486 .... 4–03, 5–22, 5–34,
                                                                          5–55, 5–60
Monosolar IQ Ltd v Woden Park Ltd [2020] EWHC 1407 (Ch) 3–08
Montrod Ltd v Grundkotter Fleischvertriebs GmbH [2001] EWCA Civ 1954; [2002] 1
  W.L.R. 1975; [2002] 3 All E.R. 697; [2002] 1 All E.R. (Comm) 257; [2002] C.L.C. 499
  CA (Civ Div) 3–45, 3–51
Moore v Shelley (1883) 8 App. Cas. 285 PC (Australia) 4–11
Moralice (London) Ltd v ED&F Man [1954] 2 Lloyd's Rep. 526 3–15
More OG Romsdal Fylkesbatar AS v Demise Charterers of the Jotunheim, Jotunheim, The
  [2004] EWHC 671 (Comm); [2005] 1 Lloyd's Rep. 181 .... 3–84, 4–04
Moriarty v Atkinson [2008] EWCA Civ 1604; [2010] 1 B.C.L.C. 142; [2009] B.P.I.R. 248;
  [2011] W.T.L.R. 1661 5–36
Moschi v Lep Air Services Ltd; sub nom. Moschi v Rolloswin Investments Ltd; Lep Air
  Services v Rolloswin Investments [1973] A.C. 331; [1972] 2 W.L.R. 1175; [1972] 2 All
  E.R. 393; (1972) 116 S.J. 372 HL 2–43
Mosconici, The. See Kinetics Technology International SpA v Cross Seas Shipping Corp
Moss v Hancock [1899] 2 Q.B. 111; 63 JP 517; 68 LJQB 657; 19 Cox CC 324; 47 WR 698;
  43 S.J. 479; 80 LT 693; 15 T.L.R. 353 DC 1–07
Mount Albert BC v Australasian Temperance & General Mutual Life Assurance Society Ltd
  [1938] A.C. 224 PC (NZ) 6–48
MP – Bilt Pte Ltd v Oey Widarto [1999] 3 S.L.R. 592 3–11
MS Fashions Ltd v Bank of Credit and Commerce International SA (In Liquidation); sub
  nom. MS Fashions Ltd v Bank of Credit and Commerce International SA (No.2); High
  Street Services v Bank of Credit and Commerce International; Impexbond v Bank of
  Credit and Commerce International [1993] Ch. 425; [1993] 3 W.L.R. 220; [1993] 3 All
  E.R. 769; [1993] B.C.C. 360; [1993] B.C.L.C. 1200; (1993) 137 S.J.L.B. 132 CA (Civ
  Div) 2–408
MSAS Global Logistics Ltd v Power Packaging Inc [2003] EWHC 1393 (Ch); Times, June
  25, 2003 .... 4–29, 4–32
MSC Mediterranean Shipping Co SA v Cottonex Anstalt [2016] EWCA Civ 789; [2017] 1
  All E.R. (Comm) 483; [2016] 2 Lloyd's Rep. 494; [2016] 2 C.L.C. 272 .... 3–19, 3–21
Mukorera v Ocean Breeze Engine and Cooling Systems HH 13-08
  Unreported 6–13
Multi Veste 226 BV v NI Summer Row Unitholder BV [2011] EWHC 2026 (Ch); 139 Con.
  L.R. 23; [2011] 33 E.G. 63 (C.S.) 4–31
Multiservice Bookbinding Ltd v Marden [1979] Ch. 84; [1978] 2 W.L.R. 535; [1978] 2 All
  E.R. 489; (1978) 35 P. & C.R. 201; (1978) 122 S.J. 210 .... 3–07, 3–36, 4–42,
                                                                      6–11, 6–16
Munro v Butt (1858) 8 E. & B. 738 3–16
MW High Tech Projects UK Ltd v Biffa Waste Services Ltd [2015] 1 C.L.C.
  449 3–49
MWB Business Exchange Centres Ltd v Rock Advertising Ltd. See Rock Advertising Ltd v
  MWB Business Exchange Centres Ltd
N Joachimson (A Firm) v Swiss Bank Corp (Costs) [1921] 3 K.B. 110; (1921) 6 Ll. L. Rep.
  435 CA 2–33, 5–46
Nadezhda Krupskaya, The. See Brown Boveri (Australia) Pty v Baltic Shipping Co

National Bank of Greece SA v Pinios Shipping Co (No.1); sub nom. Pinios Shipping Co No.
  1 v National Bank of Greece SA [1990] 1 A.C. 637; [1989] 3 W.L.R. 1330; [1990] 1 All
  E.R. 78; [1990] 1 Lloyd's Rep. 225; [1988] 2 F.T.L.R. 9; [1988] Fin. L.R. 249; [1990]
  C.C.L.R. 18; (1990) 87(4) L.S.G. 33; (1989) 139 N.L.J. 1711; (1990) 134 S.J. 261
  HL 4–42
National Crime Agency v N; sub nom. N v Royal Bank of Scotland Plc [2017] EWCA Civ
  253; [2017] 1 W.L.R. 3938; [2017] Lloyd's Rep. F.C. 232 5–42
National Housing Trust v YP Seaton & Associates Co Ltd [2015] UKPC 43; [2016] B.L.R.
  215; 162 Con. L.R. 117 4–60
National Infrastructure Development Co Ltd v Banco Santander SA [2017] EWCA Civ 27;
  [2018] 1 All E.R. (Comm) 156; [2017] 1 Lloyd's Rep. 361; [2017] 1 C.L.C. 37; [2017]
  C.I.L.L. 3939 .... 3–44, 3–50
National Merchant Buying Society Ltd v Bellamy [2012] EWHC 2563 (Ch) 3–83
National Westminister Bank Ltd v Barclays Bank International Ltd [1975] Q.B. 654; [1975]
  2 W.L.R. 12; [1974] 3 All E.R. 834; [1974] 2 Lloyd's Rep. 506; (1974) 118 S.J. 627
  QBD 3–82
Nationwide Building Society v Registry of Friendly Societies [1983] 1 W.L.R. 1226; [1983]
  3 All E.R. 296; (1984) 47 P. & C.R. 221; (1983) 80 L.S.G. 3238; (1983) 133 N.L.J. 958;
  (1983) 127 S.J. 696 3–07
Nautica Marine Limited v Trafigura Trading LLC [2020] EWHC 1986
  (Comm) 6–24
Naxos, The. *See* Cie Commerciale Sucres et Denrées v C Czarnikow Ltd
Nebel, Inc v Mid-City National Bank of Chicago 769 N.E.2d 45 (2002, Appellate Court of
  Illinois, First District) 3–05
Neil Ex p. Burden, Re (1880–81) L.R. 16 Ch. D. 675 CA 4–51
Newbigging v Adam. *See* Adam v Newbigging
North v Brown [2012] EWCA Civ 223 .... 1–05, 2–29
North Shore Ventures Ltd v Anstead Holdings Inc [2011] EWCA Civ 230; [2012] Ch. 31;
  [2011] 3 W.L.R. 628; [2011] 2 All E.R. (Comm) 1024; [2011] Bus. L.R. 1036; [2011] 2
  Lloyd's Rep. 45; [2011] B.L.R. 757 2–17
Northwest Shipping and Towage Co Pty Ltd v Commonwealth Bank of Australia (1993) 118
  C.L.R. 453 2–25
Norton v Ellam (1837) 2 M. & W. 461 .... 2–17, 4–11
Nottingham City Council v Calverton Parish Council [2015] EWHC 503 (Admin); [2015]
  P.T.S.R. 1130; [2015] A.C.D. 97 4–05
Nova (Jersey) Knit Ltd v Kammgarn Spinnerei GmbH [1977] 1 W.L.R. 713; [1977] 2 All
  E.R. 463; [1977] 1 Lloyd's Rep. 463; (1977) 121 S.J. 170 HL 5–27
Novoship (UK) Ltd v Mikhaylyuk [2014] EWCA Civ 908; [2015] Q.B. 499; [2015] 2
  W.L.R. 526; [2014] W.T.L.R. 1521; (2014) 158(28) S.J.L.B. 37 3–76
O'Connor Utilities Ltd v Revenue and Customs Commissioners [2009] EWHC 3704
  (Admin); [2010] S.T.C. 682; [2010] S.T.I. 624 4–06
Odenfeld, The. *See* Gator Shipping Corp v Trans-Asiatic Oil SA
Office of Fair Trading v Abbey National Plc [2009] UKSC 6; [2010] 1 A.C. 696; [2009] 3
  W.L.R. 1215; [2010] 1 All E.R. 667; [2010] 2 All E.R. (Comm) 945; [2010] 1 Lloyd's
  Rep. 281; [2010] 1 C.M.L.R. 44; [2010] Eu. L.R. 309; (2009) 159 N.L.J. 1702; (2009)
  153(45) S.J.L.B. 28 .... 3–29, 4–44
Office of Fair Trading v Lloyds TSB Bank Plc [2007] UKHL 48; [2008] 1 A.C. 316; [2007]
  3 W.L.R. 733; [2008] Bus. L.R. 450; [2008] 1 All E.R. 205; [2008] 1 All E.R. (Comm)
  113; [2008] 1 Lloyd's Rep. 30; (2007) 104(44) L.S.G. 31; (2007) 157 N.L.J. 1614;
  (2007) 151 S.J.L.B. 1432 HL 5–31
Olex Focas Pty Ltd v Skodaexport Co Ltd [1996] 70 A.J.L.R. 983 .... 3–45, 3–50
Olivine Industries (Pvt) Ltd v Nharara [2006] ZWSC 77 6–13
Olwine v Torrens, 344 A 2d 665 (1975) 3–08
Olympia & York Canary Wharf Ltd (No.2), Re; sub nom. Bear Stearns International Ltd v
  Adamson [1993] B.C.C. 159 .... 4–27, 4–31
Olympia Securities Commercial Plc (In Administration), Re [2017] EWHC 2807
  (Ch) 3–54
On Demand Information Plc (In Administrative Receivership) v Michael Gerson (Finance)
  Plc [2002] UKHL 13; [2003] 1 A.C. 368; [2002] 2 W.L.R. 919; [2002] 2 All E.R. 949;
  [2002] 1 All E.R. (Comm) 641; [2002] B.C.C. 673; [2002] C.L.C. 1140; (2002) 99(21)
  L.S.G. 31; (2002) 146 S.J.L.B. 110 3–84

Onfido Ltd v Blockchain Access UK Ltd [2020] EWHC 2585 3–13
Oresundsvarvet AB v Lemos (The Angelic Star), Angelica Star, The [1988] 1 Lloyd's Rep.
  122; [1988] 1 F.T.L.R. 94 .... 3–32, 3–59
Ornstein v Hickerson, 40 F. Supp. 305 (1941) 5–28
Osibanjo v Seahive Investments Ltd [2008] EWCA Civ 1282; [2009] 2 P. & C.R. 2; [2009]
  L. & T.R. 16; [2009] 1 E.G.L.R. 32; [2009] 9 E.G. 194; [2008] 47 E.G. 112 (C.S.);
  [2008] N.P.C. 127; [2009] 1 P. & C.R. DG7................................ 2–28
Otago Stations Estates Ltd v Parker [2005] 2 N.Z.L.R. 734 SC (HZ) 5–27
Ouais Group Engineering and Contracting v Saipem SpA [2013] EWHC 990
  (Comm) 3–45, 4–49
Owneast Shippin Limited v Qatar Navigation QSC [2010] EWHC 1663 (Comm); [2011] 2
  All E.R. (Comm) 76; [2011] 1 Lloyd's Rep. 350; [2010] 2 C.L.C. 42 4–04
Owners of the Eleftherotria v Owners of the Despina R; sub nom. Services Europe
  Atlantique Sud (SEAS) v Stockholms Rederi AB Svea (The Folias) [1979] A.C. 685;
  [1978] 3 W.L.R. 804; [1979] 1 All E.R. 421; [1979] 1 Lloyd's Rep. 1; (1978) 122 S.J.
  758 HL... 6–32, 6–38, 6–39,
                                                                          6–40
Owners of Turbo Electric Bulk Carrier Teh Hu v Nippon Salvage Co Ltd (The Teh Hu)
  [1970] P. 106; [1969] 3 W.L.R. 1135; [1969] 3 All E.R. 1200; [1969] 2 Lloyd's Rep.
  365; (1969) 113 S.J. 792 CA (Civ Div) 6–30
Oxigen Environmental Ltd v Mullan [2012] NIQB 17........................... 5–27
Ozalid Group (Export) Ltd v African Continental Bank Ltd [1979] 2 Lloyd's Rep.
  231 .... 6–36, 6–42
Paciocco v ANZ Banking Group Ltd [2016] HCA 28 3–34
Pacitti Jones (A Firm) v O'Brien; sub nom. O'Brien v Pacitti Jones (A Firm) [2005] CSIH
  56; 2006 S.C. 616; 2005 S.L.T. 793; [2005] I.R.L.R. 888; 2005 G.W.D. 25–483 IH (Ex
  Div) 4–06
Pammer v Reederei Karl Schluter GmbH & Co KG (C-585/08), Hotel Alpenhof GmbH v
  Heller (C-144/09) EU:C:2010:740; [2011] 2 All E.R. (Comm) 888; [2012] Bus. L.R.
  972; [2010] E.C.R. I-12527; [2012] All E.R. (EC) 34 5–40
Panama New Zealand and Australian Royal Mail Co, Re (1869–70) L.R. 5 Ch. App. 318,
  CA in Ch 3–74
Pankhania v Hackney LBC [2002] EWHC 2441 (Ch); [2002] N.P.C. 123 3–82
Pao On v Lau Yiu Long [1980] A.C. 614; [1979] 3 W.L.R. 435; [1979] 3 All E.R. 65;
  (1979) 123 S.J. 319 PC (HK) 3–83
Paragon Finance Plc (formerly National Home Loans Corp) v Nash; sub nom. Nash v
  Paragon Finance Plc; Staunton v Paragon Finance Plc; Paragon Finance Plc v Staunton
  [2001] EWCA Civ 1466; [2002] 1 W.L.R. 685; [2002] 2 All E.R. 248; [2001] 2 All E.R.
  (Comm) 1025; [2002] 2 P. & C.R. 20; (2001) 98(44) L.S.G. 36; (2001) 145 S.J.L.B. 244;
  [2002] 1 P. & C.R. DG13 CA (Civ Div) 4–43
Paragon Finance Plc (formerly National Home Loans Corp) v Pender [2005] EWCA Civ
  760; [2005] 1 W.L.R. 3412; [2005] N.P.C. 84; [2005] 2 P. & C.R. DG18 CA (Civ
  Div) 4–43
Parbulk II A/S v Heritage Maritime Ltd SA [2011] EWHC 2917 (Comm); [2012] 2 All E.R.
  (Comm) 418; [2012] 1 Lloyd's Rep. 87; (2011) 161 N.L.J. 1668 2–286
Parsons v Mather & Platt Ltd [1977] 1 W.L.R. 855; [1977] 2 All E.R. 715; (1977) 121 S.J.
  204 4–61
Page v Newman, 109 E.R. 140; (1829) 9 B. & C. 378 KB 4–39
PCE Investors Ltd v Cancer Research Ltd [2012] EWHC 884 (Ch); [2012] 2 P. & C.R. 5;
  [2012] L. & T.R. 34; [2012] 17 E.G. 110 (C.S.) 4–03
Peacock v Imagine Property Developments Ltd [2018] EWHC 1113 (TCC) 4–30
Permasteelisa Japan KK v Bouyguesstroi [2007] EWHC 3508 (QB).................. 3–49
Perrin v Morgan; sub nom. Morgan, Re; Morgan v Morgan [1943] A.C. 399,
  HL 1–02
Peter Cassidy Seed Co v Osuustukkukauppa IL [1957] 1 W.L.R. 273; [1957] 1 All E.R. 484;
  [1957] 1 Lloyd's Rep. 25; (1957) 101 S.J. 149 QBD (Comm) 6–24
Petrofina, The. See A/S Tankexpress v Compagnie Financière Belge des Petroles SA
Petrol (Passive Emissions Testing Research Organisation Laboratories) Ltd v Industrial
  Property Investment Fund [2006] EWHC 2219 (Ch) 4–30
Phibro Energy AG v Nissho Iwai Corp (The Honam Jade) [1991] 1 Lloyd's Rep. 38 CA
  (Civ Div) 4–27

Philips Hong Kong Ltd v Attorney General of Hong Kong (1993) 61 B.L.R. 41; (1993) 9
    Const. L.J. 202 PC (HK) 3–33
Phillips v Lamdin [1949] 2 K.B. 33; [1949] 1 All E.R. 770; [1949] L.J.R. 1293; (1949) 93
    S.J. 320 4–34
Phones 4U Ltd (In Administration) v EE Ltd [2018] EWHC 49 (Comm); [2018] 2 All E.R.
    (Comm) 315; [2018] Bus. L.R. 574; [2018] 1 Lloyd's Rep. 204; [2018] B.L.R. 255; 176
    Con. L.R. 199 .... 3–33, 4–34
Photo Production Ltd v Securicor Transport Ltd [1980] A.C. 827; [1980] 2 W.L.R. 283;
    [1980] 1 All E.R. 556; [1980] 1 Lloyd's Rep. 545; (1980) 124 S.J. 147
    HL 3–19
Pic-A-Pop Beverages Ltd v G & J Watt Co Ltd (1975) 52 D.L.R. (3d) 754 4–27
Piggin, Re; sub nom. Dicker v Lombank (1962) 112 L.J. 424 3–29
Pioneer Freight Futures Co Ltd (In Liquidation) v Cosco Bulk Carrier Co Ltd. *See* Lomas v
    JFB Firth Rixson Inc
Pioneer Freight Futures Co Ltd (In Liquidation) v TMT Asia Ltd [2011] EWHC 1888
    (Comm); [2011] 2 Lloyd's Rep. 565; [2011] 2 C.L.C. 225................... 3–56, 3–57
Planché v Colbourn, 131 E.R. 305; (1831) 8 Bing. 14.......................... 3–18
Plevin v Paragon Personal Finance Ltd [2014] UKSC 61; [2014] 1 W.L.R. 4222; [2015] 1
    All E.R. 625; [2015] 1 All E.R. (Comm) 1007; [2014] Bus. L.R. 1257; [2015] E.C.C. 2;
    [2015] Lloyd's Rep. I.R. 247 3–37
Point v Federal Commissioner of Taxation (Australia) (1970) 70 A.T.C. 4021 2–03
Polish Steamship Co v Atlantic Maritime Co (The Garden City) (No.2) [1985] Q.B. 41;
    [1984] 3 W.L.R. 300; [1984] 3 All E.R. 59; [1984] 2 Lloyd's Rep. 37; (1984) 81 L.S.G.
    1367; (1984) 128 S.J. 469 CA (Civ Div) 4–59, 4–60
Postlethwaite v Freeland (1879–80) L.R. 5 App. Cas. 599 HL 4–15
Power Curber International Ltd v National Bank of Kuwait SAK [1981] 1 W.L.R. 1233;
    [1981] 3 All E.R. 607; [1981] 2 Lloyd's Rep. 394; [1981] Com. L.R. 224 CA (Civ
    Div) 7–24
President of India v La Pintada Compania Navigacion SA (The La Pintada) [1985] A.C.
    104; [1984] 3 W.L.R. 10; [1984] 2 All E.R. 773; [1984] 2 Lloyd's Rep. 9; [1984]
    C.I.L.L. 110; (1984) 81 L.S.G. 1999; (1984) 128 S.J. 414 HL 4–56, 4–59
President of India v Lips Maritime Corp (The Lips); sub nom. Lips Maritime Corp v
    President of India [1988] A.C. 395; [1987] 3 W.L.R. 572; [1987] 3 All E.R. 110; [1987]
    2 Lloyd's Rep. 311; [1987] 2 F.T.L.R. 477; [1987] Fin. L.R. 313; (1987) 84 L.S.G. 2765;
    (1987) 137 N.L.J. 734; (1987) 131 S.J. 1085 HL........................ 4–56, 6–44
Price v Great Western Railway Co (1847) 16 M. & W. 244 4–58
Procter and Gamble Co v Svenska Cellulosa Aktiebolaget SCA [2012] EWCA Civ
    1413 .... 3–02, 6–02, 6–08
Progress Bulk Carriers Ltd v Tube City IMS Ltd [2012] EWHC 273 (Comm); [2012] 2 All
    E.R. (Comm) 855; [2012] 1 Lloyd's Rep. 501; [2012] 1 C.L.C. 365 3–83
Promenade Towers Mutual Housing Corp v Metropolitan Life Insurance Co (1991) 597 A.2d
    1377 4–18
Property Alliance Group Ltd v Royal Bank of Scotland Plc [2018] EWCA Civ 355; [2018] 1
    W.L.R. 3529; [2018] 2 All E.R. (Comm) 695; [2018] 2 B.C.L.C. 322 4–46
Protector Endowment Loan & Annuity Co v Grice; sub nom. Protector Loan Co v Grice
    (1879–80) L.R. 5 Q.B.D. 592 CA 3–59
Prudential Assurance Co Ltd v Revenue and Custom Commissioners [2013] EWHC 3249
    (Ch); [2014] S.T.C. 1236; [2014] 2 C.M.L.R. 10; [2013] B.T.C. 751; [2013] S.T.I.
    3391 4–56
PT Berlian Laju Tanker TBK v Nuse Shipping Ltd (The Aktor) [2008] EWHC 1330
    (Comm); [2008] 2 All E.R. (Comm) 784; [2008] 2 Lloyd's Rep. 246; [2008] 1 C.L.C.
    967 .... 5–36, 6–19, 6–21,
                                                                         6–25
PST Energy 7 Shipping LLC v OW Bunker Malta Ltd, Res Cogitans, The [2016] UKSC 23;
    [2016] A.C. 1034; [2016] 2 W.L.R. 1193; [2016] 3 All E.R. 879; [2017] 1 All E.R.
    (Comm) 1; [2016] 1 Lloyd's Rep. 589; [2016] 2 C.L.C. 1; [2016] B.P.I.R.
    973 .... 3–81, 4–22
Puerto Buitrago, The. *See* Attica Sea Carriers Corp v Ferrostaal Poseidon Bulk Reederei
    GmbHPugh v Duke of Leeds, 98 E.R. 1323; (1977) Cowp. 714 KB 4–09
Pulbrook v Lawes (1876) 1 Q.B.D. 284 3–81
Pyrmont Ltd v Schott [1939] A.C. 145; [1938] 4 All E.R. 713 PC(Gibraltar) 6–47

Quah Su-Ling v Goldman Sachs International [2015] EWHC 759 (Comm) 4–11
Quality Publications Australia Pty Ltd v Commissioner of Taxation [2012] FCA
    256 2–01
Queensland Electricity Generating Board v New Hope Collieries [1989] 1 Lloyd's Rep. 205
    PC (Aus) 3–08, 6–13
R (on the application of Bednash) v Westminster City Council [2014] EWHC 2160
    (Admin); [2014] L.L.R. 755; [2015] 2 C.L. 169 DC 4–09
R. (on the application of Camden LBC) v Parking Adjudicator [2011] EWHC 295 (Admin);
    [2011] P.T.S.R. 1391; [2011] B.L.G.R. 504 ....2–01, 2–32
R. (on the application of Cardiff City Council) v Customs and Excise Commissioners; sub
    nom. Cardiff CC v Customs and Excise Commissioners [2003] EWCA Civ 1456; [2004]
    S.T.C. 356; [2004] B.T.C. 5048; [2004] B.V.C. 108; [2003] S.T.I. 1849 CA (Civ
    Div) 2–05
R. (on the application of SRM Global Master Fund LP) v Treasury Commissioner [2009]
    EWHC 227 (Admin); [2009] B.C.C. 251; [2009] U.K.H.R.R. 712; (2009) 159 N.L.J.
    279 4–21
R. (on the application of Zaporozhchenko) v Westminster Magistrates Court [2011] EWHC
    34; [2011] 1 W.L.R. 994 .... 4–09, 4–14
R. v Lovitt (Irvine) [1912] A.C. 212 PC (Can)....................................5–46
R. v Preddy (John Crawford); R. v Slade (Mark); R. v Dhillon (Rajpaul Singh) [1996] A.C.
    815; [1996] 3 W.L.R. 255; [1996] 3 All E.R. 481; [1996] 2 Cr. App. R. 524; (1996) 160
    J.P. 677; [1996] Crim. L.R. 726; (1996) 160 J.P.N. 936; (1996) 93(31) L.S.G. 29; (1996)
    146 N.L.J. 1057; (1996) 140 S.J.L.B. 184 HL 5–36
R v Teresko (Sergejs) Unreported, 11 October 2017 Cr Ct 1–20
RA Cripps (Pharmaceutical) and Son Ltd v Wickenden [1973] 1 W.L.R. 944; [1973] 2 All
    E.R. 606; (1972) 117 S.J. 446 4–11
Radio and Allied Holdings Ltd v Bowmakers [1963] C.L.Y. 512 4–26
Raineri v Miles [1981] A.C. 1050; [1980] 2 W.L.R. 847; [1980] 2 All E.R. 145; (1981) 41 P.
    & C.R. 71; (1980) 124 S.J. 328 HL 4–24, 4–31, 4–34
Ralli Bros v Compania Naviera Sota y Aznar; sub nom. Compania Naviera Sota Y Aznar v
    Ralli Bros [1920] 2 K.B. 287; (1920) 2 Ll. L. Rep. 550 CA 5–46, 6–25, 6–26,
                                                                                    6–27
RAM Media Ltd (In Administration) v Ministry of Culture of the Hellenic Republic
    (Secretariat General of Sport) [2009] EWCA Civ 528 3–11
Raymond Construction Pte Ltd v Low Yang Tong [1996] SGHC 136 3–50
Rays, The. See Canmer International Inc v UK Mutual Steamship Assurance Association
    (Bermuda) Ltd
RD Harbottle (Mercantile) Ltd v National Westminster Bank Ltd; Harbottle (Mercantile) Ltd
    v National Westminster Bank Ltd [1978] Q.B. 146; [1977] 3 W.L.R. 752; [1977] 2 All
    E.R. 862; (1977) 121 S.J. 745 ....2–45, 3–45
RDC Concrete Pte Ltd v Sato Kogyo (S) Pte Ltd [2007] SGC 39 4–24
Regazzoni v KC Sethia (1944) Ltd; sub nom. Regazzoni v Sethia (KC) (1944) [1958] A.C.
    301; [1957] 3 W.L.R. 752; [1957] 3 All E.R. 286; [1957] 2 Lloyd's Rep. 289; (1957)
    101 S.J. 848 HL..3–24
Registrar of Companies v Stonelee Developments Ltd; Registrar of Companies v Stonelee
    Properties Ltd, 2004 S.L.T. (Sh Ct) 116; 2004 S.C.L.R. 950; 2004 G.W.D.
    22–480 4–10
Reichman v Beveridge; sub nom. Reichman v Gauntlett [2006] EWCA Civ 1659; [2007]
    Bus. L.R. 412; [2007] 1 P. & C.R. 20; [2007] L. & T.R. 18; [2007] 1 E.G.L.R. 37;
    [2007] 8 E.G. 138; [2007] 1 E.G. 92 (C.S.); (2007) 104(4) L.S.G. 35; [2006] N.P.C. 132
    CA (Civ Div) 3–21
Res Cogitans, The. See PST Energy 7 Shipping LLC v OW Bunker Malta Ltd
Reuter Hufeland & Co v Sala & Co (1879) 4 C.P.D. 239 CA 4–27
Revenue and Customs Commissioners v Taylor Clark Leisure Plc [2018] UKSC 35; [2018]
    1 W.L.R. 3803; [2018] 4 All E.R. 817; [2018] S.T.C. 1556; 2018 S.C. (U.K.S.C.) 153;
    2018 S.L.T. 1091; [2018] B.V.C. 34; [2018] L.L.R. 681; [2018] S.T.I. 1415; 2018
    G.W.D. 23-297 5–51
Richard Buxton Solicitors v Mills-Owens [2010] EWCA Civ 122; [2010] 1 W.L.R. 1997;
    [2010] 4 All E.R. 405; [2010] C.P. Rep. 26; [2010] 3 Costs L.R. 421; [2010] 2 E.G.L.R.
    73; [2010] 17 E.G. 96; [2010] 9 E.G. 166 (C.S.); (2010) 107(10) L.S.G. 15; (2010)
    154(8) S.J.L.B. 29; [2010] N.P.C. 21 3–13

Rick Dees Ltd v Larsen [2006] NZCA 25 5–36
Ridgley v Topa Thrift & Loan Association 62 Cal. Rptr. 2d 309 4–18
Rightside Properties Ltd v Gray [1975] Ch. 72; [1974] 3 W.L.R. 484; [1974] 2 All E.R.
   1169; (1974) 28 P. & C.R. 232; (1974) 118 S.J. 698 Ch D 4–14
Riverside Housing Association Ltd v White. *See* White v Riverside Housing Association Ltd
Robe River Mining Co Pty Ltd v Commissioner of Taxation [1988] FCA 303 6–18
Robertson v French, 102 E.R. 779; (1803) 4 East. 130 KB 4–21
Robey & Co v Snaefell Mining Co Ltd (1888) L.R. 20 Q.B.D. 152 2–33
Rochis Ltd v Chambers [2006] NZHC 524 3–07
Rock Advertising Ltd v MWB Business Exchange Centres Ltd; sub nom. MWB Business
   Exchange Centres Ltd v Rock Advertising Ltd [2018] UKSC 24; [2019] A.C. 119;
   [2018] 2 W.L.R. 1603; [2018] 4 All E.R. 21; [2018] 2 All E.R. (Comm) 961; [2018] 1
   C.L.C. 946; [2018] B.L.R. 479; 179 Con. L.R. 1; [2018] C.I.L.L. 4145; [2018] 2 P. &
   C.R. DG17 3–17
Rogers v Louth CC [1981] I.R. 265 SC (Ireland) 3–82
Romer & Haslam, Re [1893] 2 Q.B. 286 CA 2–25
Ropaigealach v Barclays Bank Plc [2000] QB 263; [1999] 4 All E.R. 235; [1999] 3 W.L.R.
   17, 32 H.L.R. 234; [1998] N.P.C. 167; [1998] EGCS 189, 149 N.L.J., 72 P & CR
   D32 3–73
Rosa S, The [1989] Q.B. 419; [1989] 2 W.L.R. 162; [1989] 1 All E.R. 489; [1988] 2 Lloyd's
   Rep. 574; 1989 A.M.C. 912 .... 3–034, 3–05
Rowland v Divall [1923] 2 K.B. 500, CA; 92 LJKB 1041; [1923] All E.R. Rep. 270; 67 S.J.
   703; 129 LT 757 CA 3–81
Royal Bank of Canada v W Got & Associates Electric Ltd [1993] 3 S.C.R. 408 SC
   (Canada) 4–11
Royal Products v Midland Bank [1981] 2 Lloyd's Rep. 194; [1981] Com. L.R.
   93 5–36
RSM Bentley Jennison (A Firm) v Ayton [2015] EWCA Civ 1120; [2016] 1 W.L.R. 1281;
   [2016] P.N.L.R. 10 2–42
RSPCA v Sharp [2010] EWCA Civ 1474; [2011] 1 W.L.R. 980; [2011] P.T.S.R. 942; [2011]
   S.T.C. 553; [2011] Costs L.R. Online 171; [2011] W.T.L.R. 311; 13 I.T.E.L.R. 701;
   [2011] S.T.I. 253; (2011) 155(1) S.J.L.B. 30 1–02
Rubicon Vantage International Pte Ltd v Krisenergy Ltd [2019] EWHC 2012 (Comm);
   [2020] 1 Lloyd's Rep. 383 3–42
SA Eagle Insurance Co Ltd v Hartley, 1990 (4) S.A. 833 (AD) SC (South
   Africa) 3–02
Safa Ltd v Banque du Caire [2000] 2 All E.R. (Comm) 567; [2000] 2 Lloyd's Rep. 600;
   [2000] Lloyd's Rep. Bank. 323; [2000] C.L.C. 1556 3–48
Sail Labrador Ltd v The Challenge One [1999] 1 S.C.R. 265 SC (Canada) 4–27, 4–30
Samarenko v Dawn Hill House Ltd [2011] EWCA Civ 1445; [2013] Ch. 36; [2012] 3
   W.L.R. 638; [2012] 2 All E.R. 476; [2012] 2 All E.R. (Comm) 240; [2012] 1 P. & C.R.
   14; [2011] 49 E.G. 98 (C.S.); [2011] N.P.C. 125 .... 4–26, 4–29, 4–31
Santa Clara, The. *See* Vitol SA v Norelf Ltd
Sass Ex p National Provincial Bank of England Ltd, Re [1896] 2 Q.B. 12; 65 LJQB 481; 3
   Mans 125; 44 WR 588; 40 S.J. 686; 74 LT 383; 12 T.L.R. 333 2–40
Scandinavian Trading Tanker Co AB v Flota Petrolera Ecuatoriana (The Scaptrade) [1983] 2
   A.C. 694; [1983] 3 W.L.R. 203; [1983] 2 All E.R. 763; [1983] 2 Lloyd's Rep. 253
   HL 3–84, 4–04
Scaptrade, The. *See* Scandinavian Trading Tanker Co AB v Flota Petrolera Ecuatoriana
Schnapper, Re [1936] 1 All E.R. 322 6–12
School Facility Management Ltd v Governing Body of Christ the King College [2020]
   EWHC 1118 (Comm) 3–18
Schorsch Meier GmbH v Hennin [1975] Q.B. 416; [1974] 3 W.L.R. 823; [1975] 1 All E.R.
   152; [1975] 1 Lloyd's Rep. 1; [1975] 1 C.M.L.R. 20; (1974) 118 S.J. 881 CA (Civ
   Div) 6–31
Scotland v British Credit Trust Ltd [2014] EWCA Civ 790; [2015] 1 All E.R. 708; [2015] 1
   All E.R. (Comm) 401; [2014] Bus. L.R. 1079; [2015] C.T.L.C. 25 3–37
Sea-Cargo Skips AS v State Bank of India [2013] EWHC 177 (Comm); [2013] 2 Lloyd's
   Rep. 477 3–41
Secretary of State for Defence v Spencer [2019] EWHC 1526 (Ch); [2019] 1 W.L.R.
   6065 2–11

Secured Residential Funding Plc v Douglas Goldberg Hendeles & Co (2000) 97(18) L.S.G.
  38; (2000) 97(21) L.S.G. 40; (2000) 144 S.J.L.B. 218; [2000] N.P.C. 47 CA (Civ
  Div) 5–51
Securities Exchange Commission v Shavers 2013 BL 208180 (ED Tex, 6 August 2013)
  District Court for the Eastern District of Texas 1–20
Sempra Metals Ltd (formerly Metallgesellschaft Ltd) v Inland Revenue Commissioners
  [2007] UKHL 34; [2008] 1 A.C. 561; [2007] 3 W.L.R. 354; [2008] Bus. L.R. 49; [2007]
  4 All E.R. 657; [2007] S.T.C. 1559; [2008] Eu. L.R. 1; [2007] B.T.C. 509; [2007] S.T.I.
  1865; (2007) 104(31) L.S.G. 25; (2007) 157 N.L.J. 1082; (2007) 151 S.J.L.B. 985
  HL 4–56, 4–59
Serious Fraud Office v Sweett Group Plc Unreported, February 19, 2016 Crown Court,
  Southwark 5–43
Sewing Machines Rentals v Wilson; Sewing Machines Rentals v Udeala; Morlen
  Investments v Wilson [1976] 1 W.L.R. 37; [1975] 3 All E.R. 553; (1975) 120 S.J. 47 CA
  (Civ Div) 4–51
Shah v HSBC Private Bank (UK) Ltd [2012] EWHC 1283; [2013] 1 All E.R. (Comm) 72;
  [2012] Lloyd's Rep. F.C. 507; [2013] Bus. L.R. D38 5–42
Shanning International Ltd (In Liquidation) v Lloyds TSB Bank Plc (formerly Lloyds Bank
  Plc); sub nom. Lloyds TSB Bank Plc (formerly Lloyds Bank Plc) v Rasheed Bank;
  Shanning International Ltd (In Liquidation) v Rasheed Bank [2001] UKHL 31; [2001] 1
  W.L.R. 1462; [2001] 3 C.M.L.R. 14; (2001) 98(32) L.S.G. 36 HL 3–47
Shava v Bergus Investments (Pvt) Ltd 2011 (2)ZLR 430 (HC) 6–13
Sheahan v Carrier Air Conditioning Pty Ltd (1997) 189 CLR 407 2–29
Shearer v Spring Capital Ltd [2013] EWHC 3148 (Ch) 2–17
Sheppard & Cooper Ltd v TSB Bank Plc (No.2) [1996] 2 All E.R. 654; [1996] B.C.C.
  965 4–11
Shipping Corporation of India v Jaldhi Overseas Pte Ltd 583 F3d58 (2nd Cir,
  2009) 5–46
Siemens Hearing Instruments Ltd v Friends Life Ltd [2014] EWCA Civ 382 4–30
Sim v Rotherham MBC [1987] Ch. 216; [1986] 3 W.L.R. 851; [1986] 3 All E.R. 387;
  [1986] I.C.R. 897; [1986] I.R.L.R. 391; 85 L.G.R. 128; (1986) 83 L.S.G. 3746; (1986)
  130 S.J. 839 2–07
Simmons v Swann, 275 U.S. 113 (1927) 2–01
Simon Carves Ltd v Ensus UK Ltd [2011] EWHC 657 (TCC); [2011] B.L.R. 340; 135 Con.
  L.R. 96 3–49
Siqueira v Noronha [1934] A.C. 332; [1934] All E.R. Rep. 78; [1934] 2 W.W.R. 117 PC
  (EA) 2–03
Sirius International Insurance Co (Publ) v FAI General Insurance Ltd; sub nom. Sirius
  International Insurance Corp Ltd v FAI General Insurance Co Ltd [2004] UKHL 54;
  [2004] 1 W.L.R. 3251; [2005] 1 All E.R. 191; [2005] 1 All E.R. (Comm) 117; [2005] 1
  Lloyd's Rep. 461; [2005] 1 C.L.C. 451; [2005] Lloyd's Rep. I.R. 294; (2004) 101(48)
  L.S.G. 25; (2004) 148 S.J.L.B. 1435 3–49
Sixteenth Ocean GmbH & Co KG v Société Générale [2018] EWHC 1731 (Comm); [2018]
  2 Lloyd's Rep. 465 3–18
Skatteverket v Hedqvist (C-264/14) EU:C:2015:718; [2016] S.T.C. 372; [2015] B.V.C. 34;
  [2015] S.T.I. 3240 ECJ 1–19
SL Sethia Liners v Naviagro Maritime Corp (The Kostas Melas), Kostas Melas, The [1981]
  1 Lloyd's Rep 18; [1980] Com. L.R. 3 QBD 2–11
Smales v Lea [2011] EWCA Civ 1325; 140 Con. L.R. 70; [2012] P.N.L.R. 8 3–13
Smith v Battams (1857) 26 L.J. Ex 232 2–16
Smith v Hamilton [1951] Ch. 174; [1950] 2 All E.R. 928; 66 T.L.R. (Pt 2) 937; (1950) 94
  S.J. 724 .... 4–24, 4–31
Smith v Smith [1891] 3 Ch. 550 Ch D 4–18
Sneyd Ex p. Fewings, Re (1884) L.R. 25 Ch. D. 338 CA 4–51
Société Eram Shipping Co Ltd v Compagnie Internationale de Navigation; sub nom. Société
  Eram Shipping Co Ltd v Hong Kong and Shanghai Banking Corp Ltd [2003] UKHL 30;
  [2004] 1 A.C. 260; [2003] 3 W.L.R. 21; [2003] 3 All E.R. 465; [2003] 2 All E.R.
  (Comm) 65; [2003] 2 Lloyd's Rep. 405; [2003] 1 C.L.C. 1163; [2003] I.L.Pr. 36; (2003)
  100(28) L.S.G. 31; (2003) 153 N.L.J. 948; (2003) 147 S.J.L.B. 749 HL 5–48
Société Francaise Bunge SA v Belcan NV (The Federal Huron) [1985] 3 All E.R. 378;
  [1985] 2 Lloyd's Rep. 189; [1985] Fin. L.R. 282 6–38

Solo Industries UK Ltd v Canara Bank [2001] EWCA Civ 1059; [2001] 1 W.L.R. 1800; [2001] 2 All E.R. (Comm) 217; [2001] 2 Lloyd's Rep. 578; [2001] Lloyd's Rep. Bank. 346; [2001] C.L.C. 1651; (2001) 98(29) L.S.G. 37; (2001) 145 S.J.L.B. 168 3–44
Soproma SpA v Marine & Animal By-Products Corp [1966] 1 Lloyd's Rep. 367; 116 N.L.J. 867 3–15
South West Water Services Ltd v International Computers Ltd [1999] B.L.R. 420; [1998–99] Info. T.L.R. 154; [1999–2000] Info. T.L.R. 1; [1999] I.T.C.L.R. 439; [2001] Lloyd's Rep. P.N. 353; [1999] Masons C.L.R. 400 4–03
Spar Shipping AS v Grand China Logistics Holding (Group) Co Ltd, Spar Capella, Spar Vega, Spar Draco; sub nom. Grand China Logistics Holding (Group) Co Ltd v Spar Shipping AS [2016] EWCA Civ 982; [2017] 4 All E.R. 124; [2017] 2 All E.R. (Comm) 701; [2017] Bus. L.R. 663; [2016] 2 Lloyd's Rep. 447; [2016] 2 C.L.C. 441 ....4–13, 4–24, 4–27, 4–31, 4–35
Spargo's Case. See Harmony & Montagne Tin and Copper Mining Co Re
Spectrum Plus Ltd (In Liquidation), Re; sub nom. National Westminster Bank Plc v Spectrum Plus Ltd (In Creditors Voluntary Liquidation) [2005] UKHL 41; [2005] 2 A.C. 680; [2005] 3 W.L.R. 58; [2005] 4 All E.R. 209; [2005] 2 Lloyd's Rep. 275; [2005] B.C.C. 694; [2005] 2 B.C.L.C. 269; (2005) 155 N.L.J. 1045 1–03
Spliethoff's Bevrachtingskantoor BV v Bank of China Ltd [2015] EWHC 999 (Comm); [2016] 1 All E.R. (Comm) 1034; [2015] 2 Lloyd's Rep. 123; [2015] 1 C.L.C. 651 ....3–43, 3–45
Sprint Electric Ltd v Buyer's Dream Ltd [2020] EWHC 2004 (Ch) 6–39
SS Pharmaceutical Co Ltd v Qantas Airways Ltd [1991] 1 Lloyd's Rep. 288 CA (NSW) 3–04
St Maximus Shipping Co Ltd v AP Moller-Maersk [2014] EWHC 1643 (Comm); [2014] 2 Lloyd's Rep. 377 4–03
St Vincent European General Partner Ltd v Robinson [2018] EWHC 1230 (Comm); [2019] 1 B.C.L.C. 706 2–17
Staffordshire AHA v South Staffordshire Waterworks Co [1978] 1 W.L.R. 1387; [1978] 3 All E.R. 769; 77 L.G.R. 17; (1978) 122 S.J. 331 6–13
Standard Bank London Ltd v Bank of Tokyo Ltd; Südwestdeutsche Landesbank Girozentrale v Bank of Tokyo Ltd [1995] 2 Lloyd's Rep. 169; [1995] C.L.C. 496; [1998] Masons C.L.R. Rep. 126 5–36
Standard Chartered Bank v Beam Technology (MFG) Pte Ltd [2002] 2 S.L.R. 155 3–51
Standard Chartered Bank v Ceylon Petroleum Corp [2011] EWHC 1785 (Comm) 6–25
Standard Chartered Bank v Ceylon Petroleum Corp [2011] EWHC 2094 (Comm); (2011) 108(33) L.S.G. 27 4–51
Stavrinides v Bank of Cyprus Public Co Ltd [2019] EWHC 1328 (Ch) 2–27, 5–26
Starbev GP Ltd v Interbrew Central European Holdings BV [2014] EWHC 1311 4–03
Startup v Macdonald (1843) 6 Man. & G. 593; 7 Scott NR 269; 12 LJ Ex 477; 1 LTOS 172 4–03
State of Florida v Espinoza Case No.F14-2923 (Fla. 11th Cir. 2016) 1–20
Steam Stoker Co, Re (1875) L.R. 19 Eq. 416; 44 LJ Ch 386; 23 WR 545; 32 LT 143 2–23
Stein v Blake (No.1) [1996] A.C. 243; [1995] 2 W.L.R. 710; [1995] 2 All E.R. 961; [1995] B.C.C. 543; [1995] 2 B.C.L.C. 94; (1995) 145 N.L.J. 760 HL 2–05
Stein, Forbes & Co Ltd v County Tailoring Ltd (1916) 86 L.J.K.B. 448; 13 Asp MLC 422; 115 LT 215 4–22
Stemcor UK Ltd v Global Steel Holdings Ltd [2015] EWHC 363 (Comm); [2015] 1 Lloyd's Rep. 580 ....2–07, 2–11, 4–36
Stericker v Horner 2012] B.P.I.R. 645 Ch D 4–11
Sterling Industrial Facilities v Lydiate Textiles (1962) 106 S.J. 669 CA 3–29
Stevens, Re (1929) 1 ABC 90 2–29
Stewart Gill Ltd v Horatio Myer and Co Ltd [1992] Q.B. 600; [1992] 2 W.L.R. 721; [1992] 2 All E.R. 257; 31 Con. L.R. 1; (1991) 11 Tr. L.R. 86; (1992) 142 N.L.J. 241 CA (Civ Div 3–48

Stickney v Keeble [1915] A.C. 386, HL; [1914–1915] All E.R. 73; 84 LJ Ch 259; 112 LT
664 HL 4–26
Stobart Group Ltd v Tinkler [2019] EWHC 258 (Comm) 3–22
Stocznia Gdanska SA v Latvian Shipping Co (Repudiation) [2002] EWCA Civ 889; [2002]
2 All E.R. (Comm) 768; [2002] 2 Lloyd's Rep. 436; [2003] 1 C.L.C. 282 CA (Civ
Div) 4–33
Strategic Finance Ltd (in receivership and in liquidation) v Bridgman [2013] NZCA
357 .... 2–37, 2–40
Strode v Parker (1694) 2 Vern. 316 4–51
Strydom v Vendside Ltd [2009] EWHC 2130 (QB); [2009] 6 Costs L.R. 886; (2009)
106(33) L.S.G. 16 3–36
Sugar Hut Brentwood Ltd v Norcross [2008] EWHC 2634 (Ch) 2–40
Sumpter v Hedges [1898] 1 Q.B. 673, CA; 67 LJQB 545; 46 WR 454; 42 S.J. 362; 78 LT
378 CA 3–16, 3–18
Sunrise Brokers LLP v Rodgers [2014] EWCA Civ 1373; [2015] I.C.R. 272; [2015] I.R.L.R.
57 3–19
Superstrike Ltd v Rodrigues [2013] EWCA Civ 669; [2013] 1 W.L.R. 3848; [2013] H.L.R.
42; [2013] L. & T.R. 33; [2013] 2 E.G.L.R. 91; [2013] 2 P. & C.R. DG19 2–16
Sutherland v Royal Bank of Scotland Plc 1997 S.L.T. 329; [1997] 6 Bank. L.R. 132; 1996
G.W.D. 6-290 CSOH 5–59
Swallowfalls Ltd v Monaco Yachting and Technologies SAM [2014] EWCA Civ 186;
[2014] 2 All E.R. (Comm) 185; [2014] 2 Lloyd's Rep. 50 2–17
Swift Advances Plc v Okokenu [2015] C.T.L.C. 302 CC (Central London) 3–37
Swotbooks.com Ltd v Royal Bank of Scotland Plc [2011] EWHC 2025 (QB) 3–15, 5–29
Sztejn v Henry Schroder Banking Corp, 31 N.Y.S. 2d 631 (1941) 3–44
Tadcaster Tower Brewery Co v Wilson [1897] 1 Ch. 705; 61 JP 360; 66 LJ Ch 402; 45 WR
428; 41 S.J. 387; 76 LT 459; 13 T.L.R. 295 4–29
Talent Plc v Revenue and Customs Commissioners [2008] S.T.C. (S.C.D.) 202; [2007] S.T.I.
2234 2–16
Tameside and Glossop Acute Services NHS Trust v Thompstone; sub nom. Thompstone v
Tameside and Glossop Acute Services NHS Trust; South West London Strategic HA v
De Haas; United Bristol Healthcare NHS Trust v RH; South Yorkshire Strategic HA v
Corbett [2008] EWCA Civ 5; [2008] 1 W.L.R. 2207; [2008] 2 All E.R. 537; [2008]
P.I.Q.R. Q2; (2008) 100 B.M.L.R. 113; (2008) 105(4) L.S.G. 25; (2008) 158 N.L.J. 146;
(2008) 152(5) S.J.L.B. 29 CA (Civ Div) 3–06
Tan Hung Nguyen v Luxury Design Homes Pty Ltd [2004] NSWCA 494 CA
(NSW) 3–15
Tasman Discoverer, The. *See* Dairy Containers Ltd v Tasman Orient Line CV
Taurus Petroleum Ltd v State Oil Marketing Co of Iraq [2015] EWCA Civ 835; [2016] 2 All
E.R. (Comm) 1037; [2016] 1 Lloyd's Rep. 42; [2015] C.P. Rep. 48; [2015] 2 C.L.C.
284 5–48
Tayeb v HSBC Bank Plc [2004] EWHC 1529 (Comm); [2004] 4 All E.R. 1024; [2004] 2 All
E.R. (Comm) 880; [2005] 1 C.L.C. 866; (2004) 154 N.L.J. 1217 .... 1–08, 5–22, 5–41,
5–42
Taylor v Brown, 147 U.S. 640 (1893) SC (US) 4–09
Taylor v Caldwell, 122 E.R. 309; (1863) 3 B. & S. 826; (1863) 2 New Rep. 198 Ct of
KB 3–39
Taylor v Rocky Castle Finance Pty Ltd [2014] SASFC 1 SC (South Australia) 2–01
Taylor, Re [1923] 1 Ch. 99 CA 1–02
Teh Hu, The. *See* Owners of Turbo Electric Bulk Carrier Teh Hu v Nippon Salvage Co Ltd
Tehno-Impex v Gebr Van Weelde Scheepvaart Kantoor BV [1981] Q.B. 648; [1981] 2
W.L.R. 821; [1981] 2 All E.R. 669; [1981] 1 Lloyd's Rep. 587; [1981] Com. L.R. 82;
(1981) 125 S.J. 304 CA (Civ Div) 4–59, 4–60
Telewest Communications Plc (No.1), Re [2004] EWCA Civ 728; [2005] B.C.C. 29; [2005]
1 B.C.L.C. 752 6–33
Telford Homes (Creekside) Ltd v Ampurius Nu Homes Holdings Ltd. *See* Ampurius Nu
Homes Holdings Ltd v Telford Homes (Creekside) Ltd

Tenax Steamship Co v Owners of the Motor Vessel Brimnes (The Brimnes); sub nom. Tenax
   Steamship Co v Reinante Transoceanica Navegacion SA (The Brimnes) [1975] Q.B.
   929; [1974] 3 W.L.R. 613; [1974] 3 All E.R. 88; [1974] 2 Lloyd's Rep. 241; (1974) 118
   S.J. 808 CA (Civ Div) 2–23, 4–13, 5–22,
   5–26, 5–34, 5–44, 5–51, 5–52, 5–57,
   5–60, 6–19
Tetronics (International) Ltd v HSBC Bank Plc [2018] EWHC 201 (TCC); [2018] B.L.R.
   450; 177 Con. L.R. 159 3–44
Texaco Melbourne, The. *See* Attorney General of Ghana v Texaco Overseas Tankships Ltd
Thomas v Brown (1876) 1 Q.B.D. 714 3–81
Thompson v ASDA-MFI Group Plc [1988] Ch. 241; [1988] 2 W.L.R. 1093; [1988] 2 All
   E.R. 722; [1988] I.R.L.R. 340; (1988) 132 S.J. 497 2–17
Thompson v Hudson (Appropriation of Payments) (1870–71) L.R. 6 Ch. App. 320 CA in
   Chancery 4–51
Tidal Energy Ltd v Bank of Scotland Plc [2014] EWCA Civ 1107; [2015] 2 All E.R. 15;
   [2015] 2 All E.R. (Comm) 38; [2014] Bus. L.R. 1167; [2014] 2 Lloyd's Rep. 549;
   [2014] 2 C.L.C. 124 5–22
Tilley v Bowman Ltd [1910] 1 K.B. 745; 79 LJKB 547; 17 Mans 79; [1908–10] All E.R.
   Rep. 952: 54 S.J. 342; 102 LT 318 3–78
Tilley v Thomas (1867–68) L.R. 3 Ch. App. 61; 32 JP 180; 16 WR 166; 17 LT
   422 4–26
Timber Shipping Co SA v London and Overseas Freighters; sub nom. London & Overseas
   Freighters Ltd v Timber Shipping Co SA [1972] A.C. 1; [1971] 2 W.L.R. 1360; [1971] 2
   All E.R. 599; [1971] 1 Lloyd's Rep. 523; (1971) 115 S.J. 404 HL 4–61
Titford Property Co Ltd v Cannon Street Acceptances Ltd Unreported 197) 4–21
Toms v Wilson (1862) 4 B. & S. 442, 455; 32 LJQB 382; 10 Jur NS 201; 2 New Rep 454;
   11 WR 952; 8 LT 799 4–11
Toprak Mahsulleri Ofisi v Finagrain Compagnie Commerciale Agricole et Financière SA
   [1979] 2 Lloyd's Rep. 98 CA (Civ Div) 6–24, 6–25
Tradax Export SA v Dorada Compania Naviera SA of Panama (The Lutetian) [1982] 2
   Lloyd's Rep. 140; [1982] Com. L.R. 130 4–03
Trans Trust SPRL v Danubian Trading Co Ltd [1952] 2 Q.B. 297; [1952] 1 All E.R. 970;
   [1952] 1 Lloyd's Rep. 348; [1952] 1 T.L.R. 1066; (1952) 96 S.J. 312 CA 4–55
Transoceanica Francesca, The and Nicos V, The [1987] 2 Lloyd's Rep. 155 6–39
Transpacific Eternity SA v Kanematsu Corp (The Antares III) [2002] 1 Lloyd's Rep. 233;
   [2001] All E.R. (D) 33 4–34
Travelers Casualty & Surety Co of Canada v Sun Life Assurance Co of Canada (UK) Ltd
   [2006] EWHC 2716 (Comm); [2007] Lloyd's Rep. I.R. 619 6–44
Treseder-Griffin v Co-operative Insurance Society Ltd [1956] 2 Q.B. 127; [1956] 2 W.L.R.
   866; [1956] 2 All E.R. 33; [1956] 1 Lloyd's Rep. 377; (1956) 100 S.J. 283
   CA 3–02, 3–04
Triffit Nurseries v Salads Etcetera Ltd [2000] 1 All E.R. (Comm) 737; [2000] 2 Lloyd's
   Rep. 74; [2001] B.C.C. 457; [2000] 1 B.C.L.C. 761 CA (Civ Div) 5–36
Trigg v Revenue and Customs Commissioners [2018] EWCA Civ 17; [2018] 1 W.L.R. 5180;
   [2018] 2 All E.R. 455; [2018] S.T.C. 281; [2018] B.T.C. 7; [2018] S.T.I.
   257 6–08
Trillium (Prime) Property GP Ltd v Elmfield Road Ltd [2018] EWCA Civ 1556; [2018] 2 P.
   & C.R. DG21 3–08
Trinh v Citibank, 850 F. 2d 164 (1988) 5–46
TSB Bank of Scotland Plc v Welwyn & Hatfield DC [1993] 2 Bank. L.R. 267 5–36
TTI Team Telecom International Ltd v Hutchison 3G UK Ltd [2003] EWHC 762 (TCC);
   [2003] 1 All E.R. (Comm) 914 . . . . 3–45, 3–50
Turkiye IS Bankasi AS v Bank of China [1998] 1 Lloyd's Rep. 250; [1998] C.L.C. 182 CA
   (Civ Div) 3–44, 3–45
Twinsectra Ltd v Yardley [2002] UKHL 12; [2002] 2 A.C. 164; [2002] 2 W.L.R. 802; [2002]
   2 All E.R. 377; [2002] P.N.L.R. 30; [2002] W.T.L.R. 423; [2002] 38 E.G. 204 (C.S.);
   (2002) 99(19) L.S.G. 32; (2002) 152 N.L.J. 469; (2002) 146 S.J.L.B. 84; [2002] N.P.C.
   47 2–23
UK Housing Alliance (North West) Ltd v Francis [2010] EWCA Civ 117; [2010] 3 All E.R.
   519; [2010] Bus. L.R. 1034; [2010] H.L.R. 28; [2010] 2 E.G.L.R. 81; [2010] 18 E.G.
   100; [2010] 9 E.G. 167 (C.S.); [2010] N.P.C. 23; [2010] 2 P. & C.R. DG9 . . . . 3–84, 4–04

Ukraine v Law Debenture Trust Corp Plc [2018] EWCA Civ 2026; [2019] Q.B. 1121;
  [2019] 2 W.L.R. 655; [2018] 2 C.L.C. 627 2–17
Underwood Son & Piper v Lewis [1894] 2 Q.B. 306 CA 3–13
United City Merchants (Investments) Ltd v Royal Bank of Canada (The American Accord)
  [1983] 1 A.C. 168; [1982] 2 W.L.R. 1039; [1982] 2 All E.R. 720; [1982] 2 Lloyd's Rep.
  1; [1982] Com. L.R. 142 HL 2–45, 3–24, 3–44,
  3–51
United Dominions Trust (Commercial) v Eagle Aircraft Services; sub nom. United
  Dominions Trust (Commercial) v Eagle Aviation [1968] 1 W.L.R. 74; [1968] 1 All E.R.
  104; (1967) 111 S.J. 849 CA (Civ Div) 4–30
United Railways of Havana and Regla Warehouses Ltd, Re [1961] A.C. 1007; [1960] 2
  W.L.R. 969; [1960] 2 All E.R. 332; (1960) 104 S.J. 466 HL 6–30, 6–31
United Scientific Holdings Ltd v Burnley BC; Cheapside Land Development Co Ltd v
  Messels Service Co [1978] A.C. 904; [1977] 2 W.L.R. 806; [1977] 2 All E.R. 62; 75
  L.G.R. 407; (1977) 33 P. & C.R. 220; (1977) 243 E.G. 43; (1977) 121 S.J. 223
  HL 4–26, 4–27, 4–30,
  4–31
United States of America v Faiella Case 1:14-cr-00243-JSR, New York 1–20
United States of America v Ulbricht Case 1:14-cr-00068-KBF, New York 1–20
United Trading Corp SA v Allied Arab Bank Ltd, Murray Clayton v Rafidair Bank [1985] 2
  Lloyd's Rep. 554 3–44
University of Zimbabwe v Sibanda [2014] ZWLC 21 6–13
Urban I (Blonk Street) Ltd v Ayres [2013] EWCA Civ 816; [2014] 1 W.L.R. 756; [2013]
  B.L.R. 505; [2014] 1 P. & C.R. 1; [2013] 3 E.G.L.R. 91; [2013] 29 E.G. 105
  (C.S.) 4–15, 4–24, 4–31,
  4–35
UTB LLC v Sheffield United Ltd, Blades Leisure Ltd, Re; sub nom. Sheffield United Ltd v
  UTB LLC [2019] EWHC 2322 (Ch) 2–17
Valilas v Januzaj [2014] EWCA Civ 436; [2015] 1 All E.R. (Comm) 1047; 154 Con. L.R.
  38. 4–35
Vannin Capital PCC v RBOS Shareholders Action Group Ltd [2018] EWHC 2821
  (Ch) 5–51
Vansandau v Browne 131 E.R. 667; (1832) 9 Bing. 402 Com Pl 3–13
Videocon Global Ltd v Goldman Sachs International; sub nom. Goldman Sachs International
  v Videocon Global Ltd [2016] EWCA Civ 130; [2017] 2 All E.R. (Comm) 800; [2017] 1
  B.C.L.C. 696; [2016] 1 C.L.C. 528 2–14
Vishipco Lines v Chase Manhattan Bank NA, 754 F. 2d 452 (2nd Cir. 1985) 1–07, 5–46
Vitol SA v Norelf Ltd (The Santa Clara) [1996] A.C. 800; [1996] 3 W.L.R. 105; [1996] 3
  All E.R. 193; [1996] 2 Lloyd's Rep. 225; [1996] C.L.C. 1159; (1996) 15 Tr. L.R. 347;
  (1996) 93(26) L.S.G. 19; (1996) 146 N.L.J. 957; (1996) 140 S.J.L.B. 147
  HL 3–19
Vivienne Westwood Ltd v Conduit Street Development Ltd [2017] EWHC 350 (Ch); [2017]
  L. & T.R. 23 . . . . 3–29, 3–30
Voest Alpine Intertrading GmbH v Bunwill & Co SA (Pty) Ltd [1985] 2 S.A.L.R.
  149. 6–39
Volk v Hirstlens (NZ) Ltd [1987] 1 N.Z.R.R. 385 6–44
Vossloh AG v Alpha Trains (UK) Ltd [2010] EWHC 2443 (Ch); [2011] 2 All E.R. (Comm)
  307; [2010] T.C.L.R. 8; 132 Con. L.R. 32 . . . . 2–43, 3–42
Vucicevic v Aleksic [2017] EWHC 2335 (Ch); [2017] W.T.L.R. 1545 1–02
Wadham Stringer Finance Ltd v Meaney [1981] 1 W.L.R. 39; [1980] 3 All E.R. 789; [1980]
  Com. L.R. 7; [1981] R.T.R. 152; (1980) 124 S.J. 807. . . . . 3–32, 3–59
Wadsworth v Lydell [1981] 1 W.L.R. 598; [1981] 2 All E.R. 401; (1981) 125 S.J. 309, CA
  (Civ Div) 4–55, 4–56
Walker v Texas Commerce Bank, 635 F. Supp. 678 (S.D. Tex., 1986). 5–36
Wallace v Universal Automatic Machines Co [1894] 2 Ch. 547, CA; 63 LJ Ch 598; 1 Mans
  315; 7 R 316; [1891–94] All E.R. Rep. 1156; 70 LT 852; 10 T.L.R. 501 4–36
Wallersteiner v Moir (No.2); sub nom. Moir v Wallersteiner (No.2) [1975] Q.B. 373; [1975]
  2 W.L.R. 389; [1975] 1 All E.R. 849; (1975) 119 S.J. 97 CA (Civ Div) 4–58
Ward v Kidswin (1661) Lat. 77 6–30
Warinco v Samor SpA [1979] 1 Lloyd's Rep. 450, CA (Civ Div) 3–11

Warnborough Ltd v Garmite Ltd [2006] EWHC 10 (Ch); [2007] 1 P. & C.R. 2; [2006] 3
E.G. 121 (C.S.); [2006] 2 P. & C.R. DG8 2–01
Warren v Burns [2014] EWHC 3671 (QB) 4–29, 4–34
Warren v Hill Dickinson LLP [2018] EWHC 3322 (QB); [2018] 6 Costs L.R.
1377 3–13
Webb v Fairmaner 150 E.R. 1231; (1838) 3 M. & W. 473 Ex 4–09
Webber v NHS Direct [2012] 11 WLUK 930 EAT 4–06
Weldon v GRE Linked Life Assurance Ltd [2000] 2 All E.R. (Comm) 914
QBD 5–34
Wells Fargo Asia Ltd v Citibank NA 852 F. 2d 657, 495 US 660 (1990) and 926 F. 2d 273
(2nd Cir. 1991), cert denied (1992) 505 US 1204 ....5–46, 5–48, 5–49,
6–20
Westdeutsche Landesbank Girozentrale v Islington LBC; sub nom. Islington LBC v
Westdeutsche Landesbank Girozentrale; Kleinwort Benson Ltd v Sandwell BC [1996]
A.C. 669; [1996] 2 W.L.R. 802; [1996] 2 All E.R. 961; [1996] 5 Bank. L.R. 341; [1996]
C.L.C. 990; 95 L.G.R. 1; (1996) 160 J.P. Rep. 1130; (1996) 146 N.L.J. 877; (1996) 140
S.J.L.B. 136 HL 3–16, 3–82, 4–56
Western Bulk Carriers K/S v Li Hai Maritime Inc [2005] EWHC 735 (Comm); [2005] 2
Lloyd's Rep. 389; [2005] 1 C.L.C. 704 4–03
Whitbread Group Plc v Goldapple Ltd (No.2), 2005 S.L.T. 281; 2005 S.C.L.R. 263; 2005
G.W.D. 8–114 OH 4–04
White & Carter (Councils) Ltd v McGregor [1962] A.C. 413; [1962] 2 W.L.R. 17; [1961] 3
All E.R. 1178; 1962 S.C. (H.L.) 1; 1962 S.L.T. 9; (1961) 105 S.J. 1104
HL 3–19, 3–21, 3–22
White v Riverside Housing Association Ltd; sub nom. Riverside Housing Association Ltd v
White [2007] UKHL 20; [2007] 4 All E.R. 97; [2007] H.L.R. 31; [2008] 1 P. & C.R. 13;
[2007] L. & T.R. 22; [2007] 2 E.G.L.R. 69; [2007] 29 E.G. 144; [2007] 18 E.G. 152
(C.S.); (2007) 104(19) L.S.G. 25; (2007) 151 S.J.L.B. 574; [2007] N.P.C. 46
HL 4–28
White v Shortall [2006] NSWSC 1379 4–29
Whitehead v National Westminster Bank Ltd, Times, June 9, 1982 5–3429
Whonnock Industries Ltd v National Bank of Canada (1987) 42 D.L.R. (4th) 4–11
William Clark Partnership Ltd v Dock St Pct Ltd [2015] EWHC 2923 (TCC); 163 Con. L.R.
117 3–13
Williams & Glyn's Bank Ltd v Barnes [1981] Com. L.R. 205 HC 4–11, 4–21
Williams v Burgess (1840) 10 L.J.Q.B. 10 4–14
Williams v Gibbons [1994] NZLR 273 SC (NZ) 5–27
Williams v Roffey Bros & Nicholls (Contractors) Ltd [1991] 1 QB 1; [1990] 1 All E.R. 512;
[1990] 2 W.L.R. 1153; [1990] 12 LS Gax R 36; [1989] NLJR 1712; 48 B.L.R. 75, CA;
[1989] EWCA Civ 5 3–15
Willmot v Gardner. See Henry, Re Marquess of Anglesey. Willmot v Gardner
Wilson, Smithett & Cope Ltd v Terruzzi [1976] Q.B. 683; [1976] 2 W.L.R. 418; [1976] 1
All E.R. 817; [1976] 1 Lloyd's Rep. 509; (1976) 120 S.J. 116 CA (Civ
Div) 3–24
Windermere Court Kenley RTM Co Ltd v Sinclair Gardens Investments (Kensington) Ltd
[2014] UKUT 420 (LC) 4–06, 4–14
WJ Alan & Co Ltd v El Nasr Export & Import Co [1972] 2 Q.B. 189; [1972] 2 W.L.R. 800;
[1972] 2 All E.R. 127; [1972] 1 Lloyd's Rep. 313; (1972) 116 S.J. 139 CA (Civ
Div) 2–25
Wood v TUI Travel Plc (t/a First Choice) [2017] EWCA Civ 11; [2018] Q.B. 927; [2018] 2
W.L.R. 1051; [2017] 2 All E.R. (Comm) 734; [2017] 1 Lloyd's Rep. 322; [2017]
P.I.Q.R. P8 4–22
Woodar Investment Development Ltd v Wimpey Construction UK Ltd [1980] 1 W.L.R. 277;
[1980] 1 All E.R. 571; (1980) 124 S.J. 184 HL 4–35
Woodhouse AC Israel Cocoa SA v Nigerian Produce Marketing Co Ltd; sub nom.
Woodhouse v Nigerian Produce Marketing Co Ltd [[1972] A.C. 741; [1972] 2 W.L.R.
1090; [1972] 2 All E.R. 271; [1972] 1 Lloyd's Rep. 439; (1972) 116 S.J. 329
HL..3–02, 6–02, 6–08,
6–09
Woodland v Fear 119 E.R. 1339; (1857) 7 El. & Bl. 519 ....2–33, 5–59

Woodroffes, Re (Musical Instruments) Ltd [1986] Ch. 366; [1985] 3 W.L.R. 543; [1985] 2
  All E.R. 908; [1985] P.C.C. 318; (1985) 82 L.S.G. 3170; (1985) 129 S.J.
  589 3–74
Woods v Mackenzie Hill Ltd [1975] 1 W.L.R. 613; [1975] 2 All E.R. 170; (1975) 29 P. &
  C.R. 306; (1975) 119 S.J. 187 4–31
Wright v Shawcross (1819) 2 B. & A. 501, Note 4–07
WS Tankship II BV v Kwangju Bank Ltd [2011] EWHC 3103 (Comm); [2012] C.I.L.L.
  3155 .... 2–45, 3–45
Wuhan Guoyu Logistics Group Co Ltd v Emporiki Bank of Greece SA [2012] EWCA Civ
  1629; [2013] 1 All E.R. (Comm) 1191; [2014] 1 Lloyd's Rep. 266; [2012] 2 C.L.C. 986;
  [2013] B.L.R. 74; [2013] C.I.L.L. 3300; [2013] Bus. L.R. D76 .... 2–45, 3–43, 3–49
Xena Systems Ltd v Cantideck [2013] EWPCC 1 4–56
Yam Seng Pte Ltd v International Trade Corp Ltd [2013] EWHC 111 (QB); [2013] 1 All
  E.R. (Comm) 1321; [2013] 1 Lloyd's Rep. 526; [2013] 1 C.L.C. 662; [2013] B.L.R. 147;
  146 Con. L.R. 39; [2013] Bus. L.R. D53 2–17
Yemgas FZCO v Superior Pescadores SA Panama [2014] EWHC 971 (Comm); [2014] 1
  Lloyd's Rep. 660; [2014] 1 C.L.C. 496 3–04
Yemgas FZCO v Superior Pescadores SA Panama [2016] EWCA Civ 101; [2016] 2 All E.R.
  (Comm) 104; [2016] Bus. L.R. 1033; [2016] 1 Lloyd's Rep. 561; [2016] 1 C.L.C.
  317 3–04
Yourell v Hibernian Bank Ltd [1918] A.C. 372 HL 4–42
Zim Israel Navigation Co Ltd v Effy Shipping Corp [1972] 1 Lloyd's Rep. 18 .... 2–01, 5–57
ZCCM Investments Holdings Plc v Konkola Copper Mines Plc [2017] EWHC 3288
  (Comm) 3–59, 4–52

TABLE OF STATUTES

1728	Insolvent Debtors Relief (2 Geo. 2, c.22)	1974	Consumer Credit Act
	s.13 2–06		(c.39) 3–38, 3–59, 3–60,
1734	Set-off (8 Geo. 2, c.24)		3–62, 4–18, 4–43, 5–33
	s.5 2–06		s.66 5–33
1838	Judgments Act (c.110)		s.75 . . . . 5–31, 5–33, 5–71,
	s.17 . . . . 4–61, 4–62		5–75
1870	Apportionment Act (c.35)		s.83 5–33
	s.2 . . . . 4–41, 4–51		s.84 5–33
	s.5 . . . . 4–41, 4–51		(1) 5–33
1873	Supreme Court of Judicature Act (c.66)		(2) 5–33
	s.25(7) 4–26		(3) 5–33
1882	Bills of Exchange Act (45 & 46 Vict.		(3A) 5–33
	c.61)		ss.86B–86F 3–59
	s.3(1) 4–48		s.87 3–62
	s.14(1) 4–05		(1) 3–59
	(2) 4–14		s.88 3–59
	s.46(2)(a) 6–24		s.90 3–62
	s.53(1) 2–27		s.94 . . . . 4–17, 4–20
	s.57 4–57		s.95 4–20
	(2) 6–32		s.138 4–43
	s.72(4) 6–32		ss.140A—140C 3–35, 4–43
	s.83 1–03		s.140A 3–36
	s.92 . . . . 4–05, 4–07		(1)(b) 4–43
1890	Partnership Act (c.39)		(2) 4–43
	s.24 4–40		s.140B 3–38
1925	Law of Property Act		s.171 5–33
	(c.20) 3–73	1977	Administration of Justice Act (c.38)
	s.41 4–26		s.4 6–32
	s.61 4–08		Unfair Contract Terms Act (c.50)
	s.87(1) 3–73		s.13 3–48
	s.93 3–65	1978	Interpretation Act (c.30)
	ss.101–109 3–73		Sch.1 4–08
	s.146 2–28	1979	International Monetary Fund Act (c.29)
1934	Law Reform (Miscellaneous Provisions)		s.6(2) 3–24
	Act (c.41) 6–28		Sale of Goods Act (c.54) . . . 5–31, 5–75
	s.1(2) 6–28		s.2(1) 1–21, 4–22, 5–75
	(3) 6–28		s.10 4–26
	s.3 4–60		(1) 4–27
1943	Law Reform (Frustrated Contracts) Act		(3) 4–08
	(c.40)		s.19 4–34
	s.1 3–39		s.27 3–11
1954	Currency and Bank Notes Act (c.12)		s.28 . . . . 2–45, 3–11, 3–70,
	s.1 3–02		4–22
	(4) 1–03		s.30(1) 3–13, 3–18
	Landlord and Tenant Act		s.38(1) 2–17, 3–78
	(c.56) 4–10		(b) 2–27
1968	Theft Act (c.60) 5–36		s.41(1) 3–78
1970	Administration of Justice Act (c.31)		s.45(1) 3–78
	s.44A 4–60, 4–61		s.46(1)–(2) 3–78
1971	Coinage Act (c.24)		s.48 3–78
	s.2 3–02		(3) 4–29
	Banking and Financial Dealings Act		(4) 4–31
	(c.80) 4–05		s.49 . . . . 2–17, 3–78, 4–22
	s.3(2) 4–05		(1) 3–11, 4–22
			(2) 4–22

1979	Sale of Goods Act (c.54)—*continued*	2002	Proceeds of Crime Act
	s.61(1) 3–11		(c.29) 5–11, 5–41, 5–42,
	(4) 3–78		6–20
1981	Senior Courts Act (c.54)		ss.327–330 5–41
	s.35A 4–60, 4–61		s.327 5–43
1982	Supply of Goods and Services Act (c.29)		s.329 5–43
	s.4. 4–22		Enterprise Act (c.40). 3–73
	Administration of Justice Act (c.53)	2004	Housing Act (c.34)
	s.15(1) 4–60		s.213 2–16
	Sch1 Pt 1 4–60	2006	Consumer Credit Act
1983	Currency Act (c.9)		(c.14) 3–35, 3–36, 3–38,
	s.1. 3–02		4–43
1984	County Court Act (c.28)		ss.9–12 3–59
	s.74. . . . . 4–60, 4–61		s.14. 3–59
1986	Insolvency Act (c.45) 3–61, 3–73		Companies Act (c.46)
	s.189 . . . . 4–57, 4–62		s.739 4–20
	s.239 . . . . 2–23, 5–36, 5–55		s.859H 4–36
	s.244 . . . . 2–29, 4–45	2009	Banking Act (c.1). 2–12
	s.267(2) 4–11		Pt 2 5–12
	s.322 6–33		Pt 5 . . . . 5–12, 5–68
	s.382 6–33		s.48(1)(d) 2–12
	(3) 4–36		s.206A 5–68
1988	Income and Corporation Taxes Act (c.1)	2010	Equality Act (c.15)
	s.203(1) 2–16		s.199 2–20
1989	Law of Property (Miscellaneous		Bribery Act (c.23) 5–11, 5–43
	Provisions) Act (c.34)		s.7. 5–43
	s.2. 3–81		Financial Services Act (c.28)
1992	Social Security Contributions and		s.20. . . . . 5–68, 5–72
	Benefits Act (c.4)	2011	Energy Act (c.27). 3–59
	s.6(1) 2–16	2012	Financial Services Act
1995	Private International Law		(c.21). 4–45
	(Miscellaneous Provisions) Act (c.42)	2013	Crime and Courts (c.22) 5–41
	s.5. 4–61		Financial Services (Banking Reform)
1996	Arbitration Act (c.23) 6–39		Act (c.33) 5–06
	s.20. 4–61	2015	Consumer rights Act
	s.35A. 4–60		(c15) 3–68, 4–43, 4–51,
	(5) 4–60		4–54, 5–75
	s.49. . . . . 4–60, 4–61		Pt 2 . . . . 4–44, 4–51, 5–75
	Damages Act (c.48)		s.2(9) 5–75
	s.2(8) 3–06		s.62. . . . . 5–40, 5–75
	(9) 3–06		(4) 3–35
1998	Late Payment of Commercial Debts		s.64(2) 4–44
	(Interest) Act (c.20) 3–31, 4–39,		Sch.2 Pt 1 para.5 3–35
	4–57	2018	Data Protection Act (c.12) 5–10
2000	Financial Services and Markets Act		Sanctions and Anti-Money Laundering
	(c.8) 4–18		Act (c.13) 5–41

TABLE OF STATUTORY INSTRUMENTS

1986	Insolvency Rules (SI 1986/1925) r.4.90 . . . . 2–40, 6–33		2015	Financial Services Act 2012 (Misleading Statements and Impressions) (Amendment) Order (SI 2015/369) 4–45
1991	County Courts (Interest on Judgment Debts) Order 1 (SI 1991/1184) 4–61			Payment Accounts Regulations (SI 2015/2038) 5–06
1993	Judgment Debts (Rate of Interest) Order (SI 1993/564) 4–61		2016	Insolvency (England and Wales) Rules (SI 2016/1024)
1998	Administration of Insolvent Estates of Deceased Persons Order (SI 1986/1999) 6–33			rr.14.24–14.25 . . . . 2–40 r.14.21 6–33
	Civil Procedure Rules (SI 1998/3132) Pt 16 PD 16 para.9.1 . . . . 6–36 Pt 24 . . . . 2–42, 3–21, 3–44, 4–60			r.14.24 . . . . 2–05, 2–10, 2–39, 3–77 r.14.25 . . . . 2–05, 2–10, 3–77
	Pt 37 r.2 2–17		2017	r.14.44 . . . . 2–39 Money Laundering, Terrorist Financing and Transfer of Funds (Information on the Payer) Regulations (SI 2017/692) 5–41, 5–72
1999	Unfair Terms in Consumer Contract Regulations (SI 1999/2083) 3–29, 3–35, 3–68, 4–44, 4–51, 4–54			
	s.6(2) . . . . 4–44 s.64(1)(b) . . . . 4–44 (2) . . . . 4–45 Sch.2 para.1(f) 3–35			reg.3(1)(b) . . . . 5–76 regs 18–25 . . . . 5–41 reg.18 . . . . 5–41 regs 19–40 . . . . 5–41 reg.27 5–41
	Financial Market and Insolvency (Settlement Finality) Regulations (SI 1999/2979) 5–12, 5–55			reg.28 . . . . 5–41 regs 42–45ZB . . . . 5–41 Payment Services Regulations (SI
2001	Financial Services and Markets Act 2001 (Regulated Activities) Order (SI 2001/544 . . . . 1–21 art.2 . . . . 1–21 art.5(2) 1–21			2017/752) . . . . . . 5–33, 5–36, 5–67, 5–68, 5–71 reg.2 . . . . 5–71 (1) 5–33, 5–36, 5–65 reg.23 5–67
2002	Electronic Commerce Regulations (SI 2002/2013) 5–09			reg.72 . . . . 5–33 (3) 5–33
2003	Financial Collateral Arrangements (No.2) Regulations (SI 2003/3226) 5–12			reg.74(1) . . . . 5–33 reg.75(1) 5–33 (3) 5–33
2004	Consumer Credit (Early Settlement) Regulations (SI 2004/1483) 4–20			(4) . . . . 5–33 reg.76 . . . . 5–33 (2) 5–33, 5–67
2008	Legislative Reform (Consumer Credit) Order (SI 2008/2826) 3–59			reg.77(1) . . . . 5–33 (a) 5–33
2009	Payment Services Regulations (SI 2009/209) 5–33, 5–75 reg.2 5–75			(b) . . . . 5–33 (3) 5–33 (4) 5–33
2010	Consumer Credit (EU Directive) Regulations (SI 2010/1010) reg.37 3–59			reg.100 . . . . 5–33, 5–67 Pt 8 . . . . 5–65 (3) 5–67
2011	Electronic Money Regulations (SI 2011/99) . . . . 5–67, 5–75 reg.2 . . . . 1–11, 5–75			Sch.2 para.11 . . . . 5–68 Sch.8(1) para.1(b) . . . . 5–33 Banking Act 2009 (Service Providers to Payment Systems) Order (SI
2014	Consumer Credit Act 1974 (Green Deal) (Amendment) Order (SI 2014/436) 3–59		2018	2017/1167) . . . . 5–68 Electronic Money, Payment Services and Payment Systems (Amendment and Transitional Provisions) (EU Exit)

2018 Electronic Money, Payment Services and Payment Systems (Amendment and Transitional Provisions) (EU Exit) —*continued*
Regulations 2018 (SI 2018/1201) 5–77
2019 Interchange Fee (Amendment) (EU Exit) Regulations 2019 (SI 2019/284) 5–77

Money Laundering and Terrorist Financing (Amendment) Regulations (SI 2019/1511) 5–41, 5–76
reg.4(1)(b) 5–41

TABLE OF EC AND EU LEGISLATION

Treaties and Conventions

1980 Rome Convention on the Law applicable to Contractual
Obligations 5–39
art.4 5–39

Regulations

1997 Reg.1103/97 on certain provisions relating to the introduction of the euro [1997] OJ L162/1 3–10
1998 Reg.2866/98 on euro conversion rates and the currencies of the Member States adopting the euro [1998] OJ L359/1 . . . . 3–10, 6–09
2000 Reg.1478/2000 on the conversion rates between the euro and the currencies of the Member States adopting the euro [2000] OJ L167/1 3–10
2001 44/2001 on jurisdiction and the recognition and enforcement of judgments in civil and commercial matters (Brussels 1) [2001] OJ L12/1 5–40
art.15 5–40
art.73 5–40
2006 Reg.1086/2006 amending Regulation (EC) No 2866/98 on the conversion rates between the euro and the currencies of the Member States adopting the euro [2006] OJ L195/1 3–10
2007 Reg.1134/2007 as regards the conversion rate to the euro for Malta [2007] OJ L256/1 3–10
Reg.1135/2007 as regards the conversion rate to the euro for Cyprus [2007] OJ L256/2 3–10
2008 Reg.593/2008 on the law applicable to contractual obligations (Rome I) [2008] OJ L177/6 . . . . . . 5–39, 6–07
art.3 . . . . 5–39, 6–07
art.4 . . . . 5–39, 6–07
(1)(a) 5–39
(b) 5–39
art.6(1) 5–39, 5–40
(2) 5–40
art.9(3) 5–46, 6–26
art.12(1) 3–25, 5–46, 6–08, 6–47
(a) 6–46
(b) 6–24, 6–46
(d) 6–24
(2) 6–08, 6–18, 6–26, 6–48
art.21 . . . . 5–46, 6–27
Reg.694/2008 as regards the conversion rate to the euro for Slovakia [2008] OJ L195/3 3–10
2009 Reg.924/2009 on cross-border payments in the Community [2009] OJ L266/11 2–08
2010 Reg.671/2010 as regards the conversion rate to the euro for Estonia [2010] OJ L196/4 6–10
2012 Reg.260/2012 establishing technical and business requirements for credit transfers and direct debits in euro [2012] OJ L94/22 5–08
Reg.1215/2012 on jurisdiction and the recognition and enforcement of judgments in civil and commercial matters (recast) OJ L351/1 5–40
2013 Reg.575/2013 on prudential requirements for credit institutions and investment firms [2013] OJ L176/1
art.4(1) 5–65
Reg.870/2013 as regards the conversion rate to the euro for Latvia [2013] OJ L243/1 3–10
2014 Regulation (EU) No 596/2014 on market abuse (market abuse regulation) and repealing Directive 2003/6/EC of the European Parliament and of the Council and Commission Directives 2003/124/EC, 2003/125/EC and 2004/72/EC 4–45
Reg. 851/2014 as regards the conversion rate to the euro for Lithuania [2014] OJ L233/21 3–010
Reg.910/2014 on electronic identification and trust services for electronic transactions in the internal market [2014] OJ L257/73 5–09
2015 Reg.2015/751 on interchange fees for card-based payment transactions [2015] OJ L123/1 . . . . . . 5–08, 5–09
Reg.2015/847 on information accompanying transfers of funds [2015] OJ L141/1 . . . . . . 5–41, 5–47
2016 Reg.2016/679 on the protection of natural persons with regard to the processing of personal data and on the free movement of such data [2016] OJ L119/1 5–10

Reg.2016/1011 on indices used as benchmarks in financial instruments and financial contracts or to measure the performance of investment funds and amending Directives 2008/48/EC and 2014/17/EU and Regulation (EU) No 596/2014 [2016] OJ L171/1 4–45

2018 Reg.2018/389 with regard to regulatory technical standards for strong customer authentication and common and secure open standards of communication [2018] OJ L69/23 art.11 5–33

Directives

1993 Dir.93/13 of 5 April 1993 on unfair terms in consumer contracts [1993] OJ L95/29 .... 4–53, 5–07
1998 Dir.98/26 on settlement finality in payment and securities settlement systems [1998] OJ L166/45 .... 5–11, 5–55
2000 Dir.2000/31 on certain legal aspects of information society services, in particular electronic commerce, in the Internal Market ('Directive on electronic commerce') [2000] OJ L178/1 5–09
Dir.2000/46 on the supervision of electronic money institutions [2000] OJ L275/39 art.1(3)(a) 5–65
2002 Dir.2002/47 on financial collateral arrangements [2002] OJ L168/43 5–12
2007 Dir.2007/64 on payment services (PSD I) [2007] OJ L319/1 .... 5–06, 5–65
2009 Dir.2009/110 on the taking up, pursuit and prudential supervision of the business of electronic money institutions [2009] OJ L267/7 .... 5–09, 5–10, 5–69
art.2(1) 5–65
art.7 5–10

2014 Dir.2014/49 on deposit guarantee schemes [2014] OJ L173/149 5–10
Dir.2014/92 on the comparability of fees related to payment accounts, payment account switching and access to payment accounts with basic features [2014] OJ L257/214 5–06
2015 Dir.2015/849 on the prevention of the use of the financial system for the purposes of money laundering or terrorist financing [2015] OJ L141/73 .... 5–11, 5–41
Dir.2015/2366 on payment services in the internal market (PSD II) [2015] OJ L337/35 ..... 5–06, 5–08, 5–09, 5–10, 5–33, 5–38, 5–65, 5–77
art.2 5–77
art.4(3) 5–10
(15) 5–65
(16) 5–65
art.10 5–10
art.66 5–09
art.67 5–09
arts 73-77 5–10
art.74 5–10
art.77 5–34
art.82 5–20
(1) 5–20
(2) 5–20
art.83(1) 5–20
art.97 5–33
(5) 5–67
Annex I 5–09
2017 Dir.2017/541 on combating terrorism OJ L88/6 5–47
2018 Dir.2018/843 amending Dir.2015/849 on the prevention of the use of the financial system for the purposes of money laundering or terrorist financing [2018] OJ L156/43 .... 1–20, 5–41, 5–47
Dir.2018/1673 on combating money laundering by criminal law OJ L284/22 5–41

TABLE OF INTERNATIONAL TREATIES AND CONVENTIONS

1924 International Convention for the Unification of Certain Rules relating to Bills of Lading and Protocol of Signature (Hague Rules) 3–04, 3–05
     Art.22 3–04
1945 Articles of Agreement of the International Monetary Fund (IMF)
     Art.VIII(2) 3–24
     (b) 3–24
1950 European Convention on Human Rights 3–73
1967 Council of Europe Convention on Foreign Money Liabilities 6–01
1972 Council of Europe Convention on the Place of Payment of Money Liabilities 6–01
1980 United Nations Convention on Contracts for the International Sale of Goods
     art.57 6–03
2001 Cape Town Convention on International Interests in Mobile Equipment 4–07
     Protocol Art.IX 4–07
     Art.X 4–07
2007 Luxembourg Protocol to the Convention on Interests in Mobile Equipment on Matters Specific to Rail Rolling Stock 4–07

Chapter 1

THE CONCEPT OF MONEY

1. The Concept of Money

What is money?

What is the meaning of the expression "money"? As with so many things, the answer will depend on the context or framework within which the question is asked. For an economist, the question may arise in the context of monetary, fiscal or macro-economic policy. For the lawyer, the question is likely to arise in the context of the performance of a financial obligation arising under a contract, court order or statute. Both disciplines therefore approach the subject with different viewpoints and priorities, so it is not surprising that they arrive at different answers.

1–01

The concept of money

We are naturally concerned with the *legal* definition of money. However, even within that discipline, different shades of meaning may apply in different contexts. For example, if a testator makes a simple will leaving "all my money" to his widow, this may be intended to include all the assets which he owns at the date of his death, including his real and personal property.[1] That definition would, however, be too broad when considering a financial obligation under a commercial contract; in such a case, the parties would clearly have contemplated a payment in cash or its equivalent. But money has proved to be similar to the proverbial elephant—easy to identify but rather more difficult to define. The lack of a consistent meaning of "money" was identified in *Perrin v Morgan*,[2] where the court considered that[3]:

1–02

> "... the word 'money' has not got one natural or usual meaning. It has several meanings, each of which in appropriate circumstances may be regarded as natural. In its original sense, which is also its narrowest sense, the word means 'coin' ... The question: 'Have you any money in your purse?' refers presumably to bank notes or Treasury notes, as well as to shillings and pence. A further extension would include not only coin and currency in the possession of an

---

[1] In reality, this is unrelated to any standalone definition of "money" but is directed to the task of identifying the testator's true intentions. On the point made in the text, see *Perrin v Morgan* [1943] A.C. 399 HL, followed in *Re Barnes Will Trust* [1972] 1 W.L.R. 587 Ch D; *RSPCA v Sharp* [2011] 1 W.L.R. 980; and *Vucicevic v Aleksic* [2017] EWHC 2335 (Ch).
[2] *Perrin* [1943] A.C. 399 HL.
[3] *Perrin* [1943] A.C. 399 HL at 406–407 per Viscount Simon LC.

[1]

individual, but debts owing to him, and cheques which he could pay into his banking account, or postal orders, or the like. Again, going further, it is a matter of common speech to refer to one's 'money at the bank', although in a stricter sense the bank is not holding one's own money and what one possesses is a chose in action which represents the right to require the bank to pay out sums held at the call of its customer. Sums on deposit, whether with a bank or otherwise, may be included by a further extension, but this is by no means the limit to the senses in which the word 'money' is frequently and quite naturally used in English speech. The statement: 'I have my money invested on mortgage, or in debentures, or in stocks and shares, or in savings certificates,' is not an illegitimate use of the word 'money' on which the courts are bound to frown, though it is a great extension from its original meaning to interpret it as covering securities, and, in considering the various meanings of the word 'money' in common speech, one must go even further, as any dictionary will show. The word may be used to cover the whole of an individual's personal property—sometimes, indeed, all of a person's property, whether real or personal . . . ".

It is clear, therefore, that the meaning of "money" depends on the context and can be a much wider concept than simply physical money in the sense of coins and notes,[4] although in many cases it will be much narrower than the widest possible meaning identified above, i.e. the whole of a person's property.[5] We can try to be more specific by identifying terms which cover narrower concepts of money. The term "cash" is often used to refer to physical money[6] but this term can be problematic as "cash", when not specifically limited to coins and notes, is also used in a wider sense to cover not only coins and notes in a person's possession but amounts immediately due to him.[7] For instance, it is common to refer to "cash at bank", which means a debt owed by the bank to the holder of the account[8] rather than a physical mass of coins and notes. No consistent legal meaning of "cash" has emerged, although the term would seem to exclude amounts which are not immediately payable. At least as regards bank balances, the term "bank money" is sometimes used to distinguish this from physical currency. Therefore, since the term "cash" can have a wider meaning than simply physical money,[9] the latter will be referred to as "physical cash" for the purposes of this book.[10]

---

[4] The Bank of England estimated in 2014 that only 3% of the money held by the public is currency, with the rest being bank money; "Money in the Modern Economy", *Bank of England Quarterly Bulletin*, 2014 Q1, 2.

[5] On this basis, Benjamin defines money as "consisting of (circulating) debt, together with faith that it has value"; J. Benjamin, *Financial Law* (Oxford: Oxford University Press, 2007), para.1.49.

[6] Staughton J, for instance, uses "cash" in this sense in *Libyan Arab Foreign Bank v Bankers Trust Co* [1989] Q.B. 728 QBD (Comm) at 748.

[7] See, for instance, *Re Taylor* [1923] 1 Ch. 99 CA, where Lord Sterndale MR seemed to distinguish between "cash" and "ready cash" and where he noted (at 106) that: "In the case of cash, there is no difference between 'have' and 'am entitled to' . . . ".

[8] See para.1–03 below.

[9] Indeed, in *Federal-Mogul Asbestos Personal Injury Trust v Federal Mogul Ltd (formerly T&N Plc)* [2014] EWHC 2000 (Comm), payment "as cash" was considered to cover set-off; see para.2–05. The court specifically noted that "payment 'as cash' cannot be taken literally as meaning only payment in money bills or other legal tender" (at [171]).

[10] For a fuller discussion of the concept of money, see Simon Gleeson, *The Legal Concept of Money* (Oxford: Oxford University Press, 2018).

Theories of money

For the last 60 years of the twentieth century, the law of money was dominated by the late Dr F.A. Mann. He completed five editions of *The Legal Aspect of Money*, in which he wrote[11]:

1–03

> "It is suggested that in law the quality of money is to be attributed to all chattels which, issued by the authority of the law and denominated with reference to a unit of account, are meant to serve as a universal means of exchange in the State of issue."

The emphasis on the role of the State in the issue of the currency led to the label "State Theory of Money".

It is necessary to observe at the outset that this definition focuses on money as a physical chattel—in other words, on money in the form of notes and coins. Now, in most commercial contexts, the law will be concerned with money *as a means of payment*. It was thus inevitable that the completeness of this definition would increasingly come into question as the use of physical cash falls into retreat and numerous payment transactions—especially larger ones—are completed by other means.

The definition presupposes that the State has the monopoly on the creation of money. Now, it is true that the State has a monopoly on the issue of *physical* bank notes and coin, but the process of acceptance and re-lending of deposits has the effect of creating "money" without the intervention of the State.

To this, it might be objected that bank notes and coins are money, while a bank deposit, as law students learn early on, represents only a *claim* for money against the bank concerned. This was established in *Foley v Hill*,[12] where Lord Cottenham LC stated that[13]:

> "... Money, when paid into a bank, ceases altogether to be the money of the principal ... ; it is then the money of the banker, who is bound to return an equivalent by paying a similar sum to that deposited with him when he is asked for it ... That being established to be the relative situations of banker and customer, the banker is not an agent or factor, but he is a debtor ... ."

Therefore, due to the legal nature of a bank deposit as a claim against the bank in question, it is often said that an element of credit risk is involved which does not exist for bank notes and coins.[14] This is, of course, true, but it is to be observed that a bank note does itself represent a promise to pay and, hence, a claim against the Bank of England itself. Bank of England notes incorporate a promise to pay

---

[11] Most recently in C. Proctor, Dr C. Kleiner and Dr F. Mohs (eds), *Mann on The Legal Aspect of Money*, 7th edn (Oxford: Oxford University Press, 2012), p.8.
[12] *Foley* 9 E.R. 1002 QB. The principle in *Foley* has been confirmed in a number of cases; see, for example, *Re Spectrum Plus Ltd (In Liquidation)* [2004] 2 W.L.R. 783 at [88]–[89]; and *Fanfield Ltd v Revenue and Customs Commissioners* [2011] S.F.T.D. 324 at [19].
[13] *Foley* 9 E.R. 1002 QB at [36]–[37].
[14] This aspect of the nature of a bank deposit was brought into uncomfortably sharp relief by the 2008–2009 global financial crisis.

the bearer on demand a sum equivalent to the face amount of the note, and hence constitute promissory notes for the purposes of s.83 of the Bills of Exchange Act 1882.[15]

A number of factors—including the increasing role of banking institutions in the creation of money and the growth in the use of non-physical modes of payment—led the previous editor of this book to reformulate Dr Mann's theory. As a result, para.1.68 of the current edition of *Mann* reads[16]:

> "If the requirement that money should exist in the form of a chattel is no longer tenable, then it must follow that the expression 'money' is an essentially abstract rather than a physical concept. Looking at the State theory of money in the round, it seems that the essential legal characteristics of 'money' are as follows:
> (a) It must be expressed by reference to a name and denominated by reference to a unit of account which, in each case, is prescribed by the law of the State concerned;
> (b) the currency and unit so prescribed must be intended to serve as the generally accepted measure of value and medium of exchange within the State concerned; and
> (c) the legal framework for the currency must include a central bank or monetary authority responsible for the issue of the currency, and including appropriate institutional provisions for its management through the conduct of monetary policy and the oversight of payment systems."

This move away from the physical aspect of money may draw some inferential support from the decision of the European Court of Justice in *First National Bank of Chicago v Customs and Excise Commissioners*[17] to the effect that trading in foreign currencies for a customer *is to be regarded as the provision of a service* (rather than *goods*) since money is not "tangible property".[18] A broader approach to the definition of "money" has also found favour with the Federal Court of Australia.[19]

It should be appreciated that the move away from physical cash has also led to the formulation of certain other theories of money,[20] including the "Institutional Theory of Money". This holds that money "is no more than credit against an obligor, whose acceptance as a store of value and as a means of payment by the public is dependent on a comprehensive legal framework that ensures stable purchasing power, its availability even in times of banking stress and its

---

[15] However, a person presenting a note for payment at the Bank would merely receive other lower denomination bank notes which are legal tender in exchange: see s.1(4) of the Currency and Bank Notes Act 1954. Since bank notes are legal tender, the substitute notes would discharge the promise given by the original note. The main purpose of this facility is to allow bank notes which have ceased to be legal tender to be exchanged for current bank notes.

[16] *Mann* (2012), pp.40–41. It should be said that the third aspect of the definition was adopted in the most recent edition of *Mann* and owes much to the institutional theory that is considered below.

[17] *First National Bank of Chicago v Customs and Excise Commissioners* (C-172/96) [1999] Q.B. 570 ECJ (Fifth Chamber).

[18] It is, of course, accepted that this decision was made within the framework of specific rules dealing with VAT.

[19] See *Elsinora Global Ltd v Healthscope Ltd (No.2)* [2006] FCA 18 at [55].

[20] For more detail on theories of money, including on the State theory, see *Mann* (2012), paras 1.17–1.71; Michael Bridge (ed.) et al, *The Law of Personal Property*, 2nd edn (London: Sweet & Maxwell, 2018), para.7-011. See also David Fox, *Property Rights in Money* (Oxford: Oxford University Press, 2008), paras 1.19–1.58, on legal and economic conceptions of money; Claus Zimmermann's account of legal theories of money in *A Contemporary Concept of Monetary Sovereignty* (Oxford: Oxford University Press, 2013), p.12.

functional capability to settle monetary obligations ... ".[21] Thus, the institutional theory asserts that "money": (i) is a direct or indirect claim against a central bank; (ii) is a claim which can be used by the public as a means of exchange and store of value; and (iii) represents a claim which is originated by a central bank in a manner that preserves its availability, functionality and purchasing power.[22] Although obviously formulated from a different perspective, it may be noted that the institutional theory nevertheless focuses on the legal basis for the issue and functions of money and, to that extent, it may be said to reflect some of the aspects of the State theory.[23]

By way of contrast, it may be briefly noted that the "Societary Theory of Money", another theory which has been developed, would define "money" as that which is in practice widely accepted as such, irrespective of the legal infrastructure for its issue and use. According to this theory, it is the attitude of society, rather than any formal decision by the state, which determines what constitutes money.[24]

However that may be, let us revert to the requirements of the updated definition of the State theory, as outlined above.

(1) Name and unit of account

Money must be named by, and denominated by, reference to a unit of account prescribed by the law in force in the issuing State.

1–04

Thus, if the State does not have a monopoly over *the creation of money*, it nevertheless retains a monopoly over the *design and structure of the monetary system*.

Money must be expressed by reference to a unit of account prescribed by law. Thus, a 50 pence coin has a monetary value of 50 pence and can be used in discharge of a monetary debt obligation of that amount. This is so regardless of the silver content of the coin or the market value of that content. For the same reason, a £5 note has a nominal value of that amount and can discharge an obligation of that amount, regardless of its cost or value as a piece of paper and the associated printing ink.[25]

---

[21] See Sáinz de Vicuña, "An Institutional Theory of Money" in Mario Giovanoli and Diego Devos (eds), *International Monetary and Financial Law: The Global Crisis* (Oxford: Oxford University Press, 2010); also Zimmermann, *A Contemporary Concept of Monetary Sovereignty* (2013), p.15.
[22] De Vicuña, "An Institutional Theory of Money" in Giovanoli and Devos, *International Monetary and Financial Law* (2010), paras 25.24–25.33.
[23] The State theory perhaps lays greater emphasis on the use of money in the private sphere, whilst the institutional theory focuses on the central bank and the public structures that underpin a monetary system.
[24] On the societary theory, see *Mann* (2012), para.1.29; see also Zimmermann, *A Contemporary Concept of Monetary Sovereignty* (2013), p.13. This theory is not considered further for present purposes.
[25] On this subject, see the interesting situation which arose in *Banco de Portugal v Waterlow & Sons Ltd* [1932] A.C. 452 HL. The case concerned the Portuguese Bank Note Crisis of 1925, where a fraudster convinced the defendants, a firm of printers, that he was a representative of the Banco de Portugal. The defendants, in breach of contract, delivered 580,000 forged banknotes to the fraudster, a large number of which were put into circulation. The bank subsequently withdrew the whole issue of notes and exchanged notes presented by innocent third parties for other notes. The House of Lords

Applying this definition, kruggerrands,[26] gold coins acquired by gold investors, are not "money". In contrast to the situation which arose in *First National Bank of Chicago*, they are treated as "goods" for the purposes of any applicable customs legislation.[27]

(2) Generally accepted measure of value and medium of exchange

1–05 The unit of account prescribed by the State must be intended to act as a standard measure of monetary value within the boundaries of the State concerned. In other words, the cost or value of property, goods or services is priced in terms of the selected unit of account. Since money is meant to serve as a medium of exchange, it must be available to operate as an immediate means of payment for goods, services or other assets.

This means that physical cash, and funds at bank available for immediate use, are "money" for the purposes of the present definition, since they can be used to discharge a present financial obligation. This should be contrasted with instruments such as Treasury bills, which have a nominal value but are not yet payable. These cannot be used to discharge a present financial obligation of the holder, and are thus not "money" for these purposes.[28]

If money is to serve as a general means of exchange within the issuing State, then it must be fungible in the sense that the debtor must be entitled validly to tender bank notes and coins to the requisite nominal value. The creditor must not, for example, be entitled to reject the tender on the footing that the debtor has proffered old bank notes, but the creditor would prefer crisp, new ones; all bank notes emanate from the same stable and must be capable of discharging the same obligations. In other words, all bank notes which remain legal tender must be truly fungible, and the creditor can accept them regardless of the identity or character of the payer or any other matter.[29]

Likewise, if a creditor agrees to accept payment by means of a bank transfer, the debtor can make a valid tender by arranging a transfer from any bank. The creditor could not normally decline the tender on the basis of the identity of the paying bank.

---

found the defendants liable not only for the cost of printing the genuine notes withdrawn but also the exchange value of the genuine currency given in exchange for the spurious notes.

[26] A form of gold coin first minted in South Africa in 1967 and enjoying legal tender status, but which is not officially issued by reference to a unit of account. Legal tender status was apparently conferred because, at that time, US citizens could not hold gold bullion but could hold foreign coins. The coins were never intended to form a part of the South African monetary system.

[27] See, for example, *Allgemeine Gold und Silberscheideanstalt v Customs and Excise Commissioners* [1980] Q.B. 390 CA (Civ Div) and the decision of the Supreme Court of Zimbabwe in *Bennett–Cohen v The State* (1985) (2) SA 465.

[28] They could, of course, be sold to raise money, but that is a separate matter. The European Court of Justice has held that discount cards and vouchers did not constitute "payment" for VAT purposes since they do not discharge financial obligations but simply entitle the holder to a price discount (*Granton Advertising BV v Inspecteur van der Belastingdienst Haaglanden/kantoor Den Haag* (C-461/12) [2014] S.T.C. 2375 ECJ (Fifth Chamber)).

[29] In other words, the monetary value of the cash proffered is unaffected by the person proffering it. For a similar formulation, see *North v Brown* [2012] EWCA Civ 223 at [6]: "[T]he very essence of money is that it is a depersonalised medium of exchange. It is not therefore dependent on the personality of whoever provides it . . . ." This case is discussed in more detail at para.2–29 below.

(3) Institutional framework

The requirement for an institutional framework supporting the issue of the currency is, in many ways, a natural extension of the State theory of money. A central bank or other monetary authority is required to issue, control and manage the currency.

1–06

Money as a commodity

There may be rare cases where "money" falls to be treated as a commodity or as goods, rather than as money itself. For example, a collector will wish to buy *specific* notes or coins which have a value by reference to their rarity, rather than their nominal or face value,[30] with the result that sale of goods legislation may apply to the transaction. However, transactions of this kind will generally be obvious—why, otherwise, would a person buy money for a price in excess of its nominal value? This touches on the so-called "commodity theory of money", which held that money—especially foreign money[31]—could be more broadly treated as a commodity where it was purchased or sold, e.g. as part of a foreign exchange transaction. Thus, foreign currency could be purchased or sold as an *object* of exchange, rather than a *medium* of exchange. The commodity theory of foreign money had a number of consequences. In particular, and most artificially, a failure to pay an amount due in a foreign currency was treated as a failure of *delivery*, rather than of *payment*. The remedy, therefore, was an action for breach of contract, rather than in debt—with the curious result that the creditor had to mitigate his loss when the price of goods was due in a foreign currency, but not when it was due in sterling. Despite this curiosity, and the injustice to which it could give rise, the commodity theory continued its hold even after the landmark decision in *Miliangos v George Frank (Textiles) Ltd*,[32] which allowed creditors under a contract to obtain judgment for debts in the currency of the contract. Thus, in 1985, the US Court of Appeals held that an obligation to pay foreign currency "is treated as a promise to deliver a commodity"[33] and, as late as 1996, the Court of Appeal observed that foreign bank notes held in England "are not to be regarded as legal tender, but commodities or objects of commerce".[34]

1–07

But the commodity theory now seems to have largely run its course. In *Camdex International Ltd v Bank of Zambia (No.3)*,[35] the claimants sought a garnishee order in respect of monies which a Zambian copper producer was required to pay to the Zambian central bank in return for local currency in accordance with Zambia's system of exchange control. This was resisted on the basis that: (i) the US dollars were to be paid as a commodity and not as money;

---

[30] *Moss v Hancock* [1899] 2 Q.B. 111 QBD.
[31] Whilst the domestic currency was treated as a means of exchange and, hence, as "money", foreign currencies might be treated as commodities. The commodity theory was, therefore, principally applicable to external currencies.
[32] *Miliangos v George Frank (Textiles) Ltd* [1976] A.C. 443 HL. These developments are considered in Ch.5 below.
[33] *Vishipco Lines v Chase Manhattan Bank NA* 754 F.2d 452 at 458 (2nd Cir. 1985).
[34] *A Ltd v B Bank* [1997] 6 Bank. L.R. 85 CA (Civ Div).
[35] *Camdex International Ltd v Bank of Zambia (No.3)* [1997] 6 Bank. L.R. 44 CA (Civ Div).

and (ii) accordingly, the obligation to pay those dollars was not a "debt" which was capable of being subjected to a garnishee order. In the Court of Appeal, Phillips LJ accepted that rare notes and coins could be purchased for their intrinsic—rather than their nominal—value, and that the obligation of the seller should properly be characterised as one of delivery rather than debt or payment. However, he continued[36]:

> "Beyond this, however, I do not think it helpful, or even possible, to differentiate between money as a commodity and money as a means of exchange by reference to the nature of the transaction under which it falls to be transferred. It seems to me that whether money is lent or borrowed, whether it is used to buy goods or services, or whether it is exchanged against a different currency, it retains its character as a medium of exchange. The mere fact that the identity of the currency may be a material feature of the transaction does not translate the currency into a commodity, whatever the nature of the transaction."

The result of this decision, allied with the transformation achieved by the *Miliangos* decision, is that foreign money and foreign currency obligations are to be treated on essentially the same footing as money and obligations expressed in sterling.[37] This outcome is to be welcomed on the basis of its logic and convenience.

Similarities between physical money and bank money

1–08
As noted above, money is now to be regarded as an abstract concept, rather than a physical chattel. Yet, if bank notes and coins are to be treated as essentially identical to a claim on a bank then, as a matter of principle, they ought to share some identifiable, common characteristics.

It must be said that the initial point of departure—highlighted by the financial crisis in 2008–2009—is not promising. Bank money is vulnerable to loss in consequence of the insolvency of the bank at which the relevant account is held—a risk obviously not applicable to bank notes, at any rate so long as the Bank of England remains solvent. Bank notes, on the other hand, are subject to loss through theft, fire or other mishap—risks which do not apply to bank deposits.

Yet, despite this unpromising start, there are various similarities between physical and bank money, especially in the context of their use as a medium of exchange or means of payment. The following principles apply as between parties dealing in good faith and for value in the context of a commercial transaction[38]:

(a) A recipient will generally acquire good title to bank notes and coins handed to him in settlement of a transaction. Notes and coins pass by delivery or transfer of possession and this remains the case even though the payer had no title. Bank notes are thus negotiable instruments, in that the transferee

---

[36] *Camdex* [1997] 6 Bank. L.R. 44 CA (Civ Div) at 719.
[37] For further discussion on the status of foreign money in England, see *Mann* (2012), paras 1.83–1.90.
[38] It is necessary to emphasise these qualifications. Tracing and other remedies may apply in cases of fraud or where the recipient is a volunteer.

acquires title free from any prior equities.[39] Likewise, where a payment is made by means of a bank transfer, the payee will generally acquire an indefeasible right to the funds once they have been credited to his account.[40]

(b) In order to achieve payment through the medium of bank notes, it is necessary that they should be transferred unconditionally and without reservation. Likewise, the transfer of funds to a bank account only discharges the debt if the creditor thereby receives full and unconditional access to the funds.[41]

(c) A creditor who receives notes and coins in discharge of a debt is not in any sense concerned with the character or credit standing of his debtor. Similarly, a creditor who receives payment by credit to his own bank account will be unconcerned with the state of his debtor's bank account, whether it is overdrawn or any other matter.[42] The creditor can thus treat the payment by funds transfer as "final", just as if the necessary physical bank notes had been handed to them.[43]

At least from a legal perspective, there is accordingly some basis for treating bank deposits and physical cash on the same footing and for treating both of them as "money" for the purposes of our earlier definition. They may both be used to settle monetary obligations[44] and the legal consequences—in terms of the effect and finality of payment—are essentially the same.

---

[39] See, for example, the discussion in *Banque Belge pour l'Etranger v Hambrouck* [1921] 1 K.B. 321 CA at 329.

[40] For an illustration of this point, see the decision in *Tayeb v HSBC Bank Plc* [2004] 4 All E.R. 1024, considered at para.5–22 below. However, this is only the case where parties receive the money in good faith; see, for instance, *Independent Trustee Services Ltd v GP Noble Trustees Ltd* [2013] Ch. 91, where it was held that, where a former husband had used money misappropriated from pension funds in breach of trust to make a payment to his former wife pursuant to a consent order, she lost the benefit of the bona fide purchaser for value defence when the consent order was set aside—the court considered that, prior to the setting aside of that consent order, she would have had that defence since she did not at that point have notice of the breach of trust.

[41] *Awilco of Oslo A/S v Fulvia SpA di Navigazione of Cagliari (The Chikuma)* [1981] 1 W.L.R. 314 HL, recently reiterated in *K v A* [2019] EWHC 1118 at [26] (which concerned payment being made to a fraudulent bank account following the hacking of email accounts and provision of forged payment details).

[42] Thus, if the debtor's bank has made a mistake as to the credit balance on their customer's account and has made payment when it would not otherwise have done so, this will be of no concern to the creditor and he can retain the funds remitted to him: see *Lloyds Bank Plc v Independent Insurance Co Ltd* [2000] Q.B. 110 CA (Civ Div).

[43] For a possible exception to this principle, see the discussion of the decision in *Barclays Bank Ltd v WJ Simms Son & Cooke (Southern) Ltd* [1980] Q.B. 677 QBD (Comm) in Ch.3 below.

[44] See, for instance, *Federal-Mogul Asbestos Personal Injury Trust v Federal-Mogul Ltd (formerly T&N Plc)* [2014] Lloyd's Rep. I.R. 671, where Elder J noted (at [171]) that "the reference to a payment 'as cash' cannot be taken literally as meaning only payment in money, bills or other legal tender".

2. DEVELOPMENTS IN MONEY

Some examples

1–09   Earlier parts of this chapter have focused on money in its more obviously recognised forms and their use as a means of payment. However, it is convenient at this point to examine three recent developments in this area and the extent to which they may themselves be regarded as "money" and a medium of payment.

(1)   Eurocurrencies

1–10   The expression "Eurocurrency" usually refers to a deposit denominated in a currency other than that of the country in which the account holding branch is situated.[45] By definition, therefore, Eurocurrencies are bank money, rather than physical cash. Since currencies can usually only be settled through the clearing system operating in the country of issue, the bank holding the Eurocurrency deposit will itself have a corresponding credit with a bank branch in the issuing State.[46]

This "dual account" feature creates difficulties which remained largely unexplored until the English courts had to decide *Libyan Arab Foreign Bank v Bankers Trust Co*[47] and US courts were confronted with the Wells Fargo Asia litigation.[48] In essence, the structure involves two levels of linked transactions, each of which will usually be governed by different systems of law.[49] In the *Libyan Arab Foreign Bank* case, the court held that the London branch of Bankers Trust was required to repay a Eurodollar deposit held at its London branch and governed by English law, even though the corresponding transfer across New York accounts would be unlawful under US federal law.

These cases will be considered later.[50] For immediate purposes, the question is whether Eurocurrencies can be regarded as "money", notwithstanding the particular structure just described. In principle, it seems that they should be so regarded because they can be used as a means of payment in the same way as a more straightforward and purely domestic bank deposit.[51] Against this view is the fact that their value depends on clearing and settlement mechanisms in the issuing State.[52] In any case, as in the case of an ordinary bank deposit, a

---

[45] Eurocurrencies are defined as "deposits of a specific currency outside the territory of the issuing state" in Claus Zimmermann, *A Contemporary Concept of Monetary Sovereignty* (Oxford: Oxford University Press, 2013), fn.50; see also p.76 onwards for discussion of eurocurrencies as private and transnational money.
[46] The point was made in *Citibank, N.A. v Wells Fargo Asia Ltd* (1990) 495 US 660. On the clearing of foreign currency payments, see Ch.5 below.
[47] *Libyan Arab Foreign Bank v Bankers Trust Co* [1989] Q.B. 728 QBD (Comm).
[48] See fn.46 above.
[49] Mentioned in Claus Zimmermann, *A Contemporary Concept of Monetary Sovereignty* (2013), p.78.
[50] See paras 5–44 to 5–46 below.
[51] See the above discussion and, for a more detailed consideration of Eurocurrency deposits, see *Mann* (2012), paras 1.91–1.101.
[52] Discussed in Claus Zimmermann, *A Contemporary Concept of Monetary Sovereignty* (2013), pp.78–79.

Eurodollar deposit would only acquire the status of "money" when the deposit has matured and has thus become available to the depositor for the purpose of making payments to third parties. Until that point, the deposit merely represents a future claim on the bank concerned.

(2) Electronic money

Electronic money ("e-money"), sometimes called "digital cash", may be defined as monetary value represented by a claim on the issuer which is stored on an electronic device, issued for the purpose of making payment transactions and accepted as a means of payments by undertakings other than the issuer itself.[53]

1–11

E-money is stored electronically, either on a smart card or an electronic device such as a mobile phone, or remotely in an internet payment account.[54] Payment using e-money bears some similarity to payment by way of funds transfer, because:

(a) the retailer receives immediate credit to his account;
(b) the transfer will generally be both unconditional and final; and
(c) e-money can be accepted without reference to the identity or creditworthiness of the holder.

To this extent, e-money or digital cash, although not legal tender, may also be regarded as "money" for the purposes of the definition formulated in this chapter.[55]

One form of e-money the use of which has been increasing in recent years is mobile money. Mobile money is e-money stored electronically on a mobile phone or device. Mobile money has proved particularly popular in the developing world,[56] although it has given rise to concerns around consumer protection.[57]

Importantly, e-money in its various forms, including mobile money, should not be confused with virtual currencies, since, unlike the latter, it is expressed in units of "fiat currency", a concept discussed further below.

---

[53] See the definition set out in reg.2 of the Electronic Money Regulations 2011 (SI 2011/99), discussed at para.5–75 below.
[54] On the whole subject, see *Law of Bank Payments* (2018), paras 4–053 to 4–058. Significantly, the growth of e-money has led to the development of non-bank payment systems and service providers such as PayPal—see the discussion of non-bank payment systems in Ch.5.
[55] Although Brindle and Cox suggest otherwise on a narrow definition of money since e-money is not legal tender and merchants must participate in the relevant scheme to accept it. They do, however, note that e-money, or "digital cash" as they term it, is a genuine medium of exchange unlike debit cards and cheques: *Law of Bank Payments* (2018), para.4-055.
[56] In particular, since it makes a convenient method of transferring funds available to many people excluded from formal banking systems or without internet.
[57] Discussed in further detail at para.5–10. For example, on insolvency of a mobile money provider; see e.g. Jonathan Greenacre and Ross P. Buckley, "Using Trusts to Protect Mobile Money Customers" (2014) S.J.L.S. 59, where it is suggested that trust law could be used to protect customers' funds in common law jurisdictions.

(3) Virtual currencies

1–12   It was noted earlier in this chapter that the legal definition of "money" has required development over the years, as the use of physical cash as a means of settlement has declined. Yet it was suggested that the creation of a monetary system remains the prerogative of the State and its legislature, with the result that the designation of the unit of account must be achieved through a legislative act.[58]

The increased use of so-called "virtual currencies" in recent years presents a challenge to this remaining principle.[59] The Financial Action Task Force (FATF) defines a virtual currency as[60]:

> "... a digital representation of value that can be digitally traded and functions as (1) a medium of exchange; and/or (2) a unit of account; and/or (3) a store of value, but does not have legal tender status (i.e. when tendered to a creditor, is a valid and legal offer of payment) in any jurisdiction. It is not issued nor guaranteed by any jurisdiction, and fulfils the above functions only by agreement within the community of users of the virtual currency".

Virtual currencies are distinguished from "fiat currency" (the coin and paper money of a country that is designated as its legal tender, circulates and is customarily used and accepted as a medium of exchange in the issuing country) and from e-money, defined as "a digital representation of fiat currency used to electronically transfer value denominated in fiat currency".[61] The key characteristics of a virtual currency according to this definition are that: (i) it has one or more of the following functions—medium of exchange, unit of account, and/or store of value; (ii) it is not legal tender nor issued or guaranteed by any state; and (iii) it fulfils its functions solely by agreement among its users.

1–13   In terms of the classification of virtual currencies, they are either convertible or non-convertible. Where they are convertible (or "open"), a market exists by which participants in the system may buy and sell units of the virtual currency (so their "convertibility" is not guaranteed by law).[62] Instead, they have a value in fiat currency and can be exchanged for fiat currency. Bitcoin is an example of a convertible virtual currency. Where virtual currencies are non-convertible (or "closed"), they do not have an equivalent value in fiat currency and are intended

---

[58] See the discussion at para.1–04 above.
[59] For in-depth discussion of the legal aspects of virtual currencies, including their status as money, see Sarah Green and David Fox, *Cryptocurrencies in Public and Private Law* (Oxford: Oxford University Press, 2019); Niels Vandezande, *Virtual Currencies: A Legal Framework* (Cambridge: Intarsia, 2018).
[60] FATF Report, *Virtual Currencies: Key Definitions and Potential AML/CFT Risks* (June 2014), p.4 (available at: *http://www.fatf-gafi.org/media/fatf/documents/reports/Virtual-currency-key-definitions-and-potential-aml-cft-risks.pdf* [Accessed 5 October 2020]).
[61] FATF Report (June 2014), p.4.
[62] FATF Report (June 2014), p.4.

for use in a specific virtual domain (i.e. their rules do not provide for exchange into fiat currency). Examples of non-convertible virtual currencies are Q Coins and World of Warcraft Gold.[63]

Virtual currencies can be further divided into centralised and non-centralised virtual currencies, with all non-convertible virtual currencies being centralised.[64] Convertible virtual currencies may be either centralised or decentralised. Centralised virtual currencies have a single controlling authority or "administrator" who issues and redeems the currency, establishes its rules and maintains a centralised ledger.[65] By contrast, decentralised virtual currencies (or "cryptocurrencies") are "distributed, open-source, math-based peer-to-peer virtual currencies"[66] with no central administrator and no central control. Bitcoin is an example of the latter.

For convenience, the focus of this section will be on Bitcoin, which is perhaps the best-known virtual currency, although, as noted above, there are a number of other virtual currencies which take various different forms. The currency is generally referred to as "Bitcoin" and the individual units of account as "bitcoins".

Before attempting a discussion of bitcoins as a unit of account or as a means of payment,[67] it may be helpful to provide a brief overview of Bitcoin's operation.[68] Bitcoin first appeared in early 2009 and creates an open-source, peer-to-peer digital currency. The effect of these arrangements is that: (i) payment transactions are processed directly between payer and payee without any need for an institutional intermediary; (ii) part of the controlling computer code is open to public view; and (iii) the currency exists purely in electronic form, with no notes or coins.

1–14

Dealing with these points in turn, Bitcoin, as a decentralised virtual currency, removes the intermediary from the payment system in a way that other third-party payment systems and centralised virtual currencies do not. The main issue with having a payment system without an intermediary is the "double-spending" problem, e.g. the risk that money, or in this case bitcoins, will be successfully spent more than once in two different transactions. Having an intermediary solves this problem because both parties to a transaction will have an account with that intermediary and, when one party makes a payment to another party, both parties' accounts with the intermediary will be adjusted. Bitcoin removes the need for an intermediary through a "decentralised ledger" or cryptocurrency ledger. This is a public ledger known as the "blockchain" which is

---

[63] Although there is some suggestion that World of Warcraft Gold, at least, can be converted to fiat money through player auctions—Stuart Hoegner refers to this in "What is Bitcoin?" in Jerry Brito et al, *The Law of Bitcoin* (Bloomington: iUniverse, 2015). There is therefore, at least in this sense, a "secondary market" for such currencies.
[64] FATF Report (June 2014), p.5.
[65] Examples of convertible, centralised virtual currencies include the now defunct E-gold and Liberty Reserve.
[66] FATF Report (June 2014), p.5.
[67] For a more general discussion of the legal issues in relation to Bitcoin and other virtual currencies, see Brito et al, *The Law of Bitcoin* (Bloomington: iUniverse, 2015).
[68] For a more detailed account, see Sarah Green, "Cryptocurrencies: The Underlying Technology", Ch.1 in Sarah Green and David Fox (eds), *Cryptocurrencies in Public and Private Law* (2019).

distributed among all users of Bitcoin through a peer-to-peer network. All transactions are registered in the blockchain and new transactions are checked against the blockchain to make sure the bitcoins in question have not been previously spent. This global peer-to-peer network removes the need for a centralised intermediary.[69]

With regard to the mechanics, the security of the system is maintained by the cryptographic technologies involved in Bitcoin. Transactions are publicly announced through "public key cryptography". Each coin is associated with a bitcoin user's public key. A user can transfer bitcoins to other users by creating a message (called a "transaction") attaching the intended recipient's public key to the bitcoins in question. The transferor then "signs" the transaction using his "private key", a secret number which allows the transferor to attach a digital signature to the transaction. The bitcoins are then separated from the transferor's bitcoin address and attached to another bitcoin address. The transaction is recorded in a new "block" on the blockchain (the decentralised leger), which is available to all users of the network.[70]

Bitcoins exist purely in electronic form. A system user can obtain bitcoins by: (i) paying for them in ordinary currency at the prevailing price or "exchange rate"[71]; (ii) accepting bitcoins as a method of payment for goods or services; or (iii) providing network services to validate and secure transactions in bitcoins, which are remunerated by the allocation of new bitcoins to the provider as the service expands.[72] Bitcoins are created or "issued" by way of a decentralised computer process called "mining". The operation of the Bitcoin system relies on users, known as "miners", who verify transactions and audit the blockchain. They do this by creating "hashes" (in effect, the digital equivalent of wax seals), each of which secures a specific block of transactions in the blockchain and ensures that the blockchain is not tampered with. Bitcoins are issued to miners who complete hashes as a reward for their services. They were originally produced at a rate of 50 bitcoins per new block of transactions (with one new block occurring every ten minutes) but this rate halves every four years and is subject to an

---

[69] In Corinne Zellweger-Gutknecht, "Developing the Right Regulatory Regime for Cryptocurrencies and Other Value Data", Ch.4 in Sarah Green and David Fox (eds), *Cryptocurrencies in Public and Private Law* (2019), the author comments that these assets are "data recorded by trusted forms of technology" rather than by intermediaries (at para.4.80).

[70] It has been suggested that this blockchain technology may eventually have uses beyond facilitating bitcoin transactions, for instance, "smart contracts" and securities clearing settlement. On the former, see Larry A. DiMatteo, Michel Cannarsa and Cristina Poncibo (eds), *The Cambridge Handbook of Smart Contracts, Blockchain Technology and Digital Platforms* (Cambridge: CUP, 2019). On the latter, see Charles W. Mooney Jr., "Beyond Intermediation A New (FinTech) Model for Securities Holding Infrastructures" (2020) 22 U. Pa. J. Bus. L. 386; Eva Micheler and Luke von der Heyde, "Holding, Clearing and Settling Securities through Blockchain/Distributed Ledger Technology: Creating an Efficient System by Empowering Investments" (2016) 31(11) *Journal of International Banking and Financial Law*; also Sarah Green and Ferdisha Snagg, "Intermediated Securities and Distributed Ledger Technology" in Louise Gullifer and Jennifer Payne (eds), *Intermediation and Beyond* (Hart Publishing, 2019).

[71] In practice, the exchange rate between Bitcoins and traditional currencies has often fluctuated quite significantly, as can be seen from the various Bitcoin price indexes which exist: see, for instance, the NYSE Bitcoin Index (NYXBT) (available at: *https://www.nyse.com/quote/index/NYXBT* [Accessed 5 October 2020]).

[72] This process is known as "mining".

overall cap of 21 million on the number of bitcoins (provided for in the Bitcoin protocol, which is the cryptographic "language" underlying Bitcoin).[73]

A question which is linked to the creation and transfer of bitcoins is that of how their value is determined. The price of a bitcoin is determined purely by supply and demand; by what a buyer will pay and a seller will accept in the bitcoin "marketplace". It is not set centrally and is not based on any underlying indicator such as gold. Arguably, the value of Bitcoin lies in the underlying technology and is supported by those who accept bitcoins as payment for their goods and services. It has been suggested that the potential benefits to users of bitcoins include lower transaction costs, increased privacy and no erosion of purchasing power due to inflation.[74]

As a result of this structure, it will be seen that: (i) there is thus no central body responsible for Bitcoin transactions or payments, nor are they subject to control by a central bank or other monetary authority; and (ii) payment may be achieved without the intervention (or cost) of a bank or provider of payment services.

In line with the discussion earlier in this chapter, two issues arise for discussion, namely: 1–15

(a) do Bitcoin and other virtual currencies qualify for the label "money"; and
(b) can such currencies amount to a means of settlement or payment?

Virtual currencies as "money"

It was suggested earlier in this chapter that the essential legal characteristics of money are that it is: (a) expressed by reference to, and denominated in, a unit of account prescribed by the law of the issuing State; (b) a generally accepted measure of value and medium of exchange within that State; and (c) has a legal framework including a central bank or monetary authority responsible for the currency, including its issue. In the light of this updated State theory of money, virtual currencies plainly cannot be regarded as "money". In relation to (a), virtual currencies are not linked to, or expressed in, fiat money. Moreover, (b) is not satisfied since virtual currencies are not universally accepted and are subject to substantial volatility.[75] Although arguments have been made that virtual currencies should at least in some circumstances be viewed as money since they are increasingly becoming *a* means of exchange,[76] the trust which characterises 1–16

---

[73] It was released in 2008 by Satoshi Nakamoto, the inventor of bitcoin. It is not known whether "Satoshi Nakamoto" is a person or a group, and whether the name is real or a pseudonym, although various suggestions have been made as to the identity of Satoshi Nakamoto. Craig Wright, an Australian computer scientist, claimed to be Satoshi Nakamoto in a post on his blog on 2 May 2016, but he subsequently refused to publish evidence that he created Bitcoin.
[74] See "Bitcoin: Questions, Answers and Analysis of Legal Issues" (Congressional Research Service, 13 October 2015) (available at: *https://www.fas.org/sgp/crs/misc/R43339.pdf* [Accessed 5 October 2020]), pp.5–7.
[75] Although this argument could be made about various fiat currencies; see Sarah Green, "It's Virtually Money", Ch.2 in Sarah Green and David Fox, *Cryptocurrencies in Public and Private Law* (2019), para.2.20.
[76] Although Green argues that, since virtual currencies are accepted as *a* means of exchange, they should be treated as money in some circumstances as it seems "artificial and disingenuous" to divide

fiat currencies and makes them universally accepted is lacking for virtual currencies. For (c), virtual currencies may depend upon a framework of contractual relationships between the issuer and the holder but these do not take the form of the mandatory law of the State, nor is the virtual currency part of a monetary system prescribed by a State. The State thus has no monetary or policy responsibility for virtual currencies which are effectively issued without the recourse to the State or institutional support that is implied in the context of a national currency. In addition, whilst it has been observed that demand deposits should now equally be recognised as "money", these deposits are created through recognised and regulated financial institutions. Virtual currencies cannot be regarded as akin to bank deposits for these purposes.

1–17 If virtual currencies fall outside the scope of the prevailing legal definition of "money", then it becomes necessary to consider whether the legal expression itself should be re-defined to accommodate these more recent developments. This is because the failure to recognise virtual currencies as money may cause uncertainty or have undesirable consequences, including the following three examples:

i) the taxation treatment of virtual currencies may be uncertain;
ii) regulatory measures intended to protect the public and prevent crime, including anti-money laundering and anti-terrorist financing legislation, may not apply to virtual currencies if they do not come within the definition of money; and
iii) investors in and users of Bitcoin may be unprotected.

1–18 Before discussing these three areas, it is useful to note that attempts to address them have led to the inconsistent legal categorisation of virtual currencies, not only at a cross-border level but also internally in many jurisdictions. As a starting-point, virtual currencies such as Bitcoin are generally classified in two main ways; as a currency or "money" and as a form of intangible property.[77] However, different jurisdictions may categorise them differently and, within a single jurisdiction, their categorisation may vary depending on the context.

1–19 In relation to taxation of bitcoins,[78] the dominant approach where bitcoins are held as an investment[79] appears to be to treat them as assets rather than currency and subject them to the relevant capital gains or property taxes. The US,[80]

---

mutually agreed payment obligations into those made on the basis of fiat money and those not. This is particularly the case since, in her view, bitcoins are fungible and unconsumable; paras 2.02, 2.15–2.18.

[77] For a discussion of cryptocurrencies in particular as a species of property see David Fox, "Cryptocurrencies in the Common Law of Property", Ch.6 in Sarah Green and David Fox, *Cryptocurrencies in Public and Private Law* (2019).

[78] The taxation of Bitcoin and other cryptocurrencies is discussed in Anne Fairpo, "Taxation of Cryptocurrencies", Ch.10 in Sarah Green and David Fox, *Cryptocurrencies in Public and Private Law* (2019).

[79] As opposed to being traded with a view to profit, in which case profits are subject to the relevant income tax or (in the case of companies/businesses) business or corporation tax.

[80] According to Internal Revenue Service guidance issued in March 2014. See also the updated October 2019 guidance.

Canadian,[81] Australian[82] and UK[83] tax authorities all take this approach. A notable exception to this view is found in the EU's treatment of Bitcoin for VAT purposes. The European Court of Justice considered in *Skatteverket v David Hedqvist*[84] that Bitcoin was a currency for the purpose of exempting conversions between fiat currency and Bitcoin from VAT.

However, in some jurisdictions, this approach is not consistently carried through to scenarios involving infringement of anti-money laundering legislation or other measures addressing financial crime. The US offers a good example as it is here that there have been the most prosecutions for criminal activity involving Bitcoin. Although Bitcoin is taxed as an asset, various cases have at least impliedly recognised it in the law enforcement and regulatory context as "money" in order to bring it within the scope of existing anti money laundering or other criminal laws. Examples include *Securities Exchange Commission v Shavers*,[85] where a bitcoin investment scheme was held to amount to an "investment contract" (and the SEC therefore had jurisdiction) since it involved the investment of *money* in a common enterprise with a view to profit. The court rejected Mr Shavers' argument that Bitcoin was not money because: (i) it could be used to purchase goods and services, or to pay living expenses; and (ii) it can be exchanged for conventional currencies. Bitcoin was thus accepted as money even though it is not denominated by reference to a State-mandated unit of account and it only serves as a medium of exchange among a narrow group of persons prepared to accept it. However, it has been argued that the actual question the court was considering in the *Shavers* case was whether the Bitcoin Savings and Trust investments constituted securities under federal securities law—therefore, the opinion of the court focused on the characterisation of the investments and not bitcoins as the underlying commodity.[86] In *United States of America v Faiella*,[87] the argument that Bitcoin did not constitute "money" in the context of criminal proceedings for operating an unlicensed money transmitting business and conspiracy to commit money laundering was rejected by the court on the basis that "'money' in ordinary parlance means 'something generally accepted as a medium of exchange, a measure of value, or a means of payment'. (MERRIAM-WEBSTER ONLINE, http://www.merriam-webster.com/dictionary/

1–20

---

[81] https://www.canada.ca/en/revenue-agency/programs/about-canada-revenue-agency-cra/compliance/digital-currency/cryptocurrency-guide.html [Accessed 5 October 2020].
[82] https://www.ato.gov.au/general/gen/tax-treatment-of-crypto-currencies-in-australia—specifically-bitcoin/ [Accessed 5 October 2020].
[83] https://www.gov.uk/government/publications/tax-on-cryptoassets/cryptoassets-for-individuals [Accessed 5 October 2020].
[84] *Skatteverket v Hedqvist* (C-264/14) EU:C:2015:718; [2016] S.T.C. 372.
[85] *Securities Exchange Commission v Shavers* 2013 BL 208180 (ED Tex, 6 August 2013), a decision of the District Court for the Eastern District of Texas.
[86] See David Lee Kuo Chuen (ed.), *Handbook of Digital Currency: Bitcoin, Innovation, Financial Instruments, and Big Data* (London: Elsevier, 2015), p.347. Mr Shavers pleaded guilty in September 2015 to securities fraud for defrauding investors out of an estimated $4.5 million in relation to the Bitcoin Savings and Trust.
[87] *United States of America v Faiella* Case 1:14-cr-00243-JSR, New York. A similar result was reached in *United States of America v Ulbricht*, Case 1:14-cr-00068-KBF (New York), where the court considered that "Bitcoins carry value—that is their purpose and function—and act as a medium of exchange" and the definition of "funds" was therefore wide enough to encompass them.

money ...)". Also, the legislation referred not simply to "money", but to "funds", and Bitcoin, in the court's view, clearly qualified as "money" or "funds" as it "can be easily purchased in exchange for ordinary currency, acts as a denominator of value, and is used to conduct financial transactions".

But the cases do not all go one way. In *The State of Florida v Espinoza*,[88] the argument that bitcoins should be viewed as money was unexpectedly rejected. The judge dismissed charges of operating an unlicensed money services business (later changed to being a "payment instrument seller") and of money laundering against the defendant. Judge Pooler considered that "nothing in our frame of reference allows us to accurately define or describe Bitcoin" and that, while it "may have some attributes in common with what we commonly refer to as money", it differs "in many important aspects".[89] Significantly, and in apparent contrast to the approach taken in *Faiella* and *Ulbricht* where bitcoins were accepted as "funds" and as having value and being a medium of exchange, Judge Pooler did not consider that Bitcoin came within the statutory definition of "payment instrument"[90] as having "monetary value", defined as a "medium of exchange, whether or not redeemable in currency".[91] She noted that bitcoins are not a commonly used means of exchange, their value fluctuates wildly and their high volatility means that they have limited ability to act as a store of value, another important attribute of money.[92] She also noted the lack of a central authority and backing for Bitcoin.[93] Concluding that Bitcoin had a "long way to go before it is the equivalent of money", she considered that "attempting to fit the sale of Bitcoin into a statutory scheme regulating money services business is like fitting a square peg into a round hole".[94] Instead, she held that the defendant was simply selling his property not money.

Other jurisdictions have also grappled with the issue of Bitcoin as money for the purposes of anti-money laundering or terrorist financing legislation. There has been increasing national and international recognition of the need to ensure appropriate regulation of virtual currencies. The Financial Action Task Force has issued guidance in this area addressing money laundering and terrorist financing concerns.[95] At an EU level, the gaps in existing anti-money laundering and terrorist financing legislation[96] have led to the introduction of the Fifth Anti-Money Laundering Directive.[97] It addresses anti-money laundering and terrorist financing risks due to the use of virtual currencies, including bringing

---

[88] *The State of Florida v Espinoza* Case No.F14-2923 (Fla. 11th Cir. 2016).
[89] *Espinoza* Case No.F14-2923 (Fla. 11th Cir. 2016) at 5.
[90] *Espinoza* Case No.F14-2923 (Fla. 11th Cir. 2016); s.560.103(29), Fla. Stat.
[91] *Espinoza* Case No.F14-2923 (Fla. 11th Cir. 2016); s.560.125(21), Fla. Stat.
[92] *Espinoza* Case No.F14-2923 (Fla. 11th Cir. 2016) at 5–6.
[93] *Espinoza* Case No.F14-2923 (Fla. 11th Cir. 2016) at 6.
[94] *Espinoza* Case No.F14-2923 (Fla. 11th Cir. 2016) at 6.
[95] See FATF, *Guidance for a Risk-Based Approach to Virtual Currencies* (issued in June 2015, as amended in October 2018 and updated in June 2019), together with the FATF's Interpretative Note to Recommendation 15 (INR. 15).
[96] As shown by the recent discovery of a money laundering operation using unlicensed Bitcoin ATMs in Spain; see https://www.bloomberg.com/news/articles/2019-07-11/bitcoin-atms-show-gap-in-eu-s-money-laundering-rules-police-say [Accessed 5 October 2020].
[97] Directive (EU) 2018/843 of the European Parliament and of the Council of 30 May 2018 amending Directive (EU) 2015/849 on the prevention of the use of the financial system for the purpose of

exchange service providers and custodian wallet providers within the scope of existing legislation.[98] The UK has also established a "Cryptoassets Taskforce", which has published a report setting out the UK's intended regulatory response to the challenges posed by cryptocurrencies.[99] Further, bitcoins have been confiscated in the UK under the Proceeds of Crime Act 2002.[100] Australia and Canada have both recently introduced laws regulating virtual currency exchanges. Some jurisdictions view the dangers of illicit activity to be so great that they have either banned all activities involving virtual currencies[101] or prohibited financial institutions from facilitating virtual currency transactions.[102]

The legal categorisation of Bitcoin and other virtual currencies also raises issues in relation to protection for those who invest in, and use, such currencies. The risks are significant, including of theft and loss of assets if passcodes are misplaced.[103] This was highlighted as an issue in the final report of the Cryptoassets Taskforce.[104] Nor are investors always fully informed of the risks; subsequent research by the FCA indicates a lack of awareness of the potential risks of buying cryptocurrencies.[105]

1–21

One issue which has been discussed in this context is whether Bitcoin is to be regarded as an "investment" such that the related regulatory rules regarding financial investments apply to it. For example, if Bitcoin is an asset, do advertising materials relating to the acquisition of Bitcoin amount to a regulated financial promotion in the UK? If Bitcoin is not money and its value can fluctuate in terms of other goods and commodities, one might instinctively have thought that it could be regarded as an "investment" for these purposes. However, as matters stand, it seems reasonably clear that activities involving the issue and holding of bitcoins are outside the scope of the Financial Services and Markets

---

money laundering or terrorist financing, and amending Directives 2009/138/EC and 2013/36/EU. It was adopted on 19 April 2018 and the deadline for transposition into national law was 10 January 2020.

[98] Discussed in Ch.5.
[99] *https://assets.publishing.service.gov.uk/government/uploads/system/uploads/attachment_data/file/752070/cryptoassets_taskforce_final_report_final_web.pdf* [Accessed 5 October 2020].
[100] *R. v Teresko (Sergejs)* [2018] Crim. L.R. 81. See C. Proctor, "Cryptocurrencies in the International and Public Law Conceptions of Money", Ch.3 in Sarah Green and David Fox, *Cryptocurrencies in Public and Private Law* (2019), paras 3.32–3.33 for a discussion of cryptocurrencies as criminal property in the context of money laundering.
[101] At the moment, Algeria, Morocco, Bolivia, Nepal, Pakistan and Vietnam, as well as Qatar and Bahrain when citizens are inside their borders; *https://www.loc.gov/law/help/cryptocurrency/world-survey.php#compsum* [Accessed 5 October 2020].
[102] Examples include Bangladesh, Iran, Thailand, Lithuania, Lesotho, China, and Colombia; *https://www.loc.gov/law/help/cryptocurrency/world-survey.php#compsum* [Accessed 5 October 2020]. For example, in Bangladesh, the central bank indicated in circulars issued in September 2014 and December 2017 that transacting in virtual currencies could violate foreign exchange, anti-money laundering and anti-terrorist financing legislation.
[103] Discussed in Ch.5.
[104] *https://assets.publishing.service.gov.uk/government/uploads/system/uploads/attachment_data/file/752070/cryptoassets_taskforce_final_report_final_web.pdf* [Accessed 5 October 2020].
[105] Available online at *https://www.fca.org.uk/publications/research/consumer-attitudes-and-awareness-cryptoassets-research-summary* [Accessed 5 October 2020].

Act 2001 (Regulated Activities) Order 2001.[106] For example, it would appear that Bitcoin could only constitute a regulated investment under two possible headings:

(a) the conduct of business involving the acceptance of deposits is subject to the terms of the Regulated Activities Order. However, art.5(2) of the Order defines a "deposit" as a *sum of money* that is to be repaid at a later date. If Bitcoin is not money, then it must fall outside the scope of this prohibition; and

(b) the issue of e-money is also within the scope of the Regulated Activities Order. However, the definition of "electronic money" incorporated by art.2 of the Order refers to stored *monetary* value that represents a *claim* on the issuer. Based on the description given above, it appears that Bitcoin would not meet either of these criteria—Bitcoin transactions are simply maintained on a ledger and there is no issuer against whom a claim could be established.[107]

A separate issue is protection for those who transact using virtual currencies, i.e. use them as a means of "payment". As Green identifies, contracts for the transfer of property where payment is to be made by virtual currency are not contracts for the sale of goods pursuant to s.2(1) of the Sale of Goods Act 1979, which requires that the seller agrees to transfer property in good to the buyer for a money consideration.[108] Consequently, they fall outside the protections given to parties to such contracts.[109]

1–22 The difficulties caused by the uncertain legal status of virtual currencies have led several commentators to argue for a revised definition of "money" which, at least in some contexts, is broad enough to cover virtual currencies.[110] However, notwithstanding these issues, it is submitted that they should not be included as "money". This follows in part from the fact that the volume of use of virtual currencies remains relatively limited at present but, at a more principled level, it must be observed that virtual currencies exist outside the State and central bank mechanisms designed to support a currency. In addition, the establishment of monetary and exchange rate policies are essentially governmental activities, and there is no structure for the development of such policies in relation to Bitcoin. There are also inevitable tensions between a national monetary system which is created primarily to serve as a medium of exchange and a virtual currency which, although designed to provide a similar service, is also established with a view to private profit.

---

[106] Financial Services and Markets Act 2001 (Regulated Activities) Order 2001 (SI 2001/544). See the UK Financial Conduct Authority, *Guidance on Cryptoassets*, Consultation Paper CP19/3, published January 2019.
[107] For further discussion of this, see paras 5–74 to 5–75 below.
[108] Sarah Green, "It's Virtually Money", Ch.2 in Sarah Green and David Fox, *Cryptocurrencies in Public and Private Law* (2019).
[109] In particular, the "seller" has no ability to sue for the price.
[110] Green, for example, argues for their recognition as money in a private law context, given the effects which rest on this recognition; Sarah Green, "It's Virtually Money", fn.108 above, especially paras 2.22, 2.26–2.47.

Virtual currencies as a medium of payment

If one concludes that Bitcoin and other virtual currencies are not "money", then the purist may argue that they cannot in any event be used as a means of "payment". That may well be so but, in practical terms, such an approach would be at odds with the court's objective to give effect to the commercial intention of the parties. Accordingly, it is suggested that—whether or not one elects to adorn the transaction with the "payment" label—the key question is whether the debtor has performed his obligations in accordance with the terms of the contract.

In this specific context, the analysis should therefore mirror the earlier discussion in the context of payments effected by means of a transfer to a bank account of the creditor.[111] In other words, has the payer succeeded in crediting the requisite number of bitcoins to the payee by the required deadline, such that the payee has the unconditional right to deal with and to dispose of the full benefit of the assets transferred to him?[112]

1–23

---

[111] See para.1–08 above.
[112] See *The Chikuma* [1981] 1 W.L.R. 314 HL. See also the discussion of virtual currency payments in Ch.5.

Chapter 2

THE CONCEPT OF PAYMENT

1. The Concept of Payment

What is payment?

So much for the meaning of "money"; what then of the meaning of "payment"? Usually, payment denotes the transfer of money or of a money fund, or performance of some other act tendered and accepted in discharge of a money obligation, but often the parties to a contract use the term to denote some intermediate step, such as a conditional payment or a dispatch of funds. An example of the former is payment by cheque. Here, the contractual obligation to "pay" by a certain date may by agreement or course of dealing between the parties be considered honoured by delivery of the cheque on or before that date, but the payment is not complete until the instrument has been honoured.[1] Similarly, the parties may expressly or by implication agree that the duty to pay by a certain date shall be considered performed if a remittance is dispatched to the creditor by that date,[2] but payment in the legal sense is not complete until received and adopted by the creditor or his duly authorised agent except where the creditor has agreed to bear the risk of loss during transmission.

2–01

Payment in the legal sense means a gift or loan of money or any act offered and accepted in performance of a money obligation.[3] So an act cannot constitute

---

[1] See para.5–28 below.
[2] *A/S Tankexpress v Compagnie Financière Belge des Petroles SA* [1949] A.C. 76 HL; *Zim Israel Navigation Co Ltd v Effy Shipping Corp* [1972] 1 Lloyd's Rep. 18 QBD (Comm). These two cases are briefly considered in *Warnborough Ltd v Garmite Ltd* [2007] 1 P. & C.R. 2 at [86]–[87], where the parties had departed from the agreed contractual terms and method of payment. In landlord and tenant cases: (1) the starting point is that the landlord is entitled to payment *in cash*; but (2) where it has been expressly or impliedly agreed that a cheque will suffice, the date of payment is the date on which the cheque is posted by the tenant, provided that the cheque is subsequently met on presentation: see *Beevers v Mason* (1979) 37 P. & C.R. 452 CA (Civ Div); *Coltrane v Day* [2003] 1 W.L.R. 1379 and *Avocet Industrial Estates LLP v Merol Ltd* [2012] L. & T.R. 13. It may be that the courts are indulgent to the tenant in this type of case because the consequences of forfeiture for non-payment of rent are disproportionate to the losses that may flow to the landlord as a result of a few days' delay in payment. However, if the rule just stated is to apply, the cheque as posted must be in a form that the bank is obliged to meet without further formality. Thus, for example, the cheque must comply with the terms of the mandate as to the identity and number of signatories: see *Luttenberger v North Thoresby Farms Ltd* [1993] 1 E.G.L.R. 3 Ch D.
[3] Compare the remarks of Staughton J in *Libyan Arab Foreign Bank v Bankers Trust Co* [1989] Q.B. 728 QBD (Comm), where he observed (at 764) that "every obligation in monetary terms, is to be fulfilled, either by the delivery of cash or by some other operation which the creditor demands and which the debtor is either obliged, or is content to perform". It is therefore correct to observe that

payment unless money is involved, but this requirement may be satisfied not only by the transfer of money to the creditor but also by the performance of some other act in fulfilment of an obligation to pay money.[4] The default method of satisfying a money obligation—and that on which the creditor is entitled to insist unless otherwise expressly or impliedly agreed—is, of course, by the transfer of coins and notes by way of legal tender. This, however, is highly inconvenient, not to say risky, where substantial sums are involved, and the court will readily infer an agreement to pay by some other method which is equally acceptable commercially.[5] In *R. (on the application of Camden LBC) v Parking Adjudicator*, although it was accepted "(a)s a matter of strict theory" that the only form of payment that the council in that case was obliged to accept as a matter of law was "cash in legal tender, unless they agree otherwise", the judge, Burnett J, suggested that "a council which required parking contraveners to pay cash in notes, or coins of £1 or higher value (current legal tender) would be vulnerable to challenge on grounds of irrationality".[6] The three most common alternatives to payments in physical cash—transfer to creditor's account, offset of items on a running account and set-off—will now be discussed. Netting will also be discussed as, although there is some overlap with set-off, these are different concepts.

(1) Transfer to creditor's account

2-02 The creditor requires or agrees to accept the transfer of the stipulated sum to his account with a third party or with the debtor himself.

Example 1
S sells goods to B and stipulates that payment is to be made to the credit of S's account with T Bank. Payment is considered made when T Bank accepts the instruction to credit S's account.[7]

---

obligations of payment are similar to any other form of contractual obligations—their meaning and effect are matters for the construction of the terms of the contract itself. The subject is considered by *Chitty on Contracts*, edited by H. Beale, 33rd edn (London: Sweet & Maxwell, 2018), para.21–040.

[4] For example, an obligation to advance monies pursuant to a loan agreement may be satisfied if the lender makes payment to a third party at the direction of the borrower: for an example, see *Equuscorp Pty Ltd v Glengallan Investments Pty Ltd* [2004] HCA 55 (High Court of Australia). Whatever the mode of performance, it seems clear that there must be some movement of money or settlement of accounts that improves the financial position of the creditor: see *Taylor v Rocky Castle Finance Pty Ltd* [2014] SASFC 1 (Supreme Court of South Australia).

[5] The formulation in this paragraph was approved by the Federal Court of Australia in *Quality Publications Australia Pty Ltd v Commissioner of Taxation* [2012] FCA 256 at [48]. If payment becomes impossible by such means, then the creditor may nevertheless retain his ultimate right to insist on cash, even when the sums involved are very large: see the *Libyan Arab* decision at fn.3 above. If the creditor wishes, at the last moment, to insist on payment in cash in circumstances where another means of payment would normally be used, then it may be an implied term of the contract that the debtor is allowed a grace period to obtain the cash: see the decision of the US Supreme Court in *Simmons v Swann* 275 U.S. 113 (1927).

[6] *R. (on the application of Camden LBC) v Parking Adjudicator* [2011] P.T.S.R. 1391 at [28].

[7] As to when this occurs and for discussion of the principle, see Ch.5. It will, however, always be necessary to scrutinise the contract in such cases. If the funds have been credited to an escrow account in Country A, the release of the deposit to the purchaser may not amount to payment if the purchase

Example 2
S sells his shares in his company to B. It is a term of the sale agreement that part of the purchase price shall be placed on deposit with B's Bank. Payment of that part is made when B's Bank treats S as a depositor and no longer as an unpaid seller.[8]

(2) *Offset of items on a running account*

Where transactions between two parties are by agreement recorded in a running account, showing debits on one side and credits on the other, the transactions cease to be individualised for accounting purposes, for the effect of the agreement is that, instead of settling each transaction separately, the parties will periodically strike a balance, settlement of which will discharge their respective liabilities on all the preceding transactions. In other words, "all sums paid in form one blended fund, the parts of which have no longer any distinctive existence",[9] whilst all the debit items constitute an acknowledgment of a global indebtedness. The result is that, unless otherwise agreed, the normal rule by which the debtor, or, in default of his so doing, the creditor, can appropriate a payment to whichever debt he chooses is displaced, and sums paid to the credit of the account are to be appropriated to items on the debit side in the order in which the latter occur, the earliest debit items being settled first. This is the famous rule in *Devaynes v Noble*,[10] which is of the utmost importance in banking transactions.

2–03

It is well settled that agreement and payment of a debit balance on a running account constitute payment of all the items on the account.[11] Where the creditor—at the request of the debtor—accepts that his invoice is to be debited to the running account, then that invoice is effectively treated as paid or discharged,

---

price is payable in Country B: see *Canmer International Inc v UK Mutual Steamship Assurance Association (Bermuda) Ltd (The Rays)* [2005] 2 Lloyd's Rep. 479.

[8] This would normally occur when the purchaser instructs B's Bank to release the deposit to S. Contrast the position where S's account is credited qua seller. In such a case, the credit is not intended as payment but merely acknowledges B's indebtedness to S, which remains to be discharged in the manner agreed between the parties.

[9] Commonly known as the rule in *Clayton's Case*; *Devaynes v Noble* (1816) 1 Mer. 529 Ch at 608 per Sir William Grant MR.

[10] *Devaynes v Noble* at fn.9 above.

[11] *Re Harmony & Montague Tin and Copper Mining Co, Spargo's Case* (1872–73) L.R. 8 Ch. App. 407 CA, referred to in *Investment Trust Companies (In Liquidation) v Revenue and Customs Commissioners* [2012] S.T.C. 1150; and *MJP Media Services Ltd v Revenue and Customs Commissioners* [2011] S.T.C. 2290. The Australian Tax Office (ATO) considers that a mutuality of presently existing liabilities or obligations for a certain monetary amount immediately payable between the two parties must be in existence for a payment to be affected by an agreed set-off. Thus, in the context of a self-managed superannuation fund with a surviving spouse where the surviving spouse was entitled to be paid the deceased member's benefits as a lump sum by the trustee of the fund, there was no mutuality of liabilities in respect of which the principle in *Re Harmony* might apply since the surviving spouse had no present liability to pay an amount to the trustees and so there was no set-off (see ATO ID 2015/23). Accordingly, debiting the amount of the deceased member's benefits from the deceased member's account and crediting the amount of the surviving spouse by a journal entry was not considered to constitute a payment and therefore a cashing of the deceased member's benefits as a lump sum to the spouse.

and is subsumed into the running balance.[12] Where the debtor on a balance of account expressly or by implication assents to the balance as a matter of arithmetical computation[13] but fails to pay it, the creditor can sue either on the account as an account stated, the assent to which implies a new promise to pay, or on the original transactions.[14] It would seem that appropriation does not take effect so as to constitute payment until the agreed debit balance has been paid,[15] so that if the debtor fails to pay and the creditor elects to sue on the original transactions rather than on the account, he can presumably appropriate the debtor's payments to such of the transactions as he chooses.

(3) Set-off

2–04   A third method of payment is set-off, that is, the setting of one money claim against another in or towards payment. Set-off arises between two parties who owe money to each other and has been defined as "the right of a debtor who is owed money by his creditor on another account or dealing to secure payment for what is owed to him by setting this off in reduction of his own liability".[16] For instance, in a scenario where A owes B £100, and B owes A £200, a right of set-off would allow B to apply the amount owing to it by A against the amount it owes to A, reducing its liability to A to £100.[17]

2–05   Set-off takes place without any need for a formal tender of payment by either party, since it is not necessary that the parties should "go through the form and ceremony of having the money backwards and forwards".[18] In contrast to the running account previously described and based on the agreement of the parties to pay a single debit balance when struck, set-off presupposes the maintenance of

---

[12] See *Commissioner of Taxation v Desalination Technology Pty Ltd* [2014] FCA 1120 (Federal Court of Australia) at [33], citing the second edition of this book with approval.

[13] Where the parties agree to the net debit balance not as a matter of arithmetic computation, which may later be reopened and shown to be erroneous, but by way of compromise of disputed or unliquidated claims, there is a binding accord and the debtor must pay the balance even if it transpires that less was due under the original contracts than had been thought or that such contracts were wholly or partially unenforceable.

[14] Designation of the appropriate cause of action no longer bothers the practitioner but caused a great deal of trouble in the days when formalities of pleading were more stringent. See, for example, *Callander v Howard* 138 E.R. 117 Court of Common Pleas.

[15] See, for example, the judgment of Blackburn J in *Laycock v Pickles* (1863) 4 B. & S. 397 KB at 506: "There is a real account stated when several items of claim are brought into account on either side, and, being set against one another, a balance is struck, and the consideration for the payment of the balance is the discharge of the items on each side. It is then the same as if each item was paid and a discharge given for each, and in consideration of that discharge the balance was agreed to be due. It is to be taken as if the sums had been really paid down on each side; and the balance is recoverable as if money had been really taken in satisfaction." Cited with approval in *Camillo Tank Steamship Co v Alexandria Engineering Works* (1921) 9 Ll. L. Rep. 307 HL; and *Siqueira v Noronha* [1934] A.C. 332 PC; *Point v Federal Commissioner of Taxation (Australia)* [1970] 70 ATC 4021; and *Bank of New South Wales v Brown* (1983) 151 CLR 514.

[16] *Goode and Gullifer on Legal Problems of Credit and Security*, 6th edn (London: Sweet & Maxwell, 2018), para.7-01.

[17] For a more detailed account of the law of set-off, see *Goode and Gullifer on Legal Problems of Credit and Security* (2018), Ch.7; also Rory Derham, *Derham on the Law of Set-Off*, 4th edn (Oxford: Oxford University Press, 2010).

[18] *Re Harmony* (1872–73) L.R. 8 Ch. App. 407 CA at 414.

the claim and cross-claim as two distinct items, each of which can be separately pursued. A distinction is, however, to be drawn between various types of set-off, which may have differing legal consequences.[19] In cases involving cross-claims between the same parties but which are otherwise unrelated ("independent set-off"), a debtor may set up his claim as a procedural defence but this will not amount to a discharge of his own obligation until judgment is given. In contrast, the exercise of a right of set-off may amount to substantive performance of the obligation—and hence, to "payment"—in the following cases:

1. where the claim and the cross-claim are so closely connected that it would be inequitable to enforce the claim without giving credit for the cross-claim ("transaction set-off");
2. where the contract specifically allows for the parties to set-off their respective claims ("contractual set-off"); and
3. where the right is exercised as a part of the process of a liquidation or administration[20] ("insolvency set-off"). This form of set-off may be regarded as self-executing in nature.[21]

The issue of set-off as a method of payment was specifically addressed in *Federal-Mogul Asbestos Personal Injury Trust v Federal Mogul Ltd*,[22] where the court concluded that not only was set-off payment, but a reference to payment "as cash" could include set-off.[23]

Independent set-off

Independent set-off is given primarily to avoid circuity of actions.[24] There are two types.[25] The first, referred to as statutory or legal set-off, is set-off under the rules carried over from the former Statutes of Set-off enacted in 1728[26] and 1734.[27] The second type is that applied by equity by analogy with the Statutes of Set-Off, where the conditions for statutory set-off were present except that one of the liquidated cross-claims was equitable.

In both cases, independent set-off is a purely procedural defence which does not operate to reduce or extinguish the parties' payment obligations except when judgment is given for the balance. The requirements for independent set-off are

2–06

---

[19] For a classification, see P. Wood, *English and International Set-off* (London: Sweet & Maxwell, 1989), adopted by *Goode and Gullifer on Legal Problems of Credit and Security* (2018), para.7–03.
[20] See, in particular, rr.14.24 and 14.25 of the Insolvency (England and Wales) Rules 2016.
[21] *Stein v Blake (No.1)* [1996] A.C. 243 HL. Payment by way of set-off may also be self-executing under other statutes. For an example in the context of VAT, see *R. (on the application of Cardiff City Council) v Customs and Excise Commissioners* [2004] S.T.C. 356; and *R. (on the application of Capital Accommodation (London) Ltd (In Liquidation)) v Revenue and Customs Commissioners* [2013] S.T.C. 303.
[22] *Federal-Mogul Asbestos Personal Injury Trust v Federal-Mogul Ltd (formerly T&N plc)* [2014] EWHC 2000 (Comm).
[23] *Federal-Mogul* [2014] EWHC 2000 (Comm) at [172]–[177].
[24] *Goode and Gullifer on Legal Problems of Credit and Security* (2018), paras 7–01, 7-35.
[25] *Goode and Gullifer on Legal Problems of Credit and Security* (2018), para.7–04.
[26] Insolvent Debtors Relief Act 1728 (2 Geo. 2 c.22) s.13.
[27] Set-off of Debts Act 1734 (8 Geo. 2 c.24) s.5.

that the claim and cross-claim are for sums of money or based on non-payment of money, that they are both liquidated, that they are both due when the claim is commenced and that they are mutual, i.e. due from the same parties in the same right; unlike transaction set-off, it is unnecessary for the claims to be connected to each other.[28]

Transaction set-off

2–07 Transaction set-off arises in the case of closely connected transactions and is known in England as "equitable set-off" or "abatement".[29] It is often taken to include the common law right of abatement which exists in relation to contracts for the sale of goods and for work and labour. In *The Law of Set-Off*, Derham notes that this right developed to allow a defendant in an action for the agreed price of: (i) goods sold with a warranty; or (ii) work to be performed according to a contract, to show that the goods were, by reason of non-compliance with the warranty, or the work was, in consequence of the improper performance of the contract, diminished in value or of no value.[30] At this point in time, the only right of set-off at common law was under the Statutes of Set-off, which required liquidated cross-demands. This right of abatement is now restricted to contracts for the sale of goods and for work and labour.[31]

Transaction set-off or "equitable set-off" arises where the claim and cross-claim, even if not arising from the same transaction, are so closely connected that it would be inequitable for one claim to be enforced without credit being given for the other.[32] The requirements for transaction set-off are that there is a close connection between the claim and the cross-claim, that the cross-claim is based on the non-payment of money (although this is not limited to a claim for money set-off) and that there is mutuality of claims, i.e. the claims are due from the same parties in the same right.[33] It used to be considered as a purely procedural remedy, but can now operate as a substantive defence when not precluded by the nature or the terms of any contract between the parties.[34]

---

[28] See *Goode and Gullifer on Legal Problems of Credit and Security* (2018), paras 7–04, 7–35 to 7–49, for a more detailed account of independent set-off and its operation.

[29] See P. Wood, *Principles of Insolvency Law*, 2nd edn (London: Sweet & Maxwell, 2007); *Goode and Gullifer on Legal Problems of Credit and Security* (2018), para.7–05.

[30] *Derham on the Law of Set-Off* (2010), para.2.123.

[31] See fn.27 above; Derham cites *Gilbert Ash (Northern) Ltd v Modern Engineering (Bristol) Ltd* [1974] AC 689 HL at 717 (Lord Diplock); *Aries Tanker Corp v Total Transport Ltd (The Aries)* [1977] 1 W.L.R. 185 HL at 190; *Sim v Rotherham MBC* [1987] Ch. 216 Ch D at 258–259; *Mellowes Archital Ltd v Bell Projects Ltd* 87 B.L.R. 26 CA (Civ Div) at 37.

[32] *Derham on the Law of Set-Off* (2010), paras 4.30 and 18.25, with para.18.25 approved in *Stemcor UK Ltd v Global Steel Holdings Ltd* [2015] EWHC 363 (Comm) at [35].

[33] See *Goode and Gullifer on Legal Problems of Credit and Security* (2018), paras 7–50 to 7–64, and cases cited therein for further information on transaction set-off and its requirements.

[34] See *Derham on the Law of Set-Off* (2010), para.4.29 and cases cited therein; also *Goode on Legal Problems of Credit and Security* (2018), para.7–54.

Contractual set-off

Contractual set-off is provided for expressly by agreement of the parties. It has been defined as "a set-off created by contract where such set-off would not otherwise arise".[35] Its existence is an illustration of the general rule in English law that parties are usually free to make their own contractual arrangements. They can, for instance, agree that their obligations will be set off against each other and only the balance payable (e.g. that their obligations are owed only on a net basis). Contractual set-off operates as a substantive defence and has the effects provided for by the parties, i.e. it may extinguish or reduce the claim depending on what the parties have agreed.[36] The parties can override the usual requirement of mutuality of debts by, for example, providing that debts due from a parent company's subsidiary can be set off against the amount owing to the parent company. It should be noted that on the insolvency of one of the contractual parties, contractual set-off is generally disapplied and insolvency set-off applies instead.[37]

2–08

Other rights with an effect analogous to set-off

Certain rights exist which, although different from set-off, have an analogous effect. Derham discusses two such rights[38]; combination of bank accounts and the rule in *Cherry v Boultbee*.[39] Combination of bank accounts, also referred to as "current account set-off", refers to a bank's right to combine the various accounts held by a customer and consider them as a single debt (thus setting off a debit balance on one account against a credit balance on the other).[40] The rule in *Cherry v Boultbee* is relevant where a person who is entitled to receive a distribution from a fund is also under an obligation to contribute to the fund. The administrator of the fund can direct the person to satisfy his entitlement to a distribution from the fund from his obligation to contribute to the fund (in this sense, an "asset" of the fund).

2–09

Insolvency set-off

Set-off is very important in an insolvency scenario.[41] If insolvency set-off was not available and there were cross-demands owing between a creditor and an insolvent debtor, the creditor would have to pay his own debt in full while

2–10

---

[35] P. Wood, *Title Finance, Derivatives, Securitisations, Set-off and Netting* (London: Sweet & Maxwell, 1995), p.112.
[36] *Goode and Gullifer on Legal Problems of Credit and Security* (2018), para.7–06.
[37] This is the result of the application of the anti-deprivation principle and the pari passu principle; see *Goode and Gullifer on Legal Problems of Credit and Security* (2018), para.7–98 for more information.
[38] *Derham on the Law of Set-Off* (2010), para.1.12.
[39] *Cherry v Boultbee* 41 E.R. 171 Ch D.
[40] *Goode and Gullifer on Legal Problems of Credit and Security* (2018), para.7–07. See paras 7–31 to 7–34 for further information on current account set-off.
[41] For a detailed discussion of insolvency set-off, see *Goode and Gullifer on Legal Problems of Credit and Security* (2018), paras 7–79 to 7–103.

receiving a dividend only along with other creditors from the debtor. Mandatory insolvency set-off (on administrative or winding-up) is provided for in rr.14.24 and 14.25 of the Insolvency (England and Wales) Rules 2016. Insolvency set-off operates as a substantive rule of law and does not depend on the creditor taking any procedural steps.[42]

When is payment deemed to occur?

2–11   Where set-off can of itself amount to payment, it may be necessary to ask at what point payment is deemed to occur. It seems clear that the mere *existence* of a right of set-off does not reduce or discharge the primary debt; this occurs only when the right is *exercised*. The point could be important where the creditor wishes to terminate a contract for non-payment or holds security and wishes to take enforcement proceedings; is he entitled to do so or is the debt already discharged? Two separate questions have to be distinguished: (1) at what point does a right of set-off operate as substantive defence; and (2) at what point does it extinguish or reduce a claim to payment?

On the first point, *Fearns (t/a Autopaint International) v Anglo-Dutch Paint & Chemical Co Ltd*[43] clarified the operation of transaction (equitable) set-off as a substantive defence. While it confirmed that set-off operated as a substantive defence,[44] it was held that this was not automatic as had been indicated in previous cases[45] and, on the contrary, there must be a positive *assertion* of the set-off by the debtor.[46] Set-off, when asserted, will therefore operate as a defence to a claim for payment, and the exercise of associated rights such as termination and enforcement, so long as it is asserted on reasonable grounds and in good faith.[47]

On the second point, the assertion of set-off is not sufficient in itself to extinguish or reduce a claim to payment, as confirmed in the *Fearns* case.[48] In *Fearns*, the court had to consider the precise time at which a claim and cross-claim were converted into the same currency. It was held that equitable set-off does not extinguish or reduce the claim or cross-claim until judgment or agreement.[49] This, therefore, was the point of conversion.

---

[42] *Stein* [1996] A.C. 243 HL.
[43] *Fearns (t/a Autopaint International) v Anglo-Dutch Paint & Chemical Co Ltd* [2011] 1 W.L.R. 366 Ch D.
[44] *Fearns* [2011] 1 W.L.R. 366 at [21]–[23].
[45] *Goode and Gullifer on Legal Problems of Credit and Security* (2018), para.7.-58, especially fn.284 and the cases cited therein.
[46] On the whole subject, see *Goode and Gullifer on Legal Problems of Credit and Security* (2018), paras 7–58 to 7–59.
[47] Even if the amount or validity of the cross-claim is uncertain; *SL Sethia Liners Ltd v Naviagro Maritime Corp (The Kostas Melas)* [1981] 1 Lloyd's Rep 18 at 26–27; *Modern Trading Co Ltd v Swale Building and Construction Ltd* (1990) 24 Con. L.R. 59.
[48] *Fearns* [2011] 1 W.L.R. 366 at [30], [34]–[35].
[49] *Fearns* [2011] 1 W.L.R. 366 at [50(1)], approved in *Stemcor UK Ltd v Global Steel Holdings Ltd* [2015] 1 Lloyd's Rep. 580 at [34] and applied in *Secretary of State for Defence v Spencer* [2019] EWHC 1526 (Ch). For discussion of this case, see *Goode and Gullifer on Legal Problems of Credit and Security* (2018), para.7-59.

(1) Netting

Although "set-off" and "netting" are sometimes treated as being interchangeable terms, netting has a different meaning when used in a financial context. It describes the contractual arrangements used to consolidate the mutual claims of different parties into a single net balance. There are a number of statutory definitions of netting; the Banking Act 2009, for instance, defines "netting arrangements" as[50]:

2–12

> "... arrangements under which a number of claims or obligations can be converted into a net claim or obligation and include, in particular, 'close-out' netting arrangements, under which actual or theoretical debts are calculated during the course of a contract for the purpose of enabling them to be set off against each other or to be converted into a net debt".

The two main types of netting are settlement or "payment" netting and "close-out" netting. Payment netting occurs during the normal operation of the contract and involves the parties setting off amounts owed to give a single net sum which is payable by one party to the other. For many agreements, a net sum will usually be payable in respect of amounts owed on the same date and in the same currency.[51] "Close-out" netting, on the other hand, referred to in the definition above, occurs where the contract under which payments are made is terminated or "closed out", usually due to default by one party, for instance, because of non-payment or insolvency, or the exercise of termination rights. Close-out netting, depending on the terms of the contract, involves either[52]:

(i) the acceleration of the parties' obligations so they become immediately due and expressed as an obligation to pay an amount representing the original obligation's estimated current value or replacement cost, or being terminated and replaced by an obligation to pay that amount; or

(ii) an account being taken of what is due from each party to the other party in respect of such obligations and a net sum equal to the balance of the account being payable by the party from whom the larger amount is due to the other party.

The use of close-out netting can substantially reduce the exposures of contractual parties to each other and close-out netting is therefore viewed as being extremely important in the financial markets. Its effective operation is considered crucial to maintain financial stability and reduce systemic risk. However, the effectiveness of close-out netting on the insolvency of a contractual party depends on various legal techniques, some of which have been subject to challenge (as discussed below).[53]

---

[50] Banking Act 2009 s.48(1)(d).
[51] For instance, this is the case for the ISDA Master Agreement (discussed below).
[52] See *Goode and Gullifer on Legal Problems of Credit and Security* (2018), para.7-09.
[53] See *Goode and Gullifer on Legal Problems of Credit and Security* (2018), para.7-101, for an overview of the vulnerabilities of close-out netting on insolvency.

The ISDA Master Agreement

2–13 A master agreement is often used in order to facilitate payment and close-out netting. There are a number of standard form master agreements for different types of contracts which have been developed to facilitate netting. The most well-known is that published by the International Swaps and Derivatives Association Inc (ISDA), an industry association for participants in the derivatives markets. This master agreement, referred to as the ISDA Master Agreement, is a standard form template document agreed by two parties to document derivatives transactions. Since it covers all transactions to which it is specified as applying, it removes the need to enter into a new agreement or renegotiate terms each time a transaction is entered into since the terms of the ISDA Master Agreement between the parties apply automatically.

The ISDA Master Agreement framework includes the master agreement itself, a schedule, confirmations which set out the specific terms for each transaction and often (but not always) credit support documentation, of which the credit support annex (CSA) is the most common for English law transactions.[54] The master agreement is a pre-printed document which is never amended beyond inserting the parties' names. Any changes are made in the schedule, which provides for elections, additions and amendments to be made to the master agreement by the parties. The schedule does not, however, contain the commercial terms for a particular transaction, which are set out in the confirmation for that transaction. Credit support documentation such as the CSA is optional and is used where one or both parties agree to provide collateral to the other party to cover any exposures. The CSA contains the terms relating to the provision of collateral, including its posting and return and types of acceptable collateral.

2–14 The ISDA Master Agreement is intended to operate on a "single agreement" basis, i.e. all transactions entered into pursuant to its terms form part of one single agreement.[55] It provides for the netting of all sums due on a given day and in a given currency between the parties.[56] It also provides for close-out netting; for instance, on termination of transactions under the 2002 ISDA Master Agreement, a single "Early Termination Amount" is payable by one party to the other party. The "single agreement" structure is intended to ensure netting operates effectively on insolvency and prevent the "cherry-picking" of particular transactions by insolvency officials. In *BNP Paribas v Wockhardt EU Operations (Swiss) AG*,[57] it was considered that this approach was acceptable on the basis of party autonomy and freedom of contract as reflecting the substance of the legal relations into which the parties had chosen to enter.[58]

---

[54] ISDA has produced a number of forms of master agreements over the years, but, for English law transactions, the two which are generally used are the 1992 ISDA Master Agreement and the 2002 ISDA Master Agreement. The most common credit support document presently used is the 1995 ISDA Credit Support Annex.
[55] 1992 and 2002 ISDA Master Agreement s.1(c).
[56] 1992 and 2002 ISDA Master Agreement s.2(c).
[57] *BNP Paribas v Wockhardt EU Operations (Swiss) AG* 132 Con. L.R. 177.
[58] *BNP Paribas* 132 Con. L.R. 177 at [24], applied in *Videocon Ltd v Goldman Sachs International* [2016] EWCA Civ 130 at [51].

However, netting in this respect is limited to transactions actually under the ISDA Master Agreement itself and cannot be combined with other set-off rights. In *MHB-Bank AG v Shanpark Ltd*,[59] which considered the relationship between the payment netting and close-out netting provisions of the 1992 ISDA Master Agreement and a contractual set-off provision which had been added by the parties in the schedule, the court held that the ISDA netting provisions are limited to amounts due under the terms of the agreement itself. Therefore, amounts payable under any other agreement (in the present case, an unliquidated damages claim for mis-selling) could only reduce the amount payable pursuant to the master agreement in question (termed the "Early Termination Amount" in the contractual set-off provision added by the parties) to the extent that they could be set off according to the usual rules. It was held by Cooke J that netting and "set-off" were "different concepts" for the purposes of the ISDA Master Agreement; netting "relates to sums due under" the agreement, whether during its life or after termination, whereas set-off, as used, allowed "amounts payable under any other agreement to reduce the Early Termination Amount, which is in itself the result of close-out netting".[60]

2–15 The other aspect of the ISDA Master Agreement intended to facilitate close-out netting is the "flawed asset" clause which makes each party's performance conditional on there being no default by the other party. If there is a default, the non-defaulting party can withhold performance.[61] This protects the non-defaulting party while deciding whether or not to trigger the close-out netting provisions, as the non-defaulting party does not have to make payments or deliveries in the meantime. The effectiveness of the "flawed asset" clause was confirmed by the Court of Appeal in *Lomas v JFB Firth Rixson Inc*,[62] where its effect was held to be to suspend any obligations of the non-defaulting party to make payments or deliveries arising subsequently to the default until either the default in question is cured or close-out netting occurs.

Despite decisions indicating the effectiveness of the "single agreement" and "flawed asset" approaches, remaining uncertainty over the effectiveness of certain netting arrangements has led to the introduction of specific legislation to preserve netting arrangements in certain scenarios.[63]

2–16 The above methods of payment, though the most common alternatives to payment in cash, are not exhaustive. It is also possible to discharge monetary obligations by the tender and acceptance of services or of goods or other tangible

---

[59] *MHB-Bank AG v Shanpark Ltd* [2016] 1 B.C.L.C. 527.
[60] *MHB-Bank* [2016] 1 B.C.L.C. 527 at [33].
[61] 1992 and 2002 ISDA Master Agreement s.2(a)(iii).
[62] *Lomas v JFB Firth Rixson Inc* [2012] 2 All E.R. (Comm) 1076. The decision in *Lomas* was applied outside the ISDA Master Agreement context in *Mercuria Energy Trading PTE Ltd v Citibank NA* [2015] EWHC 1481 (Comm), in circumstances where the repo master agreement in question specified that, whilst there was a termination event which was continuing, the other party could refuse to make any payments or deliveries until the corresponding payment or delivery of the other party had been irrevocably and unconditionally settled in full. The court held (at [132]) that the approach taken by the Court of Appeal in *Lomas* applied equally to this clause (at [132]).
[63] See *Goode and Gullifer on Legal Problems of Credit and Security* (2018), paras 7–102 to 7–103, for an overview of the statutory provisions which have been brought in to preserve close-out netting arrangements.

non-money assets,[64] but this is unusual.[65] "Payment" may also mean different things in different contexts, such as the tax context,[66] but we are concerned here with the discharge of monetary obligations.

To constitute payment, it is not necessary that the money be handed over, or the claim transferred, to the creditor; equally effective is payment or transfer to a third party at the request or direction of the creditor.[67] Likewise, a deduction from a sum which would otherwise be due to the debtor or a reduction in or discharge of his liability may constitute payment.[68]

In determining whether payment has been made, it is important to identify the contractual relationship under discussion. For example, if the debtor's bank transfers funds to the creditor's bank at a given date ("value date") with instructions to pay the creditor, or credit his account, at a later date ("payment date"), there is a payment between the two banks on the value date but no payment as between debtor and creditor until the payment date.[69] Again, if a bank discounts a bill of exchange for its customer, the payee, that is a purchase of the bill by the bank, not a payment of it, and whilst the bank's payment of the purchase price (whether in cash or by credit to its customer's account) involves a

---

[64] See *Elmdene Estates Ltd v White* [1959] 2 All E.R. 605 CA at 610–611, where Lord Evershed MR noted that "the word 'payment' in itself is one which, in an appropriate context, may cover many ways of discharging obligations. It may even ... include a discharge not by money payment at all but by what is called 'payment in kind'" (approved in *Hanoman v Southwark LBC (No 2)* [2009] 1 W.L.R. 1367; *Smith v Battams* (1857) 26 L.J. Ex. 232.

[65] The typical part exchange transaction in which, say, a motorcar is sold and the buyer's car taken in part exchange, is not a true case of acceptance of goods towards payment of a money obligation, since on a proper analysis that which is applied in part satisfaction of the price of the new car is not the old car but the agreed part exchange allowance. That is to say, delivery of the old car in "part exchange" generates a reciprocal contract of sale under which the price, as represented by the part exchange allowance, is set off against the price of the new car.

[66] See, for instance, *Aberdeen Asset Management Plc v Revenue and Customers Commissioners* [2014] S.T.C. 438, where the Scottish Court of Session reversed the decision of the Upper Tribunal that the transfer of shares in a "money box company" did not constitute a "payment" for PAYE purposes, holding that the transfer of shares in a money box company to an employee was a "payment" within the meaning of s.203(1) of the Income and Corporation Taxes Act 1988. This was in the context of a scheme that was apparently "designed to deliver cash or its equivalent to certain employees" (at [30]) and where the employees "had total practical control over the disposal of the funds that had been paid into the money box companies" (at [36]).

[67] E.g. in *Talent Plc v Revenue and Customs Commissioners* [2008] S.T.C. (S.C.D.) 202 Special Commissioners, it was held that contributions by an employer to a funded unapproved retirement benefit scheme and life assurance scheme for the benefit of an employee were not payments in kind but earnings for the purposes of liability for national insurance contributions. The court considered that, although s.6(1) of the Social Security Contributions and Benefits Act 1992 required earnings to be "paid", there was no indication in the primary legislation that there was intended to be any limitations on the "usual wide meaning" given to "payment" in cases such as *Elmdene Estates*.

[68] See e.g. *Elmdene Estates Ltd v White* [1959] 2 All E.R. 605 CA; *Hanoman v Southwark LBC (No 2)* [2009] 1 W.L.R. 1367; *Superstrike Ltd v Rodrigues* [2013] 1 W.L.R. 3848. In *Superstrike* [2013] 1 W.L.R. 3848, the court, applying *Elmdene*, held that, in the context of tenancy deposit schemes, a deposit did not have to be "physically received" through payment by cash, cheque, bank transfer etc, for there to have been payment and receipt of a deposit for the purposes of s.213 of the Housing Act 2004.

[69] See para.5–26 below.

transfer of funds as between the bank and its customer, it does not in any way discharge the bill, upon which the acceptor continues to be liable until payment has been made in due course.

Payment distinguished from other acts

(1) Tender

Payment is a consensual act and thus requires the accord of both creditor and debtor.[70] A tender which is not made in conformity with the contract[71] between the parties is of no effect if rejected by the creditor but produces payment if accepted by him as a valid payment.[72] Conversely, an unaccepted tender, even if fully complying with the contract, is not payment, despite the fact that the creditor's refusal to accept payment is a breach of duty. Hence, where acceptance is under the control of the creditor or his agent—as where payment is required to be tendered directly to the creditor or agent—the creditor is in a position to frustrate payment by refusing the tender and by instructing his agent to refuse a tender made to the agent. Instructive on this point is the case of *Colley v Overseas Exporters (1919) Ltd*.[73]

2–17

The plaintiff made a contract for the sale of a quantity of unascertained goods to the defendant f.o.b. Liverpool. The plaintiff sent goods to the docks but owing to a series of misfortunes the defendant was not able to nominate a vessel able to take them. The plaintiff's application for summary judgment for the price was dismissed on the ground that the property in goods sold f.o.b. did not pass until shipment, and the passing of the property was a pre-requisite of the right to sue for the price under the Sale of Goods Act 1979. The fact that the transfer of the property was prevented by the defendants' own breach (albeit unintentional) did not stop them from contending that the property had not passed. Accordingly, the plaintiff's proper remedy was damages, for which purpose he would have to amend his writ.

This decision appears at first sight to be in conflict with the Scottish case of *Mackay v Dick*,[74] where goods were sold but the buyer had a right to test them and return them if they failed the test. The buyer having wrongfully prevented the test from taking place meant that the seller was to be held entitled to sue for the

---

[70] The corresponding statement in the first edition of this work (Roy Goode, *Payment Obligations in Commercial and Financial Transactions*, 1st edn (London: Sweet & Maxwell, 1983)) was cited with approval by Gloster J in *Canmer International Inc v UK Mutual Steamship Assurance Association (Bermuda) Ltd (The Rays)* [2005] 2 Lloyd's Rep. 479 at [53]. See also *Chitty* (2018), para.21–075. The same point has been accepted by the Federal Court of Australia: *ABB Australia Pty Ltd v Commissioner of Taxation* [2007] FCA 1063.

[71] In other words, the amount tendered must be the full amount payable under the contract and the tender must be either: (1) unconditional (*Mitchell v King* 172 E.R. 1223, referred to in *St Vincent European General Partner Ltd v Robinson* [2018] EWHC 1230 (Comm) at [60]); or (2) subject only to such conditions as the contract may allow.

[72] As to what constitutes acceptance, see paras 2–24 to 2–25 below.

[73] *Colley v Overseas Exporters (1919) Ltd* [1921] 3 K.B. 302 KBD. The position may be different in other countries: see Paul Evans, "FOB and CIF Contracts" (1996) 67 A.L.J. 844.

[74] *Mackay v Dick* (1881) 6 App. Cas. 251 HL. See also *Thompson v ASDA-MFI Group Plc* [1988] Ch. 241 Ch D.

price. Lord Blackburn noted that "a party cannot invoke a right to cancel or terminate a contract for non-fulfilment of a condition precedent where that party caused the condition precedent not to be fulfilled".[75] But the important point about that case is that the contract was for the sale of specific goods, in which the property passed to the buyer under the contract, subject to a resolutive condition (i.e. a condition subsequent) by which the buyer could revest them in the seller if they failed the test. McCardie J noted in *Colley* itself that[76]:

> "... a clear distinction exists between cases where the default of the buyer has occurred after the property has passed and cases where that default has been before the property has passed. To the former cases *Mackay v. Dick* may be applied on appropriate facts. To the latter cases *Mackay v. Dick* does not apply so as to enable the buyer to recover the price as distinguished from damages for breach of contract."

Since, in *Mackay*, performance of the test was not a condition precedent to the passing of the property, there was no obstacle to the seller's claim to the price. This is a separate matter to the second category of cases distinguished by McCardie J, where property has not passed. There is some authority at common law, including in *Mackay* itself, for the position that a person wrongfully prevented from rendering contractual performance may sue for breach of the contract. Lord Blackburn stated in *Mackay* that[77]:

> "... as a general rule ... where in a written contract it appears that both parties have agreed that something shall be done, which cannot effectively be done unless both concur in doing it, the construction of the contract is that each agrees to do all that is necessary to be done on his part for the carrying out of that thing, though there may be no express words to that effect."

Lord Blackburn's statement has been referred to in a number of subsequent cases as indicating that a duty to cooperate, or at least not to prevent performance, may be implied into a contract depending on its terms, breach of which will give rise to a claim for damages.[78] However, this depends on the circumstances[79] and is separate from the right to sue for the price in sale of goods cases, which is

---

[75] *Mackay* (1881) 6 App. Cas. 251 HL at 263.
[76] *Colley v Overseas Exporters (1919) Ltd* [1921] 3 K.B. 302 KBD at 310.
[77] *Mackay* (1881) 6 App. Cas. 251 HL at 263.
[78] See, for example, the Court of Appeal's judgment in *Swallowfields Ltd v Monaco Yachting and Technologies SAM* [2014] 2 All E.R. (Comm) 185, where a claim for summary judgment was rejected since it was arguable that a duty to co-operate would be implied into any contract for the performance of which cooperation is required, such as a ship-building contract and related loan agreements (at [32]–[33]). See also *F&C Alternative Investments (Holdings) Ltd v Barthelemy* [2012] Ch. 613; *Hudson Bay Apparel Brands LLC v Umbro International Ltd* [2010] E.T.M.R. 15; *General Trading Co (Holdings) Ltd v Richmond Corp Ltd* [2008] 2 Lloyd's Rep. 475; *The Law Debenture Trust Corporation plc v Ukraine* [2019] QB 1121 at [207]; *UTB LLC v Sheffield United Ltd* [2019] EWHC 2322 (Ch) at [229]. It may be that, following Leggatt J's judgment in *Yam Seng Pte Ltd v International Trade Corporation Ltd* [2013] 1 C.L.C. 662 and subsequent cases which suggest that a duty of good faith may be implied into certain "relational" categories of contract, the English courts are more willing to imply duties to cooperate as an aspect of good faith (see *Yam Seng* at [140]) but that remains to be seen.
[79] As the Court of Appeal made clear in *The Law Debenture Trust Corporation plc v Ukraine* [2019] Q.B. 1121: "The implication of such a term, and, perhaps more importantly its scope, will depend on the contract under consideration, and in particular its express terms". This was applied recently in *Magdeev v Tsvetkov* [2020] EWHC 887 (Comm) at [370]–[372].

"conditional on the passing of property or the inclusion of express terms in the contract providing for the price to be payable on a day certain".[80]

Nevertheless, acceptance of payment is not always under the creditor's control, and sometimes it is possible for the debtor to make payment against the creditor's wishes, as where the contract or the law empowers the debtor to pay by way of set-off or by payment to a third party who is not subject to the creditor's instructions.

Whilst an unaccepted tender is not payment, a valid tender[81] does produce certain legal effects. In the first place, it precludes the creditor from asserting that the debtor was in breach of his payment obligation, for plainly the creditor, having frustrated payment, cannot complain of non-payment produced by his own wrongful act. Secondly, if the debtor is sued for payment, he can set up the defence of tender by paying the sum in question into court and serving a defence pleading the tender and the payment into court and asserting his continued willingness to make payment. This deprives the creditor of any right to interest[82] or damages[83] and he will usually be ordered to pay the defendant's costs.[84] In order that these may be provided for, the creditor is not entitled to withdraw the money in court except on an order, and this will generally provide for the defendant's costs, after taxation or assessment, to be deducted from the sum in court, the balance being paid out to the claimant. Thirdly, tender of the price under a contract of sale of goods has the effect that the seller is no longer an unpaid seller for the purpose of the Sale of Goods Act and thus ceases to be entitled to exercise a lien, a right to withhold delivery or a right of resale.[85] Fourthly, where under a contract of sale the property in the goods is to pass to the buyer on payment, the court will usually infer an intention that tender of payment is to have the same effect.[86]

---

[80] Sale of Goods Act 1979 s.49. See further discussion of this point at para.4–22 below; also *Benjamin's Sale of Goods*, 10th edn (London: Sweet & Maxwell, 2017), para.16-023.
[81] See generally *Chitty* (2018), paras 21–085 to 21–098.
[82] But interest will continue to run unless the debtor keeps the money ready for payment without making a profit on it (*Edmondson v Copland* [1911] 2 Ch. 301 Ch D), except in "exceptional" cases (as held by the Privy Council in *Cukurova Finance International Ltd v Alfa Telecom Turkey Ltd* [2015] 2 W.L.R. 875). In the *Cukurova* case, the circumstances were held to be "exceptional" where a mortgagee appropriated charged shares and then refused to accept prompt tender of full repayment of the loan. However, there was a disagreement among the Privy Council as to the reasoning; while the majority accepted Cukurova's argument that appropriation discharged the due debt, the minority rejected this but considered (agreeing with the majority) that rejection of a valid tender by a mortgagee stopped interest on the loan running, provided that the borrower set aside the sums due to the lender. It was noted in *Shearer v Spring Capital Ltd* [2013] EWHC 3148 (Ch) that the authorities on tender were hard to reconcile and the principles on tenders "provide opportunities for gaming on both sides" (at [127]).
[83] *Norton v Ellam* 150 E.R. 839 Court of Exchequer. In *North Shore Ventures Ltd v Anstead Holdings Inc* [2010] EWHC 1485 (Ch), which concerned liability for default interest, the court considered there must at least have been "an unconditional offer of payment (by whatever means)" and relief from liability would be "for no longer than the refusal to accept payment continued" (at [266]).
[84] *Griffith v Ystradyfodwg School Board* (1890) 24 Q.B.D. 307 QBD. But payment into court is essential: Civil Procedure Rules 1998 (CPR), Pt 37 r.2.
[85] Sale of Goods Act 1979 s.38(1).
[86] *Mirabita v Imperial Ottoman Bank* (1878) 3 Ex. D. 164 CA; and cf. *City Motors (1933) Pty v Southern Aerial Super Service Pty* 106 C.L.R. 477 HC.

(2) Exchange

2–18 Since payment involves either the transfer of money or the discharge of a money obligation, a pure exchange, in which the rights of the parties are not fixed by reference to any money sum, does not involve payment. Thus, an exchange of a motor cycle for a refrigerator is not a payment, merely a barter.[87]

(3) Purchase of a claim

2–19 A distinction is to be drawn between purchase of a claim and payment in discharge of a claim. Thus a person negotiating a bill of exchange does not pay the bill, he pays for it; the purchaser of a contract right does not, in handing over the purchase price, discharge the obligation of the debtor to the assignor, he buys it.

(4) Loans

2–20 The completion of a loan arrangement involves the advance of funds to the borrower and this is achieved by payment or transfer of the requisite amounts to the borrower or to a third party at his direction.[88] If such payment is made and there are no circumstances suggesting a different transaction (such as a purchase or a gift), then the factual background may give rise to a presumed obligation of repayment.[89]

(5) Advance against a projected transfer of funds

2–21 Only the debtor or his duly authorised agent can pay the debt. If a third party without authority makes a payment to the creditor in anticipation of reimbursement from the debtor or his agent, this is not payment as between debtor and creditor but an advance by the third party from his own funds, and payment as between debtor and creditor is not made until the third party has received the expected reimbursement or his act of payment has in some other way been ratified by the debtor.[90]

(6) Commitment to pay

2–22 It is important to distinguish actual payment from a mere commitment to pay. At a certain point, a debtor's instruction to his bank to make a payment to his creditor, or the bank's undertaking to the creditor or his agent to make payment

---

[87] Compare the analysis of a part exchange transaction; see fn.65 above.
[88] See the discussion at para.2–02 above.
[89] See, for example, *FBC Construction Co Ltd v Ben Lee* [2014] 2 HKLRD 1054 (Hong Kong Court of Appeal), and authorities there cited. Although not if the presumption of advancement applies and there is no evidence that the transfer is not a gift (though this presumption is due to be abolished when s.199 of the Equality Act 2010 is brought into force); see, for example, *Farrell v Burden* [2019] EWHC 3671 (QB).
[90] See the discussion of this subject at para.5–51 below.

on behalf of the debtor, becomes irrevocable.[91] But this does not of itself constitute payment, which occurs only when the instruction or undertaking is implemented. So the issue of a cheque commits the drawer to payment but payment is not made until the cheque has been cleared.[92]

Similarly, the intimation of a credit transfer by one bank to another commits the former to pay the latter but payment is not effected until the requisite debit and credit entries have been initiated in the accounts of the two banks at the Central Bank—in England, the Bank of England.[93] Payment coincides with commitment only where the normal sequence—authority to pay followed by the transfer of funds—is reversed, and funds are transferred in anticipation of a payment authority which is subsequently given. In that case, payment takes effect when the authority to pay is received. Thus, a cheque is paid when the time for stopping it has passed without the cheque being returned[94]; and where the creditor's bank transfers funds to its customer in anticipation of a request from the debtor's bank to do so, payment by the debtor to the creditor takes place when the request is received by the creditor's bank or the payment otherwise ratified by the debtor or his agent.[95] Similarly, creditors are not bound, in the absence of agreement by them, to accept promissory notes by way of payment.[96]

(7) Transfer which reserves an interest to the debtor or his agent

Since payment involves either a gift or loan or the discharge of a money obligation, it follows that a transfer of coins or notes or a credit to an account cannot amount to payment unless what is transferred to the creditor is freely at his disposal and ceases to be subject to the interest or control of the debtor or his paying agent. In the recent case of *K v A*,[97] it was reiterated that a payment to discharge an obligation to pay in cash must give the payee "the unconditional and unfettered right to the immediate use of the funds".[98] It is thus obvious that the delivery of coins or notes by the debtor to be held in specie for the debtor and returned to him in due course or applied at his direction cannot constitute payment of the debt. This is not because such coins or notes lack the character of money (for, as we have seen, money obligations may be discharged by the accepted tender of any type of asset[99]) but because the coins or notes do not pass into the beneficial (or even the legal) ownership of the creditor and therefore cannot be applied by him in discharge of the debt.

2–23

---

[91] As to when this occurs, see para.5–55 below.
[92] See para.5–28 below.
[93] See paras 5–20 and 5–21 below.
[94] See para.5–17 below.
[95] See para.5–51 below.
[96] *Child Maintenance and Enforcement Commission v Wilson* 2014 S.L.T. 46. See also *McLeod v Prestige Finance Ltd* [2016] CSOH 69, aff'd [2016] CSIH 87, where it was held that a creditor was not obliged to accept as valid payment cheques drawn on "WeRe Bank", an unregulated entity identified as being of concern by the FCA. Referring to *Wilson*, it was noted (at [17]) that the creditor was "entitled to refuse to accept payment otherwise than in legal tender".
[97] *K v A* [2019] EWHC 1118 (Comm).
[98] *K v A* [2019] EWHC 1118 (Comm) at [26], with reference to *The Brimnes* [1973] 1 W.L.R. 386.
[99] See para.2–01 above.

Somewhat less obvious is the fact that, even where coins or notes are transferred as money fungibles, the transfer does not constitute payment where its terms impose on the creditor a duty to hold the money as a distinct fund for the debtor or a third party. In this case, legal title to the coins or notes passes to the creditor, but, while he is entitled to retain or apply as he thinks fit the specific coins or notes handed to him, the money they represent is not freely available to him, since he is obliged to keep a fund of equivalent amount separate from his own moneys and to account for this to the debtor or to the third party for whom it is required to be held. Hence the transfer of money to be held on trust for the debtor,[100] or to be applied for a specific purpose which fails, producing a resulting trust in the debtor's favour,[101] or to be held to the order of the debtor pending fulfilment of a condition precedent, does not constitute payment so long as the trust continues or the condition remains unsatisfied.

Similarly, where the debtor's bank transfers funds to the creditor's bank for the account of the creditor but with a pay date later than the date of the transfer, unconditional payment to the creditor does not take effect until the specified pay date, even if the creditor can withdraw the money on payment of a small amount of interest. This highly unusual situation actually happened in *Awilco of Oslo A/S v Fulvia SpA di Navigazione of Cagliari (The Chikuma)*,[102] where, under Italian law, the effect of such stipulation was that, while the creditor became entitled to use the money immediately, interest would be payable on any use prior to the pay

---

[100] *Re Kayford Ltd (In Liquidation)* [1975] 1 W.L.R. 279 Ch D. For a Canadian decision which goes the other way, see *Re H.B. Haina & Associates Inc* (1978) D.L.R. (2d) 262. *Re Kayford* has been criticised on the ground that, as the debtor paid the money outright in the first instance and it was the creditor who then subjected it to a trust, the trust was prima facie a preference within s.239 of the Insolvency Act 1986. See William Goodhart and Gareth Jones, "The Infiltration of Equitable Doctrine into English Commercial Law" (1980) 43 M.L.R. 489 at 495 and following. The judgment of Megarry J indicates that, "on the facts of the case counsel for the joint liquidators was unable to contend that any question of a fraudulent preference arose. If one leaves on one side any case in which an insolvent company seeks to declare a trust in favour of creditors, one is concerned here with the question not of preferring creditors but of preventing those who pay money from becoming creditors, by making them beneficiaries under a trust" (at 606). Insofar as this suggests that the moneys were subject to a trust at the time of payment, the criticism is well founded. However, it does not follow that the establishment of the trust by the company was a fraudulent preference. The relevant question is the intention of the debtor. There is a difference between accepting money with the intention of treating it as the free assets of the recipient, the decision to create a trust being formed later, and an intention from the outset, and before the money is ever received, to subject it to a trust at the time of its receipt. In the later case, the recipient, knowing that he might well be unable to supply the goods for which the sums were paid, might well feel that to accept the payments and retain them for his own benefit would verge on fraudulent trading. It may be added that the *Re Kayford* decision was applied in *Re Branston & Gothard Ltd* [1999] 1 All E.R. (Comm) 289 Ch D, although the inference of a trust in that case was much stronger because the company was a regulated financial services company dealing with client money.

[101] See *Barclays Bank Ltd v Quistclose Investments Ltd* [1970] A.C. 567 HL, although note that there are conflicting views (both judicial and academic) about the legal basis for the trust in that case. *Twinsectra Ltd v Yardley* [2002] 2 A.C. 164, a subsequent "Quistclose trust" case, suggested that the correct analysis was that a resulting trust existed from the outset. The Quistclose trust was recently considered in *Challinor v Bellis* [2015] EWCA Civ 59; [2016] W.T.L.R. 43, where the Court of Appeal agreed it was a species of resulting trust but found intention to create an express trust (which subsequently fails) on the part of the transferor to be necessary.

[102] *Awilco of Oslo A/S v Fulvia SpA di Navigazione of Cagliari (The Chikuma)* [1981] 1 W.L.R. 314 HL. See also the earlier decision in *Re Steam Stoker Co* (1874–75) L.R. 19 Eq. 416 Ch.

date and no interest would be credited to him prior to that date if he left the money on deposit. The House of Lords held that, in these circumstances, whilst the interest payable or foregone might be very small in relation to the amount of money in question, the money could not be said to be freely at the disposal of the creditor. In consequence, the debtor was in breach by failing to make a timely payment, with a potentially huge liability in damages.[103]

However, a condition precedent to the release of money to the creditor must be distinguished from an outright payment upon a condition subsequent requiring repayment if a stated event occurs. In this case, the payment takes effect immediately and the occurrence of the condition entitles the debtor to recover the money.[104] The dishonoured cheque is a case in point. Cheques passing through the clearing system are credited to the collecting bank and debited to the paying bank in anticipation of the cheque being met, and funds are transferred from one bank to the other on the same day by entry in the records of the Bank of England before the cheque has even been presented for payment at the branch on which it is drawn. If the cheque is subsequently dishonoured, the paying bank will debit back the item to the collecting bank through the system and this will be reflected in the ensuing settlement between the two banks, consummated by another entry at the Bank of England. The original transfer of funds was not subject to any condition precedent in favour of the paying bank; the transfer was complete when the entries were initiated at the Bank of England, and dishonour of the cheque simply entitled the paying bank to a refund. In the unlikely event of the collecting bank going into liquidation before making the refund, the paying bank would be left to prove in the winding-up as an unsecured creditor.

What constitutes acceptance of a tender?

In most cases, the tender of payment and acceptance of the tender are simultaneous and there is no difficulty in seeing that payment has been made. But mere receipt of a tender does not necessarily take effect immediately as an acceptance. Two cases deserve particular mention.

2–24

(1) Conditional acceptance

Where a cheque or other bill of exchange is accepted in payment of a money obligation, the presumption is that the acceptance is conditional on the cheque or bill being met, so that if it is dishonoured the payee, if still the holder, may either sue on the instrument or treat the cause of action on the underlying transaction as having revived.[105] It is commonly said that the instrument is accepted as

2–25

---

[103] This also demonstrates that the doctrine of substantial performance does not apply to monetary obligations.
[104] But the creditor is not obliged to accept a tender subject to such a condition (*Chitty* (2018), para.21–093), though the mere fact that the debtor reserves a right to dispute the amount due or claim repayment does not invalidate the tender if he does not require the creditor to agree to this (*Chitty* (2018), para.21–094).
[105] *Re Romer & Haslam* [1893] 2 Q.B. 286 CA; see also *Michael Aronis & Aronis Nominees Pty Ltd (trading as Welland Tyrepower) v Hallett Brick Industries Ltd* [1999] SASC 92.

conditional payment,[106] but whilst acceptance of the instrument suspends the creditor's right of action on the original consideration pending maturity of the instrument, it is clear that the issue of the instrument does not operate as an assignment of funds in the hands of the drawee,[107] and is therefore not payment in any real sense. So in *Re Hone (A Bankrupt)*,[108] Harman J held that where a cheque was given to a rating authority in payment of rates and a receiving order was made against the drawer after issue of the cheque but before its collection by the rating authority's bank, payment was made on collection of the cheque, not on its issue, and the proceeds of the cheque were therefore recoverable by the trustee in bankruptcy on the footing that payment had taken place after the date of the receiving order.[109] Where the cheque is duly honoured on presentation, then payment is deemed to have been received as at the date in which the creditor received the cheque.[110]

Similarly, where the seller of goods is to receive payment under a bank letter of credit, acceptance of the letter of credit as payment is presumed to be conditional on the bank honouring the credit, failing which the seller's rights against the buyer for payment of the price revive.[111] Again, if the debtor's bank sends a banker's payment to the creditor's bank for the account of the creditor, the acceptance of this as payment is conditional on the payment order being met through the Clearing House settlement procedure and entry in the accounts of the two banks at the Bank of England. If the debtor's bank were to become insolvent before that time, the creditor's bank would be entitled to reverse the credit made conditionally to the creditor's account, and the debt would not be paid.[112]

(2) Receipt by the creditor's agent

2–26 Where money or a cheque is tendered to and received by the creditor's agent, two questions arise. Is receipt by the agent receipt by the creditor? If so, does the agent's receipt also constitute acceptance by the creditor? The answer to both these questions turns on the agent's actual or ostensible authority.

2–27 **(a) Unauthorised receipt.** If the agent had neither actual nor ostensible authority even to receive the money, his receipt is not that of the creditor and, if

---

[106] See, for example, Sale of Goods Act 1979 s.38(1)(b) and the discussion at para.5–28 below.
[107] Bills of Exchange Act 1882 s.53(1); see Halsbury's Laws of England, 5th edn (London: LexisNexis), Vol.13, paras 38 and 79.
[108] *Re Hone (A Bankrupt)* [1951] Ch. 85 Ch D.
[109] Current commercial practice regards payment by direct debit in the same way as payment by cheque. Hence, the cancellation of a direct debit has legal effects similar to the dishonour or countermand of a cheque: *Esso Petroleum Co Ltd v Milton* [1997] 1 W.L.R. 938 CA (Civ Div).
[110] *Homes v Smith* [2000] Lloyd's Rep. Bank. 139 CA (Civ Div). Where there is express or implied agreement that cheques will be accepted as payment due to a consistent course of dealing which indicates an agreement to accept cheques, tendering a cheque can constitute payment; *Avocet Industrial Estates LLP v Merol Ltd* [2012] L. & T.R. 13.
[111] See *WJ Alan & Co Ltd v El Nasr Export & Import Co* [1972] 2 Q.B. 189 CA (Civ Div) at 212 per Lord Denning MR; see also *ED&F Man Ltd v Nigerian Sweets & Confectionary Co* [1977] 2 Lloyd's Rep. 50 QBD (Comm) at 55–56; *Northwest Shipping and Towage Co Pty Ltd v Commonwealth Bank of Australia* (1993) 118 CLR 453 at 463.
[112] See further at para.5–55 below.

the agent fails to account to the creditor, the debtor will have to pay a second time, to the creditor directly. This was the fate of the defendant bank in *Cleveland Manufacturing Co Ltd v Muslim Commercial Bank Ltd*.[113] The defendants had issued a letter of credit to the plaintiffs and, relying on the fact that the shipping documents had been prepared by an employee of the plaintiffs' agent, who also signed the draft on behalf of the plaintiffs, the defendants made payment under the letter of credit to the agent. The latter became insolvent without having accounted for the payment to the plaintiffs. The court held that the acts of the agent did not entitle the defendants to treat him as authorised to receive payment, and the plaintiffs were accordingly entitled to judgment for the sum payable under the letter of credit.

(b) Authorised receipt. Where the agent is authorised to receive payment (as where the debtor is instructed by the creditor to remit the money to the creditor's bank), then whether such receipt also constitutes acceptance of the tender giving rise to payment depends partly on the terms on which it was received and partly on the extent of the agent's actual or apparent authority to receive payment. The agent, like his principal, the creditor, may impose a condition precedent to treating receipt of the money as payment. Where he does so, there is no payment until the condition is fulfilled. In other cases, it is necessary to look at the agent's actual or apparent authority. If he was authorised, or held out by the creditor as authorised, to accept payment on behalf of the creditor, then payment to the agent is payment to the creditor even if (unbeknown to the creditor, or known to him but unbeknown to the agent) the debtor had committed some breach of duty which would have entitled the creditor to refuse a tender of payment.[114] Where, on the other hand, the agent is authorised merely to receive the sum tendered pending the creditor's instructions and has no actual or ostensible authority to accept the tender as payment, then payment will not be deemed made unless and until the creditor has approved it, either expressly or implicitly, e.g. by failing to repudiate it within a reasonable time.[115] The principle is neatly illustrated by the contrasting decisions in *Central Estates (Belgravia)*

2–28

---

[113] *Cleveland Manufacturing Co Ltd v Muslim Commercial Bank Ltd* [1981] 2 Lloyd's Rep. 646 QBD (Comm), a case which turns principally on the question of apparent or ostensible authority; see also *British Bank of the Middle East v Sun Life Assurance Co of Canada (UK)* [1983] 2 Lloyd's Rep. 9 HL where there was a failure to establish ostensible authority. In *Stavrinides v Bank of Cyprus Public Co Ltd* [2019] EWHC 1328 (Ch), a letter agreeing to write off substantial bank borrowings for a lesser sum was a forgery since the relationship management who signed it did not have actual or ostensible authority to bind the bank.

[114] A person authorised to accept a tender has no implied authority to accept a cheque in payment, unless it can be shown that it is usual in the ordinary course of the particular business to accept payment by cheque: *Blumberg v Life Interests and Reversionary Securities Corp* [1897] 1 Ch. 171 Ch D affirmed [1898] 1 Ch. 27 CA, a case involving the completion of a real estate transaction. It must be very questionable whether the basic rule has significant modern application; it would surely be overshadowed by the exception. Standard conditions of sale for real property transactions now in any event provide for payment by means of bank transfer: see *Emmet and Farrand on Title*, 19th edn (London: Sweet & Maxwell), Vol.1, para.8.010.

[115] *Mardorf Peach & Co Ltd v Attica Sea Carriers Corp of Liberia (The Laconia)* [1977] A.C. 850 HL.

The Concept of Payment

Ltd v Woolgar (No.2)[116] and *Mardorf Peach & Co Ltd v Attica Sea Carriers Corp of Liberia (The Laconia)*.[117] In the former case:

The defendant had committed a breach of a covenant in his lease with the claimant, as the result of which the plaintiffs' agents managing the estate served a notice on the defendant tenant under s.146 of the Law of Property Act 1925 as a prelude to forfeiture of the lease. One of the partners in the firm of agents circulated a memorandum to the staff informing them of the decision to forfeit the lease and stating that no rent should be demanded or accepted from the tenant. The memorandum did not reach a subordinate clerk, who, in ignorance of the tenant's breach and of the decision to forfeit the lease, sent a rent demand to the tenant and upon receiving the rent issued a receipt. The Court of Appeal, reversing the decision of the trial judge on this point, held that since the landlords, through their agents, had done an act which unequivocally recognised the continuance of the lease after the landlords had knowledge of the ground of forfeiture, they had waived the forfeiture, and it was irrelevant that they had not intended to do so and that in paying the rent the tenant knew that their decision to forfeit remained unchanged. The crucial point here, of course, was that the agents were managing the property and had authority to accept rent, not merely to receive it. Hence their demand for and acceptance of the rent had the same effect as if the rent had been demanded and accepted by the landlords themselves.

It has subsequently been held in a High Court case that there is no binding authority that an unambiguous demand for (as opposed to acceptance of) rent operates as an automatic waiver of the right to forfeiture and that, even if this principle existed in landlord and tenant law, it was at least questionable whether it should be extended beyond this field.[118] In *Osibanjo v Seahive Investments Ltd*,[119] the Court of Appeal found that, where a landlord had accepted a cheque from a tenant which the tenant had tendered with a view in part to avoiding a bankruptcy order, it had not waived its right to forfeit the tenant's lease. Mummery LJ commented that "for waiver of forfeiture it must... be shown that the payment was accepted and that it was accepted as rent by the landlord".[120] On the facts, the landlord only accepted part of the sum realised by processing the cheque, which related to the bankruptcy debt, which was paid by the tenant to secure the dismissal of the bankruptcy petition, and returned the balance to the tenant and, when the tenant sent a further cheque, did not bank it. It was held that processing the cheque was not in itself conclusive of the question whether the payment was accepted as rent.

By contrast, in *The Laconia*[121]:

A charterparty provided that, failing the punctual and regular payment of the hire, the owners were to be at liberty to withdraw the vessel from the service of the charterers. Payments were to be made into the owners' account at their bank. The final payment fell due on a Sunday, when the banks were closed, and the

---

[116] *Central Estates (Belgravia) Ltd v Woolgar (No.2)* [1972] 1 W.L.R. 1048 CA (Civ Div).
[117] See fn.115 above.
[118] *Parbulk II A/S v Heritage Maritime Ltd SA* [2012] 2 All E.R. (Comm) 418 at [22].
[119] *Osibanjo v Seahive Investments Ltd* [2009] 2 P. & C.R. 2.
[120] *Osibanjo* [2009] 2 P. & C.R. 2 at [22].
[121] *The Laconia* [1977] A.C. 850 HL, overruling *Empresa Cubana de Fletes v Lagonisi Shipping Co Ltd (The Georgios* C) [1971] 1 Q.B. 488 CA (Civ Div).

charterers arranged for their own bank to issue a payment order to the owners' bank on the Monday. The payment order was delivered by hand to the owners' bank at about 15.00 and received by the latter, who informed the owners. The owners thereupon instructed the bank to return the payment. Some four hours later, the owners gave notice to the charterers withdrawing the vessel for non-payment of hire. On behalf of the charterers, it was conceded that payment should have been made on the Friday (the last business day before the due date) but contended that the breach had been waived by the owners' acceptance of the late tender through their agents, their bankers, who had received it without objection. This contention was rejected by the arbitrators, whose decision was upheld on a special case stated but reversed by the Court of Appeal, on the ground that, by accepting the late payment, the owners' bankers had as their agents waived the breach.

On appeal, the House of Lords restored the original decision, holding that a provision for punctual payment had to be strictly complied with, and that, whilst the owners could waive the breach by accepting a late tender as timeous, their bankers had but a limited authority as agents, namely to receive money and obtain instructions, not to accept it so as to affect legal relations between their customers and the charterers, still less to accept a late tender. Accordingly, their acts in delivering the payment order and crediting the owners' account were of a ministerial, and thus of a provisional and reversible, character. Since the owners had instructed their bank to return the payment as soon as it came to their notice, there had been no waiver and the vessel had been effectively withdrawn. The *Woolgar* decision[122] was to be distinguished in that it involved estate agents with powers of management, whereas, in the present case, the owners' bank had no authority to waive or remedy late tender.

It remains only to note that actual authority to accept a late payment is not essential; it suffices if the agent acted within his apparent authority in so doing. In this context, and in contrast to the position which arose in *The Laconia*, the creditor probably clothes his bank with actual authority to accept the payment on behalf of the creditor by naming the bank in the underlying contract, even though the bank will not know whether the transfer is indeed compliant.[123]

Payment by a third party

An accepted tender made not by the debtor personally but by a third party is effective as payment only if the person making the tender was under a duty to pay (e.g. as co-contractor or surety) or had actual or ostensible authority from the debtor to do so or if the debtor later ratifies the payment, expressly or by implication.[124] Thus, if A is indebted to B but, at B's direction, A makes the

2–29

---

[122] *Central Estates (Belgravia) Ltd v Woolgar (No.2)* [1972] 1 W.L.R. 1048 CA (Civ Div).
[123] *Dovey v Bank of New Zealand* [2003] 3 NZLR 650 (Court of Appeal, New Zealand), noted in Michael Brindle and Raymond Cox (eds), *Law of Bank Payments*, 5th edn (London: Sweet & Maxwell, 2018), para.3–134.
[124] For a discussion of this point, see Peter Birks and Jack Beatson, "Unrequested Payment of Another's Debt" (1976) 92 L.Q.R. 188.

necessary payment to C (who is himself a creditor of B), then B's debt to C is thereby discharged to the extent of the payment made by A.[125]

The matter was approached from a slightly different perspective by the Court of Appeal in *North v Brown*.[126] In that case, Mr Brown agreed to lend to his wife's grandmother, a Mrs Clothier, a sum of £200 per month for an extended period. The agreement was formalised in writing and was made between Mr Brown and Mrs Clothier personally. Despite this, Mr Brown arranged for the loan instalments to be advanced by a company controlled by him. When he demanded payment from Mrs Clothier's personal representatives following her death, they resisted the claim on the simple bases that: (i) Mr Brown had not made the advances himself; and (ii) he was therefore not entitled to repayment. At first instance, this defence had been upheld on the basis that the loan contract required Mr Brown to make the advances and he was not entitled to delegate that obligation to another person. However, the Court of Appeal upheld Mr Brown's claim, stating that he had performed his payment obligations vicariously through the company and there could be no objection to that type of performance where the contract involved the payment of money (as opposed to the performance of some other service).[127] Consequently, Mr Brown had performed his loan obligations and was entitled to repayment.

In contrast, a party who, without actual or ostensible authority to do so, voluntarily pays another's debt cannot change the relations of creditor and debtor against the wishes of the latter, who is entitled to retain control over the discharge of his own indebtedness without having it satisfied by the officious (or malicious) intervention of a stranger. If the rule were otherwise, a debtor might not only find himself exposed to a new creditor who was much tougher than the original one—a situation which can in any event result from assignment of the debt—but might be seriously prejudiced in the conduct of his business, e.g. through reduction of his liquidity or premature discharge of a monetary liability, the interest on which attracted tax relief.

Yet, it must be noted that there is a slightly curious departure from this rule where a third party pays the debt pursuant to some statutory or contractual obligation owed by it to the creditor, and this remains the case even though: (i) the payer will have voluntarily assumed any contractual obligation in this respect; and (ii) the payer is not acting as agent for the debtor. This point is illustrated by the decision of the Court of Appeal in *Ibrahim v Barclays Bank Plc*.[128] The case involved LDV Group, a van manufacturer based in the Midlands. It had run into cashflow difficulties and was on the point of insolvency. One of its Far Eastern distributors, Weststar, was willing to consider an acquisition of LDV although, following a due diligence process, this proved to be abortive. Whilst negotiations were ongoing, and in order to afford LDV some breathing space during that period, Weststar arranged for a bank to issue a standby letter of credit to Barclays, which was willing to provide a loan facility to LDV on that basis. When LDV

---

[125] *Re Stevens* (1929) 1 ABC 90; *Sheahan v Carrier Air Conditioning Pty Ltd* (1997) 189 CLR 407.
[126] *North v Brown* [2012] EWCA Civ 223.
[127] On vicarious performance generally, see *Chitty* (2018), paras 19–082 to 19–085. As there noted, it is not always easy to distinguish between situations involving vicarious performance and performance through an agent.
[128] *Ibrahim v Barclays Bank Plc* [2013] Ch. 400.

subsequently went into administration, Barclays made demand for payment on the issuing bank. After analysing earlier case law in this area, the Court of Appeal concluded that payment by the issuing bank under the credit had the effect of fully discharging LDV's corresponding debt obligation to Barclays because: (i) payment under the credit was compulsory as far as the issuing bank was concerned; and (ii) the terms of the credit made it clear that it was intended to form a means of payment in respect of the LDV debt. The court made it clear that, where payment is made under compulsion—even pursuant to a voluntarily assumed contractual obligation—this would have the effect of fully discharging the primary debt. Additionally, the court confirmed that this type of case is separate from that discussed in the last paragraph, noting that "where the case is one of payment under compulsion, questions of agency, authority and ratification do not... arise".[129]

It should be said that—at least where the obligation to pay is imposed as a result of a contractual obligation assumed by the payer vis-a-vis the creditor—there would seem to be no basis on which the payer could recover the amount of the payment from the primary debtor. The payer is not acting as agent for the debtor and is thus not entitled to an indemnity.

A deliberate officious payment of another's debt is relatively rare. More often than not, such payment is made by mistake or pursuant to an agreement with the creditor not concluded at the debtor's request[130] or some interest of the payer falling short of a legal obligation. For example, a bank may misinterpret its customer's instructions or may inadvertently pay a cheque after receipt of instructions to stop payment. In international financing, a bank may intervene to make a payment by way of participation in a syndicated loan already concluded or in accordance with a pro rata sharing agreement with another creditor. The general rule in cases of mistake is that the third party is entitled to recover the payment, at any rate if made under mistake, unless the payee has changed his position in reliance on the payment.[131] In other cases, the third party is not entitled to an indemnity from the creditor, who never asked him to intervene, but has the usual right of subrogation if he pays the debt. However, this is not the case if the debt is paid under legal compulsion. Thus, in *Ibrahim*,[132] the Court of Appeal held that, where a third party paid a creditor under legal compulsion, such as a letter of credit, on account of a debt owed by a debtor, this would automatically discharge the debtor's debt, and so there would be no rights of subrogation to which the third party would be entitled.

---

[129] *Ibrahim* [2013] Ch. 400 at [50]. In *Electricity Supply Nominees Ltd v Thorn EMI Retail Ltd* (1992) 63 P. & C.R. 143 CA (Civ Div), the compulsion to pay arose as a result of a statutory obligation.

[130] As where the seller of receivables guarantees payment by the debtors or a dealer selling goods to a finance house to be let on hire-purchase to the dealer's customer gives recourse.

[131] See, for example, *Barclays Bank Ltd v WJ Simms Son & Cooke (Southern) Ltd* [1980] Q.B. 677 (payment of stopped cheque); *Chase Manhattan Bank NA v Israel-British Bank (London) Ltd* [1981] Ch. 105 Ch D (mistaken duplication of payment); also more recent cases including *Jones v Churcher* [2009] 2 Lloyd's Rep. 94. See further para.3–82.

[132] *Ibrahim* [2013] Ch. 400.

The payment obligation

2–30 Given that the payment obligation will be contained within a contract, it must follow that questions touching the performance of that obligation—e.g. its amount, the due date, the mode of performance and similar matters—are matters to be derived from the construction of the contract itself.[133] The present section deals with various issues that may arise in this context.

(1) Time when payment is due

2–31 Payment must be made at the time, or within the period, stipulated in the contract. If no period is fixed, the obligation is usually to pay on performance of the act which is the consideration for the payment, subject to any contrary custom or usage. Late payment is a breach, though the consequences of late payment depend on whether time of payment is or has become of the essence. Early payment is prima facie permissible but it is not uncommon for financial agreements to exclude or restrict prepayment or to impose a premium for exercise of the right of prepayment.[134] Stipulations as to time are considered in Ch.4.

(2) Due mode of payment

2–32 This depends on the terms of the contract and on custom and usage. Prima facie the creditor is entitled to be paid in legal tender and thus to reject, for example, cheques and even bankers' drafts. But in modern commerce such a presumption is easily displaced, e.g. by evidence of contrary usage or of a prior course of dealing between the parties in which the creditor has consistently accepted payment by cheque. A usage negating the duty to pay by legal tender is particularly likely where the sum is large. It is scarcely reasonable to suppose that the payment of millions of pounds is to be made in £50 notes, yet this may be the ultimate position if payment by other means becomes impossible.[135] In *K v A*,[136] the court considered that "an obligation to pay cash, against the background of modern banking practice, permits any method of transferring funds, providing it is equivalent to cash, that is to say it gives the payee the unconditional and

---

[133] See *Chitty* (2018), para.21–040, citing *Re Charge Card Services Ltd (No.2)* [1989] Ch. 497 CA (Civ Div). See also *Kaupthing Singer & Friedlander Ltd (In Administration) v UBS AG* [2014] EWHC 2450 (Comm) at [63], where this approach is taken.
[134] i.e. to compensate the financier for the loss of interest as a result of the shortened maturity period.
[135] *Libyan Arab* [1989] Q.B. 728 QBD (Comm) at 755, where Staughton J referred to the difficulties in paying $131 million in cash. He noted that there would be "formidable counting and security operations" involved in paying that sum by dollar bills (of which he considered it unlikely that the defendants would be able to obtain a sufficient amount in Europe) and similar "counting and security problems" in paying using sterling notes. Other aspects of this case are discussed at para.5–45. Although it was accepted in *R. (on the application of Camden LBC) v Parking Adjudicator* [2011] P.T.S.R. 1391 that "[a]s a matter of strict theory" it might be right that the only form of payment a creditor is obliged to accept is "cash in legal tender", Burnett J thought (at [28]) that a local council which "required parking contraveners to pay cash in notes, or coins of £1 or higher value (current legal tender) would be vulnerable to challenge on grounds of rationality".
[136] *K v A* [2019] EWHC 1118 (Comm).

unfettered right to the immediate use of the funds". Payment by cheque may in any event be good tender if no objection is made to it.[137]

Where a contract governed by English law provides for payment in England in foreign currency, there is a presumption that the debtor has the option of paying in sterling.[138]

(3) Due place of payment

Prima facie it is for the debtor to seek out his creditor and pay him where he may be found.[139] Again, this may be rebutted by the express or implied terms of the contract or by usage or a course of dealing. A bank need only repay a deposit on demand[140] and is not obliged to honour a cheque presented at a branch other than that at which the drawer maintains his account.[141] The debt is payable only in the branch in which the account is kept.[142] There are many reasons why the contractual place of payment may be legally significant. For example, the fact that payment was due in England suffices to give the English court jurisdiction over the claim; an English court will not enforce a payment stipulation where payment would be illegal under the law of the State where it is to be made, at any rate if English law is the applicable law.[143] In international financial transactions where different time zones are involved, the relevant time of payment is the time in the place where payment is to be made.

2–33

Typical channels of payment

The time and place where payment is to be considered made, and the legal ability or otherwise of the debtor to honour his commitments in the face of governmental blocking of accounts, depend in no small measure on the payment mechanism selected for the particular transaction. In some cases, it may be necessary to examine this in the most minute detail in order to see at exactly what point funds become transferred or committed.[144]

2–34

The contractual channel of payment is to be ascertained by examining the terms of the contract. Frequently, however, this is not spelled out, the parties being content to leave it to their bankers to make suitable arrangements. The simplest case is that of transfer direct from debtor to creditor. The debtor may,

---

[137] *Jones v Arthur* (1840) 8 Dowl. 442; *Cohen v Roche* [1927] 1 K.B. 169 KBD.
[138] See para.6–19.
[139] *Robey & Co v Snaefell Mining Co Ltd* (1887) 20 Q.B.D. 152 QBD.
[140] *N Joachimson (A Firm) v Swiss Bank Corp (Costs)* [1921] 3 K.B. 110 CA.
[141] *Woodland v Fear* 119 E.R. 1339 KB. It seems that this remains the rule, notwithstanding the fact that banks now frequently pay cheques drawn on other branches since it is now much easier to check balances than was formerly the case.
[142] *N Joachimson* [1921] 3 K.B. 110 CA; *Arab Bank Ltd v Barclays Bank (Dominion, Colonial and Overseas)* [1954] A.C. 495 HL. See also *Chitty* (2018), para.34–311: "[t]he debt... is payable only on demand at the branch in which the account is kept". *Chitty* notes (at fn.981) that this rule is "ripe for review in light of modern technology and business practices..." and that the courts in overseas jurisdictions seem prepared to jettison the rule (*Damayanti Kantilal Doshi v Indian Bank* [1999] 4 S.L.R. 1 Singapore CA at 11).
[143] See para.5–55.
[144] See para.6–24.

however, choose to pay through his bank or other agent, whilst the creditor may stipulate that payment is to be made to his bank or other agent. Where payment is to be both made and received by a bank, the transferor bank may transfer the funds to the transferee bank directly or through one or more correspondents of one or both banks; and the ultimate inter-bank settlement will be by the striking of a balance on the totality of dealings between the two banks through a clearing house, followed by settlement of the balance by transfer in the books of their clearing agents or, where the two banks are themselves clearing banks, in the books of the Central Bank. Such inter-bank settlements give rise to peculiar problems where one of the banks participating in the clearing defaults on an item. Issues of this kind will be considered in more detail in Ch.5 below.

Non-cash payment mechanisms fall into one of two categories: credit transfers and debit collections.[145] Credit transfers are initiated by an instruction from the debtor to his bank to make a payment to the creditor or his bank. Debit collections are initiated by the creditor, who instructs the bank to collect (whether on a cheque or otherwise) a sum of money from the debtor or the debtor's bank or alternatively, with authority from the debtor, instructs the debtor's bank direct (direct debit). The distinction is of legal as well as practical significance. In the case of a credit transfer, the paying bank already knows it has the authority of its customer, the debtor, when notifying the transfer and knows or assumes that the account is in funds or within an agreed drawing limit. It is therefore appropriate that such notification should commit the bank to pay. By contrast, on a debit collection, the paying bank must be given the opportunity to verify the payment instruction and to check that the account is in funds. Since the clearing process requires immediate debit and credit entries for convenient accounting, the paying bank cannot sensibly be irrevocably committed by such entries before the verification has been carried out, in the way it can in the case of a credit transfer. The paying bank is therefore given a limited time within which to return the item, if the account is not in funds or payment has been countermanded, and to recover from the collecting bank, in a balance of account, the payment it has made.

Time when payment considered made

2–35 Although the fact of payment is more often in issue than the time of payment, there are situations in which, whilst it is accepted that payment has been made, something turns on when it was made. This is relevant (inter alia) to the calculation of interest and to the time at which a currency conversion must be computed in relation to a foreign money dealing.

It should be emphasised that we are concerned here with the point of time when actual payment takes place as the result of transfer of money or performance of some other act which constitutes a pro tanto discharge of a claim. This is entirely distinct from the question at what moment a payment instruction given by the debtor to his bank, or a payment undertaking given by the debtor's bank to the creditor or the creditor's bank, becomes irrevocable.

---

[145] Credit card and certain other types of payment media are disregarded for present purposes.

The Concept of Payment

As noted earlier, a binding commitment to pay is not the same as payment itself.[146]

The previous analysis of what does and does not constitute payment also provides an answer, in many cases, to the question at what moment payment is to be considered complete. Where money (coins or notes) is tendered direct to the creditor and taken by him, payment is immediate unless the money is paid or accepted subject to a condition precedent imposed by one of the parties or to a trust imposed by the debtor, in which event payment is deferred until the condition is satisfied or the trust comes to an end so as to leave the money at the free disposal of the creditor. Where the debtor tenders and the creditor accepts a cheque, payment is complete when the sum of money embodied in the cheque is at the creditor's disposal. When this occurs depends on the circumstances, and in particular on whether debtor and creditor bank at different banks—so that the cheque has to go through the clearing system—or at different branches of the same bank or at the same branch.[147] Similarly, the time when a credit transfer takes effect as payment depends on whether the transaction is "in-house" or involves two banks.[148]

2. Categories of Payment Obligation

We may now turn to consider the different methods of classifying payment obligations and the significance of each of the classifications.

2–36

Existing and contingent obligations

An existing payment obligation is one to which the debtor is committed, even if it has not yet matured. A contingent obligation is one which may or may not have to be performed, being dependent on the occurrence of a future uncertain event.[149] An example is a guarantee, which creates an obligation that is purely contingent so long as the debtor has not made default. Similarly, from the creditor's

2–37

---

[146] See para.2–22.
[147] See para.5–17 below.
[148] See para.5–26 below.
[149] The distinction between an actual and a contingent liability was considered by the Canadian Supreme Court in *McLarty v R* [2008] 2 SCR 79, where the issue was important because a claimed tax deduction was available only on the basis of an actual monetary liability incurred for the purposes of meeting exploration expenses. The court held that a liability is contingent if the payment obligation becomes effective on the occurrence of a particular event that may never occur. The fact that the debtor may well lack the resources to meet the obligation if it arises and/or that the security for that obligation may prove to be inadequate will not transform an actual obligation into a contingent one. For a comparable decision, see *Industries Perron Inc v R* [2013] FCA 176 (Federal Court of Appeal, Canada). See also the New Zealand Court of Appeal case of *Strategic Finance Ltd (In Receivership and In Liquidation) v Bridgman* [2013] NZCA 357, which references the second edition of this book in relation to the difference between existing and contingent rights and obligations, concluding that a contingent payment obligation is not a "monetary obligation" as " . . . [t]ypically, an existing right to payment is one which is definite, even if maturing in the future, whereas a contingent claim is one which may not materialise. The latter does not therefore constitute an existing monetary obligation. There is no existing liability to pay and no matching legally enforceable right to receive" (at [62]–[63]).

viewpoint an existing right to payment is one which is definite, even if maturing in the future, whereas a contingent claim is one which may or may not materialise. The distinction between existing and contingent rights and obligations is material in at least four respects.

(1) Legal assignability

2–38 An existing debt, even if payable in the future, is considered to be a presently owned asset of the creditor and is thus capable of statutory assignment.[150] By contrast, a contingent claim is a pure expectancy and can only be assigned in equity.[151] The point is not of great importance since the difference in effect between a statutory assignment and an equitable assignment is largely procedural.

(2) Amount for which provable

2–39 An existing claim is provable at its face value in a winding-up of the debtor but if it has not become due at the time of any declaration of dividend, it is discounted for the purpose of calculating the dividend entitlement. Claims which are purely contingent or sound only in damages may likewise be proved, but must be appropriately valued.[152]

(3) Eligibility for set-off in insolvency

2–40 Creditors may lodge a proof in an administration, liquidation or bankruptcy even though their claims have not yet matured or are of a contingent nature, although a guarantor will have to pay the relevant debt as a condition.[153] Where a company in administration or liquidation or the bankrupt has an unmatured or contingent claim, then this may likewise be set-off against the creditor's proof, but the remaining balance will only be payable to the insolvent estate when the maturity date arrives or the relevant contingency occurs.[154]

---

[150] *G. & T. Earle (1925) Ltd v Hemsworth R.D.C.* (1928) 140 L.T. 69; *Hughes v Pump House Hotel Co Ltd (No.1)* [1902] 2 K.B. 190 CA.

[151] See *Chitty* (2018), paras 19–028 to 19–030. Consideration is required for agreements to assign pure expectancies, since they cannot be the subject of an actual assignment.

[152] Insolvency (England and Wales) Rules 2016 rr.14.2 and 14.44.

[153] *Re Sass Ex p. National Provincial Bank of England Ltd* [1896] 2 Q.B. 12 QBD; *Sugar Hut Brentwood Ltd v Norcross* [2008] EWHC 2634 (Ch) at [36].

[154] See Insolvency (England and Wales) Rules 2016 rr.14.24–14.25. Prior to the revisions to what was previously r.4.90 of the Insolvency Rules 1986, set-off was not available to the insolvent company or bankrupt in this situation: *MS Fashions Ltd v Bank of Credit and Commerce International SA (In Liquidation)* [1993] Ch. 425 CA (Civ Div). See also: (1) the decision of the High Court of Australia in *Day & Dent Constructions Pty Ltd v North Australian Properties Pty Ltd* (1982) 40 ALR 399; (2) the discussion in Roy Goode and Kristen van Zwieten, *Goode on Principles of Corporate Insolvency*, 5th edn (London: Sweet & Maxwell, 2018), paras 9.37–9.38; and (3) the decision of the New Zealand Court of Appeal in *Strategic Finance Ltd (In Receivership and In Liquidation) v Bridgman* [2013] NZCA 357 at [62] (where the analysis in this paragraph was cited with approval).

(4) Status in relation to contractual set-off

It is not uncommon for banking and related documents to confer on the banker or other financier by contract the right to set-off even contingent claims against money due to the depositor or other party. But since by definition a contingent claim is unascertained, the right of set-off cannot be intended to be immediate, except where one can infer from the agreement an intention to allow the creditor to set off an ascertainable maximum liability. In most cases, a contractual set-off in relation to a contingent claim implies a two-stage process, the first being that the creditor has the right to withhold payment of the customer's credit balance until the contingency has occurred and the cross-claim has been quantified, and the second stage, the exercise of the set-off by applying the quantified claim in diminution or extinction of the customer's credit balance.[155]

2–41

Liquidated and unliquidated obligations

A liquidated claim is a claim for an established amount, e.g. the amount due on repayment of a loan or for the price of goods. An unliquidated claim is a claim which requires assessment by the court, e.g. a claim for damages in tort or for breach of contract. The significance of the distinction between the two is seen at its sharpest focus by comparing a debt claim with a claim for unliquidated damages for breach of contract.

2–42

(1) A debt claim is for a definite agreed amount. Therefore, no assessment is required and final judgment may be entered in favour of the creditor if the debtor fails to notify his intention to defend (a default judgment) or if, on an application for summary judgment, the claimant satisfies the court that there is no defence to the claim.[156] A judgment for unliquidated damages, on the other hand, is an interlocutory judgment for damages to be assessed, and the judgment does not become final or enforceable until after assessment. Prior to that time, it is effective solely on the issue of liability.

(2) Since, by definition, the amount of a debt is fixed and ascertained, the claimant is entitled to judgment for the amount of the debt without being under any obligation to show that he has suffered loss. It follows that the rules as to remoteness of loss and measure of damages, including mitigation of loss, do not apply.[157] Damages, on the other hand, have to be assessed on the basis of what it is reasonable to allow the claimant to recover for the loss he establishes, and the claimant will not be entitled to recover for loss which he has brought upon himself, whether by needless or unreasonable expenditure or by failing to take reasonable steps to mitigate his loss by securing alternative performance elsewhere.

---

[155] See *Goode and Gullifer on Legal Problems of Credit and Security* (2018), para.7–23.

[156] Civil Procedure Rules Pt 24.

[157] However, in exceptional cases the court may hold that a party had no legitimate interest in continuing a contract against the wishes of the other party and that his proper remedy is damages, not a claim for money earned under the contract. See paras 3–19 to 3–22 below.

(3) A plea of tender is available only in relation to a liquidated claim.[158] It is open to the parties to prescribe by the terms of their contract the payment of an agreed sum as liquidated damages, but the sum fixed will be recoverable only if it is not penal. The rule used to be that the sum fixed had to be a genuine and reasonable pre-estimate of the loss likely to flow from the breach, but this has changed as result of the Supreme Court's judgment in *Makdessi v Cavendish Square Holding BV* and, as a result, the test is now whether the clause in question "is a secondary obligation which imposes a detriment on the contract-breaker out of all proportion to any legitimate interest of the innocent party in the enforcement of the primary obligation".[159]

Primary and secondary obligations

2–43   Payment obligations imposed by a contract may be primary or secondary. A primary payment obligation is that which the creditor exacts by way of the desired performance. But if the debtor defaults, he also incurs a secondary liability in damages in addition to or in substitution for the primary remedy. The distinction has been canvassed in cases on guarantees, where the surety has unsuccessfully argued that his guarantee applied only to the debtor's primary liability and did not extend to any secondary liability resulting from the creditor's exercise of a right to terminate the contract on account of the debtor's default.[160]

Principal and accessory obligations

2–44   A principal payment obligation is one which stands on its own; an accessory obligation is one which is measured by reference to the obligation of a third party. If two people undertake joint and several liability for payment of a debt, each is

---

[158] *Davys v Richardson* (1888) 21 Q.B.D. 202 CA, followed in *RSM Bentley Jennison (A Firm) v Ayton* [2016] 1 W.L.R. 1281.
[159] *Makdessi v Cavendish Square Holding BV* [2015] 3 W.L.R. 1373 at [32]. See paras 3–28 to 3–35 for further discussion of the penalty rule.
[160] *Moschi v Lep Air Services Ltd* [1973] A.C. 331 HL, applied in cases including *Vossloh AG v Alpha Trains (UK) Ltd* [2011] 2 All E.R. (Comm) 307 (at [23]) and *McGuinness v Norwich and Peterborough Building Society* [2011] 1 W.L.R. 613 (at [21]). See also *Hyundai Heavy Industries Co Ltd v Papadopoulos* [1980] 1 W.L.R. 1129 HL and *Associated British Ports v Ferryways NV* [2009] 1 Lloyd's Rep. 595. In the latter, Field J (at [1]) discusses the difference between a guarantee and indemnity in terms of primary and secondary liability: "A guarantee is ... a promise to 'answer for the debt, default or miscarriage of another person'. There must be another person who is primarily liable. The liability of the guarantor is secondary. By an indemnity, on the other hand, the surety assumes a primary liability... Because the liability of a guarantor is secondary, it is usually discharged by a bilateral variation of the contract between the creditor and the debtor. In the absence of an express provision to the contrary in the contract of guarantee, the giving of time by the creditor to the debtor will generally discharge the guarantor. However, it will not have that effect if the suretyship is one of indemnity; the liability, being a primary liability, survives." For more information on the law relating to guarantees, see G. Andrews and R. Millett, *Law of Guarantees*, 6th edn (London: Sweet & Maxwell, 2011). See also the ICC Uniform Rules for Demand Guarantees (URDG 758, 2010 Revision) and G. Affaki and R. Goode, *Guide to Uniform Rules for Demand Guarantees URDG 758* (2011), available at: *https://icckauppa.fi/wp-content/uploads/sites/26/2016/05/702-icc-guide-to-icc-uniform-rules-for-demand-guarantees-urdg-758.pdf* [Accessed 23 October 2020].

fully liable as principal. If, on the other hand, one person guarantees another's debt, the liability of the surety is accessory only, so that, unless otherwise agreed, it cannot be any greater than that of the principal debtor, is suspended so long as the rights against the principal debtor are suspended and is discharged if the principal is released or if the terms of the principal contract are altered to the detriment of the surety.[161]

Obligations supported by consideration and abstract obligations

Most payment obligations arise from the conventional contract in which the payment undertaking is supported by consideration in the form of a counter-promise or performance of an act by the intended payee. If the payment undertaking and the counter-promise are mutually dependent obligations, the duty to pay need not be performed unless the promisee is ready and willing to perform his own obligations,[162] whilst if payment is made and the payee gives no performance on his side at all, or no performance of legal value, the payer can recover his money as paid on a total failure of consideration.

2–45

There are, however, some payment undertakings which are not supported by consideration but are abstract in character.[163] An early example is the promise under seal, the old style bond, which is enforceable because a seal imports consideration. More recent instruments are the irrevocable letter of credit and the on-demand performance bond or guarantee. These are interesting from a legal viewpoint because they are enforceable as promises even though not under seal or supported by consideration. They therefore defy the general principle of contract law which declines to give legal effect, except by way of estoppel, to voluntary undertakings not by deed. English law has never rationalised this result; indeed, there is no decided case in which the voluntary nature of the undertaking has ever been put in issue, but the courts have tacitly assumed that a bank can be sued on an irrevocable letter of credit and on a performance bond despite the want of consideration. We can ascribe this to the binding force of mercantile custom. These abstract undertakings therefore have the characteristic that, being unsupported by consideration, they cannot be nullified or in any way affected by a failure of consideration. So an irrevocable credit is enforceable by the seller beneficiary even if he has committed a flagrant breach of the underlying sale contract,[164] unless he has been guilty of fraud.[165] Similarly, when a bank issues an unconditional performance bond or guarantee to a beneficiary to secure

---

[161] See *Goode and Gullifer on Legal Problems of Credit and Security* (2018), para.8–14.
[162] See, for example, the Sale of Goods Act 1979 s.28.
[163] See para.3–40 on abstract payment obligations.
[164] *Hamzeh Malas & Sons v British Imex Industries Ltd* [1958] 2 Q.B. 127 CA; *Discount Records Ltd v Barclays Bank Ltd* [1975] 1 W.L.R. 315 Ch D; *Alternative Power Solution Ltd v Central Electricity Board* [2015] 1 W.L.R. 697 (at [68]); *Wuhan Guoyu Logistics Group Co Ltd v Emporiki Bank of Greece SA* [2014] 1 All E.R. (Comm) 870 (at [21]–[22]); *WS Tankship II BV v Kwangju Bank Ltd* [2012] C.I.L.L. 3155; *Meritz Fire & Marine Insurance Co Ltd v Jan de Nul NV* [2011] 1 All E.R. (Comm) 1049.
[165] Fraud by a third party for whose acts the beneficiary is not responsible is not a defence to payment (*United City Merchants (Investments) Ltd v Royal Bank of Canada (The American Accord)* [1983] 1 A.C. 168 HL).

performance of the obligations of the bank's customer under a supply or construction contract, the bank is obliged to pay the beneficiary on demand, in the absence of fraud, even if the customer has not defaulted in his obligations or was entitled to withhold performance because of the beneficiary's own breach.[166]

Bilateral and unilateral obligations

2–46   The consideration for the debtor's promise may be a counter-promise by the creditor, generating a bilateral contract, or performance of an act by the creditor ("act" here including forbearance from an act), giving rise to a unilateral contract. For example, B may undertake to buy a car from S for £5,000 in consideration of S's undertaking to sell the car for that sum. This is a bilateral contract because both parties assume an obligation. By contrast, if G agrees to guarantee repayment of advances by L to B, this is usually a unilateral contract, since as a rule only G makes a promise. L does not give any undertaking to G to make advances to B. The consideration for G's guarantee is not a promise by L to make an advance but the act of making it. Performance of that act is not an obligation on L, merely a condition of G's own obligation. So, in the typical case a guarantee, even when printed, signed, sealed and delivered, is not a contract at the time of its signature; it is merely an offer (and in the case of a continuing guarantee, a standing offer) by the surety to the creditor that if an advance is made and the debtor defaults, the surety will pay. In the case of a continuing guarantee, that offer is accepted by conduct each time the creditor makes an advance within the scope of the guarantee. The guarantee document thus represents a set of uniform terms applicable to each of a series of separate contracts generated by each advance. It follows that the surety is free to terminate his guarantee at any time as to future advances, for in relation to these, his offer has not been accepted and there is therefore no contract.

---

[166] *Edward Owen Engineering Ltd v Barclays Bank International Ltd* [1978] Q.B. 159 CA (Civ Div); *RD Harbottle (Mercantile) Ltd v National Westminster Bank Ltd* [1978] Q.B. 146 QBD; *Howe Richardson Scale Co v Polimex-Cekop* [1978] 1 Lloyd's Rep. 161 CA (Civ Div). See paras 3–40 to 3–48 for a discussion of potential differences to a claim on an abstract payment obligation.

Chapter 3

THE RIGHT TO PAYMENT AND THE DEFENCES TO A PAYMENT CLAIM

In this section, we shall examine four topics: (i) the creditor's right to payment, and the conditions that have to be satisfied before payment can be recovered; (ii) the common defences to a liquidated claim; (iii) the principal remedies open to the creditor for non-payment; and (iv) the circumstances in which the debtor may recover a payment he has made. Once again, we shall see that principles may be more easily stated than applied and that there are aspects of the payment obligation on which the law is both unclear and unsatisfactory.

3–01

1. THE RIGHT TO PAYMENT

The principle of nominalism

Prima facie, the creditor is entitled to be paid in legal tender[1] to the nominal value of the currency of the account, without regard to changes in the purchasing power of that currency, whether internal (through inflation or deflation) or external (through a change in the rate of exchange of that currency in relation to another currency used by the creditor). In other words, the parties are not entitled or obliged to demand and receive payment according to the real value of the money of account at due payment date compared with its value at contract date, they are merely concerned with the nominal value specified in the contract. This principle of nominalism, which applies across the world, was well described by Denning LJ in *Treseder-Griffin v Cooperative Insurance Society Ltd*[2]:

3–02

---

[1] Legal tender refers, of course, to physical cash which the creditor is by law bound to accept. On the meaning of "legal tender", see the Currency and Bank Notes Act 1954 s.1, the Coinage Act 1971 s.2, and the Currency Act 1983 s.1. In practice, the right to payment of large sums in physical cash will be waived by the creditor, either by an express term of the contract, by sending his bank account details to the debtor, or by accepting some other mode of performance when proffered.

[2] *Treseder-Griffin v Cooperative Insurance Society Ltd* [1956] 2 Q.B. 127 CA at 144. The case concerned a covenant to pay yearly rent of £1,900 in gold sterling or Bank of England notes to equivalent value. The Court of Appeal (Harman LJ dissenting) held that the rent payable was £1,900 per annum, not the gold value of 475 gold sovereigns a quarter. See also *Woodhouse AC Israel Cocoa Ltd SA v Nigerian Produce Marketing Co Ltd* [1971] 2 Q.B. 23 CA (Civ Div), affirmed [1972] A.C. 741 HL, and *Procter and Gamble Co v Svenska Cellulosa Aktiebolaget SCA* [2012] EWHC 498 (Ch), affirmed [2012] EWCA Civ 1413. The principle seems to be recognised in the domestic law of every country. In relation to the US, see the decisions of the Supreme Court in *Knox v Lee* and *Parker v Davis* (1970) 12 Wall (79) US 457 (the so-called "Legal Tender Cases"). For an application of the principle by the Supreme Court of South Africa (Appellate Division) in the context of a claim for special damages in a personal injury claim, see *SA Eagle Insurance Co Ltd v Hartley* 1990 (4) SA 833

"A man who stipulates for a pound must take a pound when payment is made, whatever the pound is worth at that time. Sterling is the constant unit of value by which in the eye of the law everything else is measured. Prices of commodities may go up or down, other currencies may go up and down, but sterling remains the same."

A modern restatement of the principle is to be found in the leading textbook on private international law[3]:

"Rule 259:
A debt expressed in the currency of any country involves an obligation to pay the nominal amount of the debt in whatever is legal tender at the time of payment according to the law of the country in whose currency the debt is expressed (*lex monetae*), irrespective of any fluctuations which may have occurred in the value of that currency in terms of sterling or any other currency, of gold, or of any commodities between the time when the debt was incurred and the time of the payment."

The principle of nominalism is subject to the qualifications that the contract may provide for the currency of payment to be different from the currency of account, and that, even where the currency of payment and account are both foreign currencies, the debtor may still pay either in the foreign currency or in sterling, converted at the date of payment.[4] *Procter and Gamble Co v Svenska Cellulosa Aktiebolaget SCA*[5] is an example of the former, with the contract providing for a price in euros but payment in sterling. The court declined to find an implied term that the exchange rate was fixed in circumstances where it had declined over the course of the contract.

It should be noted that the principle of nominalism flows from the presumed intention of the parties in relation to the contracted monetary obligation. So far as English law is concerned, it follows that its application can be varied by the express provisions of the contract.[6] Since inflation has been an ever present evil, it is unsurprising that investors in long-term bonds and similar instruments have attempted to protect themselves from it and have thus—consciously or otherwise—departed from the principle of nominalism. The ensuing paragraphs consider the techniques which have been adopted for that purpose.

Revalorisation

3–03   Due to the principle of nominalism, a creditor to a money obligation assumes the risk that the amount he is repaid, as specified in the contract, will be worth less at the time of payment. Over the years, creditors have resorted to various revalorisation devices to guard against depreciation in the value of money

---

(AD). For an in-depth discussion of the principle, see C. Proctor, Dr C. Kleiner and Dr F. Mohs (eds), *Mann on the Legal Aspect of Money*, 7th edn (Oxford: Oxford University Press, 2012), Ch.9.

[3] *Dicey, Morris & Collins on the Conflict of Laws*, edited by Lord Collins of Mapesbury et al, 15th edn (London: Sweet & Maxwell, 2012), r.259. Given the subject matter of the text, the rule is stated in terms of foreign currencies, but the formulation would apply equally to obligations expressed in sterling.

[4] *Law of Bank Payments*, 5th edn (London: Sweet & Maxwell, 2018), para.2–006.

[5] *Procter and Gamble Co v Svenska Cellulosa Aktiebolaget SCA* [2012] EWHC 498 (Ch), affirmed [2012] EWCA Civ 1413.

[6] On the whole subject of nominalism, see *Mann* (2012), Chs 9–13.

promised to them. The doctrine of revalorisation is concerned to ensure that the debtor's obligation is not to repay the same nominal amount but to repay money of a particular value.

(1)   Gold clauses

Historically, gold clauses are the most well-known example of a revalorisation device. Gold clauses—or more precisely, gold value clauses—involve the debtor undertaking to discharge his indebtedness by repaying such amount of sterling (or other designated currency) as could be purchased with the gold equivalent of the debt at the time of the contract.[7] The effect is to link the amount of the repayment obligation to the change in the value of gold between the date of contract and the date of repayment. If, as was usually the case, gold went up in value in relation to the relevant currency, the debtor's obligation in that currency was pro tanto increased. Such clauses, which would seem to be perfectly valid in the absence of legislation to the contrary,[8] no doubt worked well enough while gold was a standard by reference to which the value of national currencies was fixed, but with the demonetisation of gold[9] it ceased to be a useful yardstick, for, as a pure commodity having no par value in relation to a currency, its price fluctuated too widely to provide a safe measure of obligation either for the creditor or for the debtor.

3–04

For the reasons given above, gold clauses are now obsolete in ordinary commercial contracts. However, like the proverbial bad penny, they do insist on turning up occasionally. Most case law in the relatively recent past has arisen from transport conventions concluded in the early part of the twentieth century, and which still remain in force. The issues may be contractual, in the sense that (for example) claims may arise in respect of bills of lading which incorporate the Hague Rules of 1924.[10] For this reason, the relevant cases merit a brief discussion. The Australian courts have considered two cases involving "gold value" clauses. In the first case, *Brown Boveri (Australia) Pty v Baltic Shipping Co (The Nadezhda Krupskaya)*,[11] the relevant bill of lading incorporated the Hague Rules, which provided for the liability of the carrier to be limited to a sum "in pounds sterling", which was "to be taken to be its gold value". The New South Wales Court of Appeal awarded damages in Australian dollars, calculated by reference to the price of gold as expressed in sterling. In the second case, which involved carriage by air and, hence, the Warsaw Convention, the same court noted that, under art.22 of the Convention:

---

[7] For a detailed description, see *Mann* (2012), paras 11.05–11.33 and literature there cited; also *Chitty* (2018), paras 21–071 to 21–073.

[8] Despite the contrary view expressed by Denning LJ in *Treseder-Griffin* [1956] 2 Q.B. 122 at 145. See also *Mann* (2012), paras 11.25–11.26. In 1933, gold clauses were rendered inoperative by the US Congress, but were later allowed for contracts entered into after 27 October 1977 (see USC s.5188(d)(2)).

[9] i.e. on the 1971 collapse of the system of exchange rate parities established by the Bretton Woods Agreement in the immediate post-war era.

[10] i.e. as contained in the 1924 International Convention for the Unification of Certain Rules relating to Bills of Lading and Protocol of Signature.

[11] *Brown Boveri (Australia) Pty v Baltic Shipping Co (The Nadezhda Krupskaya)* [1989] 1 Lloyd's Rep. 518 CA.

"... the liability of the carrier is limited to a sum of two hundred and fifty francs per kilogramme the sums referred to in this Article shall be deemed to refer to a currency unit consisting of gold of millesimal fineness nine hundred. Conversions of the sums into national currency other than gold shall in the case of judicial proceedings be made according to the gold value of such currencies as at the date of judgment".

The court thus applied the market value of gold by reference to an official price quotation.[12]

An English court, dealing with a bill of lading subject to the Hague Rules, has likewise held that references to "gold sterling" are to a *standard of value*, rather than a mere means of payment. The limit on the carrier's liability was thus to be determined by reference to the gold (rather than the nominal or "paper") value of sterling. In the result, one "gold" pound sterling was held to be equivalent to £66.30 in paper money.[13] With regard to the time of conversion, it was held in a recent bill of lading case that the correct time for converting the gold value into the nominal value of the currency was (applying the Hague Rules) the date of delivery (or, in the case of loss, the date when the goods ought to have been delivered as this was when the loss crystallised and the cause of action accrued).[14]

3–05 Finally, in an appeal from New Zealand, the Privy Council[15] likewise reasserted that references in the Hague Rules to "sterling" include its gold value. However, the "gold" provisions of the Hague Rules were disapplied on the specific facts, because the bill of lading explicitly stated that the carrier's liability under the Hague Rules "shall be deemed to be £100 sterling, lawful money of the United Kingdom" (i.e. "paper" money rather than gold).

Subject always to the express terms of the contract, it follows that the gold value provision has generally succeeded in protecting the effective value of the limits against the depreciation in value of paper money. It might be thought, therefore, that, apart from the specialist conventions considered above cases, questions touching gold value clauses are now highly unlikely to arise in practice. Whilst this statement is broadly true, it is pertinent to note that gold clauses have come before the US courts in recent years, and completeness requires a brief explanation of these cases. During the Great Depression of the 1930s, there was no doubt that gold clauses could cause severe hardship for debtors. As a result, a Joint Resolution of Congress[16] declared such clauses to be contrary to public policy and allowed for settlement of all monetary obligations at their US dollar face value. The result was that gold clauses largely went out of fashion for an extended period. However, with effect from 28 October 1977, Congress amended the Joint Resolution so that "obligations issued... after" the date of the

---

[12] *SS Pharmaceutical Co Ltd v Qantas Airways Ltd* [1991] 1 Lloyd's Rep. 288 CA.
[13] *The Rosa S* [1989] Q.B. 419 QBD (Admlty).
[14] *Yemgas FZCO v Superior Pescadores SA Panama* [2014] 1 Lloyd's Rep. 660 at [59], affirmed [2016] EWCA Civ 101. Although the Court of Appeal did not find it necessary to express a view on the date of conversion, it concurred with the first instance approach (at [41]).
[15] *Dairy Containers Ltd v Tasman Orient Line CV (The Tasman Discoverer)* [2005] 1 W.L.R. 215 applying the decision in *The Rosa S* at fn.11 above.
[16] Gold Clause Joint Resolution of June 5, 1933, Cr. 48 § 1, 48 Stat. 112, 113 (1933) (codified at 31 U.S.C. § 463).

amendment would no longer be subject to the ban on gold clauses.[17] The plain intention of this language was that *historical* gold clauses would not be revived, and the reference to "issue date" no doubt reflects the fact that gold clauses were mostly found in long-dated bonds. However, gold clauses had also been fashionable in long-term leases, and American legal ingenuity turned its mind to the possibility of reviving such clauses. Thus, in cases in which ancient gold clause leases had been reaffirmed or novated after 1977, it was held that a new obligation had been "issued" by the tenant, with the result that the landlord was thenceforth entitled to recover rent by reference to the gold value clause.[18]

(2) Indexation

A more modern and more satisfactory method of protecting the creditor against loss in value of the payment obligation is to link the obligation to some established index considered by the creditor to be the most suitable for his purpose. 3–06

Those who have lived through periods of high inflation will readily understand the purposes of, and the need for, indexation as a *general* concept. The question is: how should the appropriate index be identified? References to a general rate of inflation will often conceal the fact that the rate applicable to *particular* commodities or services may vary widely. Retail or consumer price indices are thus useful but they necessarily imply a significant degree of averaging and, in any event, the range of goods and services forming a part of the "basket" is necessarily selective.

Considerable care is required in the drafting of indexation clauses. In particular, what is the nature of the inflationary risk against which the creditor seeks protection? In the context of wage bargaining, pensions or similar "household" payments, protection is really being sought against rises in the general or broader cost of living across a variety of products and services, with the result that a retail or consumer-based index will usually be most appropriate. However, in many commercial cases, the creditor will be concerned with the increased cost of *particular* commodities, rather than inflation affecting the economy *as a whole*. Consequently, a specialist index needs to be adopted in cases of this kind.[19] Where this kind of index is used, provision should be made

---

[17] Act of Oct. 28, 1977, Pub. L. No. 95-147, § 4(c), 91 Stat. 1227, 1229 (codified as amended at 31 U.S.C.A § 5118(d)(2) (1983).
[18] See in particular *Nebel, Inc v Mid-City National Bank of Chicago* 769 N.E.2d 45 (2002, Appellate Court of Illinois, First District) and *216 Jamaica Avenue, LLC v S & R Playhouse Realty Co* 540 F.3d 433 (12 June 2008, US Court of Appeals, 6th Cir.). For further discussion of these cases, see *Mann* (2012), para.12.27.
[19] See, for example, the situation which arose in the *Esso Exploration* and *Queensland Electricity Generating Board* cases, discussed at fnn.17 and 24 below. Although a case involving damages in tort (rather than in contract), it is instructive to compare the decision in *Tameside and Glossop Acute Services NHS Trust v Thompstone* [2008] EWCA Civ 5. The Trust was liable for damages to a child as a result of injuries sustained during birth. An order was made for periodical payments to cover future medical care. Under ss.2(8) and 2(9) of the Damages Act 1996, an order for periodical payments "shall be treated as providing for the amount of payments to vary by reference to the retail price index", but the court is allowed to disapply or modify the application of that section. Insofar as the periodic payments were linked to the requirement for future medical care, the court linked the

for an alternative index to be brought into operation if the index originally selected is abolished or significantly modified. The importance of such a provision became clear when the Bank of England abolished its minimum lending rate, to which many monetary obligations were linked and which also featured in statutory instruments, although it was generally thought to be an implied term of the contract that one could instead refer to the substitute or most nearly corresponding rate. Though minimum lending rate was used as a base for interest rates, the same problems arise where an index used to measure a repayment of principal is abolished.[20]

3–07 If the creditor wishes to protect the value of his money in relation to other currencies, he may stipulate that the payment obligation is to be adjusted by reference to changes in the value of sterling (or other currency of account) in relation to a designated foreign currency. The validity of such indexation clauses was upheld by Browne-Wilkinson J in *Multiservice Bookbinding Ltd v Marden*,[21] where the creditor's foresight paid handsome dividends.

The plaintiff made a loan of £36,000 to the defendant, the repayment obligation being linked to the Swiss franc. Sterling fell in value substantially in relation to the Swiss franc between the date of the loan and the due repayment date, with the result that, under the terms of the loan agreement, the defendant became liable to repay the principal sum of £87,588.

The court rejected the defendant's contention that the indexation clause was contrary to public policy. Index-linking was common and was motivated by the perfectly legitimate desire of the creditor to preserve the real value of the debt.[22] Even if the bargain were unreasonable, that would not justify its being disturbed by the court. The defendant had to show that the bargain was unconscionable in the sense of being imposed in a morally reprehensible manner. That was not so in the present case, for apart from other considerations the defendant had taken independent legal advice. The plaintiff was therefore entitled to judgment for the amount claimed.

It may be noted that the contract at issue in *Multiservice Bookbinding* was of a purely domestic character. The loan was made in sterling by a UK lender to the UK borrowers for the purchase of assets in England. In spite of the purely domestic nature of the arrangements, Browne-Wilkinson J felt unable to hold that the Swiss franc indexation clause was contrary to public policy. In *Rochis Ltd v*

---

payments to an index reflecting the earnings of care assistants, since that would be most likely to reflect the actual funding required over the relevant period.

[20] For a case in which prices in a very specialised energy market ceased to be available with the result that a purported price revision by the seller proved to be effective, see *Esso Exploration & Production UK Ltd v Electricity Supply Board* [2004] EWHC 723 (Comm), discussed in J. Baily and R. Lidgate, "LNG Price Reviews: A Sign of the Times" (2014) 7(2) J.W.E.L. & B. 140. Although concerned with the price of commodities rather than the value of money, the case demonstrates both the importance and the difficulty of drafting adequate "fallback" provisions in this type of case.

[21] *Multiservice Bookbinding Ltd v Marden* [1979] Ch. 84 Ch D.

[22] Whether the linking of a sterling debt to the value of the Swiss franc does have the effect of preserving the proper value of a sterling amount may be open to question. It may be argued that a sterling debt can legitimately be linked to a UK domestic index but that a link to a foreign currency is purely speculative and thus should be void on public policy grounds: see R.A. Bowles, (1981) 131 N.L.J. 4, noted by *Chitty* (2018), para.21–074.

Chambers,[23] the New Zealand Court of Appeal was confronted with a contract between New Zealand nationals for the sale and purchase of land in New Zealand. The price was likewise expressed in New Zealand dollars, but the vendors must have been concerned about a possible weakening of the local dollar. The price was accordingly indexed to the US dollar. The decision in fact deals with damages payable on late completion but both the parties and the court appear to have proceeded on the footing that the indexation clause was intrinsically valid. It is unfortunate that the public policy issue was not considered, but perhaps the issue was seen as foreclosed by the *Multiservice Bookbinding* decision. At least insofar as English law is concerned, however, it would be difficult to challenge such clauses on such grounds for the following reasons:

- the UK Government itself has occasionally issued index-linked Treasury Stock, thus suggesting that such clauses do not meet with objection at that level;
- at various times, collective wage bargaining agreements have included indexation provisions to protect union members against the rising cost of living[24]; and
- an English court has decided that a building society can make loans on terms that the repayment of the principal sum is index-linked.[25]

In the light of these points and the *Multiservice Bookbinding* decision, challenges to the validity of indexation clauses cannot be based on general considerations but will need to be fact specific—e.g. on the basis that the creditor misrepresented the effect of the provision or otherwise acted in an unconscionable or oppressive manner.

Indeed, leaving aside difficulties which have arisen in specific cases,[26] the courts have generally striven to uphold indexation clauses in commercial contracts and, in some cases, have even gone so far as to imply the necessary terms. In *Queensland Electricity Generating Board v New Hope Collieries*,[27] a long-term coal supply contract required that periodic price variations "shall be agreed between the parties". This clause was asking for trouble because no mechanics were provided in the event of a failure to agree. However, the Privy Council implied terms into the contract to the effect that: (i) the revised pricing should be fair and reasonable; (ii) the parties should use reasonable endeavours to agree the

3–08

---

[23] *Rochis Ltd v Chambers* [2006] NZHC 524.
[24] See *Australian Workers Union v Commonwealth Railway Commission* (1933) 49 CLR 589.
[25] *Nationwide Building Society v Registry of Friendly Societies* [1983] 1 W.L.R. 1226 Ch D. It should be said, however, that the various instances just noted all related to a *domestic* price index. The *Multiservice Bookbinding* case may thus remain open to challenge at a later date on the basis that the link to a foreign currency is not a bona fide attempt to protect the creditor against gyrations in the domestic economy, and that a local index should be used instead. On that basis, public policy arguments could be invoked against the Swiss franc hedge. That said, Multiservice Bookbinding seems to meet with general approval and the prospects of a successful challenge must therefore be at the lower end of the scale.
[26] See the *Esso Exploration* case at fn.20 above.
[27] *Queensland Electricity Generating Board v New Hope Collieries* [1989] 1 Lloyd's Rep. 205 PC.

price revision; and (iii) in the absence of agreement, the parties would take all steps necessary for the appointment of an arbitrator.[28]

The bar is likely to be high for a successful challenge and the courts may uphold clauses which prove very onerous for one of the parties. Although not directly concerning an indexation clause, this is demonstrated by the Supreme Court's approach in *Arnold v Britton*.[29] The case concerned the correct interpretation of five different versions of a service charge clause used in different leases entered into for 99 years between 1977 and 2000. Despite the differences in drafting, the court construed these provisions in the same way and held that the lessees were liable to pay the lessors a fixed sum in the first year of the lease and, after that, a fixed sum rising at a rate of 10% per annum on a compound basis. Although a literal interpretation of the clauses would result in a service charge of over £1 million being due for the last year of the 99-year term for one of the leases, the clauses were upheld. The Supreme Court considered that the meaning of the terms was clear and "commercial common sense is not to be invoked retrospectively".[30] Therefore, the "mere fact that a contractual arrangement, if interpreted according to its natural language, has worked out badly, or even disastrously, for one of the parties" was not considered "a reason for departing from the natural language".[31] However, the recent case of *Monosolar IQ Ltd v Woden Park Ltd*[32] demonstrates that there may be limits to this approach where there is a clear mistake in the drafting of the clause so it does not reflect the parties' intentions. In this case, such a mistake was found since the result produced by the formula as drafted produced was "wholly illogical".[33]

It may be added that courts in the US have taken a slightly different line and have held that the amounts payable under an indexation clause should be added to the interest charge, and will thus be unenforceable if they exceed the limits imposed by the local usury laws.[34]

(3) The euro

3–09   The introduction of the euro posed an issue for the principle of nominalism, since the latter implies that obligations expressed in a certain currency will need to be fulfilled at their face value for the agreed amounts. It has been noted that, where a group of countries with independent monetary systems replace their existing currencies with a common currency, it is the *lex monetae* which determines legal

---

[28] A similar robust approach has been adopted in other parts of the Commonwealth: see, for example, *Calvan Consolidated Oil and Gas Co Ltd v Manning* [1959] S.C.R. 253 (Supreme Court of Canada); *Attorney-General v Barker Bros Ltd* [1976] 2 NZLR 495; *Booker Industries Pty Ltd v Wilson Parking (Qld) Pty Ltd* (1982) 56 ALJR 825; and *Barbcraft Pty Ltd v Geobel Pty Ltd* [2003] VCAT 1700.
[29] *Arnold v Britton* [2015] A.C. 1619.
[30] *Arnold* [2015] A.C. 1619 at [19].
[31] *Arnold* [2015] A.C. 1619 at [19]. This approach has been applied in subsequent cases including *Trillium (Prime) Property GP Ltd v Elmfield Road Ltd* [2018] EWCA Civ 1556.
[32] *Monosolar IQ Ltd v Woden Park Ltd* [2020] EWHC 1407 (Ch).
[33] *Monosolar* [2020] EWHC 1407 (Ch) at [54].
[34] See, for example, the decision of the Supreme Court of Tennessee in *Aztec Properties Inc v Union Planters National Bank of Memphis* 530 S.W.2d 756 (1975) and the Pennsylvanian decision in *Olwine v Torrens* 344 A.2d 665 (1975).

tender, and that, in the case of the euro, European law has become the *lex monetae* for the participating Member States.³⁵

The euro became the currency of the 11 original participating Member States on 1 January 1999 and was introduced in physical form on 1 January 2002, when bank notes and coins denominated in euros became legal tender. It is currently the official currency of 19 of the 28 Member States of the EU,³⁶ and is also used by a number of other countries and territories. The dates on which the national currencies replaced by the euro ceased to be legal tender varied between Member States, with the earliest being in Germany (31 December 2001).

Monetary obligations such as payment obligations do not become impossible to perform simply because the currency in which they are denominated ceases to exist; instead, the relationship between the old currency and new currency is determined by the *lex monetae*.³⁷ The *lex monetae* in the case of the Eurozone countries would be European law. At the time the euro was introduced, legislation was passed fixing irrevocably the rate of exchange between the euro and the former currencies of the original participating Member States.³⁸ Similarly, the rate of exchange has been fixed between the euro and the currencies of those Member States which have subsequently adopted the euro.³⁹ The continuity of contracts was specifically addressed; in the absence of express provision to the contrary in the parties' agreement, the introduction of the euro did not discharge or excuse the performance of the contractual obligation nor give a party the right unilaterally to alter or terminate any contract term.⁴⁰

3–10

The European sovereign debt crisis that has been taking place since 2009 led to much discussion as to the potential effect on payment obligations if a participating Member State were to leave the Eurozone and, in particular, the risk that monetary obligations currently expressed in euros would be redenominated in the new currency of a departing Member State (which would presumably be much devalued).⁴¹ Since the euro would still exist following the departure of a

---

³⁵ *Dicey, Morris & Collins* (2012), para.37–011. See *Mann* (2012), paras 13.03–13.08 for more information on the *lex monetae* principle.

³⁶ As specified on the EU website available at: *https://europa.eu/european-union/about-eu/money/euro_en* [Accessed 13 October 2020].

³⁷ *Dicey, Morris & Collins* (2012), para.37–014.

³⁸ Regulation 2866/98 on the conversion rates between the euro and the currencies of the Member States adopting the euro ([1998] OJ L359/1).

³⁹ See reg.1478/2000 on the conversion rates between the euro and the currencies of the Member States adopting the euro [2000] OJ L167/1 (Greece), reg.1086/2006 amending reg.2866/98 on the conversion rates between the euro and the currencies of the Member States adopting the euro [2006] OJ L195/1 (Slovenia), reg.1135/2007 amending reg.2866/98 as regards the conversion rate to the euro for Cyprus [2007] OJ L256/2, reg.1134/2007 amending reg.2866/98 as regards the conversion rate to the euro for Malta [2007] OJ L256/1, reg.694/2008 amending reg.2866/98 as regards the conversion rate to the euro for Slovakia [2008] OJ L195/3, reg.671/2010 amending reg.2866/98 as regards the conversion rate to the euro for Estonia [2010] OJ L196/4, reg.870/2013 amending reg.2866/98 as regards the conversion rate to the euro for Latvia [2013] OJ L243/1), and reg.851/2014 amending reg.2866/98 as regards the conversion rate to the euro for Lithuania ([2014] OJ L233/21), all of which amend reg.2866/98.

⁴⁰ Regulation 1103/97 on certain provisions relating to the introduction of the euro ([1997] OJ L162/1).

⁴¹ For an in-depth view of the potential consequences, see Tolek Petch, *Legal Implications of the Eurozone Crisis: Debt Restructuring, Sovereign Default and Euro Zone* (Alpan aan de Rijn: Kluwar

participating Member State, the default position would be that obligations expressed in euros would remain denominated in euros. However, new legislation would be likely to be passed to govern both the withdrawal of the Member State in question from the Eurozone and also the conversion of certain obligations expressed in euros into obligations in the new currency. The effect of such legislation would depend on the *lex monetae* which would apply to the relevant contract in these circumstances, which is likely to depend on the circumstances in relation to each individual contract, in particular, the governing law. The outcome would likely be different if the euro were to be abandoned altogether and replaced by a number of different currencies. Again, the consequences of this would depend on the applicable *lex monetae*, which might prove difficult for the English courts to ascertain.[42]

Payment must be earned

3–11 The creditor is entitled to be paid only where the conditions of payment prescribed by the contract or by statute have been fulfilled. Thus, in a contract for the sale of goods, payment and delivery are concurrent conditions, unless otherwise agreed, so that the seller is not entitled to recover the price unless he is ready and willing to give possession of the goods to the buyer.[43] Although the obligation to pay the price may have arisen, the seller can normally only sue for the price where property in the goods has passed to the buyer and he has wrongfully neglected or refused to pay the price.[44] Performance of a condition precedent to payment is not dispensed with even where it is the debtor's own breach that has obstructed performance,[45] though, to the extent to which the debtor has benefited from partial performance by the creditor, he may in such a case be sued for the value of that partial performance in a restitutionary claim.[46]

Whilst the creditor must earn the contract sum by performance of all obligations correlative to the debtor's payment obligation, it does not follow that this entails completion of all, or indeed any, of the creditor's contractual duties. This will only be the case if the contract is an "entire contract" under which the creditor must perform all of his obligations in order for the debtor to be obliged to make payment. Where this is not the case, performance is required only of those obligations on which the debtor's duty to pay is dependent. Whether these

---

Law International, 2014), Ch.5. See also Eugenio Bruno (ed.), *Sovereign Debt and Debt Restructuring: Legal, Financial and Regulatory Aspects* (London: Globe Business Publishing Ltd, 2013); Rutsel Silvestre J. Martha, *The Financial Obligation in International Law* (Oxford: Oxford University Press, 2015); Jean Pisani-Ferry, *The Euro Crisis and Its Aftermath* (Oxford: Oxford University Press, 2014).

[42] On this topic, see *Law of Bank Payments* (2018), para.2–025; *Dicey, Morris & Collins* (2012), para.37–014.

[43] Sale of Goods Act 1979 s.28. Under s.27 of that Act, it is the duty of the seller to deliver the goods in accordance with the contract and, correspondingly, it is the duty of the buyer to pay the price. Note that "delivery" is not necessarily the same as the transfer of ownership and risk, since s.61(1) defines delivery as the transfer of possession from seller to buyer. See also E. McKendrick (ed), *Goode on Commercial Law*, 5th edn (London: Penguin, 2016), paras 15.10–15.11.

[44] Section 49(1) of the 1979 Act. Otherwise, the seller may be limited to an action for damages.

[45] See para.2–17 above.

[46] See para.3–18 below.

represent all or only part or none at all of the creditor's total contractual commitments depends on the terms of the contract. It is, for example, open to the parties to agree that the creditor shall be paid the entire contract sum in advance or after partial performance. Again, the contract may allow the creditor to spread or divide his performance and to receive separate payment for each part or division of performance. For example, a building contract commonly provides for stage payments against architect's certificates, entitling the builder to the amount certified as he completes the stage of the works to which each certificate relates.[47] Similarly, a contract for the sale of goods may permit or require the seller to deliver by instalments, each instalment to be separately paid for.[48] Delivery of an instalment entitles the creditor to be paid for it whether or not he has fulfilled his obligations as regards the other instalments, except where his default in relation to these constitutes a repudiation of the contract as a whole.[49] Furthermore, it is not necessarily the case that the debtor is entitled to withhold payment simply because the contract provides for payment in instalments; the fulfilment of the relevant obligations by the creditor must be a condition precedent to receiving a particular instalment.[50]

A provision for payment in advance does not, of course, entitle the creditor to get money for nothing. The debtor must perform first, but if the creditor then wholly fails to perform his own obligations, the payment can be recovered as made on a total failure of consideration,[51] whilst if the creditor only partially performs, he incurs a liability to pay damages.

In most cases, no question of law arises as to the creditor's right to be paid; the issue is usually one of fact as to whether he has in fact performed the acts upon which his right to payment depends. There are, however, two questions of law that periodically cause difficulty. The first is whether, and in what circumstances, the creditor can claim pro rata payment for partial performance where the contract makes no provision, expressly or by implication, for such payment. The second is whether a creditor who is able to perform his part of the contract without the co-operation of the debtor can recover the contract price if he proceeds to perform against the debtor's wishes.

---

[47] For a case of this kind in which the buyer's (ultimately unsuccessful) arguments against the claim for a stage payment did not want for ingenuity, see the decision of the High Court of Singapore in *MP-Bilt Pte Ltd v Oey Widarto* [1999] 3 S.L.R. 592.

[48] *Foxholes Nursing Home Ltd v Accora Ltd* [2013] EWHC 3712.

[49] i.e. the contract as a whole is not separable or divisible: see *Chitty* (2018), paras 21–028 and 24–045 to 24–046. See also *Mersey Steel & Iron Co Ltd v Naylor Benzon & Co* (1884) 9 App. Cas. 434 HL per Lord Blackburn at 443–444; *Warinco v Samor SpA* [1977] 2 Lloyd's Rep. 582 QBD (Comm) per Donaldson J at 588, reversed by the Court of Appeal [1979] 1 Lloyd's Rep. 450 CA (Civ Div) but only on the application of the law to the facts.

[50] Thus, there was no right to withhold a payment in *RAM Media Ltd (In Administration) v Ministry of Culture of the Hellenic Republic (Secretariat General of Sport)* [2008] EWHC 1835 (QB), affirmed [2009] EWCA Civ 528, which concerned the organization of a football awards ceremony. Although the contract provided for payment in instalments, the court found there was no direct relationship between the instalments to be paid and the services to be provided.

[51] See para.3–81 below.

Partial performance

3-12 It should be emphasised that we are dealing here not with the case of divisible contracts, the terms of which allow the creditor to perform in stages and be paid for each stage as it is carried out, but with situations in which the creditor seeks payment where he has not fully performed and the payment obligation itself is indivisible. The principles applicable are the same whether the contract is a bilateral one in which the creditor has undertaken to perform the acts generating the right to payment or is a unilateral contract in which no such undertaking has been given and performance of the designated acts is merely a condition of the creditor's right to be paid.

(1) The principle of complete performance

3-13 Unless the contract otherwise provides, expressly or by implication, the creditor is not entitled to be paid until he has completed performance of the acts for which payment is to be made. Partial performance does not entitle the creditor to payment pro rata, for that is not the basis of the parties' bargain. If an owner of land asks a builder to erect a house for £100,000 and there is no provision for stage payments, the builder cannot sue the owner for £50,000 when he has reached the halfway point. Similarly, if the seller of goods tenders less than the contract quantity, he is not entitled to payment of the price unless the buyer chooses to accept what is tendered.[52] The root decision on entire contracts is *Cutter v Powell*.[53]

The defendant agreed to pay Cutter 30 guineas for serving as second mate on the defendant's vessel for a journey from Kingston, Jamaica, to Liverpool. Halfway through the voyage, Cutter died and his widow claimed a proportion of the agreed sum on a quantum meruit. The claim was dismissed on the ground that the agreement was an entire contract which did not entitle the deceased or his personal representative to pro rata payment for partial performance.

At first sight, the decision seems a harsh one. However, it is clear that the court was strongly influenced by the fact that the stipulated sum was nearly four times what the deceased could normally have expected as a wage if paid by the month. Since he had chosen to bargain for substantial payment for a complete voyage rather than a wage calculated on a time basis, there was no scope for implying a term for pro rata payment.[54] He had elected for an entire contract, taking a chance in return for a larger payment, and his widow could not change the basis of the bargain.[55]

---

[52] In which case the buyer must pay for the goods at the contract rate (1979 Act s.30(1)).
[53] *Cutter v Powell* 101 E.R. 573 KB.
[54] If such a term can be implied then this will obviously mitigate potential hardship to the creditor. For a case in which such a term was applied (distinguishing *Cutter*) see *Forney v Bushe* [1954] C.L.Y. 3183 CC.
[55] The decision would be different now because wages are deemed to accrue from day to day: Apportionment Act 1870 s.2. "Day" in this context means a calendar day, not working day; *Hartley v King Edward VI College* [2017] UKSC 39 at [31]. On the whole subject, see *Chitty* (2018), paras 21-28 to 21-039.

An interesting example of where entire performance has been required by the courts is in relation to solicitors' retainers. These are prima facie "entire contracts" and solicitors who terminate retainers without good cause or reasonable grounds may lose the right to payment.[56] Interestingly, the same approach is not necessarily taken in relation to other contracts for professional services, where there is no assumption that such contracts are entire contracts. In *Smales v Lea*,[57] a case involving a surveyor's contract of engagement, the Court of Appeal considered that it is relatively unusual in the "modern construction of contracts and contracts of retainer for professional services" for the client to have no obligation to make payment unless the contractor or professional firm has performed every single one of their obligations.[58] In the absence of an express term stating that it was an entire contract or that no payment would be due until all obligations had been performed, the contract in question was held not to be an entire contract.[59] A similar conclusion was reached in the recent case of *Onfido Ltd v Blockchain Access UK Ltd*.[60] The claimant sought summary judgment in respect of two invoices which the defendant, a cryptocurrency dealer, had failed to pay for verification services provided by the claimant. The defendant disputed the quality of the services provided and argued that the agreement was an entire obligation that required the claimant to demonstrate it that it had at least substantially performed all its obligations in the month for which payment was claimed (a matter which could not be determined in the summary application). The court rejected the defendant's argument, finding no evidence that there was a condition precedent to payment that services were to be performed wholly or substantially non-defectively.

There are four cases in which the creditor can claim payment at the contract rate for less than full performance of an entire contract. The first is where he has substantially performed and the contract is not one calling for exact performance as a pre-requisite of payment. The second is where the debtor voluntarily accepts the benefit of partial performance. The third is where the debtor in some other way waives further performance, having received a substantial part of the consideration for his payment undertaking. The fourth is where the debtor obstructs completion.

3–14

---

[56] *Vansandau v Browne* 131 E.R. 667 Court of Common Pleas; *Underwood Son & Piper v Lewis* [1894] 2 Q.B. 306 CA; *Richard Buxton Solicitors v Mills-Owens* [2010] EWCA Civ 122; *Gill v Heer Manak Solicitors* [2018] EWHC 2881 (QB); *Gallacher v Emerald Law* unreported 15 January 2019 QBD (Sheffield). However, solicitors may suspend a retainer pending payment without losing the right to payment; *Cawdery Kaye Fireman & Taylor v Minkin* [2012] EWCA Civ 546. Moreover, the courts have held that conditional fee arrangements may be novated with the client's consent without the right to payment being lost: *Budana v Leeds Teaching Hospitals NHS Trust* [2017] EWCA Civ 1980; *Warren v Hill Dickinson LLP* [2018] EWHC 3322 (QB).
[57] *Smales v Lea* 140 Con. L.R. 70; see also *William Clark Partnership Ltd v Dock St Pct Ltd* [2015] EWHC 2923 (TCC), which concerned professional construction services.
[58] *Smales v Lea* 140 Con. L.R. 70 at [43].
[59] *Smales v Lea* 140 Con. L.R. 70 at [34]–[44].
[60] *Onfido Ltd v Blockchain Access UK Ltd* [2020] EWHC 2585. See also *Donovan v Grainmarket Asset Management LLP* [2020] EWHC 17 (Comm).

(2) The doctrine of substantial performance

3–15 Since it is hard for mere mortals to achieve perfection, a creditor who substantially performs his part of the contract, leaving only a small amount undone or improperly done, will usually be entitled to recover the contract price less a deduction for the uncompleted or defective performance. So in *H Dakin & Co v Lee*,[61] a builder who carried out building works except for a small number of defective or uncompleted items was held entitled to the contract price less a deduction. Similarly, in *Hoenig v Isaacs*,[62] where the contract price of certain works was £750 and the cost of remedying defects was £55, the plaintiff recovered the contract price less the £55. The position is otherwise where there has not been substantial performance and the debtor does not voluntarily accept the benefit of the partial performance or otherwise waive his right to require completion of performance. Thus, in *Bolton v Mahadeva*[63]:

The plaintiff contracted to supply and install a heating system. The system was defective, so that the heat was inadequate and fumes were given off. The contract price was £560 and the cost of remedying the defects was £174.50. It was held that there had been no substantial performance, so that the plaintiff was not entitled to be paid anything.

The case illustrates the point that, as a general rule, the debtor can retain the benefit of partly performed services without payment, since services cannot be returned so that the debtor's acceptance of them cannot be regarded as voluntary.[64]

Even substantial performance will not entitle the creditor to payment where precise performance is a condition of the contract. Thus, if goods tendered under a contract of sale fail to conform to the contract description, the buyer is entitled to reject them even if the degree of non-conformity is small and will not cause the buyer any loss.[65] Again, the doctrine of strict compliance applies to the tender of documents under a letter of credit, and even a minor non-conformity entitles (indeed obliges) the bank to refuse payment unless its customer gives authority to pay.[66] If the contact expressly provides that the creditor must satisfy a particular

---

[61] *H Dakin & Co v Lee* [1916] 1 K.B. 566 CA, applied in *Kiely & Sons v Medcraft* (1965) 109 S.J. 829 CA.

[62] *Hoenig v Isaacs* [1952] 2 All E.R. 176 CA. The decision has been applied on a number of occasions: see, for example, *Williams v Roffey Bros & Nicholls (Contractors) Ltd* [1991] 1 Q.B. 1 CA (Civ Div); *Tan Hung Nguyen v Luxury Design Homes Pty Ltd* [2004] NSWCA 494 (New South Wales Court of Appeal); *Foxholes Nursing Home* [2013] EWHC 3712 (Ch).

[63] *Bolton v Mahadeva* [1972] 1 W.L.R. 1009; applied in *Brown v West Midlands Patio Doors Ltd* [1997] C.L.Y. 933 CC.

[64] See para.3–16 below.

[65] *Arcos Ltd v EA Ronaasen & Son* [1933] A.C. 470 HL. More recently, see *Hazlewood Grocery Ltd v Lion Foods Ltd* [2007] EWHC 1887 (QB), where chili powder sold with measurable quantities of a non-permitted additive was found not to be reasonably fit for its purpose or of satisfactory quality, because—as in fact happened—it was likely that the Food Standards Agency would prohibit its sale. This was so even though the contamination was minor and was not harmful to human health. The seller was thus not entitled to any payment on account of the price.

[66] *Equitable Trust Co of New York v Dawson Partners Ltd* (1927) 27 Ll. L. Rep. 49 HL; *Swotbooks.com Ltd v Royal Bank of Scotland Plc* [2011] EWHC 2025 (QB); *Fortis Bank SA/NV v Indian Overseas Bank* [2010] 1 Lloyd's Rep. 227; *Moralice (London) Ltd v ED&F Man* [1954] 2 Lloyd's Rep. 526 QBD; approved in *Soproma SpA v Marine & Animal By-Products Corp* [1966] 1

condition or requirement in order for payment to be due, the creditor will not be entitled to payment unless this is satisfied.[67]

(3) Voluntary acceptance of partial performance

It is open to the debtor to waive his right to demand completion of performance as a pre-requisite of payment. One common form of waiver is by voluntary acceptance[68] of the benefit of the creditor's partial performance. The general rule here is that acceptance is voluntary only if the debtor has the choice of returning the benefit he has received.

3–16

Accordingly, whilst a buyer of goods who chooses to retain a tender of less than the contract quantity must pay for them at the contract rate,[69] one who receives a benefit in the form of partial performance of a contract for the provision of services need not pay for them, even if he completes the work himself or by another party, for services cannot be returned and the debtor therefore has no choice in the matter. The distinction between goods and services is neatly illustrated by the well-known case of *Sumpter v Hedges*,[70] where work was abandoned when only partially carried out and the defendant finished it himself, using the plaintiff's materials. The plaintiff was held entitled to recover the cost of the materials, which the defendant could have returned, but nothing else. Similarly, in *Munro v Butt*,[71] it was held that, where work done on the defendant's land was left uncompleted and he finished it himself, he did not have to pay for what was done. His receipt of a benefit was involuntary, since he could not return the services provided and could not be expected to leave his land impaired by a half-finished building.

Though the logic of the *Sumpter v Hedges* principle may seem compelling, its rigidity can produce results offending one's sense of justice. It is all very well to say that a party who fails to complete performance has only himself to blame but there are cases, falling short of frustration of the contract, where for one reason or another the creditor is unable to complete and the debtor secures a windfall. It was for this reason that the Law Commission, in its *Report on Pecuniary Restitution on Breach of Contract*,[72] made the sensible recommendation that where the creditor has conferred a valuable benefit on the debtor but is unable to complete the contract, which is treated by the debtor as no longer on foot, then, unless otherwise agreed between the parties, the creditor should be entitled to recover a reasonable sum for his partial performance, reduced or extinguished by any set-off the debtor might have for damages for breach of contract.[73] To that

---

Lloyd's Rep. 367 QBD (Comm). Note that the beneficiary has the right to rectify the errors within set time periods: art.16 of the Uniform Customs and Practice for Documentary Credits (2006 Revision).
[67] See e.g. *Diamandis v Wills* [2015] EWHC 312 (Ch), where there was no right to payment because it was an express condition that the creditor would submit an invoice, which he had not done.
[68] Note that "acceptance" connotes something more positive than "receipt": see *Chitty* (2018), para.21–036.
[69] Sale of Goods Act s.30(1).
[70] *Sumpter v Hedges* [1898] 1 Q.B. 673 CA.
[71] *Munro v Butt* 120 E.R. 275 QB.
[72] Law Commission, *Report on Pecuniary Restitution on Breach of Contract* (1983), Law Com. No.121.
[73] Law Commission, *Report on Pecuniary Restitution on Breach of Contract*, para.2.37.

end, the Commission proposed a Law Reform (Lump Sum Contracts) Act but the recommendations of the report have not been implemented.

The validity of *Sumpter v Hedges* was reconfirmed in *Cleveland Bridge UK Ltd v Multiplex Constructions (UK) Ltd*.[74] The parties had entered into construction contracts relating to Wembley Stadium. Cleveland failed to complete the contract but significant quantities of steel supplied by it remained on site. Cleveland had also undertaken a significant amount of work on that steel, including fabrication and painting work. The court applied *Sumpter v Hedges* to the extent that Multiplex could have returned the steel but instead elected to make use of that material in the continuing works. Instinctively, one would have thought that the amount to be paid by Multiplex should be increased by the value added to the steel by the fabrication and painting work, but the point had not been sufficiently pleaded and was not pursued. Interestingly, however, the claimants sought to circumvent *Sumpter v Hedges* on the basis that the decision had now been superseded by later developments. In particular, it was argued that Multiplex would be unjustly enriched by its retention of the benefit of Cleveland's work on the project and that the claimant was thus entitled to restitution of the value of the work that it had done. This argument—based on the House of Lords' decision in *Westdeutsche Landesbank Girozentrale v Islington LBC*[75]—was decisively rejected and *Sumpter v Hedges* was held to remain good law, in spite of academic criticism that has been levelled at it.[76]

(4) Other waiver of right to demand completion

3–17 If the debtor does any other act indicating an intention to waive completion of performance as a pre-requisite of payment—as where he changes his mind and decides that he wishes to have the rest of the work carried out in a different way or not to have it done at all—the creditor is entitled to be paid an appropriate proportion of the contract price.[77] This is subject to the qualification that the debtor must have received a significant part of the consideration for his payment.

---

[74] *Cleveland Bridge UK Ltd v Multiplex Constructions (UK) Ltd* [2008] EWHC 2220 (TCC), affirmed on this point in [2010] EWCA Civ 139.

[75] *Westdeutsche Landesbank Girozentrale v Islington LBC* [1996] A.C. 669 HL.

[76] See, for instance, the sources listed in fn.6 of Ben McFarlane and Robert Stevens, "In Defence of *Sumpter v Hedges*" (2002) 118 L.Q.R. 569, where disapproval is referred to as being "almost uniform amongst leading unjust enrichment scholars" (at 569). Stevens and McFarlane present the contrary view and argue in favour of *Sumpter v Hedges*.

[77] See *Chitty* (2018), para.21–036. See also the recent case of *Barton v Gwyn-Jones* [2019] EWCA Civ 1999, where a quantum meruit was awarded to a claimant who introduced a potential buyer to the defendant for a commercial property on the basis that he would receive a £1.2 million fee if the property was sold for £6.5 million. The property eventually sold for £6 million and the defendant refused to pay him anything. Although the court awarded the claimant £435,000 as the reasonable value of his services, this decision has been criticised on the basis that, contrary to what the court found, the risk that the target price would not be reached had in fact been allocated by the contract (to the claimant) and therefore the decision undermined the express terms of the contract; William Day and Graham Virgo, "Risks on the contract/unjust enrichment borderline" (2020) 136 L.Q.R. 349. Contrast the basis of the restitutionary claim which arises where the debtor obstructs performance. See below at para.3–18.

A purported waiver of a right to have any part of the benefit contracted for is equivalent to a promise of a gift and is unenforceable for want of consideration.[78]

Debtor's obstruction of performance

We have seen that where the debtor obstructs completion of performance, the creditor is still not entitled to sue for the contract sum, his remedy being in damages.[79] However, where his part performance has been of some benefit to the debtor, an alternative remedy is open to the creditor, namely a restitutionary claim for the value of what he has done.[80] This remedy is to be distinguished from a claim on the contract where the debtor waives completion. In the latter case, the creditor's remedy is contractual and his monetary entitlement is a due proportion of the contract sum. The value of what he has done is not relevant as such; the basis of his entitlement is the contract price. Where, for example, a buyer contracts to buy for £10,000 a quantity of goods worth only £2,000 and when half the contract quantity is tendered and the buyer chooses to accept the tender instead of exercising his right to reject, the seller is entitled to payment at the contract rate,[81] and thus to receive £5,000, not the £1,000 which the goods tendered are worth. By contrast, the quantum meruit to which the creditor is entitled for partial performance where completion is wrongfully prevented by the debtor is the *value* of what he has supplied or done.[82] The contract price as such is irrelevant, since the claim is not on the contract but is based on unjust enrichment, and presupposes that the contract has become ineffective.[83] "Value" in this case does not necessarily mean the market value of the goods or services, but rather their value to the defendant. The Supreme Court accepted in *Benedetti v Sawiris*[84] that, although the starting point for valuing the enrichment is the

3–18

---

[78] See the well-known decision in *Foakes v Beer* (1884) 9 App. Cas. 605 HL, which continues to be applied; examples include *Collier v P & MJ Wright (Holdings) Ltd* [2007] EWCA Civ 1329 and *Blackstar (Isle of Man) Ltd v Imperium Trust Co Ltd* [2016] EWHC 3216 (Ch). See also P. Birks, "No Consideration: Restitution after Void Contracts" (1993) 23(2) WALR 195–234. Note that the question of what constitutes valid consideration, and in particular the extent to which "practical", as opposed to legal benefit, is valid consideration, is currently a vexed one following the Court of Appeal's decision in *MWB Business Exchange Centres Ltd v Rock Advertising Ltd* [2016] EWCA Civ 553 that the concept could apply to promises to pay less or render lesser performance (overturned by the Supreme Court on other grounds, [2018] UKSC 24). See *Chitty* (2018), para.4–006.
[79] See para.2–17 above.
[80] It should be carefully noted that this type of restitutionary claim is only available in the event of a breach *by the debtor* which prevents performance. As noted above in relation to *Sumpter v Hedges*, no such remedy is available in the context of a breach *by the creditor*.
[81] 1979 Act s.30(1).
[82] *Planché v Colburn* 172 E.R. 876 Assizes; *Benedetti v Sawiris* [2014] A.C. 938. See *Chitty* (2018), paras 29–019 to 29–025 on establishing and valuing enrichment, applied in subsequent cases including *Sixteenth Ocean GmbH & Co KG v Société Générale* [2018] EWHC 1731 (Comm); *Barton v Gwyn-Jones* [2019] EWCA Civ 1999; and *Dowman Imports Ltd v 2 Toobz Ltd* [2020] EWHC 291 (Comm).
[83] See e.g. *School Facility Management Ltd v Governing Body of Christ the King College* [2020] EWHC 1118 (Comm) at [425]–[431], where the contract price was not considered to bear any relation to the market value and so was not the basis for valuing the enrichment.
[84] *Benedetti* [2014] A.C. 938.

"objective market value, or market price",[85] it might sometimes be open to a defendant to invoke subjective devaluation of a benefit to reduce the quantum meruit payable, i.e. argue that the benefit conferred on him was not worth as much as its market value.[86]

Performance against the debtor's wishes

3–19   This brings us to the second of the two problems raised earlier, namely the creditor's right to payment where he is able to perform without the debtor's co-operation and proceeds with performance against the debtor's wishes. From the debtor's viewpoint, the creditor's performance may have no value whatsoever since the debtor no longer wants it and told the creditor so before he performed. Is the debtor still liable for the contract price? In most cases, yes. Where one party to a contract repudiates it, the other has the choice of holding the contract open for performance. He cannot have termination thrust upon him by the unilateral act of the contract-breaker.[87] This right is traditionally viewed as subject to two qualifications: (i) that he is able to perform his own obligations without the co-operation of the contract-breaker; and (ii) that he has a "legitimate interest" in continuing performance.[88] This is the effect of the majority decision of the House of Lords in *White & Carter (Councils) Ltd v McGregor*.[89]

The plaintiffs were in the business of supplying litter bins to local authorities, being paid not by the authorities but by traders advertising on the bins. The defendants concluded a three-year contract with the plaintiffs for the display of advertising on litter bins and then sought to cancel the contract on the day it was made. The plaintiffs refused to accept the repudiation, and on the defendants' failure to pay the first instalment, the plaintiffs exercised their right to call up the whole amount due pursuant to an acceleration clause in the contract.

---

[85] *Benedetti* [2014] A.C. 938 at [15].
[86] *Benedetti* [2014] A.C. 938 at [18]–[19]; discussed *Chitty* (2018), para.29–025. However, it was considered (at [21]) that the burden of proof would fall on the defendant to prove he did not subjectively value the benefit or valued it at less than the market price. Note that the Supreme Court did not consider that recognition should be given to *subjective revaluation*, i.e. the claimant should not be entitled to invoke the defendant's subjective willingness to pay a higher sum for the benefit as a reason for valuing the benefit at a higher rate (at [29]–[33]). Therefore, account is not taken of any potential "consumer surplus".
[87] The innocent party has the choice of holding the other party to the contract or accepting the repudiation and claiming damages. These are obviously inconsistent rights and the innocent party must make an election. On this subject, see *Vitol SA v Norelf Ltd (The Santa Clara)* [1996] A.C. 800 HL and A.M. Sheppard, "Demystifying the Right of Election in Contract Law" (2007) J.B.L. 442. For recent cases confirming this, see *Geys v Societe Generale* [2013] 1 A.C. 523; *Sunrise Brokers LLP v Rodgers* [2014] I.R.L.R. 780, affirmed [2015] I.C.R. 272; *Le Puy Ltd v Potter* [2015] I.R.L.R. 554; and *MSC Mediterranean Shipping Co SA v Cottonex Anstalt* [2016] EWCA Civ 789. If the innocent party accepts the repudiation, the contract comes to an end and he can claim damages in respect of the losses flowing from early termination: see *Photo Production Ltd v Securicor Transport Ltd* [1980] A.C. 827 HL.
[88] These are more properly viewed as restrictions on the right to claim the contract price, rather than on the innocent party's right to affirm; see *Chitty* (2018), para.27–006, and cases cited therein.
[89] *White & Carter (Councils) Ltd v McGregor* [1962] A.C. 413 HL, discussed in *Chitty* (2018), para.27–006, and confirmed.

It was held (Lord Morton of Henryton and Lord Keith of Avonholm dissenting) that the plaintiffs were entitled to succeed. They were under no duty to accept the defendant's repudiation, nor were they obliged to take steps in mitigation of their loss after the repudiation, for the mitigation rule applied only to claims for damages and was not relevant where the plaintiff's claim was for money earned under the contract.

The first qualification to the right to claim the contract price is that the innocent party must be able to perform without the defendant's co-operation. It is not always clear what will constitute performance in this regard and the distinctions involved can be relatively fine. For instance, it was held in *Isabella Shipowner SA v Shagang Shipping Co Ltd (The Aquafaith)*,[90] reversing the arbitrator's decision, that the owners of a vessel could perform a time charter by keeping the ship ready and waiting for the charterer's orders; it was suggested that the same is not true of a demise charter since the latter cannot be performed without the charterer's co-operation as it involves the transfer of possession of the vessel to the charterer.[91] In contracts where the price becomes payable irrespective of the innocent party's performance of his outstanding obligations, he may recover the price.[92]

3–20

The decision of the majority in *White & Carter* is controversial.[93] Those who defend it maintain that it is fully in accordance with long-established principle. Opponents of the decision argue that one of the functions of contract law is, or should be, to discourage economic waste, and that it is wrong to saddle a contracting party with the price of a performance he did not want when the innocent party has a perfectly good remedy in damages for loss that he could not have avoided by taking reasonable steps in mitigation. Even in *White & Carter*, the majority suggested a second qualification to the right to claim the contract price; that there might be extreme cases in which the innocent party had no "legitimate interest" in continuing performance rather than accepting damages.[94] Lord Reid instanced the case put in argument of an expert engaged by a company to go abroad and prepare a report, the contract being repudiated before anything was done. Should the expert be allowed to waste thousands of pounds preparing a report which the company no longer wanted and to exact his contractual fee?[95]

3–21

Either solution causes hardship to one of the parties. Thus it is not necessarily straightforward to determine what constitutes a "legitimate interest" which permits the innocent party to continue performance. A defendant saddled with a huge bill for a performance that the innocent party knew before he started was no longer required can quite fairly argue that this is economically wasteful and does not promote sensible market behaviour. The innocent party can with equal

---

[90] *Isabella Shipowner SA v Shagang Shipping Co Ltd (The Aquafaith)* [2012] 2 All E.R. (Comm) 461.
[91] At [40], distinguishing *Attica Sea Carriers Corp v Ferrostaal Poseidon Bulk Reederei GmbH (The Puerto Buitrago)* [1976] 1 Lloyd's Rep. 250 CA (Civ Div).
[92] See *Chitty* (2018), para.27–007 and cases mentioned therein.
[93] See, for example, discussions in D. Winterton, "Reconsidering *White & Carter v McGregor*" [2013] L.M.C.L.Q. 5; and J. Morgan, "Smuggling Mitigation into *White & Carter v McGregor*: Time to Come Clean?" [2015] L.M.C.L.Q. 575.
[94] *White & Carter* [1962] A.C. 413 HL at 431. This requirement has been accepted and applied subsequently by the courts; see *Chitty* (2018), para.27–008 and cases mentioned therein.
[95] *White & Carter* [1962] A.C. 413 HL at 431.

justification retort that it is unfair to expect him to accept damages, since, quite apart from the fact that performance may carry with it important incidental benefits (e.g. enhancement of reputation, the establishment of useful business contacts), it is much more burdensome on him to claim damages, necessitating proof of loss and subjecting him to the duty to mitigate, than to recover an agreed contract sum for which final judgment may be speedily obtained where there is no arguable defence to the claim.[96] In the final analysis, the question is one of degree. Prima facie, the innocent party is entitled to use self-help to obtain what is in effect specific performance of his contract. He is only precluded from doing so where the loss to the defendant in enforcing performance would be disproportionate to the benefit that such enforcement would bring him, having regard to the steps that the innocent party could take to mitigate his loss by offering performance to a third party instead of to the defendant.

Attica Sea Carriers Corp v Ferrostaal Poseidon Bulk Reederei GmbH[97] offers an example. Where a vessel was let under a charterparty and the charterers, being under a duty to return it in good repair, allowed it to get into such a bad state that it was estimated that putting it into good order as required by the charterparty would cost £2 million (following which the vessel would only be worth £1 million so repairs would be quite uneconomic), the owners declined to accept redelivery and argued the ship could only validly be delivered when in a proper condition and so the charterparty remained in force and hire remained payable. The Court of Appeal rejected this, holding, first, that the duty to repair was not a condition precedent to the right to redeliver, and secondly, even if this were not so, it was unreasonable for the owners not to accept the charterers' repudiation so their proper course again was to sue for damages. Lord Denning MR pointed out that, if the position were otherwise, the charterers would either be committed to paying hire charges for years to come while the vessel lay idle or useless or would be compelled to do repairs costing twice as much as the vessel was worth in its repaired state. For the owners to continue the contract in such circumstances was wholly unreasonable.[98] More recently, the Court of Appeal suggested in *MSC Mediterranean Shipping Company SA v Cottonex Anstalt*,[99] in the context of a claim for demurrage for containers detained by customs authorities in Bangladesh which could not be redelivered by the defendant, that it would have been unreasonable for the plaintiff to insist on further performance in circumstances where the demurrage considerably exceeded the value of the containers.[100] Nevertheless, in the ordinary case, the owner of a vessel is entitled to insist that

---

[96] The Civil Procedure Rules 1998 (CPR), Pt 24.

[97] *The Puerto Buitrago* [1976] 1 Lloyd's Rep. 250. Whether or not the creditor can complete the performance of the contract without the debtor's co-operation, and whether or not the creditor has acted unreasonably, may raise difficult questions of fact and law. For a more recent case where the creditor was found to have acted reasonably and was thus entitled to full payment of the contract sum, see *Ministry of Sound (Ireland) Ltd v World Online Ltd* [2003] 2 All E.R. (Comm) 823. Final judgment was not, however, given because of the existence of other competing claims under the contract.

[98] For a similar decision relying on the "no legitimate interest" exception to the *White & Carter* principle, see *Clea Shipping Corp v Bulk Oil International Ltd (The Alaskan Trader) (No.2)* [1984] 1 All E.R. 129 QBD (Comm).

[99] *MSC Mediterranean Shipping Co SA v Cottonex Anstalt* [2016] EWCA Civ 789.

[100] Obiter, as the contract was ultimately found to be discharged by frustration in any case.

the vessel should remain on hire for the originally agreed period and is not obliged to accept re-delivery of the vessel in breach of the charterer's obligations.[101]

The onus is on the defendant to show there is no "legitimate interest" and the standard is high. Consistently with the essential principles in *White & Carter,* Cooke J held in *The Aquafaith,* after reviewing the authorities, that "[t]he effect of the authorities is that an innocent party will have no legitimate interest in maintaining the contract if damages are an adequate remedy and his insistence on maintaining the contract can be described as 'wholly unreasonable', 'extremely unreasonable' or, perhaps, in my words, 'perverse'".[102] It has, for example, been held that—in the absence of any authority allowing a landlord to claim loss of future rent by way of damages following wrongful repudiation of a lease—it is reasonable for the landlord to refuse to accept repudiation in the first place, and to hold the tenant to his rental obligations even though the tenant has no further use for the premises.[103] It therefore appears that only exceptionally will an innocent party have no legitimate interest in affirming the contract.[104] Moreover, there is no obligation on the innocent party to act in good faith. The Court of Appeal in *MSC Mediterranean Shipping* rejected the suggestion that good faith principles should apply in determining whether the innocent party has a legitimate interest in performing rather than claiming damages.[105]

It is now clear following the Supreme Court's decision in *Geys v Société Générale*[106] that a repudiatory breach does not automatically terminate a contract of employment without the innocent party having the chance to affirm, a matter on which there was previously some uncertainty:

3–22

The plaintiff was employed by the defendant bank, which could dismiss him with three months' written notice or terminate his employment with immediate effect by making a payment in lieu of notice. The bank summarily dismissed the plaintiff in breach of contract and later made a payment in lieu of notice into his bank account. It sent the plaintiff details of the payment, which the plaintiff did not see until around three weeks after the payment was sent. The plaintiff informed the bank before he received the details that he had decided to affirm the contract. Two days later, the bank wrote to the plaintiff saying it had exercised its

---

[101] *The Aquafaith* [2012] 2 All E.R. (Comm) 461, where a "no legitimate interest" defence was rejected.

[102] *The Aquafaith* [2012] 2 All E.R. (Comm) 461 at [44]. This reflects previous judicial statements, including that of Kerr J in *Gator Shipping Corp v Trans-Asiatic Oil SA (The Odenfeld)* [1978] 2 Lloyd's Rep. 357 QBD (Comm) at 374 that "any fetter on the innocent party's right of election whether or not to accept the repudiation will only be applied in extreme cases, *viz;* where damages would be an adequate remedy and where an election to keep the contract alive would be wholly unreasonable".

[103] *Reichman v Beveridge* [2007] Bus. L.R. 412.

[104] Indeed, the "no legitimate interest" test has been subject to criticism on the basis that it is unclear when it will be satisfied. See, for instance, J.W. Carter, "*White and Carter v McGregor*—How Unreasonable?" (2012) 128 L.Q.R. 490, where the qualification is criticised as "a puzzle" (at 491) and it is noted that it is "difficult to envisage any situation in which it could seriously be argued that a plaintiff has no legitimate interest to prefer a claim in debt over a claim in damages" (at 492).

[105] *MSC Mediterranean Shipping* at [2016] EWCA Civ 789 at [45] (per Moore-Bick LJ).

[106] *Geys v Société Générale* [2013] 1 A.C. 523, applied in *Feltham Management Ltd v Feltham* [2017] 12 WLUK 641.

right to terminate his employment with immediate effect and had made a payment in lieu of notice. An issue arose over when the contract was terminated, which was important in calculating the termination payment due to the plaintiff.

The Supreme Court held (Lord Sumption dissenting) that the standard contractual principle that the innocent party can elect whether to accept the breach or affirm the contract also applied in the employment context. Thus, a repudiatory breach did not terminate the contract unless the innocent party elected to accept the repudiation and it was not until the plaintiff was deemed to have received the bank's letter that the contractual right to terminate by the payment in lieu of notice method had been validly exercised (which substantially increased the plaintiff's termination payment). The Supreme Court rejected the argument that, in the employment context, repudiation automatically terminated the contact. It considered that the overall effect of this view was to reward a wrongful repudiator of a contract of employment with a date of termination which he had chosen, no doubt as being most beneficial to him and most detrimental to the innocent party.[107]

The decision in *Geys* is open to criticism since it suggests that it is not necessary for the innocent party to be able to perform his own obligations without the defendant's co-operation in order to affirm the contract.[108] Indeed, this was one of the bases on which Lord Sumption dissented, stating that "the innocent party cannot meaningfully be said to have a right to treat the contract as subsisting if he cannot perform it and the law will not allow him to enforce it".[109] In addition to this, Lord Sumption considered that employment relationships have "significant social and economic implications" and "when it comes to enforcing an unwanted relationship of employer and employee, there are altogether more sensitive considerations involved than those governing most other more contractual bargains".[110] To the extent that it was necessary to prevent the bank from profiting from its own wrong and protect the plaintiff, he considered these as "proper functions of an award of damages".[111] The case has received a mixed response.[112] On the one hand, it has been argued that particular features of employment contacts, such as inequality of bargaining power, inevitable incompleteness and (usually) indeterminate length mean general contract law principles are "unsuitable" for resolving employment disputes.[113] There has also been judicial recognition that employment contacts are different from other

---

[107] *Geys* [2013] 1 A.C. 523 at [66] per Lord Wilson.
[108] Indeed, in *Stobart Group Ltd v Tinkler* [2019] EWHC 258 (Comm), the court would not have granted a declaration that the employee (in this case, the former chief executive) remained an employee of the company had it found that he had been improperly dismissed since it is "inappropriate to force parties into relations demanding close personal trust and confidence" (at [535]), hence the usual bar on specific performance in relation to contracts for personal services. On the facts, the dismissal was justified in any case.
[109] *Geys* [2013] 1 A.C. 523 at [139].
[110] *Geys* [2013] 1 A.C. 523 at [118].
[111] *Geys* [2013] 1 A.C. 523 at [140].
[112] G. Pitt, "Crisis or Stasis in the Contract of Employment?" (2012–13) 12 C.I.L. 193; A. Blackham, "Uncertain Junctions between Employment and Contract Law" (2013) 72 C.L.J. 269; D. Cabrelli and R. Zahn, "The Elective and Automatic Theories of Termination in the Common Law of the Contract of Employment; Conundrum Resolved?" (2013) 76 M.L.R. 1106; I. Smith, "Rich Pickings" (2013) 163 N.L.J. 57.
[113] H. Collins, *Employment Law,* 2nd edn (Oxford: Oxford University Press, 2010), p.6.

contracts.[114] Conversely, others argue that general contract law principles, including those relating to repudiation and affirmation, are flexible enough to deal with employment contracts.[115] While the argument that automatic termination would permit the contract-breaker to take advantage of breaching the contract in order to put itself in a better position has some merit, the decision in *Geys* does seem to suggest that, contrary to what had previously been assumed from *White & Carter* and subsequent cases, the innocent party can affirm a contract even in circumstances where he cannot perform his own obligations. It should be noted that an employee's claim will, of course, be limited to sums which would have accrued during his notice period.[116]

2. Defences to a Liquidated Claim

Factors vitiating the contract as a whole

A claim on a contract may, of course, be defeated by any defence which impugns the contract as a whole. For example, the contract may be void by statute or for want of *consensus ad idem* or consideration; voidable on account of misrepresentation, duress or undue influence; or unenforceable through failure to comply with a formality prescribed by statute or through expiry of the prescribed period of limitation. Such general defences are fully examined in the contract textbooks and require no further discussion here.

3–23

There is, however, one general defence which is not known as widely as it should be, namely that the contract is unenforceable because it contravenes the provisions of art.VIII(2)(b) of the Agreement made at Bretton Woods in 1944 relating to the establishment and operation of the International Monetary Fund. Article VIII(2) of the IMF Agreement, effectuated by Order in Council,[117] provides as follows:

3–24

> "Exchange contracts which involve the currency of any member and which are contrary to the exchange control regulations of that member maintained or imposed consistently with this Agreement shall be unenforceable in the territories of any member."

The purpose of art.VIII(2) is to secure mutual respect among Member States for regulatory steps taken by each member to safeguard its currency resources,[118] typically by restricting the export of its own currency or the holding of foreign

---

[114] See, for instance, Lord Steyn's statement in *Johnson v Unisys Ltd* [2003] 1 A.C. 518 that "[i]t is no longer right to equate a contract of employment with commercial contracts".
[115] See G. Pitt, "Crisis or Stasis in the Contract of Employment?" (2012–13) 12 C.I.L. 193.
[116] *Johnson v Unisys Ltd* [2001] UKHL 13; *Botham v Ministry of Defence* [2012] 2 A.C. 22.
[117] Bretton Woods Agreement Order in Council 1946, made under the Bretton Woods Agreements Act 1945 and continued in force by virtue of the International Monetary Fund Act 1979 s.6(2). It must be said that exchange controls are generally in retreat. The "free movement of capital" rules in the EU Treaty would prevent the imposition of exchange controls in EU Member States except in very exceptional circumstances. Nevertheless, States in various parts of the world continue to impose controls of this kind.
[118] See generally, *Mann* (2012), Ch.15; also *Dicey, Morris & Collins* (2012), r.264 and discussion thereof.

currency by its own residents. There has been considerable discussion both in this country and abroad as to the meaning and scope of art.VIII(2) but, so far as the UK is concerned, the authorities now firmly establish the narrowest of the possible interpretations. In particular, a contract is not an exchange contract merely because it in some way affects the currency resources of a Member State. To be an exchange contract, the agreement must be one which provides for the exchange of one currency for another. So a contract of sale which involves the payment of foreign currency in breach of a Member State's exchange control regulations is not an exchange contract except to the extent to which it is a disguise for a currency exchange. The narrow view of the meaning of "exchange contract"—at least so far as the English courts are concerned—was established by the Court of Appeal in *Wilson, Smithett & Cope Ltd v Terruzzi*[119] and was subsequently endorsed by the House of Lords in *United City Merchants (Investments) Ltd v Royal Bank of Canada (The American Accord)*[120]:

An English company contracted to sell to a Peruvian company plant and machinery for the manufacture of fibreglass. Payment was to be made in London under a confirmed irrevocable transferable credit, 20% of the invoiced price being payable on opening of the credit, 70% on presentation of the shipping documents and the balance on completion of erection of the plant.[121] At the buyer's request, the seller sent an invoice for double the agreed contract price. The purpose of this was to enable the buyer to get US dollars out of Peru in breach of Peruvian exchange control regulations. The seller agreed with the buyer to remit the excess half of the payment to the buyer's associate company at its bank in Florida. The defendants as confirming bank paid the initial 20%, half of which was remitted to Florida as agreed, but refused to pay the balance on the ground that the bill of lading contained a false statement of the date of shipment on board.

The plaintiffs as transferees of the credit brought proceedings to recover the balance payable. The trial judge dismissed the claim on the ground that the sale transaction at an inflated price was a disguised monetary transaction and was unenforceable under art.VIII(2) of the Bretton Woods Agreement. The Court of Appeal, whose decision on this point[122] was upheld by the House of Lords, held that the sale was a monetary transaction only in relation to the excess of the invoice price over the genuine price and that, as regards the half of the price that was genuinely payable, the letter of credit was enforceable. Giving the leading speech in the House of Lords, Lord Diplock stated that an exchange contract was a contract for exchange of currencies and did not include a contract of sale under

---

[119] *Wilson, Smithett & Cope Ltd v Terruzzi* [1976] Q.B. 683 CA (Civ Div).
[120] *United City Merchants (Investments) Ltd v Royal Bank of Canada (The American Accord)* [1983] 1 A.C. 168 HL.
[121] An odd provision in a letter of credit since, by virtue of the well-known autonomy principle (on which see para.3–36 below), parties to a letter of credit transaction deal in documents, not in facts (Uniform Customs and Practice for Documentary Credits art.8(a)). It may be that the letter of credit in fact called for a certificate of completion as one of the documents to be presented. This is not clear from the reports.
[122] On the separate question whether the documents could be rejected as not conforming to the credit where the bill of lading had been fraudulently altered by someone other than the beneficiary or his agent, the House of Lords gave a negative answer, reversing the decision of the Court of Appeal on this point.

which the buyer had to convert one currency into another to enable him to pay the purchase price, except so far as the transaction was a disguised monetary transaction, in the present case as to the excess over the genuine sale price.[123]

This narrow approach to the expression "exchange contract" is no doubt in part motivated by a desire to enforce contractual obligations wherever possible and has recently been applied in *Deutsche Bank AG v Unitech Global Ltd*.[124] Unitech, an Indian company which had guaranteed a US dollar obligation of its UK subsidiary, had not obtained the required Indian exchange control to do so. It may be assumed that Unitech would have to use Indian rupees to purchase any US dollars that were necessary to meet a call under the guarantee and, in the absence of the exchange control approval, such a purchase would be unlawful under Indian law. It was therefore argued that the guarantee was an "exchange contract" for the purposes of art.VIII(2)(b). However, the court rejected this argument because: (i) the court was not obliged to inquire into Unitech's sources of US dollar funding for payments under the guarantee; and (ii) in any event, a guarantee was not an "exchange contract" because it did not involve an exchange of currencies—it was simply a unilateral obligation to pay in US dollars.

It must be said that courts in other countries have adopted a much broader view of the meaning of exchange contracts; it may, therefore, be argued that the English approach fails to give effect to art.VIII(2)(b) in domestic law. However that may be, it must not be overlooked that a breach of foreign exchange control laws may also have other consequences. For example:

3–25

(a) if the contract is governed by the laws of the country which imposes the exchange controls, then the contract may be unenforceable in England[125]; and
(b) if the contract forms part of a wider scheme to flout the laws of a friendly foreign State, then the contract will be contrary to public policy and will be unenforceable, even if governed by English law.[126]

---

[123] This decision has attracted some criticism. See *Mann* (2012), para.15.17 and sources there mentioned.
[124] *Deutsche Bank AG v Unitech Global Ltd* [2014] 2 All E.R. (Comm) 268.
[125] i.e. in accordance with art.12(1) of reg.593/2008 on the law applicable to contractual obligations (Rome I) [2008] OJ L177/6.
[126] i.e. in accordance with the principles in *Foster v Driscoll* [1929] 1 K.B. 470 CA; and *Regazzoni v KC Sethia (1944) Ltd* [1958] A.C. 301 HL, as more recently reaffirmed in *Ispahani v Bank Melli Iran* [1998] Lloyd's Rep. Bank. 133 CA (Civ Div); *Mahonia Ltd v West LB AG* [2004] EWHC 1938 (Comm); and *Beijing Jianlong Heavy Industry Group v Golden Ocean Group Ltd* [2013] 2 All E.R. (Comm) 436. The mere fact that the issue of a guarantee required Chinese exchange control approval—which was not obtained—was held to be insufficient to invoke the *Regazzoni* principle in *Emeraldian LP v Wellmix Shipping Ltd (The Vine)* [2011] 1 Lloyd's Rep. 301. For a discussion of earlier proceedings in the *Mahonia* litigation, see C. Proctor, "Enron, Letters of Credit and the Anatomy Principle" (2004) 19(6) B.J.I.B. & F.L. 204.

Leaving aside art.VIII(2)(b), it should be noted that a contract governed by English law will generally be enforceable in this country notwithstanding any contravention of the foreign exchange control laws of the country in which the debtor is resident.[127]

Payment stipulation unenforceable as such

3–26 There are various grounds upon which a debtor who is not able to attack the contract as a whole can impugn the efficacy of the payment stipulation.

(1) Illegality under foreign law

3–27 Where payment would be illegal under a relevant foreign law, this may preclude the creditor from recovering it in proceedings in England. The topic is complex and is dealt with in the last chapter of this work.[128]

(2) Penalty

3–28 The parties may agree that, in the event of a breach of the contract by the debtor, he shall pay an agreed sum as liquidated damages. Prior to *Cavendish Square Holding BV v Makdessi*,[129] such a provision would be enforceable only where the stipulated sum was a genuine pre-estimate of the loss likely to flow from the breach—as opposed to, for example, being imposed *in terrorem* to dissuade the debtor from committing a breach or as a penalty for so doing—and was reasonable as viewed at the time of the contract.[130] However, in *Cavendish Square v Makdessi*, the Supreme Court fundamentally rewrote the law on penalties, holding that the genuine pre-estimate of loss test had been applied too artificially and that the law on penalties had become "the prisoner of artificial categorisation", the result of unsatisfactory distinctions being drawn between a penalty and a genuine pre-estimate of loss and a genuine pre-estimate of loss and a deterrent.[131] Lords Neuberger and Sumption considered the real question to be whether a contractual provision "is penal, not whether it is a pre-estimate of loss" and reformulated the test for a penalty to focus on "whether the impugned provision is a secondary obligation which imposes a detriment on the

---

[127] See *Kleinwort Sons & Co v Ungarische Baumwolle Industrie AG* [1939] 2 K.B. 678 CA; *Deutsche Bank AG v Unitech Global Ltd* [2016] EWCA Civ 119.
[128] See paras 6–24 to 6–27 below, dealing with supervening illegality.
[129] *Cavendish Square Holding BV v Makdessi* [2015] 3 W.L.R. 1373.
[130] The *locus classicus* on penalty clauses is the judgment of Lord Dunedin in *Dunlop Pneumatic Tyre Co Ltd v New Garage & Motor Co Ltd* [1915] A.C. 79 HL at 86–88 which, as described in *Cavendish Square v Makdessi*, "achieved the status of a quasi-statutory code in the subsequent case law" (at [22]). The key distinction made was between: (1) a liquidated damages clause, which provides a realistic estimate of the loss likely to flow from the breach, and is hence enforceable; and (2) a penalty clause, which is designed to force the borrower to perform the contract for fear of unfair consequences, and which is hence unenforceable. Lord Dunedin noted that "[t]he essence of a penalty is a payment of money stipulated *in terrorem* of the offending party; the essence of liquidated damages is a genuine covenanted pre-estimate of damage".
[131] *Cavendish Square* [2015] 3 W.L.R. 1373 at [33].

contract-breaker *out of all proportion* to any *legitimate interest* of the innocent party in the enforcement of the primary obligation".[132]

The "threshold" question for engaging the rule against penalties is whether the clause in question imposes "in substance a secondary obligation engaged upon breach of a primary contractual obligation".[133] The rule against penalties does not apply to a sum payable otherwise than on a breach of contract by the party from whom recovery is sought.[134] Hence, despite dicta to the contrary,[135] it has no application to a clause which provides for payment of a specified sum by the debtor upon his lawfully terminating the contract,[136] or to a sum payable on termination on insolvency[137] or on the occurrence of some other non-breach event. Similarly, it does not apply to clauses by which a party undertakes to make an agreed payment, or give an indemnity, in respect of loss caused by the breach of contract of a third party.[138] The Supreme Court in *Cavendish Square* confirmed this position and declined to extend the penalty rule to contexts other than breaches of contract, holding that "[t]here is no freestanding equitable jurisdiction

3–29

---

[132] *Cavendish Square* [2015] 3 W.L.R. 1373 at [32]. See *Chitty* (2018), paras 26–178 to 26–204, for more information on the law of penalties.

[133] *Vivienne Westwood v Conduit Street* [2017] EWHC 350 (Ch) at [41], referring to *Cavendish Square* [2015] 3 W.L.R. 1373.

[134] For examples of where the penalty jurisdiction has not been triggered, see *Edgeworth Capital* [2016] EWCA Civ 412 (the Court of Appeal held that a fee triggered by the occurrence of a "payment event" was not a penalty as it had nothing to do with damages for breach of contract); *Brown's Bay Resort* [2016] UKPC 10 (the Privy Council held that a fee payable on the interruption of a lease was not a substitute for common law damages for breach of contract but a contractual charge or fee); *Holyoake v Candy* [2017] EWHC 3397 (Ch) (early repayment fees, extension fees and "double interest" charges on previously accrued interest as a condition of extending the loan in question were not penal since they were not triggered by breach).

[135] See *Bridge v Campbell Discount Co Ltd* [1962] A.C. 600 per Lord Denning at 629–631 and per Lord Devlin at 634.

[136] *Goulston Discount Co v Harman* (1962) 106 S.J. 369 CA. A clause which provides for a fee when the borrower elects to make a voluntary prepayment under a loan agreement is thus not open to challenge on "penalty" grounds.

[137] In *Granor Finance v Liquidator of Eastore* 1974 S.L.T. 296 Court of Session (Outer House), a company took machinery under a hire-purchase agreement from a finance company. It was stipulated that voluntary liquidation of the hirer would terminate the agreement and entitle the finance company to repossess the machinery as well as to claim a termination fee. When the hirer did go into voluntary liquidation, the liquidator resisted the claim for the fee as penal and unenforceable. However, since there was no breach of contract, the law of penalty and liquidated damages did not apply. The finance company was accordingly entitled to enforce the termination fee provisions. This decision was applied and followed in *EFT Commercial Ltd v Security Charge Ltd (No.1)* 1992 S.C. 414 Court of Session (Inner House, First Division) and, for a decision to similar effect, see *Lombard North Central Plc v Brooks* [1999] B.P.I.R. 701. However, in an English county court decision, such a provision has been held void as contrary to a fundamental principle of bankruptcy law (*Re Piggin* (1962) 112 L.J. 424 CC), though this appears against the weight of the previous case law. It may, however, be possible to re-open such provisions on the basis that the credit transaction is "extortionate" for the purposes of s.244 of the Insolvency Act 1986. Additional avenues of challenge may also be open to consumers—see below.

[138] *Sterling Industrial Facilities v Lydiate Textiles* (1962) 106 S.J. 669 CA; *Export Credits Guarantee Department v Universal Oil Products Co* [1983] 1 W.L.R. 399 HL. The latter decision has most recently been applied in the "bank charges" litigation brought by the OFT against major banks, where the court granted a declaration to the effect that bank charges for unauthorised overdrafts were not amenable to a "fairness" review under the Unfair Terms in Consumer Contract Regulations 1999 (SI 1999/2083): see *Office of Fair Trading v Abbey National Plc* [2010] 1 A.C. 696.

to render unenforceable as penalties stipulations operative as a result of events which do not entail a breach of contract".[139] However, the distinction between a primary obligation and a penalty payable on breach is not always straightforward and appears in some cases to depend on fine drafting distinctions rather than differences of substance.[140]

3–30　Where the jurisdiction against penalties is engaged, the position post-*Cavendish* is that a provision which: (a) imposes a detriment upon breach which is not a genuine pre-estimate of the likely loss; and/or (b) is aimed at deterring the other party from breaching the contract, may nonetheless be valid if: (i) the innocent party has a legitimate interest in deterring the breach rather than simply claiming damages; and (ii) the provision is not extravagant and unconscionable in proportion to that interest (i.e. penal).[141] Uncertainty persists over what constitutes a "legitimate interest" and when a detriment will be considered "out of all proportion" to the innocent party's legitimate interest, including the extent to which the pre-*Cavendish* case law is useful in determining this.[142] In relation to the "legitimate interest" requirement,[143] Lords Neuberger and Sumption indicated that there should be a legitimate interest in obtaining *performance*, not just damages.[144] In *Vivienne Westwood Ltd v Conduit Street Development Ltd*, it was suggested that this required a legitimate interest beyond pecuniary compensation for any loss caused by the particular breach.[145] In many cases where such provisions have been successfully enforced, it appears that the inadequacy of damages as a deterrent to breach because of the difficulty of proving loss has been a factor.[146] In the banking context, it was accepted in *Lordsvale Finance Plc v Bank of Zambia*[147] that a clause requiring a higher rate of interest on default could be "commercially justified" since the defaulting borrower represents a greater credit risk and "money is more expensive for a less good credit risk".[148] That this also satisfies the "legitimate interest" requirement post-*Cavendish* was

---

[139] *Cavendish Square* [2015] 3 W.L.R. 1373 at [241]. A wider approach to the penalty rule has been advocated for and is taken in some other jurisdictions; discussed at para.3–34 below.
[140] Compare e.g. *Vivienne Westwood v Conduit Street* [2017] EWHC 350 (Ch) (penalty found where a clause in a side letter providing for payment of a lower rent permitted the landlord to terminate the side letter and require payment of a higher rent in tbe main lease if the tenant's obligations were not complied with) with *Edgeworth Capital (Luxembourg) Sarl v Ramblas Investments BV* [2016] EWCA Civ 412 (no penalty where a clause provided for the payment of a fee on default).
[141] See *Chitty* (2018), para.26–213.
[142] On this topic, see *Chitty* (2018), paras 26–213 to 26–225 on "legitimate interest" and 26–226 to 26–229 on "extravagant and unconscionable". The "legitimate interest" requirement has also been addressed by the Scottish Law Commission in its *Discussion Paper on Penalty Clauses No. 162* (206) and its *Report on Review of Contract Law: Formation, Interpretation, Remedies for Breach of Contract, and Penalty Clauses No. 252* (2018), paras 20.20–20.26.
[143] Discussed *Chitty* (2018), paras 26–213 to 26–225. The "legitimate interest" requirement has also been addressed by the Scottish Law Commission in its *Discussion Paper on Penalty Clauses No. 162* (206) and its *Report on Review of Contract Law: Formation, Interpretation, Remedies for Breach of Contract, and Penalty Clauses No. 252* (2018), paras 20.20–20.26.
[144] *Cavendish v Makdessi* [2015] UKSC 67 at [28].
[145] *Vivienne Westwood Ltd v Conduit Street Development Ltd* [2017] EWHC 350 (Ch) at [49].
[146] *Chitty* (2018), para.26–215.
[147] *Lordsvale Finance Plc v Bank of Zambia* [1996] Q.B. 752 QBD.
[148] *Lordsvale Finance Plc v Bank of Zambia* [1996] Q.B. 752 QBD at 762–764, discussed in *Chitty* (2018), para.26–219A.

confirmed in *Cargill International Trading Pte Ltd v Uttam Galva Steels Ltd* on the basis that "it is self-evident ... that there is a good commercial justification for charging a higher rate of interest on an advance of money after a default in repayment".[149] Therefore, lenders charging default interest rates will almost certainly be able to demonstrate a legitimate interest.

The second requirement is that the provision is not "wholly disproportionate" or "extravagant and unconscionable" in relation to that legitimate interest.[150] Prior to *Cavendish Square*, *Lordsvale Finance Plc v Bank of Zambia*[151] indicated that an increase of 1% in the interest margin following a payment default was enforceable as a fair reflection of the greater credit risk incurred by the bank as a result of the default.[152] It was unclear whether default margins greater than 1% would be enforceable, although the Hong Kong Admiralty Court upheld a 2% penalty rate payable on default under a loan secured by a ship mortgage, on the footing that liquidated damages clauses should be enforced unless they are unconscionable, oppressive or extravagant.[153] Following *Cavendish*, lenders have much more leeway to impose higher default margins so long as they are not penal in the sense that they can be commercially justified. In *Cargill International Trading Pte Ltd v Uttam Galva Steels Ltd*,[154] for example, a "default compensation" rate of one month LIBOR plus 12% was not viewed as out of proportion, exorbitant or unconscionable.

3–31

However, there may still be cases where the secondary liability imposed is clearly disproportionate to the innocent party's legitimate interest in securing performance. Before *Cavendish*, a rate equivalent to 260% per annum on amounts due under a sportswear supply contract was, unsurprisingly, held to be a penalty,[155] and it is likely that the same finding would be made under the new test. In *Hayfin Opal Luxco 3 SARL v Windermere VII CMBS Plc*, it was considered obiter that a provision under which further interest accrued and was payable on unpaid interest would be penal since "the almost inevitable result that could be anticipated at the time of contract would be a multiplication of the unpaid amount by a very sizeable factor to arrive at a sum many times the amount that would adequately compensate the innocent party for being kept out of its money."[156] Thus, "in any conventional terms", this would be regarded as "exorbitant (if not extortionate)".[157] How should it be determined whether a particular case crosses the line? Snowden J provided some guidance in *Hayfin Opal* on factors which would or would not suggest that a particular provision was

---

[149] *Cargill International Trading Pte Ltd v Uttam Galva Steels Ltd* [2019] EWHC 476 (Comm) at [50].
[150] On this topic, see *Chitty* (2018), paras 26–226 to 26–229.
[151] *Lordsvale Finance Plc v Bank of Zambia* [1996] Q.B. 752 QBD.
[152] The decision in *Lordsvale* has met with general approval—see, for example, *Makdessi v Cavendish Square Holdings BV* [2013] EWCA Civ 1529; and *Aodhcon LLP v Bridgeco Ltd* [2014] 2 All E.R. (Comm) 928.
[153] *Re Mandarin Container* [2004] 3 HKLRD 554.
[154] *Cargill International Trading Pte Ltd v Uttam Galva Steels Ltd* [2019] EWHC 476 (Comm).
[155] *Jeancharm Ltd (t/a Beaver International) v Barnet Football Club Ltd* 92 Con. L.R. 26.
[156] *Hayfin Opal* [2016] EWHC 782 (Ch) at [140].
[157] *Hayfin Opal* [2016] EWHC 782 (Ch) at [140].

penal. He suggested that the following would be irrelevant[158]: the subjective intentions of the parties to provide a deterrent; the actual effect of the provision as a deterrent; the contract-breaker's ability to pay the specified amount (lack of financial resources on the contract-breaker's part cannot turn an otherwise unobjectionable clause into a penalty clause and vice versa); and the source from which the contract breaker was to pay the amount. Instead, the penalty doctrine "must be founded upon objective reference to some norm" and "focuses on the lack of proportionality between the amount of the secondary liability imposed and the innocent party's legitimate interest in performance of the primary obligation".[159] The statutory background may be relevant in making the assessment. In *First Personnel Services Ltd v Halford Ltd*,[160] a contractual rate of interest of 2% per month on late payments was considered penal as there was a lack of commercial justification for it being above the "commercial norm"[161] or the rate payable under the Late Payment of Commercial Debts (Interest) Act 1998.[162]

3–32   Previously, care had to be taken in drafting default interest clauses, in particular to ensure the default rate was payable only from the date of default until actual payment. In this context, agreements allowing the creditor to accelerate the principal indebtedness and also to claim interest for the entire, originally contracted period of the loan were held, pre-*Cavendish*, to be unenforceable as a penalty[163] and it is suggested here that this will generally continue to be the case since, in most cases, the amount payable will be disproportionate to the loss suffered by the innocent party. However, acceleration clauses which do not provide for unaccrued interest but simply that the loan itself and accrued interest are payable are likely to be enforceable.[164]

3–33   Whereas a creditor who elects to accept the debtor's repudiation as terminating the contract can include as part of his claim for damages the loss of the profit he would have earned if the contract had been fully performed, even though (in a sense) that loss results from the creditor's own act of termination, this does not apply where the creditor exercises a contractual right to terminate for a breach which is not repudiatory in character.[165] It was therefore suggested previously in

---

[158] *Hayfin Opal* [2016] EWHC 782 (Ch) at [142].
[159] *Hayfin Opal* [2016] EWHC 782 (Ch) at [142].
[160] *First Personnel Services Ltd v Halford Ltd* [2016] EWHC 3220 (Ch).
[161] *First Personnel* [2016] EWHC 3220 (Ch) at [163].
[162] Approved in *Makdessi v Cavendish Square Holdings BV* [2013] EWCA Civ 1529 and *Aodhcon LLP v Bridgeco Ltd* [2014] 2 All E.R. (Comm) 928.
[163] See *County Leasing Ltd v East* [2007] EWHC 2907 (QB) for an example. However, this is not the case where the clause applies for payment of unaccrued interest on events other than breach, e.g. early repayment; *Holyoake v Candy* [2017] EWHC 3397 (Ch).
[164] See e.g. *Oresundsvarvet AB v Lemos (The Angelic Star)* [1988] 1 Lloyd's Rep 122; *Wadham Stringer Finance Ltd v Meaney* [1981] 1 W.L.R. 39 QBD.
[165] *Financings Ltd v Baldock* [1963] 2 Q.B. 104 CA, confirmed recently in *Phones 4 U Ltd (in administration) v EE Ltd* [2018] EWHC 49 (Comm). See also *Capital Finance Co Ltd v Donati* (1977) 121 S.J. 270 CA (Civ Div), approved in *AMEV-UDC Finance v Austin* (1987) 68 ALR 185 (High Court of Australia) and applied in *Kelly v Sovereign Leasing* [1995] C.L.Y. 720. In the *AMEV-UDC* case, the court specifically noted that, where the lessor under a hiring contract terminates for non-fundamental (or non-repudiatiory) breach, they can recover losses flowing from the lessor's breach, but they cannot recover losses flowing from termination, since that is the lessor's own

this book[166] that it followed that, if the creditor stipulated for payment of a liquidated sum designed to compensate him for loss of the bargain on termination even in cases of non-repudiatory breach by the debtor, the stipulation would be unenforceable as a penalty since it would have the effect of giving the creditor more than he could have recovered at common law,[167] although there was case law suggesting this could be avoided by careful drafting of the contract.[168] Following *Cavendish*, it is questionable whether this is still the position. Since the test now applied is whether the provision is disproportionate to the innocent party's legitimate interest not whether it goes beyond a genuine pre-estimate of loss, this would seem inconsistent with the argument that a provision allowing recovery of damages unavailable at common law is automatically a penalty.

The decision in *Cavendish* has attracted much discussion.[169] On a pragmatic level, it has been argued that, rather than clarifying the law, it has made it more uncertain.[170] Moreover, some oppose the decision in principle either on the grounds that the Supreme Court should have gone further and abolished the doctrine against penalties as an infringement of freedom of contract[171] or, conversely, that the doctrine should have been expanded beyond breaches of contract, a step explicitly rejected in *Cavendish* itself.[172] A wider scope for the

3–34

---

unilateral act. The *Baldock* decision has thus been widely approved and applied. However, for a criticism see B. Opeskin, "Damages for Breach of Contract Terminated under Express Terms" [1990] L.Q.R. 293.

[166] In the second edition: Roy Goode and Charles Proctor, *Goode on Payment Obligations in Commercial and Financial Transactions*, 2nd edn (London: Sweet & Maxwell, 2009) relying on *Baldock* above.

[167] *Goode on Payment Obligations in Commercial and Financial Transactions* (2009) relying on *Baldock* above. The Privy Council in *Philips Hong Kong Ltd v Attorney General of Hong Kong* (1993) 61 B.L.R. 49 cited with approval Dickson J's view in the Canadian case of *Elsey v J.G. Collins Insurance Agencies Ltd* (1978) 83 D.L.R. (3d) 1 at 15 that: "The power to strike down a penalty clause is a blatant interference with freedom of contract and is designed for the sole purpose of providing relief against oppression for the party having to pay the stipulated sum. It has no place where there is no oppression."

[168] *Lombard North Central Plc v Butterworth* [1987] Q.B. 527 CA (Civ Div), followed in *BNP Paribas v Wockhardt EU Operations (Swiss) AG* [2009] EWHC 3116 (Comm).

[169] See, for instance, Edwin Peel, "Unjustified Penalties or an Unjustified Rule against Penalties?" (2014) 130 L.Q.R. 365; Lorna Richardson, "Commercial Justification for Penalty Clauses: The Death of the Old Dichotomy" (2015) 19 Edin. L.R. 119; Gareth Eagles, Edward Attenborough and Adam Wallin, "The Reformulated Rule against Penalties and Its Impact on Finance Documents" (2016) 31 B.J.I.B. & F.L. 23; William Day, "A Pyrrhic Victory for the Doctrine against Penalties: *Makdessi v Cavendish Square Holding BV*" [2016] J.B.L. 115; Jonathan Morgan, "The Penalty Clause Doctrine: Unlovable but Untouchable" (2016) 75 Cambridge L.J. 11.

[170] See e.g. A. Summers, "Unresolved Issues in the Law on Penalties" (2017) *Lloyds Maritime and Commercial Law Quarterly* 95.

[171] Which the Supreme Court declined to do, recognising a number of reasons why the doctrine should be maintained, including that the rule is found in almost all major systems of law and is aimed at preventing the contract-breaker having to pay a sum out of all proportion to the loss suffered by the innocent party, as well as concerns about inequality of bargaining power; Lord Neuberger and Lord Sumption (at [32] and [37]), Lord Mance (at [164]–[167]) and Lord Hodge (at [262]–[265]). There was also some indication that abolition should be for Parliament.

[172] *Cavendish Square* [2015] 3 W.L.R. 1373 at [12]–[14] (Lords Neuberger and Sumption), [129] (Lord Mance) and [239] (Lord Hodge).

penalty doctrine has found favour in Australia,[173] although the New Zealand courts have preferred to follow the narrower *Cavendish* approach.[174] The Scottish Law Commission previously suggested extending it beyond cases where the operation of the "penalty" depends on a breach of contract to include cases where it is imposed if there is early termination of the contract or the party performs or fails to perform in a particular way,[175] but ultimately appears to have concluded that no reform should presently be undertaken.[176] On balance, the *Cavendish* restatement indicates an increased respect for parties' freedom of contract which removes the need to make often fine distinctions between penalties and genuine pre-estimates of loss without entirely abandoning protection for the contract-breaker. This seems a reasonable position.

3–35 In consumer contracts, a penalty clause may be challenged "if, contrary to the requirements of good faith, it causes a significant imbalance in the parties' rights and obligations, to the detriment of the consumer".[177] However, in relation to consumer credit agreements entered into after 6 April 2007, the borrower is perhaps more likely to challenge a penalty interest clause or similar fee or charge under the "unfair relationships" test in s.140A–140C of the Consumer Credit Act 1974.[178]

(3) Unconscionable bargain[179]

3–36 The court has a general equitable jurisdiction to reopen a contract as harsh and unconscionable. However, the burden on the party seeking to set aside the contract is a heavy one and has rarely been successfully discharged in recent times. In *Multiservice Bookbinding*,[180] Browne-Wilkinson J, in a general survey of the equitable jurisdiction, pointed out that it was not sufficient for the plaintiff to show that the contract terms are hard or even unreasonable. What he has to establish is that they are oppressive in the sense of being imposed in a morally

---

[173] *Andrews v ANZ Banking Group Ltd* [2012] HCA 30; *Paciocco v ANZ Banking Group Ltd* [2016] HCA 28.
[174] *127 Hobson Street v Honey Bees Preschool* [2019] NZCA 122.
[175] Scottish Law Commission, *Discussion Paper on Penalty Clauses No. 162* (2016), paras 5.2–5.11; see also its earlier *Report on Penalty Clauses No. 171* (1999).
[176] Scottish Law Commission, *Report on Review of Contract Law: Formation, Interpretation, Remedies for Breach, and Penalty Clauses No. 252* (2018), paras 2.22–2.24, Pt 5.
[177] See s.62(4) of the Consumer Rights Act 2015. The Consumer Rights Act 2015 replaces the Unfair Terms in Consumer Contracts Regulations (SI 1999/2083), which have been revoked. Schedule 2 Pt 1 para.5 to the Consumer Rights Act 2015 (replacing para.1(f) of Sch.2 to the Regulations), specifically contemplates that a term "which has the object or effect of requiring that, where the consumer decides not to conclude or perform the contract, the consumer must pay the trade a disproportionately high sum in compensation or for services which have not been supplied" may be regarded as unfair for these purposes.
[178] As inserted by the Consumer Credit Act 2006.
[179] See Roy Goode, *Consumer Credit Law and Practice* (New York: LexisNexis, 2015), Ch.47, for a detailed account of the law relating to challenging extortionate bargains and unfair relationships.
[180] *Multiservice Bookbinding* [1979] Ch. 84 Ch D, applied in *Liddle v Cree* [2011] EWHC 3294 (Ch) (at [92]) and in *Strydom v Vendside Ltd* [2009] EWHC 2130 (QB) (at [39]). In the *Strydom* case, it was indicated (at [39]) that the question of whether the bargain was oppressive should be determined at the time the contract was entered into and from the perspective of the defendant.

reprehensible manner.[181] This principle was reiterated by Peter Millett QC (sitting as a Deputy High Court Judge) in *Alec Lobb (Garages) Ltd v Total Oil Great Britain Ltd*[182]:

> "If the cases are examined, it will be seen that three elements have almost invariably been present before the court has interfered. First, one party has been at a serious disadvantage to the other, whether through poverty, or ignorance, or lack of advice, or otherwise, so that circumstances existed of which unfair advantage could be taken. Secondly, this weakness of the one party has been exploited by the other in some morally culpable manner. And thirdly, the resulting transaction has been, not merely hard or improvident, but overreaching and oppressive. In short, there must, in my judgement, be some impropriety, both in the conduct of the stronger party and in the terms of the transaction itself (though the former may often be inferred from the latter in the absence of an innocent explanation) which in the traditional phrase 'shocks the conscience of the court', and makes it against equity and good conscience of the stronger party to retain the benefit of a transaction he has unfairly obtained."

Although these requirements have subsequently been applied with varying stringency,[183] recent cases have reiterated their necessity,[184] as "[g]enerally speaking, the law will not intervene to save people from making improvident bargains".[185]

(4) Unfair credit relationships

Different considerations apply to the statutory power of the court to reopen a credit agreement where the relationship between the creditor and the debtor arising out of the agreement is unfair to the debtor.[186] Under s.140A of the 1974 Act, as amended by the Consumer Credit Act 2006, a relationship may be unfair to the debtor because of one or more of the following:

3–37

(a) any of the terms of the agreement or any related agreement;
(b) the way in which the creditor has exercised or enforced any of his rights under the agreement or any related agreement; and
(c) any other thing done (or not done) by, or on behalf of, the creditor (whether occurring before or after the making of the agreement or any related agreement).[187]

It is unfortunate that the Government resisted all attempts to introduce into the Consumer Credit Bill 2006 a provision setting out the criteria to be applied by the court in determining whether a relationship is unfair. However, the case law to

---

[181] *Multiservice Bookbinding* [1979] Ch. 84 Ch D at 109–110 per Browne-Wilkinson J.
[182] *Alec Lobb (Garages) Ltd v Total Oil Great Britain Ltd* [1983] 1 All E.R. 944 at 961, applied in *Strydom* [2009] EWHC 2130 (QB) at [36]–[37].
[183] As discussed in *Chitty* (2018), paras 8–134 to 8–142. In particular, it is noted that the requirement that the claimant be "poor and ignorant" has been broadly interpreted in some cases (at para.8–137).
[184] See e.g. *Libyan Investment Authority v Goldman Sachs International* [2016] EWHC 2530 (Ch); *Minder Music Ltd v Sharples* [2015] EWHC 1454 (IPEC); *Liddle v Cree* [2011] EWHC 3294 (Ch).
[185] *Libyan Investment Authority v Goldman Sachs International* [2016] EWHC 2530 (Ch), at [132].
[186] See s.140A–C of the 1974 Act as inserted by the 2006 Act replacing ss.137–140 of the 1974 Act relating to extortionate credit bargains.
[187] 1974 Act s.140A.

date offers some assistance. In *Plevin v Paragon Personal Finance Ltd*,[188] the Supreme Court held that the relationship between a lender and a borrower was unfair because of a failure by the lender to disclose to the borrower that the loan broker would receive a very substantial commission for arranging the associated payment protection insurance.[189] The courts have, however, decided that the relationship does not become "unfair" for these purposes merely because the lender makes demand for repayment when due, seeks to enforce payment or makes customary reports to credit reference agencies, since these are part of the ordinary steps involved in recovering payment.[190] It is clear from *Plevin* that there does not need to be a breach of a regulatory duty for a relationship to be unfair,[191] but instead, the test under s.140A is a broader one of fairness applied to the particular debtor/creditor relationship.[192] There have been a number of cases since *Plevin* which have considered this and they reiterate the position of the Supreme Court in *Plevin* that s.140A is framed in wide terms and its application "must depend on the court's judgment of all the relevant facts".[193] A useful list of factors which the authorities suggest are likely to be relevant is found in Hamblen J's judgment in *Deutsche Bank (Suisse) SA v Khan*[194]:

(1) In relation to the fairness of the terms themselves: (a) whether the term is commonplace and/or in the nature of the product in question; (b) whether there are sound commercial reasons for the term; (c) whether it represents a legitimate and proportionate attempt by the creditor to protect its position; (d) to the extent that it is solely for the benefit of the lender, whether it exists to protect him from a risk which the debtor does not face; (e) the scale of the lending and whether commercial or quasi-commercial in nature (high value commercial lending arrangements being less likely to be found unfair than consumer agreements); (f) the strength of the debtor's

---

[188] *Plevin v Paragon Personal Finance Ltd* [2014] 1 W.L.R. 4222, followed in *McMullon v Secure the Bridge Ltd* [2015] EWCA Civ 884; and applied in *Swift Advances Plc v Okokenu* [2015] C.T.L.C. 302 CC.

[189] For a broadly similar decision, see *Scotland v British Credit Trust Ltd* [2015] 1 All E.R. 708.

[190] *McGuffick v Royal Bank of Scotland Plc* [2010] 1 All E.R. 634. However, this is assuming that the agreement is not irredeemably unenforceable in the first place; *Grace v Black Horse Ltd* [2015] 3 All E.R. 223; *Re London Scottish Finance Ltd (In Administration)* [2014] Bus. L.R. 424. This may cause an issue if a breach which leads to an agreement becoming unenforceable is "curable" so that the agreement then becomes enforceable again: see the discussion of this in *Carey v HSBC Bank Plc* [2010] Bus. L.R. 1142 (at [130]–[131]).

[191] *Plevin* [2014] 1 W.L.R. 4222 at [16], concluding that the Court of Appeal's decision in *Harrison v Black Horse Ltd* [2012] E.C.C. 7 was wrongly decided.

[192] *Plevin* [2014] 1 W.L.R. 4222 at [17].

[193] *Plevin* [2014] 1 W.L.R. 4222 at [10]. See, for example, *Swift Advances plc v Okokenu* [2015] C.T.L.C. 302 CC, which held that, in determining fairness, the court was required to look at the whole of the transaction from the point of view of both the debtor and the creditor ([42]). In *McMullon v Secure the Bridge Ltd* [2015] EWCA Civ 884, the Court of Appeal cited Lord Sumption's judgment and noted that the application of s.140A is dependent on the court's "judgment of all the relevant facts" ([11]).

[194] *Deutsche Bank (Suisse) SA v Khan* [2013] EWHC 482 (Comm) at [345]–[346]. This guidance has been followed in subsequent cases, including *Holyoake v Candy* [2017] EWHC 3397 (Ch) (at [490]); and *Carney v NM Rothschild & Sons Ltd* [2018] EWHC 959 (Comm) (at [55]).

bargaining position; and (g) whether the terms are individually negotiated or pro forma terms and, if the latter, whether presented on a "take it or leave it" basis.

(2) In relation to the creditor's conduct before and at the time of formation: (a) whether the creditor applied any pressure on the borrowers to execute the agreement; (b) whether the creditor understood and had reasonable grounds to believe that the borrower had experience of the relevant arrangements and had available to him the advice of solicitors; (c) whether the creditor had any reason to think that the debtor had not read or understood the terms; and (d) whether the debtor demurred at the time of formation over the terms now suggested to be unfair.

(3) In relation to the creditor's conduct following formation and leading up to enforcement: (a) whether any demand was prompted by an "improper motive" or was the consequence of an "arbitrary decision"; (b) whether the creditor has shown patience and, before leaping to enforcement, has taken steps in the hope of reaching some form of accommodation; and (c) whether the debtor has resisted attempts at accommodation by raising unfounded claims against the creditor.

This may be contrasted with the experience acquired under the earlier "extortionate credit bargains" provisions of the 1974 Act[195] which largely focused on the cost of credit, rather than the broader aspects of the relationship. 3–38

Where the court finds a contract to be unfair, it has a range of powers, including orders requiring the repayment of sums transferred under the contract or the alteration of its terms.[196]

Frustration of the contract

Where a contract is frustrated, e.g. because something occurs after its formation which makes performance impossible or renders the obligation to perform radically different from that originally undertaken[197] supervening illegality or accidental destruction of the subject-matter,[198] the contract comes to an end and each party is required to return benefits received under the contract less any expenses incurred in performing it.[199] A question of some difficulty is whether it is possible for a pure money obligation to be frustrated, and if so, where the creditor then stands. This problem is most likely to arise in relation to a foreign money obligation and it is therefore considered in the final chapter.[200] 3–39

---

[195] Under those rules, the court would not intervene merely because the rate of interest was high; the rate had to be grossly exorbitant or the transaction otherwise had to contravene ordinary principles of fair dealing. The court might decline to intervene if the debtor had misled the creditor as to his financial position: *Ketley v Scott* [1981] I.C.R. 241 Ch D.

[196] Section 140B of the Consumer Credit Act 1974, as inserted by the 2006 Act.

[197] See the definition of frustration in *Chitty* (2018), para.23-001.

[198] *Metropolitan Water Board v Dick Kerr & Co Ltd* [1918] A.C. 119 HL; *Taylor v Caldwell* 122 E.R. 309 KB.

[199] Law Reform (Frustrated Contracts) Act 1943 s.1. See *BP Exploration Co (Libya) Ltd v Hunt (No.2)* [1983] 2 A.C. 352 HL.

[200] See para.6–28 below.

The challenges caused for many businesses and individuals by the COVID-19 pandemic and related business shutdowns since March 2020 may result in increased attempts to rely on the doctrine of frustration to avoid payment obligations.[201]

Abstract payment obligations

3–40 An abstract payment obligation is, as we have seen, one that is undertaken without consideration and is enforceable either by the custom of merchants or because it is by deed.[202] Since no consideration is furnished, it follows that there can be no defence of failure of consideration. Moreover, in the typical case, the beneficiary of the payment obligation does not himself undertake any commitment to the promisor.[203] He may be required to present documents in order to be paid, but such presentation is not a contractual obligation, merely a condition of his right to collect payment. It follows that most of the defences available to a payment claim on a contract of the normal bilateral kind supported by consideration do not avail the debtor whose undertaking is abstract in character. Typical cases are the irrevocable letter of credit and the on-demand performance bond or guarantee. However, this is a developing area. For instance, over the past few years, the bank payment obligation (which essentially constitutes an irrevocable conditional undertaking to pay given between banks and which the International Chamber of Commerce (ICC) suggests can be seen as an "electronic letters of credit"[204]) has been presented as an alternative to the conventional letters of credit. The ICC published the ICC Uniform Rules for Bank Payment Obligations (URBPO) in 2013.

A bank issuing or confirming a letter of credit commits itself to payment on due presentation of the specified shipping documents and is not concerned with the underlying contract of sale or its performance. This is emphasised in two separate provisions of the Uniform Customs and Practice for Documentary Credits (2006 Revision—UCP 600). Article 4(a) tells us that:

---

[201] However, given the strict criteria for frustration, in particular around the question of foreseability of the frustrating event (see *Chitty* (2018), para.23-009), it is not clear whether such attempts would succeed, at least in the absence of a force majeure clause which covered it in the contract. The UK Government published general guidance on how contractual parties should respond to the COVID-19 situation in May 2020; see Cabinet Office, *Guidance on responsible contractual behaviour in the performance and enforcement of contracts impacted by the Covid-19 emergency*, available at: https://assets.publishing.service.gov.uk/government/uploads/system/uploads/attachment_data/file/883737/_Covid-19_and_Responsible_Contractual_Behaviour__web_final___7_May_.pdf] [Accessed 10 November 2020].

[202] See para.2–45 above. In view of the "autonomy principle" discussed below, it is not possible to argue that performance by the promisee of his obligations under a collateral or underlying contract should be regarded as consideration for the abstract obligation.

[203] See para.3–40 above. See also *Goode on Commercial Law* (2016), paras 35.49–35.51 for discussion of the issue which the lack of consideration poses for ordinary contract law principles. See also R. Goode, "Abstract Payment Obligations" in *Essays for Patrick Atiyah*, edited by P. Cane and J. Stephen (Oxford: Oxford University Press, 1991).

[204] Although this description is questioned on the grounds of key legal differences between the two instruments, in particular, the beneficiary's lack of an underlying claim against the issuing bank if the confirming bank fails to pay; see G. Wynne and H.Fearn, "The bank payment obligation: will it replace the traditional letter of credit—now, or ever?" (2014) 2 JIBFL 102.

"Credits, by their nature, are separate transactions from the sales or other contracts on which they may be based and banks are in no way concerned with or bound by such contracts."

This is the so-called autonomy principle[205] reinforced by art.5: "In documentary credit operations all parties concerned deal in documents and not in goods." The courts have repeatedly held that, in the absence of fraud or illegality, the bank must pay against a conforming tender even if the seller has broken his contract by shipping goods that are defective, not in accordance with the contract description or deficient in quantity. The court will refuse to grant an injunction to restrain the beneficiary from presenting his documents or the bank from paying against them unless the beneficiary[206] has been guilty of fraud or payment would be illegal under the relevant law.[207]

Particularly in the case of on-demand performance bonds or guarantees, there can sometimes be difficulties in determining whether these are intended to be abstract payment obligations or ordinary guarantees subject to the usual limitations. The typical on-demand bond requires the bank to pay the beneficiary on demand, either without any evidence of its customer's default on the underlying transaction or against a certificate of default by the beneficiary himself.[208] The question of whether it is necessary for a demand to be accompanied by a statement demonstrating the basis on which the demand is made (e.g. a breach of contract by the customer) has been held to depend on the construction of the contract itself,[209] although it was noted by the Court of Appeal in the same case that a construction requiring a demand to set out the breach is:

3–41

---

[205] On the autonomy principle, see generally A. Malik and D. Quest, *Jack: Documentary Credits*, 4th edn (Haywards Heath: Tottel Publishing, 2009), paras 1.34–1.36. For a valuable survey of the principle in the specific context of guarantees, see G. Affaki, *A User's Handbook to the Uniform Rules on Demand Guarantees* (France: ICC Publishing S.A., 2001). See also the discussion of the autonomy principle in *Goode on Commercial Law* (2016), paras 35.52 et seq., especially at 35.54 and 35.115–35.117 where it is argued that the Court of Appeal has carried the principle of autonomy too far and has elevated a principle designed for the protection of banks into one protecting the beneficiary who in good faith presents forged or fraudulent documents which appear to conform to the credit. The principle is not necessarily restricted to bonds issued by financial institutions: see *Marubeni Hong Kong and South China Ltd v Mongolia* [2005] 1 W.L.R. 2497 CA (Civ Div).

[206] i.e. the seller himself. The fact that some other party involved in the transaction has been guilty of fraud will not prevent the seller from collecting payment under the credit, provided that he has not been complicit in the fraud.

[207] As to the relevant law, see para.6–24 below.

[208] The form of demand must, of course, comply with the requirements of the performance bond itself. On the required extent of compliance, see *IE Contractors Ltd v Lloyds Bank Plc* [1990] 2 Lloyd's Rep. 496 CA (Civ Div). On the difficulties posed by this case in the context of the fraud exception, see P. Howcroft, "Performance Bonds—The Tide Turns against the Banks" (1990) 5(1) J.I.B.L. 17. If the bond states that it is payable "on your written demand in the event that the supplier fails to execute the contract in perfect performance", then it is probably safest to assume that a valid demand should include an explicit statement to that effect: see *Esal (Commodities) Ltd and Reltor Ltd v Oriental Credit Ltd and Wells Fargo Bank NA* [1985] 2 Lloyd's Rep. 546 CA (Civ Div). In *Sea-Cargo Skips AS v State Bank of India* [2013] 2 Lloyd's Rep. 477, it was held that a demand did not have to repeat the precise words of the refund guarantee under which it was made, but it had to be clear to the guarantor on the face of the documents that it was compliant; in *East Ayrshire Council v Zurich Insurance Plc* [2014] CSOH 102, by contrast, the Scottish Court of Session held that, where a certificate of default had failed to include one of the necessary requirements as agreed between the parties, the pursuer could not expect the defender to make payment in terms of a restoration bond.

[209] *IE Contractors* [1990] 2 Lloyd's Rep. 496 CA (Civ Div).

"A construction which one would wish to adopt, since it requires the beneficiary to state in plain terms that which he must, if honest, be prepared to assert—and may place him in peril of a charge of obtaining money by deception if it is untrue to his knowledge."[210]

It should be noted that the ICC Uniform Rules for Demand Guarantees, intended to reflect standard international practice in the use of demand guarantees, include a requirement that a demand must be supported by a written statement of breach indicating the nature of the breach, even if not required by the guarantee, unless this requirement is expressly excluded.[211]

3–42　However, it is not always clear what falls into the on-demand bond category and the approach taken by the courts in recent cases to determining whether a guarantee is an on-demand bond or guarantee is not necessarily consistent. Further, the division may not be a binary one; a recent Scottish case has indicated that there may be "hybrid" instruments with features of both.[212] To date, a distinction has been drawn between cases outside the banking context and cases concerning instruments issued by banks. In *Marubeni Hong Kong & South China Ltd v Mongolia*,[213] it was considered that, outside the banking context, there was a strong presumption against an instrument being interpreted as being on demand in the absence of appropriate language in the wording of the instrument to displace the presumption.[214] The *Marubeni* presumption has been subject to criticism on various grounds, including that there is no reason why performance bonds cannot be used in other contexts.[215] Moreover, it is unclear from subsequent cases what strength of wording is required to displace the presumption.[216] Generally, the courts will give effect to clear words indicating an on demand guarantee or performance bond, even if the instrument is not labelled as such. Thus, the Court of Appeal in *IIG Capital LLC v Van der Merwe*[217] found that the presumption was displaced due to the wording used in a director's guarantee that the third party was liable as principal debtor and the certificate of the amount payable by the third party would be conclusive in the absence of manifest error, even though the wording was commonly used in guarantees throughout the market. Similarly, in *Meritz Fire & Marine Insurance Co Ltd v Jan de Nul NV*,[218] the court looked at the substance of the instruments as a whole when finding that advance payment guarantees issued by an insurance company guaranteeing the repayment of payments made under shipbuilding contracts were performance bonds or demand guarantees (on which the insurance company was

---

[210] See fn.208 above.
[211] Article 15(a) of the ICC Uniform Rules for Demand Guarantees. The ICC Uniform Rules were first issued in 1992 (URDG 458) and substantially revised in 2010 (URDG 758). For a comprehensive treatment of URDG 758, see Georges Affaki and Roy Goode, *Guide to ICC Uniform Rules for Demand Guarantees* (URDG 758) (2011), ICC Publication No.702E.
[212] *Buchan Biogas Ltd v BSG Civil Engineering Ltd* [2020] CSOH 42.
[213] *Marubeni Hong Kong & South China Ltd v Mongolia* [2005] 1 W.L.R. 2497.
[214] *Marubeni* [2005] 1 W.L.R. 2497 at [30]–[31].
[215] See L. Gullifer and J. Payne, *Corporate Finance Law: Principles and Policy*, 2nd edn (London: Bloomsbury, 2015), p.243.
[216] See T. Evans, "Guarantees and Performance Bonds: Problems of Drafting and Interpretation" [2013] B.J.I.B. & F.L. 614, where it is argued that the presumption has been inconsistently applied.
[217] *IIG Capital LLC v Van der Merwe* [2008] 2 All E.R. (Comm) 1173, discussed in P. McGrath, "The Nature of Modern Guarantees: IIG v Van Der Merwes" [2009] *Corporate Rescue and Insolvency* 10.
[218] *Meritz Fire & Marine Insurance Co Ltd v Jan de Nul NV* [2011] 1 All E.R. (Comm) 1049.

liable without regard to the underlying contracts). By contrast, the presumption was not displaced in *Carey Value Added SL v Grupo Urvasco SA*,[219] where the court considered that a deed of guarantee and indemnity did not contain language appropriate to a demand bond imposing a primary liability on the guarantor and so dismissed an application for summary judgment. In *Carey*, *IIG Capital* was distinguished, and the court picked up on a number of factors indicating that the deed did not amount to an on demand bond; e.g. although obligations were expressly described as being "primary", the obligations of the guarantor were the same as or co-extensive with the obligations of the principal debtor and so "not indicative of the unqualified liability which arises under a demand bond"[220] and it was arguable that, if the contract was rescinded, there would be no liability under the guarantee,[221] As a result, the *Marubeni* presumption had not been rebutted. In *Vossloh AG v Alpha Trains (UK) Ltd*,[222] the presumption was not rebutted even though this seemed to be the intention of the parties. The claimant train company entered into an agreement with the defendant's subsidiary for the manufacture, operation and servicing of trains. The defendant company provided a guarantee in relation to its subsidiary's operations. The claimant later tried to recover over 7 million from the defendant on the grounds of defectiveness of some of the trains supplied. The issue arose as to whether the presumption that the contract was not a performance bond was rebutted. The court held that it was not, despite the inclusion of an on-demand payment clause, a waiver of defences clause and a conclusive evidence clause.

Where the presumption is displaced and it is accepted that the instrument in question imposes autonomous liabilities, the presumption will not apply to limit the extent of those liabilities and instead the correct approach is to "begin simply by considering the words the parties chose to use to record their agreement, free from any antecedent presumption …".[223]

Within the banking context, it appears that the opposite presumption applies, subject to certain conditions. This is set out in para.34.4 of *Paget's Law of Banking* (11th edn):

3–43

> "Where an instrument (i) relates to an underlying transaction between parties in different jurisdictions, (ii) is issued by a bank, (iii) contains an undertaking to pay 'on demand' (with or without the words 'first' and/or 'written') and (iv) does not contain clauses excluding or limiting the defences available to a guarantor, it will almost always be construed as a demand guarantee."

In *Wuhan Guoyu Logistics Group Co Ltd v Emporiki Bank of Greece SA*,[224] the Court of Appeal, after reviewing the authorities, overturned the first instance decision that the instrument in question was a guarantee and applied the *Paget* presumption to find that it was actually a performance bond. Although the *Paget*

---

[219] *Carey Value Added SL v Grupo Urvasco SA* [2011] 2 All E.R. (Comm) 140.
[220] *IIG Capital* [2008] 2 All E.R. (Comm) 1173 at [37].
[221] *IIG Capital* [2008] 2 All E.R. (Comm) 1173 at [42].
[222] *Vossloh AG v Alpha Trains (UK) Ltd* [2011] 2 All E.R. (Comm) 307.
[223] *Rubicon Vantage International Pte Ltd v Krisenergy Ltd* [2019] EWHC 2012 (Comm) at [18] (per Nicholas Vineall QC).
[224] *Wuhan Guoyu Logistics Group Co Ltd v Emporiki Bank of Greece SA* [2013] 1 All E.R. (Comm) 1191.

presumption is not intended to be conclusive and can be criticised on the grounds that the intention is not inferred from the words used by the parties,[225] it does appear, at least in the banking context, that it should be applied in determining whether an instrument is a performance bond or a guarantee. In *Bitumen Invest SA v Richmond Mercantile Limited FZC*,[226] a document labelled a "Deed of Guarantee" in the context of a transaction "in the nature of a financing transaction" was found to be an on demand guarantee. Uncertainty remains around the strength of the weight which should be given to the presumption and the evidence which will be required to displace it. It is clear that the labelling used by the parties is not determinative; the court should look instead at the substance and context.[227] However, it was held in *Caterpillar Motoren GmbH & Co KG v Mutual Benefits Assurance Co*[228] that, even when the four factors exist, it is necessary to example the background and the language of the instrument to see whether the reasonable man would consider the presumption to be rebutted.[229] Conversely, it has been held that non-compliance with the fourth *Paget* factor is not inconsistent with the existence of a performance bond.[230]

What defences, then, are available to a claim on an abstract payment obligation? There appear to be at least four, though only the first of these has so far been the subject of an extensive body of case law.

(1) Fraud of the beneficiary

3–44 Where the beneficiary has been guilty of fraud, either himself[231] or by his agent, the bank is entitled, and if it is aware of the fraud, obliged, to withhold payment.[232] But the fraud of a third party is irrelevant. So, on presentation of documents by a beneficiary who was unaware that the ship's loading broker had fraudulently misstated the date of shipment on the bill of lading, the bank was held liable to pay, the broker not being the beneficiary's agent.[233] In the case of fraud by the beneficiary or his agent, the bank must withhold payment where the evidence is clear but it is not obliged to investigate a mere suspicion.

In cases of suspected but unproven fraud, the bank has a choice: it can pay, relying on the absence of compelling evidence, or it can withhold payment in the hope that, by the time the case comes to court, it will have secured the necessary evidence. The latter step is risky on two counts. First, if the bank does not get the

---

[225] Evans, "Guarantees and Performance Bonds" [2013] B.J.I.B. & F.L. 614.
[226] *Bitumen Invest SA v Richmond Mercantile Limited FZC* [2016] EWHC 2957 (Comm).
[227] See *Spliethoff's Bevrachtingskantoor BV v Bank of China Ltd* [2015] EWHC 999 (Comm) at [84], where Carr J said in relation to the relevant obligations, "[l]abelling plays no part in *"Paget's presumption*. I prefer to look at the substance and international and commercial context".
[228] *Caterpillar Motoren GmbH & Co KG v Mutual Benefits Assurance Co* [2016] 2 All E.R. (Comm) 322.
[229] *Caterpillar Motoren* [2016] 2 All E.R. (Comm) 322 at [13] and [15].
[230] *Caterpillar Motoren* [2016] 2 All E.R. (Comm) 322 at [21]; *Spliethoff's Bevrachtingskantoor BV* at [81].
[231] See *United City Merchants (Investments) Ltd v Royal Bank of Canada (The American Accord)* [1983] 1 A.C. 168 HL.
[232] *Sztejn v Henry Schroder Banking Corp* 31 N.Y.S.2d 631 (1941); *Discount Records Ltd v Barclays Bank Ltd* [1975] 1 W.L.R. 315 Ch D; *The American Accord* [1983] 1 A.C. 168 HL.
[233] *The American Accord* [1983] 1 A.C. 168 HL.

evidence it needs, it will be held in breach of duty both to the beneficiary and to its customer. Secondly, the smooth running of the documentary credit system depends on the assurance of payment by the relevant bank, and the system would be undermined if banks began to acquire the reputation for being too ready to withhold payment on mere suspicion.

So what standard of knowledge would entitle the bank to withhold payment? The courts have held that payment cannot be withheld on the basis of mere allegations of fraud or dishonesty without production of real evidence.[234] Prior to the Privy Council decision in *Alternative Power Solution Ltd v Central Electricity Board*,[235] it had seemed that the applicant for a credit who wished to prevent the bank from paying out must show that he had a real prospect of being able to prove that the beneficiary did not honestly believe that it had the right to call the bond and that the issuing bank was aware of that fact.[236] However, the Privy Council's decision indicates that the standard is higher than this for cases involving injunctive relief. It rejected the trial judge's conclusion that a "a serious prima facie arguable case that there might be an attempt to defraud" was sufficient for an injunction, instead finding that an interlocutory injunction to prevent payment under a letter of credit should only be granted if "it is seriously arguable that, on the material available, 'the only realistic inference is that [the beneficiary] could not honestly have believed in the validity of its demands' ... and the bank was aware of this fact"[237] It considered that "seriously arguable" was intended to be "a significantly more stringent test than good arguable case, let alone serious issue to be tried".[238] This approach has been applied subsequently in a first instance case,[239] although it appears that the lower standard still applies to a bank resisting a claim for summary judgment under CPR 24 for failure to pay.[240]

It appears therefore that only "established fraud" will allow payment to be withheld.[241] Most cases where an injunction to prevent the bank paying is sought involve the beneficiary presenting a claim which it knows to be invalid and

---

[234] *Turkiye IS Bankasi AS v Bank of China* [1996] 2 Lloyd's Rep. 611 QBD (Comm); *Enka Insaat Ve Sanayi AS v Banca Popolare dell'Alto Adige SpA* [2009] C.I.L.L. 2777; *AES-3C Maritza East 1 E00D v Credit Agricole Corporate and Investment Bank* [2011] B.L.R. 249.
[235] *Alternative Power Solution Ltd v Central Electricity Board* [2014] UKPC 31.
[236] For this formulation of the fraud exception, see *Banque Saudi Fransi v Lear Siegler Services Inc* [2007] 1 All E.R. (Comm) 67.
[237] *Alternative Power Solution Ltd v Central Electricity Board* [2015] 1 W.L.R. 697 at [59], referring to Ackner LJ's formulation of the standard in *United Trading Corp SA v Allied Arab Bank Ltd* [1985] 2 Lloyd's Rep. 554 at 561.
[238] *Alternative Power Solution Ltd* [2015] 1 W.L.R. 697 at [59]. The Privy Council endorsed Mance LJ's statement in *Solo Industries UK Ltd v Canara Bank* [2001] 1 W.L.R. 1800 at [32] that "[t]he defence ... of established fraud known to the bank, is, by its nature, one which, if it is good at all, must be capable of being established with clarity at the interlocutory stage".
[239] In *Tetronics (International) Ltd v HSBC Bank Plc* [2018] EWHC 201 (TCC), it was accepted as representing the applicable law at [23]–[24].
[240] In *National Infrastructure Development Company Ltd v Banco Santander S.A.* [2017] EWCA Civ 27, the Court of Appeal considered that the trial judge had set the bar too high by apparently applying the "seriously arguable" standard in the *Alternative Power* case and that the correct test was the "real prospect" test in CPR 24 (approving Teare J's judgment in *Enka Insaat ve Sanayi AS v Banco Popolare dell'Alto Adige SpA* [2009] EWHC 2410 (Comm) at [24]–[250]).
[241] This terminology was used in *Solo Industries UK Ltd v Canara Bank* [2001] 1 W.L.R. 1800 at [31].

representing it to the bank as a valid claim.[242] It is not sufficient that there is a dispute under the contract since the abstract payment obligation is separate from the contract. So, in *Hamzeh Malas & Sons v British Imex Industries Ltd*,[243] where reinforced steel rods were to be supplied in two instalments and paid for under two letters of credit, the buyer's application to restrain presentation of documents under the second letter of credit on the ground that the seller had repudiated the contract by supplying rods not of the contract quality in the first instalment was dismissed. The banker's payment obligation was absolute and did not in any way turn on whether the buyer was liable to the seller for the price.

A more extreme example is offered by the decision in *Discount Records*[244]:

> The plaintiff contracted to purchase a number of discs and cassettes, payment to be made under an irrevocable credit. On arrival of the consignment the plaintiff discovered that some crates were empty, some were filled with rubbish or packing and many others were short on quantity or filled with goods different from those ordered. The plaintiff sought an injunction to restrain the bank from paying because of the seller's fraud The court held that, whilst established fraud was an exception to the normal rule that the payment obligation under a letter of credit is absolute, the mere allegation of fraud was not sufficient.

3–45 At first sight, it seems surprising that the evidence adduced in *Discount Records* was not considered strong enough to make out a convincing case of fraud, sufficient at least for the grant of an interlocutory injunction. There is, however, one crucial point which has tactical implications for the litigation lawyer. The action was brought against the bank alone; the allegedly fraudulent seller was not made a party to the proceedings. The defendant bank, understandably enough, put in no evidence on the fraud issue, since the facts were not within their knowledge. The seller had no opportunity to do so as it was not a party to the action. In these circumstances, the court was obviously unable to regard the evidence as going beyond an unproven allegation of fraud. The moral for the claimant's lawyers in such cases is obvious: make the allegedly fraudulent beneficiary a party to the proceedings wherever possible. Similar principles as for letters of credit apply to the unconditional, or on-demand, performance bond[245] or guarantee.[246] In the absence of fraud,[247] the court will not restrain payment by the bank even where

---

[242] Parker LJ refers to this as "common law fraud" in *GKN Contractors v Lloyds Bank Plc* 1986 WL 40833.

[243] *Hamzeh Malas & Sons v British Imex Industries Ltd* [1958] 2 Q.B. 127 CA.

[244] *Discount Records* [1975] 1 W.L.R. 315.

[245] For an example, see the Australian decision in *Olex Focas Pty Ltd v Skodaexport Co Ltd* [1996] 70 AJLR 983.

[246] Although the expression "guarantee" is used, a performance bond or demand guarantee is not a secondary or ancillary obligation. The applicant creates an autonomous obligation to pay the specified amount against demand or the production of evidential documents stipulated in the performance guarantee itself see the third and fourth limb of *Paget*'s presumption above. See also recent reiterations of the primary nature of the obligation in *Caterpillar Motoren* [2016] 2 All E.R. (Comm) 322 at [25]–[26]; *Spliethoff* [2016] 1 All E.R. (Comm) 1034 at [69]. In *WS Tankship II BV v Kwangju Bank Ltd* [2012] C.I.L.L. 3155, it was considered that the rules as to discharge of a surety on the basis of material variation, forbearance or non-disclosure had no application to demand guarantees.

[247] In the case of a *standby* letter of credit, it appears that the fraud exception may apply if the applicant—to the knowledge of the beneficiary—procured the issue of the credit for an unlawful purpose. On this subject, see *Mahonia Ltd v JP Morgan Chase Bank (No.1)* [2003] 2 Lloyd's Rep. 911. Courts in other Commonwealth jurisdictions have held that a call under a documentary credit

there is clear evidence that its customer is not in default and that the call on the bond is unreasonable.²⁴⁸ It has been recognised that on-demand performance bonds are on the same footing as letters of credit as regards the burden of proof of fraud which the bank must discharge²⁴⁹; following *Alternative Power*, this would appear to be the more stringent standard that it is seriously arguable that the only realistic inference is that fraud of which the bank is aware, at least where injunctive relief is concerned although a lower standard applies for summary judgment.²⁵⁰

(2) Innocent misrepresentation

If the opening or confirmation of the credit was obtained by innocent misrepresentation, then on general principles of contract law the bank can rescind the contract and decline payment. In practice, this is unlikely to occur. A court would be most unlikely to accept that a credit should be rescinded in this type of case unless the beneficiary himself had been responsible for the misrepresentation. To hold the credit to be voidable on the basis of a misrepresentation made by the applicant would be contrary to principle and would be unjust to the beneficiary, who may have changed his position in reliance on the document.

3–46

(3) Illegality

Where payment would be illegal under the relevant law, the bank can and must refuse to pay. What the relevant law is will be discussed later.²⁵¹ There will,

3–47

---

may be restrained if the demand would be unconscionable: in the case of Australia, *Olex Focas* (1996) 70 ALJR 983 and, in the case of Singapore, see *Kvaerner Singapore Pte Ltd v UDL Shipbuilding (Singapore) Pte Ltd* [1993] 3 S.L.R. 350; and *Bocotra Construction Pte Ltd v AG (No.2)* [1995] 2 S.L.R. 733 (although the Singapore Court of Appeal has recently recognized the parties' contractual right to exclude unconscionability as a ground for non-payment, which arguably largely nullifies the unconscionability exception; *CKR Contract Services Pte v Asplenium Land Pte Ltd* [2015] 3 SLR 1041 (CA), discussed in Garth C Wooler, "The New 'Asplenium' Clause—Unconscionability Unwound?" (2016) Sing JLS 169). These decisions need to be treated with care since they detract from the autonomy principle.

²⁴⁸ *Edward Owen Engineering Ltd v Barclays Bank International Ltd* [1978] Q.B. 159 CA (Civ Div); *RD Harbottle (Mercantile) Ltd v National Westminster Bank Ltd* [1978] Q.B. 146 QBD. The decision in *Edward Owen* has been cited and followed on numerous occasions: see, for example, *Bolivinter Oil SA v Chase Manhattan Bank NA* [1984] 1 W.L.R. 392 CA (Civ Div); *Deutsche Ruckversicherung AG v Walbrook Insurance Co Ltd* [1995] 1 W.L.R. 1017 QBD (Comm) affirmed [1996] 1 W.L.R. 1152 CA (Civ Div). Given the need to demonstrate that fraud is the only realistic inference from the circumstances (see the discussion of *Alternative Power Solutions* above), the existence of a mere contractual dispute as to the beneficiary's entitlement to draw on the bond will not justify an injunction: see *TTI Team Telecom International Ltd v Hutchison 3G UK Ltd* [2003] 1 All E.R. (Comm) 914; *Ouais Group Engineering and Contracting v Saipem SpA* [2013] EWHC 990 (Comm). Likewise, the mere fact that a document presented in order to obtain payment under the credit had been signed without authority does not exonerate the bank from payment under the credit, unless the circumstances are known to the bank and provide clear evidence of fraud: *Montrod Ltd v Grundkotter Fleischvertriebs GmbH* [2002] 1 W.L.R. 1975 CA (Civ Div).

²⁴⁹ *Turkiye IS Bankasi AS v Bank of China* [1998] 1 Lloyd's Rep. 250 CA (Civ Div); *Enka Insaat* [2009] C.I.L.L. 2777.

²⁵⁰ See further, *Law of Bank Payments* (2018), paras 7-105, 7-108 to 7-112.

²⁵¹ See para.6–24 below.

however, be instances in which enforcement will be manifestly contrary to the public policy of the forum, and payment will not be enforced in any event.[252]

(4) Set-off

3–48   Whilst the bank is not entitled to plead a set-off available to its customer against the beneficiary, if the bank itself has a cross-claim against the beneficiary which is appropriate for set-off,[253] there seems no reason why it cannot exercise the set-off even against a claim on a documentary credit.[254] However, the right of set-off would apply only where the paying bank was involved as principal, incurring a commitment by virtue of issuing or confirming the credit. A correspondent bank acting merely as advising bank, and therefore paying as agent for the issuing bank, could not rely on its own cross-claim to withhold payment.[255] The position appears to be essentially the same for a guarantor. The Supreme Court of Victoria has held that a guarantor has no defence to a claim for payment under his guarantee merely because the primary debtor has a cross-claim in damages against the beneficiary of the guarantee under the terms of the underlying commercial contract.[256] Standard forms of guarantee—and indeed many other forms of financial documents—will contain express provisions requiring payment to be made without deduction on account of any set-off or counterclaim.[257] However, there may come a point at which the making of a demand under the guarantee is fraudulent, e.g. where the creditor has manifestly failed to perform his obligations and has thus not earned the payment.

Breach of an underlying restriction in the contract?

3–49   The autonomy principle has always been regarded as central to letters of credit and on-demand bonds and guarantees. However, it has been suggested that a recent line of cases has brought the scope of the autonomy principle into question by indicating that there may be a defence to payment where there is a restriction in the underlying contact which prevents the credit or performance bond from

---

[252] See, for example, *Mahonia* [2003] 2 Lloyd's Rep. 911, and *Shanning International Ltd (In Liquidation) v Lloyds TSB Bank Plc (formerly Lloyds Bank Plc)* [2001] 1 W.L.R. 1462, where payment would have contravened sanctions legislation.
[253] See *Goode and Gullifer on Legal Problems of Credit and Security* (2018), Ch.7.
[254] See *Hong Kong and Shanghai Banking Corp v Kloeckner & Co AG* [1990] 2 Q.B. 514 QBD (Comm) and *Safa Ltd v Banque du Caire* [2000] 2 All E.R. (Comm) 567 CA (Civ Div).
[255] See C. Proctor, *International Payment Obligations—A Legal Perspective* (London: Butterworths, 1997), pp.144–146.
[256] In *Indrisie v General Credit* [1985] V.R. 251, applying the decision in *British Anzani (Felixstone) Ltd v International Marine Management (UK) Ltd* [1980] Q.B. 137 QBD.
[257] Provisions of this kind were given effect in accordance with their terms in *Continental Illinois National Bank & Trust Co of Chicago v Papanicolaou* [1986] 2 Lloyd's Rep. 441 CA (Civ Div), and see *IIG Capital* [2008] 2 All E.R. (Comm) 1173 at [11] where they were contained in one party's standard terms of business. Such clauses may be subject to challenge on the basis of the "reasonableness" test in s.13 of the Unfair Contract Terms Act 1977: see *Stewart Gill Ltd v Horatio Myer and Co Ltd* [1992] Q.B. 600 CA (Civ Div), but were been found to be reasonable in *FG Wilson (Engineering) Ltd v John Holt & Company (Liverpool) Limited* [2012] EWHC 2477 (Comm) (reversed by the Court of Appeal on other grounds [2013] EWCA Civ 1232).

being called upon.²⁵⁸ In *Sirius International Insurance Co (Publ) v FAI General Insurance Ltd*, the Court of Appeal accepted that calls under on-demand securities could be restrained where there was a breach of an express restriction in the underlying contract and such a restriction had been "positively established".²⁵⁹ The "positively established" requirement was applied by Ramsay J in *Permasteelisa Japan KK v Bouyguesstroi*²⁶⁰ in relation to a call on a bond, where it was not considered to cover cases where there was only a "serious, arguable case" that it was positively established that the party was not entitled to draw down.²⁶¹ The requirement appeared to have been diluted in *Simon Carves Ltd v Ensus UK Ltd*,²⁶² where Akenhead J required only a "strong case" that the bond in question was not valid. In this case, the relevant question was the extent to which a party might be prevented from seeking payment under an on-demand bond by the terms of the contract in respect of which the bond was provided as security. Akenhead J considered that while, in the absence of fraud, a bank would not be prevented from paying out under an on-demand bond provided there had been compliance with the bond conditions, in circumstances where the contract clearly and expressly prevented the beneficiary from making a demand on the bond, the court could issue an injunction preventing it from doing so. Akenhead J viewed this as constituting a second exception to the autonomy principle. The "strong case" approach in *Simon Carves* was applied in *Doosan Babcock Ltd v Comercializadora De Equipos Y Materiales Mabe Lda (formerly Mabe Chile Lda)*,²⁶³ where it was accepted that this constituted an extension to the law.²⁶⁴ It was further suggested in *Doosan Babcock* that a lesser standard of a "realistic prospect of success" might apply to situations in which a call under on-demand security could be said to fall under the principle that no party should benefit from its own wrong.²⁶⁵

However, subsequent cases have retreated from this position. In *MW High Tech Projects UK Ltd v Biffa Waste Services Ltd*,²⁶⁶ Stuart-Smith J rejected the "strong case" approach and adopted the "positively established" test established by the Court of Appeal in the *Sirius* case and applied by Ramsay J in the *Permasteelisa* case, on the grounds that this was "in accordance with the substance of the decisions of higher authority".²⁶⁷ He noted that "[i]t seems to me, both on principle and authority, that the only established exceptions to the

---

²⁵⁸ See *Chitty* (2018), paras 34–508 to 34–509 on restrictions on the beneficiary's right to call or payment.
²⁵⁹ *Sirius International Insurance Co (Publ) v FAI General Insurance Ltd* [2003] 1 W.L.R. 2214 at [30]. Its decision was subsequently reversed by the House of Lords but on another ground.
²⁶⁰ *Permasteelisa Japan KK v Bouyguesstroi* [2007] EWHC 3508 (QB).
²⁶¹ *Permasteelisa Japan KK* [2007] EWHC 3508 (QB) at [51].
²⁶² *Simon Carves Ltd v Ensus UK Ltd* [2011] B.L.R. 340.
²⁶³ *Doosan Babcock Ltd v Comercializadora De Equipos Y Materiales Mabe Lda (formerly Mabe Chile Lda)* [2014] 1 Lloyd's Rep. 464. It was also followed in *Ouais Group Engineering and Contracting v Saipem SpA* [2013] EWHC 990 (Comm).
²⁶⁴ *Doosan Babcock* [2014] 1 Lloyd's Rep. 464 at [34].
²⁶⁵ *Doosan Babcock* [2014] 1 Lloyd's Rep. 464 at [40].
²⁶⁶ *MW High Tech Projects UK Ltd v Biffa Waste Services Ltd* [2015] 1 C.L.C. 449, discussed in D. Cashmore, "On Demand Bonds—Pay Now, Argue Later" (2015) 26(5) Cons. Law 17 and P. Cassidy and J. Otoo, "Interaction between On-demand Bonds and the Underlying Contract Revisited by the English High Court" [2015] F. & C.L. 5.
²⁶⁷ *MW High Tech* [2015] 1 C.L.C. 449 at [34].

rule that the court will not intervene should be where there is a seriously arguable case of fraud, or it has been clearly established that the beneficiary is precluded from making a call by the terms of the contract".[268] Although narrowing the scope of the *Sirius* exception, he did therefore accept its existence.

The existence of a defence to payment based on restrictions in the underlying contract, however narrow, has been the subject of much comment as to its effect on the autonomy principle.[269] However, it should be noted that that these cases concerned injunctions against the beneficiary to prevent them from making demands or to compel them to withdraw demands and that fraud remains the only established basis upon which a party can obtain an injunction restricting a *bank* from paying pursuant to a letter of credit or performance bond.[270] This was reiterated in *Wuhan Guoyo Logistics Group Co Ltd v Emporiki Bank of Greece SA*, where the Court of Appeal noted that[271]:

> "It is critical to the efficacy of these financial arrangements that as between beneficiary and bank the position crystallises as at presentation of documents or demand as the case may be, and that it is only in the case of fraudulent presentation of demand by the beneficiary that the bank can resist payment against an apparently conforming presentation or demand."

The Privy Council in *Mauri Garments Trading and Marketing Ltd v Mauritius Commercial Bank Ltd*[272] reaffirmed the independence of obligations under a letter of indemnity. The claimant had entered into a contract to buy shirts from a company, which required a bank guarantee to be issued. A letter of credit was issued by a third-party bank, Banque S.G. Warburg, in favour of the defendant bank. The defendant bank, having put the company into receivership, made a demand under the letter of indemnity for more than was actually due under the contract from the claimant to the company. The Privy Council upheld the trial judge's dismissal of the claimant's claim on the basis that the obligation of the issuing bank to pay under the letter of indemnity was independent from the underlying sale and purchase contract between the buyer and seller and that any adjustment that required to be made regarding the purchase price of the raw materials was a matter between the buyer and seller. A separate argument that the seller had a tort claim against the defendant bank for claiming more than it knew to be due from the seller to the buyer was dismissed by the Privy Council. Lord Mance considered that[273]:

---

[268] *MW High Tech* [2015] 1 C.L.C. 449 at [34].

[269] See, for instance, D. Metzger, T. Steadman and E. Brotherton, "On-demand Bonds: Is the Lifeblood of International Commerce Still Flowing Freely?" [2014–15] F. & C.L. 4; J. Chuah, "Documentary credit—Derogation from Principle of Autonomy on the Basis that the Terms of Draw-down have not been Met" [2003] F. & C.L. 5; C. Chatterjee and A. Lefcovitch, "The Principle of Autonomy of Letters of Credit is Sacrosanct in Nature" (2003) 5(1) J.I.B.R. 72; C. Hare, "Not so Black and White: The Limits of the Autonomy Principle" (2004) 63(2) C.L.J. 288; N. Enonchong, "The Problem of Abusive Calls on Demand Guarantees" (2007) 1 L.M.C.L.Q. 83.

[270] This view is also taken in G.M. Andrews and R. Millett, *Law of Guarantees*, 7th edn (London: Sweet & Maxwell, 2015), para.16–001.

[271] *Wuhan Guoyo Logistics Group Co Ltd v Emporiki Bank of Greece SA* [2014] 1 All E.R. (Comm) 870 at [22] per Tomlinson LJ. See also *Tetronics (International) Ltd v HSBC Bank Plc* [2018] EWHC 201 (TCC).

[272] *Mauri Garments Trading and Marketing Ltd v Mauritius Commercial Bank Ltd* [2015] UKPC 14.

[273] *Mauri Garments* [2015] UKPC 14 at [14].

"...[w]here parties have... entered into carefully structured contractual arrangements, involving two separate and autonomous contracts each between different parties to the other, it is impossible for the law to recognise tortious duties outside and cutting across the terms and performance of these contracts".[274]

The suggestion, therefore, that the availability of an injunction against the beneficiary somehow undermines the autonomy of a demand guarantee is misconceived. All the autonomy principle involves is that *the bank* is not concerned with the relationship between the customer and the beneficiary. The latter relationship itself does not attract the autonomy principle. The grant of relief in such cases is based on the long-established principle that the court can grant a quia timet injunction to restrain a threatened breach of contract.

Should English law accept a wider range of defences?

There has been some movement in English law towards accepting a wider range of defences than at present.[275] In *TTI Team Telecom International Ltd v Hutchison 3G UK Ltd*,[276] which concerned a performance bond in a construction contract, the court held that the bank would be entitled not to pay if there was a "breach of faith" by the beneficiary established by clear evidence. However, as has been pointed out, it is unclear whether "breach of faith" as elaborated in the *TTI Team Telecom* case adds much to the already established defences of fraud and breach of a restriction in the underlying contract.[277]

In other jurisdictions, the courts have been willing to go much further. For example, the Singapore courts have long accepted "unconscionability" as a general ground for granting an injunction including against the issuing or paying bank,[278] although the scope of this ground is arguably much reduced by the Singapore Court of Appeal's decision in *CKR Contract Services Pte Ltd v Asplenium Land Pte Ltd* that the parties can agree terms limiting the circumstances in which an injunction may be sought.[279] In relation to what constitutes unconscionability, the Singapore Court of Appeal indicated that it did not think it was possible to define it other than to give very broad indications.[280] However, it referred to the following passage in *Raymond Construction Pte Ltd v Low Yang Tong*[281]:

3–50

---

[274] *Mauri Garments* [2015] UKPC 14 at [14].
[275] See Andrews and Millett, *Law of Guarantees* (2011), para.16–032 and the cases cited therein.
[276] *TTI Team* [2003] 1 All E.R. (Comm) 914.
[277] See discussion of this point in *Law of Bank Payments* (2018), para.7–101.
[278] *GHL Pte Ltd v Unitrack Building Construction Pte Ltd* [1999] 3 S.L.R. 44; *Dauphin Offshore Engineering & Trading Pte Ltd v The Private Office of HRH Sheikh Sultan bin Khalifa bin Zayed Al Nahyan* [2000] 1 S.L.R. 117; affirmed in *JBE Properties Pte Ltd v Gammon Pte Ltd* [2011] 2 S.L.R. 47. In *GHL*, the court considered (at [16]) the decision in *Bocotra Construction Pte Ltd v AG* [1995] 2 S.L.R. 262 that "whether there is fraud or unconscionability is the sole consideration in applications for injunctions restraining payment or calls on bonds to be granted" to be a "conscious departure" from the English position. Knowles J acknowledged in *National Infrastructure Development Co Ltd* [2016] EWHC 2990 (Comm) that "the position under Singapore law is, it appears different" at [27].
[279] *CKR Contract Services Pte Ltd v Asplenium Land Pte Ltd* [2015] SGCA 24.
[280] *Dauphin* [2000] 1 S.L.R. 117.
[281] *Raymond Construction Pte Ltd v Low Yang Tong* [1996] SGHC 136 at [5].

"[T]he concept of unconscionability ... involves unfairness, as distinct from dishonesty or fraud, or conduct of a kind so reprehensible or lacking in good faith that a court of conscience would either restrain the party or refuse to assist the party. Mere breaches of contract by the party in question... would not by themselves be unconscionable."

In Australia, the courts have also been willing to issue injunctions against payment on a wider range of grounds, such as that the making of the demand by the beneficiary was inconsistent with the provision of the Trade Practices Act 1974.[282] Australian courts have also adopted the concept of unconscionability as a separate ground for restraining the enforcement of on-demand guarantees in reliance on the Australian Consumer Law (ACL).[283] It is unlikely that English law will proceed down this route any time soon. Indeed, in *National Infrastructure Development Co Ltd v Banco Santander SA*,[284] Knowles J refused to develop the law to recognise an exception for unconscionable conduct in relation to standby letters of credit.[285]

3–51 Separately, arguments have been made for a nullity defence where the underlying documents are forged or the underlying transaction void for some reason,[286] which it was held is not part of English law in *Montrod Ltd v Grundkotter Fleischvertriebs GmbH*.[287] This question was left open by the House of Lord's decision in *United City Merchants (Investments) Ltd v Royal Bank of Canada (The American Accord)*,[288] where the House of Lords held that a bank was required to accept and pay against a bill of lading even though there was a false statement in the bill of lading. The case concerned a fraudulent backdating of the date of shipment; however, the fraud was not on the part of the beneficiary hence the fraud exception did not apply. In that case, however, the House of Lords did not consider that the bill of lading in that case was a nullity. Lord Diplock's view was that[289]:

---

[282] See *Olex Focus Pty Ltd v Skodaexport Co Ltd* [1996] 70 ALJR 983; *Boral Framework and Scaffolding Pty Ltd v Action Makers Ltd* [2003] NSWSC 713, discussed by W.M. Dixon, "As Good as Cash? The Diminution of the Autonomy Principle" (2004) 32(6) *Australian Business Law Review* 391–406; *Clough Engineering Ltd v Oil and Natural Gas Corporation Ltd (No. 2)* (2008) FCAFC 136.

[283] Now Sch.2 to the Competition and Consumer Act 2010. The ACL states that "[a] person must not, in trade or commerce, engage in conduct that is unconscionable, within the meaning of the unwritten law, from time to time". See the recent cases of *Clough Engineering Ltd v Oil and Natural Gas Corp Ltd* (2008) 249 ALR 458 (the court examined whether the beneficiary's demand on the bank guarantee was "unconscionable", but concluded that there was no unconscionable conduct) and *Board Solutions Australia Pty Ltd v Westpac Banking Corp* [2009] VSC 474 (the Supreme Court of Victoria reiterated that "unconscionable" conduct on the part of a beneficiary is a ground upon which a call on a demand guarantee can be restrained in Australia).

[284] *National Infrastructure Development Co Ltd v Banco Santander SA* [2016] EWHC 2990 (Comm) (aff'd [2017] EWCA Civ 27).

[285] *National Infrastructure Development Co Ltd* [2016] EWHC 2990 (Comm) at [26]–[27].

[286] Since the fraud exception would not apply if this was unknown to the beneficiary or the beneficiary had not acted fraudulently for some other reason. See K. Donnelly, "Nothing for Nothing: A Nullity Exception in Letters of Credit?" [2008] J.B.L. 316.

[287] *Montrod Ltd v Grundkotter Fleischvertriebs GmbH* [2002] 1 W.L.R. 1975.

[288] *The American Accord* [1983] 1 A.C. 168 HL.

[289] *The American Accord* [1983] 1 A.C. 168 HL at 188.

> "[T]he bill of lading with the wrong date of loading placed on it by the carrier's agent was far from being a nullity. It was a valid transferable receipt for the goods giving the holder a right to claim them at their destination... and was evidence of the terms of the contract under which they were being carried."

The case is therefore authority for the proposition that, where a document appears on its face to be in accordance with the terms and conditions of the instrument, the bank is required to make payment even if it knows that one of the documents is false or has been made fraudulently. Although the outcome of *The American Accord* can be justified on the basis that the bill of lading in question was genuine, but simply contained false information, Lord Diplock's reasoning can be questioned on the grounds that a number of the propositions he made are untenable.[290] To discuss one in particular, the proposition that the bank may not be entitled to withhold payment even if the documents presented are forged conflates the principles that the documents must constitute a complying presentation and that fraud is only a defence if on the part of the beneficiary or his agent. Although a bank may have a defence if it pays against forged documents which appear on their face to constitute a complying presentation, this is not the same as saying that the beneficiary has a right to payment against forged documents. On a common sense level, forged documents cannot rationally be treated as constituting a complying presentation.

Lord Diplock's approach in *The American Accord* was subsequently applied in the Court of Appeal's decision in *Montrod* that the nullity of documents was not an independent ground for a bank to refuse payment. The court held that a beneficiary who tendered documents in good faith was entitled to payment even if the documents were fraudulent or devoid of commercial value. The Court of Appeal reached its decision on the basis that a general nullity defence would make "undesirable inroads into the principle of autonomy and negotiability universally recognised in relation to letter of credit transactions".[291] The decision is unfortunate, as it means that a bank could be in the position of having to pay against documents which it is aware are not genuine and have no commercial value. This approach has not been universally adopted; for instance, a nullity exception has been recognised by the courts in Singapore in respect of forged documents.[292]

3. REMEDIES FOR NON-PAYMENT

The creditor's remedies where the debtor defaults in payment may be one of two kinds: those given by the express terms of the contract and those conferred by law.

3–52

---

[290] See further, *Goode and McKendrick on Commercial Law* (2020), pp.1104–1107.
[291] *The American Accord* [1983] 1 A.C. 168 HL at [58].
[292] *Standard Chartered Bank v Beam Technology (MFG) Pte Ltd* [2002] 2 S.L.R. 155. On this topic, see Dora Neo, "A Nullity Exception in Letter of Credit Transactions?" (2014) *Singapore Journal of Legal Studies* 46.

Express contractual provisions

3–53 In any sizeable transaction, the well-drawn contract will make detailed provision for remedies on default. Among the many forms of contractual remedy to be found in agreements, the following deserve brief mention.

(1) Withholding of performance

3–54 The creditor may stipulate that some or all of his own obligations are to be dependent on payment or performance by the debtor. Provisions of this sort which make a contractual right to payment conditional upon performance are sometimes referred to as "flawed asset" provisions.[293]

The insolvency of Lehman Brothers spawned litigation on the validity of such provisions (as well as many other issues). Lehman was party to a large number of interest rate swap contracts executed on the standard form documentation issued by ISDA.[294] Under such transactions, one party agrees to pay to the other on stipulated dates a floating rate of interest by reference to LIBOR,[295] whilst the other party pays interest at a pre-agreed fixed rate.[296] The ISDA documentation contains a series of default clauses that allow the non-defaulting party to terminate the transaction. In addition, s.2(a)(iii) of the ISDA Master Agreement provides that the payment obligations of each party are subject to the condition precedent that no "Event of Default or Potential Event of Default with respect to the other party has occurred and is continuing...". In *Lomas v JFB Firth Rixson Inc*, a case brought by the administrators of Lehman, the Court of Appeal held that the clause merely had suspensory effect,[297] and that the amounts unpaid by the non-defaulting party could all become payable at a later date if the defaulting party managed to cure the default.[298] Payment at that time would be due even if the cure only occurred after the scheduled expiry of the transaction.[299] Of course, where, as in the *Lomas* case, the default was caused by insolvency, it is very unlikely that the defaulting counterparty will ever be able to remedy that situation. The result would be that the suspensory provision would be likely to continue on a permanent basis.

---

[293] See H. Beale, M. Bridge, L. Gullifer and E. Lomnicka, *The Law of Security and Title-Based Financing*, 3rd edn (Oxford: Oxford University Press, 2018), para.8.88; *Goode and Gullifer on Legal Problems of Credit and Security* (2018), para.7–21 (which deals with the relationship between netting and the "flawed asset" provision in s.2(a)(iii) of the ISDA Master Agreement); also L. Gullifer, "Flawed Assets" in G. Virgo and S. Worthington (eds), *Commercial Remedies: Resolving Controversies* (Cambridge: CUP, 2017). See also para.2–13 above.
[294] See para.2–13 above.
[295] Now being phased out; see paras 4–45 to 4–47.
[296] In practice, a net payment would be made by one party.
[297] *Lomas v JFB Firth Rixson Inc* [2012] 2 All E.R. (Comm) 1076 at [30].
[298] The court was principally concerned with the 1992 ISDA Master Agreement; it is possible that a different approach could be taken in relation to s.2(a)(iii) of the 2002 ISDA Master Agreement. Also, note that the suspensory effect of s.2(a)(iii) does not apply to accrued obligations; *Mercuria Energy Trading PTE Ltd v Citibank* NA [2015] EWHC 1481 (Comm), applying *Lomas* [2012] 2 All E.R. (Comm) 1076.
[299] To this extent, the decision overrules the earlier judgment in cl.2(a)(iii) in *Marine Trade SA v Pioneer Freight Futures Co Ltd BVI* [2010] Lloyd's Rep. 631, which decided that the defaulting creditor simply lost the right to payment altogether if he was in default when the payment fell due.

The fact that, in many cases, it might not be possible for the defaulting party ever to cure the default has raised questions as to whether a non-defaulting party could rely on it indefinitely to suspend its obligation to make payments and deliveries without closing out its transactions when it was "out of the money", i.e. owed money to the defaulting party. In *Enron Australia Finance Pty Ltd v TXU Electricity Ltd*,[300] the New South Wales Supreme Court held that the non-defaulting party could not be forced to close out by designating an early termination date under the agreement.[301] This meant that s.2(a)(iii) essentially operated as a "walkaway clause" which effectively removed the defaulting party's right to payment. The Court of Appeal also took this position in *Lomas*, declining to imply a term that the non-defaulting party's obligations were suspended only for a reasonable time to enable that party to decide whether to terminate or to continue to perform its payment obligations.[302] The contract therefore continues in full force and effect. However, if the non-defaulting party later commits a default, the other party will then be able to serve notice and close out regardless of its own continuing default.[303]

As a related matter, it must be considered whether "dependent performance" provisions of this kind infringe the "anti-deprivation" rule in insolvency, which vitiates any arrangement by a company to forego any of its assets in the event of its own liquidation. This rule is intended to support the principle that the assets of an insolvent company should be distributed on a pari passu basis to all of its creditors. In *Belmont Park Investments Pty Ltd v BNY Corporate Trustee Services Ltd*,[304] the Supreme Court held that s.2(a)(iii) was a reasonable response to the risks posed by counterparty insolvency and, hence, did not infringe the principles just described.[305] A different approach has been taken in relation to s.2(a)(iii) in the US. In *Lehman Brothers Holdings Inc v Metavante*,[306] Peck J considered that the non-defaulting party was not entitled to rely on s.2(a)(iii) to withhold payments indefinitely as part of the "safe harbour" provision of the US Bankruptcy Code where it had not attempted to terminate the agreement or apply any close-out netting. It was held that a non-defaulting party must decide whether or not to terminate within a reasonable time and that to indefinitely suspend payment obligations amounted to a modification of the parties' contractual rights which was in contravention of the US Bankruptcy Code.[307]

3–55

---

[300] *Enron Australia Finance Pty Ltd v TXU Electricity Ltd* [2003] NSWSC 1169.
[301] The non-defaulting party had this right pursuant to s.6(a) of the 1992 ISDA Master Agreement.
[302] *Lomas* [2012] 2 All E.R. (Comm) 1076 at [39]–[42].
[303] *Re Olympia Securities Commercial Plc (In Administration)* [2017] EWHC 2807 (Ch).
[304] *Belmont Park Investments Pty Ltd v BNY Corporate Trustee Services Ltd* [2012] 1 A.C. 383.
[305] For a more detailed discussion of the decision and reasoning in this case, see R. Goode, "Perpetual Trustee and Flip Clauses in Swap Transactions" (2011) 127 L.Q.R. 1; and R. Goode, "Flip clauses: The End of the Affair?' (2012) 128 L.Q.R. 171.
[306] *Lehman Brothers Holdings Inc v Metavante* Case No.08-13555 (JMP), Bankr SDNY, 15 September 2009.
[307] But note that US bankruptcy law takes a completely different approach to clauses which allow a party to terminate a contract upon the commencement of bankruptcy proceedings in relation to a counterparty (known as ipso facto clauses), which are essentially prohibited in the absence of a "safe harbour" provision.

In response to widespread concern about the decision in *Lomas*,[308] ISDA published an amendment to s.2(a)(iii) aimed at addressing the problem of delay by allowing the parties to set a time limit after which the effect of s.2(a)(iii) comes to an end.[309]

3–56　A further, related issue which has arisen in the context of the Lehman litigation is the interaction of the "flawed asset" provision in s.2(a)(iii) with the netting provisions in the ISDA documentation,[310] and, in particular, whether s.2(a)(iii) applies on a "net" or "gross" basis. In *Marine Trade SA v Pioneer Freight Futures Co Ltd BVI*,[311] Flaux J considered that it applied on a gross basis; the non-defaulting party was entitled to withhold payment to the defaulting party whilst enforcing the defaulting party's payment obligation in full. Although amounts owing under an ISDA Master Agreement are normally netted against each other to give a single amount payable,[312] Flaux J considered that credit only had to be given for amounts that were payable not for amounts not payable due to the condition precedent in s.2(a)(iii) not being fulfilled. The issue arose subsequently in *Pioneer Freight Futures Co Ltd (In Liquidation) v Cosco Bulk Carrier Co Ltd*,[313] where Flaux J adopted the same approach as in *Marine Trade SA v Pioneer Freight*, holding that netting is not available to a defaulting party and the "gross" basis applies. However, the opposite approach was taken in *Pioneer Freight Futures Company Ltd (In Liquidation) v TMT Asia Ltd*,[314] where Gloster J considered that the "net" basis and not the "gross" basis should apply. She noted that she could not see

> "... any sensible commercial justification or rationale for a construction of section 2 of ISDA 92 which enables a Non-defaulting Party to claim against a Defaulting Party on a gross basis. It appears to be wholly contrary to the ethos of ISDA 92 ... and the clear commercial purpose of the parties that all amounts outstanding under all Transactions subject to one ISDA 92 Master Agreement should be subject to automatic payment netting in respect of payments due on the same date. It emasculates the netting provisions ... in the very circumstances where they may be most needed: namely where a Defaulting Party in the money may have to wait a long time for payment of what is owing to it (for example, until cure of its own Event of Default, or potential Event of Default, or Early Termination), and where it may well itself be subject to cash flow constraints, or other financial pressures. On the contrary, it confers a wholly unmerited (in commercial terms) benefit on the Non-defaulting Party. Such a construction would, in my mind, fundamentally change the financial structure of the relationship".[315]

---

[308] The UK Treasury, for instance, called for ISDA to find a "market solution" to limit s.2(a)(iii)'s operation to a "reasonable period" in December 2009 (HM Treasury, *Establishing resolution arrangements for investment banks* (16 December 2009), Consultation Paper).
[309] See C. Gurney, "Calling Time on Section 2(a)(iii) of the ISDA Master Agreement: ISDA Publishes an Amendment" (2014) 29(8) B.J.I.B. & F.L. 520; E. Murray, "Lomas v Firth Rixson: 'As You Were!'" (2013) 8(4) *Capital Markets Law Journal* 395.
[310] See para.2–13 above.
[311] *Marine Trade* [2010] Lloyd's Rep. 631.
[312] See para.2–14 above.
[313] *Pioneer Freight Futures Co Ltd (In Liquidation) v Cosco Bulk Carrier Co Ltd* [2011] 2 All E.R. (Comm) 1079.
[314] *Pioneer Freight Futures Company Ltd (In Liquidation) v TMT Asia Ltd* [2011] 2 Lloyd's Rep. 565.
[315] *TMT Asia* [2011] 2 Lloyd's Rep. 565 at [44].

The Court of Appeal in *Lomas* (which involved a joint appeal in relation to four cases including *Britannia Bulk Plc (In Liquidation) v Bulk Trading SA* which concerned a number of ISDA interpretation points),[316] declined to accept the gross basis interpretation of s.2(a)(iii) and instead followed Gloster J's approach in *TMT Asia*.[317] The Court of Appeal considered that the purpose of the netting provisions in the ISDA Master Agreement was to "re-formulate the content of the obligations which arise as at each payment date" so only the net sum is payable.[318] Therefore, the non-defaulting party could only be required to pay the net sum.

In relation to other provisions which provide for the withholding of performance, it was held in *Re Bank of Credit and Commerce International SA (In Liquidation) (No.8)*[319] that a bank could enter into a "charge-back" arrangement with a customer, despite the conceptual difficulties with a bank taking security over what is essentially a debt owed by it to its customer.[320] It has been suggested that, in the unlikely event that a "charge-back" was not properly registered,[321] a bank would be able to rely on a suitably drafted "flawed asset" clause to argue that its debt to its customer was a conditional obligation dependent on the customer fulfilling his own obligations to the bank.[322]

3–57

(2) Interest on overdue payments

Many contracts provide expressly for interest on overdue payments. The rate should be specified and interest should be expressed as calculated from day to day and made to run after as well as before judgment, in order to avoid merger of the contractual provision in the judgment, which would restrict the creditor to interest at the rate from time to time carried by judgment debts. Stipulations for payment of overdue interest must not be wholly disproportionate to the interest of the creditor in enforcing the primary obligation since otherwise they may be unenforceable as penalties.[323]

3–58

(3) Acceleration of liability[324]

Where payment is to be made by instalments, the contract may contain an acceleration clause calling up the full outstanding balance if default is made in

3–59

---

[316] *Lomas* [2012] 2 All E.R. (Comm) 1076.
[317] See the discussion of this point in *Lomas* [2012] 2 All E.R. (Comm) 1076 at [70]–[79].
[318] *TMT Asia* [2011] 2 Lloyd's Rep. 565 at [77].
[319] *Re Bank of Credit and Commerce International SA (In Liquidation) (No.8)* [1998] A.C. 214 HL.
[320] See para.1–02 above on the nature of account balances. Indeed, in an earlier case, *Re Charge Card Services Ltd (No.2)* [1987] Ch. 150 Ch D (Comp), Millett J considered that it was "conceptually impossible" for a bank to take a charge over assets held in its own accounts (at [175]–[176]).
[321] As a registrable charge under s.860 of the Companies Act 2006.
[322] Beale et al, *The Law of Security and Title-Based Financing* (2018), para.8.90. However, it is suggested in para.8.91 that the drafting of the clause in the *Bank of Credit* case did not achieve this.
[323] See discussion of the penalty rule and its reformulation in the *Cavendish Square* case above at paras 3–28 to 3–34.
[324] See R. Goode, "Acceleration Clauses" [1982] J.B.L. 148; also *Chitty* (2018), para.26-232.

payment of an instalment or if some other, specified default occurs.[325] Such clauses are most common in loan agreements, deferred purchase agreements and similar contracts where the creditor is taking a longer-term risk on performance by the debtor. Acceleration clauses are of two kinds: those which are triggered automatically by the occurrence of the default or other specified event and those which confer on the creditor the right to call up the outstanding balance if he chooses. Automatic acceleration clauses have largely fallen out of favour because they deprive the creditor of control.[326] It is usually much better to leave him with the choice of action when default occurs. The creditor must, of course, make up his mind; if he continues to accept instalments, he will be held to have waived his right to invoke the acceleration clause.

Reliance on an acceleration clause presupposes that the agreement is still on foot. The creditor cannot, for example, terminate a hire-purchase agreement for default by the debtor and then call up the remaining instalments. A clause purporting to give him this right would be struck down as penal because rent as such is payable only so long as the debtor has the right to use the hired goods and cannot be charged after the agreement has come to an end. What the creditor can do is provide for the payment of an agreed sum as liquidated damages in the event of termination for default, but this must be so drafted as not to offend the rule against penalties,[327] and in the case of termination of the agreement, this requires credit to be given for the value of the repossessed goods in addition to a discount for acceleration of the payment liability consequent on replacement of future rentals by present damages.[328] If, however, the creditor wishes to invoke an acceleration clause he must keep the agreement alive. Where he exercises his right to call for accelerated payment and *then* desires to terminate, he is faced with a choice. Enforcement of the acceleration clause in effect compels the debtor to complete the contract and thus debars termination of the contract and a consequential claim for damages for loss of future profits. Alternatively the creditor can exercise a right to terminate the contract, in which case he gives up his right to sue for the accelerated payment—for by terminating he deprives the debtor of the quid pro quo for his payment obligation as regards the future period covered by the accelerated payment—and is restricted to a claim in damages.[329]

---

[325] Such provisions are, in principle, enforceable: see *Lumley v Simmons* (1887) 34 Ch. D. 698 CA.

[326] Automatic acceleration clauses on insolvency of the counterparty are now mainly found in swap contracts, and are designed to support the operation of netting and set-off arrangements at the point of insolvency. These provisions and their operation are of a highly technical nature and are beyond the scope of this work.

[327] See para.3–28 above.

[328] Indeed, even if credit is given for these items, a clause calling up the full outstanding balance will usually be held as a penalty where the debtor did not repudiate the contract, on the ground that since a hire-purchase agreement in normal form entitles the debtor to terminate at any time by notice to the creditor, a clause fixing liquidated damages on the assumption that but for the breach the agreement would have run its full course will give the creditor a greater sum that the debtor could have been compelled to pay if he had not broken the agreement. The exception for cases where the debtor repudiates is generally recognised as anomalous. For a full discussion, see R. Goode, *Hire-Purchase Law and Practice*, 2nd edn (London: Butterworths, 1970), Ch.18.

[329] In Goode, "Acceleration Clauses" [1982] J.B.L. 148, Professor Goode suggested (at pp.152–153) that, after termination by the creditor, the sum payable under the acceleration clause could be adjusted by the court in exercise of its equitable power to grant relief against forfeiture. Further consideration persuaded him that the correct answer is not relief against forfeiture (which in any event might not be

An acceleration clause does not offend the rule against penalties insofar as it is restricted to the outstanding balance of principal. The debtor is not being required to pay a penny more than he contracted to pay at the outset, he merely has to pay it sooner.[330] The position is otherwise, however, as regards interest or charges. These are payable by the debtor for his use of the creditor's money, and cease to be payable when the creditor has exercised a right to call for repayment of the outstanding balance of principal. So an acceleration clause will be penal if it purports to give the creditor a right to unaccrued interest on a loan[331] or unaccrued charges on a hire-purchase,[332] or a conditional sale[333] agreement. Where interest or charges are pre-computed, the acceleration clause must provide for a discount or rebate in respect of the unexpired period of the agreement under some suitable formula.[334]

Under the terms of the Consumer Credit Act 1974, a creditor under a regulated agreement is required to serve at least 14 days' notice before enforcing an acceleration clause and the debtor can cure the default during this period by paying the arrears.[335]

(4) Enforcement of security

Where security has been taken, the security instrument will typically provide for enforcement of the security in the event of default, e.g. by empowering the creditor to take possession of the security or appoint a receiver and to sell the security and recover any remaining deficiency from the debtor. The enforcement of security taken in connection within a regulated agreement is subject to notice and other requirements under the Consumer Credit Act 1974.

3–60

---

appropriate as to moneys not yet paid to the creditor) but election of remedies. Acceleration of liability being dependent on the continuance of the contract, termination for subsequent or continuing breach constitutes the adoption of an alternative and inconsistent remedy which negates the operation of the acceleration clause.

[330] *Protector Endowment Loan & Annuity Co v Grice* (1880) 5 Q.B.D. 592 CA. See also *Oresundsvarvet AB v Lemos (The Angelic Star)* [1988] 1 Lloyd's Rep. 122 CA (Civ Div); *Edgeworth Capital (Luxembourg) Sarl v Ramblas Investments BV* [2015] EWHC 150 (Comm) (upheld [2016] EWCA Civ 412 although this point was not referred to) at [67]; and *ZCCM Investments Holdings Plc v Konkola Copper Mines Plc* [2017] EWHC 3288 (Comm) at [37].

[331] See Goode, "Acceleration Clauses" [1982] J.B.L. 148, 150.

[332] There is no authority on the effect of an acceleration clause in a hire-purchase agreement, no doubt because it is unusual to find such clauses in hire-purchase agreements. The probable effect is to convert the agreement into a conditional sale agreement, in which case the *Wadham Stringer* decision (at fn.282) applies.

[333] *Wadham Stringer Finance Ltd v Meaney* [1981] 1 W.L.R. 39 QBD.

[334] See *Wadham Stringer*, at fn.282 above, where the formula used was held reasonable.

[335] Consumer Credit Act 1974 ss.87(1) and 88 as amended by the Consumer Credit Act 2006 s.14, and the Consumer Credit (EU Directive) Regulations 2010 (SI 2010/1010) Pt 2 reg.37. For other notices now required where the debtor is in default, see the Consumer Credit Act s.86B–F as inserted by the Consumer Credit Act 2006 ss.9–12, and as amended by the Legislative Reform (Consumer Credit) Order 2008/2826, the Energy Act 2011 and the Consumer Credit Act 1974 (Green Deal) (Amendment) Order 2014/436.

(5) Crystallisation of floating charge

3–61 A creditor who takes a floating charge may provide for crystallisation of the charge upon the occurrence of stated events.[336] Like an acceleration clause, a crystallisation clause may be automatic or may simply empower the creditor to crystallise by notice on the occurrence of the designated event. Crystallisation converts a floating charge to a fixed charge and therefore removes the authority of the debtor to deal with the assets which are the subject of the charge without the consent of the creditor.[337] There is now some judicial endorsement of the validity of automatic crystallisation clauses[338] but they should be drafted carefully as they can all too often produce results which are not wanted either by the debtor or by the creditor.[339]

Provisions of this kind became common during the 1970s and 1980s, but their popularity is now on the wane.[340]

(6) Termination and/or repossession

3–62 The contract may provide for termination on default and, where the contract relates to goods supplied on hire, hire-purchase or conditional sale, repossession of the goods. Alternatively, it may permit repossession without termination of the agreement as a whole, though this device nowadays has little to commend it. Where an agreement falls within the scope of the Consumer Credit Act 1974, a default notice must in any event be served on the debtor or hirer before the creditor can accelerate the indebtedness or enforce any security.[341] Furthermore, in the case of hire purchase and conditional sale agreements, a court order will be required if the debtor has already paid more than one-third of the purchase price.[342]

---

[336] See *Goode and Gullifer on Legal Problems of Credit and Security* (2018), Chs 4 and 5; and Beale et al, *The Law of Security and Title-Based Financing* (2018), paras 6-66 to 6-141, for an overview of the law relating to the floating charge, including crystallisation; also *Goode and McKendrick on Commercial Law* (2020), paras 25-15 to 25-32, on crystallisation.

[337] *Goode and Gullifer on Legal Problems of Credit and Security* (2018), para.4-31; see also Beale et al, *The Law of Security and Title-Based Financing* (2018), para.6-78.

[338] *Re Brightlife Ltd* [1987] Ch. 200 Ch D (Comp). Automatic crystallisation has also been upheld in New Zealand and Australia; see *Re Manurewa Transport Ltd* [1971] N.Z.L.R. 909, *Deputy Commissioner of Taxation v Horsburgh* [1984] V.R. 773; *DFC Financial Services Ltd v Coffey* [1991] 2 N.Z.L.R. 513; *Cavacich v Riordan* [1994] N.Z.L.R. 502; *Fire Nymph Products Ltd v Heating Centre Pty Ltd* (1992) 7 A.C.S.R. 365. See also the Irish Supreme Court decision on semi-automatic crystallisation in *Re JD Brian Ltd (In Liquidation)* [2015] IESC 62, especially at [71]–[72].

[339] See *Goode and Gullifer on Legal Problems of Credit and Security* (2018), paras 4-55 to 4-59, discussing the decision in *Re Brightlife* and highlighting potential issues with automatic crystallisation clauses; see also Beale et al, *The Law of Security and Title-Based Financing* (2018), paras 6-86 to 6-96.

[340] *Goode and Gullifer on Legal Problems of Credit and Security* (2018), para.4-53. This is especially so given the removal of the temptation to use automatic crystallisation to protect against subordination to preferential creditors on insolvency by the Insolvency Act 1986; this point is discussed in *Goode and Gullifer*, para.5-73.

[341] Consumer Credit Act 1974 s.87.

[342] Consumer Credit Act 1974 s.90.

(7) Liquidated damages

Liquidated damages provisions have already been mentioned.[343]

3–63

(8) Enforcement of rights under separate agreement: the cross-default/material adverse change clauses

Particularly common in international financial agreements is the cross-default clause which entitles the creditor to exercise a range of default remedies where the debtor defaults in his obligations under some other agreement, whether with the creditor or with a third party. The clause is designed to ensure that a lender who has been paid to date is not obliged to bide his time whilst the borrower's financial condition is obviously deteriorating and other creditors are taking enforcement action against the borrower.

3–64

Equally common is the "material adverse change" clause (or "MAC" clause), under which the lender can call in the loan if there occurs a material change in the borrower's business or financial condition which, in the opinion of the lender, may adversely affect the borrower's ability to perform its obligations under the agreement. This "broad brush" provision is obviously designed to cover circumstances not covered by more specific default clauses, but it obviously involves a degree of judgment or appreciation.[344] Nevertheless, these clauses are not completely open-textured. In *Grupo Hotelero Urvasco v Carey Value Added SL*, the leading English case on the interpretation of such clauses, the court provided the following guidance[345]:

(i) if the MAC clause requires a change in the borrower's "financial condition", regard should be had primarily to its financial information, though other information, such as missed debt payments, may be relevant as to whether a material adverse change has occurred. If the clause refers to the borrower's "business or financial condition", this covers a broader scope and a wider range of matters can be considered;
(ii) evidence of "external economic or market changes" will not generally be sufficient to trigger a MAC clause;
(iii) the adverse change must be "material in a substantial way to the borrower's ability to perform the transaction in question", in this case to repay the loan. It must "significantly" affect this ability;
(iv) pre-existing circumstances will not generally give rise to a material adverse change. The lender cannot rely on circumstances that it was aware of when the agreement was entered into unless conditions worsen in a way that makes them "materially different in nature";

---

[343] See para.2–42 above.
[344] For litigation involving this type of clause, see *BNP Paribas SA v Yukos Oil Co* [2005] EWHC 1321 (Ch). A tax judgment of some US $3.3 billion had been issued against Yukos, and its assets had been frozen by court order. Unsurprisingly, the court held that the lenders were justified in terminating the facility in reliance on the material adverse change clause.
[345] *Grupo Hotelero Urvasco v Carey Value Added SL* [2013] EWHC 1039 (Comm) at [334]–[364].

(v) the impact of the event causing the change must not be temporary (even if the event itself is); and
(vi) the burden of proof is on the party seeking to trigger the clause.

In relation to the last point, it was emphasised in *Decura IM Investments LLP v UBS AG London Branch*[346] that the onus of proof is on the party seeking to establish a material adverse change. For instance, the production of internal forecasts as to future earnings demonstrating a worsening financial position for the future will not necessarily be sufficient since—other considerations apart—the forecasts may prove inaccurate.[347]

Ultimately, determining whether there is a material adverse change will involve an exercise of judgment and might in a marginal case be a point on which views could reasonably differ.[348] The issue of MAC clauses may become more relevant in the coming months due to the significant financial and business consequences for many borrowers caused by the COVID-19 pandemic.[349] As a general rule, however, lenders are reluctant to invoke MAC clauses if there is any doubt due to the reputational and financial consequences if invocation turns out to be unjustified.[350]

(9) Consolidation of liabilities

3–65 The agreement may provide that the debtor is not to be entitled to discharge his obligations under it without also tendering the balance outstanding under other agreements with the creditor. Such a provision appears to be perfectly valid. In the case of a mortgage over land, the right of consolidation is excluded but it may be reinstated by an express term in the security documents.[351]

(10) Set-off

3–66 Many agreements reinforce the equitable right of set-off by expressly empowering a party to set off cross-claims against his indebtedness to the other.[352] Clauses of this kind will generally be valid, at least so long as the contracting parties remain solvent.

(11) Right of repurchase/resale

3–67 Occasionally agreements involving the sale of an asset empower the seller to repurchase it—usually at the original price—if the buyer defaults. A provision of this kind is perfectly valid except where the purported sale and repurchase are a

---

[346] *Decura IM Investments LLP v UBS AG London Branch* [2015] EWHC 171 (Comm).
[347] *Ipsos SA v Dentsu Aegis Network Ltd (formerly Aegis Group Plc)* [2015] EWHC 1726 (Comm).
[348] *Kitcatt v MMS UK Holdings* [2017] EWHC 675 at [207].
[349] See discussion of this in James Green et al, "Coronavirus: the impact on financing transactions" (2020) 5 JIBFL 287.
[350] As pointed out in *Grupo Hotelero Urvasco v Carey Value Added SL* [2013] EWHC 1039 at [334].
[351] Law of Property Act 1925 s.93.
[352] See *Goode and Gullifer on Legal Problems of Credit and Security* (2018), paras 7–17 to 7–30 and 7–89 to 7–95. See also paras 2–07 to 2–08 above.

cloak for a loan to the "seller" on the security of his asset. More common are agreements conferring on the buyer a right to require repurchase by the seller. Such a provision is common in block discounting and factoring agreements.

(12) Indemnity against costs and liabilities

Finally, the debtor may agree to indemnify the creditor against costs and liabilities incurred by the latter as the result of the debtor's default. Subject to the application of rules designed for the protection of consumers,[353] such indemnities are in principle valid and, in practice, may do little more than reflect the creditor's right to damages flowing from the debtor's breach. The amount which may be claimed under such an indemnity may also be subject to limitations. It is probably to be implied that the expenses must be reasonably incurred and must be fair in amount. Furthermore, where the indemnity relates to legal expenses on enforcement, the indemnity is likely to be unenforceable to the extent to which costs actually incurred by the creditor exceed the allowable costs as taxed by the court.

3–68

Default remedies given by law

Even where the agreement is silent, the law gives a number of remedies to the creditor against a defaulting debtor.

3–69

(1) Withholding of performance

The creditor is entitled to withhold performance of any obligation correlative to the debtor's duty to pay. So on a contract of sale the seller need not be ready with the goods unless and until the buyer is ready and willing to tender the price.[354]

3–70

(2) Interest on overdue payments

In certain cases interest may be claimed by the creditor as of right, or awarded him by way of damages or pursuant to some discretion of the court, even without a contractual stipulation for interest.[355]

3–71

(3) Damages without termination of agreement

On the debtor's default in payment the creditor may, without exercising any right he may have to terminate the agreement, recover damages for loss resulting from the breach. Where the loss is confined to loss of use of his money the creditor's remedy will usually be to claim interest,[356] but in certain circumstances he may

3–72

---

[353] In particular, indemnity clauses may be amenable to challenge under the Consumer Rights Act 2015, which replaces the Unfair Terms in Consumer Contracts Regulations 1999 (SI 1999/2083).
[354] Sale of Goods Act 1979 s.28. See *Goode and McKendrick on Commercial Law* (2020), paras 3.153–3.154, on the withholding of performance.
[355] See para.4–51 below.
[356] See para.6–43 below.

have a substantial claim for damages. For example, if, as the result of the delay in payment currency which would otherwise have been available to the creditor has diminished in value and this result could reasonably have been contemplated by the debtor at the time of the contract, the loss may be recoverable.[357] Again, where the debtor has undertaken to perform an act involving payment to a third party, e.g. an insurer for insurance of goods, the creditor may make the payment and recover it as damages.

In practice, a claim for damages usually goes hand in hand with termination of the contract, since a creditor is reluctant to maintain contractual relations with a debtor he has to sue.[358] As will be seen, termination itself has an important effect on the quantification of damages.

(4) Enforcement of security

3–73 Except where the contract or statute otherwise provides, a legal mortgagee is entitled to possession even before default[359] and it is possible that a similar right is available to an equitable mortgagee.[360] A chargee by way of legal mortgage has the same rights and remedies as a legal mortgagee,[361] but other chargees require a court order in order to take possession.[362] The Law of Property Act 1925 contains provisions for sale and the appointment of a receiver,[363] though in practice these are usually replaced by express provisions of the mortgage deed. A mortgagee whose mortgagor has defaulted can also apply for foreclosure, but the remedy is rarely exercised.[364]

---

[357] See para.4–51 below.

[358] At least, this will be the case in contracts for the supply of goods and services. But agreements of a banking and financial nature will usually contain their own provisions for acceleration, default interest and similar matters. In such cases, the creditor will usually wish to keep the agreement on foot and will rely on the remedies which are internal to the agreement itself.

[359] *Four-Maids Ltd v Dudley Marshall (Properties) Ltd* [1957] Ch. 317 Ch D. This decision has been cited with approval on a number of occasions—see, for example, *Ropaigealach v Barclays Bank Plc* [2000] Q.B. 263 CA (Civ Div); *Credit & Mercantile Plc v Marks* [2005] Ch. 81.

[360] See H. Wade, "An Equitable Mortgagee's Right to Possession" (1955) 71 L.Q.R. 204; Charles Harpum, Stuart Bridge and Martin Dixon, *Megarry & Wade: Law of Real Property*, 8th edn (London: Sweet & Maxwell, 2012), para.25–046.

[361] Law of Property Act 1925 s.87(1).

[362] *Garfitt v Allen* (1887) 37 Ch. D. 48.

[363] Law of Property Act 1925 ss.101–109. The exercise of the statutory power of sale created by s.101 has been held—unsurprisingly—not to constitute a deprivation of property in contravention of the European Convention on Human Rights: *Horsham Properties Group Ltd v Clark* [2009] 1 W.L.R. 1255. The Law of Property Act 1925 receivership is of income and is to be contrasted with the modern administrative receivership by which an administrative receiver (formerly described as a receiver and manager) takes over control of the debtor company's enterprise. The cases in which a receiver can be appointed have been severely curtailed by the Insolvency Act 1986, as amended by the Enterprise Act 2002, which provides for an administration procedure designed to benefit all creditors.

[364] See Beale et al, *The Law of Security and Title-Based Financing* (2018), paras 6.01–6.16, for more information on mortgages and the rights and remedies available to mortgagees.

(5) Crystallisation of floating charge

A floating charge crystallises as a matter of law when the debtor company goes into receivership,[365] liquidation[366] or ceases to carry on business.[367] Administration per se does not, as a matter of law, cause a floating charge to crystallise since it is not incompatible with the continuance of the debtor company as a going concern.[368]

3–74

(6) Termination of agreement

Default in payment entitles the creditor to terminate the agreement where it has not been fully executed[369] and time of payment is of the essence or the default is so serious or persistent as to constitute a repudiation of the contract. But prima facie time of payment is not of the essence, even in a commercial contract,[370] unless so agreed.

3–75

(7) Damages resulting from termination

Where the creditor exercises a right to terminate the agreement because of the debtor's repudiatory breach he is entitled to recover, in addition to any special damages, an amount representing the profit he would have earned if the contract had been fully performed. Though the loss results immediately from the creditor's own act of termination, it is nevertheless considered reasonable that this should be laid at the debtor's door, since the creditor cannot be expected to hold open a contract that has been repudiated. The position is otherwise where the creditor exercises a *contractual* right to terminate for a non-repudiatory breach.[371]

3–76

It follows that the creditor's election to affirm on the one hand or terminate on the other radically affects the measure of damages:

> "A lets equipment to B on lease for five years at a rent of £100 a month. By the end of the first year B has paid only £500 in rent. If A elects to keep the lease on foot, all he is entitled to is the arrears of rent and interest on those arrears by way of damages. If there is further default, he will have to institute fresh proceedings. Where, however, A exercises his right to terminate the

---

[365] *Evans v Rival Granite Quarries Ltd* [1910] 2 K.B. 979 CA. In the case of appointment by the court, application to the court to appoint a receiver causes the charge to crystallise (per Vaughan Williams LJ at 986).

[366] *Re Colonial Trusts Corp Ex p. Bradshaw* (1879) 15 Ch. D. 465; *Re Panama, New Zealand and Australian Royal Mail Co* (1870) 5 Ch. App. 318.

[367] See *Re Woodroffes (Musical Instruments) Ltd* [1986] Ch. 366 Ch D; and other cases noted in Goode and Gullifer on *Legal Problems of Credit and Security* (2018), para.4.35.

[368] Goode and Gullifer on *Legal Problems of Credit and Security* (2018), para.4-37; this view is also taken on balance in *Lightman and Moss: The Law of Administrators and Receivers of Companies*, edited by G. Lightman et al, 5th edn (London: Sweet & Maxwell, 2014), para.3–62.

[369] The position is otherwise where it has been fully executed, as on a sale of goods where both property and possession have passed to the buyer.

[370] See para.4–27.

[371] See para.4–34.

lease by reason of B's repudiation, A can recover in full the profit he would have earned over the remaining four years of the lease, less what he receives or would have received by taking reasonable steps to mitigate his loss."[372]

In some circumstances where the debtor has made a profit due to his breach of contract, the creditor may be able to claim an account of profits made by the debtor. In *Novoship (UK) Ltd v Mikhaylyuk*,[373] the Court of Appeal held that the remedy of account of profits was available against the defendant who had dishonestly assisted in another's breach of fiduciary duty by bribing them.

(8) Set-off

3–77 A creditor may usually set-off the debt against a liquidated amount due from him to his debtor, even if the claim and cross-claim arise out of separate contracts.[374] Set-off in bankruptcy or winding-up is automatic where the statutory requirement of mutuality is met.[375]

(9) Remedies of unpaid seller under the Sale of Goods Act

3–78 Where the buyer defaults in payment the seller's best remedy is to sue for the price, assuming the buyer is good for the money.[376] Even where damages are available as an alternative, as on the buyer's repudiation, an action for the price is preferable, where the statutory conditions are satisfied,[377] since the seller then has to do no more than prove the contract and fulfilment of the above conditions, and avoids having to establish his loss or deal with the question of mitigation. However, there are certain remedies which the unpaid seller[378] is entitled to exercise either before the price has become payable or by way of securing it after the price has become due or as an alternative to the price. If still in possession of the goods, the seller has a lien (or if property has not passed to the buyer, a right to withhold delivery) until tender of payment, except where the seller agreed to give credit.[379] Where the buyer has become insolvent[380] after dispatch of the goods to him and while they are still in transit,[381] the seller may stop them by repossession or by notice to the carrier,[382] though he then becomes liable to the carrier for any unpaid freight.[383] In certain cases, the seller may resell the goods

---

[372] For example, by reletting the repossessed equipment.
[373] *Novoship (UK) Ltd v Mikhaylyuk* [2015] Q.B. 499 CA (Civ Div).
[374] See para.2–07 above.
[375] See para.2–10 above and the Insolvency (England and Wales) Rules 2016 rr.14.24 and 14.25.
[376] If he is not, repossession and sale will be preferable, assuming that the buyer has not acquired both ownership and possession.
[377] See Sale of Goods Act 1979 s.49.
[378] As defined by s.38(1) of the Sale of Goods Act 1979.
[379] Sale of Goods Act 1979 s.41(1).
[380] As to the meaning of this, see Sale of Goods Act 1979 s.61(4).
[381] See Sale of Goods Act 1979 s.45(1).
[382] Sale of Goods Act 1979 s.46(1)–(2).
[383] *Booth Steamship Co Ltd v Cargo Fleet Iron Co Ltd* [1916] 2 K.B. 570 CA. The decision also confirms that, pending payment of the freight, the carrier has a lien on the goods.

and recover any loss as damages,[384] but this remedy is not available where both property and possession have passed to the buyer.

There is one exceptional case in which the seller can get his goods back even after possession and ownership have passed to the buyer. This is where the sale was induced by the buyer's misrepresentation or fraud. The typical case is where the buyer gives a cheque in payment knowing that it will be dishonoured. In this case, instead of suing for the price or for damages the seller may rescind the contract of sale ab initio, in which event ownership automatically revests in him. The beauty of this remedy is that it is available even after the buyer has become bankrupt, as his trustee cannot stand in any better position than the buyer himself.[385] Rescission normally requires notice to the buyer, repossession or an order of the court; but, where communication to the buyer is impossible because he has deliberately removed himself, other acts by the seller manifesting an intention to rescind (e.g. contacting the police with a view to tracing the goods) suffice.[386]

4. The Recovery of Payments Made

Prima facie a payment made is irrecoverable. The onus is on the payer to show grounds for obtaining repayment from the payee. There are various circumstances in which recovery is allowed. It is impossible to classify these exhaustively, but some of the principal grounds of repayment are set out below. For a detailed treatment, see the eighth edition of that excellent work, retitled *The Law of Unjust Enrichment*, by Goff and Jones.[387]

3–79

Payment made on a condition subsequent

The first and obvious case of entitlement to repayment is where the parties have agreed that repayment shall be made on the occurrence of an event which later takes place. Such conditions subsequent are common in banking transactions. For example, a bank making payment through the clearing system to another bank in respect of a cheque not yet presented[388] is entitled to recover the payment if the cheque is dishonoured. The courts have also had to consider the meaning of payment of a letter of credit "under reserve". In *Banque de l'Indochine et de Suez SA v JH Rayner (Mincing Lane) Ltd*,[389] the Court of Appeal, reversing the decision of the judge at first instance, held that the object of payment under reserve was to enable the bank, though of opinion that the documents were not in order, to make payment to the beneficiary with the assurance that the beneficiary would repay the money if the bank's principal declined to take up the documents,

3–80

---

[384] Sale of Goods Act 1979 s.48.
[385] *Re Eastgate Ex p. Ward* [1905] 1 K.B. 465; *Tilley v Bowman Ltd* [1910] 1 K.B. 745.
[386] *Car & Universal Finance Co Ltd v Caldwell* [1965] 1 Q.B. 525 CA.
[387] Charles Mitchell, Paul Mitchell and Stephen Watterson (eds), *Goff & Jones: The Law of Unjust Enrichment*, 9th edn (London: Sweet & Maxwell, 2016).
[388] See para.2–23 above and para.5–19 below.
[389] *Banque de l'Indochine et de Suez SA v JH Rayner (Mincing Lane) Ltd* [1983] 2 W.L.R. 841 QBD (Comm); and [1983] Q.B. 711 CA (Civ Div).

whether or not his refusal to accept them was justified. The court pointed out that situations arose in which bank and beneficiary hoped or believed that the documents would be acceptable to the buyer and wished to avoid disrupting the transaction, but that in paying under reserve the bank could not be expected to engage in a dispute with its principal as to whether the documents were or were not conforming, or to be put in the position of having to sue its principal if reimbursement were refused. Accordingly, a confirming bank paying under reserve could recover the payment if its principal, the issuing bank, declined to accept the documents, and the issuing bank paying under reserve could likewise recover its payment if the buyer refused to take up the documents, even if it transpired that the documents were in order after all. In that event, the bank would ultimately have to pay.

Total failure of consideration

3–81   Where the debtor has received no part of the consideration for which his payment was made then as an alternative to suing for damages for breach of contract he can claim the return of his money as paid on a total failure of consideration. This can arise in a variety of situations. The creditor may have wholly failed to perform his part of the bargain. In that connection, the fundamental obligation of a seller under a contract of sale is to transfer ownership, and if the seller lacks title, there is considered to be a total failure of consideration even if the buyer has enjoyed possession of the goods for a substantial period.[390] It follows that the buyer can recover the whole of the price without deduction for his use of the goods.[391] Other cases in which there is total failure of consideration are where the supposed contract proves to be void, where the contract becomes ineffective because of rescission ab initio[392] or because the contract being unenforceable against a party,[393] he chooses to decline to perform it.[394]

Payment under mistake

3–82   It was for a long time believed that money paid under a mistake of law was irrecoverable, at any rate where it is paid in settlement of an honest claim.[395] By contrast, money paid under a mistake of fact was prima facie recoverable. This

---

[390] *Rowland v Divall* [1923] 2 K.B. 500 CA; cited with approval in *Guinness Mahon & Co Ltd v Kensington & Chelsea RLBC* [1999] Q.B. 215 CA (Civ Div) and applied in *The Res Cogitans* [2015] 2 Lloyd's Rep. 563.

[391] See fn.334 above. The Law Commission decided not to recommend any change in this rule. See the Law Commission, *Pecuniary Restitution on Breach of Contract* (1983), Law Com. No.121, Pt III, Report No.65.

[392] *Adam v Newbigging* (1886) 34 Ch. D. 582 CA.

[393] For example, for want of compliance with statutory formalities, such as those prescribed by s.2 of the Law of Property (Miscellaneous Provisions) Act 1989.

[394] *Thomas v Brown* (1876) 1 Q.B.D. 714; *Pulbrook v Lawes* (1876) 1 Q.B.D. 284.

[395] It was otherwise where the payee was responsible for the mistake (*Rogers v Louth CC* [1981] I.R. 265 SC). It should be appreciated that the claim is not made in equity, and thus does not depend upon the existence of a fiduciary relationship. Nor does it depend on the mistakenly paid funds remaining in the hands of the recipient: *Agip (Africa) Ltd v Jackson* [1991] Ch. 547 CA (Civ Div).

arcane distinction, which was at times difficult to apply, was finally put to rest by the majority decision of the House of Lords in *Kleinwort Benson Ltd v Lincoln City Council*.[396] Kleinwort had made a number of payments to the Council in the mistaken belief that a swap agreement was valid[397] and it was able to recover those payments on that footing. The rules applicable to the recovery of money paid under a mistake of fact or of law are now placed on essentially the same footing.[398] In a case dealing with a mistake of fact, the situations in which recovery will be denied were summarised as follows by Goff J in his comprehensive review of the authorities in *Barclays Bank Ltd v WJ Simms Son & Cooke (Southern) Ltd*[399]:

> "His claim may however fail if (a) the payer intends that the payee shall have the money at all events, whether the fact be true or false, or is deemed in law to so intend; or (b) the payment is made for good consideration, in particular if the money is paid to discharge, and does discharge, a debt owed to the payee (or a principal on whose behalf he is authorised to receive the payment) by the payer or by a third party by whom he is authorised to discharge the debt; or (c) the payee has changed his position in good faith, or is deemed in law to have done so."

Hence a mistaken double payment can be recovered,[400] and a bank paying a forged cheque is entitled to recover the payment from the payee, and from the collecting bank, and is not deemed to warrant the genuineness of the cheque to the holder.[401] A bank has even been held entitled to recover money paid on a cheque through inadvertence after payment had been stopped by the drawer, the cheque having been given to meet an architect's certificate in respect of building works carried out by the payee.[402] This decision is open to criticism on several grounds: that it took no account of the bank's ostensible authority to pay or the debtor's change of position in giving up the cheque; and that its effect is to undermine the finality of payment of a debt that was due. However, the decision does not seem to have been challenged in later cases. In contrast, if the payment is made on the basis of a mistaken belief that the customer has adequate funds to make the payment, then the payment will not be recoverable. This situation arose

---

[396] *Kleinwort Benson Ltd v Lincoln City Council* [1999] 2 A.C. 349 HL.
[397] In fact, such agreements were later found to be beyond the powers of a local authority and void accordingly. See *Hazell v Hammersmith and Fulham LBC* [1992] 2 A.C. 1 HL. See also *Westdeutsche Landesbank* [1996] A.C. 669 HL.
[398] It also used to be the case that a mistake had to relate to a matter of *fact* (s opposed to a matter of *law*) if it was to form the basis for the rescission of the contract. However, in parallel with the *Kleinwort Benson* decision, this distinction has now been discredited: see *Pankhania v Hackney LBC* [2002] N.P.C. 123 and *Mears Ltd v Shoreline Housing Ltd* 160 Con. L.R. 157 QBD (TCC).
[399] *Barclays Bank Ltd v WJ Simms Son & Cooke (Southern) Ltd* [1980] 1 Q.B. 677 QBD (Comm) at 695. For a criticism of this case, see R. Goode, "The Bank's Right to Recover Money Paid on a Stopped Cheque" (1981) 97 L.Q.R. 254, and see para.5–24 below. For a case where recovery was denied on grounds of estoppel and change of position, see *Avon CC v Howlett* [1983] 1 W.L.R. 605 CA (Civ Div). That change of position and the provision of good consideration in the context of a bona fide purchase are good defences to a recovery claim of this kind; this was confirmed in *Lipkin Gorman v Karpnale Ltd* [1991] 2 A.C. 548 HL.
[400] *Chase Manhattan Bank NA v Israel-British Bank (London) Ltd* [1981] 1 Ch. 105 Ch D; *Jones v Churcher* [2009] 2 Lloyd's Rep. 94. See Mitchell, *Goff and Jones: The Law of Unjust Enrichment* (2011), Ch.9, for more information on mistake as a ground for restitution.
[401] *National Westminister Bank Ltd v Barclays Bank International Ltd* [1975] Q.B. 654.
[402] *WJ Simms* [1980] 1 Q.B. 677 QBD (Comm). See further paras 5–28 to 5–29 below.

in *Lloyds Bank Plc v Independent Insurance Co Ltd*,[403] where the bank mistakenly believed that the customer had adequate funds because of a recent large credit which, however, was provisional and the item was subsequently dishonoured. The bank could not recover the payment because: (i) the customer's request to make the payments impliedly included a request for any overdraft facility which was necessary for that purpose; (ii) in making the payment, the bank impliedly agreed to that request; and (iii) since the payment was made with the authority of the customer, it had the effect of discharging the obligation of the customer under the underlying commercial contract. In that situation, it would be unreasonable to require the creditor to refund the payment. Given that his debt claim against the customer would have been discharged, it could not be said that he was unjustly enriched by retaining the payment.

A similar decision appears to have been reached in *Fairfield Sentry Ltd (In Liquidation) v Migani*,[404] which concerned a fraud where the Bernard L. Madoff Investment Securities LLC, a mutual fund, had placed investors' money in a Ponzi scheme. Investors were entitled to withdraw funds by redeeming their shares under the provisions of the fund's articles of association and the redemption amount was calculated using the NAV per share. When the High Court of the British Virgin Islands ordered the fund to be wound up in July 2009, the fund's liquidators brought proceedings against members of the fund who had redeemed some or all of their shares prior to the suspension of the determination of the fund's NAV per share in December 2008 (after which no further redemptions could be made). The liquidators' claim was based on the argument that payments had been made to these investors in the mistaken belief that the assets were as stated by the fund, whereas there were in fact no such assets. The Privy Council allowed the investors' appeal on the basis that a payee could not be said to be unjustly enriched if he was entitled to receive the sum paid to him and that the true effect of the redemption terms in the articles was that the fund was obliged to pay the NAV per share determined by the directors at the time, not the NAV per share ascertained in the light of information which subsequently became available about the fund's fraud.

In the final analysis, therefore, the recoverability of a payment made by a bank by mistake under those circumstances will depend to a significant extent on whether or not the payment was made with the customer's authority.[405] A payment made under a forged transfer request necessarily lacks the authorisation of the customer and—subject to "change of position" and other defences noted above—the bank should be able to recover from the payee under such circumstances.[406] Still more interesting is the ruling in *Chase Manhattan Bank NA v Israel-British Bank (London) Ltd* that money paid under a mistake of fact can be recovered by way of a *proprietary* claim, so that repayment may be obtained from the payee's estate even if the payee has meanwhile become bankrupt or gone into liquidation. The "money" in this context refers, of course,

---

[403] *Lloyds Bank Plc v Independent Insurance Co Ltd* [2000] Q.B. 110 CA (Civ Div).
[404] *Fairfield Sentry Ltd (In Liquidation) v Migani* [2014] 1 C.L.C. 611.
[405] On this subject, see *Crantrave Ltd (In Liquidation) v Lloyds Bank Plc* [2000] Q.B. 917 CA (Civ Div) and the discussion in *Law of Bank Payments* (2018), para.3–142.
[406] See, for example, *Agip* [1991] Ch. 547 CA (Civ Div). See the discussion in *Law of Bank Payments* (2018), para.3–117.

to a money *fund* available to be followed in a tracing action, not to coins or notes in specie. The precise status of this decision is, however, uncertain; some of the reasoning which led the court to this conclusion was doubted by the House of Lords in *Westdeutsche Landesbank*,[407] although it was felt that the decision may have been correct on other grounds.

Payment under economic duress

A payment is recoverable if made under duress. This is not confined to physical duress but extends to economic duress, that is, commercial pressure so coercive of the payer's will as to vitiate his consent to the payment or to the transaction under which it was made.[408] However, duress can only be invoked if the pressure that was applied was illegitimate under the circumstances. Thus, where a debtor company was in default and the creditor was entitled to withdraw the facility, the directors' guarantees given to stave off an immediate demand were not procured by duress. The lender was not in breach of its contract by threatening to withdraw the facility, or in seeking alternative forms of cover.[409]

3–83

Equitable relief against forfeiture

Where it would be unconscionable for the payee to retain the payment made to him, the court has an equitable jurisdiction to grant relief against forfeiture of the payment and to order return of the money to the payer.[410] However, the Court of Appeal has held[411] that this jurisdiction does not exist in relation to normal arm's length commercial transactions between parties of equal bargaining power except in the case of a contract relating to land, e.g. a commercial lease or a mortgage. The need of the businessman for certainty in his commercial dealings—the case in question concerned withdrawal of a vessel supplied under a charterparty, for non-payment of hire—meant that it was not sufficient for the court to declare that its equitable jurisdiction would rarely be exercised in commercial disputes; it was necessary to go further and hold that the court had no jurisdiction at all.[412] Nevertheless, this limitation has not stood the test of time or, at least, the scope of

3–84

---

[407] *Westdeutsche Landesbank* [1996] A.C. 669 HL.
[408] *Pao On v Lau Yiu Long* [1980] A.C. 614 PC; *Dimskal Shipping Co SA v International Transport Federation(The Evia Luck) (No.2)* [1992] 2 A.C. 152 HL. The threat will usually consist of an indication that the party will breach its contract or commit some other unlawful act, although note the situation that arose in *Progress Bulk Carriers Ltd v Tube City IMS Ltd* [2012] 2 All E.R. (Comm) 855.
[409] *National Merchant Buying Society Ltd v Bellamy* [2012] EWHC 2563 (Ch).
[410] See *Chitty* (2018), para.4–086.
[411] *Scandinavian Trading Tanker Co AB v Flota Petrolera Ecuatoriana (The Scaptrade)* [1983] 1 All E.R. 301 CA (Civ Div), affirmed by the House of Lords [1983] 2 A.C. 694 HL. See fn.356 below. The decision has subsequently been followed—see, for example, *UK Housing Alliance (North West) Ltd v Francis* [2010] 3 All E.R. 519. Although ultimately distinguished, the decision is also discussed at some length in *LauritzenCool AB v Lady Navigation Inc* [2005] 1 W.L.R. 3686.
[412] *The Scaptrade* [1983] 1 All E.R. 301 per Goff LJ at 309. On appeal, the judgment of Goff LJ was referred to with approval by Lord Diplock ([1983] 2 A.C. 694 HL), whose own speech was, however, carefully confined to cases of time charter.

the rule has been clarified. For example, in *The Jotunheim*,[413] it was held that the charterer under a bareboat charter had a property interest in the vessel and that relief against forfeiture was in principle available (although it was not granted on the facts of the case). Equally, in *Cukurova Finance International Ltd v Alfa Telecom Turkey Ltd*,[414] the Privy Council decided that the court's jurisdiction to grant relief from forfeiture was not restricted to contracts or arrangements relating solely to real estate. In that case, a chargor had created security over shares owned by it and, following a default, the chargee enforced its security by appropriating those shares. The court held that it had jurisdiction to grant equitable relief against forfeiture on conditions (e.g. that overdue payments were brought up to date). The court appeared to believe that the forfeiture of the shares would be disproportionate given the nature of the default. In *On Demand Information Plc (In Administrative Receivership) v Michael Gerson (Finance) Plc*,[415] it was indicated that there does not need to be a proprietary interest in the narrow sense for relief against forfeiture to be granted, but a real interest in the sense of a "financial interest" was sufficient. The House of Lords held relief from forfeiture was available in relation to chattel leases, even though chattel leases do not create a proprietary interest and the goods in this particular case had been sold. It was the borrower's interest in the surplus value of the goods above the outstanding debt, rather than in the goods themselves, which was being protected. This position has again been confirmed by the now Supreme Court in the recent case of *Manchester Ship Canal Co Ltd v Vauxhall Motors UK Ltd*,[416] where it was held that relief against forfeiture could extend to a possessory right over land in the form of a licence, given the rights in question were perpetual in nature.

---

[413] *The Jotunheim* [2005] 1 Lloyd's Rep. 181.
[414] *Cukurova Finance International Ltd v Alfa Telecom Turkey Ltd* [2015] 2 W.L.R. 875.
[415] *On Demand Information Plc (In Administrative Receivership) v Michael Gerson (Finance) Plc* [2003] 1 A.C. 368.
[416] *Manchester Ship Canal Co Ltd v Vauxhall Motors UK Ltd* [2019] UKSC 46.

CHAPTER 4

STIPULATIONS AS TO TIME: INTEREST

1. THE SIGNIFICANCE OF STIPULATIONS AS TO TIME

Few aspects of the duty to pay have caused so much litigation as the interpretation and effect of stipulations as to time. In the great majority of cases, the issue comes before the court because the creditor has relied on delay in payment as a ground for terminating the debtor's contract. A typical scenario is provided by the charterparty. The owner, alleging that the charterer has been late with a payment, withdraws the vessel. There may be a variety of underlying reasons: substantial delay in payment which is likely to recur; a series of minor but irritating delays as a result of which the creditor is constantly having to monitor payments; and a rise in freight and hire rates, rendering the charterparty less profitable than it was and encouraging the owner to find a reason for withdrawing the vessel so that he can let it out on more favourable terms, either to the same charterer or to a new one. For his part, the charterer may advance a series of arguments to show that withdrawal of the vessel by the owner was improper. First, he may contend that, as a matter of contract or course of dealing, complete payment was not required, merely an earlier step, e.g. dispatch of payment, which was taken in due time. Secondly, he may argue that, as a matter of law, payment was made within the time prescribed by the contract, and that the charterer was premature in terminating the contract. Thirdly, he may seek to persuade the court that, on the facts, payment was made earlier than at the time contended for by the owner and was effected in due time. This may involve detailed investigation into the payment mechanism, particularly in the case of inter-bank transfers, where the court has sometimes been concerned with a delay not of days but of hours or even minutes. Finally, the charterer may plead that, even if he was late, the time of payment was not of the essence or the delay was "technical" and that he is protected by an anti-technicality clause.

4–01

Lawful termination of a contract can have serious, sometime ruinous, consequences for the debtor, whilst a creditor who "jumps the gun" and gives a premature notice of termination may find himself exposed to a substantial claim for damages for breach of contract. So even small delays, or apparent delays, may have a profound impact on the parties' rights and liabilities, and it is for this reason that stipulations as to time have assumed such importance in English commercial transactions.

2. EXPRESS STIPULATIONS AS TO TIME

The computation of time[1]

(1) The significance of time computations

4–02 Time computations are material for a range of purposes.

In loan agreements, computations of dates and time periods may be material for a number of purposes, including:

- the duration of interest periods, which are often expressed as one month or multiples of it;
- the dates on which principal instalments are payable which, again, are frequently expressed as periods of months from the date of the agreement; and
- the duration of grace periods in the event of a payment or other default.

And, as we have seen, the computation of time is most material to the question of breach and remedies, including the triggering of an acceleration clause and the right of the creditor to terminate the agreement.

We may now turn to consider some of the important rules relating to the computation of time.

(2) The witching hour

4–03 Where payment falls due on or by a stated date, then, prima facie, the debtor has until midnight at the end of that date in which to tender payment. This rule was settled a long time ago in *Startup v Macdonald*.[2] It was emphatically affirmed by the Court of Appeal and the House of Lords in *Afovos Shipping Co SA v R Pagnan & Fratelli (The Afovos)*,[3] yet another decision on withdrawal of a vessel under a charterparty.

The charterparty concluded between O and C provided that O was not to be at liberty to withdraw the vessel for non-payment of hire without giving C 48 hours' notice of their intention to do so, during which time C could remedy the breach by tendering the amount due. Owing to the fact that one of O's telex numbers in the telex directory had been given up without the directory being corrected, and the failure of C's bank to check that its credit transfer instruction covering the payment of hire due had reached its proper destination, payment was not made on the due date, 14 June 1979. The mistake was not discovered until after that date. Meanwhile, at 16.40 on 14 June, O gave 48 hours' notice of intention to withdraw

---

[1] For a short but useful discussion and a collection of cases, see "Time, Gentlemen, Please: But What Time Is It?" [1986] *Conveyancer and Property Lawyer* 306.
[2] *Startup v Macdonald* 134 E.R. 1029 Court of Common Pleas.
[3] *Afovos Shipping Co SA v R Pagnan & Fratelli (The Afovos)* [1982] 3 All E.R. 18 CA (Civ Div), affirmed [1983] 1 W.L.R. 195 HL; applied in *South West Water Services Ltd v International Computers Ltd* [1999] B.L.R. 420 QBD (TCC). For a decision of the Federal Court of Australia on termination notices and the application of the decision in *The Afovos*, see *Amman Aviation Pty Ltd v Comonwealth of Australia* [1990] FCA 55.

the vessel, pursuant to the anti-technicality clause, and after expiry of the notice, when the hire remained unpaid, notified C, that the vessel was withdrawn.

The Court of Appeal, whose decision was upheld by the House of Lords, held that the anti-technicality notice by O was given prematurely, and was thus ineffective. The notice could not validly have been given until C was in default, and this did not occur until midnight on 14–15 June. The court rejected the argument that the time for payment had expired at the close of banking hours on 14 June, pointing out that the business hours of a bank might vary from country to country and from bank to bank, and that, with such momentous consequences following from non-payment, it was important that the expiry of time should be fixed at the certain time of midnight rather than the uncertain time of a bank's closing hours.[4] The court considered that, despite the fact that the payment would not be processed that day as a matter of normal banking practice, the general rule of law applied that "a default only occurs at midnight on the due date for payment".[5] The court rejected O's argument that the notice was validly given because it was obvious that C would not be able to pay in time, holding that the notice could not be given in advance of midnight even if the owners could see beforehand that the transfer could be processed on that day.[6]

Charterparty cases have continued to occupy the courts. In *Tradax Export SA v Dorada Compania Naviera SA of Panama (The Lutetian)*[7] the owner—in accordance with the terms of the contract—gave three days' notice that payment of the charter hire had not been received. The charterers paid the bulk of the hire well within the three-day period, but made a deduction in respect of four days *anticipated* off-hire. The owners did not query this deduction until well into the third day when it was apparently too late for the charterers to make the additional payment; the owners thereupon withdrew the vessel for non-payment. Bingham J held that they were entitled to do so. The three-day notice period had been valid in accordance with the terms of the contract. It was for the charterers to ensure full payment by the required date, and it was not incumbent on the owners to do further chasing or to query short payment. In the event, however, the withdrawal of the vessel was found to be invalid because the vessel had been withdrawn before the third day of notice had expired.[8] Similarly, in the landlord and tenant context, *Avocet Industrial Estates LLP v Merol Ltd*,[9] a break notice issued by a tenant was held to be invalid as the tenant had failed to pay default interest and the lease stated that a break notice would be invalid unless any payment due under the lease was paid. This was despite the fact that the landlord had not made a demand for default interest, as the court did not consider that a demand in relation to default interest was necessary and, additionally, it was unlikely that

---

[4] Contrast *Momm v Barclays Bank International Ltd* [1977] Q.B. 790 QBD (Comm), where the court observed that, in cases involving payment through the banking system, the "day" ends at the close of banking hours.

[5] *The Afovos* [1982] 3 All E.R. 18 CA (Civ Div) at 21.

[6] *The Afovos* [1982] 3 All E.R. 18 CA (Civ Div) at 22.

[7] *Tradax Export SA v Dorada Compania Naviera SA of Panama (The Lutetian)* [1982] 2 Lloyd's Rep. 140 QBD (Comm).

[8] The court applied the decision in *The Afovos* in this respect.

[9] *Avocet Industrial Estates LLP v Merol Ltd* [2012] L. & T.R. 13. See also *PCE Investors Ltd v Cancer Research Ltd UK* [2012] 2 P. & C.R. 5.

there would have been any real practical difficulty in the tenant knowing what sum it had to pay even without a demand. It appears that the position may be different if some kind of estoppel can be raised which means that one party has a duty to bring certain facts to the attention of the other party.[10]

Additional case law has further demonstrated the need for owners to take particular care when seeking to terminate the charterparty. For example, *Western Bulk Carriers K/S v Li Hai Maritime Inc*,[11] involved the charter of a bulk carrier under a New York Produce Exchange Form. In making payment of an instalment of hire, the charterers deducted a US $500 cancellation fee incurred at a particular point and for which they held the owners responsible. The charterers were not entitled to make that deduction. The so called "anti-technicality" clause in the document required the owners to give "72 hours official notice in writing and not withdraw the vessel if the hire is paid or the alleged breach is rectified within the 72 hours allowed for from time the owners served such notice".

Unfortunately for them, the owners simply gave notice that the vessel would be withdrawn within 72 hours. They made no reference to the nature of the breach or the fact that it was up to the charterer to remedy the breach within the grace period. Whilst the court accepted that one should not adopt an excessively technical approach to the construction of such notices (which were, after all, given under an "anti-technicality" clause), the notice did nevertheless have to meet the requirements of the contract. This one did not, with the result that the owners were liable for wrongful withdrawal of the vessel and incurred a liability in damages in excess of US $2,000,000.[12]

4–04 It may be noted that the charterparty itself and any notice given pursuant to it require careful interpretation in this type of case, not least because a time charterparty[13] gives the charterer no proprietary interest in the vessel, with the result that the court is unable to grant relief from forfeiture.[14] As a result, the essential validity of any termination notice is likely to come under much closer scrutiny than would otherwise be the case. In contrast, it has been specifically

---

[10] See Bingham J's dictum in *The Lutetian* (at 157) that a duty to speak may arise because "a reasonable man would expect the person against whom the estoppel is raised, acting honestly and responsibly, to bring the true facts to the attention of the other party known by him to be under a mistake as to their respective rights and obligations", referred to in cases including *St Maximus Shipping Co Ltd v AP Moller-Maersk A/S* [2014] 2 Lloyd's Rep. 377 (at [50]); and *Starbev GP Ltd v Interbrew Central European Holdings BV* [2014] EWHC 1311 (Comm) (at [129]). However, no such duty was found in these cases.

[11] *Western Bulk Carriers K/S v Li Hai Maritime Inc* [2005] 2 Lloyd's Rep. 389.

[12] Damages for wrongful withdrawal of the vessel are calculated by reference to the excess cost of chartering a replacement vessel for the remainder of the charterparty: see *Koch Marine Inc v d'Amica Societa di Navigazione arl (The Elena d'Amico)* [1980] 1 Lloyd's Rep. 75 QBD (Comm) (at 87), applied in *Bunge SA v Nideria BV (formerly Nidera Handelscompagnie BV)* [2015] 3 All E.R. 1082, *Mitsui Osk Lines Ltd v Salgaocar Mining Industries Private Ltd* [2015] 2 Lloyd's Rep. 518; and *Glory Wealth Shipping Pte Ltd v North China Shipping Ltd (The North Prince)* [2011] 1 All E.R. (Comm) 641.

[13] Other than a charterparty by way of demise.

[14] See *Scandinavian Trading Tanker Co AB v Flota Petrolera Ecuatoriana (The Scaptrade)* [1983] 2 A.C. 694 HL, applied in *UK Housing Alliance (North West) Ltd v Francis* [2010] 3 All E.R. 519 (at [11]), *Owneast Shipping Ltd v Qatar Navigation QSC* [2011] 2 All E.R. (Comm) 76 (at [8]); and mentioned in *Lancore Services Ltd v Barclays Bank Plc* [2008] 1 C.L.C. 1039 (at [104]). The comment on this point is subject to the earlier discussion on this point at para.3–84 above.

confirmed that relief from forfeiture is available in the context of a bareboat or demise charter, because the charterer is effectively in the same position as a lessee.[15]

Although many of the most difficult cases in this sphere have arisen in shipping cases, the general principles illustrated by them do have more general application.[16] The extent of the court's jurisdiction to grant relief from forfeiture has been considered in a number of cases in recent years, notably *Cukurova Finance International Ltd v Alfa Telecom Turkey Ltd*,[17] where the Privy Council considered that there was "no principled basis upon which the jurisdiction can be limited to real property" as opposed to other types of property as well and that it could be applied regardless of the type of property concerned, although it did only apply where "what is in question is forfeiture of proprietary or possessory rights, as opposed to merely contractual rights...".[18] Where the transfer of possessory as opposed to proprietary rights is concerned, it seems that the relief jurisdiction does not apply if a bare possessory right is only transferred for a proportion of the economic life of the property in question.[19]

(3) Payment falling due on non-business day

In procedural law, an applicant whose time for instituting proceedings expires on a day when the court offices are closed has until the next day they are open to issue his writ.[20] No such relief is available at common law to a debtor whose payment obligation falls due on a non-business day, when the banks are closed and the creditor is not at his office. In such a case, the debtor must pay earlier, not

4–05

---

[15] *More OG Romsdal Fylkesbatar AS v Demise Charterers of the Jotunheim* [2005] 1 Lloyd's Rep. 181, discussed at para.3–84 above.
[16] For example, in a landlord and tenant context, see the decision of the Court of Session, Outer House in *Whitbread Group Plc v Goldapple Ltd (No.2)* 2005 S.L.T. 281.
[17] *Cukurova Finance International Ltd v Alfa Telecom Turkey Ltd* [2015] 2 W.L.R. 875.
[18] *Cukurova* [2015] 2 W.L.R. 875 at [92] and [94], confirmed in the recent Court of Appeal decision of *Manchester Ship Canal Co Ltd v Vauxhall Motors UK Ltd* [2018] EWCA Civ 1100 at [35]–[56], where relief was granted in relation to a licence in perpetuity to discharge surface water and trade effluent into the Manchester Ship Canal which gave possessory rights over the drainage infrastructure.
[19] See *Celestial Aviation Trading 71 Ltd v Paramount Airways Private Ltd* [2011] 1 All E.R. (Comm) 259, where *The Scaptrade* was considered. Hamblen J accepted that this makes it clear that relief against forfeiture is generally limited to contracts which involve the transfer of proprietary or possessory rights (at [48]). However, while acknowledging that the leases in the case, while not involving the transfer of proprietary rights, did involve the transfer of possessory rights (at [49]), Hamblen J ultimately considered that applying the relief jurisdiction to contracts transferring a bare possessory right for only a proportion of the economic life of the chattel (as opposed to cases involving a right to "indefinite" possession of the chattels) "would represent a major extension of the existing authority" (at [57]) which was not justified by reasons of legal policy, in particular the need for certainty (at [83]).
[20] *Kaur v S Russell & Sons Ltd* [1973] Q.B. 336 CA (Civ Div); *The Clifford Maersk* [1982] 1 W.L.R. 1292 QBD (Admlty); *Nottingham City Council v Calverton Parish Council* [2015] P.T.S.R. 1130.

later.[21] There is a statutory exception in the case of bills of exchange. A bill of exchange falling due on a non-business day[22] is payable on the succeeding business day.[23]

(4) The corresponding date rule

4-06 A provision for payment "not more than X months after" a given date means that, where possible, one chooses as the due date the corresponding day of the month of expiry of the stated period, ignoring differences in the length of the two months concerned. Where the month of expiry has fewer days than the month which commences the period, the due date is the last day of the month of expiry.[24] Thus:

(a)   one month after 27 January is 27 February;
(b)   one month after 31 January is 28 February (29 February in a leap year); and
(c)   four months after 31 May is 30 September.

Time starts to run at midnight after the end of the day on which the stated period commences, i.e. that day is excluded when making the computation—and expires at midnight after the end of the corresponding date applicable under the rule.

(5) "Day"

4-07 Agreements and statutes will frequently contain references to a period of "days". In the absence of any contrary indication, a "day" is the period spanning midnight to midnight and not simply 24 hours.[25] Whether reference to a "day" refers to any day or is limited to business days will obviously depend upon the true construction of the document at issue. If "business day" is meant, then it would obviously be wise to say so explicitly. In agreements including cross-border financial relationships, even a further degree of reinforcement may be required; precisely *where* must it be a business day? Where a UK bank is due to make an advance in US dollars, it is common to stipulate that such an obligation is only required to be performed on a day on which both London and New York are open, so that both the necessary administrative work can be done in London and the payment can be cleared in New York. A statutory example of this problem is

---

[21] *Mardorf Peach & Co Ltd v Attica Sea Carriers Corp of Liberia (The Laconia)* [1977] A.C. 850 HL.
[22] See Bills of Exchange Act 1882 s.92; Banking and Financial Dealings Act 1971.
[23] Bills of Exchange Act 1882 s.14(1), as amended by the Banking and Financial Dealings Act 1971 s.3(2).
[24] *Dodds v Walker* [1981] 1 W.L.R. 1027 HL, applied in *Windermere Court Kenley RTM Co Ltd v Sinclair Gardens Investments (Kensington) Ltd* [2014] UKUT 420 (LC), *Webber v NHS Direct* 2012 WL 5995896; *O'Connor Utilities Ltd v Revenue and Customs Commissioners* [2010] S.T.C. 682; and *Matthew v Sedman* [2019] EWCA Civ 475. See also *Pacitti Jones (A Firm) v O'Brien* 2006 S.C. 616.
[25] *Cartwright v MacCormack* [1963] 1 W.L.R. 18 CA.

offered by s.92 of the Bills of Exchange Act 1882, which requires notice of dishonour to be given within "three days". Weekends and holidays are thus included within the calculation.[26]

Difficulties of this kind continue to occupy the legislative process, and to give rise to disagreements. For example, the Cape Town Convention on International Interests in Mobile Equipment 2001 includes a Protocol on matters specific to aircraft equipment. Articles IX and X of that Protocol deal with remedies and provide for the giving of notice and filing of applications in terms of "working days".[27] Yet, in a context which must be regarded as essentially similar, the 2007 Luxembourg Protocol on railway rolling stock works by reference to "calendar days" on the ground that "working day" begs the question as to *where* it must be a working day. "Working Days" vary not only from one country to another but sometimes even from one part of a country to another part, making it difficult for the "non-local" party to know when a prescribed period expires.

(6) "Month"

Prima facie, "month" means a calendar month, so that the fact that different months may comprise different numbers of days is, in principle, irrelevant.[28]

4–08

(7) "From" or "after" a stated date

A provision for payment "from" a specified date will generally exclude that date unless it is stated to be inclusive,[29] and it appears that "after" will have the same effect.[30] However, it must be appreciated that every expression must be construed in its context with a view to giving effect to the intention of the parties. As Lord Mansfield noted in *Pugh v Duke of Leeds*,[31] "the sense of the word 'from' must always depend on the context and the subject-matter, whether it shall be construed inclusive or exclusive of the *terminus a quo*". Where, instead of "from", a time period is expressed to "start with" a particular date, the date will be included.[32]

4–09

---

[26] See *Hawkes, Assignees of Day, Bankrupts v Salter* 130 E.R. 944 Court of Common Pleas; *Wright v Shawcross* (1819) 2 B. & A. 501, Note.

[27] On the application of this Convention, see Professor Sir R. Goode, *Official Commentary on the Convention on International Interests in Mobile Equipment and the Protocol thereto on Matters Specific to Aircraft Equipment*, 4th edn (UNIDROIT, 2019).

[28] Law of Property Act 1925 s.61; Sale of Goods Act 1979 s.10(3); Interpretation Act 1978 Sch.1. But this refers to periods within the same calendar month, and thus does not affect the application of the "corresponding date" rule where a period spans two or more months.

[29] *Cartwright v MacCormack* [1963] 1 W.L.R. 18 CA, followed in *Re Figgis* [1969] 1 Ch. 123 Ch D, where the unhappy question was whether the testator's wife had been "living at the expiration of a period of three months from my death". See also *Webb v Fairmaner* 150 E.R. 1231 Court of Exchequer (where a writ for price issued on 5 December 1837 for the price in respect of a contract for the sale of goods which were to be paid for in two months from 5 October 1837 was held to be premature; the debtor was entitled to pay at any time up to midnight on 5 December 1837).

[30] *R. (on the application of Bednash) v Westminster City Council* [2014] EWHC 2160 (Admin) (the wording "three months after that date" excluded the date on which the relevant notice was received).

[31] 98 E.R. 1323 KB. This observation found favour with the US Supreme Court in *Taylor v Brown* 147 U.S. 640 (1893).

[32] *R. (on the application of Zaporozhchenko) v Westminster Magistrates Court* [2011] 1 W.L.R. 994.

Moreover, the interpretation may be governed by express terms of the contract. For example, art.3(d)(i) of the ICC Uniform Rules for Demand Guarantees 2010,[33] which have effect by incorporation into demand guarantees, provides that "from" includes the date mentioned. By contrast, art.3 of the ICC Uniform Customs and Practice for Documentary Credits[34] states that, when used to determine a maturity date, "from" excludes the date mentioned, though, if used to determine a period of shipment, it includes the date.

(8) "Not later than X days before" a stated date

4–10 Where payment is to be made not later than a given number of days before a specified date, one must count backwards from the date in question, which must itself be excluded in making the computation.[35] So if payment is due "not later than three days before February 1", it must be made by midnight on 28–29 January.[36]

(9) "On demand"

4–11 A provision for payment on demand entitles the debtor to have a reasonable time: (a) to verify the authority of the collector to collect payment, where he is not the creditor; and (b) physically to get the money. It does not, however, allow for a period to raise finance. Three cases illustrate the rule quite neatly. In *Toms v Wilson*,[37] a bailiff called at the debtor's house to present the creditor's demand for payment of £200 due under a bill of sale and interest which had not been calculated. The bailiff did not say that he was authorised to receive payment. Payment not being forthcoming, the bailiff seized the goods. It was held that the seizure was unlawful. In *Moore v Shelley*,[38] where payment was demanded by the wife of one of the plaintiffs, the defendant was held entitled to an opportunity to enquire into her authority to receive the money. Finally, in *RA Cripps (Pharmaceutical) & Son Ltd v Wickenden*,[39] where a charge authorised the debenture holder to appoint a receiver after making a demand for the money due, it was held that the only time to which the debtor was entitled was what was

---

[33] G. Affaki and R. Goode, *Guide to Uniform Rules for Demand Guarantees URDG 758* (2011), available at: *https://icckauppa.fi/wp-content/uploads/sites/26/2016/05/702-icc-guide-to-icc-uniform-rules-for-demand-guarantees-urdg-758.pdf* [Accessed 23 October 2020].
[34] ICC Uniform Customs and Practice for Documentary Credits (UCP 600), 2007 Revision.
[35] *Carapanayoti & Co Ltd v Comptoir Commercial Andre & Cie SA* [1972] 1 Lloyd's Rep. 139 CA (Civ Div).
[36] *Carapanayoti* [1972] 1 Lloyd's Rep. 139 CA (Civ Div) at 142. For a similar decision based on time periods for the filing of accounts at Companies House, see *Registrar of Companies v Stonelee Developments Ltd* 2004 S.L.T. (Sh Ct) 116 Sheriff Principal and, for a case on the time periods allowed for the service of notices under the Landlord and Tenant Act 1954, see *EJ Riley Investments Ltd v Eurostile Holdings Ltd* [1985] 1 W.L.R. 1139 CA (Civ Div).
[37] *Toms v Wilson* 122 E.R. 524 QB.
[38] *Moore v Shelley* (1883) 8 App. Cas. 285 PC.
[39] *RA Cripps (Pharmaceutical) & Son Ltd v Wickenden* [1973] 1 W.L.R. 944 Ch D. This decision has been followed on a number of occasions. See, for example, *Bank of Baroda v Panessar* [1987] Ch. 335 Ch D. To similar effect, see *Williams & Glyn's Bank Ltd v Barnes* [1981] Com. L.R. 205 HC; *Bank of Ireland v AMCD (Property Holdings) Ltd* [2001] 2 All E.R. (Comm) 894 Ch D.

needed to get the money from a convenient place. He was not entitled to an opportunity to raise the funds. In that case, an appointment made two hours after demand was held to be reasonable.[40] The defendant did not have the money and there was no question of his procuring it from a place where it was available. The creditor may therefore treat the debtor's default as occurring immediately if, in response to it, the debtor confirms that the necessary funds are not available.[41] The essential test of a "reasonable time" to meet the demand is that the debtor must be able to implement the necessary transfer mechanics to arrange payment from an existing bank account with a sufficient credit balance or overdraft limit.[42] Thus, if, exceptionally, a demand were made over a weekend, the creditor would have to wait until the next banking day to allow the debtor to complete payment.

This issue, together with the cases above, was considered in *Quah v Goldman Sachs International*,[43] where the defendant bank demanded repayment of an on-demand loan from the claimant in the early hours of the morning and, having given the claimant the morning to repay, issued a default notice the same day. The court, dismissing the claimant's application to amend her claim to raise this issue, considered that it was well established that the time required to effect the mechanics of repayment before the making of a declaration of default might be exceptionally short.[44]

It may be added that, where payment is due "on demand", the service of proceedings may constitute an adequate demand for these purposes, at any rate unless the contract specifically provides for prior notice.[45] As a matter of ordinary language, it does seem odd that no "demand" is necessary to crystallise the right to repayment where the payment obligation appears to be subject to that condition precedent. Happily, this anomaly is not taken too far; where the obligation arises from a guarantee, a written notice of demand is required before proceedings can be served.[46] However, no demand is required if the guarantee gives rise to a liquidated debt liability rather than an unliquidated obligation in damages. In *McGuinness v Norwich and Peterborough Building Society*,[47] it was held that, where a guarantor guaranteed that "all money and liabilities owing... will be paid and satisfied when due" and the guarantee contained a promise by the guarantor to pay the principal sum and interest if the debtor failed to pay his

---

[40] Not all Commonwealth legal systems adopt such a draconian view. For example, a Canadian court has held that a "reasonable time" for this purpose may encompass a few days: *Whonnock Industries Ltd v National Bank of Canada* (1987) 42 DLR (4th), and the Canadian Supreme Court has upheld an award of exemplary damages against a bank which required full repayment by 15.00 on the day of demand, which was found to be unreasonable in the circumstances: see *Royal Bank of Canada v W Got & Associates Electric Ltd* [1993] 3 SCR 408. In *Bank of Montreal v Carnival National Leasing Ltd* [2011] O.J. No.671, the Ontario Superior Court considered (at [13]) that, although what was reasonable will vary depending on the circumstances, such time will generally be "of short duration" and would not encompass "anything approaching 30 days".
[41] *Sheppard & Cooper Ltd v TSB Bank Plc (No.2)* [1996] 2 All E.R. 654 Ch D.
[42] In the context of a margin call, see *Quah v Goldman Sachs International* [2015] EWHC 759 (Comm) and cases there cited.
[43] *Quah* [2015] EWHC 759 (Comm).
[44] *Quah* [2015] EWHC 759 (Comm) [61]–[62].
[45] See *Norton v Ellam* 150 E.R. 839 Court of Exchequer.
[46] See *Lloyds Bank Ltd v Margolis* [1954] 1 W.L.R. 644 Ch D; *Habib Bank Ltd v Tailor* [1982] 1 W.L.R. 1218 CA (Civ Div).
[47] *McGuinness v Norwich and Peterborough Building Society* [2012] 2 All E.R. (Comm) 265.

mortgage liabilities, the creditor had a claim in debt in a pre-agreed amount, which constituted a liability in debt to the creditor within the meaning of s.267(2)(b) of the Insolvency Act 1986 and therefore the creditor could petition for bankruptcy. The Court of Appeal considered that, on its proper construction, the guarantee reflected the status of the guarantor as principal debtor by making it clear that his liability was concurrent with the borrower's and not contingent upon it. As a result, the guarantor's liability under the guarantee created a debt within the meaning of s.267(2)(b) of the Insolvency Act 1986. This approach has been followed in subsequent cases.[48]

Likewise, where a demand notice is stated to have the contractual effect of *accelerating* the later liabilities, a written demand is required to crystallise the outstanding instalments before proceedings can be issued in respect of them.[49]

(10) "On or about" a given date

4–12 The phrase "on or about" a specified date allows the debtor a little tolerance but not much. The precise construction will depend on the circumstances. For instance, in a long-term contract, the court might feel disposed to construe such a phrase more liberally than where the contract period is relatively short.

The issue has been considered in several Australian cases: in *Blackett v Clutterbuck Brothers (Adelaide) Ltd*,[50] one to three days after the due date was considered to be the maximum. This and other authorities were considered in *Mackenzie v Kentcade Properties Pty Ltd*, where the Supreme Court of Queensland considered that the authorities "serve to illustrate that, in some contexts, the word 'on' or its synonym 'upon' does not stipulate a time for something to be done".[51] Instead, the court considered the issue to be "what reason and good sense require in the context of the present contract".[52] In the context of a put option agreement to sell management rights to a resort developer on the occurrence of a "Put Option Event", which included breaches of the put option agreement, one question was whether the resort developer had allegedly breached the put option agreement by not giving notice "on" the execution of a contract with a buyer for the sale of a lot. The court, concluding that it was in breach, considered that: "An interpretation of 'on' which requires the notice to be given on the date of the relevant occurrence or within a few days thereafter accords with the ordinary meaning of the word 'on', while allowing for the exigency that it may not be possible for a notice to be given on the very same day that the contract is executed."[53] A similar question was considered by the

---

[48] See, for instance, *Dunbar Assets Plc v Fowler* [2013] B.P.I.R. 46 Ch D (Bankruptcy Court); *Lombard North Central Plc v Blower* [2014] I.L.Pr. 46; *Law Society v Blavo* [2018] EWCA Civ 2250. See *Stericker v Horner* [2012] B.P.I.R. 645 Ch D; *Doherty v Fannigan Holdings Ltd* [2018] EWCA Civ 1615; and *Davies v Revelan Estates (Wigston) Ltd* [2019] B.P.I.R. 1102 for examples of where no liquidated debt liability was found.
[49] *Esso Petroleum Co Ltd v Alstonbridge Properties Ltd* [1975] 1 W.L.R. 1474 Ch D; *Bank of Baroda v Patel* [1996] 1 Lloyd's Rep. 391 QBD.
[50] *Blackett v Clutterbuck Brothers (Adelaide) Ltd* [1923] SASR 301.
[51] *Mackenzie v Kentcade Properties Pty Ltd* [2012] QSC 299 at [27].
[52] *Mackenzie* [2012] QSC 299 at [28].
[53] *Mackenzie* [2012] QSC 299 at [37].

Supreme Court of Tasmania in *Edwards v Stock*[54] in relation to limitation of actions and when time began to run where money was borrowed "on or about 1 September 1986". The court concluded that a day "on or about 1 September" was probably before September, in the same way that "on or about 12 September" would probably be a reference to a day after 6 September.[55]

Under art.3 of the ICC Uniform Customs and Practice for Documentary Credits, "on or about" is to be interpreted as a stipulation that an event is to occur during a period of five calendar days before until five calendar days after the specified date, both start and end dates included.

(11) "Punctual", "punctually"

The word "punctual" or "punctually" does not indicate any tolerance in favour of the debtor; on the contrary, it requires him to make payment on the due date.[56]

4–13

(12) "Within X days after" a stated date, after sight or the happening of an event

Where this phrase is used, the stated date is excluded in making the computation,[57] as is the last date of the specified period.[58] So a provision for payment within seven days after 1 January requires payment to be made by midnight on 8–9 January.[59]

4–14

---

[54] *Edwards v Stock* [2008] TASSC 12.

[55] *Edwards* [2008] TASSC 12 at [25].

[56] *Maclaine v Gatty* [1921] 1 A.C. 376 HL; *A/S Tankexpress v Compagnie Financiere Belge des Petroles SA* [1949] A.C. 76 HL; *The Laconia* [1977] A.C. 850 HL. But provision for punctual payment does not mean that time of payment is necessarily of the essence in the sense that any delay will entitle the creditor to terminate the agreement (see para.4–28 below). The word "punctual" neither adds to nor detracts from the word "payment" (*Maclaine*), signifying merely that failure to pay on the date stated will be a breach. The expression was also used in the contract in *Tenax Steamship Co v Owners of the Motor Vessel Brimnes (The Brimnes)* [1975] Q.B. 929 CA (Civ Div). While Flaux J took a different view of "punctual" in *Kuwait Rocks Co v AMN Bulkcarriers Inc* [2013] 2 All E.R. (Comm) 689 QBD (Comm), considering that an obligation to make punctual payment of hire was a condition of the contract, rather than the word "punctual" adding little or nothing to the word "payment" (at [114]), *Kuwait Rocks* was overruled in *Spar Shipping AS v Grand China Logistics Holding (Group) Co Ltd* [2016] EWCA Civ 982.

[57] *Williams v Burgess* 113 E.R. 955 KB; *Dodds* [1981] 1 W.L.R. 1027 HL, applied in *Windermere* [2014] UKUT 420 (LC). It is submitted that this rule remains valid in contractual cases but a different approach to the subject may be adopted where a matter of statutory interpretation is involved: see *Zaporozhchenko* [2011] 1 W.L.R. 994.

[58] *Rightside Properties Ltd v Gray* [1975] Ch. 72 Ch D. Similarly, art.3 of Affaki and Goode, *Guide to Uniform Rules for Demand Guarantees URDG 758* (2011) specifies that, in relation to a period after a given date or event, the stated date or the date of that event is to be excluded, while adding that the last date of that period is to be included.

[59] Bills of Exchange Act 1882 s.14(2). See also *Campbell v French and Hobson* 101 E.R. 510 KB; *Manorlike Ltd v Le Vitas Travel Agency and Consultative Services* [1986] 1 All E.R. 573 CA (Civ Div).

(13) "Within a reasonable time"

4–15 This expression is frequently found in, or implied into, commercial contracts.[60] What is "reasonable" in a particular case will obviously depend on an appreciation of the contract and the customs of the market in which the parties operate and the presumed expectations of the parties.[61] Cases of this kind will inevitably be highly fact-sensitive and will involve an analysis of the conduct of the parties to allocate responsibility for any delay which may be relevant. Failure to complete within a reasonable time may give rise to a claim for damages but will not necessarily be repudiatory, if the party concerned demonstrates an intention to complete the contract and is allocating sufficient resources to that purpose.

(14) "Till", "until"

4–16 Where it is provided that payment may be made "till" or "until" a particular date, this generally includes the whole of the day named.[62]

Right to Prepay

4–17 To begin with matters of terminology, prepayment of a debt occurs at the election of the debtor to discharge the debt early, to which he may suffer a penalty in the form of interest or termination fee.[63] Acceleration, on the other hand, occurs at the election of the creditor as a result of non-payment or some other breach of the contract on the part of the debtor.

The present section deals with voluntary prepayment at the election of the debtor.[64] For these purposes, it is important to refer to the terms of the contract in order to distinguish between those cases where the contract is silent as to prepayment and those contracts which specifically exclude or restrict prepayment.

---

[60] *Postlethwaite v Freeland* (1880) 5 App. Cas. 599 HL and other cases cited by *Chitty on Contracts*, 33rd edn (London: Sweet & Maxwell, 2018), para.21–021.

[61] For an illustration, see *Astea (UK) Ltd v Time Group Ltd* [2003] EWHC 725 (TCC). The court noted that "within a reasonable time" does not have a meaning equivalent to "as quickly as possible". This has been approved by the Court of Appeal in *Urban I (Blonk Street) Ltd v Ayres* [2014] 1 W.L.R. 756 at [49]. See also the Privy Council's decision in *Francis v Vista del Mar Development Ltd* [2019] UKPC 14 in relation to what constituted a "reasonable time" in which to exercise an option.

[62] *Isaacs v Royal Insurance Co* (1869–70) L.R. 5 Ex. 296 Court of Exchequer.

[63] Where the agreement is regulated by the Consumer Credit Act 1974 (as amended), the debtor has a general right of prepayment at any time: see s.94 of the Act. Beyond this, however, a clause stipulating for a prepayment fee in the event of a voluntary decision by the borrower to terminate the contract prematurely cannot be challenged as a penalty, since the obligation to pay does not flow from a breach of contract by the borrower. See the discussion at para.3–29 above.

[64] On acceleration by the creditor, see para.3–59 above.

(1) Contract silent

4–18 There is a somewhat curious rule of mortgage law[65] that the mortgagor cannot redeem the mortgage before the due date, even if he tenders full interest,[66] except where the mortgagee has taken possession[67] or the mortgage is repayable on demand[68]; whilst a right to redeem after the due date is equitable only, so that, except in the above two cases, the mortgagor must normally give six months' notice of his intention to redeem or pay six months interest in lieu of notice.[69] The mortgagor must therefore get his timing right: payment *on* the due date, not before, is what he must tender if he wishes to redeem against the creditor's wishes. Outside the somewhat specialised and occasionally arcane field of real estate, the law is more flexible. Unless the contract otherwise provides, the debtor is entitled to accelerate payment[70] by tender of the amount due, with interest or charges to the *due* date of payment, except where the deferment of payment until the contractual payment date is a stipulation in favour of the creditor as well as the debtor.[71] Where it is in favour of the debtor only, as will usually be the case, the debtor can waive the stipulation and pay early, at any rate so long as he tenders the full sum that would be payable on the due date, without deducting unaccrued interest or charges. Hence, prima facie, the hirer under a hire-purchase agreement and the buyer under an instalment sale agreement[72] can settle ahead of time, a right now given by statute in relation to regulated consumer credit agreements.[73]

(2) Contract precluding or restricting prepayment

4–19 It is open to the parties to agree that the debtor shall not have the right to prepay, or that his right of prepayment is to be restricted or is to be exercisable only on

---

[65] On mortgages generally, see P. Morgan, *Fisher & Lightwood's Law of Mortgage*, 14th edn (London: LexisNexis, 2014) and *Halsbury's Laws of England*, 7th edn (London: LexisNexis), Vol.77.
[66] *Brown v Cole* 60 E.R. 424 Ch. The right to prepay must be distinguished from the right (or "equity") of redemption, which is exerciseable by the borrower only once the contractual date for repayment has arrived: see *Halsbury's Laws of England*, Vol.77, para.304. The rule in *Brown v Cole* is generally accepted in the US: see *Promenade Towers Mutual Housing Corp v Metropolitan Life Insurance Co* (1991) 597 A.2d 1377; and *Ridgley v Topa Thrift & Loan Association* 62 Cal. Rptr. 2d 309 at 318. Inevitably, however, differences in practice have arisen. The Pennsylvania Supreme Court has observed that "where a mortgage note is silent as to the right of prepayment, there arises a presumption that the debt may be prepaid": *Mahoney v Furches* 468 A.2d 458 (Pa 1983) at 461.
[67] *Bovill v Endle* [1896] 1 Ch. 648 Ch D.
[68] *GA Investments Pty Ltd v Standard Insurance Co Ltd* [1964] WAR 264.
[69] *Smith v Smith* [1891] 3 Ch. 550 Ch D; *Johnson v Evans* (1889) 61 L.T. 18.
[70] *Lancashire Waggon Co Ltd v Nuttall* (1879) 42 L.T. 465.
[71] A potential example being where interest rates are negative, so that the creditor incurs costs as a result of holding the money, as has been happening in Switzerland since 2014.
[72] *Lancashire Waggon* at fn.68 above. It seems that the position would be different in a complex commercial transaction, e.g. a syndicated loan.
[73] See below. Most first mortgages of residential property for personal occupation are now no longer within the scope of the Consumer Credit Act 1974, but are governed by the Financial Services and Markets Act 2000.

payment of a premium for early settlement.[74] Even in mortgage transactions, the right to redeem can validly be postponed for a substantial period so long as the transaction is not thereby rendered unconscionable.[75] In relation to debentures issued by companies, s.739 of the Companies Act 2006 expressly provides that they are not to be invalid by reason only that they are made irredeemable or redeemable only on the happening of a contingency, however remote, or on the expiration of a period, however long, notwithstanding any rule of equity to the contrary.

(3) Prepayment by statute

4–20 Section 94 of the Consumer Credit Act 1974 gives the debtor under a regulated consumer credit agreement a right to prepay his indebtedness, whilst s.95 prescribes a rebate for early settlement in accordance with regulations made under that section.[76]

3. IMPLIED TERMS AS TO TIME

Bank loan or overdraft

4–21 Prima facie, a bank loan or overdraft is repayable on demand,[77] but this presumption is displaced by an express or implied term to the contrary. In particular, the court may find that, in order to give business efficacy to the

---

[74] *Knightsbridge Estates Trust Ltd v Byrne* [1939] Ch. 441 CA, affirmed [1940] A.C. 613 HL. See also *Brighton and Hove City Council v Audus* [2010] 1 All E.R. (Comm), where, although the court considered that a condition which is a clog on the contractual and equitable right to redeem would be void, not just voidable, no such clog was found where a nephew had "loaned" his aunt and uncle money to buy their council house and they granted two charges in favour of him, one for the purchase price of £12,375, and the second to "secure to the lender the benefit of any capital appreciation of the property". Morgan J found that the arrangement did not involve a loan or create a security interest as there was no intention that the loan should be repaid. Instead, the nephew was to be the owner, with his rights subordinate to the agreement that the couple could remain in occupation for the remainder of their lives.

[75] *Knightsbridge Estates* [1939] Ch. 441 CA at 459.

[76] See the Consumer Credit (Early Settlement) Regulations 2004 (SI 2004/1483).

[77] *Titford Property Co Ltd v Cannon Street Acceptances Ltd* unreported 22 May 1975 Ch D, Goff J; *Williams & Glyn's Bank Ltd v Barnes* (1981) Com. L.R. 205 HC, Gibson J. These decisions have occasionally encouraged other borrowers to argue that an overdraft is not repayable on demand, but, in *Lloyds Bank Plc v Lampert* [1999] 1 All E.R. (Comm) 161 CA (Civ Div), the Court of Appeal held that the words "the amount borrowed will be repayable in full on demand, but it is the Bank's present intention to make the facility available to you until 31 December 1996" meant precisely what they said. The statement of intention did not overrule the bank's general right of demand. For an essentially similar decision, see *Bank of Ireland v AMCD (Property Holdings) Ltd* [2001] 2 All E.R. (Comm) 894 Ch D. See also *Arora* (1981) 2 Co. Law 23. See also *Carey Group Plc v AIB Group (UK) Plc* [2012] Ch. 304 Ch D, where the terms of an overdraft facility expressly contemplated that a demand might be made before to the termination of the facility, and *Hall v Royal Bank of Scotland Plc* [2009] EWHC 3163 (QB), where it was held that a bank had not breached its duty of care or contractual obligations by refusing to extend a customer's overdraft facilities in circumstances where it was repayable on demand and there was nothing to suggest that the bank's right to demand repayment was restricted. It was held in *R. (on the application of SRM Global Master Fund LP) v Treasury Commissioner* [2009] B.C.C. 251, that it was settled law that "where a facility letter provides that a loan is 'repayable on

contract, it is necessary to imply a term that the loan or overdraft shall not be called in before a given date or event or without reasonable notice. An example is offered by the unreported decision of Gibson J in *Williams and Glyn's Bank Ltd v Barnes*,[78] where a facility letter from the bank to its customer provided for an increase in the facility to £11 million on "the usual banking conditions" to enable the customer to meet its obligations under various bills of exchange on their maturity. It was held that, to give business efficacy to the contract, a term was to be implied that the bank could not require repayment of its advance until the payment of the last of the bills and the expiry of reasonable notice. The reference to "usual banking conditions" was insufficient to negate the inference that the bank was not free to require repayment on demand.

A not uncommon problem in banking and finance transactions is a conflict, or apparent conflict, between provisions as to time of repayment in one document and those contained in another document—and sometimes even the same document—relating to the same transaction. Typical is the case where the facility letter provides for, say, repayment in 12 months and then proceeds to incorporate by reference the lender's standard form of charge which provides for repayment on demand. How is the conflict to be resolved? The normal rule of interpretation is that the general yields to the particular, and the standard term gives way to the term specifically negotiated.[79] Accordingly, the specific terms of a facility letter will take precedence over the inconsistent terms of the lender's standard security document unless, on a proper construction of the facility letter, the apparently inconsistent term in that letter is to take effect subject to the security instrument. Sometimes, of course, the two provisions taken together produce nonsense and the court has to disregard one as repugnant to the other. In *Titford Property Co Ltd v Cannon Street Acceptances Ltd*,[80] the inconsistency was not between one document and another but between two separate provisions of the facility letter. The first of these provided for an overdraft facility for a period of 12 months while the second stated that all moneys due were repayable on demand. Plainly, it was not possible to give effect to both provisions; and Goff J held that the stipulation as to repayment on demand was to be rejected, for otherwise the customer could be led into a disastrous position in reliance on the prior statement as to the duration of the facility. The stipulation as to repayment on demand was repugnant to the purpose of the transaction and was to be disregarded. However, it does not follow that in every case a provision for payment on demand gives way to a provision for a term loan. The contract must be construed as a whole, and, reading the two provisions together, the court may conclude that the intention is to give the debtor a facility for the stated period or duration of the

---

demand', that provision prevails even though there are other provisions in the facility agreement indicating that the bank intends to make the facility available until a specific date..." (citing the *Lampert* and *Bank of Ireland* cases) (at [139]).

[78] At fn.77 above.

[79] *Robertson v French* (1803) 4 East 130 KB at 136 per Lord Ellenborough CJ. The rule has been applied in many subsequent cases. See, for example, *Gesellschaft Burgerlichen Rechts v Stockholms Rederi AB Svea (The Brabant)* [1967] 1 Q.B. 588 QBD (Comm); *Bayoil SA v Seawind Tankers Corp (The Leonidas)* [2001] 1 All E.R. (Comm) 392 QBD (Comm); *Cubitt Building & Interiors Ltd v Richardson Roofing (Industrial) Ltd* [2008] B.L.R. 354.

[80] *Titford Property* unreported May 22 1975 Ch D.

Sale of goods

4–22 Unless otherwise agreed, delivery and payment under a contract of sale of goods are concurrent conditions, so that the seller cannot claim payment unless he is ready and willing to tender delivery.[82] However, there is a further requirement that must be satisfied. Section 49 of the Sale of Goods Act 1979 requires that either property in the goods must have passed to the buyer (s.49(1)) or the price must be payable on a day certain irrespective of delivery and that day must have arrived (s.49(2)).

Where no provision is made for a date certain, the seller only has an action for the price if property has passed in accordance with s.49(1). This means that the seller, even if ready to tender delivery, cannot claim the price if the property has not passed, and this is so even if it is the buyer's breach that has prevented the transfer of the property.[83] It is, however, open to the seller to stipulate that the price is payable before delivery, and the seller may sue for the price at that point.[84]

The requirement in s.49(1) for property to have passed in order for the seller to be able to sue for the price has given rise to difficulties in recent cases involving retention of title (ROT) clauses where the goods are likely to be consumed or resold before payment is made. ROT clauses typically provide that property in goods does not pass to the buyer until the buyer has paid the purchase price. On this basis, it has been held by the Court of Appeal in *Caterpillar (NI) Ltd (formerly FG Wilson (Engineering) Ltd) v John Holt & Co (Liverpool) Ltd,* that a seller on ROT terms where the goods were resold before payment was made could not sue for the price[85]; although this conclusion is now in doubt following obiter dicta in the Supreme Court decision of *The Res Cogitans*, as will be discussed below.[86]

In *Wilson v Holt* it was held that, where a seller sold generators to a customer on credit on ROT terms and the customer would sub-sell to its Nigerian subsidiary before paying the seller, the seller could not bring a claim for the price within s.49 since its claim would have to comply with the condition in s.49(1) that property in the goods had passed to the buyer. The Court of Appeal in *Wilson v Holt* took the view that s.49 was mandatory and intended to specify the only circumstances in which a seller could maintain an action for the price.

---

[81] *Barnes* (1981) Com. L.R. 205 HC, and other cases referred to in fn.77 above.
[82] Sale of Goods Act 1979 s.28.
[83] *Colley v Overseas Exporters (1919) Ltd* [1921] 3 K.B. 302 KBD; *Caterpillar (NI) Ltd (formerly FG Wilson (Engineering) Ltd) v John Holt & Co (Liverpool) Ltd* [2014] 1 W.L.R. 2365. See para.2–15 above.
[84] The contract may, however, have to be carefully drafted to achieve this result: see the discussion in *Henderson & Keay Ltd v AM Carmichael Ltd* 1956 S.L.T. (Notes) 58 Court of Session (Outer House).
[85] *Wilson v Holt* [2014] 1 W.L.R. 2365.
[86] *PST Energy 7 Shipping LLC v OW Bunker Malta Ltd (The Res Cogitans)* [2016] 2 W.L.R. 1193.

This view has been subject to much criticism and suggestions were subsequently made that s.49 should either been reinterpreted or reformed.[87] Given that the effect of the Court of Appeal's view was that an obligation to pay the purchase price may have arisen (in *Wilson v Holt*, the buyer was obliged to pay within "30 days from date of invoice") but the seller still had no action for the price unless the parties have agreed that payment will occur on "a day certain", the criticisms appeared well founded. In the ROT context, the decision has the potential to lead to commercially undesirable consequences and cause uncertainty for sellers who supply goods on credit terms. At least when the buyer is solvent, such sellers will want to be able to sue non-paying buyers for the price rather than relying on their proprietary rights. As a wider point, it seemed strange that parties to a contract could specify that there should be an action for the price in circumstances other than those in s.49. Popplewell J at first instance and Longmore LJ in the Court of Appeal both considered that the requirement that property must have passed if s.49(2) did not apply was correct,[88] apparently on the basis that the buyer should not have to pay until he had received what he was paying for. However, they did not analyse precisely what the buyer in this contract was paying for, e.g. possession of the goods or property in the goods. It has been argued that the real evil which s.49(2) is intended to guard against is a seller who fails to deliver the goods but still sues for the price.[89] In addition, it was not clear that the seller would have a claim for damages in this scenario as an alternative to an action for the price, which would present "windfall" concerns. Longmore LJ had noted in *Wilson v Holt* that "English law does not normally allow a claim for damages for failure to pay money" and that there was a "logical difficulty" in holding that the buyer was in breach of contract in failing to pay the price if the price is itself not due because property in the goods has never passed.[90] The solution suggested by Longmore LJ was that ROT sellers provide for payment on "a day certain" to bring their contracts within s.49(2).[91] However, since this would have required that payment be made on a specified date or within a specified period (as discussed below), the requirement would not be met where the determination of the date for payment depended on an action by one of the contract parties after the date of the contract, as it did in *Wilson v Holt* (in this case, the seller issuing the invoice). Therefore, since it might be commercially difficult for sellers to stipulate actual dates in the contract, this "solution" is clearly unsatisfactory.

The practical implications of the decision in *Wilson v Holt* were clearly highlighted in *The Res Cogitans*,[92] where the Supreme Court criticised the view that s.49 was mandatory in obiter dicta.[93] By way of background, a supplier had

---

[87] See, for instance, Louise Gullifer, "The Interpretation of Retention of Title Clauses: Some Difficulties" [2014] L.M.C.L.Q. 564.
[88] *Wilson v Holt* [2013] 1 All E.R. (Comm) 223 at [41]; and [2014] 1 W.L.R. 2365 at [52].
[89] Louise Gullifer, "The Interpretation of Retention of Title Clauses: Some Difficulties" (2014) 4 L.M.C.L.Q. 564 at 576–577; "'Sales' on Retention of Title Terms: Is the English Law Analysis Broken?" (2017) 133 L.Q.R. 244.
[90] *Wilson v Holt* [2014] 1 W.L.R. 2365 at [55].
[91] *Wilson v Holt* [2014] 1 W.L.R. 2365 at [44].
[92] *The Res Cogitans* [2016] UKSC 23.
[93] *The Res Cogitans* [2016] UKSC 23 at [41]–[58].

sold bunkers of oil to some shipowners on credit but the shipowners had the right to use the bunkers for propulsion of the vessel before payment. The contract contained an ROT clause whereby property in the bunkers would not pass to the shipowners until they were paid for. The bunkers were delivered and consumed before the expiration of the 60-day credit period. The shipowners failed to pay on the payment date. They argued that, since the bunkers had already been consumed by the payment date, property in the bunkers had never passed to them and the supplier had no claim for the price under s.49(1). Relying on *Wilson v Holt*, they also claimed that the supplier had no claim for the price as a contract debt at common law, since the price of goods sold cannot be recovered except pursuant to s.49. The suppliers counter-argued that the contract was not a "contract of sale of goods" within the Sale of Goods Act 1979 and was instead a supply contract, so they could claim the contract amount as a liquidated debt.

At first instance, Males J agreed with the suppliers.[94] His decision was unanimously upheld by the Court of Appeal,[95] which considered that the contract could not be a contract of sale of goods since the "essential nature" of the contract was that goods were to be "delivered to the owners as bailees with a licence to consume them ... coupled with an agreement to sell any quantity remaining at the date of payment ...".[96] The Court of Appeal considered that this was outside the definition of a contract of sale of goods in s.2(1) of the Sale of Goods Act, which defines a contract of sale of goods as a "contract by which the seller transfers or agrees to transfer the property in goods to the buyer for a money consideration, called the price". It is significant to note that both Males J and the Court of Appeal were bound by the decision in *Wilson v Holt* and so, had they found that the contract was a contract for the sale of goods within the 1979 Act, the suppliers would have had no claim for the price.

The Supreme Court upheld the Court of Appeal's finding that the contract was not a contract for the sale of goods within s.2(1). However, it further considered in obiter dicta that s.49 was not a "complete code of situations in which the price may be recoverable under a contract of sale" and therefore would have been no bar to a claim by the seller for payment of the agreed price.[97] Lord Mance noted that, had the contract been one of sale, he would have overruled *Wilson v Holt* and found that the price in the instant case was recoverable by virtue of the express terms of the contract in the event which had occurred, namely, the complete consumption of the bunkers.[98] Therefore, it was not necessary for the Supreme Court to find that the contract was a supply contract.

While the Supreme Court's finding that s.49 is not mandatory is welcome in light of the difficulties presented by the alternative view, its decision in *The Res Cogitans* that the contract in question was not one for the sale of goods is more controversial. Lord Mance noted that the contract in question was:

> "in substance an agreement with two aspects: first, to permit consumption prior to any payment and (once the theory of a nanosecond transfer of property is, rightly, rejected) without any

---

[94] *The Res Cogitans* [2015] 2 Lloyd's Rep. 563.
[95] *The Res Cogitans* [2016] 2 W.L.R. 1072.
[96] *The Res Cogitans* [2016] 2 W.L.R. 1072 at [33].
[97] *The Res Cogitans* [2016] 2 W.L.R. 1193 at [58] and [60].
[98] *The Res Cogitans* [2016] 2 W.L.R. 1193 at [58].

property ever passing in the bunkers consumed; and, second, but only if and so far as the bunkers remained unconsumed, to transfer the property in the bunkers so remaining to the owners in return for the owners paying the price. But in this latter connection it is to be noted that the price does not here refer to the price of the bunkers in respect of which property was passing, it refers to the price payable for all the bunkers, whether consumed before or remaining at the time of its payment."[99]

The Supreme Court rejected the argument that the contract was a contract of sale since it was an agreement to transfer property, conditional on the bunkers being unburdened when payment was made. It considered that this would categorise the whole agreement by reference to only one possibility relating to one part of the bunkers (e.g. that some would be unconsumed at the time payment was due or made) that there was no condition governing the transfer of property in the bunkers before payment and that the agreement was a single contract to pay a single "price" for all bunkers not later than 60 days after delivery, whether consumed or not and could not "sensibly be treated as divisible".[100] It also rejected the Court of Appeal's suggestion that the contract could be analysed as a contract of sale to the extent it provided for the transfer of property in any surviving bunkers at the time of payment.[101]

However, the outcome of the case appears to be that the Sale of Goods Act does not apply to contracts on ROT terms where the goods are likely to be consumed or sold on prior to payment. This appears incorrect in principle as well as potentially having undesirable practical consequences. It is not an essential ingredient of a contract of sale that the seller should be legally or physically able to transfer ownership. A person may make an *agreement for sale* of goods to which he has neither title nor a right to dispose or which he knows have ceased to exist. Moreover, it seems logical despite the Supreme Court's rejection of the "nanosecond transfer of property" theory that, where the buyer is given a right to consum the goods before property has passed, such consumption triggers the passing of property, as at that point the seller can no longer assert a proprietary interest as regards what has been consumed. This view would seem more in keeping with the commercial expectations of parties contracting on ROT terms.

In *Wood v TUI Travel Plc (t/a First Choice)*,[102] the Court of Appeal rejected an attempt to apply this theory outside the context of ROT clauses in sales of goods. Where a couple who booked an all-inclusive holiday had contracted food poisoning from the food, the travel company attempted to argue that there was no intention that property in the food and drink would pass to customers until it was consumed (and therefore there would be no transfer, since it would no longer exist), such that s.4 of the Supply of Goods and Services Act 1982 would not apply. This argument was rejected on the basis that property in the goods passed to the customers when it was served to them, while the situation in *The Res Cogitans* depended on the relationship between the ROT clause and right to consume.[103]

---

[99] *The Res Cogitans* [2016] 2 W.L.R. 1193 at [28].
[100] *The Res Cogitans* [2016] 2 W.L.R. 1193 at [29].
[101] *The Res Cogitans* [2016] 2 W.L.R. 1193 at [31].
[102] *Wood v TUI Travel Plc (t/a First Choice)* [2017] EWCA Civ 11.
[103] *Wood v TUI Travel* [2017] EWCA Civ 11 at [25].

If property has not passed, the "day certain" requirement in s.49(2) must be met for the seller to be able to sue for the price.[104] What is meant by "a day certain" is not altogether clear, but the phrase would seem to require that the contract should specify either a date on or by which or a period at the end of which payment is to be made. It is not sufficient to provide for payment on invoice[105] or against documents.[106] The meaning of "a day certain" was discussed at first instance in *The Res Cogitans*[107] where Males J considered (disagreeing with the decision of the arbitrators) that provision for payment to be made within a fixed period (in this case, 60 days after delivery) would be sufficient to satisfy the requirement.[108] Ultimately, however, it was not necessary for Males J to decide the point since it was found (as discussed above) that the contract in question was not a contract for the sale of goods within the Sale of Goods Act. The Supreme Court considered that, although these words could be "construed liberally", they were not of "indefinite expansion"[109] but did not give further guidance.

Supply of services

4–23   Unless otherwise agreed, payment under a contract for services is due when the services have been performed and the debtor has had an opportunity to check that the work has been properly carried out.[110]

4. TERMINATION OF CONTRACT FOR DELAY IN PAYMENT

4–24   The remedies of the creditor where the debtor fails to pay on the due date depend on the terms of the contract and on what is implied by law where the contract makes no provision. Every failure to pay on the due date is a breach of contract entitling the creditor to damages, either as an alternative to a claim for the contract price[111] or in addition to such claim. But the remedy in which the creditor is likely to be most interested is termination of the agreement, with or without a consequential claim for damages. In what circumstances does delay in payment entitle the creditor to treat the contract as discharged?

It is strange that, despite all the litigation that has raged over this question, conceptual difficulties continue to plague us. These are in large measure due to the fact that so many of the cases involve conveyancing transactions and that, for many years, conveyancers had somehow got into the habit of believing their contracts to be immune from general principles of contract law. All too often,

---

[104] Subject, it is submitted following the Supreme Court decision in *The Res Cogitans*, to any express rights seller has to sue for the price pursuant to the contract.
[105] *Henderson & Keay* 1956 S.L.T. (Notes) 58 Court of Session (Outer House); *Wilson v Holt* [2014] 1 W.L.R. 2365.
[106] *Stein Forbes & Co Ltd v County Tailoring Co Ltd* (1916) 86 L.J.K.B. 448 KB.
[107] *The Res Cogitans* [2015] 2 Lloyd's Rep. 563.
[108] *The Res Cogitans* [2015] 2 Lloyd's Rep. 563 at [73].
[109] *The Res Cogitans* [2016] 2 W.L.R. 1193 at [50].
[110] *Hughes v Lenny* 151 E.R. 79 Court of Exchequer.
[111] It will rarely be in the creditor's interest to pursue this alternative in view of the great advantages of an action for money earned over a claim for damages. See para.2–40 above.

they have been reinforced in this view by unguarded judicial utterances and it has been left to the House of Lords to remind the profession that a conveyancing contract is to be interpreted like any other contract and is governed by the same general principles. Thus, for years, it was thought that the remedy for a purchaser's failure to complete was rescission ab initio, which was inconsistent with a claim for damages,[112] whereas it is elementary contract law that rescission ab initio is given not for breach but for some external factor (misrepresentation, duress, undue influence etc) constituting an improper inducement by the guilty party to the innocent party to enter into the contract and entitling the latter to avoid it from the beginning. The remedy for non-performance is not rescission and restitution but termination and damages.[113] Again, the fact that time of completion is prima facie not of the essence, so that failure to complete on the due date does not by itself entitle the innocent party to terminate the contract, led courts and textbook writers to conclude that a party who did not complete on the specified completion date was not guilty of breach of contract at all until the lapse of a reasonable time—a manifest non sequitur which persisted until finally put to rest by the House of Lords in *Raineri v Miles*.[114] From this sprang what seems to be the equally erroneous notion that a reasonable time must be allowed to elapse after the specified completion date before the innocent party can serve a notice, making time of the essence.[115]

What, then, is the present law concerning the innocent party's right to bring the contract to an end because of delay by the other party in making payment? In Grand *China Logistics Holding (Group) Co Ltd v Spar Shipping AS*,[116] Sir Terence Etherton MR described references to time being "of the essence" as being used in "two very different senses" in our jurisprudence[117]:

> "On the one hand, it is used to describe a contractual time condition any breach of which is a repudiatory breach entitling the other party to bring the contract to an end. On the other hand, in the context of a provision for service of a notice making time of the essence, typically in a conveyancing contract, subject always to the express terms of the contract it means fixing the

---

[112] The error arose through misuse of the word "rescission", which was no doubt used as a convenient shorthand expression but, in this context, should have been taken to mean acceptance of the defaulting party's repudiation, producing termination of the contract, not cancellation from the beginning. The error was not put right until the decision of the House of Lords in *Johnson v Agnew* [1980] A.C. 367 HL, overruling a line of prior authority.

[113] The point is highlighted with clarity in *Howard-Jones v Tate* [2012] 1 All E.R. 369. It is true that total non-performance by one party entitles the other to recover payments he has made as money paid on a total failure of consideration, but he is not obliged to pursue this restitutionary remedy and may simply take the more usual course and terminate the contract and sue for damages.

[114] *Raineri v Miles* [1981] A.C. 1050 HL, applied in *RDC Concrete Pte Ltd v Sato Kogyo (S) Pte Ltd* [2007] SGCA 39; *Cochrane (Decorators) v Sarabandi* (1983) 133 N.L.J. 588 QBD (Official Referee); *Fitzpatrick v Sarcon (No.177) Ltd* [2012] NICh 10 (although the Court of Appeal reversed the trial judge's ruling that time was of the essence in the contract and held that the purchaser was not entitled to rescind; [2014] N.I. 35 CA). That the law in this area had unquestionably fallen into a confused and unhappy state was acknowledged by the Court of Appeal in *Urban I* [2014] 1 W.L.R. 756.

[115] *Green v Sevin* (1879) 13 Ch. D. 589; *Smith v Hamilton* [1951] Ch. 174 Ch D. See para.4–31 below. The decision in *Hamilton* was finally overruled in *Behzadi v Shaftesbury Hotels Ltd* [1992] Ch. 1 CA (Civ Div).

[116] *Grand China Logistics Holding (Group) Co Ltd v Spar Shipping AS* [2016] EWCA Civ 982.

[117] *Spar Shipping* [2016] EWCA Civ 982 at [104].

time beyond which equity will not intervene to prevent the innocent party being entitled to treat the contract as at an end if the innocent party would otherwise be entitled at law to do so."

This indicates that there are two conceptually distinct situations in which the innocent party can terminate a contract for non-payment due to time being "of the essence".[118] The first is where the time of payment is of the essence from the outset of the contract. The second is where the innocent party serves a notice making time of the essence in accordance with the contract. This bears some discussion since, as was discussed in the first and second editions of this book, it used to be thought that the innocent party could make time of the essence by reasonable notice given after the due date of payment had passed until *Urban I (Blonk Street) Ltd v Ayres*[119] challenged the notion that a notice can turn an innominate term into a condition. Finally, of course, the debtor's default may be so grave or persistent as to constitute a repudiation of the contract.[120]

Shipping and charterparty cases have continued to provide a source of difficulty and it may be useful to examine two recent cases dealing with the non-payment of hire. In *The Astra*,[121] the charterers ran into financial difficulties. They indicated that they would have to declare bankruptcy unless the owners agreed a reduction in the level of the contractual hire. In addition, they frequently paid late.

Time of the essence from the outset

(1) Significance of time as of the essence

4–25   The statement that time is of the essence means that the parties are to be taken to attach such importance to punctual payment that any delay, however brief, is to entitle the creditor to treat the contract as at an end.[122]

---

[118] As Popplewell J suggested at first instance in the *Spar Shipping* case.
[119] *Urban 1 (Blonk Street) Ltd v Ayres* [2014] 1 W.L.R. 756.
[120] Discussed below at 4–35.
[121] *The Astra* [2013] EWHC 865.
[122] Whether the delay amounts to a repudiation of the contract for the purpose of computing damages is a separate question. Termination of a contract for default pursuant to an express provision of the contract is not in all cases to be equated with acceptance of a repudiation. See para.3–70 above. It should be emphasised that the frequent use of the standard expression "time is of the essence in this agreement" is not especially helpful, since many contracts will contain a multiplicity of obligations of different levels of importance, and it cannot seriously be argued that time is of the essence of *all* of them: see *British & Commonwealth Holdings Plc v Quadrex Holdings Inc* [1989] Q.B. 842 CA (Civ Div). Yet, if the time of payment is stipulated to be of the essence, then the court must give effect to that clause as a condition of the contract. The consequences of that decision are evident from the decision in *Lombard North Central Plc v Butterworth* [1987] Q.B. 527 CA (Civ Div), where a clause making time of the essence was held to have the effect of making the time of payment a condition of the contract, with the result that: (i) the relevant breach went to the root of the contract; (ii) the lessor had a contractual right to terminate the contract; and (iii) the lessor was entitled to recover damages for loss of the entire transaction, including the benefit of future payment streams, despite the penalty rule which would have made a penalty provision in the contract unenforceable—although see paras 3–28 to 3–33 above for subsequent changes to the penalty rule.

(2) When is time of payment of the essence from the outset?

At law, time was originally considered to be of the essence in relation to any stipulated performance constituting a condition of the contract.[123] Equity, however, took a more relaxed attitude towards performance and considered that the stipulation of a time for performance did not make adherence to that time crucial (in the sense of precluding a late tender of performance) except where it was apparent from the terms of the contract, its nature or the surrounding circumstances that the parties intended time to be of the essence.[124] The common law in turn began to move away from its strict position, and it became recognised that timely performance might be more important for some types of obligation than for others. For example, in a contract for the sale of goods between merchants, late delivery might ordinarily be expected to have far more adverse consequences for the buyer than late payment for the seller.[125] The principles of equity and law relating to time have been brought together in what is now s.41 of the Law of Property Act 1925[126]:

4–26

> "Stipulations in a contract, as to time or otherwise, which according to rules of equity are not deemed to be or to have become of the essence of the contract, are also construed and have effect at law in accordance with the same rules."

Therefore, it appears that the equitable rules prevail.[127] There has been much debate regarding the basis of the equitable rules as to time. In some of the cases, these rules have been treated as a particular manifestation of the equitable jurisdiction to grant relief against forfeiture,[128] whilst, in others, the judges have declared that equity must give effect to the intention of the parties and that the question is one of the construction of the contract.[129] The difference between the

---

[123] For a comprehensive review of the authorities, see the speech of Lord Simon in *United Scientific Holdings Ltd v Burnley BC* [1978] A.C. 904 HL. In what circumstances performance of a designated act *was* a condition of the contract was a much debated question. In the early days of the common law, after bilateral contracts had become recognised, the respective undertakings of the parties were usually treated as independent of each other, on the premise that the consideration for each party's promise was not the performance by the other party but merely his counter-promise. Later, the pendulum swung the other way and undertakings began to be more strictly construed and treated as conditions. Under the influence of equity, this strict approach was relaxed, and there was a tendency to move away from the rule engendered by the requirements of pleading that each party's readiness to perform at the appointed time was a condition precedent to the other's duty to perform.
[124] *Stickney v Keeble* [1915] A.C. 386 HL at 415–416 per Lord Parker; *United Scientific Holdings* at fn.110 above. See also *Martindale v Smith* 113 E.R. 1181 QB; *Mersey Steel & Iron Co Ltd v Naylor Benzon & Co* (1884) 9 App. Cas. 434 HL; *Bunge Corp v Tradax Export SA* [1981] 1 W.L.R. 711 HL. Time has generally been held not to be of the essence in contracts for the sale of land. For US authorities to this effect, see the decision of the New York Court of Appeals in *ADC Orange Inc v Coyote Acres Inc* 2006 NY Slip Op 07520.
[125] A fact reflected in s.10 of the Sale of Goods Act 1979. See also *Decro-Wall International SA v Practitioners in Marketing* [1971] 1 W.L.R. 361 CA (Civ Div).
[126] Re-enacting s.25(7) of the Supreme Court of Judicature Act 1873.
[127] As acknowledged by Lord Simon in *United Scientific Holdings Ltd* [1978] A.C. 904 HL at 943, in discussing the effect of s.41. Also, see *Chitty* (2018), para.21–012.
[128] *Tilley v Thomas* (1867–68) L.R. 3 Ch. App. 61 CA (Ch); *Lennon v Napper* (1802) 2 Sch. & Lef. 682.
[129] George Northcore, *Fry: A Treatise on Specific Performance*, 6th edn (London: Stevens and Sons, 1921), para.1075, quoted with approval by Buckley LJ in *United Scientific Holdings Ltd v Burnley BC*

two approaches is more apparent than real, a fact which becomes evident if we bear in mind that construction of a contract involves not merely its interpretation as a matter of language but its legal effect.[130] Where the intention of the parties was to make time of the essence, equity followed the law in giving effect to that intention. Where, however, the parties' intention was not made manifest by the terms of the contract, the subject matter or the surrounding circumstances, the common law regarded failure to perform on time as absolving the innocent party from his own duty of performance, whilst equity would grant relief against the strictness of the common law rule and give specific performance despite the applicant's delay in performing his part of the contract. It is in this sense of determining the legal effect of a contract that equity "construed" the contract differently from the common law.

With these preliminary remarks, we can turn to the modern rules dealing with the circumstances in which time of payment is to be considered of the essence. It should be noted that it is potentially inaccurate to talk of time being "of the essence of the contract" as a whole, since time may be of the essence for particular terms in the contract but not for the entire contract.[131] Therefore, the question in each case is whether the time is of the essence in relation to the particular term which has been breached. This is a matter of interpretation in the context of the contract as a whole.[132]

(a) Prima facie, time of payment is not of the essence

4–27 The presumption is that time of payment is not of the essence, so that delay in payment does not of itself entitle the creditor to treat the contract as being at an end.[133] In the case of sale of goods, this presumption is enshrined in s.10(1) of the Sale of Goods Act 1979, a provision which reflects a rule of the common law applicable to contracts generally,[134] save those which by their nature necessitate strict performance of the payment obligation.

While it has sometimes been asserted that time is always of the essence in relation to "mercantile" contracts, it was made clear in the *Spar Shipping* case that this does not generally apply to the time of payment.[135] Moreover, this is not

---

[1976] Ch. 128 CA (Civ Div) at 141, and by Roskill LJ at 147; *Raineri* [1981] A.C. 1050 HL at 1074, per Viscount Dilhorne. On contracts for the sale of land, see C.J. Rossiter, "The Essence of Punctuality: Termination of Contracts for the Sale of Land for Late Performance and Relief in Equity" [2001] UNSWLJ 10. The construction approach appears to have been taken in *Samarenko v Dawn Hill House Ltd* [2013] Ch. 36 CA (Civ Div), where it was held that failure to make timely payment of a deposit amounted to repudiatory breach and any presumption that time was not of the essence was rebutted.

[130] *Amin Rasheed Shipping Corp v Kuwait Insurance Co (The Al Wahab)* [1984] A.C. 50 HL.
[131] See *Chitty* (2018), para.21–011 and cases cited therein.
[132] *Samarenko* [2013] Ch. 36 CA (Civ Div) at [9].
[133] See *Chitty* (2018), para.21–013; *Halsbury's Laws of England*, Vol.22, para.502.
[134] See, for example, *Radio & Allied (Holdings) v Bowmakers Guardian*, 15 June 1963 and *Pic-A-Pop Beverages Ltd v G&J Watt Co Ltd* (1975) 52 D.L.R. (3d) 754 (noted by *Halsbury's Laws of England*, Vol.22, fn.20).
[135] *Spar Shipping* [2016] EWCA Civ 982 at [56].

necessarily the case even as regards stipulations other than payment,[136] and whilst it is true that, in the more common types of commercial contract, timely performance of many non-money stipulations is generally considered crucial, e.g. delivery[137] and notice of readiness to load,[138] payment has usually been treated differently.[139] An examination of the modern cases on termination of a contract for delay in performance shows that, on each occasion, the court was concerned with a non-money stipulation or with a payment undertaking of which punctual performance was made of the essence by the express terms of the contract. As a rule, time of payment is not of the essence even in commercial contracts.[140] The Canadian Supreme Court held, in the context of an option to purchase a vessel, that time is not of the essence of the contract unless the parties have expressly made it so or the nature of the property or the circumstances of the contract create such a presumption.[141] An exception is payment under a letter of credit against shipping documents.[142]

Nevertheless, as the House of Lords affirmed in *United Scientific Holdings Ltd v Burnley BC*,[143] whilst time will not generally be of the essence in commercial contracts, it will be so if: (i) the parties expressly state that time limits require strict compliance; or (ii) the nature of the subject matter or the surrounding circumstances demonstrate that the time of payment was of the essence. To this it may be added that time will often be of the essence for option agreements and that, in other cases, the innocent party may be able to make time of the essence by notice to the defaulting party to that effect. It is necessary to consider each of these various alternatives in turn.

---

[136] See *Bunge Corp v Tradax Export SA* [1981] 2 All E.R. 540 HL at 553 per Lord Roskill; *United Scientific Holdings* [1978] A.C. 904 HL at 950 per Lord Salmon. See also *Cie Commercial Sucres et Denrées v C Czarnikow Ltd (The Naxos)* [1990] 1 W.L.R. 1337 HL; and *Re Olympia & York Canary Wharf Ltd (No.2)* [1993] B.C.C. 159 Ch D (Comp).

[137] *Bowes v Shand* (1877) 2 App. Cas. 455 HL; *Reuter Hufeland & Co v Sala & Co* (1879) 4 C.P.D. 239 CA; *Hartley v Hymans* [1920] 3 K.B. 475.

[138] *Bunge* at fn.136 above.

[139] See William Norman Raeburn and Leonard Charles Thomas, *Blackburn on Sale*, 3rd edn (London: Stevens and Sons, 1910), p.244: "In mercantile contracts, stipulations as to time (*except as regards time of payment*) are usually of the essence of the contract" (emphasis added). This passage was quoted with approval by McCardie J in *Hartley* [1920] 3 K.B. 475 at 484. See to the same effect Megaw LJ in *Bunge* [1981] 2 All E.R. 540 HL at 534. A similar formulation was approved by Lord Wilberforce in the same case: [1981] 2 All E.R. 540 at 542 HL. See also *Phibro Energy AG v Nissho Iwai Corp (The Honam Jade)* [1991] 1 Lloyd's Rep. 38 CA (Civ Div).

[140] It may well be that time will be of critical importance in loan contracts, in the sense that repayment will be expected on the precise due date. But it is of not "of the essence" in the sense that late payment will necessarily be a repudiatory breach on the part of the borrower. This point will normally be theoretical since the agreement will contain its own remedies in the event that payment is not made when due (although see *Lombard North Central Plc v Butterworth* [1987] Q.B. 527 CA (Civ Div)).

[141] *Sail Labrador Ltd v The Challenge One* [1999] 1 S.C.R. 265, applying the decision in *Tankexpress* [1949] A.C. 76 HL.

[142] See *Bunge* [1981] 2 All E.R. 540 HL at 549 per Lord Roskill, mentioned in *Kuwait Rocks Co v AMN Bulkcarriers Inc* [2013] 2 All E.R. (Comm) 689 at [85]. The question of time has rarely been put in issue in such cases, where the argument has generally centred upon whether and in what circumstances the bank is entitled to refuse payment.

[143] *United Scientific Holdings* [1978] A.C. 904 HL.

(b) Time is of the essence where expressly stipulated

4-28 If the contract provides that time of payment is to be of the essence,[144] whether by using those words or by empowering the creditor to determine the contract if payment is not made in due time, the creditor is entitled to reject a late tender and to treat the contract as being at an end.[145] The court has no discretion to extend the time, and, in the case of commercial contracts, even the general equitable jurisdiction to grant relief against forfeiture is restricted.[146] But is time of the essence? Expressions such as "in no event later than" a stipulated date will not of themselves make time of the essence,[147] although it will obviously always be necessary to review the contract as a whole to ascertain the meanings of particular words. Likewise, a clause entitling a landlord to increase the annual rent "with effect from the first Monday in each June" subject to four weeks prior notice was held to imply that the rent could be increased once a year. Provided that the increase only took place four weeks from the date of the notice, the landlord did not lose his right to a review merely because he failed to serve the notice at the appropriate time in early May.[148] If a contract stipulates for payment by a due date and then allows for a few days grace period, then it may be possible to infer that time is of the essence with respect to that payment as soon as the grace period expires.[149] But, in practical terms, if the performance of particular obligations is intended to be of the essence of the agreement, then this should be expressly and unequivocally stated.

(c) Nature of contract or circumstances may make time of the essence

4-29 Even in the absence of an express stipulation, the court may infer from the nature of the contract or the surrounding circumstances that the time of payment is to be of the essence. Typical are cases in which the contract relates to an asset which is of a speculative nature,[150] fluctuates in value,[151] comprises perishables,[152] or is a business which is being sold as a going concern in such circumstances that delay might cause serious prejudice or inconvenience.[153] In such cases, punctual payment by the transferee is as much of the essence as punctual completion by

---

[144] Where time of payment is stipulated to be of the essence, a breach of a condition as to time will generally amount to repudiation without reference to the seriousness of the breach: see *Lombard North Central* [1987] Q.B. 527 CA (Civ Div).

[145] *The Laconia* [1977] A.C. 850 HL, overruling *Empresa Cubana de Fletes v Lagonisi Shipping Co Ltd* [1971] 1 Q.B. 488 CA (Civ Div) and followed in *The Astra* [2013] 2 All E.R. (Comm) 689. This is on the assumption that the creditor has not waived the breach. See para.4-36 below.

[146] See para.3-84 above.

[147] *ADC Orange Inc v Coyote Acres Inc* 2000 NY Slip Op 07699.

[148] *White v Riverside Housing Association Ltd* [2007] 4 All E.R. 97 HL.

[149] See *The Astra* [2013] 2 All E.R. (Comm) 689. The case is discussed at para.4-40 below.

[150] *Hare v Nicoll* [1966] 2 Q.B. 130 CA, applied in *MSAS Global Logistics Ltd v Power Packaging Inc* [2003] EWHC 1393 (Ch).

[151] *Hare v Nicoll* at fn.150 above. See also *White v Shortall* [2006] NSWSC 1379, Supreme Court of New South Wales (Equity Division) (time of essence in contract for sale of listed shares, since price may fluctuate daily).

[152] Sale of Goods Act 1979 s.48(3).

[153] Several of the cases have concerned public houses. See, for example, *Tadcaster Tower Brewery Co v Wilson* [1897] 1 Ch. 705 Ch D; *Lock v Bell* [1931] 1 Ch. 35 Ch D.

the transferor.[154] Time is usually of the essence in relation to contractual provisions in contracts for the sale of land, for instance, payment of a deposit in respect of a contract for the sale of land,[155] but also the exercise of contractual rights to rescind a sale of land due to, for instance, failure to obtain landlord consent[156] or failure to obtain planning permission.[157] In contrast, a contract for the supply of an IT system and associated services will not normally carry the implication that time is of the essence.[158] Neither will employment contracts or similar contracts such as agency agreements[159] or management contracts.[160]

(d) Time is of the essence with regard to payment for exercise of an option

An entirely distinct principle governs the exercise of options. The grant of an option creates a unilateral contract,[161] in which the grantor's offer to dispose of the subject-matter of the option is accepted not by counter-promise but by performance of the acts stipulated as the conditions for exercise of the option.[162] Until those acts are performed, there is no acceptance of the offer; and since acceptance of an offer is ineffective unless made in accordance with the terms of the offer, a purported acceptance which is late is no acceptance at all unless the offer or chooses to treat it as valid. It follows that, where an option is exercisable by tender of a stipulated option payment, the grantor of the option is entitled to reject a late tender and to regard the option as having lapsed.[163] This has

4–30

---

[154] See *Hare v Nicoll* [1966] 2 Q.B. 130 CA at 289 per Willmer LJ, rejecting the contrary argument of counsel for the claimant.
[155] *Samarenko* [2013] Ch. 36 CA (Civ Div), followed in *Hardy v Griffiths* [2014] EWHC 3947 (Ch).
[156] *Alchemy Estates Ltd v Astor* [2009] 1 W.L.R. 940.
[157] *Get Nominees Ltd v Trinity Welsh Homes Ltd* [2014] EWHC 4737 (Ch).
[158] See, for example, the decision of the Hong Kong court in *Hong Kong Society for Rehablitation v Cadia Ho* [2003] HKCFI 752.
[159] *Crocs Europe BV v Anderson (t/a Spectrum Agencies (A Partnership))* [2013] 1 Lloyd's Rep. 1.
[160] *Warren v Burns* [2014] EWHC 3671 (QB).
[161] Though it may form part of a wider bilateral contract, as in an agreement for a lease where the tenant also takes an option to purchase the freehold.
[162] *United Scientific Holdings* [1978] A.C. 904 HL at 945 per Lord Simon; *United Dominions Trust (Commercial) v Eagle Aircraft Services* [1968] 1 W.L.R. 74 CA (Civ Div). Note, however, that once the *option* has been validly exercised, there will come into existence a *contract* for the sale of the land, and time will not usually be of the essence of that contract, at least from the outset: on this point, see *Ahmed v Wingrove* [2007] 31 E.G. 81 (C.S.) at [9]. Care must be taken in identifying those acts which are conditions precedent to the option being exercised; see *Peacock v Imagine Property Developments Ltd* [2018] EWHC 1113 (TCC), where payment of the deposit was not a condition precedent to the valid exercise of the option.
[163] See the cases mentioned in the previous footnote and *Hare v Nicoll* [1966] 2 Q.B. 130 CA, which adopted the other common ground for treating time as of the essence in relation to the exercise of an option, viz that an option is a privilege. This is surely a rather unreal approach. An option is part and parcel of the total bargain; there seems little justification for treating it as any more a privilege than any other contractual right. *Hare v Nicoll* was followed in *Di Luca v Juraise (Springs) Ltd* (2000) 79 P. & C.R. 193 CA (Civ Div). An attempt—based on the construction of the option agreement—to argue that the option could be validly exercised without payment of the associated fee failed in *Haugland Tankers AS v RMK Marine Gemi Yapim Sanayii ve Deniz Tasimaciligi Isletmesi AS* [2005] 1 All E.R. (Comm) 679.

subsequently been affirmed in other cases.[164] Thus, a claim for specific performance of an option to take a lease necessarily had to fail when the option notice was not accompanied by a cheque for the exercise price.[165] Nevertheless, as noted earlier, the Canadian Supreme Court has held that time was not of the essence in relation to an option to purchase a vessel.[166] It must be doubtful whether the English courts would follow this decision in this particular context.

(e) Making time of the essence by notice

4–31 It was previously thought that, where time was not initially of the essence, the innocent party could make it so by giving reasonable notice, after default in payment, requiring the sum to be paid. If payment was not tendered by the time the notice expires, the creditor could terminate the contract. However, this view now appears incorrect following recent case-law indicating that a notice purporting to make time of the essence where the contract is silent as to this cannot turn an innominate term into a condition.[167]

In *Urban 1 (Blonk Street) Ltd v Ayres*, Sir Terence Etherton C considered that:

> "Statements in many of the cases and some textbooks that the service of a notice to complete makes time of the essence in equity are incorrect. Absent any relevant express provisions in the contract ... it is contrary to all principle for one party to be able unilaterally to transform one type of contractual provision (namely, an innominate term or a warranty in the strict sense) into something different (a condition in the strict sense) . . . ."

Thus, it appears that, unless the contract provides for a notice to be served making time of the essence (the second sense of time "of the essence" set out in *Spar Shipping*,[168] serving notice will not turn a time provision into a condition).

However, even if serving notice cannot make time a condition of the contract, there must come a point at which the delay is treated as repudiatory. It is not clear why failure to comply with a notice to complete which allows performance up to that point should not establish repudiation and, in this sense, the Court of Appeal's decision that this is not the case in *Urban 1* does not seem in line with the previous authorities on this point, where the notice was considered to operate as evidence that the promisee considered a reasonable time for performance to have elapsed and therefore that it was reasonable to require the contract to be performed and, if this did not occur, to treat repudiation as having occurred.[169]

If time can be made of the essence by notice, in the sense that failure to comply with the notice is likely to result in a repudiatory breach, a question still not finally resolved is whether the creditor can give the notice immediately as

---

[164] *Haugland Tankers* [2005] 1 All E.R. (Comm) 679.
[165] See *Petrol (Passive Emissions Testing Research Organisation Laboratories) Ltd v Industrial Property Investment Fund* [2006] EWHC 2219 (Ch). The exercise notice in respect of the option must comply in all respects with the requirements of the primary document under which it is granted: see *Siemens Hearing Instruments Ltd v Friends Life Ltd* [2015] 1 All E.R. (Comm) 1068.
[166] *Sail Labrador* [1999] 1 S.C.R. 265.
[167] See e.g. *Urban 1 (Blonk Street) Ltd v Ayres* [2014] 1 W.L.R. 756; also *Samarenko* [2013] Ch. 36 CA (Civ Div); and *Ampurius NU Homes Holdings Ltd v Telford Homes (Creekside) Ltd* [2013] 4 All E.R. 377.
[168] *Spar Shipping* [2016] EWCA Civ 982 at [104].
[169] See, for instance, *United Scientific Holdings* [1978] A.C. 904 HL at 146–147 (per Lord Simon).

default occurs or whether he must allow a reasonable time to elapse before doing so. There is certainly something odd about a requirement that the creditor must allow his debtor not one reasonable period but two before he can exercise his right to terminate the agreement. Nevertheless, there are several conveyancing cases in which it has been held that the innocent party must go through this two-stage process and that a notice to complete, albeit of reasonable length, is premature if given before the lapse of a reasonable time after the date fixed for completion. The root decision, relied on in subsequent cases, is *Green v Sevin*,[170] where the matter was put in the following way by that distinguished judge, Fry J:

> "It has been argued that there is a right in either party to a contract by notice so to engraft time as to make it of the essence of the contract where it has not originally been of the essence, independently of delay on the part of him to whom the notice is given. In my view there is no such right. It is plain upon principle, as it appears to me, that there can be no such right. That which is not of the essence of the original contract is not to be made so by the volition of one of the parties, unless the other has done something which gives a right to the other to make it so. You cannot make a new contract at the will of one of the contracting parties. There must have been such improper conduct on the part of the other as to justify the rescission of the contract *sub modo*, that is, if a reasonable notice be not complied with."

What was overlooked in some of the subsequent cases was that the contract under consideration in *Green v Sevin* was an open contract which did not fix any completion date. Accordingly, the non-performing party was not in breach at all until the lapse of a reasonable time, and notice making time of the essence could not, of course, be served on a party before he was in default. Unfortunately, the principle correctly applied by Fry J in *Green v Sevin* was erroneously extended to contracts with a fixed completion date by Harman J in *Smith v Hamilton*,[171] whose decision received the *imprimatur* of Lord Simon in *United Scientific Holdings*.[172] Now, this extension to contracts in which the date for completion was fixed becomes explicable if we bear in mind that, until 1980, when *Raineri*[173] was decided, there was a widespread belief that a completion date in a contract relating to land was not legally the due date but merely a "target" date, a sort of best estimate of when the parties expected to complete, so that a party would not be in default at all unless he failed to complete within a reasonable time after the specified completion date.[174] In other words, not only was the date for completion not treated as of the essence of the contract, it was not even regarded as a firm contractual date. Thus, we have several judicial utterances to the effect that the defendant's obligation was to complete on the day fixed or

---

[170] *Sevin* (1879) 13 Ch. D. 589. The decision was cited with approval by the Privy Council in *Chaitlal v Ramlal* [2004] 1 P. & C.R. 1 PC.
[171] *Hamilton* [1951] Ch. 174 Ch D. This decision is no longer good law; see fn.115 above and fn.175 below.
[172] *United Scientific Holdings* [1978] A.C. 904 HL at 946. Contrast the speech of Lord Diplock at 928, stating that the innocent party may serve his notice as soon as the specified time for performance had elapsed.
[173] *Raineri* [1981] A.C. 1050 HL.
[174] It was also common to refer to "rescission" of the contract if the buyer failed to complete, when in fact the seller intended to accept the repudiation and sue for damages: see *Buckland v Farmer & Moody* [1979] 3 1 W.L.R. 221 CA (Civ Div).

within a reasonable time thereafter[175] and a ruling that, until the lapse of that reasonable time, the defendant was not even liable in damages for failing to complete on the specified date for completion. Given this premise, it is perfectly understandable that the courts should insist on the lapse of a reasonable time from the stipulated completion date before service of a notice to complete, for, until then, the defendant was not in default and had therefore not been guilty of improper conduct justifying a notice making time of the essence. Now that *Raineri* has exposed the fallacy of this premise, and has shown that a completion date specified in a contract is not a mere target date but means exactly what it says, a party who fails to complete on that date will immediately be in default, and it will then be open to the innocent party to serve a completion notice without waiting for any further time to elapse. The two-stage requirement, disapproved both in legal literature[176] and in the decision of the High Court of Australia in *Louinder v Leis*,[177] is not, and never has been, good law. The Court of Appeal decision in *British & Commonwealth Holdings Plc v Quadrex Holdings Inc*[178] confirms the modern and correct approach to this issue. A contract for the sale and purchase of shares in a subsidiary provided for completion as soon as reasonably practicable after certain preliminary conditions had been met. Since no fixed completion date was stated in the contract, time could not be seen as the essence in completion. However, given the commercial nature of the agreement, it was open to the creditor to make time of the essence by serving reasonable notice to complete once the conditions had been satisfied. This was so even though, at the time of the notice, the debtor had not yet been guilty of unreasonable or improper delay. It follows that time may be made of the essence by notice of reasonable length served as soon as default has occurred or, in the case of an "open" contract, as soon as any necessary conditions precedent have been met.[179]

What constitutes reasonable notice depends on all the circumstances, including the period of delay that has already elapsed and the conduct of the parties in requesting or giving assurances of payment. In transactions relating to land, a period of 28 days has become conventional.[180] Of all obligations, payment is the easiest to perform and a notice making time of payment of the essence may therefore be justifiably shorter in length than, say, a notice requiring the construction and delivery of property or goods. Where the contract itself specifies

---

[175] See, for example, *Hamilton* [1951] Ch. 174 Ch D; *Babacomp Ltd v Rightside Properties Ltd* [1973] 3 All E.R. 873 Ch D at 875 per Goff J; *Woods v Mackenzie Hill Ltd* [1975] 1 W.L.R. 613 Ch D at 615 per Megarry J. To this extent, these cases can no longer be regarded as good law in the light of *Behzadi* [1992] Ch. 1 CA (Civ Div) (see fn.115 above).
[176] C. Emery, "The Date Fixed for Completion" [1978] Conv. 144; J. Farrand, *Contract and Conveyance*, 4th edn (London: Sweet & Maxwell, 1983), Ch.IX, p.185. Mr Emery's reasoning is adopted in the text. See also A. Sydenham, "Unreasonable Delay—Something of a Long-stop on the Service of a Notice to Complete" [1980] 44 Conv. 19.
[177] *Louinder v Leis* (1982) 56 ALJR 433. See (1983) 99 L.Q.R. 5.
[178] *British & Commonwealth* [1989] Q.B. 842 CA (Civ Div).
[179] A rule that was always applicable to contracts of sale of goods. See now Sale of Goods Act 1979 s.48(4).
[180] A similar period of notice was employed by the creditor in the *British & Commonwealth* case, at fn.178 above.

the period of notice, it is not open to the defaulting party to say that a notice allowing that period is unreasonably short.[181]

If the purchaser of land has been guilty of inordinate delay, then the court may infer that he has repudiated the contract even in the absence of a notice to complete (or "time of the essence" notice).[182] The seller may then terminate the contract and sue for damages without further formality. However, this will depend upon an assessment of the evidence and delay of itself may not be sufficient to prove repudiation to the buyer. The seller will therefore usually be best advised to serve such a notice.[183]

A notice which is intended to make time of the essence must be clear and unequivocal as to its purpose.[184] In *HDK Ltd (t/a Unique Home) v Sunshine Ventures Ltd*, it was found, in the context of a contract for building works, that correspondence urging the defendant "to complete the work to the requisite standard as soon as possible" and "complete the outstanding works as a matter of urgency" failed to address the "necessary ingredients of a notice making time of the essence".[185] The court considered that[186]:

> "Plainly it is not enough to write to the party in default without giving any particular indication of what the communication is supposed to be about or what consequences may follow depending upon what happens after receipt of communication."

Instead, the court considered that the notice must clearly convey that, unless the notice is complied with, the party giving the notice will treat the contract between the parties as at an end.[187] In addition, it was considered that a date for compliance should be specified and this should be sufficiently in the future as to give the recipient of the notice a reasonable time for compliance.[188] In *Multi Veste 226 BV v NI Summer Row Unitholder BV*,[189] time was successfully made of the essence under a development contract where the developers' solicitors gave notice that any failure by the investors to fulfil their obligation to provide guarantees would be treated as a repudiatory breach.

The effect of giving notice making time of the essence is not the same as if time is of the essence from the outset of the contract. As Sir Terence Etherton C noted in *Urban 1 (Blonk Street) Ltd v Ayres*,[190] one party cannot unilaterally alter

---

[181] *Cumberland Court (Brighton) Ltd v Taylor* [1964] Ch. 29 Ch D.
[182] *Farrant v Oliver* (1922) 91 L. J. Ch. 758; *Accuba Ltd v Allied Shoe Repairs Ltd* [1975] 1 W.L.R. 1559 Ch D; *Behzadi* [1992] Ch. 1 CA (Civ Div).
[183] As the seller discovered to her cost in *Graham v Pitkin* [1992] 1 W.L.R. 403 PC.
[184] A requirement which seems not to have been met in *Chaitlal* [2004] 1 P. & C.R. 1 PC.
[185] *HDK Ltd (t/a Unique Home) v Sunshine Ventures Ltd* [2009] EWHC 2866 (QB) at [87]–[88].
[186] *HDK* [2009] EWHC 2866 (QB) at [88].
[187] *HDK* [2009] EWHC 2866 (QB) at [89].
[188] *HDK* [2009] EWHC 2866 (QB) at [89].
[189] *Multi Veste 226 BV v NI Summer Row Unitholder BV* [2011] EWHC 2026 (Ch).
[190] *Urban I* [2014] 1 W.L.R. 756 at [44].

the contract to transform an innominate term or warranty into a condition. Thus, failure to comply with the notice will not necessarily trigger the right to terminate.[191]

In *Urban I,* it was considered that the effect of a valid written notice was to bring to an end "the possibility of equity's intervention by the grant of specific performance to the contract-breaker".[192] Whether the innocent party can terminate depends on their ordinary legal rights, i.e. whether there is a repudiatory breach.[193]

Waiver of stipulation making time of the essence

4–32 The creditor may, of course, waive a stipulation making time of the essence, either expressly or by conduct, e.g. in pressing for payment or otherwise holding the contract open for performance.[194] However, it is now established that the creditor does not lose his right to terminate the contract, in a case where time is of the essence, merely because the debtor gets in a late tender before the creditor has exercised his right of termination.[195] The creditor is entitled to refuse the late tender and to determine the contract for non-payment. Similarly, if a course of dealing has been established by which a party will not insist on performance by the contractually agreed date so long as performance occurs very shortly afterwards, the party may not be obliged to accept performance where there is more than a short delay.[196]

Acceptance of debtor's repudiation

4–33 If the buyer has repudiated the contract—either expressly or by inordinate delay in payment[197]—then it is open to the seller to accept the repudiation and sue for damages.

As an alternative formulation, it has been said that a failure to pay particular instalments will constitute a repudiation by the debtor if it is such as to justifiably destroy the creditor's confidence in the debtor's credit-worthiness.[198]

Nevertheless, the seller needs to exercise some care in selecting his remedies, since they may affect his entitlement to damages. If the contract contains

---

[191] *Re Olympia* [1993] B.C.C. 159 Ch D (Comp) (at 171–172); *Dalkia Utilities Services Plc v Celtech International Ltd* [2006] 1 Lloyd's Rep. 599 QBD (Comm) (at [131(d)]); *Multi* 139 Con. L.R. 23 (at [193]–[202]); *Urban 1 (Blonk Street) Ltd v Ayres* [2013] EWCA Civ 816 (at para.44). See also *Chitty*, para 21–018, and cases cited therein.
[192] *Urban I* [2014] 1 W.L.R. 756 at [44].
[193] See the discussion of what constitutes a repudiatory breach at para.4–35 below.
[194] *Luck v White* (1973) 26 P. & C.R. 89 Ch D; *Charles Rickards Ltd v Oppenheim* [1950] 1 K.B. 616 CA (where the default was by the seller of goods). See also *MSAS Global* [2003] EWHC 1393 (Ch).
[195] See fn.145 above.
[196] *Leeds City Council v Waco UK Ltd* [2015] T.C.L.R. 5.
[197] See the case mentioned in fn.145 above.
[198] See *Decro-Wall International SA v Practitioners in Marketing* [1971] 1 W.L.R. 361 CA (Civ Div) (where, however, the non-payments in question were held not to constitute a repudiatory breach). The decision has been considered on a number of occasions: see, for example, *Alan Auld Associates Ltd v Rick Pollard Associates* [2008] B.L.R. 419.

provisions for termination in the event of non-payment, together with clauses settling the respective obligations of the parties, the seller, may have to decide whether it should: (i) rely on the right of termination and accept the contractual entitlement; or (ii) treat the non-payment as a repudiation of the contract; and sue for damages on that basis.[199]

Other consequences of non-payment

A contract may contain other provisions which may be engaged by a failure to pay. For example, a contract may confer upon the parties a mutual right of termination in the event of a "material breach" by the other party. A failure to pay three consecutive instalments under a contract will almost invariably constitute a "material breach" for these purposes, and the debtor cannot plead his own impecuniosity as a defence.[200] Parties should beware relying on contractual termination rights which do not depend on breach by the other party, however, since if they terminate in reliance upon such rights (such as rights to terminate where insolvency proceedings are commenced), damages for repudiatory breach may be unavailable even if there has been such a breach by the other party.[201] A failure to pay under a contract may also have wider consequences. For example, if property in goods is only to pass upon payment or the seller has otherwise reserved a right of disposal pending fulfilment of contract conditions,[202] then the goods may remain the property of the creditor in the event of insolvency, with the result that the creditor is effectively "secured" on these goods for the purposes of the liquidation process.[203]

4–34

Finally, if time is not "of the essence" or that stipulation is waived on any occasion, then the creditor may not be entitled to terminate the contract on the basis of the relevant breach but will retain his entitlement to damages in respect of it.[204]

Non-payment as a repudiatory breach

A repudiatory breach of contract is one which entitles the innocent party to terminate the contract. This is sometimes referred to as a "fundamental" breach of contract; the view taken in this book is that the use of the latter term causes unnecessary confusion and therefore references to fundamental breach in this context should be avoided. Breaches will generally be regarded as repudiatory in three circumstances:

4–35

---

[199] For a fairly complex illustration of this dilemma, see *Stocznia Gdanska SA v Latvian Shipping Co (Repudiation)* [2002] 2 All E.R. (Comm) 768.
[200] *Dalkia Utilities* [2006] 1 Lloyd's Rep. 599 QBD (Comm), cited with approval in *Warren* [2014] EWHC 3671 (QB). For a similar decision on "material breach", see *Fortman Holdings Ltd v Modem Holdings Ltd* [2001] EWCA Civ 1235.
[201] *Phones 4U Ltd (in administration) v EE Ltd* [2018] EWHC 49 (Comm).
[202] i.e. in accordance with s.19 of the Sale of Goods Act 1979.
[203] See, for example, *Mitsui & Co Ltd v Flota Mercante Grancolombiana SA (The Ciudad de Pasto and The Ciudad de Neiva)* [1988] 1 W.L.R. 1145 CA (Civ Div), approved in *Transpacific Eternity SA v Kanemetsa Corp (The Antares III)* [2002] 1 Lloyd's Rep. 233 QBD (Comm).
[204] *Phillips v Lamdin* [1949] 2 K.B. 33; *Rainieri* [1981] A.C. 1050 HL.

(i) if they relate to a condition of the contract;
(ii) if they relate to an "innominate term" of the contract and the effects are sufficient serious; or
(iii) if the breach involves the defendant evidencing an intention to abandon the contact.

Each of these circumstances requires further explanation. In relation to the first circumstance, a breach of contract is generally repudiatory if the term breached is a condition of the contract. Not all contractual terms are equally important, and therefore failure to perform different types of terms has different consequences. In *Urban I*, the court considered that it was necessary to distinguish between three types of "contractual time provisions"[205]:

> "They are those which are conditions in the technical sense that any breach of them, however slight, is a repudiatory breach of contract which entitles the other party to terminate the contract immediately; those which are warranties in the technical sense that any breach of them, however serious, will only ever entitle the other party to damages and not to terminate the contract; and those which are so-called innominate terms, breach of which will only be a repudiation of the contract entitling the other party to terminate the contract if the breach deprives him or her of substantially the whole benefit which it was intended they should obtain from the contract or, in simpler language, which goes to the root of the contract... It is a matter to be determined on ordinary principles of contractual interpretation into which of those categories the term falls."

If a term is a condition in the "technical sense", as opposed to a warranty or innominate term,[206] breach is generally considered repudiatory, entitling the innocent party to terminate it. However, whether a particular term is a condition or not is not always a straightforward enquiry. Conditions are said to be terms if they "go to the root of the contract". Stipulations that time is of the essence are generally considered to go to the root of the contract.[207] However, what about payment terms where time is not expressly specified to be of the essence?

Shipping and charterparty cases have continued to provide a source of difficulty, although it is to be hoped that the Court of Appeal's decision in *Spar Shipping*[208] provides a degree of clarity in this regard.

In the earlier case of *The Astra*,[209] which involved frequent late payments by the charterers where they had run into financial difficulties, Flaux J had found that non-payment of hire on the due date amounted to a breach of condition, which entitled the owner to terminate the charter and to claim damages in respect of the remaining period.[210] It is fair to say that this decision caused some surprise in the shipping industry and academic disquiet.[211] The court could have reached

---

[205] *Urban I* [2014] 1 W.L.R. 756 at [44(1)].
[206] The concept of "innominate" or "indeterminate" terms was developed by Diplock LJ in *Hongkong Fir Shipping Co Ltd v Kawasaki Kisen Kaisha Ltd (The Hongkong Fir)* [1962] 2 Q.B. 26 CA.
[207] See *Lombard North Central* [1987] Q.B. 527 CA (Civ Div) at 535.
[208] *Spar Shipping AS* [2016] EWCA Civ 982.
[209] *Kuwait Rocks Co v AMN Bulkcarriers Inc (The Astra)* [2013] EWHC 865 (Comm).
[210] Flaux J considered that the payment clause went to the root of the contract—and, hence, was a condition—because only a limited grace period was allowed and the document contained explicit withdrawal, termination and compensation rights in the event that hire was not paid; *The Astra* [2013] EWHC 865 (Comm) at [109], [111]–[113] and [120].
[211] For a summary of various views, see *Spar Shipping* [2016] EWCA Civ 982 at [39].

the same outcome on the basis that the persistent breaches of the contract by the charterer amounted to a repudiatory breach,[212] without holding that the obligation to pay hire was a condition.

The same issue arose in *Spar Shipping*. At first instance,[213] Popplewell J declined to follow *The Astra* on this point. Spar, the owner of three supramax bulk carriers, had let them on long-term leases to a subsidiary of the defendant, who had issued a guarantee in respect of the obligations under the contract. The charterers defaulted in respect of a number of payments and ultimately went into liquidation. Popplewell J held that this amounted to a repudiatory breach of contract which the owner was entitled to accept. The owner was therefore entitled to damages to cover its losses in respect of the remaining period of the charter. In the light of the charterer's insolvency, Spar sought to recover those losses from the defendant guarantor. However, on the condition point, Popplewell J reached a different conclusion from Flaux J,[214] noting various observations of the Supreme Court to the effect that payment of hire does not amount to a condition of the contract.[215] Prior to the Court of Appeal's judgment, therefore, the question whether the obligation to pay hire was a condition or an innominate or intermediate term was a matter of some uncertainty.

The Court of Appeal, agreeing with Popplewell J, answered this question in the negative, concurring with the "general view" of the market that the obligation to pay punctual hire is not, without more, a condition of the contract.[216] In the absence of clear evidence that on the construction of the contract the parties' intention was that the term should be a condition, it was an innominate term (the meaning of which is discussed further below), trivial breaches of which would not give rise to a right to terminate.[217] It therefore seems that the obligation to pay hire is not, without more, a condition of the contract.

Although the parties' own description of a term as a "condition" will generally be important in determining its status,[218] it is not necessarily the case that this will be decisive if, for instance, the court does not consider that the parties could have intended breach of the term to give rise to a right to terminate the contract. Thus, in *L Schuler AG v Wickman Machine Tool Sales Ltd*, the House of Lords refused to find that a term was a condition where it was expressly stated to be "a condition of this agreement", on the basis that it would lead to a very unreasonable result and "the more unreasonable the result the more unlikely it is that the parties can have intended it...".[219] The corollary of this is that, even if a term is not described as a "condition", the courts may find it to be a condition if

---

[212] *The Astra* [2013] EWHC 865 (Comm) at [28], where Flaux J found an intention to deprive the owner of a substantial portion of the benefit of the contract.
[213] *Spar Shipping AS v Grand China Logistics Holding (Group) Co Ltd* [2015] EWHC 718 (Comm).
[214] In particular, he found that the mere existence of a right of termination for breach of an obligation did not automatically elevate that obligation to a condition of the contract: *Spar Shipping* [2015] EWHC 718 (Comm) at [104].
[215] For example, *ENE 1 Kos Ltd v Petroleo Brasileiro SA Petrobras (The Kos)* [2012] 2 A.C. 164, discussed in by Popplewell J at first instance in *Spar Shipping* at [151]–[153].
[216] *Spar Shipping* [2016] EWCA Civ 982 at [63].
[217] Although, on the facts in question, the Court of Appeal found that the charterers' conduct was repudiatory and therefore their appeal was dismissed.
[218] See *Lombard North Central* [1987] Q.B. 527 CA (Civ Div) (at 535–537).
[219] *L Schuler AG v Wickman Machine Tool Sales Ltd* [1974] A.C. 235 HL at 251 (per Lord Reid).

it is clear that the parties intended the consequences for breach to be those which would usually follow from breach of a condition. Thus, in *BNP Paribas v Wockhardt EU Operations (Swiss) AG*,[220] the court considered the early termination provisions in the ISDA Master Agreement. It was held that, while the agreement did not use the word "condition", it specified that non-payment or non-delivery should have the consequences which would follow from breach of condition, including entitlement to terminate, and the parties therefore had to be taken to have agreed that the term in question was a condition.

In relation to the second circumstance in which there can be a repudiatory breach, whilst it may be clear that some terms are not sufficiently important that breach should give rise to a right to terminate (e.g. they are "warranties" in the technical sense), a third category of "innominate" or "intermediate" terms was recognised by Diplock LJ in *Hongkong Fir Shipping Co Ltd v Kawasaki Kisen Kaisha Ltd (The Hongkong Fir)*.[221] Whether breach of these terms is repudiatory depends on the seriousness of the consequences of the breach. There is currently some conflict in the authorities in relation to the test for repudiatory breach of an innominate term; in particular, whether the test is that the innocent party is deprived of "substantially the whole benefit" which it was the intention of the parties that he should obtain from the contact[222] or only a "substantial part" of the benefit of the contract.[223]

This uncertainty was acknowledged by the Court of Appeal in *Telford Homes (Creekside) Ltd v Ampurius Nu Homes Holdings Ltd*.[224] The case involved a claimant who had contracted to take 999 year leases of commercial premises in a new development in Greenwich. When the development was delayed, the claimant sought to argue this amounted to repudiatory breach. Although acknowledging the tension over the test to be applied, the Court of Appeal did not appear to think it was necessary to resolve the point. Lewison LJ considered that, whichever test was adopted, the starting-point was to consider the benefit the injured party intended to obtain from performance of the contract, and then the effect of the breach on the injured party.[225] In the instant case, the Court of Appeal did not find that a delay of one year in delivery of the development deprived the claimant of "a substantial part (let alone substantially the whole) benefit of the contract".[226] In *Federal Commerce & Navigation Co Ltd v Molena*

---

[220] *BNP Paribas v Wockhardt EU Operations (Swiss) AG* 132 Con. L.R. 177.
[221] *The Hongkong Fir* [1962] 2 Q.B. 26 CA.
[222] The test put forward by Lord Diplock in *The Hongkong Fir*, at fn.221 above.
[223] Applied by Buckley LJ in *Decro-Wall* [1971] 1 W.L.R. 361. Buckley LJ's formulation of this test was approved in *Federal Commerce & Navigation Co Ltd v Molena Alpha Inc (The Nanfri)* [1979] A.C. 757 HL.
[224] *Telford Homes (Creekside) Ltd v Ampurius Nu Homes Holdings Ltd* [2013] 4 All E.R. 377 (at [48]–[50]).
[225] *Telford Homes* [2013] 4 All E.R. 377 at [51]–[52]. This approach has been applied in subsequent cases and was accepted as the "starting-point" when considering the seriousness of the breach by the Court of Appeal in *Spar Shipping* [2016] EWCA Civ 982 at [77].
[226] *Telford Homes* [2013] 4 All E.R. 377 at [69].

Alpha Inc (The Nanfri), a House of Lords case, Lord Wilberforce seemed to suggest the difference between the two formulations was not significant[227]:

> "The difference in expression between these two last formulations does not, in my opinion, reflect a divergence of principle, but arises from and is related to the particular contract under consideration; they represent, in other words, applications to different contracts, of the common principle that, to amount to repudiation a breach must go to the root of the contract."

Despite this, it is possible to find cases where the application of one test rather than the other may have affected the outcome. *Valilas v Januzaj*,[228] for instance, involved the deliberate withholding of payments by a dentist to the owner of his practice. The majority in the Court of Appeal, applying the "substantially the whole benefit" test, found that there had not been a repudiatory breach since the owner of the practice could expect to receive the money in the end and had other sources of income; his only likely loss was the loss of the use of the money which could be adequately compensated in damages. However, Underhill J, dissenting, appeared to adopt the "substantial part of the benefit" test in holding that total non-performance was not required,[229] although his analysis focused primarily on the deliberate nature of the breaches (discussed below). The majority view in *Valilas* has been applied in subsequent cases.[230] In any event, it is clear that, whichever test is applied, the bar is a high one. The following two cases involving late payments illustrate how the assessment of the court may differ depending on the circumstances. In *Decro-Wall International SA v Practitioners in Marketing*,[231] there had been a series of late payments by the defendants to their suppliers, but no repudiatory breach was found since the delays were very short (the average period of delay was eight days), the suppliers incurred only minimal interest losses which they could recover from the defendants and the suppliers had no reason to doubt they would receive payment in full. By contrast, repudiatory breach was found in *Alan Auld Associates Ltd v Rick Pollard Associates*,[232] where a company had repeatedly delayed payments to a chartered engineer employed on an advisory basis. It was considered significant that the contract was analogous to a contract of employment. The work provided the engineer's only income and the delays involved were "substantial, persistent and cynical".[233]

Finally, a breach will be repudiatory if it involves the defendant evidencing an intention to abandon the contract.[234] Therefore, there will be no repudiation if the defendant seeks to rely on a term of the contract.[235] However, repudiation can

---

[227] *The Nanfri* [1979] AC 757 HL 779. This was referred to by Leweson LJ in *Telford Homes*, who acknowledged, however, that it was difficult to be sure what was meant by going to "the root of the contract" (at [50]).
[228] *Valilas v Januzaj* [2014] EWCA Civ 436.
[229] *Valilas* [2014] EWCA Civ 436 at [34].
[230] See e.g. *Green Deal Marketing Southern Ltd v Economy Energy Trading Ltd* [2019] EWHC 507 (Ch) at [125], although note that it has also been suggested that it may be too "onerous": *C21 London Estates Ltd v Maurice Macneill Iona Ltd* [2017] EWHC 998 (Ch) at [86].
[231] *Decro-Wall* [1971] 1 W.L.R. 361.
[232] *Alan Auld* [2008] B.L.R. 419.
[233] *Alan Auld* [2008] B.L.R. 419 at [20].
[234] *Woodar Investment Development Ltd v Wimpey Construction UK Ltd* [1980]1 W.L.R. 277 HL.
[235] See fn.234 above.

include declaring an intention to perform the contract in a manner which is substantially inconsistent with the contract terms. In *The Nanfri*,[236] the charterers of a vessel had made deductions from the hire which the owners did not accept. The owners therefore instructed the master not to sign any freight prepaid bills of lading and withdrew the authority of the charterers and their agents to do so. The House of Lords held that this was repudiation of the charters, which had been accepted by the charterers. In *Valilas*, Underhill J considered it significant in his finding of repudiatory breach that the claimant had deliberately not performed the contract.[237] However, a genuine but mistaken view about the effect of issuing notices of rescission on the validity of a contract is not repudiatory breach. In *Eminence Property Developments Ltd v Heaney*,[238] the Court of Appeal held that an innocent mistake made by a party in calculating the completion date in notices to complete in reliance upon which it issued notices of rescission was not a repudiatory breach as it did not demonstrate a clear intention by the party not to perform its obligations. It should be noted that the Court of Appeal emphasised that whether or not there has been a repudiatory breach is "highly fact sensitive".[239]

5. ACCELERATION OF LIABILITY

4–36   We considered earlier the effect of contractual provisions entitling the creditor to accelerated payment, and noted the need to provide in acceleration clauses for a rebate of unearned interest or charges, or otherwise to ensure that the debtor is not being made liable for post-termination interest.[240] It should be noted that there are cases in which liability is automatically accelerated by statute or subordinate legislation. For example, where a charge created by a company becomes void for non-registration, the money secured by the charge becomes immediately payable.[241] Again, if the debtor becomes bankrupt or goes into winding-up, the creditor may prove even for debts not then due.[242]

---

[236] *The Nanfri* [1979] AC 757 HL. See also *Spar Shipping* [2016] EWCA Civ 982, where the court considered that payment in arrears not in advance could constitute repudiatory breach.
[237] *Valilas* [2014] EWCA Civ 436 at [33]–[35] and [40].
[238] *Eminence Property Developments Ltd v Heaney* [2010] EWCA Civ 1168.
[239] *Eminence Property* [2010] EWCA Civ 1168 at [62].
[240] See above at para.3–59.
[241] Companies Act 2006 s.859H. The same is true in common law as regards moneys secured by a floating charge when the debtor company goes into winding-up (*Wallace v Universal Automatic Machine Co* [1894] 2 Ch. 547 CA). The effect of s.859H is unclear where the obligation secured by the charge is itself contingent, e.g. because it secures a counter indemnity obligation in respect of a performance bond or guarantee facility.
[242] In defining a "bankruptcy debt", s.382(3) of the Insolvency Act 1986 provides that: "For the purposes of references to a debt or liability, it is immaterial whether the debt or liability is present or future, whether it is certain or contingent or whether its amount is fixed or liquidated." Following *Fearns (t/a Autopaint International) v Anglo-Dutch Paint & Chemical Co Ltd* [2011] 1 W.L.R. 366, applied in *Stemcor UK Ltd v Global Steel Holdings Ltd* [2015] 1 Lloyd's Rep. 580, it appears that the existence of an equitable right of set-off which exceeds the accelerated debt does not operate to negate the validity of the acceleration as the two claims cannot be netted off except by agreement or by a court judgment: see para.2–11 where this is discussed in more detail. On the whole subject, see *Goode and Gullifer on Legal Problems of Credit and Security* (2018), paras 7–57 to 7–59.

6. INTEREST ON CONTRACT DEBTS

We must now turn to the important topic of interest. The right to interest can be very valuable to the creditor, particularly when interest rates are high. Of course, the debtor may get into such difficulties that he cannot repay the principal indebtedness, let alone interest; yet even in this case a right to interest may prove beneficial, as where there is a surety who is able to pay and/or real security to which the creditor can resort. At the very least, it will serve to maximise the amount which may form the subject of a proof of debt in the event of a liquidation.

4–37

The law governing the creditor's entitlement to interest is complicated, not so much because of theoretical problems as because the treatment of interest is diffused over numerous cases and a considerable number of statutes.

Interest phases

There are three different phases of interest: pre-default interest, i.e. interest payable on a debt for the period up to the date on which the debt falls due; default interest, i.e. interest from the time of default to the time of judgment; and judgment interest, i.e. interest payable on a judgment debt. Different rules govern each phase. Each of these will be considered in turn, as well as the special rules as to interest which apply on the debtor's insolvency or winding-up.

4–38

Sources of the right to interest

Historically, English law gave no general right to interest[243] on a debt or money loan in the absence of express agreement, or custom in business dealings.[244] Therefore, if interest is to be recovered, some source of the right to it must be established. The four principal sources are: contract, express or implied,[245] to pay interest; equity; Admiralty law[246]; and statute or subordinate legislation. In the absence of some such source, interest is not recoverable even on money that is overdue. Moreover, the common law at one time refused to recognise even the availability of interest by way of general damages for failure to pay money, although thankfully this curious position has now been remedied.[247]

4–39

---

[243] Interest is now payable on certain overdue commercial debts—see the Late Payment of Commercial Debts (Interest) Act 1998.
[244] See, for example, *Lloyds Bank Plc v Voller* [2000] 2 All E.R. (Comm) 978 CA (Civ Div) applied in *Emerald Meats (London) Ltd v AIB Group (UK) Plc* [2002] EWCA Civ 460.
[245] For example, if a customer has an agreed overdraft facility then the rate will be stipulated in the relevant agreement. If there is no express agreement then, by drawing a cheque beyond available funds, the account holder impliedly requests an overdraft on the bank's standard terms as to interest, demand etc. The contract comes into being when the bank impliedly accepts the offer by meeting the cheque: see *Voller* [2000] 2 All E.R. (Comm) 978 CA (Civ Div).
[246] At least, this was at one time thought to be the case—see below.
[247] See *Page v Newman* 109 E.R. 140 KB; *London Chatham & Dover Railway Co v South Eastern Railway Co* [1893] A.C. 429 HL. For the current position, see para.4–56 below.

Pre-default interest

4–40 Pre-default interest is recoverable on a debt only where statute so provides or there is an express or implied contractual provision to that effect. An example of a statutory provision is s.24 of the Partnership Act 1890, which gives a partner a right to % per annum interest on advances for the purpose of the partnership beyond the capital he agreed to subscribe. Most claims to pre-default interest are based on contract. As in the case of other contractual undertakings, a term as to payment of interest may be implied from the circumstances or from custom or usage or a prior course of dealing between the parties. So interest is payable on a bank loan or overdraft by the custom of bankers[248]; and, if interest has regularly been debited to a party without objection by him, his agreement to pay interest may be inferred.[249]

(1) Accrual of interest

4–41 Interest accrues at the contract rate from day to day.[250] In relation to a current account, the amount by reference to which interest may be charged should obviously be reduced when items credited to the account are cleared. However, the duration of the clearing cycle is a matter of contract and will usually be governed by the bank's standard terms and conditions.[251]

(2) Simple or compound?

4–42 Interest may be simple or compound. Simple interest is calculated only on the principal amount of a loan. The formula for simple interest can be expressed as follows:

Simple interest = Principal Amount x Interest Rate x Loan Term

Therefore, simple interest on a loan of £1 million with an interest rate of 4% per annum and a term of five years would be calculated as follows:

1,000,000 x 0.04 x 5

The annual interest would be £40,000 and total simple interest over the term of the loan would be £200,000.

Where it is agreed that compound interest should be charged, this involves an agreement that interest should be capitalised from time to time. Compound interest therefore includes "interest on interest". It is calculated not only on the

---

[248] *Gwyn v Godby* 128 E.R. 363 Court of Common Pleas. For a banker's right to charge interest, see generally *Halsbury's Laws of England*, Vol.48, para.285; the right is limited to simple interest at a reasonable rate.
[249] *Re Marquis of Anglesey* [1901] 2 Ch. 548 CA.
[250] Apportionment Act 1870 ss.2 and 5.
[251] For a case in which this issue arose, see *Emerald Meats* [2002] EWCA Civ 460.

principal amount but also on accumulated interest from previous interest periods. The formula for calculating compound interest can be expressed as follows:

Compound interest = Principal Amount $(1+ \text{Interest Rate})^{\text{Number of Compounding Periods}}$ − Principal Amount

Using the above example, if compound interest was calculated for the same £1 million loan, with interest compounded on an annual basis, the calculation would be as follows:

$$[1,000,000 (1 + 0.04)^5] - 1,000,000$$

The total amount of compound interest charged over the term of the loan would be £216,652.90, so £16,652.90 more than if only simple interest was charged on the loan. Therefore, whether or not compound interest is payable is a matter of some significance. Prima facie, only simple interest is payable during the normal loan period; the debtor is liable for compound interest only where there is an express or implied term to that effect.[252] Again, such a term may be implied from custom or course of dealing.[253] Bankers traditionally compound interest on overdrafts, and it has been accepted that interest may be capitalised at three-month intervals.[254] It is also an implied term of the banker–customer contract that interest may be compounded until final payment of all sums due. The right does not come to an end merely because demand is made or the broader relationship is brought to an end.[255] The periodicity of compounding can be settled by the express terms of the contract. In *Multiservice Bookbinding Ltd v Marden*,[256] one of the many unusual features of the loan was that interest was capitalised every 21 days. Despite this and the payment of a premium coupled with indexation of the principal to the Swiss franc, the court refused to disturb the loan transaction.[257]

(3) Variable rate interest

It is common for lenders to provide for a variable rate of interest, e.g. a rate linked to a given bank's base rate. Such provisions are usually valid and enforceable in accordance with their terms, at any rate in the context of corporate and commercial contracts. Floating rate interest clauses may be subject to limitations under the Consumer Credit Act 1974 for certain types of contracts

4–43

---

[252] *Fergusson v Fyffe* 8 E.R. 49 HL. The right to capitalise interest can be implied into the banker–customer relationship by banking custom—see *National Bank of Greece SA v Pinios Shipping Co No.1* [1990] 1 A.C. 637 HL and *Kitchen v HSBC Bank Plc* [2000] 1 All E.R. (Comm) 787 CA (Civ Div).
[253] *Yourell v Hibernian Bank Ltd* [1918] A.C. 372 HL; *Deutsche Bank und Disconto-Gesellschaft v Banque des Marchands de Moscou* (1931) 4 LDAB 293.
[254] *Kitchen* [2000] 1 All E.R. (Comm) 787 CA (Civ Div).
[255] *National Bank of Greece* [1990] 1 A.C. 637 HL.
[256] *Multiservice Bookbinding Ltd v Marden* [1979] Ch. 84 Ch D. The broader aspects of the decision are considered at para.3–07 above.
[257] It should be noted that this section is limited to *contractual* provisions for compound interest. On compound interest by way of *damages*, see para.4–56 below.

entered into by individuals (but it is proposed to leave that subject out of account for present purposes). In one case, *Paragon Finance Plc (formerly National Home Loans Corp) v Nash*,[258] the lender had a discretion to vary the interest rate from time to time. The lender failed to adjust its rates in line with reductions made by the Bank of England. The Court of Appeal held that the discretion to vary rates is not unfettered; it was an implied term that the discretion should be exercised honestly and in good faith, and that the lender should not act capriciously, arbitrarily or unreasonably. However, the lender's own cost of funding remained high because of its financial difficulties; as a result, there was no breach of the implied term even though, as a result, the borrower did not benefit from a broader environment of lower interest rates. Furthermore, the court found that there was no power to reopen a consumer credit agreement on the footing that post-contractual variations in interest rates resulted in an "extortionate credit bargain" for the purposes of s.138 of the Consumer Credit Act 1974.[259] These provisions have now been substituted by significantly broader provisions dealing with "unfair credit relationships".[260] These provisions potentially allow the court to intervene in cases similar to *Paragon Finance,* because the manner in which the creditor fixes the interest rate could be unfair to the debtor. As in *Paragon Finance,* however, it seems that the court would have to take into account any financial problems affecting the creditor.[261]

4–44 Aside from interest rates, however, banks may make other charges for unauthorised overdrafts. It is not clear whether terms allowing for such charges would fall foul of consumer protection legislation. Before the Supreme Court decision in *Office of Fair Trading v Abbey National Plc*,[262] it was thought that such arrangements might be amenable to challenge for unfairness under the Unfair Terms in Consumer Contracts Regulations 1999.[263] However, the Supreme Court allowed Abbey National's appeal against the Court of Appeal's decision that such charges were unfair under the 1999 Regulations on the basis that they came within the "price and remuneration" exception contained in the 1999 Regulations.[264] However, the 1999 Regulations have since been replaced with Pt 2 of the Consumer Rights Act 2015. Although this contains an equivalent exemption, the wording is different in that it applies to terms where "the assessment is of the appropriateness of the price payable under the contract by comparison with the goods, digital content or services supplied".[265] The 2015 Act

---

[258] *Paragon Finance Plc (formerly National Home Loans Corp) v Nash* [2002] 1 W.L.R. 685.
[259] It may be thought that this leaves something of a gap in the protection afforded by the 1974 Act. However, the position is mitigated by the implied term described in the text. For other cases, see *Paragon Finance Plc (formerly National Home Loans Corp) v Pender* [2005] 1 W.L.R. 3412; and *Broadwick Financial Services Ltd v Spencer* [2002] 1 All E.R. (Comm) 446 CA (Civ Div). The Court of Appeal decision in *Lombard Tricity Finance v Paton* [1989] 1 All E.R. 918 CA (Civ Div) can no longer be considered good law.
[260] See ss.140A–140C of the 1974 Act, as inserted by the Consumer Credit Act 2006.
[261] On these points, see ss.140A(1)(b) and 140A(2) of the 1974 Act.
[262] *Office of Fair Trading v Abbey National Plc* [2010] 1 A.C. 696, overruling the Court of Appeal's decision in [2009] 2 W.L.R. 1286.
[263] Unfair Terms in Consumer Contracts Regulations 1999 (SI 1999/2083).
[264] In reg.6(2) of the 1999 Regulations.
[265] Section 64(1)(b) of the 1999 Regulations. However, it also introduces another requirement that the term must be "transparent and prominent" to be excluded; s.64(2).

also introduces another requirement that the term must be "transparent and prominent" to be excluded.[266] Therefore, it is possible that the *Office of Fair Trading* case would be decided differently under the 2015 Act if any terms allowing charges for unauthorised overdrafts were found not to comply with the "transparent and prominent" requirement since they had not been highlighted to consumers when entering into the relevant agreement.

Loan agreements will obviously provide the basis on which interest is to be calculated and paid. Occasionally, this will be a fixed percentage rate throughout the life of the loan. Much more commonly, the rate will be variable since the lender will want a return which matches its own (variable) cost of funding throughout the life of the facility. Subject to certain specialised exceptions,[267] variable rate clauses are essentially valid according to their own terms. Provisions of this kind will usually provide for interest to be calculated by reference to either: (i) the bank's published base rate; or (ii) a money market reference rate such as the London Interbank Offered Rate (LIBOR).

4–45

Money market reference rates are intended to represent the rates at which banks lend to each other on an unsecured basis and are often used to calculate interest payments on loan agreements. For example, LIBOR, the most well-known reference rate, is intended to represent the rate at which banks lend to each other in the London market. LIBOR was traditionally calculated by asking a reference panel of between 11 and 18 banks to quote rates based on the following question[268]:

> "At what rate could you borrow funds, were you to do so by asking for and then accepting interbank offers in a reasonable market size just prior to 11 am London time?"

An average of the quoted rates was then derived. LIBOR has to date been themain global benchmark used to calculate interest rates in loan agreements and financial products such as derivatives.

However, confidence in LIBOR has been steadily eroded since the "credit crunch" in 2007 at the start of the 2007–2008 global financial crisis, necessitating far-reaching reforms. During the this time, banks started to hoard their own liquidity and virtually stopped lending to each other, making it difficult to derive a figure for LIBOR. The subsequent LIBOR and Euribor rigging scandal, which started in June 2012, exacerbated this decline in confidence. It was found that there had been widespread manipulation of LIBOR and Euribor rates by a number of contributor banks. Instead of quoting the rates which they were actually paying, or would expect to pay, to borrow from other banks, some banks manipulated the rates for their own purposes. In particular, there were allegations that some banks had deliberately understated their own borrowing costs in order to disguise their weak financial position during the financial crisis. Another reason for fixing LIBOR was to benefit the banks' own derivatives positions;

---

[266] Section 64(2) of the 2015 Act.
[267] See, for example, s.244 of the Insolvency Act 1986, which allows the court to reopen extortionate credit transactions.
[268] See the ICE website available at: *https://www.theice.com/iba/libor* [Accessed 14 October 2020].

there was evidence of rates being pushed higher or lower depending on specific exposures in relation to the banks' interest rate swaps.

In response to calls for reform, HM Treasury commissioned an independent review of LIBOR and the *Wheatley Review*[269] was published on 28 September 2012. It set out a comprehensive plan for reform, including removal of LIBOR from the control of the BBA, increased regulatory oversight, reducing the number of LIBOR fixings to only five currencies (GBP, EUR, JPY, CHF and USD) and requiring quotations not only to be verifiable but also reflective of actual transactions and real borrowing costs. Notably, the *Wheatley Review* did not advocate abolishing the reference rate, noting that

> "... transition to a new benchmark or benchmarks would pose an unacceptably high risk of significant financial instability, and risk large-scale litigation between parties holding contracts that reference LIBOR".[270]

All the recommendations of the *Wheatley Review* were accepted and implemented and responsibility for LIBOR transferred from the BBA to Intercontinental Exchange Benchmark Administration Ltd, a subsidiary of Intercontinental Exchange (ICE). Further, the Financial Services Act 2012 created two new offences relating to "benchmark manipulation".[271] Reference rates have also been subjected to regulation at EU level, with the Benchmarks Regulation[272] being introduced in 2014 and an offence for manipulation of benchmarks added to the Market Abuse Regulation 2014.[273]

Despite these measures, LIBOR is to be phased out in 2021 and alternatives are presently being sought. The *Wheatley Review* highlighted five criteria which a benchmark should meet in order to be acceptable as a LIBOR replacement: (i) it must be resilient to stress and illiquidity; (ii) have a liquid underlying market across multiple currencies; (iii) avoid too much complexity; (iv) have a measurable history to allow past comparison for pricing and risk models; and (v) cover all maturities.[274] The chosen alternative for LIBOR is SONIA (the overnight interest rate in the wholesale markets), although another available

---

[269] *The Wheatley Review of LIBOR: Final Report* (8 September 2012), available at: *https://assets. publishing.service.gov.uk/government/uploads/system/uploads/attachment_data/file/191762/ wheatley_review_libor_finalreport_280912.pdf* [Accessed 23 October 2020].

[270] *Wheatley Review*, para.1–12 above.

[271] Financial Services Act 2012 s.91(a) (making false or misleading statements) and (b) (acts or conduct creating a false or misleading impression). These offences originally only covered LIBOR, but seven additional benchmarks including SONIA have since been brought within their scope by the Financial Services Act 2012 (Misleading Statements and Impressions) (Amendment) Order 2015 (SI 2015/369).

[272] Regulation (EU) 2016/1011 of the European Parliament and of the Council of 8 June 2016 on indices used as benchmarks in financial instruments and financial contracts or to measure the performance of investment funds and amending Directives 2008/48/EC and 2014/17/EU and Regulation (EU) No 596/2014.

[273] Regulation (EU) No 596/2014 of the European Parliament and of the Council of 16 April 2014 on market abuse (market abuse regulation) and repealing Directive 2003/6/EC of the European Parliament and of the Council and Commission Directives 2003/124/EC, 2003/125/EC and 2004/72/EC. The offence is found in s.44.

[274] *Wheatley Review*, para.6.22.

benchmark rate is the OIS (Overnight Indexed Swap) rate.[275] The main objection to these measures is that they do not represent actual bank funding costs but it is questionable whether LIBOR currently represents this in any case. Indeed, a major reason for abolishing LIBOR is the unwillingness of banks to continue to provide reference rates.

One question considered after the manipulation of LIBOR became public was whether it had any contractual consequences for contracts where it was used as a reference rate. Here, a distinction must be drawn between contracts in which one party was a panel bank implicated in the rigging of LIBOR, and contracts where neither party was a panel bank. In relation to the former, some customers brought claims against implicated banks alleging implied and fraudulent misrepresentation about the integrity of LIBOR. In *Graiseley Properties Ltd v Barclays Bank Plc and Deutsche Bank AG v Unitech Global Ltd*,[276] the Court of Appeal allowed parties in proceedings against Barclays and Deutsche Bank, both implicated in LIBOR rigging, to amend their pleadings to allege that the banks had made implied representations as to the efficiency or non-manipulation of LIBOR. Longmore LJ considered that[277]

4–46

> "... the banks did propose the use of LIBOR and it must be arguable that, at the very least, they were representing that their own participation in the setting of the rate was an honest one".

He also questioned the notion that there was no implied representation on the basis that "doing nothing cannot amount to an implied representation", noting that arguably the banks did not do nothing but proposed transactions intended to be governed by LIBOR which is "conduct just as much as a customer's conduct in sitting down in a restaurant amounts to a representation that he is able to pay for his meal".[278] On this basis, it was arguable that the borrowers could rescind the contracts in question for misrepresentation[279]:

> "If the day after the contracts had been made, the banks had told their counterparties that they had been manipulating LIBOR in the past and intended to do so in the future, but would be happy to pay any loss that their borrowers could prove, the borrower would (arguably) be sufficiently horrified so as to think he would be entitled to rescind the deal. The law should strive to uphold the reasonable expectations of honest men and women."

However, this position was not ultimately tested in court. Barclays settled, and the continuation of Unitech Global's claim against Deutsche Bank was made condition on its paying $120 million into court (since this was the minimum it would owe Deutsche Bank even if its LIBOR defence were to be successful).

In order for a reference bank to be liable to a customer, there must be clear evidence of its involvement in manipulating LIBOR. In *Property Alliance Group*

---

[275] OIS is the only unsecured money market index calculated on actual transactions. On the difficulties of choosing a LIBOR alternative, see the *Wheatley Review*, B.36–B.37; also Rebecca Tabb and Joseph Grundfest, "Alternatives to LIBOR" (2013) 8 *Capital Markets Law Journal* 229.
[276] *Graiseley Properties Ltd v Barclays Bank Plc and Deutsche Bank AG v Unitech Global Ltd* [2013] EWCA Civ 1372 CA (Civ Div).
[277] *Graiseley Properties* [2013] EWCA Civ 1372 CA (Civ Div) at [27].
[278] *Graiseley Properties* [2013] EWCA Civ 1372 CA (Civ Div) at [28].
[279] *Graiseley Properties* [2013] EWCA Civ 1372 CA (Civ Div) at [30].

Ltd v Royal Bank of Scotland plc,[280] RBS provided loans and other financial products to PAG over a period spanning more than a decade. This included interest rate swaps priced by reference to a LIBOR benchmark. After the relationship between PAG and RBS broke down, PAG brought proceedings against RBS on a number of grounds including implied representations in relation to LIBOR. Although the Court of Appeal disagreed with PAG's claims on the substance of those representations, it found that RBS had impliedly represented that it was not manipulating and did not intend to manipulate LIBOR. However, this representation had not been breached since the first instance judge found that RBS had not be demonstrated to be actually manipulating LIBOR. Further, in *Marme Inversiones 2007 SL v NatWest Markets plc*,[281] decided subsequently in relation to EURIBOR, the court would have been prepared to find a narrow, implied representation along the lines of that in the *Property Alliance Group* case (i.e. that Natwest was not itself manipulating and did not intend to manipulate or attempt to manipulate EURIBOR) from Natwest's conduct in "going along" with the interest rate swaps concerned.[282] However, in that case, Marme did not argue for such a representation, it was found that there would have been no reliance in any case and, in any case, Marme had affirmed the swaps. Importantly, the court agreed with Asplin J's view in the *Property Alliance Group* case that it was necessary for implied representations to show that the claimant was aware that the representation had been made,[283] which may prove an insuperable barrier to cases of this kind succeeding.

So what about the position where neither party was implicated in the manipulation of LIBOR? Plainly, the contract cannot have been frustrated, because the other obligations created remain valid and capable of performance.[284] The borrower may well feel aggrieved if it believes that the manipulation may have worked to its disadvantage. Yet, there would be no basis to "look behind" the screen rates or unravel the commercial bargain which the parties have made. Although the parties expected that the screen rate would reflect underlying market conditions, there was no explicit, contractual guarantee that this would be the case.

In line with the advice offered above in the context of indexation clauses,[285] standard loan documentation allows the lender to vary the interest basis if the screen rate does not represent its own actual cost of funding. However, it is perhaps safe to assume that banks would only have invoked that clause if the screen rate was perceived to be too low rather than too high; these provisions are, in any event, designed to be used in cases of market disruption, when funding costs will inevitably be higher.

4–47   The second, perhaps more important, question concerns the contractual consequences of the intended abolition of LIBOR by the end of 2021 for existing

---

[280] *Property Alliance Group Ltd v Royal Bank of Scotland plc* [2018] EWCA Civ 355.
[281] *Marme Inversiones 2007 SL v NatWest Markets plc* [2019] EWHC 366.
[282] *Marme Inversiones* [2019] EWHC 366 (Comm) at [158].
[283] *Marme Inversiones* [2019] EWHC 366 (Comm) at [286]–[288].
[284] For example, the duty to repay the principal sum. At least where the contract is a single and divisible transaction, the doctrine of frustration cannot apply to parts of the contract. It applies to the whole of the contract, or it does not apply at all.
[285] See paras 3–06 to 3–08 above.

contracts relying on the reference rate. LIBOR has previously been described as "the world's most important number",[286] since it is used as a reference rate in so many financial contracts including term and syndicated loans, overdrafts, debt securities derivatives and structured financial transactions. The *Wheatley Review* had cautioned against abolishing LIBOR due to the "unacceptably high risk of significant financial instability" and risk of "large scale litigation between parties holding contracts that reference LIBOR".[287] On the basis, with its phasing out imminent, it is apposite to make some observations about how these contracts may be affected.

As discussed above, LIBOR is used to calculate the interest rate in many of these contracts. Therefore, in the absence of suitable fallbacks or alternatives, many contracts linked to LIBOR will cease to function properly since it will be impossible to determine the interest payments that should be made under these contracts. The first option for contract parties in this scenario is to negotiate an alternative to LIBOR. Indeed, many contracts entered into since the issues with LIBOR became apparent include provisions allowing for transition to a new benchmark should LIBOR be abolished. These often taken the form of "replacement of screen rate" clauses setting out what should happen if a "screen rate" such as LIBOR becomes unavailable.[288] For older contracts or those not containing transitional provisions, the UK government has made it clear that it expects most contract parties to renegotiate and amend their contracts by the end of 2021. This process is already underway. For example, in relation to swaps and derivatives, ISDA has produced a protocol to allow derivatives contracts which reference LIBOR to transition to new "risk-free-rates".[289] While it is likely to be in the interests of the parties to negotiate an alternative to LIBOR to prevent uncertainty over the continued operation of their contract, as discussed below, this may prove difficult due to the fact that any alternative is likely to be more beneficial for one party than the other. Consequently, negotiation on this issue may prove difficult without broader negotiation of the contract as a whole.

There are therefore two scenarios which need to be provided for: (i) where it is impossible for the parties to amend or renegotiate the contract; and (ii) where they fail to do so. In relation to the first of these, a category of so-described "tough legacy contracts" has been identified by the Bank of England's Working Group on Sterling Risk-Free Rates which do not have any fallbacks for when LIBOR is abolished and for which renegotiation and amendment are likely to be impossible.[290] This category may include certain derivatives contracts, bonds,

---

[286] David Enrich and Max Colchester, "Before Scandal, Clash Over Control of Libor" (11 September 2012), *Wall St. Journal*, available at: http://online.wsj.com/article/SB10000872396390443847404577631404235329424.html [Accessed 14 October 2020].

[287] *Wheatley Review*, 1.12.

[288] For an example, see the Working Group on Sterling Risk-Free Reference Rates, *Syndicated loan replacement of screen rate clause* (released 25 May 2018) (available online at: https://www.bankofengland.co.uk/-/media/boe/files/markets/benchmarks/risk-free-reference-rates-replacement-of-screen-rate-clause.pdf [Accessed 7 September 2020]).

[289] Available online at: http://assets.isda.org/media/3062e7b4/08268161-pdf/ [Accessed 10 November 2020].

[290] See Bank of England Working Group on Sterling Risk-Free Rates, *Paper on the identification of Tough Legacy issues* (available online at: https://www.bankofengland.co.uk/-/media/boe/files/markets/benchmarks/paper-on-the-identification-of-tough-legacy-issues.pdf [Accessed 7 September 2020]).

syndicated and bilateral loans and mortgages.[291] In order to address the issue of tough legacy contracts, the UK government plans to give the FCA legislative powers to force a change in the methodology for LIBOR to create a new "synthetic LIBOR" which can be used for these contracts.[292]

In cases not involving "tough legacy contracts" where parties fail to renegotiate and amend their contracts to refer to an alternative reference rate, what will happen? The FCA has made it clear that synthetic Libor will only be available for tough legacy contracts where it "considers this appropriate", not generally for new or existing contracts outside this, not generally for new and existing contracts outside this specific category. Assuming synthetic LIBOR is not available, after LIBOR's abolition there will be no basis for the calculation of payments to be made under contracts which is likely to lead to contractual disputes if the parties are unable to agree an alternative. It is possible that the courts may try to use principles of contractual interpretation or implication of terms to resolve any disputes, but this may prove difficult.[293] If a court is unable to "fill the gap" in the parties' agreement using these methods, the contract may be frustrated on the ground that it has become commercially impossible to perform.[294]

4–48 The use of variable or floating interest rates may have consequences in other contexts. For example, a floating rate note or certificate of deposit is outside the Bills of Exchange Act 1882, since it does not provide for payment of "a sum certain in money" within s.3(1) of the Act. The effect of the subsection is that the amount to be paid must be determinable from the instrument itself, without reference to external factors. On the other hand, it seems equally clear that, by mercantile usage, a floating rate note or certificate of deposit is a negotiable instrument. An instrument can acquire negotiable character in this way quite quickly, because it is the volume of usage which is determinative, rather than the period for which the usage has been current.[295]

(4) Cessation of interest

4–49 Interest continues to run only for the period and in the conditions prescribed by the contract. So in the ordinary way a bond, note or certificate of deposit ceases to

---

[291] Discussed in the *Working Group on Sterling Risk-Free Rates Paper*, pp.3–6.
[292] As set out in a statement by the Chancellor, Rishi Sunak, on 23 June 2020 (available online at: *https://questions-statements.parliament.uk/written-statements/detail/2020-06-23/HCWS307* [Accessed 7 September 2020])
[293] For example, in interpretation of contracts, the court aims to identify the intentions of the parties and it is unlikely that parties choosing LIBOR intended the interest rate under their contract to be calculated by reference to a completely different benchmark, especially one that is "forward-looking". For implications of terms in fact, it is necessary to show that the term reflects the parties' intentions. For further discussion of these points, see Arwen Handley "Risky business: UK litigation and regulatory risks of LIBOR cessation" (2020) 2 JIBFL 103.
[294] The usual requirements of frustration will need to be met, including whether the frustrating event has caused performance to become radically different from that originally undertaken: see *Chitty* (2018), Ch.23 for more detail.
[295] *Edelstein v Schuler & Co* [1902] 2 K.B. 144 KBD (Comm) at 154 per Bingham J.

carry interest after the specified maturity date,[296] and a holder who defers presentment of the instrument at maturity is simply losing money.

Default interest

The creditor's position in relation to default interest is a little complicated. There are two categories of case to be considered. The first is where the creditor is entitled to interest as of right, by contract (express or implied), statute or as damages. The second is where the court has a discretion to award him interest, in exercise of its equitable, Admiralty or statutory jurisdiction to give interest where it considers it proper to do so.

4–50

(1) Default interest recoverable as of right

(a) Contract. Default interest is recoverable where the contract between the creditor and the debtor so provides, either expressly or by implication from usage, a prior course of dealing or other circumstances indicating a common intention, that interest shall run after payment of the debt has become due. However, the mere fact that the contract provides for pre-default interest does not of itself imply that interest is to continue to run after default[297] and, in the absence of an express or implied term for overdue interest, the creditor can claim interest only as a head of damages[298] or as a matter of judicial discretion (where exercisable)[299] or by statute; and such interest will not necessarily be given at the contract rate.[300] So, where the advance is significant, the prudent creditor will ensure that the contract makes express provision for default interest. It is common to provide for default interest to accrue from day to day, though strictly this is unnecessary as such accrual occurs by statute anyway.[301] Much more important is to stipulate that interest shall continue to run after judgment until payment of the debt. If this is not done, the contractual provisions as to debt and interest will merge in the judgment,[302] which will carry interest only at the prescribed judgment rate.[303]

4–51

It was formerly thought to be a general principle of equity that the court will not enforce a provision by which the contractual rate of interest is made to

---

[296] At least provided that the full amount payable on redemption is made available to the appointed paying agent by that date.
[297] Thus, if the contract specifically states that interest accrues only up to a specified date, it will cease to accrue on that date even if default is made with respect to the principal sum; *Cook v Fowler* (1874–75) L.R. 7 H.L. 27. Even if this decision is correct, it is submitted that the court should readily fill the gap by an appropriate implied term. Modern banking documentation invariably provides for the payment of default interest. But this is frequently not the case for other types of commercial contract.
[298] See para.4–56 below.
[299] See para.4–60 below.
[300] *Cook v Fowler* (1874–75) L.R. 7 H.L. 27.
[301] Apportionment Act 1870 ss.2 and 5.
[302] *Re Sneyd Ex p. Fewings* (1883) 25 Ch. D. 338 CA; *Sewing Machines Rentals v Wilson* [1976] 1 W.L.R. 37 CA (Civ Div); *Standard Chartered Bank v Ceylon Petroleum Corp* (2011) 108(33) L.S.G. 27.
[303] See para.4–61 below.

increase substantially in the event of the debtor's default. Such a provision was considered penal.[304] The technique, frequently adopted in mortgages and sanctioned by the courts, was to set a higher level of *pre-default* interest than that actually required and then provide for reduction of the rate in the event of punctual payment.[305] The reduction in rate for punctual payment is then considered in the nature of an indulgence, to be given only on strict performance by the debtor.[306] It is hardly necessary to emphasise the artificiality of this structure, which depends on a primary stipulation for a rate of interest which the creditor does not expect to receive. The position is now different following the Supreme Court's decision in *Cavendish Square Holding BV v Makdessi*,[307] which makes it much more likely that a provision stipulating an increased rate of interest in the event of the debtor's default will be enforceable. The Supreme Court reformulated the penalty test so that, instead of focusing on whether a contractual provision is a genuine pre-estimate of loss, it focuses instead on whether the provision imposes a detriment on the contract-breaker which is "out of all proportion to any legitimate interest of the innocent party in the enforcement of the primary obligation".[308] As a result, such provisions will not be considered penal unless clearly disproportionate.

It has always been common practice in international loan agreements to provide for an increase in the rate of interest in the event of default and there is very good reason for this procedure. A debtor who goes into default becomes a higher risk for which the creditor understandably feels entitled to be compensated, in addition to which the extra supervision of the loan necessitated by default involves extra time and expense. Of course, these considerations are not peculiar to international transactions or even to commercial loans involving no foreign element; they are capable of applying to any loan, and, if given too much weight, could undermine the penalty rule altogether. Nevertheless, it is suggested that the court should not be too astute to carry over an equitable doctrine, applied typically in the case of private mortgages, to international loan transactions between substantial corporations operating in a market where there is a well-recognised custom of charging a default rate higher than the pre-default contract rate. Even before the Supreme Court's decision in *Cavendish Square*, this expectation was largely borne out by recent case law. In *Lordsvale Finance*

---

[304] *Strode v Parker* 23 E.R. 804 Ch; *Thompson v Hudson (Appropriation of Payments)* (1870–71) L.R. 6 Ch. App. 320 CA (Ch); *Dunlop Pneumatic Tyre Co Ltd v New Garage & Motor Co Ltd* [1915] A.C. 79 HL at 86. The reservation of a right to have full payment of money actually due on an existing contract, should there be a failure to pay a smaller sum on a certain day, cannot be treated as a penalty. Where the borrower is a consumer, a term for payment of a higher rate of interest on default could potentially be challenged as "unfair" and therefore not binding on the consumer under the Consumer Rights Act 2015; see *Falco Finance Ltd v Gough* (1999) 17 Tr. L.R. 526 County Court (decided under the 1999 Regulations, which was replaced by Pt 2 of the 2015 Act). See para.4–53 below.

[305] *Thompson v Hudson* (1870–71) L.R. 6 Ch. App. 320 CA (Ch). See also *Astley v Weldon* (1801) 2 Bos. & P. 346 Court Common Pleas at 353 and *Re Neil Ex p. Burden* (1881) 16 Ch. D. 675 CA.

[306] See the cases mentioned in the previous footnote: fn.305.

[307] *Cavendish Square Holding BV v Makdessi* [2015] 3 W.L.R. 1373. See paras 4–51 to 4–52 for further discussion of this decision.

[308] *Cavendish Square* [2015] 3 W.L.R. 1373 at [32].

Plc v Bank of Zambia,[309] an enhancement of 1% in the basic interest rate was considered to be justified because of the increased risk inherent in a facility which has gone into default; it did not constitute a penalty because the higher rate applied *prospectively* from the occurrence of the payment default. However, it was considered in that case that default interest would generally constitute a penalty where the higher rate was applied retrospectively, or to balances outstanding prior to the occurrence of the default; whether this would still be the case post-*Cavendish Square* is unclear and will depend on whether this is considered "out of all proportion" to the creditor's legitimate interest.

It should be noted that the Supreme Court in *Cavendish Square* expressly declined to abolish the equitable rule against penalties. Therefore, while creditors now have more flexibility in drafting their default interest provisions, such provisions, there are still limits. For instance, it is possible to identify cases decided under the previous law where the same outcome would be likely to be reached today. For instance, in a case decided under the previous law, clauses in a renegotiated credit agreement which contained onerous provisions for termination with significantly higher sums payable as a result of the default were struck down as a penalty[310]; unless the lender could argue this was proportionate, it is likely the same result would be reached today. Likewise, where a loan agreement provided for payment of all interest due under a 20-year facility upon default, it was entirely unsurprising that the court struck down that clause as a penalty and the same outcome would be likely to be reached following *Cavendish Square*.[311]

It was suggested in the second edition of this book that an enhanced rate of interest was required to be proportionate to the increased risk on the loan in question.[312] Following *Cavendish Square*, strict proportionality may not be required; instead, the question appears to be whether the penalty is wholly disproportionate or "out of all proportion". This is clearly a harder test for a debtor to satisfy. There are some provisions which would arguably have been penalties under the previous law which may now fall outside the scope of the equitable rule against penalties. For instance, while an additional default margin of 1% was sanctioned in the *Lordsvale* case, it was unclear whether higher figures were acceptable. The Hong Kong Admiralty Court in *Re Mandarin Containers*[313] refused to strike down a default margin of 2%, observing that the contractual bargain should be upheld unless the liquidated damages clause could be characterised as unconscionable, oppressive or extortionate; following *Cavendish*, much higher figures than 2% have been considered acceptable so long as not wholly disproportionate. For example, an increase of 4% was upheld,[314] as

4–52

---

[309] *Lordsvale Finance Plc v Bank of Zambia* [1996] Q.B. 752. See also the US decision in *Citibank NA v Nyland and the Republic of the Philippines* 878 F. 2d 620 (2d Cir. 1989).
[310] *Donegal International Ltd v Zambia* [2007] 1 Lloyd's Rep. 397.
[311] *County Leasing Ltd v East* [2007] EWHC 2907 (QB).
[312] *Goode on Payment Obligations in Commercial and Financial Transactions*, edited by Charles Proctor, 2nd edn (London: Sweet & Maxwell, 2009), para.3–46.
[313] *Re Mandarin Containers* [2004] 3 HKLRD 554.
[314] *ICICI Bank UK Plc v Assam Oil Co Ltd* [2019] EWHC 750 (Comm).

have default rates of LIBOR plus 10% and LIBOR plus 12%.[315] It seems the courts are unlikely to strike down a clause unless the rate is "evidently extravagant".[316] Similarly, at least in some markets, it is the practice to charge the increased rate of interest from the occurrence of any breach of the agreement (i.e. and not merely from a *payment* default). While previously this would have been likely to be unenforceable since the types of breach[317] which may occur under a credit agreement are many and varied, ranging from the highly material to the trivial, and therefore it would have been hard to see how a flat rate increase could be a reasonable pre-estimate of the creditor's loss in every such a case, following *Cavendish Square* a creditor would presumably only need to demonstrate such an increase was not wholly disproportionate given, for instance, increased risk and supervision costs. However, limits still exist and increased rate should not be disproportionate to the innocent party's interest in securing performance.[318]

4–53 The fairness of provisions for default interest was considered by the European Court of Justice (ECJ) in the recent case of *Aziz v Caixa d'Estalvis de Catalunya, Tarragona i Manresa (Catalunyacaixa)*.[319] One issue referred by the Spanish courts to the ECJ was the concept of "unfair term" within the meaning of the Unfair Contract Terms Directive,[320] and, in particular, the criteria to determine the fairness of three provisions in a loan agreement, including one providing for the charging of default interest. The ECJ considered the opinion of Advocate General Kokott and endorsed her analysis in a number of respects, including her view that the requirement that the "significant imbalance" should be contrary to good faith was included in order to limit the Directive's inroads into the principle of freedom of contract. She also recognised that, in many cases, parties have a legitimate interest in organising their contractual relations in a manner which derogates from the rules of national law. Advocate General Kokott suggested looking at factors including[321]:

> "Whether such contractual terms are common, that is to say they are used regularly in legal relations in similar contracts, or are surprising, whether there is an objective reason for the term and whether, despite the shift in the contractual balance in favour of the user of the term in relation to the substance of the term in question, the consumer is not left without protection."

In relation to default interest, she considered that default interest could be justified in serving to encourage compliance with the borrower's obligations[322]:

---

[315] *ZCCM Investment Holdings Plc v Konkola Copper Mines Plc* [2017] EWHC 3288 (Comm); and *Cargill International Trading Pte Ltd v Uttam Galva Steels Ltd* [2019] EWHC 476 (Comm) respectively.
[316] This language is used in *ZCCM Investment Holdings* [2017] EWHC 3288 (Comm) at [38]. It was significant in *Cargill International* [2019] EWHC 476 (Comm) that there was market evidence that the rate was comparable to commercially available rates.
[317] Ignoring non-payment for these purposes.
[318] See, for instance, *Hayfin Opal Luxco 3 SARL v Windermere VII CMBS Plc* [2016] EWHC 782 (Ch), discussed at para.3–31 above.
[319] *Aziz v Caixa d'Estalvis de Catalunya, Tarragona i Manresa (Catalunyacaixa)* (C-415/11) [2013] 3 C.M.L.R. 5 ECJ.
[320] Directive 93/13 on unfair terms in consumer contracts [1993] OJ L95/29.
[321] *Aziz* (C-415/11) [2013] 3 C.M.L.R. 5 ECJ at [AG75].
[322] *Aziz* (C-415/11) [2013] 3 C.M.L.R. 5 ECJ at [AG87].

"If default interest is intended merely as flat-rate compensation for damage caused by default, a default interest rate will be substantially excessive if it is much higher than the accepted actual damage caused by default. It is clear, however, that a high default interest rate motivates the debtor not to default on his contractual obligations and to rectify quickly any default which has already occurred. If default interest under national law is intended to encourage observance of the agreement and thus the maintenance of payment behaviour, it should be regarded as unfair only if it is much higher than is necessary to achieve that aim."

4–54 A provision for interest—which will usually be default interest—to continue even after judgment until actual payment will often result in a higher rate of interest than may be awarded pursuant to the various statutory powers. Nevertheless, it is fair and reasonable for the contract to reserve the commercial rate until actual payment, and the intervention of a judgment does not alter that fact. Such a provision is therefore unlikely to be successfully challenged as a penalty. It has also been held that a clause to this effect is not to be regarded as "unfair" for the purposes of the 1999 Regulations (now replaced by the 2015 Act).[323] This is an eminently sensible result. It is hardly reasonable to expect the creditor to accept a lower rate of interest merely because the debtor has forced him to seek judgment.

4–55 **(b) Damages.** The attitude of the English courts to the award of interest by way of damages for late payment of a monetary debt has developed over time. The history can best be described as tortuous.

In 1893, the House of Lords in *London Chatham & Dover Railway Co v South Eastern Railway Co*[324] decided that at common law a court had no power to award interest by way of damages for late payment. To the modern eye, the decision is wholly unconvincing. The court will award damages for late delivery of an asset; why, correspondingly, should it not award damages for late payment of the purchase price? Yet, no doubt in part because of its high authority, this unhappy decision proved very difficult to bury.[325]

Some 60 years later, the Court of Appeal ventured to suggest that, when a special loss can be foreseen at the time of the contract, it may be recoverable by way of damages for late payment.[326] It took a further 30 years for a later Court of Appeal in *Wadsworth v Lydell*[327] to hold that, on the late completion of a property transaction, interest could be recovered by the seller on the basis that the purchaser knew that his seller was buying another property and would thus suffer funding and other costs as a result of the buyer's default. It followed that interest could be recovered by way of damages, because of the special circumstances known to the buyer.[328] This was certainly a step in the right direction, yet it must surely have been obvious that interest ought to be recoverable by way of damages

---

[323] *Director General of Fair Trading v First National Bank Plc* [2002] 1 A.C. 481, discussed in *Cavendish Square Holdings BV v Makdessi* [2015] 3 W.L.R. 1373.
[324] *London Chatham & Dover Railway* [1893] A.C. 429 HL.
[325] It was followed on a number of occasions: see, for example, the decision of the Privy Council in *Johnson v The King* [1904] A.C. 817 PC.
[326] *Trans Trust SPRL v Danubian Trading Co Ltd* [1952] Q.B. 297 CA.
[327] *Wadsworth v Lydell* [1981] 1 W.L.R. 598 CA (Civ Div).
[328] i.e under the second limb of the rule in *Hadley v Baxendale* 156 E.R. 145 Court of Exchequer.

arising in the ordinary course, since late payment automatically causes a loss to the creditor—either because he cannot repay his own lender or because he cannot place the relevant funds on deposit.[329]

4–56 Yet, in spite of the gap between legal principle and commercial reality, the House of Lords missed its first opportunity to overrule the *London Chatham* decision. In *President of India v La Pintada Compania Navigacion SA (The La Pintada)*,[330] the House of Lords merely approved the decision in *Wadsworth,* with the result that the recovery of interest under the first limb of the rule in *Hadley v Baxendale* remained foreclosed.[331] A further opportunity to discard the old rule was declined by the House of Lords in *Westdeutsche Landesbank Girozentrale v Islington LBC*.[332]

For all practical purposes, however, these anomalies have been laid to rest by the decision of the House of Lords in *Sempra Metals Ltd (formerly Metallgesellschaft Ltd) v Inland Revenue Commissioners*.[333] Although the proceedings were not directly concerned with *contractual* damages,[334] the House of Lords took the opportunity to review the whole area in depth. In summary the House of Lords:

i. overruled the *London Chatham & Dover Railway* decision, holding that the court could indeed award interest by way of damages under the first limb of the rule in *Hadley*; and
ii. departed from the earlier decision of the House in *Westdeutsche Landesbank Girozentrale v Islington LBC*[335] and held that the court had jurisdiction to award compound (and not merely, simple) interest, where that course was justified by the circumstances of the case.

---

[329] i.e. such loses should be recoverable as losses incurred in the ordinary course, in accordance with the first limb of the rule in *Hadley* 156 E.R. 145 Court of Exchequer.

[330] *President of India v La Pintada Compania Navigacion SA (The La Pintada)* [1985] 1 A.C. 104 HL.

[331] It appears from *President of India v Lips Maritime Corp (The Lips)* [1988] A.C. 395 HL that the House of Lords had not wished to bring the common law into conflict with the discretionary right to award interest under various statutes. This seems to be an inadequate reason to maintain an untenable principle.

[332] *Westdeutsche Landesbank Girozentrale v Islington LBC* [1996] A.C. 669 HL. This case has been applied or followed in a number of subsequent cases, including *Littlewoods Retail Ltd v Revenue and Customs Commissioners* [2014] S.T.C. 1761, *Prudential Assurance Co Ltd v Revenue and Custom Commissioners* [2014] S.T.C. 1236, *Xena Systems Ltd v Cantideck* [2013] F.S.R. 41, *John Wilkins (Motor Engineers) Ltd v Revenue and Customs Commissioners* [2011] 1 All E.R. 339 (where it was considered that the decision in *Sempra Metals* (at fn.333 below) raised a realistic possibility of a claim for compound interest on overpayments of VAT) and *FJ Chalke Ltd v Revenue and Customs Commissioners* [2009] S.T.C. 2027.

[333] *Sempra Metals Ltd (formerly Metallgesellschaft Ltd) v Inland Revenue Commissioners* [2008] 1 A.C. 561.

[334] The case was in fact concerned with the payment of interest by the tax authorities after they had been required to refund taxes levied in contravention of EU law.

[335] *Islington* [1996] A.C. 669 HL. *JSC BTA Bank v Ablyazov (Granton Action)* [2013] EWHC 867 (Comm) and *Corbett v Gaskin* unreported 21 April 2008 Oxford CC are two examples of cases where the claimant was unable to prove his loss.

Although it will remain incumbent on the claimant to prove his loss, it is nevertheless satisfactory that he will be able to recover compound interest if that does indeed represent his loss.[336] This will frequently be the case because there is a cost to funding both principal and interest obligations.

The *Sempra Metals* decision must therefore be regarded as a welcome development so far as English law is concerned.[337] Nevertheless, it must be said that, on both aspects of the decision, courts in other common law jurisdictions have been significantly ahead of the English curve. In particular:

i. some 25 years ago, the High Court of Australia in *Hungerfords v Walker*[338] elected to disregard the decision in the *London Chatham & Dover Railway* case, holding that interest costs arose in the normal course following breach of a payment obligation. Such losses were accordingly recoverable under the first limb of the rule in *Hadley*, with the practical consequence that the claimant is not required to prove that interest costs were within the specific contemplation of the parties when the contract was made[339]; and

ii. in 2002, the Supreme Court of Canada in *Bank of America Canada v Mutual Trust Co*[340] noted that compound interest was "the norm" in financial markets and that simple interest makes an artificial distinction between the cost of funding principal and interest. In contrast, compound interest treats each dollar as a dollar and takes into account the funding costs associated with it.

The *Sempra Metals* decision is therefore satisfactory but, in many respects, the House of Lords was merely playing "catch up" with the more practical and realistic approach already adopted in other common law countries.

(c) Statute. There are certain statutory provisions by which the creditor is entitled to default interest as of right. For example, in the winding-up of a company, any surplus available after the payment of proved debts is to be applied in the payment of interest on the debt since the commencement of the winding-up.[341] This applies to all debts, whether or not they were originally interest bearing.

4–57

Section 57 of the Bills of Exchange Act 1882 provides that, following the dishonour of a bill of exchange, the holder may recover "liquidated damages" consisting of: (i) the face amount of the bill; (ii) the expenses included in noting and protest; and (iii) interest from the date on which the bill was payable.

---

[336] It may be added that the courts of equity could make awards of compound interest but this was usually confined to cases of fraud or breach of fiduciary duty or only where the trustee had made a personal profit.

[337] The decision is in line with a recommendation of the Law Commission to the effect that courts should have the power to award compound interest in order "to compensate claimants more accurately for being kept out of their money": see Law Commission, *Report on Pre-Judgment Interest on Debt and Damages (Compound Interest)* (February 2004), Law Com. No.287.

[338] *Hungerfords v Walker* 171 C.L.R. 125 HC.

[339] Although it should not be forgotten that the interest is awarded by way of damages and not the rule on remoteness, mitigation etc will therefore apply.

[340] *Bank of America Canada v Mutual Trust Co* [2002] 2 S.C.R. 601.

[341] Insolvency Act 1986 s.189.

In a commercial contract for the sale of goods or provision of services between two parties acting in the course of business, the law implies a term to the effect that a debt carries simple interest. This rule[342] was designed to prevent large corporations from using their small suppliers as a source of free credit. It is not clear how far this legislation has been effective in practice.

(2) Default interest recoverable in the discretion of the court

4–58   **(a) Equitable jurisdiction.**   Even without an express stipulation, a mortgage or charge is considered in equity to carry with it a right to interest from the due repayment date,[343] either as an implied term of the mortgage or charge[344] or by way of damages for detention of the creditor's money,[345] and there are numerous other cases in which the court will exercise its discretion to award interest in equity, usually because the defendant has abused a fiduciary relationship with the claimant.[346] Interest will also be ordered as a condition of redemption.[347] But the equitable jurisdiction does not extend to a simple contract debt.[348]

4–59   **(b) Admiralty jurisdiction.**   It had long been thought that the court had an equitable jurisdiction in Admiralty cases to award interest as damages for the late payment of freight and demurrage. That jurisdiction was specifically confirmed by the Court of Appeal in *Tehno-Impex v Gebr van Weelde Scheepvart Kantoor BV*.[349] Subsequently, however, the House of Lords rejected the *Tehno-Impex* decision in *The La Pintada*,[350] in part because it felt unable to overrule the earlier decision of the House in the *London Chatham v Dover Railway* case,[351] and evidently did not feel able to apply a special exception to Admiralty claims. However, the House has now departed from *La Pintada* itself in *Sempra Metals Ltd v Inland Revenue Commissioners*.[352] Perhaps the best way forward is to assume that no special rules should be applied in the context of Admiralty cases, and the courts hearing such cases should apply general rules as to damages for late payment of money. This should be a satisfactory solution now that those rules have been placed on a logical and consistent footing by the decision in *Sempra Metals* itself.

---

[342] Introduced by the Late Payment of Commercial Debts (Interest) Act 1998, on which see *Chitty* (2018), para.26–277.

[343] *Re Kerr's Policy* (1869) L.R. 8 Eq. 331 Ch; *Cityland & Property (Holdings) Ltd v Dabrah* [1968] Ch. 166.

[344] *Re Kerr's Policy* at fn.343 above.

[345] *Price v Great Western Railway Company* 153 E.R. 1179 Court of Exchequer; *Cook v Fowler* (1874–75) L.R. 7 H.L. 27.

[346] See *Wallersteiner v Moir (No.2)* [1975] Q.B. 373 CA (Civ Div).

[347] See para.4–17 above.

[348] *Alex Lawrie Factors Ltd v Modern Injection Moulds Ltd* [1981] 3 All E.R. 658 QBD.

[349] *Tehno-Impex v Gebr van Weelde Scheepvart Kantoor BV* [1981] Q.B. 648 CA (Civ Div). For a decision to similar effect, see *Polish Steam Ship Co v Atlantic Maritime Co (The Garden City) (No.2)* [1985] Q.B. 41 CA (Civ Div).

[350] *The La Pintada* [1985] 1 A.C. 104 HL.

[351] See the discussion at para.4–56 above.

[352] *Sempra Metals* [2008] 1 A.C. 561. The decision has been applied on a number of subsequent occasions—see, for example, *Littlewoods Retail Ltd v Revenue and Customs Commissioners* [2016] Ch. 373 and other cases referred to in fn.332 above.

(c) Statutory jurisdiction. Section 35A of the Senior Courts Act 1981,[353] **4–60** replacing s.3 of the Law Reform (Miscellaneous Provisions) Act 1934, confers a general jurisdiction on the High Court, in proceedings for recovery of a debt or damages, to include in any sum for which judgment is given simple interest at such rate as the court thinks fit or as rules of court may provide, on all or any part of the debt or damages for which judgment is given, or payment is made. The County Court enjoys the same power under s.74 of the County Court Act 1984. Section 49 of the Arbitration Act 1996 allows the same discretion to an arbitrator, with the refinement that simple or compound interest may be awarded.[354] The period for which interest may be awarded is from accrual of the cause of action to the date of payment (in the case of any sum paid before judgment) or the date of judgment (in the case of the sum for which judgment is given). Interest may be given for all or any part of that period. Section 35A gives the creditor greater protection than its predecessor in that the creditor may now obtain interest on sums paid prior to judgment, whereas previously the court could award interest only in respect of the amount for which judgment was given.[355] However, if the amount of the claim is reduced prior to the date of judgment as a result of a recovery from some other party who is also liable, the court cannot award interest on that particular amount for the period in respect of which it was outstanding; s.35A only allows for the award of interest on the judgment sum.[356] As before,[357] the statutory provisions are not confined to judgment at a full trial, a fact brought out more clearly in the new section. The discretion is exercisable when giving summary judgment or judgment in default; in these cases, the applicant obtains final judgment for the debt itself and an interlocutory judgment for interest to be assessed.[358] There is no power to award interest under the section where no judgment has been given, e.g. where the applicant elects to accept money paid into the court; nor can the court award interest in respect of a period prior to accrual of the cause of action or after the date of judgment. Post-judgment interest is dealt with by separate legislation.[359] Further, the court's powers under s.35A are not exercisable where interest is already payable for the period in question, whether by virtue of contract or otherwise.[360]

As noted, the power to award interest under s.35A is discretionary, so when should that discretion be exercised in favour of the claimant? The court should usually award interest "on the simple commercial basis that if the money had

---

[353] Inserted by Administration of Justice Act 1982 s.15(1) and Sch.1 Pt.1, and partially implementing the recommendations of Law Commission, *Report on Interest*, at fn.337 above.

[354] Though arbitrators in other common law jurisdictions may not have a discretion to award compound interest in light of previous case-law including the majority decision in *Tehno-Impex* [1981] Q.B. 684 CA (Civ Div) in the absence of specific legislation having been introduced; see the Privy Council decision in *National Housing Trust v YP Seaton & Associates Co Ltd* [2015] UKPC 43 on the Jamaican position.

[355] *Hepworth v Owners of the Medina Princess (The Medina Princess)* [1962] 2 Lloyd's Rep. 17 Probate, Divorce & Admiralty Division.

[356] *IM Properties Plc v Cape & Dalgleish* [1999] Q.B. 297 CA (Civ Div).

[357] See *Gardener Steel v Sheffield Brothers (Profiles)* [1978] 1 W.L.R. 916 CA (Civ Div) (interest on summary judgment under R.S.C. Order 14, the forerunner to CPR Pt 24); *Alex Lawrie* at fn.313 above (judgment in default).

[358] As in *Alex Lawrie* [1981] 3 All E.R. 658 QBD.

[359] See para.4–61 below.

[360] Section 35A(4) of the Arbitration Act 1996.

been paid at the appropriate time, the other side would have had use of it".[361] But care must be taken to ensure that the claimant does not receive double compensation. For example, there should be no award of interest if the purchaser is late in completing the acquisition of the freehold of a rented property, since the seller will continue to receive rent during the period of the delay.[362] The rate at which interest is awarded is entirely within the discretion of the court, but, without prejudice to this power, rules of court may provide for a rate of interest by reference to the prevailing rate of interest carried by judgment debts.[363] Commercial court practice is to award interest at 1% above base rate,[364] but a different rate may be used in appropriate cases.

Apart from the above general statutory provisions, there are numerous special statutes providing for interest on overdue amounts.[365]

Judgment interest

4–61   Judgments in the High Court carry interest under s.17 of the Judgments Act 1838 at such rate as is from time to time prescribed by order.[366] Where judgment is given in a foreign currency, the court has the discretion to apply such a rate of interest as it thinks fit.[367]

Interest on a High Court judgment debt runs from the date of pronouncement of the judgment, even if it is not formally entered up until a later date.[368] Similarly, interest on a judgment for damages to be assessed is payable as from the date the judgment is pronounced, not from the date on which the damages are subsequently quantified.[369] It was previously thought that interest on costs ran only from the date of the taxing master's certificate,[370] but the House of Lords held in *Hunt v RM Douglas (Roofing) Ltd*[371] that an order for the payment of costs to be taxed was a judgment debt and interest ran on the costs from the date when judgment was pronounced.

In relation to arbitrations, s.20 of the Arbitration Act 1950 gave an arbitrator power to award interest but it was held that this power was not entirely discretionary and, in particular, did not entitle him to give interest at a rate higher

---

[361] *AB Kemp v Tolland (t/a James Tolland & Co)* [1956] 2 Lloyd's Rep. 681 QBD at 691, noted in *Chitty* (2018), para.26–282.
[362] Or at least, any award made against the purchaser should give credit for the rental receipts.
[363] Section 35A(5) of the Arbitration Act 1996.
[364] *The Garden City* [1985] Q.B. 41 CA (Civ Div); *Metal Box Ltd v Currys Ltd* [1988] 1 W.L.R. 175 QBD.
[365] See, for example, s.44A of the Administration of Justice Act 1970.
[366] The current rate is 8% (Judgment Debts (Rate of Interest) Order 1993 (SI 1993/564), amending s.17 of the Judgments Act 1838). Similar arrangements apply in the County Court; see County Courts Act 1984 s.74, and the County Courts (Interest on Judgment Debts) Order 1991 (SI 1991/1184) (as amended).
[367] Section 44A of the Administration of Justice Act 1970, as inserted by s.5 of the Private International Law (Miscellaneous Provisions) Act 1995.
[368] *Parsons v Mather & Platt Ltd* [1977] 1 W.L.R. 855 QBD; *Erven Warnink BV v J Townsend & Sons (Hull) Ltd (No.2)* [1982] 3 All E.R. 312 CA (Civ Div); Senior Courts Act 1981 s.35A.
[369] See the authorities noted in the previous footnote: fn.368.
[370] *Erven Warnink* at fn.332 above.
[371] *Hunt v RM Douglas (Roofing) Ltd* [1990] 1 A.C. 398 HL, overruling *Erven Warnink* [1982] 3 All E.R. 312 CA (Civ Div).

than that carried by a judgment debt; his choice was limited to leaving interest to run at the judgment rate or refusing interest altogether.[372] This has now been reversed by s.49 of the Arbitration Act 1996, which allows the parties to agree on the tribunal's power to award interest but, subject to that, allows for the award of interest on a simple or compound basis at such rates as appear to meet the justice of the case.

Effect of insolvency or liquidation on right to interest

As a general principle, a creditor will be entitled to prove in the liquidation of a company for his debt plus contractual interest accrued up to the date of insolvency.[373] However, if the rate of interest is excessive then the liquidator may challenge the transaction as "extortionate credit bargain" and ask the court to set a revised interest rate.[374]

4–62

The position for post-insolvency interest is now governed by s.189 of the Insolvency Act 1986.[375] If it transpires that the assets of the company have been sufficient to pay out all debts which have been proved—including any pre-insolvency interest included in any proofs—then interest is to be paid on all such debts before any funds can find their way to the shareholders. Interest is to be paid in respect of all debts, even if they were not contractually expressed to be interest bearing.[376] The applicable interest rate is the higher of: (i) the rate applicable to judgments[377]; and (ii) the contractual or other rate which would have applied apart from the winding-up.

Interest clauses—some drafting considerations

From what has gone before, it will be apparent that there are several points which the draftsman of a contract who wishes to provide for interest would do well to bear in mind:

4–63

(1) although, following *Cavendish Square v Makdessi*, default interest provisions are more likely to be upheld, care should be taken in drafting them to ensure they are not manifestly excessive or out of all proportion to any legitimate interest of the innocent party in enforcing the contract[378];
(2) interest should be expressed to run at the specified rate both after as well as before any judgment[379];

---

[372] *Timber Shipping Co SA v London and Overseas Freighters* [1972] A.C. 1 HL.
[373] Section 189 of the Insolvency Act 1986.
[374] This section has already been briefly noted: see para.4–43 above.
[375] This section applies only rarely in practice.
[376] Where there is a surplus on completion of the administration, then creditors who claimed in the process can claim further interest until the actual date of payment. Equally, creditors who have suffered loss as a result of the requirement to convert their claims into sterling can likewise seek to recover those losses out of the surplus: see *Re Lehman Brothers International (Europe) (In Administration)* [2016] Ch. 50 (the so-called "*Lehman Waterfall*" case).
[377] See s.17 of the Judgments Act 1838, discussed at para.4–61 above.
[378] See para.4–51 above.
[379] See para.4–51 above.

(3) all sums payable under the agreement (not merely the main indebtedness) should be expressed to carry interest; and
(4) stipulated interest rates should no longer be linked to LIBOR and, if they are, transitional provisions should be included in the contract. Where interest rates are index-linked, make provision to cover the eventuality of abolition of the index.[380]

---

[380] See paras 4–43 to 4–44 above.

Chapter 5

THE LEGAL IMPLICATIONS OF PAYMENTS THROUGH BANKING AND NON-BANK SYSTEMS

1. The Changing Payments Landscape

The present chapter considers the various legal questions that may arise when payment of a debt is not made using physical cash but through the medium of banks or other payment service providers or payment systems, by credit card or by other cashless means.[1] It considers a range of issues which may arise both for domestic and international payments.[2]

5–01

Two initial points may be made in relation to how the background against which such payments are made has been transformed in recent years. The first is that the legal landscape against which payments are made has changed substantially over the past couple of decades at a national, EU and international level. As a general observation, there has been a move away from viewing payment systems as essentially "private law" contractual arrangements between various large banks, financial institutions and systems providers towards viewing them more as "public utilities". This is evident in the increased regulation of payment systems and promotion of competition in this sector. Although a detailed analysis of specific measures is beyond the scope of this work, there is no doubt that legislative and regulatory interventions have assumed greater importance in determining the legal position (including rights and remedies) of parties making or receiving payments. Therefore some of the main legislative and regulatory measures and developments will be briefly outlined below.

5–02

The second related point is the rapid pace of innovation and technological development within the payments sector. In particular, the development and evolution of new payment methods and technologies has, to some extent, left the law struggling to catch up. One example is the increasing use of "non-bank" payment systems and service providers, which will be briefly addressed later in this chapter, Although many of the legal issues which will concern the parties remain similar to those arising for bank payments, they also raise their own complications.

5–03

---

[1] Leading works in this field have been produced by Benjamin Geva—see, in particular, *The Law of Electronic Funds Transfers* (New York: Matthew Bender) and *Bank Collections and Payment Transactions—Comparative Study of Legal Aspects* (Oxford: Oxford University Press, 2001).
[2] For convenience, references in this chapter to "C" and "CB" are to the creditor and his bank. Likewise, "D" and "DB" to the debtor and his bank.

2. LEGISLATIVE AND REGULATORY BACKGROUND

5–04 Finally, the potential impact of the UK's exit from the EU (Brexit) will be considered. Following a majority vote in favour of leaving the EU on 23 June 2016, the UK government formally notified the EU of the UK's intention to withdraw on 29 March 2017. At the time of writing, the UK is in an extended transition period with Brexit scheduled to occur on 31 December 2020. It is presently unclear how Brexit will affect this area of law, but some suggestions will be made below.[3]

2. LEGISLATIVE AND REGULATORY BACKGROUND

5–05 This section is intended to give a brief overview of some of the main legislative and regulatory measures and developments which apply to the payments sector. Specific aspects of these will only be explored to the extent that they affect the payment obligations between the parties.[4]

5–06 As an initial point, the past couple of decades have seen a move away from self-regulation of payments—in the past largely dominated by big banks—towards a more competition-focused, "public utility" view of payment services and systems. For example, at an EU level, efforts to make cross-border payments more efficient were originally self-regulatory. In particular, the Single European Payments Area (SEPA) initiative was proposed from 2000, and launched in 2008, and aimed at creating an effective cross-border infrastructure for euro payments so that electronic payments in the eurozone could be made as easily as domestic payments.[5] However, it had become apparent by then that self-regulation alone would not achieve SEPA's aims since some degree of harmonisation of the rights of payment service users and the obligations of payment service providers would be required. Thus, the EU also implemented a more "top down" regulatory approach. Hence the introduction of, among other things, the first Payment Services Directive (PSD I)[6] in 2007, now replaced by the second Payment Services Directive (PSD II).[7] A "public utility" view of payment and banking services is also evident in the Payment Accounts Directive,[8] which seeks to improve access to such services by giving all consumers legally resident in the

---

[3] See para.5–77.
[4] For a more detailed overview of these various measures, see *Law of Bank Payments*, 5th edn (London: Sweet & Maxwell, 2018), especially paras 1–024 to 1–030.
[5] See Ruth Wandhöfer, *EU payments integration: the tale of SEPA, PSD and other milestones along the road* (Basingstoke: Houndmills, 2010) for more information about SEPA and payments integration in the EU.
[6] Directive 2007/64/EC of the European Parliament and of the Council of 13 November 2007 on payment services in the internal market amending Directives 97/7/EC, 2002/65/EC, 2005/60/EC and 2006/48/EC and repealing Directive 97/5/EC.
[7] Directive 2015/2366/EU of the European Parliament and of the Council of 25 November 2015 on payment services in the internal market, amending Directives 2002/65/EC, 2009/110/EC and 2013/36/EU and Regulation (EU) No 1093/2010, and repealing Directive 2007/64/EC, the requirements of which are largely implemented in the UK through the Payment Services Regulations 2017 (SI 2017/752). Most of PSD II was required to be implemented by EU countries by January 2018.
[8] Payment Accounts Directive 2014/92 on the comparability of fees related to payment accounts, payment account switching and access to payment accounts with basic features [2014] OJ L257/214, implemented in the UK via the Payment Accounts Regulations 2015 (SI 2015/2038).

EU the right to certain bank accounts, including those who might not have been able to access such services in the past due to due diligence requirements.[9]

In the UK, the payments industry prior to 2013 was essentially self-regulating by agreement with the FCA via the Payments Council[10] until the Financial Services (Banking Reform) Act 2013 created a new Payment Systems Regulator (PSR) as a subsidiary of the FCA to regulate payment transactions in the UK. The PSR now oversees the main payment systems in the UK.

5–07 It is useful to note the plurality of aims behind the various regulatory developments: these include reducing obstacles to cross-border payments, protecting consumers, promoting competition in the provision of payment systems, combating crime and ensuring the stability of payment systems. Each of these will be discussed in turn. That conflicts have on occasion arisen between securing these different aims will be evident in parts of the ensuing discussion.

Reducing obstacles to cross-border payments

5–08 The area of payments law has long been of concern to the EU, largely because of the view taken by EU institutions that the benefits of the euro as the single European currency can only be fully realised if it can flow freely and at equal cost across the entire Eurozone. This, in turn, means that the terms and conditions (including, above all, the cost) of domestic and cross-border transfers should be harmonised, and greater competition introduced into the market for payments. Although initially the EU's approach was a "soft law" one which promoted self-regulation by the banks to achieve these goals, the drive towards harmonisation has ultimately resulted in various legislative and regulatory interventions.

The main measure in reducing obstacles to cross border payments in the EU is PSD II, which seeks to harmonise important aspects of the EU legal framework for payments and extend its scope to cover previously unregulated non-bank payment services.[11] In relation to euro payments, the Cross-Border Payments Regulation[12] seeks to regulate charges on euro payments between Member States,

---

[9] Including asylum seekers and those without a fixed address or residence permit. This development does, however, give rise to potential concerns regarding anti-money laundering and counterterrorist financial controls. The impact of anti-money laundering legislation is discussed at para.5–36 below.
[10] Which had been criticised for lack of transparency, stifling competition and failing properly to serve the interests of consumers; see the Treasury Select Committee, *Ninth Report on Competition and Choice in Retail Banking* (April 2011), available at: *http://www.publications.parliament.uk/pa/cm201011/cmselect/cmtreasy/612/61202.htm* [Accessed 12 October 2020]. See also the HM Treasury Consultation, *Opening up UK payments* (March 2013), which proposed the establishment of a new regulatory body, available at: *https://www.gov.uk/government/uploads/system/uploads/attachment_data/file/221903/consult_opening_up_uk_payments.pdf* [Accessed 12 October 2020].
[11] Discussed at para.5–65 below.
[12] Regulation (EC) No 924/2009 of the European Parliament and of the Council of 16 September 2009 on cross-border payments in the Community and repealing Regulation (EC) No 2560/2001. This applies to payments between eurozone members. It has recently been revised by Regulation (EU) 2019/518 of the European Parliament and of the Council of 19 March 2019 to cover charges for cross-border payments in euros from non-euro area Member States as well as eurozone members.

while the SEPA Regulation[13] sets out conduct and information requirements for payments. Also relevant here is the Interchange Fee Regulation 2015,[14] which harmonises credit card issuers' fees to merchants.

Promoting competition and addressing innovation in the payments industry

5–09 The continual stream of technological developments in payment services over the past couple of decades has necessitated new regulation intended both to support and encourage these new developments and promote competition from non-bank payment services providers, while also seeking to regulate new payment services appropriately. The first significant EU measure introduced in 2000 was the Electronic Commerce Directive,[15] which brought in a harmonised framework for e-commerce. It requires, among other things, that Member States ensure that their legal systems permit electronic contracts to ensure the validity of contracts concluded online.[16] Since then, a number of other measures have been introduced which are intended to promote competition by providing a framework for non-bank service providers to provide payment services.[17] In particular, PSD II's objectives include contributing to a more integrated and efficient European payments market, improving the level playing field for payment service providers (including new players) and encouraging lower prices for payments. In this respect, it allows certain licensed non-bank third party providers (TPPs) to provide payment services by intermediating between banks, merchants and consumers. PSD II covers two types of TPP—"payment initiation services",

---

[13] Regulation (EU) No 260/2012 of the European Parliament and of the Council of 14 March 2012 establishing technical and business requirements for credit transfers and direct debits in euro and amending Regulation (EC) No 924/2009, OJ L 94, as amended by Regulation (EU) No 248/2014.

[14] Regulation (EU) 2015/751 of the European Parliament and of the Council of 29 April 2015 on interchange fees for card-based payment transactions.

[15] Directive 2000/31 on certain legal aspects of information society services, in particular electronic commerce, in the Internal Market [2000] OJ L178/1, implemented in the UK through the Electronic Commerce Regulations 2002 (SI 2002/2013).

[16] Although the 2002 Regulations do not cover this point specifically as the Government considered that this requirement was already met under the existing law. In Law Commission, *Electronic Commerce: Formal Requirements in Commercial Transactions* (December 2011), the Law Commission found that, in England and Wales, statutory requirements in statutes for "writing" and a "signature" are generally capable of being satisfied by e-mails and by website trading (available at: http://www.lawcom.gov.uk/wp-content/uploads/2015/09/electronic_commerce_advice.pdf [Accessed 12 October 2020]). The Electronic Commerce Directive will not apply after Brexit: https://www.gov.uk/guidance/the-ecommerce-directive-after-the-transition-period [Accessed 10 November 2020].

[17] Other significant measures besides PSD II include Directive 2009/110 on the taking up, pursuit and prudential supervision of the business of electronic money institutions amending Directives 2005/60 and 2006/48 and repealing Directive 2000/46 [2009] OJ L267/7 (the Second Electronic Money Directive), which sets out the legal framework for issuing e-money in the EU; reg.751/2015 of the European Parliament and of the Council of 29 April 2015 on interchange fees for card-based payment transactions [2015] OJ L123/1 (the Interchange Fee Regulation), which caps interchange fees paid by merchants to card issuers in respect of transactions made by their customers; reg.910/2014 on electronic identification and trust services for electronic transactions in the internal market and repealing Directive 1999/93 [2014] OJ L257/73 (the Electronic Signature and Trust Services Regulation) which provides a framework for the use of e-signatures and other online authentication methods.

which initiate direct payments between consumers and merchants,[18] and "account information services," which provide information on payment accounts held by a service user.[19] PSD II both facilitates the provision of services by these non-bank services, primarily by requiring banks to provide the necessary customer access and information to them to operate,[20] but it also imposes conduct of business requirements to ensure that they are appropriately regulated.[21] In the UK, the Competition and Markets Authority is seeking to implement "Open Banking" following a retail banking investigation in which it found that established banks do not have to compete hard enough for customers' business. The aim is for consumers and small businesses to be able to share their data securely with other banks and third parties so they can more easily access new payment services.[22]

Ensuring consumer protection

A further regulatory aim in this area is to ensure an adequate level of consumer protection for the users of payment services. There are various concerns in this area, including data protection, payment fraud and insolvency of a payment service provider.

5–10

First, although PSD II and Open Banking have the potential to benefit consumers through increased competition and availability of new services, they have data protection implications. The EU recognises the importance of protecting personal data in the General Data Protection Regulation,[23] the framework for the implementation of which in the UK is set out in the Data Protection Act 2018. These measures require banks to safeguard their customers' personal information, which may conflict with their obligations under PSD II to facilitate TPP access to customer accounts.

Payment fraud, always an issue particularly for card payments, has increased with the rise of electronic payments, particularly over the internet, since there is increased potential for consumers' details to be intercepted and used fraudulently. Ensuring that customers are adequately protected, especially with the rise in non-bank service providers, has been an important regulatory aim. To help protect consumers, PSD II mandates "Strong Customer Authentication" (SCA) to

---

[18] Thus circumventing the need for card payments. This has potential benefits for both merchants, as it may reduce their costs substantially, and also customers, who no longer require a debit or credit card to make online payments.

[19] See the list of payment services in Annex I of PSD II.

[20] For example, PSD II, arts 66 and 67 require banks and other account servicing payment service providers to cooperate with TPPs and provide TPPs with access to payment accounts when the payer gives consent.

[21] PSD II.

[22] In particular, by requiring nine banks to deliver an Open Banking Application Programming Interface (API) Standard, to provide a framework for third party software to authenticate, access data and initiate payments. See further HM Treasury Open Banking Working Group report, *The Open Banking Standard* (February 2016), available at: *http://www.paymentsforum.uk/sites/default/files/documents/Background%20Document%20No.%202%20-%20The%20Open%20Banking%20Standard%20-%20Full%20Report.pdf* [Accessed 22 September 2020].

[23] Regulation (EU) 2016/679 of the European Parliament and of the Council of 27 April 2016 on the protection of natural persons with regard to the processing of personal data and on the free movement of such data, and repealing Directive 95/46/EC.

attempt to decrease payment fraud.[24] This requires providers of payment services to use two independent elements, either knowledge, property or personal attributes, to authenticate customers.[25] If fraud does occur, PSD II sets out liability rules for unauthorised transactions, with losses above a certain threshold generally falling on the payment service provider or bank.[26]

Moreover, consumer funds may be at risk if a service provider becomes insolvent. The EU requires Member States to guarantee bank deposits up to a certain level, with harmonised rules under the Deposit Guarantee Schemes Directive.[27] The same protections do not apply to the customers of electronic money institutions and non-bank payment services. Instead, there is a "safeguarding" requirement on them either to segregate or insure customers' funds which falls short of the protection offered for bank deposits.[28]

Dealing with financial crime

5–11 Developments in payment services and systems have necessitated updates to laws intended to prevent financial crime, including money laundering, bribery and financing of terrorism. Money laundering is currently regulated at an EU level by the Fourth Anti-Money Laundering Directive,[29] which imposes cross-border controls and is intended to combat money laundering and terrorist financing. However, a Fifth Anti-Money Laundering Directive[30] entered into force in July 2018 which amended the Fourth Anti-Money Laundering Directive and which the UK implemented on 10 January 2020.[31] This extends the anti-money laundering regime to virtual currencies by imposing obligation on exchange platforms providing exchange services between virtual currencies and fiat money ("virtual currency exchange platforms") and also entities providing currency storage or

---

[24] This requires consumers to provide two peoples of information to prove their identity, e.g. a mobile phone, a PIN code or a fingerprint. The deadline for migration to SCA has been set for 31 December 2020.

[25] See PSD II art.4(3), which defines SCA as: "authentication based on the use of two or more elements categorised as knowledge (something only the user knows), possession (something only the user possesses) and inherence (something the user is) that are independent".

[26] See PSD II arts 73–77. Article 74 limits the amount the payer could be obliged to pay to €50 except in cases of fraud or gross negligence.

[27] Directive 2014/49/EU of the European Parliament and of the Council of 16 April 2014 on deposit guarantee schemes (recast). The Financial Services Compensation Scheme is the UK's deposit guarantee scheme. Deposits in the UK are currently covered up to £85,000 per individual per financial institution.

[28] For e-money institutions, see Directive 2009/110/EC of the European Parliament and of the Council of 16 September 2009 on the taking up, pursuit and prudential supervision of the business of electronic money institutions amending Directives 2005/60/EC and 2006/48/EC and repealing Directive 2000/46/EC, especially art.7; for non-bank payment service providers, see PSD II art.10.

[29] Directive 2015/849 on the prevention of the use of the financial system for the purposes of money laundering or terrorist financing, amending Regulation 648/2012 of the European Parliament and of the Council, and repealing Directive 2005/60 of the European Parliament and of the Directive 2006/70 [2015] OJ L141/73.

[30] Directive 2015/849 on the prevention of the use of the financial system for the purposes of money laundering or terrorist financing, amending reg.648/2012 of the European Parliament and of the Council, and repealing Directive 2005/60 of the European Parliament and of the Directive 2006/70 [2015] OJ L141/73.

[31] The impact of anti-money laundering legislation is discussed in more detail at para.5–41 below.

transfer services ("custodian wallet providers"). The UK addresses bribery through a combination of the Bribery Act 2010 and the Proceeds of Crime Act 2002.[32]

Ensuring stability of payment systems

Many of the measures affecting payment services are aimed at ensuring the stability of payment services. At a European level, the Settlement Finality Directive[33]—implemented in the UK through the Financial Market and Insolvency (Settlement Finality) Regulations 1999[34]—is intended to protect the integrity of the settlement procedures established by "designated" payment and securities settlement systems if a participant in a designated system becomes insolvent by providing that the procedures of that system take precedence over national insolvency law rules in the event of conflict. In addition, the Financial Collateral Arrangements (No.2) Regulations 2003,[35] which implement the Directive on Financial Collateral Arrangements,[36] play a role in ensuring the stability of payment and settlement systems by facilitating the provision of financial collateral and disapplying certain formalities rules and national insolvency law provisions which might otherwise impede the effectiveness of financial collateral arrangements.[37]

5–12

As well as these EU-wide measures, Pt V of the Banking Act 2009 gives the Bank of England extensive powers to oversee inter-bank payment systems which are recognised by the Treasury as systemically important. "Recognised payment systems" include BACS, CHAPS and Faster Payments, among others.[38] Special provision is made in Pt II of the 2009 Act for the insolvency of payment services providers.

3. PAYMENTS THROUGH THE BANKING SYSTEM

Payments until recently have almost always involved a bank in some capacity.[39] Although the use of non-bank payment services and systems is increasing, most payments still rely on banks to some degree and banks are at the centre of national and international payment systems.

5–13

---

[32] See further para.5–43 below.
[33] Directive 98/26 on settlement finality in payment and securities settlement systems [1998] OJ L166/45.
[34] Financial Market and Insolvency (Settlement Finality) Regulations 1999 (SI 1999/2979).
[35] Financial Collateral Arrangements (No.2) Regulations 2003 (SI 2003/3226).
[36] Directive 2002/47 on financial collateral arrangements [2002] OJ L168/43.
[37] A detailed discussion of these measures is beyond the scope of this book: see *Goode and Gullifer on Legal Problems of Credit and Security* (2018), Ch.6 on both the Settlement Finality Directive and the Directive on Financial Collateral as implemented in the UK.
[38] For the complete list, see the Bank of England's website available at: *http://www.bankofengland.co.uk/financialstability/Pages/fmis/supervised_sys/rps.aspx.*
[39] On this topic, see *Law of Bank Payments* (2018), para.1–018.

Structure of a national payments system

5–14 The present edition of *Goode on Commercial Law* identifies[40] various components which characterise a developed payments system structure:

(1) an inter-bank communications network for the online electronic transmission of large (wholesale) payment orders and associated messages[41];
(2) a clearing house for the physical exchange of paper-based payment orders (bills, cheques, bank giro payments) and the netting of matured payment obligations;
(3) an automated clearing house for the batch processing of large-volume off-line, mainly low value (retail) payment orders; and
(4) the involvement of the central bank as the vehicle for the settlement of dealings between the banks participating in clearing (settlement banks) by means of transfers in the books of the central bank, where all settlement banks hold an account.

The present section examines some of the legal issues which affect the use of these systems.

Structure of inter-bank payment systems

5–15 It is not possible to understand the occasionally obscure legal issues which arise in relation to inter-bank payment systems without a basic knowledge of the machinery through which settlements are effected.

It is proposed to consider separately the structural issues arising in the context of:

(1) domestic transactions in sterling; and
(2) international transactions involving foreign currencies.

Domestic transactions

5–16 It is important to understand the role played by the clearing banks in the context of the payment system. With the exception of "in-house" transfers,[42] this follows from the fact that, ultimately, inter-bank transfers are settled on an account held at the Bank of England, and such accounts are maintained only by a designated group of institutions.[43]

---

[40] Ewan McKendrick (ed.), *Goode and McKendrick on Commercial Law*, 6th edn (London: LexisNexis Butterworth, 2020), para.18.
[41] See the discussion of CHAPS below.
[42] See para.5–17 below.
[43] Thus, if a customer has an account with a non-clearing institution such as a building society, a further step will be added into the chain of transactions described below because that institution will need to complete the transaction through the agency of a clearing bank. This serves to add a further link to the chain of transactions but it does not fundamentally affect the general principles about to be discussed.

In-house transfers

The simplest case is where debtor and creditor happen to keep an account with the same institution, so that the transaction is entirely "in-house".

5–17

Where the debtor and creditor have their accounts at the same branch of a bank or financial institution, the amount involved will be debited from the debtor's account, with the corresponding amount being credited to the account of the creditor. Since this does not involve any external transfer of funds, there is no necessary requirement for the involvement of a clearing bank.[44] The absence of any movement of funds does, however, mean that special rules are required to determine at what point the transfer from debtor to creditor is to be regarded as complete—in other words, at what precise point of time was payment made and the debt discharged?[45]

The position becomes slightly more complex where the debtor and the creditor have accounts at different branches of the same bank. The transfer remains in-house, in the sense that no other bank is involved and the transfer does not need to go through the clearing system. In the case of a cheque, it will be the duty of the collecting bank to present the cheque for payment to the debtor's branch since, in law, different branches of the bank are for some purposes treated as separate entities.[46] Presentation is achieved through the bank's own clearing department which will pass the cheque on to the paying bank. The formal clearing system is thus not involved in the payment of such a cheque.[47]

The process involved in transfers of the types just described, and the flow of instructions and payments, are represented by the diagrams below.

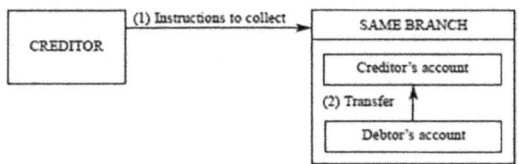

Fig.1(a): In-house cheque collection where debtor and creditor bank at same branch

---

[44] Or, if the institution concerned is a clearing bank, for any transfer of funds across its Bank of England account.

[45] On this point, see paras 5–50 to 5–55 below.

[46] See fig.2(a) and (b) below. As the late Lord Chorley observed, this is not because they are different entities in the normal legal sense but because it is an implied term of the banker–customer relationship that the payment of cheques and the effecting of certain and other transactions are to be carried out at a particular branch, typically, the branch where the customer maintains his account: see R.S.T. Chorley and P.E. Smart, *Leading Cases in the Law of Banking*, 6th edn (London: Sweet & Maxwell, 1990), p.372. This rule flows from the fact that the customer's account records would, in the past, only have been readily available at that branch. Technological developments may be rendering this rule obsolete.

[47] *Law of Bank Payments* (2018), paras 6–070 to 6–071.

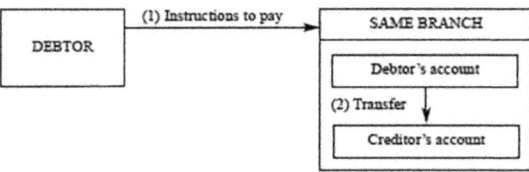

Fig.1(b): In-house credit transfer where debtor and creditor bank at same branch

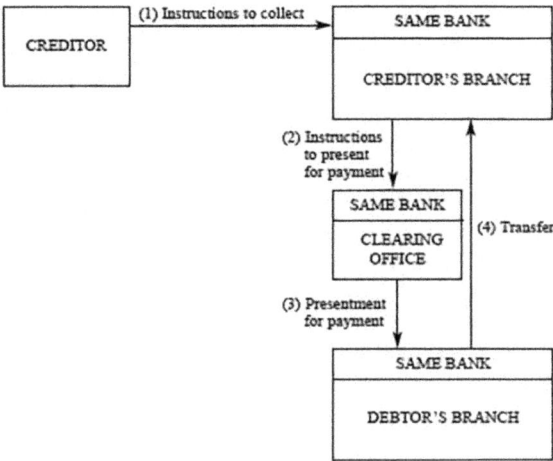

Fig.2(a): In-house cheque collection where debtor and creditor bank at different branches of same bank

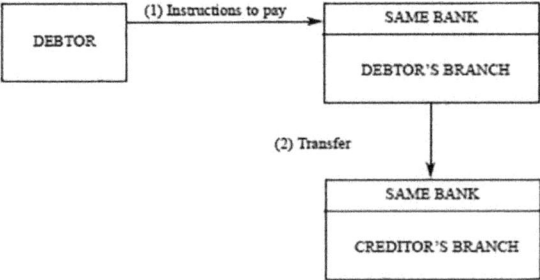

Fig.2(b): In-house credit transfer where debtor and creditor bank at different branches of same bank

External transfers

5–18 Let us now consider the position where the debtor and creditor have accounts at different clearing banks.[48]

Cheques

5–19 First of all, the process of domestic cheque clearance requires consideration.[49] This process is managed by the Cheque and Credit Clearing Company Ltd, an industry body whose members are known as the UK clearing banks. Prior to the introduction of "cheque imaging" in 2017 which may significantly speed up the process,[50] there was already a commitment on the part of banks subscribing to the now replaced Banking Codes[51] to meet standardised maximum time limits for clearing customer cheques, the "2–4–6" commitments for current accounts and the "2–6–6" commitments for savings accounts.[52] Thus, the presentation of a sterling cheque would be handled as follows:

(1) *Date of Presentation ("D")*: the creditor presents the debtor's cheque to his own bank for collection. The funds will usually be shown as a credit to the account on that day, although they will not immediately be available for withdrawal. The cheque will immediately be sent to the clearing centre operated by the collecting bank. Details of the amount of the cheque and the drawer are sent electronically to the paying bank, with the physical cheque being handed over some time later[53];

(2) *D + 2:* the creditor receives value on *D + 2*. In other words, the collecting bank recognises the payment so that, for example, any overdraft will be effectively reduced on that day and his obligation to pay interest will be adjusted accordingly. Correspondingly, the debtor's bank will recognise the payment, so that any credit balance will be reduced (or, as the case may be, his overdraft will be increased) with effect from that date. In addition, the Cheque and Credit Clearing Company Ltd will calculate the net amount

---

[48] As noted above, where a party has his account at a *non-clearing* institution, that institution will need to act through the agency of a clearing bank in order to complete or accept the transfer.

[49] This will be a relatively brief discussion because, with the growing popularity of instruments such as cards and direct debits, the use of cheques has been declining in the UK for the past twenty years; see the Cheque & Credit Clearing Company, *The Great British Cheque Report* (2009), available at: *https://www.chequeandcredit.co.uk/sites/default/files/the_great_british_cheque_report_0.pdf* [Accessed 12 October 2020]. Despite this, cheques are still widely used; in 2018, 346 million cheques were used in the UK with a total value of £442 billion and 75% of businesses reported receiving a cheque payment in the last month in spring 2018; see *https://www.chequeandcredit.co.uk/information-hub/facts-and-figures/key-facts-and-figures-0*.

[50] This removes the need for cheques to be physically transferred between banks and building societies.

[51] A self-regulatory regime replaced in November 2009 by what is now the Financial Conduct Authority (FCA) Banking and Payments Conduct Regime.

[52] The reference is to days in the clearing process. A fuller description is given in the publication mentioned in the preceding footnote.

[53] Provision of the electronic information does not absolve the paying bank from its duty to ensure that the cheque is regular (e.g. properly signed), so that it can be sure that it is paying in accordance with its mandate.

payable by the banks to each other based upon the total value of the cheques drawn on each of them. Those balances are then settled by the clearing banks through their respective accounts held at the Bank of England;

(3) *D + 4:* at this point, the funds in the creditor's account will be "cleared for withdrawal", in the sense that the creditor will now be entitled to make use of the credited funds by means of withdrawal or transfer; and

(4) *D + 6:* at this point, the creditor has certainty of funds. If the credit has not been reversed by this date,[54] then the credit entry cannot thereafter be reversed unless the creditor has been a party to some fraudulent design in relation to the cheque. This stage of the cycle is apparently referred to in banking circles as "clearing for fate". As will be seen, however, the entirety of the cheque clearing cycle bears only a limited relationship to the date on which payment is deemed to have been made as between debtor and creditor.[55]

The process involved in the collection of a cheque and the consequences of its dishonour are illustrated by the set of diagrams set out below.

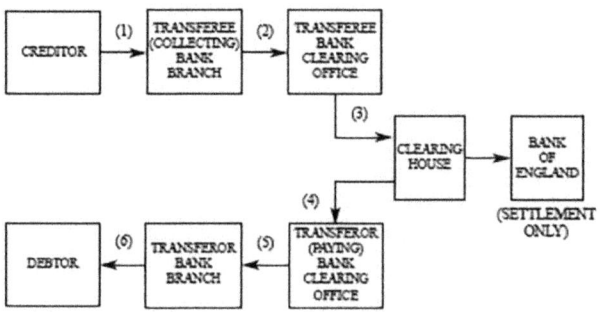

Fig.3(a): Cheque cleared through General Clearing

The Payments Council had announced in 2009 that the cheque clearing system would be closing in 2018 due to the declining use of cheques. However, this decision was reversed in 2011. It is now the PSR's responsibility to regulate cheque payment systems, including the Cheque and Credit Clearing Company Ltd.[56]

---

[54] For example, as a result of some technical defect in the cheque, or as a result of dishonour or countermand: see fig.3(b) below.

[55] See para.5–50 below. As will be seen, payment is deemed to occur when the cheque is handed over to the creditor, conditionally on the cheque being met upon presentation.

[56] On the PSR, see para.5–06 above.

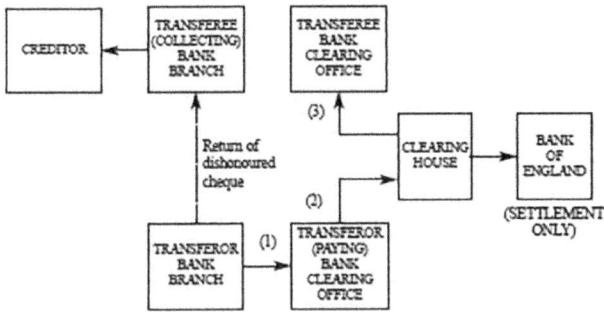

Fig.3(b): Return of dishonoured cheque presented through General Clearing (Numbered arrows show claim form in respect of cheque)

Electronic funds transfers

An electronic funds transfer involves the transfer of money from one bank account to another bank account by electronic means.[57] As part of the implementation of SEPA, and in particular the drive towards increased efficiency of payment systems in the EU, PSD II sets out time limits for the execution of payments. These are not limited to transactions in euros, but apply to payments in euros, domestic payments and transactions involving only one currency conversion between the euro and the currency of a Member State outside the Eurozone.[58] PSD II requires the payment to be credited to the account of the customer's payment service provider by the end of the next business day ($D + 1$).[59] The $D + 1$ rule also applies by default to transactions in other currencies unless the parties agree otherwise.[60] For transactions entirely within the European Economic Area, there is a limit of four business days.[61]

5–20

Domestic transfers and settlement

Various systems are available for electronic funds transfers within the UK. These include:

5–21

(1) BACS (Bankers Automated Clearing Services): this was the first UK electronic clearing system and was established in 1968. It is principally used for the settlement of direct debit and standing orders, and for the payment of salaries. Although BACS deals with a larger volume of payments than other UK payment systems,[62] their individual values tend to

---

[57] The concept is discussed in more detail at paras 5–35 to 5–36 below.
[58] PSD II art.82(1).
[59] PSD II art.83(1).
[60] PSD II art.82.
[61] PSD II art.82(2).
[62] Approximately 6.4 billion transactions in 2018; see *https://www.bankofengland.co.uk/-/media/boe/files/payments/chaps/annual-summary-of-payment-statistics-2018.pdf* [Accessed 12 October 2020].

be relatively low. For that reason, payments made through BACS do not seem to have given rise to any reported litigation and it is not proposed to consider this system further[63];

(2) Faster Payments: a system established in 2008 to provide more rapid clearing times for payments made by phone, internet or standing order. The Faster Payments system was an industry initiative set up by 13 banks and building societies to run in conjunction with existing payment systems. There is a payment limit of £250,000 via this system, although individual banks and building societies may set their own limits and limits may differ depending on the type of account from which money is sent[64]; and

(3) CHAPS (Clearing House Automated Payment System): CHAPS was established in 1984 and handles higher value payments.[65] It was originally a same-day settlement system in the sense that accounts would be credited at the end of the day following a process of net settlement among all of the participating banks. However, in line with developments in payment systems generally, CHAPS switched to real time gross settlement (RTGS) in 1996, meaning that payments are made gross immediately following receipt of payment instructions, without any delay pending a net settlement calculation at the end of the business day. CHAPS now settles sterling payments on the same "real time" basis. Measured by value, CHAPS is the main cashless payment system in the UK and the value of CHAPS transactions processed in 2018 was approximately £83.5 trillion.[66]

BACS and Faster Payments are run by Pay.UK, formerly the New Payment System Operator (NPSO).[67] CHAPS is run by the Bank of England.

The CHAPS system

5–22 It is convenient to examine the CHAPS briefly.[68] For the lawyer, it is perhaps attractive to adopt the description of CHAPS sterling which was formulated by Colman J for the purpose of considering a dispute involving a payment through that system in *Tayeb v HSBC Bank Plc*.[69] The case concerned whether the defendant bank had been entitled to return a large CHAPS payment that it had

---

[63] For a description of BACS and its clearing cycle, see *Law of Bank Payments* (2018), paras 3–023 to 3–033.

[64] For details of this system, see https://www.fasterpayments.org.uk/how-faster-payments-works [Accessed 12 October 2020].

[65] See the CHAPS website at https://www.bankofengland.co.uk/payment-and-settlement/chaps [Accessed 5 August 2020] for more information about CHAPS, including the legal and regulatory landscape.

[66] See https://www.bankofengland.co.uk/-/media/boe/files/payments/chaps/annual-summary-of-payment-statistics-2018.pdf [Accessed 12 October 2020].

[67] Which also runs the Cheque and Credit Clearing Company. The operators of these payment systems were consolidated into the NPSO in 2018.

[68] For further details on CHAPS, and for further discussions of the European Central Bank's TARGET system, the EBA Euro Clearing and Settlement System, see *Law of Bank Payments* (2018), Ch.3. The latter systems are briefly mentioned at para.5–24 below.

[69] *Tayeb v HSBC Bank Plc* [2004] 4 All E.R. 1024. The sections about to be quoted are taken from [10]–[14] of the judgment. References in this extract to a "LAK" mean a "logical acknowledgment" which informs the debtor's bank that payment has been received and credited to the transferee's

received to the bank which had paid it due to money laundering concerns. Colman J summarised matters as follows:

> "As described in Ellinger, Lomnicka & Hooley: Modern Banking Law, 3rd Edn, p480:
>
>> 'CHAPS sterling commenced operation as a same day value electronic credit transfer system in 1984. In 1996 CHAPS Sterling converted to a real time gross settlement system. This means that payments clear during the day on which they are made, within a short period after the payer's bank issues the payment instruction, rather than by netting off against all other relevant payments at the end of the day.'
>
> The immediate clearing of such payments is an extremely important advantage of CHAPS because it enables transactions involving the transfer of property, including foreign exchange and securities, to be completed on the same day. There is, as between a transferee bank and its transferee account holder, normally a crediting of the customer's account immediately following electronic acknowledgment in respect of the transfer.
>
> Both HSBC and Barclays were CHAPS settlement members and as such were bound by the CHAPS rules... It is important to note that payments under the system were required to be:
>
>> 'an irrevocable, guaranteed unconditional sterling payment for settlement in real time across members' settlement accounts at the Bank of England.'
>
> Further, by sending a LAK each member agreed, after authentication, to give same day value to its payee customer.
>
> The CHAPS system works in the following manner:
>
> CHAPS settlement members are provided with special computer software known as gateways. The gateways handle all communications between participating banks and security. The gateways are linked to and accessible from the member's own internal computer systems and they can communicate with the gateways of other participants over telecommunication links.
>
> A critical feature of CHAPS is that every payment is settled across the payer's bank's and the payee's bank's accounts at the Bank of England before any payment notification is sent to the payee's bank. The sequence of events is as follows:
>
> (1) The payer's bank initiates a payment transaction on its computer system;
> (2) The payer's bank's computer causes a settlement request to be sent to the Bank of England. This includes details of the payee's bank and account number;
> (3) If there are sufficient funds in the payer's bank's account at the Bank of England, the payment is settled by the Bank of England debiting the payer's bank's account and crediting the payee's bank's account;
> (4) The Bank of England sends a confirmation of settlement to the payer's bank's account;
> (5) On receipt of confirmation from the Bank of England, the payer's bank's gateway automatically sends a payment message to the payee's bank;
> (6) On receipt of the payment message, the payee's bank immediately transmits a LAK to the payer's bank. This follows authentication;
> (7) Mechanisms exist to ensure that inter-bank settlement can take place even where there is a temporary shortage of liquidity. However, in every such case, settlement occurs before the payee's bank receives any notification of the payment."

Part of the bank's defence to the customer's claim for the repayment of his deposit was to the effect that:

---

account. The substance of the dispute in that case involved the application of anti-money laundering legislation to the banker–customer relationship. That aspect of the case is accordingly considered at paras 5–43 to 5–44 below.

(i) it had until the end of the value date to decide whether to accept the funds remitted to it[70]; and
(ii) it had decided to block remittance into the account before the close of business that day and ultimately returned the funds to the payer.

Accordingly, it had never actually accepted the transfer.

However, these arguments could not prevail because a LAK had been despatched, confirming that the payment had been credited to Mr Tayeb's account.[71] Furthermore, CHAPS rules provided for the return of unapplied payments and transfers made in error but they made no provision for the return of other payments which had been authenticated by means of a LAK. Absent proof of fraud or illegality, it followed that transfers effected through CHAPS should be regarded as irreversible once a LAK had been transmitted.

Quite apart from the need to have a broad understanding of funds transfer systems for the purposes of the ensuing discussion, it follows from *Tayeb* that the operation of these systems may have an impact on the substantive rights and obligations of creditor and debtor vis-à-vis their respective banks. In some respects, it appears from this decision that the account holder is entitled to the benefit of the "irrevocable payment" provisions of the CHAPS rules, even though he is not directly party to them.

But this rule cuts both ways, as illustrated by the decision in *Tidal Energy Ltd v Bank of Scotland Plc*.[72] Tidal Energy completed a CHAPS transfer form requesting the bank to make a payment to a supplier. The CHAPS form specified: (i) the name of the payee; (ii) the payee's bank; (iii) the sort code; and (iv) the payee's account number. The form also included a disclaimer so that the bank would not be liable for "losses, interruptions or errors in transmission of payment" that were not attributable to the bank's negligence. There was an error in the account number specified on the form, with the result that the funds went to the wrong payee and, with the inevitability of these matters, the funds had been withdrawn from the receiving account by the time the mistake was discovered. Tidal Energy then sought restoration of its account on the basis that payments had not been made to the stated beneficiary in accordance with its instructions. It was demonstrated by evidence that normal banking practice was to make CHAPS payments solely in reliance on the identity of the recipient bank, the sort code and the account number—the name of the beneficiary was ignored for these purposes. This was in part to ensure that payments could be processed quickly—the very purpose of CHAPS—but the decision can also be justified on other, practical grounds.[73] As noted in the context of *Tayeb* (above), a customer who elects to use

---

[70] The bank relied on the authority of *Momm v Barclays Bank International Ltd* [1977] Q.B. 790 QBD (Comm) for this purpose.

[71] This may have been of some importance because, in view of the size of the remittance, the LAK could not be automatically authenticated and the direct involvement of the receiving bank's staff was therefore required.

[72] *Tidal Energy Ltd v Bank of Scotland Plc* [2015] 2 All E.R. 15. Tidal Energy were granted permission to appeal to the Supreme Court but the appeal did not go ahead.

[73] For example, the system is automated, so what is to be the position if my account title is "V S Dixon" but the payer inserts my name as "Victoria Dixon", or mis-spells my name as "Dickson"? Issues of this kind would presumably require manual checking and significantly slow down the payment process.

CHAPS is bound by the normal banking practices surrounding the operation of that system. The result was that the bank had complied with the customer's instructions in the normal way and was thus not obliged to restore Tidal Energy's account. It should be noted that the decision in *Tidal Energy* has been criticised for allowing banking practice, even if not known to the customer, to be incorporated into the contract between the customer and bank.[74]

As will be seen from some of the cases discussed in an international context,[75] the precise time at which payment is received can be a matter of dispute, even to a matter of minutes. It is at this point appropriate to refer to a decision of the Supreme Court of New Zealand in *Brett Ronald Larsen v Rick Dees Ltd*.[76] Rick Dees had contracted to purchase a number of land units from Mr Larsen. Dees had paid a deposit to Mr Larsen's solicitors, but was late in paying the balance of the purchase price. Larsen sent a completion notice that set a final deadline for completion of 17.00 on 5 March 2004. On that final day, Dees's solicitors attempted to contact Larsen's representatives to confirm that they would complete on that day, but they were unable to reach the person handling the deal. However, in line with the terms of the completion notice, Dees deposited cleared funds into the nominated solicitors' trust account by 16.54 that day. Larsen's solicitors sent a fax cancelling the contract at 17.03, not knowing that the funds had by then reached the trust account. Clause 3.7 of the contract stipulated that: "... On the settlement date ... the purchaser shall pay or satisfy the balance of the purchase price ... and the vendor shall concurrently hand to the purchaser [all title documents].... ." In spite of this wording, the Supreme Court effectively implied in cl.3.7: (a) an obligation on the purchaser to notify the vendor that funds had been credited to the trust account; and (b) a right for the vendor to assume that payment had not been received until the purchaser's notification has been received. This outcome is unfortunate at several levels:

(1) first, the wording of cl.3.7 provided no warrant for such an implied term, nor was it necessary to give business efficacy to the contract. It would have been a simple matter for the vendor's solicitors to call their own bank at 17.00 to ascertain whether or not the funds had arrived in the trust account;
(2) secondly, even if such a term was to be implied, it should have been formulated in the sense that the purchaser had to use *reasonable endeavours* to notify the vendor of payment because the purchaser cannot procure that the vendor or his representatives are available to receive the notification. Indeed, this was the very problem in this case, because the vendor's solicitor was engaged in other meetings and his fax machine was engaged at the relevant time; and

---

[74] See, for example, Gerard McMeel, "What is Payment in the 21st Century?" (2014) 11 B.J.I.B. & F.L. 675; Tom K.C. Ng, "Misdirected funds and the bank's right to debit the originator's account" (2015) 131 LQR 202.

[75] See, for example, the discussion of *The Brimnes* at para.5–44 below.

[76] *Brett Ronald Larsen v Rick Dees Ltd* [2007] NZSC 39. The criticisms that are about to be made must be tempered by the fact that the decision relates to real estate conveyancing transactions in New Zealand, of which the present writer has no experience. For further discussion of this case, see David McLauchlan, "Timely Payment by No Settlement: A Necessary Requirement of Notification?" (2008) 14 *New Zealand Business Law Quarterly* 37.

(3) in any event, the judgment overlooks the fact that the solicitor's bank had been nominated to accept *tender* of the purchase price.[77] Consequently, the vendor's own agent was aware that payment had been tendered at 16.54. This knowledge should have been imputed to the vendor himself. Payment should thus have been complete at that point because the vendor had no contractual right to reject the payment.[78]

Foreign currency transfers and settlement

5–23   Essentially similar mechanisms apply to foreign currency transfers and the discharge of foreign money obligations.[79] However:

(1) the settlement of a foreign currency transaction will generally take place through the clearing system in the country of the currency concerned[80]; and
(2) additional institutions will be involved in the chain of transactions because of the need to access the local clearing system in the country of issue.

By way of illustration, suppose that D is a UK-based purchaser of goods from C, a French-based exporter. The price of goods is, however, denominated in US dollars.[81] D holds a US dollar account with its London bank, whilst C holds a similar account in Paris. D is due to make a substantial payment under the supply contract. The following steps would be taken:

(1) D instructs his London bank to credit the Paris account of C;
(2) in order to achieve that objective, D's London bank instructs its New York correspondent bank to credit the New York correspondent of the Paris bank;
(3) for that purpose, the New York correspondent sends a message to CHIPS (Clearing House Interbank Payments System), the US dollar clearing system, requesting it to credit the New York correspondent of the Paris bank;
(4) the transfer is settled on accounts held by the respective correspondent banks with the US Federal Reserve Bank;
(5) upon clearance, CHIPS generates a payment message to the New York correspondent of the Paris bank;
(6) the New York correspondent sends a payment confirmation to the Paris bank; and

---

[77] Compare the discussion at para.5–51 below.
[78] It is submitted that the dissenting judgment of Elias CJ—to the effect that there was no notification obligation—is to be preferred.
[79] For a valuable review of some of the issues and case law, see R. Bollen, "A Review of the Legal Nature of International Payments (with Special Reference to Australian Law and Practice)" (2007) 22 J.I.B.L.R. 318.
[80] This may not be necessary where both the debtor's and the creditor's UK banks use the same correspondent bank in the country of issue, so that the ultimate transfer is achieved by in-house "netting". Compare the discussion of "in house" transfers at para.5–17 above.
[81] Many markets, including oil amongst others, are priced in US dollars regardless of the location of the individual parties.

(7) the Paris bank sends a credit advice to C.[82]

The processes involved in settling US dollars via London accounts are illustrated by the two scenarios in the diagrams set out below.

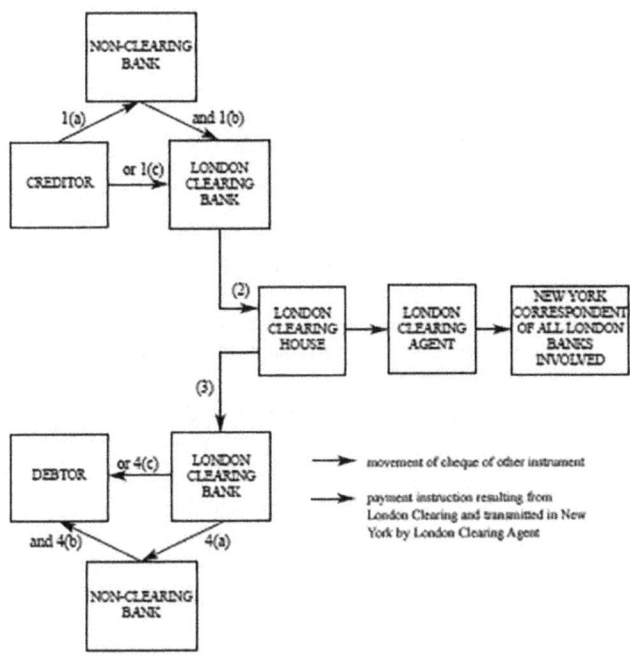

Fig.6(a): London US dollar clearing where transfers in New York are in-house

It will be obvious that, especially for high value payments, there is a need for a highly secure message transmission system on which banks can rely. This is especially the case in a highly automated payment system. For many international payment instructions, this service is provided by SWIFT (Society for Worldwide Interbank Financial Telecommunications). SWIFT does not hold or transfer funds, but acts as the carrier of information between financial institutions— operating systems designed to secure the confidentiality and integrity of that data.

It is perhaps worth briefly mentioning TARGET2, the main cross-border inter-bank payment system for euros. TARGET2 replaced TARGET in November 2007. TARGET (the Trans-European Automated Real-time Gross Settlement Express Transfer System) was introduced in 1999 to link the national central banks of each Member State and support the euro by making cross-border payments more efficient. TARGET2 takes this project further by creating a Single

5–24

---

[82] It will be seen that a series of transfers are required to achieve the ultimate payment. Although they form part of a chain, each payment is legally separate and independent. The consequences of this state of affairs are well illustrated by the decision in *European Bank Ltd v Citibank Ltd* [2004] NSWCA 76. The case is considered at paras 5–47 to 5–49 below.

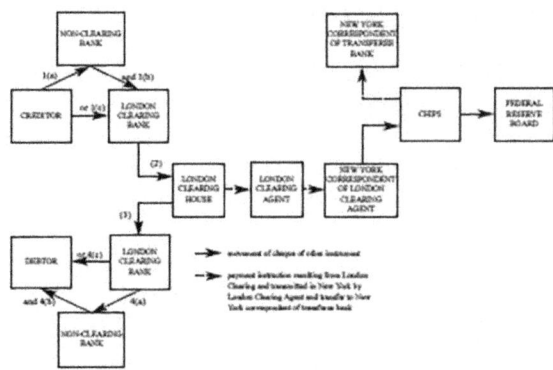

Fig.6(b): London US dollar clearing where transfers in New York are inter-bank

Shared Platform to connect the national central banks of Member States. Payments of any amount can be made through TARGET2; there are no upper or lower limits.[83] It is run by the Eurosystem (the monetary authority of the euro area comprising the European Central Bank and the national central banks of Eurozone members).[84] The development of other options for euro transfers, including TARGET2 and the "EURO1", "STEP1" and "STEP2" systems operated by EBA Clearing,[85] resulted in declining volumes of transactions through the CHAPS euro system, which was terminated in 2008.

Against this very brief and general background, it is possible to examine some of the legal implications of the various forms of non-cash payment available through the banking system.

Legal implications of payments through the banking system

5–25   The present section considers the various legal issues which may arise when payment is made through the medium of banks representing the debtor and the creditor respectively.

Whilst the *number* of transactions which are settled in cash no doubt remains large in absolute terms and payment systems offered by institutions other than banks are increasingly being used, the banking system clearly settles the greatest *value* of transactions. The reasons for this are not far to seek; the transfer of large amounts of money needs to be—so far as possible—secure, swift and risk-free. The handling of large sums in physical cash plainly meets none of these requirements. The present section accordingly considers the various means by

---

[83] For a detailed discussion of TARGET and TARGET2, see *Law of Bank Payments* (2018), paras 3–057 to 3–060.

[84] The Eurosystem also operates T2S (TARGET2-Securities), a new European securities settlement system which aims to harmonise securities settlement infrastructure in Europe. It incorporates non-Eurozone Member States although the Bank of England decided not to participate; *Law of Bank Payments* (2018), para.3–053; Dermot Turing, *Clearing and Settlement*, 2nd edn (Haywards Heath: Bloomsbury, 2016), para.2.24.

[85] For more information on EURO1, STEP1 and STEP2, see *Law of Bank Payments* (2018), paras 3–061 to 3–067.

which payment can be made through bank payment systems.[86] Non-bank payment systems, which are increasingly being used as an alternative to bank payment systems, will be discussed further below.[87]

It is necessary to emphasise that the present work is not directly or principally concerned with the law of banking; it is concerned with payment as between a debtor and creditor in respect of their own commercial transaction. So far as possible, it is thus proposed to focus on the contractual relationship between the debtor and creditor and the manner in which their monetary obligations are discharged. References to any banking law issues are thus for the purposes of explanation only and are not intended to provide an exhaustive analysis.

It is proposed to examine the following issues in relation to cashless payment:

(1) legal effect of payments through third parties;
(2) payment by cheque;
(3) payment by credit card/debit card;
(4) payment by standing order or direct debit;
(5) payment by means of funds transfer;
(6) internet payments;
(7) the impact of anti-money laundering legislation;
(8) the impact of anti-bribery legislation;
(9) special features of international funds transfers; and
(10) the international expropriation of deposits.

(1) Legal effect of payments through third parties

It is necessary at the outset to briefly consider the consequences of payments made with the assistance of third parties such as banks or other agents.

5–26

If a debtor (D) hands over notes and coins to his creditor (C), then that transaction takes place between principals and thus plainly operates to discharge the debt to the relevant extent. If, however, an agent of D hands over the necessary funds, then, on ordinary agency principles, this will only discharge the debt if the agent acted with D's authority (actual or ostensible) or if he purported to do so and his actions were ratified by D. Similarly, payment to an agent of C will only operate to discharge the debt if the agent had C's authority to accept the payment, or if he purported to do and his acceptance is later ratified by C.[88] These rather dry statements of agency law potentially have significant consequences where payment is made through the banking system. For example:

(a) D may instruct DB (D's bank) to make payment to C via CB (C's bank). If the requested payment is made to CB and it has authority to receive that payment, then this constitutes a discharge of D's debt to C. If CB becomes

---

[86] See *Law of Bank Payments* (2018) for a valuable overview of various methods of non-cash payment.
[87] See paras 5–62 to 5–76 below.
[88] See the discussion at para.2–27 above; also *British Bank of the Middle East v Sun Life Assurance Co of Canada (UK)* [1983] 2 Lloyd's Rep. 9 HL; and *Stavrinides v Bank of Cyprus Public Co Ltd* [2019] EWHC 1328 (Ch).

insolvent before C can access and utilise these funds, then that is C's misfortune but it does not affect the fact that D's obligations have been fully performed;

(b) D may instruct DB to make payment to CB out of funds to be remitted by D to CB. If CB elects to credit C's account before receiving funds from DB, then this will not have the effect of discharging D's debt to C, because CB has acted outside the scope of the authority given by DB. Payment as between D and C will only occur when the designated funds are received by CB[89]; and

(c) in the situation described in (b) above, CB credits C's account but advises that the credit is "under reserve" and may be reversed if corresponding funds are not received from DB. In the normal course, this cannot discharge D's obligation to C since a payment obligation must be performed unconditionally.

In each case, the scope of the agent's authority will require careful examination. For example, in the normal situation, CB will have authority to accept a *tender* of payment made by DB on behalf of D by means of a payment through the banking system. However, CB will have no authority to accept *payment* on behalf of C. Payment thus only occurs where C himself—or someone else on his behalf with the requisite authority—accepts the transfer as a payment. This may happen as a result of an express, communicated acceptance. More often, however, it will be inferred from the creditor's retention of the funds after he has become aware of the transfer. The important consequence is that the receipt of funds by CB does not imply a waiver of any breach as to the time of payment[90]; it thus remains open to the creditor to reject the funds on the basis that the tender does not comply with the contract.[91] The creditor must, of course, act promptly in rejecting the funds since otherwise he may be taken to have accepted any payment and waived any breach associated with its timing.[92]

(2) Payment by cheque

5–27 It is often said that—absent an express or implied contractual term—a creditor is not obliged to accept a cheque tendered in payment of a debt.[93] Yet the point is

---

[89] Again, D's debt can only be discharged by someone acting on his behalf in making the payment, or who purports to do so and his payment is later ratified by D.

[90] This is only logical. The bank will usually have no knowledge of the contract under which the payment is made. How, then, could its conduct in receiving the funds amount to a waiver of obligations to which it is not party and of which it is wholly unaware?

[91] *Mardorf Peach & Co Ltd v Attica Sea Carriers Corp of Liberia* (*The Laconia*) [1977] A.C. 850 HL. It was previously thought that receipt by CB did involve acceptance of the *payment*: see *Tenax Steamship Co v Owners of the Motor Vessel Brimnes (The Brimnes)* [1975] Q.B. 929 CA (Civ Div). However, in the absence of special terms in the underlying contract, this view can no longer stand; the bank's functions are "purely ministerial".

[92] See e.g. *Kaupthing Singer & Friedlander Ltd (In Administration) v UBS AG* [2014] EWHC 2450 (Comm) (where funds were mistakenly received by parent company, failure by C to draw D's attention to the mistake led to a finding of estoppel by convention).

[93] See, for instance, *Libyan Arab Foreign Bank v Bankers Trust Co* [1989] Q.B. 728 QBD (Comm), where it was held the claimants were entitled to cash payment. However, the creditor may impliedly

largely theoretical.[94] Unless the creditor has some particular reason for asserting that payment has not been duly made or the actual time of receipt of the funds is otherwise critical,[95] he will usually accept any recognised form of payment.

Since it is intended that cheques or similar instruments of payment should be regarded as "equivalent to cash", the creditor is—in the absence of fraud— entitled to judgment for the face amount of the dishonoured cheque regardless of any dispute relating to the underlying commercial contract.[96]

(a) Consequences of accepting payment by cheque

However, what are the more immediate consequences for a creditor who accepts a cheque proffered to him in payment?[97]   5–28

First, the cheque is accepted subject to the condition subsequent that it is duly paid on presentation. Payment is thus "provisional"—and not "payment" in any real sense—until the cheque is fully cleared.[98] This is so obvious that no further explanation is required.

Secondly, assuming that the cheque is subsequently met, the contractual payment is deemed to have been made on (or "relates back" to) the date on which the cheque is tendered.[99] In the absence of some express contractual term, the creditor can accordingly have no right to claim interest or damages from the debtor in respect of the period during which the cheque is being cleared through the system.[100]

Thirdly, if the creditor accepts the cheque tendered to him, this will effectively suspend any right of action which he has under the contract in respect of the non-payment of the sums concerned. He cannot blow hot and cold by taking the

---

agree to accept payment by cheque; see e.g. *Homes v Smith* [2000] Lloyd's Rep. Bank. 139 at 143 CA; *Avocet Industrial Estates LLP v Merol Ltd* [2011] EWHC 3422 (Ch).

[94] Yet not entirely so, for it remains the case that the creditor can decline to accept a personal cheque as a means of payment: see the decision of the New Zealand Supreme Court in *Otago Station Estates Ltd v Parker* [2005] 2 NZLR 734, where the court found that payment had to be made by means of "legal tender, bank cheque or other cleared funds". It is not clear that this observation was necessary for the decision. The court held that there was an implied term in contracts for the sale of land that the deposit should be paid by banker's cheque (as opposed to a personal cheque), and then it seems to have equated banker's cheques with "legal tender". In strict terms, this is incorrect, although, in *Williams v Gibbons* [1994] NZLR 273, the New Zealand Supreme Court had held that a banker's cheque was the "practical equivalent" of legal tender in the context of real estate transactions.

[95] For example, as in the charterparty cases discussed in Ch.4 above.

[96] See, for example, *Nova (Jersey) Knit Ltd v Kammgarn Spinnerei GmbH* [1977] 1 W.L.R. 713 HL; *Oxigen Environmental Ltd v Mullan* [2012] NIQB 17.

[97] For a detailed analysis of cheques, see *Law of Bank Payments* (2018), Ch.7.

[98] See para.2–27 above.

[99] See *Law of Bank Payments* (2018), paras 6–319 to 6–324, especially para.6–324, on discharge of the underlying debt owed by D to C. There may be a considerable delay between the date on which payment is conditionally made and the date on which funds are actually received, especially if the creditor is tardy in presenting the cheque to his bank. In terms of the cheque clearing cycle discussed at para.5–19 above, it is submitted that the condition subsequent is only met on $D + 6$ when the creditor has an unchallengeable right to the funds and the credit to his account has become irreversible.

[100] Where DB is itself the creditor and a third-party cheque is presented in reduction of the overdraft, the clearance period is a matter of contract between the debtor and his bank: see *Emerald Meats (London) Ltd v AIB Group (UK) Plc* [2002] EWCA Civ 460.

cheque and yet seeking to exercise remedies on the footing that payment has not yet been cleared through the system.[101] A creditor who accepted a cheque and yet elected to sign judgement in default thus not only had his judgement set aside, but was also made liable for the debtor's costs.[102]

5–29 These general principles are, hopefully, uncontroversial. But the agency considerations noted at the beginning of this chapter must not be overlooked. A paying bank which meets a cheque in accordance with its mandate will be acting within the scope of its authority and, in the vast majority of cases, no difficulty will arise. But the paying bank may have no authority to pay the cheque if it has been specifically countermanded or if the bank has received notice of the customer's death. What is the position if DB erroneously pays the cheque under such circumstances? Can C retain the funds which have been credited to his account and—which is much the same question—does the payment discharge the underlying debt between D and C? Alternatively, if he wishes to reject the payment and terminate the underlying contract, can C argue that the payment was made without authority and that it accordingly does not operate to discharge D's debt?

On the assumption that C was unaware of the revocation of authority, the better view appears to be that the paying bank has ostensible authority to make the payment. By delivery to C of a cheque drawn on DB, D will have impliedly represented that DB has authority to pay that cheque. Accordingly, he should be estopped from denying the authority of his own bank. In *B. Liggett (Liverpool) Ltd v Barclays Bank Ltd*,[103] the bank, having effectively discharged the customer's debt on his behalf, was held to be entitled to be subrogated in equity to the claims of the creditors themselves. However, the decision in this case does not appear consistent with the decision in *Barclays Bank Ltd v WJ Simms Son & Cooke (Southern) Ltd*.[104] where it was held that a bank could recover money paid on a cheque through inadvertence after payment was stopped by the drawer from the payee, although it was considered in that case that the bank's claim might fail if the payment was made for good consideration and discharges a pre-existing debt,[105] C therefore faces the possibility of being subject to a claim for repayment from the paying bank.

There is also a conceptual difficulty here. The bank has paid the cheque in breach of its mandate and thus had no actual authority to pay the debt. As has been seen, the obligation owing by D to C would not normally be discharged

---

[101] *Cohen v Hale* (1878) 3 Q.B.D. 371; *ED&F Man Ltd v Nigerian Sweets & Confectionery Co* [1977] 2 Lloyd's Rep. 50 QBD (Comm); *Homes v Smith* [2000] Lloyd's Rep. Bank. 139 CA (Civ Div); *Coltrane v Day* [2003] 1 W.L.R. 1379 CA (Civ Div). This is perhaps a legally more accurate way of saying that the payment by cheque is to be regarded as "provisional": see above. The position is the same in the US: *Ornstein v Hickerson* 40 F. Supp. 305 (1941). In *Re Hone (A Bankrupt)* [1951] Ch. 85 Ch D, it was held in the context of the Bankruptcy Act 1914 that "payment" in the case of payment by a cheque did not mean the date when the cheque was handed to the payee, but the date when the money was collected, but this was doubted by the Court of Appeal in *Homes v Smith*.
[102] *Bolt & Nut Co (Tipton) Ltd v Rowlands Nicholls & Co Ltd* [1964] 2 Q.B. 10 CA. The cheque was honoured after judgment had been signed.
[103] *B. Liggett (Liverpool) Ltd v Barclays Bank Ltd* [1928] 1 K.B. 48.
[104] *Barclays Bank Ltd v WJ Simms Son & Cooke (Southern) Ltd* [1980] Q.B. 677 QBD (Comm). See the discussion and criticism of this case at para.3–76 above.
[105] *WJ Simms* [1980] Q.B. 677 QBD (Comm) at 695.

under these circumstances.¹⁰⁶ Although the decision in *Liggett* was followed in *HJ Symons & Co v Barclays Bank Plc*¹⁰⁷ and does appear to accord with the justice of the case, subsequent cases have suggested that subrogation is only allowed where the paying bank has been expressly authorised to make the payment or the payment has been ratified.¹⁰⁸ For instance, the Court of Appeal in *Crantrave Ltd (In Liquidation) v Lloyds Bank Plc*¹⁰⁹ followed an earlier decision, *Re Cleadon Trust Ltd*,¹¹⁰ to find on the facts that:

> "... in the absence of authorisation or ratification by the company of the bank's payment to the third party, the 'mere fact' that the bank's payment enured to the benefit of the company does not establish an equity in favour of the bank against the company."

The Court of Appeal also considered that, even if *Liggett* was followed, it would be necessary to establish that the company's legal liability to the company's creditor had been discharged in order for there to be subrogation, and that this would require either authorisation or ratification.¹¹¹

(b) Use of cheque cards

In retail transactions, the use of cheques has been declining for some years, largely as a result of the greater convenience offered by credit and debit cards. From a high point of four billion payments by cheque in 1990,¹¹² cheque usage has declined to approximately 400 million in 2018–19.¹¹³ Until recently, it used to be the case that a payee accepting a cheque would almost invariably require that the cheque was supported by a cheque card. This was a natural precaution for a retailer; there is always the danger that a cheque will be dishonoured on presentation for want of funds in the account. Furthermore, in the ordinary retail situation, the seller would be dealing with a customer whom he did not know and had no reason to trust.

5–30

From the late 1960s, and in order to facilitate the use of cheques in retail transactions,¹¹⁴ banks began to issue cheque cards; in view of their purpose, they were frequently, if slightly misleadingly, referred to as "cheque guarantee cards". Leaving aside the details of the cheque card schemes,¹¹⁵ it is well known that the

---

¹⁰⁶ See para.5–26 above.
¹⁰⁷ *HJ Symonds & Co v Barclays Bank Plc* [2003] EWHC 1249 (Comm).
¹⁰⁸ See, for instance, the Court of Appeal decision in *Re Cleadon Trust Ltd* [1939] Ch. 286 CA, applied by the Court of Appeal in *Crantrave Ltd (In Liquidation) v Lloyds Bank Plc* [2000] Q.B. 917 CA (Civ Div) and the High Court in *Swotbooks.com Ltd v Royal Bank of Scotland* [2011] EWHC 2025 (QB).
¹⁰⁹ *Crantrave* [2000] Q.B. 917 CA (Civ Div) at 923F.
¹¹⁰ *Re Cleadon Trust Ltd* [1939] Ch. 286 CA.
¹¹¹ *Crantrave* [2000] Q.B. 917 CA (Civ Div) at 923F.
¹¹² Available at: *http://researchbriefings.files.parliament.uk/documents/SN05318/SN05318.pdf* [Accessed 24 August 2020].
¹¹³ See the UK Payments Market Summary 2019 (June 2019), available at: *http://ukfinance.org.uk/sites/default/files/uploads/pdf/UK-Finance-UK-Payment-Markets-Report-2019-SUMMARY.pdf*.
¹¹⁴ Note that cards are only issued to individuals, and not to corporate entities.
¹¹⁵ For a helpful discussion of how these cards operated, see the 4th edition of *Law of Bank Payments*, para.4–003.

bank "guaranteed" that a cheque up to the amount stated on the card[116] will be paid on presentation regardless of the state of the customer's account and irrespective of any purported countermand. The effect was that the retailer took a risk of non-payment on a well-known bank, rather than on the customer himself.[117]

In terms of a formal legal analysis, the cheque card constituted an open offer to any retailer that the bank would meet any cheque up to the stated amount, provided that the terms of the scheme were met. By issuing the card to the account holder, the bank clothed him with authority to convey that offer to retailers on behalf of the bank. It was formerly held that a bank was obliged to meet a "guaranteed" cheque provided that the signature on the cheque and the cheque card *appeared* to correspond, with the result that the bank would have to meet a forged cheque.[118] It seems clear that the bank could not debit the customer's account in such a case, at any rate unless he had been in some way complicit in, or had facilitated the fraud. Subsequent changes to the terms of the cheque card scheme may have had the effect that the retailer bears a greater proportion of the risk of forgery or fraud in this type of case.[119] Be that as it may, these issues are now of historical interest only since the cheque card scheme was closed in June 2011 by the Payments Council as a result in a decline in use of guaranteed cheques. It had been intended that the use of cheques would be phased out but that decision was reversed.[120] However, there are no plans to reinstate the cheque card scheme.

(3) Payment by credit card/debit card

(a) Credit cards

5–31   What are the legal implications of a payment made by means of a credit card?

The fundamental question in this respect is the relationship between the customer and the supplier or company. Perhaps inevitably, this question arose for decision in a case involving the insolvency of the "trusted" issuer of the card. In *Re Charge Card Services Ltd (No.2)*,[121] the company issued cards which were used to pay for fuel purchases at participating petrol stations. At the point at which the company became insolvent, it had outstanding liabilities to garages which had sold fuel on the faith of the card. Equally, some of those purchasers of fuel had outstanding obligations to reimburse the company. The question was: could the various garages recover outstanding amounts from those cardholders, or did the claim to such moneys continue to reside with the insolvent issuer?

Of course, if "payment" by card was found, as in the case of a cheque, to be conditional on receipt by the garage of a subsequent remittance from the issuing

---

[116] Usually £50, £100 or £250.
[117] See, for example, the commentary in *Re Charge Card Services Ltd (No.2)* [1987] Ch. 150 Ch D (Companies Ct), affirmed [1989] Ch. 497 CA (Civ Div).
[118] *First Sport Ltd v Barclays Bank Plc* [1993] 1 W.L.R. 1229 CA (Civ Div).
[119] For a discussion, see the 4th edition of *Law of Bank Payments*, para.4–008.
[120] See para.5–19 above.
[121] *Re Charge Card Services* [1987] Ch. 150 Ch D (Companies Ct), affirmed [1989] Ch. 497 CA (Civ Div).

company, then clearly the garage would retain its right of recourse against the original purchaser. However, the court held that cheques and credit cards are not analogous modes of payment. Where a creditor accepts a cheque, he realises that this is subject to clearance through the system and he may have obtained the comfort of a cheque card (see above). Nevertheless, he receives an instrument which is signed by the drawer/debtor and the payment obligation continues to reside with that individual; cheque guarantee cards aside, the bank owes no obligation to pay the cheque in the absence of sufficient funds. In contrast, the issuer of the card is contractually obliged to make the necessary payment to the supplier. The retailer therefore accepts the card in anticipation that, in a few weeks' time, he will receive from the card issuer the purchase price of the fuel, subject to deduction of commissions and charges levied by the issuer.[122] Under these circumstances, the court held that the acceptance of a credit card constitutes the *unconditional* discharge of the debtor or customer.[123] In consideration of that release, the issuing company assumes a corresponding obligation to pay the retailer in accordance with the merchant conditions. The cardholder does, of course, become liable to make *full* payment to the issuing company following receipt of his statement. Against the background of this contractual matrix, the insolvent issuing company remained entitled to collect amounts owing to it by its cardholders. The retailers had no claim against the customers, and were thus left to join the queue and rank as unsecured creditors on a pari passu basis.

The court further held that the customer's liability to the garage was discharged when the account of the garage with the card issuer is credited (i.e. and not at the later date when the garage is actually paid by the issuer). Given the use of modern technology, this may mean that, as between debtor and creditor, the time of payment for a credit card transaction is the point of time at which it is electronically approved by the card issuer.[124]

(b) Debit cards

Like a credit card, a debit card is a form of "plastic money".[125] In terms of technology, debit card transactions are processed by the EFTPOS system:

5–32

---

[122] This is a fundamental distinction. In the case of a cheque, the retailer expects to receive the full amount of the price by payment from the customer's bank account. In a credit card transaction, the retailer accepts that he will receive a *lesser* price from the issuing company, but nevertheless agrees to accept the card in the expectation that this will increase the volume of sales. This tends to reinforce the impression that the retailer is looking *exclusively* to the issuing company for payment.

[123] As pointed out by the court, the transaction still involves the payment of the *price* for goods and it is from the obligation to pay the *price* that the customer is discharged. The analogy is necessary to ensure that the contract falls within the Sale of Goods Act 1979, since such a contract must involve a *monetary* consideration.

[124] See the discussion of this point in *Law of Bank Payments* (2018), paras 4–029 to 4–031, 4–035. It may be noted in passing that, where a transaction is financed through the use of a credit card, s.75 of the Consumer Credit Act 1974 renders the creditor jointly and severally liable for any misrepresentation or breach of contract by the supplier. Whilst the 1974 Act only applies to *credit agreements* in the UK, s.75 can be invoked regardless of the law applicable to the underlying supply contract or the place in which it is made: see *Office of Fair Trading v Lloyds TSB Bank Plc* [2008] 1 A.C. 316.

[125] For a full description of the development and use of debit cards, see *Law of Bank Payments* (2018), paras 4–003 to 4–031.

Electronic Funds Transfer at Point of Sale.[126] This title neatly describes the underlying objective. When the retailer accepts the debit card at the time of the sale, the card is "swiped" into a device which is linked to the issuing bank's computer. In very simple terms, this process will result in a message back to the retailer confirming the transaction and that payment will be debited to the customer and credited to the account of the retailer.

So far as the retailer is concerned, the transaction creates a contract between itself and the customer's bank, to the effect that the payment has been or will be made to the retailer's account. Payment is therefore confirmed at the point of sale, although it is believed that such payments can take a few days to clear in practice. In relation to whether debit cards constitute *unconditional* payment, it is logical to assume that the position is the same as for credit cards and debit cards are to be treated as akin to cash.[127]

(c) Fraud and the use of cards

5–33 As noted earlier, plastic money has grown in popularity in part because of the difficulty and the risk of loss involved in carrying large amounts of cash. Yet plastic money suffers from its own insecurity. The simple theft of credit and debit cards is now less obviously lucrative provided that the holder has maintained the confidentiality of his PIN number. But the copying of cards—including the PIN—at the point of use has become a major criminal enterprise. These two types of fraud—resulting from cloning and theft—require separate consideration.

Where a card has been "cloned" and a replica has been produced and used, it seems clear that the original cardholder himself cannot have any liability for the resultant expenditure. So long as the cardholder is innocent of any connivance in the fraud, he will be in the same position as an account holder whose cheques have been forged. The card issuer or bank has to suffer the loss since it has paid without the customer's authority.

Where, in contrast, a debit or credit card has been stolen, the position becomes more complex. The position for debit cards is set out in the Payment Services Regulations 2017.[128] These cover "payment instruments"[129] generally and provide that both the customer and the payment service provider may face liability for unauthorised payments depending on the circumstances. In summary:

(i) where a payment was not authorised, the bank should refund it as soon as practicable[130]; however,

---

[126] Discussed in *Law of Bank Payments* (2018), paras 4-004 to 4-005.
[127] See *Law of Bank Payments* (2018), paras 4-029 to 4-031 for a discussion of the legal consequences of debit card payments.
[128] Which implement the PSD II into UK law.
[129] "Payment instrument" is defined as a "personalised device" or "personalised set of procedures agreed between the payment service user and the payment service provider", used by the payment service user in order to "initiate a payment order": reg.2(1) of the 2017 Regulations.
[130] 2017 Regulations reg.76. Under reg.76(2), the refund must be provided no later than the end of the business day following the day on which it became aware of the unauthorized transaction.

(ii) the customer has an obligation to "take all reasonable steps" to keep the personalised security credentials, e.g. PIN, of a payment instrument safe[131];
(iii) the customer is only entitled to a refund if it notifies the bank "without undue delay" on becoming aware of any unauthorised payment transaction, and in any event no later than 13 months after the debit date[132];
(iv) the bank may require the customer to be liable up to a maximum of £35 for any losses incurred in respect of authorised payment transactions arising from the use of a lost or stolen payment instrument, or the misappropriation of a payment instrument,[133] unless the loss, theft or misappropriation was not detectable by the customer prior to payment, except where the customer acted fraudulently.[134]
(v) the customer is liable for all unauthorised transactions if he has acted fraudulently, or has failed deliberately or with gross negligence to comply with his obligations in relation to the payment instrument, including to notify the bank without undue delay on becoming aware of its loss, theft, misappropriation or unauthorised use and to take all reasonable steps to keep the personalised security credentials safe[135]; and
(vi) the customer is not liable for any losses incurred arising after it has notified the bank of the loss, theft, misappropriation or unauthorised use of the payment instrument, if the bank has failed to provide the means for the customer to make the notification or if a card has been used in connection with a distance contract.[136]

The burden of proof is on the bank to prove that a transaction was authorised or correctly carried out if the customer denies this.[137] The burden of proof is also on the bank to prove that the customer was at fault in not keeping the payment instrument safe.[138]

The Consumer Credit Act 1974 sets out the position in relation to fraudulent misuse of credit cards.[139] In particular, s.83 provides that a credit card holder is not liable for fraudulent misuse of the card. The customer may be liable to the extent of £35 for loss arising after losing possession of the credit card,[140] but is not liable for losses after giving oral or written notice that the card has been lost or stolen or is liable to misuse for another other reason to the card issuer or if there is a distance contract.[141] The most significant difference between the two regimes is that there is no equivalent to the liability of the cardholder under the

---

[131] 2017 Regulations reg.72(3).
[132] 2017 Regulations reg.74(1).
[133] 2017 Regulations reg.77(1).
[134] 2017 Regulations reg.77(1)(a) and (b).
[135] 2017 Regulations regs 72 and 77(3).
[136] 2017 Regulations reg.77(4).
[137] 2017 Regulations reg.75(1).
[138] 2017 Regulations reg.75(3) and (4).
[139] The 2017 Regulations apply to debit and credit cards generally, but certain provisions are disapplied where the 1974 Act applies. The relevant provisions of the 1974 Act are ss.66, 83, 84 and 171.
[140] Consumer Credit Act 1974 s.84(1). The £35 limit was brought into line with the limit for debit cards by the 2017 Regulations Sch.8(1), para.1(b).
[141] Consumer Credit Act 1974 ss.84(3), (3A).

[213]

2017 Regulations for either intentionally or grossly negligently failing to comply with his obligation to keep the payment instrument safe. In addition, under the 2017 Regulations, any transaction must be challenged within 13 months at the latest whereas the 1974 Act does not impose an absolute cut-off point. These changes are to the benefit of the customer. Further, s.75 of the 1974 Act makes issuers of credit cards joint and severally liable to the consumer in respect of any misrepresentation claim or breach of contract claim which a consumer may have in relation to a transaction valued between £100 and £30,000. On the other hand, under the 1974 Act, the customer can be made liable without limit for use of the card by someone who acquired possession with their consent, until they give notice that it is lost or stolen or otherwise liable to be misused.[142]

The rise of "contactless" payments poses security risks in relation to credit and debit cards. Included in many new credit, debit or prepaid cards, it allows the customer to make purchases up to a certain value, presently £45,[143] simply by holding the card against a card reader without having to enter their PIN. A specific exemption from the Strong Customer Authentication requirement introduced by PSD II[144] has been introduced for contactless payments.[145] However, this gives rise to an increased risk of fraud as no PIN is required and contactless payment involves transactions being approved "offline" without being referred to the account provider for authorisation. This latter point means there is the potential for fraudulent transactions to continue to be made even after the card is cancelled. Although consumers will be entitled to a refund in line with the provisions of the 2017 Regulations and the 1974 Act which are discussed above, they will still have to comply with the safety, notification and other requirements outlined above and may in addition have to continue monitoring their payment records after cancelling a stolen card for additional unauthorised transactions.

(4) Payment by standing order or direct debit

5–34 Standing orders and direct debits are familiar forms of payment instructions given by a customer to his bank.

Standing orders are an instruction to pay a *fixed* amount at regular intervals. They presuppose that the amount payable will not vary over the period of the instruction. More common, in the modern context, is the direct debit. This, again, begins with an instruction from the customer to debit his account. However, the bank is instructed to transfer such amounts as the named creditor may from time

---

[142] Consumer Credit Act 1974 s.84(2).
[143] Increased from £30 on 1 April 2020; the changes were expedited by UK Finance due to the Covid-19 outbreak.
[144] PSD II art.97, implemented in the 2017 Regulations reg.100. SCA requires payment service providers to use two independent elements—knowledge, property or personal attributes—to authenticate payment transactions.
[145] Commission Delegated Regulation (EU) 2018/389 of 27 November 2017 supplementing Directive (EU) 2015/2366 of the European Parliament and of the Council with regard to regulatory technical standards for strong customer authentication and common and secure open standards of communication (SCA-RTS) art.11.

to time request.[146] Standing orders are therefore described as "push" or "credit" transfers (since the customer initiates the payment) while direct debits are described as "pull" or debit transfers (since the creditor instructs his own bank to collect money from the customer's bank).[147]

It should be noted that—unlike the arrangements evidenced by a cheque card—standing orders and direct debits are merely instructions given by the customer to his own bank. The bank gives no undertaking or guarantee to the beneficiary of the arrangement. Furthermore, the bank may decline the payment if there are insufficient funds in the account on the due date for payment. It is under no obligation to pay the relevant amount at a later date if the account comes into funds.[148] Due to the bilateral nature of the original instruction, it can be revoked by the customer at any time.[149]

A few substantive points may be made about payment instruments of this kind:

i. payments due under a direct debit are intended to be as close as possible to cash as the law can make them.[150] Consequently, it has been decided that a creditor is entitled to judgment against the debtor for amounts which ought to have been made under such an agreement. Any counterclaim or set-off must accordingly be disregarded for these purposes,[151] at any rate if the cross-claim is unliquidated or is not sufficiently closely connected with the payment transaction.[152] This is so even though in the ordinary course of events, an instruction to transfer funds is not normally regarded as a negotiable instrument and thus does not acquire "cash equivalent" status[153]; and

ii. it appears that the provision of a direct debit instruction to the creditor constitutes a valid tender in respect of the payment obligations concerned. The creditor must therefore seek to draw on the instruction before it seeks to exercise any remedy flowing from non-payment.[154]

---

[146] See *Mercedes-Benz Finance Ltd v Clydesdale Bank Plc* 1997 S.L.T. 905 Court of Session (Outer House). Such an instruction is obviously open to abuse, but banks operate a direct debit guarantee scheme to protect customers in such an eventuality.

[147] Described in *Law of Bank Payments* (2018), paras 3–004 to 3–005.

[148] *Whitehead v National Westminster Bank Ltd*, Times 9 June 1982, noted in *Law of Bank Payments* (2018), para.3–004.

[149] Revocation may amount to breach of contract between the customer and the relevant supplier or creditor, but that is a separate matter.

[150] This replicates the position with cheques: see para.5–22 above. Although it should be noted that PSD II gives an unconditional right of refund for direct debits up to 8 weeks following payment; art.77.

[151] See *Esso Petroleum Co Ltd v Milton* [1997] 1 W.L.R. 938 CA (Civ Div).

[152] Set-off may be available where the payment was due to be made for goods which have been lawfully rejected, so that the account holder is not liable to pay, or is entitled to recover the price as a liquidated sum.

[153] *The Brimnes* [1975] Q.B. 929 CA (Civ Div), discussed in *Law of Bank Payments* (2018), paras 3–089 to 3–090.

[154] See *Weldon v GRE Linked Life Assurance Ltd* [2000] 2 All E.R. 914 (Comm).

In these cases, it appears that payment is deemed to be made between the debtor and the creditor at the point of time at which the creditor's bank receives the relevant remittance.[155] It is not necessary that the bank should have noted that amount on the creditor's account.[156]

(5) Payment by means of funds transfer

5–35 Leaving aside the specific instruments discussed in the earlier part of this chapter, a customer may independently instruct his bank to make a specific payment by means of a transfer to his creditor's bank account. While the instruments discussed above may tend to involve retail transactions for individuals, larger amounts are likely to be the subject of specific instructions in relation to commercial or financial transactions.

5–36 In relation to the legal nature of a funds transfer, it had in the past been asserted that, when a customer instructs his bank to effect a transfer from his account, he thereby effects an assignment of the relevant proportion of his credit balance.[157]

It is true that a customer's credit balance with his bank is in the nature of a debt,[158] and the notion that a transfer operates as an assignment accordingly has superficial appeal. Nevertheless, this proposition cannot be accepted. Apart from other considerations, the transfer does not confer on the payee the rights of a creditor against the payer's bank. On a proper analysis, the instruction requires the bank to reduce its own debt to the customer and to transfer a sum to the payee's bank such that his own debt claim against his bank is correspondingly increased.[159]

A funds transfer—however convenient the terminology may be—thus does not involve the "transfer" of property from one person to another. Based on the analysis given above, the transaction involves the *extinction* of the debtor's rights against his own bank and the *creation* of a new (albeit) corresponding right of the creditor against his own bank. As a result, in *R. v Preddy (John Crawford)*,[160] defendants who had fraudulently procured the transfer of funds as part of a dishonest mortgage scheme could not be convicted of obtaining property "belonging to another" for the purposes of the Theft Act 1968.[161]

---

[155] As noted earlier, the creditor's bank must have actual or ostensible authority to receive the payment.

[156] This rule applies in this, as in other contexts: see the discussion of the decisions in *Delbreuck & Co v Manufacturers Hanover Trust Co* 609 F.2d 1047 (1979) affirming 464 F. Supp. 989 (1979) and *Momm* [1977] Q.B. 790 QBD (Comm) at para.5–51 below. Questions touching the time of payment are considered in more detail at paras 5–50 to 5–56 below.

[157] On this subject, see *Law of Bank Payments* (2018), paras 3–087 to 3–088 and materials there cited.

[158] *Foley v Hill* 9 E.R. 1002 QB.

[159] For a discussion of the legal nature of a funds transfer (or payment) instruction, see *Royal Products v Midland Bank* [1981] 2 Lloyd's Rep. 194 QBD. See also *Law of Bank Payments* (2018), paras 3–086 to 3–091.

[160] *R. v Preddy (John Crawford)* [1996] A.C. 815 HL.

[161] The 1968 Act was subsequently amended to deal with this apparent anomaly. Nevertheless, it is submitted that the outcome of *Preddy* is unattractive and, in some respects, contrary to common sense. There would be no difficulty for the respondent lender to recover the misappropriated funds from the account into which they had been paid (i.e. by way of a tracing claim). This necessarily involves the

It may be added that, as a result of this analysis, the transmission of a funds transfer instruction to a bank will not normally have the effect of creating any security or trust over the relevant amount in favour of the payee.[162] The payee might, of course, have an interest in arguing to the contrary if the instruction is countermanded—e.g. by an administrator appointed shortly after the instruction is given; a proprietary claim has obvious advantages over an unsecured claim in such a situation. The funds transfer instruction is simply a direction to the bank to deal with the customer's funds in a particular way. In the absence of very special circumstances, no intention to create a security or trust can be read into the instruction itself.[163] This view of a funds transfer accords with the definition of "payment order" in the 2017 Regulations as "any instrument by a payer or a payee to their respective payment services provider requesting the execution of a payment transaction".[164]

It may also be added that the bank owes various duties to its customer in executing the transfer.[165] However, these are of no direct relevance to the settlement of the payment obligation as between debtor and creditor, and they are accordingly left out of account for present purposes.

It remains to consider whether payment by bank transfer has the effect of discharging D's debt to C. In this context, ordinary agency principles apply. Payment by credit to CB will constitute a discharge of the debt if CB has actual or ostensible authority to accept payment on behalf of C. However, D needs to take some care in this area. The mere fact that, to D's knowledge, C has a particular

5–37

---

conclusion that the funds are the "property" of the lender. Why should this conclusion hold for the purposes of the civil law but not for the purposes of the 1968 Act? On the whole subject, see *Goode on Commercial Law* (2010), p.492.

[162] See, for instance, *Moriarty v Atkinson* [2010] 1 B.C.L.C. 142, applied in *Re Global Trader Europe Ltd (In Liquidation)* [2009] 2 B.C.L.C. 18.

[163] Whilst the transfer instruction will not *of itself* create a trust in favour of C over the debt represented by D's account with DB, it may be part of a chain of evidence which suggests that D intended to earmark the balance for C and, hence, to create a trust over the account in favour of C. Such cases will naturally be highly fact-specific and the bank itself will only be affected by the trust if it receives notice whilst the account remains in credit. If a trust is created in this way at the point of insolvency, it may be open to challenge as a preference under s.239 of the Insolvency Act 1986 although, again, this will involve a fact-sensitive inquiry. For illustrations of the difficulties of establishing a trust of this type of case, see *Bailey v Angove Triffit Nurseries v Salads Etcetera Ltd* [2000] 1 All E.R. (Comm) 737 CA (Civ Div); and *Re D&D Wines International Ltd (In liquidation)* [2014] EWCA Civ 215. For an illustration of when a trust might be found, see *Brazzill v Willoughby* [2010] 2 B.C.L.C. 259 CA (Civ Div).

[164] 2017 Regulations reg.2(1).

[165] For instance, under the 2017 Regulations. See *Law of Bank Payments* (2018), paras 3–092 to 3–107 (dealing with the 2009 Regulations, which have now been superseded by the 2017 Regulations). The use of electronic means of communication does also have some incidental consequences for the customer. For example, a bank which pays a forged cheque cannot debit the customer, however convincing the forgery may be. But if a fraudster obtains access to the passcodes and sends electronic instructions to the bank, it is submitted that the bank can debit the account, at least provided that the bank has not acted negligently: compare *Standard Bank London Ltd v Bank of Tokyo Ltd* [1995] 2 Lloyd's Rep. 169 QBD (Comm). This seems to be in line with the US decision in *Walker v Texas Commerce Bank* 635 F. Supp. 678 (S.D. Tex, 1986), which effectively required banks to implement commercially reasonable systems for the verification of such payment instructions. The decision is noted in B. Geva, *Bank Collections and Payment Instructions—A Comparative Legal Analysis* (Oxford: Oxford University Press, 2001).

account with CB does not itself clothe CB with authority to receive payment. For example, it is entirely insufficient to discharge D's debt to CB simply for CB to receive unconditional use of the funds.[166] Furthermore, payment to CB will plainly not discharge the debt if C has previously directed D to make payment to a different account.[167] Of course, such a transfer will nevertheless amount to payment if, having become aware of it, C expressly or impliedly ratifies the acceptance of the payment.[168]

The precise point in time at which payment occurs raises separate issues and is more conveniently considered later.[169]

(6) Internet payments

5–38 In recent years, the internet has become a popular means of searching for and purchasing goods. It requires no journey into town and a wider choice is likely to be available. The internet does not of itself create an independent means of payment. Rather, it creates a means for the transmission of information which may include credit card or other details.

As with other forms of remote payment,[170] this carries an increased risk of fraud. PSD II attempts to reduce this risk by introducing special security requirements for remote payments which providers of payment services must comply with.[171]

Whilst direct provision of credit or debit card details perhaps remains the most common form of payment over the internet, the lack of flexibility around card payments, in particular to make person-to-person (P2P) payments, has given rise to alternative payment methods.[172] However, and whichever method is used, the

---

[166] *K v A* [2019] EWHC 1118 (Comm).
[167] For an illustration of these principles, see *Customs & Excise Commissioners v National Westminster Bank Plc (Authorisation: Mistake)* [2003] 1 All E.R. (Comm) 327; and *PT Berlian Laju Tanker TBK v Nuse Shipping Ltd (The Aktor)* [2008] 2 All E.R. (Comm) 784, and contrast the decision of the Court of Appeal of New Zealand in *Rick Dees Ltd v Larsen* [2006] NZCA 25, discussed at para.5–22.
[168] For an example, see *TSB Bank of Scotland Plc v Welwyn Hatfield DC* [1993] 2 Bank L.R. 267.
[169] See paras 5–46 to 5–51 below.
[170] See the distinction which is often made between "cardholder present" and "cardholder not present" transactions using debit an credit cards. Cardholder present transactions (for example, ATMs, chip and pin and contactless) involve cards being used in face-to-face transactions. Cardholder not present transactions, including internet card payments, involve remote entry of the payment information on the card. The fraud risk is much higher for cardholder not present transactions, especially those over the internet where fraud is more difficult to detect: see *Law of Bank Payments* (2018), para.5-044.
[171] These include, for example, "dynamic linking", under which an authentication code specific to a particular transaction must be used, and measures to ensure that only the user is associated with the personalised security credentials (such as online login details or personal identification numbers (PINs) (SCA-RTS arts 24 and 25).
[172] See discussion of this in *Law of Bank Payments* (2018), para.5–020. See also below at paras 5–62 to 5–76 for a brief discussion of the legal implications of non-bank payment systems.

issue which is relevant for this section is: how and when does payment occur as between the debtor/buyer and creditor/seller when payment is made over the internet?[173]

This question depends in large measure upon the law which governs questions touching the performance of the contract. It has been seen that, where the arrangements are of a purely domestic nature and are thus governed by English law, the use of a credit card has the effect of discharging the debtor and conferring upon the creditor a claim for payment as against the card issuer.[174] But a contract for the purchase of goods over the internet may involve a UK consumer and a foreign supplier.

From the perspective of the UK consumer, the application of English law would be highly convenient. As far as he is concerned, payment is made once the transaction has been confirmed by the issuing company. He is entitled to his goods regardless of any difficulties which the supplier may subsequently encounter in recovering payment from the card issuer. He is not liable to pay a second time in such a case.

5–39

However, other systems of law might adopt a different view. They may hold that the consumer remains responsible for payment if his intended payment method fails for some reason. So it may be of particular importance to determine which system of law governs the contract at hand.[175]

Rome I[176] has much to say on this subject.[177] In a commercial contract, the agreement will usually be governed by the law chosen by the parties,[178] but failing such a choice, it will normally be governed by a system of law associated with the supplier—usually the law of the country in which the relevant branch of the supplier is situated.[179] However, where, as will often be the case where a payment is made over the internet, the transaction involves a consumer, this rule is displaced to protect the consumer.[180] Rome I then comprises a number of rules which affect both the identification and the application of the governing law of the contract. These may be important for a variety of reasons, but the present discussion is concerned in particular with the question of payment as between debtor and creditor. Narrowing the line of inquiry still further, can the consumer

---

[173] More generally on internet payments, see *Law of Bank Payments* (2018), Ch.5. For a general discussion of the law relating to the internet, including electronic commerce, in the EU, see Andrej Savin, *EU Internet Law* (Cheltenham: Edward Elgar, 2017).
[174] See the discussion of the decision in *Re Charge Card Services* at para.5–31 above.
[175] See *Law of Bank Payments* (2018), paras 5–002 to 5–007 on proper law and jurisdiction in relation to internet payments.
[176] Regulation 593/2008 on the law applicable to contractual obligations (Rome I) [2008] OJ L177/6 (Rome I)
[177] At least for contracts concluded after 17 December 2009; the Convention on the Law Applicable to Contractual Obligations 1980 (Rome Convention) to contracts concluded before that date.
[178] Rome I art.3.
[179] Rome I art.4. Articles 4(1)(a) and (b) provides for contracts for the sale of goods or supply of services to be governed by the law of the country of the seller's or supplier's habitual residence. Where the Rome Convention applies, the governing law will generally, in the absence of an express choice of law clause, be the law of the country where the seller has its principal place of business or the place of business through which performance is to be effected: Rome Convention, art.4.
[180] Under Rome 1 art.6(1).

be confident that payment through the use of the credit card will constitute a final discharge of his obligations? There may be two reasons why this might not be so:

i. the applicable law may preserve the supplier's right of recourse to the customer in the event of a failure of the card issuer; or
ii. the supplier's terms and conditions may include an explicit term imposing liability on the customer in such a situation.[181]

How, then, does one identify the applicable law in relation to a contract between an English consumer and a foreign supplier where that contract is concluded over the internet and a credit card payment is made through that medium?

5–40   In the absence of an express choice of law, a consumer contract will be governed by the law of the country in which the consumer has his habitual residence if the supplier pursues his commercial activities in England or "by any means, directs such activities to that country or to several countries including that country".[182] Consistently with EU legislation in the sphere of distance selling, it is stated that the quoted condition is not satisfied merely because an internet site is accessible in a particular country.[183] However, it is submitted that the condition is satisfied where, additionally, a contract may be concluded and a credit card payment made via the site. On this basis, and in the absence of an explicit choice of law, it would follow that such a contract would be governed by English law. The consumer could therefore be confident that the use of his credit card constituted a final discharge of his payment obligation.[184]

It is, however, likely that the supplier's terms and conditions will include an explicit choice of law—usually that of the country in which the supplier itself carries on business and with which it is therefore most familiar.[185] Under the circumstances described in the last paragraph, such a choice would be valid but it cannot deprive the consumer of protection afforded to him by the mandatory rules

---

[181] Whilst it is impossible to say how common such provisions are in practice, they cannot, in the experience of the present writer, be entirely ruled out.

[182] Rome I art.6(1).

[183] It is submitted that the condition of art.6(1) would not be met if the site is accessible in England but merely provides an address or contact details for further information. This view seems to be consistent with the joint declaration of the EU Commission and Council of Ministers on the consumer provisions of Council reg.44/2001 on jurisdiction and the recognition and enforcement of judgments in civil and commercial matters [2001] OJ L12/1 (the Brussels I Regulation). The Brussels I has now been replaced by Regulation (EU) 1215/2012 of the European Parliament and of the Council on jurisdiction and the recognition and enforcement of judgments in civil and commercial matters (recast) (the Recast Brussels Regulation). The Declaration (Joint Declaration of the Council and the Commission on arts 15 and 73 of reg.44/2001) (available at: *http://data.consilium.europa.eu/doc/document/ST-14139-2000-INIT/en/pdf* [Accessed 26 August 2020] states that "the mere fact that an internet site is accessible is not significant [for the specific consumer rules] to be applicable, although a factor will be that this internet site solicits the conclusion of distance contracts and that a contract has actual been concluded at a distance, by whatever means. In this respect, the language or currency which the website uses does not constitute a relevant factor". See also joined cases *Pammer v Reederei Karl Schlüter* (C-585/08) and *Hotel Alpenhof v Heller* (C-144/09).

[184] i.e. in line with *Re Charge Card Services*. discussed at para.5-31 above.

[185] If the supplier's terms and conditions are to bind the consumer, then they must, of course, be made available on the supplier's site.

of English law.[186] The difficulty here is that, whilst the English courts regard payment by credit card as a final discharge, this is not a statutory or mandatory rule of consumer protection. Consequently, if a term of the contract or the applicable law itself imposes liability on the consumer to pay directly to the supplier on the failure of the card issuer, then that term is in principle valid and binding. If sued in the English courts, the consumer would have to seek an alternative means of defence. He could, for example, seek to challenge the contract term on the basis that it is to be regarded as unfair and detrimental to the consumer.[187]

(7) The impact of anti-money laundering legislation

The UK and most other countries place considerable importance on the battle against the laundering of the proceeds of criminal activity.[188] At an EU level, there are measures in place to combat money laundering. The Fourth Anti-Money Laundering Directive,[189] repealing an earlier directive, was passed in 2015 with an implementation deadline of 2017 for Member States. It was amended by the Fifth Anti-Money Laundering Directive,[190] with Member States required to implement the changes this made by January 2020. Further, the Sixth Anti-Money Laundering Directive,[191] which comes into force in December 2020 and which must be implemented by Member States by June 2021, will expand the number of money-laundering offences,[192] extend criminal liability for money laundering to include "enablers" and legal persons and introduce tougher criminal sanctions. Currently, the UK implements the EU directives through a combination of the Money Laundering, Terrorist Financing and Transfer of Funds (Information on the Payer) Regulations 2017 (the Money Laundering Regulations 2017),[193] as amended by the Money Laundering and Terrorist Financing (Amendment) Regulations 2019 to implement the Fifth Anti-Money Laundering

5–41

---

[186] Rome I art.6(2).
[187] See s.62 of the Consumer Rights Act 2015.
[188] The same may be said of funds destined to finance terrorist activity. However, these rules raise slightly different issues since the funds which are being transferred are not necessarily criminal *in their origin*. It is not proposed to consider that aspect further in the present context. Questions touching terrorist funding are, however, briefly considered under "International Expropriation of Deposits".
[189] Directive (EU) 2015/849 of the European Parliament and of the Council of 20 May 2015 on the prevention of the use of the financing system for the purposes of money laundering or terrorist financing.
[190] Directive (EU) 2018/843 of the European Parliament and of the Council of 30 May 2018 amending Directive (EU) 2015/849 on the prevention of the use of the financial system for the purpose of money laundering or terrorist financing, and amending Directives 2009/138/EC and 2013/36/EU.
[191] Directive (EU) 2018/1673 of the European Parliament and of the Council of 23 October 2018 on combating money laundering by criminal law.
[192] In particular, cyber-crime will be included for the first time.
[193] Money Laundering, Terrorist Financing and Transfer of Funds (Information on the Payer) Regulations 2017 (SI 2017/692).

Directive,[194] the Proceeds of Crime Act 2002 (POCA) and the Terrorism Act 2000. However, the uncertain impact of Brexit means the law in this area is in flux.[195]

The Money Laundering Regulations 2017 require banks to conduct a risk assessment to identify the risks of money laundering and terrorist financing which they face[196] and implement policies, controls and procedures to mitigate and manage these risks,[197] including customer due diligence to verify the identity of those with whom they wish to establish a business relationship.[198] They contain measures to ensure legal entities, including trusts, obtain and hold adequate, accurate and up-to-date information regarding their beneficial owners.[199] The Money Laundering and Terrorist Financing (Amendment) Regulations 2019, among other things, extend the EU anti-money laundering regime to include virtual currency or "cryptoasset" dealers and custodian wallet providers.[200] Also of significance is the updated Wire Transfer Regulation,[201] which requires funds transfers by payment service providers to be accompanied by certain information to ensure that the identity of both payer and payee is clear.

From the perspective of the present discussion, however, it is more important to note the provisions of ss.327–330 of POCA. In essence, a person commits an offence if he is in possession of the proceeds of crime, or if he assists another to retain or enjoy the benefit of such proceeds. Banks accordingly put in place training processes to enable their staff to spot suspicious transactions, and reporting procedures to ensure that such transactions can be reported to the Serious Organised Crime Agency (merged into the National Crime Agency in 2013).[202]

But what, in practical terms, is a bank required to do if it receives a remittance of funds into the customer's account and then forms the view that they may be suspect? It is true that POCA creates criminal offences which may be committed by bank employees if they knowingly assist in the transfer of criminal property. But equally, the bank owes contractual obligations to the customer. How are these potential conflicts to be resolved? This issue is neatly addressed by the decision in *Tayeb*.[203]

---

[194] Money Laundering and Terrorist Financing (Amendment) Regulations 2019. These came into force on 10 January 2020, with the exception of certain amendments in relation to anonymous prepaid cards (which came into force on 10 July 2020) and bank account portals and cryptoasset businesses (which will come into force on 10 September 2020).
[195] In particular, the UK has passed the Sanctions and Anti-Money Laundering Act 2018 to enable it to regulate money laundering on the occurrence of Brexit.
[196] Money Laundering Regulations 2017 reg.18.
[197] Money Laundering Regulations 2017 regs 19–40.
[198] Money Laundering Regulations 2017 regs 27 and 28.
[199] Money Laundering Regulations 2017 regs 42–45ZB.
[200] Money Laundering and Terrorist Financing (Amendment) Regulations 2019 reg.4(1)(b).
[201] Regulation 2015/847 on information accompanying transfers of funds and repealing Regulation1781/2006 [2015] OJ L141/1. This entered into force on 26 June 2017, together with the Fourth Anti-Money Laundering Directive.
[202] By the Crime and Courts Act 2013. Internal processes of this kind are a statutory requirement: see the Money Laundering Regulations 2017, especially regs 18–25.
[203] *Tayeb* [2004] 4 All E.R. 1024. This case has already been considered in another context at para.5–22 above.

The bank received a sizeable remittance into a customer's account which was said to represent the proceeds of sale of a domain name. The originator of the remittance was a Libyan entity, and the bank was understandably suspicious of the transaction. Unable to allay those suspicions, the bank felt itself to be in danger of committing a money laundering offence if it made the funds available for use by the customer. It accordingly returned the funds to the remitting bank. However, it subsequently transpired that the transaction was perfectly legitimate and the purchaser—having obtained title to the domain name as part of the completion process—declined to retransfer the purchase price. The seller accordingly sued the bank for payment of the sums deposited into his account.

5–42

Upon receipt of the funds and their credit to the customer's account, the bank becomes a debtor to the customer for the amount concerned. Unsurprisingly, there is no express or implied term of the banker–customer contract which entitles the bank unilaterally to cancel that debt by returning the funds to the bank which originally remitted them. The bank therefore argued that it was obliged to return the funds in order to avoid the commission of a money laundering offence under POCA.

The court rejected this argument. The bank did not necessarily commit an offence if it simply held the funds, blocked the account when it formed its suspicions and made the necessary report to the Serious Organised Crime Agency, as required by the provisions of POCA.[204] Since the return of the funds was not *necessary* to avoid the commission of a money laundering offence, it followed that the bank's unilateral decision to take that step did not relieve the bank of its debt obligation to its customer.

The case illustrates the importance of determining whether, and at what point of time, funds have been credited to the customer's account so that the bank's debt obligation becomes "crystallised". However, it also demonstrates the difficulties inherent in reconciling the fight against money laundering with the bank's contractual obligations to its customer. Nevertheless, and whatever those problems may have been in the past, it is submitted that *Tayeb* offers a satisfactory solution and provides a clear guidance for a bank confronted with this type of situation. It has also been held that, where a bank has genuine suspicions of money laundering, there is an implied term in the bank–customer contract permitting it to refuse to execute a payment instruction pending consent from the National Crime Agency under POCA.[205] Moreover, although POCA does not oust the court's jurisdiction to order injunctive relief, courts should not generally intervene to injunct a bank to operate an account and carry out payment instructions where the POCA consent regime applies.[206]

---

[204] POCA ss.327–330.
[205] *Shah v HSBC Private Bank (UK) Ltd* [2013] 1 All E.R. (Comm) 72. However, banks need to take care since where there is no evidence that there are genuine suspicions of money laundering, the bank may potentially be liable for breach of contract, breach of data protection laws and defamation; *Lonsdale v National Westminster Bank Plc* [2018] EWHC 1843 (QB).
[206] *National Crime Agency v N* [2017] EWCA Civ 253.

(8) The impact of anti-bribery legislation

5–43   The Bribery Act 2010 operates alongside POCA. In force since July 2011, it was introduced to update the previous law which was seen as anachronistic and out-of-date. It replaces all previous bribery provisions with new offences of bribery, accepting bribes, bribery of foreign public officials, and failure of a commercial organisation to prevent bribery on its behalf. The introduction of the Bribery Act 2010 means that parties making payments need to be sure they are not giving, promising or accepting a "financial or other advantage" where that would constitute or lead to "improper performance" of their or another's duties. In addition, there is a strict liability offence for companies of failing to prevent bribery, although it is a defence for the company to show that it has adequate procedures in place to prevent bribery.

The first corporate conviction under the Bribery Act was in *Serious Fraud Office v Sweett Group Plc*.[207] Sweett Group was fined approximately £2.35 million for failing to prevent bribery by an associated person under s.7 of the Bribery Act. The case concerned the payment of a bribe by a wholly owned subsidiary of Sweett Group, CSI, to an individual in order to win a project management and cost consultancy contract worth £1.6 billion to CSI in relation to the building of a hotel in Dubai. Although CSI was a separate legal identity, the bribery was deemed to be for the benefit of Sweett Group since the judge considered that CSI was not autonomously operated but was effectively operated by Sweett Group. Sweett Group pleaded guilty to failing to prevent an associated person making bribes on its behalf. Sweett Group also admitted it did not have adequate procedures for the purpose of the defence in s.2 of the Bribery Act, despite having in place an anti-bribery statement, an ethics policy and providing its staff (including those of its subsidiaries) with anti-bribery training. This was due to its lack of early self-reporting, genuine co-operation with the Serious Fraud Office and adequate controls and procedures. Since then, there have been a number of successful prosecutions under the Bribery Act 2010, as well as "deferred prosecution orders" (DPAs), of which Rolls Royce's is perhaps the most high profile.[208] Rolls Royce was ordered to pay approximately £500 million to the Serious Fraud Office due to fraud, bribery and corruption offences by two subsidiaries over more than 25 years, including failure to prevent bribery under s.7 of the Bribery Act 2010.

In addition to the Bribery Act offences, paying or assisting with the payment of a bribe could potentially be an offence in relation to concealing or acquiring, using or possessing criminal property under POCA.[209]

---

[207] *Serious Fraud Office v Sweett Group Plc* unreported 19 February 2016 Crown Court Southwark.
[208] DPAs allow for a discounted fine and avoidance of criminal prosecution; the Serious Fraud Office has also entered into DPAs with Standard Bank, XYZ Limited and Tesco Plc.
[209] Sections 327 and 329 of POCA.

(9) Special features of international funds transfers

5–44 This section and the ensuing one examine some of the difficulties which may arise specifically in the context of international banking relationships.[210]

As has been noted earlier, a payment in a particular currency generally has to be completed, ultimately, by a transfer between banks located in the issuing country and through its clearing system. This has a variety of legal consequences, some of which are discussed below. But, at its most basic level, this requirement may have consequences in terms of the time of payment, since different centres obviously operate in different time zones. The point is graphically illustrated by the factual background to the decision in *The Brimnes*. The debtor under a charterparty was obliged to pay hire in US dollars. He instructed his London bank to make the payment, and they in turn transmitted payment instruction to the creditor's New York bank at 10.53 BST. Owing to the time differences, the instruction was only actioned some five hours later—approximately 20 minutes after the owner had given notice withdrawing the vessel.[211]

More fundamentally, banks involved in cross-border business are subject to all the other problems common to international transfers, including exchange controls, the blocking of payment by "freeze" legislation or government action and—in some situations—exchange losses resulting from currency fluctuations.

5–45 The first edition of this book noted[212] some of the difficulties which may have been caused by blocking legislation introduced with reference to the 1979 Iran hostage crisis. On 14 September 1979, the President of the US made an Executive Order blocking all the property of the Government of Iran, its instrumentalities and entities (including the Central Bank of Iran) which were or would come within the possession or control of persons subject to the jurisdiction of the US.[213] The dispute was settled but, otherwise, the English courts would have had to decide whether to order repayment of US dollar accounts maintained in London. The view was expressed that the debt obligations represented by such accounts should remain enforceable in accordance with their terms, because the English courts would not give extra-territorial effect to the Executive Order. The US side, however, argued that, in the Eurocurrency market, it was well understood that deposits could not be withdrawn in cash but had to be settled by

---

[210] On the difficulties posed by the absence of international harmonisation of the law on payment systems, see T.C. Baxter and S. Heller, "Core Legal Principles across Major Large-Value Credit Transfer Systems" in M. Giovanoli (ed.), *International Monetary Law—Issues for the New Millennium* (Oxford: Oxford University Press, 2000). For an excellent and wide-ranging discussion of the whole subject, see B. Geva, *The Law of Electronic Funds Transfer* (New York: Matthew Bender, 1992), Ch.4.

[211] In *The Brimnes* [1974] 2 Lloyd's Rep. 241, this point was considered crucial, since the law was then understood to be that receipt by the creditor's bank constituted acceptance by the creditor and thus a waiver of any antecedent breach by the debtor. But in truth, the bank's functions are purely ministerial and its actions cannot constitute acceptance of the payment for the purposes of the underlying contract of which it will have no knowledge. Acceptance or rejection of the payment thus remains the prerogative of the creditor himself: see *The Laconia* [1977] A.C. 850 HL at 871 per Lord Wilberforce.

[212] Roy Goode, *Payment Obligations in Commercial and Financial Transactions*, 1st edn (London: Sweet & Maxwell, 1983), p.94.

[213] Executive Order No.12170, 44 Fed. Reg. 65729 (1979).

inter-bank transfer through the clearing system and central bank of the country whose currency is involved. So, in the case of Eurodollar deposits, payment was due in, or at least through, New York. Accordingly, the argument went, the Executive Order thereby validly prevented payment abroad of blocked Iranian deposits, not because the Order was extra territorial in its operation but because it prohibited the taking of steps within the US (i.e. through CHIPS in New York) to implement instructions for the transfer of a dollar deposit located outside the US.

This issue has subsequently received judicial consideration both in England and in the US.

In England, sanctions imposed unilaterally[214] by the US against Libya afforded an opportunity for the English courts to consider their impact on US dollar deposit accounts held with the London branch of a US bank. At the risk of oversimplifying a fairly complex case, the decision in *Libyan Arab Foreign Bank v Bankers Trust Co*[215] involved US dollar deposits held by a Libyan bank with the London branch of Bankers Trust, a US institution. In January 1986, President Reagan imposed sanctions against Libya in terms very similar to the Iranian Executive Order noted above. The Order accordingly prohibited the repayment of the London dollar deposits since Bankers Trust was obviously subject to US jurisdiction. Could the English court compel Bankers Trust to repay the deposits to a Libyan entity, given that repayment would ultimately involve an unlawful transfer in New York?

5–46   The court found that:

i. the London bank accounts were governed by English law[216];
ii. an Executive Order under US law plainly could not vary or discharge a contract governed by English law[217];
iii. although the English courts would not enforce a contract where the steps necessary for performance were illegal in the place in which they were required to be taken,[218] this rule did not apply in the present case since London was the place of performance; and
iv. the bank accordingly had the option of delivering US dollars *in cash* in London, thus avoiding the need for a New York transfer[219] or making payment in the sterling countervalue—thus avoiding the need for any action to be taken in New York.[220]

---

[214] It is necessary to emphasise that the sanctions were a unilateral, US measure. Had the sanctions been imposed by the UN or the EU, they would have been incorporated into UK law and the English courts would have been obliged to apply for them for that reason.
[215] *Libyan Arab* [1989] Q.B. 728 QBD (Comm).
[216] This accords with the general rule of private international law to the effect that a bank account is governed by the law of the country in which the account-holding branch is situated.
[217] On this point, see now Rome I art.12(1).
[218] This is the rule in *Ralli Bros v Compania Naviera Sota y Aznar* [1920] 2 K.B. 287 CA. The rule has now effectively been transformed into a general rule of private international law: see Rome I art.9(3).
[219] This is one of the most controversial aspects of the decision since, given the huge amounts involved, such deposits are never repaid in cash. However, the court rejected the view that an implied term of the contract required payment to be made exclusively through CHIPS.
[220] Where a debtor is to pay a foreign currency obligation in England, he has the option to pay in sterling at the prevailing exchange rate.

This decision demonstrates the importance of identifying the due place of payment because, as has been shown, the law of that place may have an impact on the enforceability of the bank's repayment obligation. This will, however, usually be the place where the account is held. In the *Libyan Arab* case, New York may be described as the *place of settlement* but, given the analysis adopted above, illegality in that place does not detract from the validity and enforceability of the bank's obligation to repay the deposit.[221] London was the *due place of payment*.

The difficulties confronting the economy of the Philippines during the 1980s provided the backdrop for the US litigation in *Wells Fargo Asia Ltd v Citibank NA*.[222] Wells Fargo placed a US dollar deposit with the Manila branch of Citibank. Owing to its financial difficulties, the Government of the Philippines blocked the repayment of certain foreign obligations including the deposit. Wells Fargo accordingly sued Citibank for repayment in the New York courts. Now, whilst it is true that a bank is liable *as a corporate whole* for obligations contracted by its worldwide branches,[223] whether or not a *particular* obligation is in fact due and repayable must be a matter determined by reference to the law applicable to the deposit contract.[224] So far as English law is concerned, the court would have found that: (i) the deposit contract was governed by the law of the Philippines[225]; (ii) the deposit was repayable at the Manila branch, where it had originally been placed[226]; and (iii) repayment of the deposit was accordingly suspended for the duration of the freeze.[227] However, the US Court of Appeals held that the deposit agreement was governed by New York law, with the necessary consequence that the deposit was repayable in spite of the Philippines freeze. In the absence of any agreement as to the place of payment, the creditor

---

[221] For further English litigation involving the Libyan freeze, see *Libyan Arab Foreign Bank v Manufacturers Hanover Trust (No.2)* [1989] 1 Lloyd's Rep. 608 QBD (Comm). More recently, the approach in *Libyan Arab Foreign Bank v Bankers Trust Co* was endorsed at first instance in *Lamesa Investments Ltd v Cynergy Bank Ltd* [2019] EWHC 1877 (Comm) at [11], where the beneficial owner of L, the lender, became a "blocked person" under the US Ukraine Freedom Support Act 2014, s.5(b), with the result that foreign financial institutions were liable to have sanctions imposed on them if they knowingly facilitated financial transactions with that person. However, C's suspension of payments to L was permitted even though payment was not contrary to the law of the place of payment due to a contractual provision allowing non-payment to comply with mandatory provisions of law, regulation or order of any "court of competent jurisdiction"; the decision was upheld by the Court of Appeal on different reasoning in [2020] EWCA Civ 821.

[222] For the various stages of the litigation, see 852 F.2d 657, 495 US 660 (1990) and 926 F.2d 273 (2nd Cir. 1991), cert denied (1992) 505 US 1204.

[223] *R. v Lovitt (Irvine)* [1912] A.C. 212. This is so even though, for some purposes, branches in different countries are treated as separate banks. For example, a bank in Country A may confirm a letter of credit issued by its own bank in Country B: see Uniform Customs and Practices for Documentary Credits (ICC publication UCP 600) art.3.

[224] So far as English law is concerned, see Rome I art.12(1). For earlier case law to similar effect, see, for example, *N Joachimson (A Firm) v Swiss Bank Corp (Costs)* [1921] 3 K.B. 110 CA; *Arab Bank Ltd v Barclays Bank (Dominion, Colonial and Overseas)* [1954] A.C. 495 HL.

[225] See the rule of private international law mentioned in fn.188 above.

[226] i.e. as in the *Hanover Trust* case above at fn.221.

[227] This conclusion could only be avoided if the Philippine legislation was manifestly incompatible with English public policy, e.g. on the basis that it was not a genuine economic measure but was designed to discriminate against particular countries and creditors: see Rome I art.21; *Re Claim by Helbert Wagg & Co Ltd* [1956] Ch. 323 Ch D.

was entitled to collect payment from the New York head office of Citibank.[228] This decision offered the prospect of US banks having to meet all of their foreign obligations in New York even though the corresponding assets at foreign branches were inaccessible. Perhaps unsurprisingly, the US Government recognised (at least implicitly) the merit of the English approach to these matters and legislated to the effect that head offices of US banks are not liable for the blocked obligations of their overseas branches if "the branch cannot repay the deposit due to: (i) an act of war, insurrection or civil strife; or (ii) an action by a foreign government or instrumentality (whether de jure or de facto) in the country in which the branch is located".[229]

This review demonstrates the difficulties caused by freezes, sanctions, blocking orders and similar measures, bearing in mind that US dollar obligations ultimately have to be cleared in New York. Despite these difficulties, the decision of the English court in the *Libyan Arab* case appears to be correct as a matter of principle. It would not be reasonable that the US could effectively block the performance of worldwide obligations merely because the US dollar is used as a medium in a large number of international transactions.

Similar, but not identical, problems have arisen in the US with respect to federal legislation that entitles victims of State-sponsored terrorism to recover damages from the State concerned.[230] In *Hausler v JP Morgan Chase, N.A.*[231] Cuba had made various electronic transfers to creditors via Cuban and then US banks. A victim of Cuban action sought to arrest the funds so transferred on the basis that they were "assets" of Cuba and, hence, available to meet a terrorism judgment obtained against that country. The court decided that the payments had not been directly remitted by Cuba and that the "midstream" electronic belonged neither to the payer nor to the payee, but to the bank in possession of those funds. Since the funds were not assets of Cuba, they could not be subjected to garnishee proceedings to satisfy the judgment debt.[232]

(10) International expropriation of deposits

5–47 Reference has already been made to the international fight against terrorism and legislation designed to inhibit such activity by choking off its sources of funding. This battle unsurprisingly assumed a particular urgency in the period following the 9/11 attacks in 2001 and has become urgent again following further terrorist attacks in recent years in Europe and beyond. At a general level, it has been recognised that effective steps need to be taken to combat the financing of terrorism. In the EU, terrorist financing is addressed through the Fourth

---

[228] For earlier cases in a similar vein, see *Vishipco Lines v Chase Manhattan Bank* 660 F. 2d 976 (1982); *Trinh v Citibank* 850 F.2d 1164 (1988).
[229] See the US Code Title 12 s.633. The application of that general rule may be negated by contract.
[230] See the Terrorism Risk Insurance Act 2002 (28 USC s.1610). The Act has recently been extended by the Terrorism Risk Insurance Program Reauthorization Act 2015, passed by the House of Representatives on 7 January 2015, and will now run until 2020.
[231] *Hausler v JP Morgan Chase, N.A.* 12-1264(L).
[232] In this respect, the court relied in part on the decision in *Shipping Corp of India v Jaldhi Overseas Pte Ltd* 583 F.3d 58 (2nd Cir. 2009), which includes a discussion of various aspects of electronic funds transfers.

Anti-Money Laundering Directive, as amended by the Fifth Anti-Money Laundering Directive, and the updated Wire Transfer Regulation.[233] The amendments made by the Fifth Anti-Money Laundering Directive implement the European Commission's action plan to combat terrorist financing.[234] The EU regime requires banks and other "obliged entities" to apply enhanced vigilance to transactions involving high-risk third countries.[235] Further, the Directive on Combating Terrorism, introduced in 2017, makes financing terrorism a criminal offence.[236]

Of central importance in the present context is the US PATRIOT ACT.[237] The Act is important because it seeks to use the banking system to exercise a form of extra territorial or "long arm" jurisdiction over foreign financial institutions with banking relationships with US banks. Under s.317 of the Act, where a person has been involved in a financial transaction occurring wholly or partly in the US which constitutes unlawful activity,[238] the funds involved thereby become liable to forfeiture. The "long arm" issues are raised by s.319 of the Act, which uses the banking system to extend the territorial reach of the legislation. Where funds liable to forfeiture under s.317 are held by a bank *outside* the US, then the corresponding amount of money may be seized from an inter-bank account of that institution held with a bank within the US. Section 319 reads:

> "For the purpose of a forfeiture under this section ... if funds are deposited into an account at a foreign bank, and that foreign bank has an interbank account in the United States with a covered financial institution ... the funds shall be deemed to have been deposited into the interbank account in the United States and any restraining order, seizure warrant or arrest warrant in *rem* regarding the funds may be served on the covered financial institution and funds in the interbank account, up to the value of the funds deposited into the account at the foreign bank, may be restrained, seized or arrested. It shall not be necessary for the Government to establish that the funds are directly traceable to the funds that were deposited into the foreign bank."

So, in summary, if a targeted person has an account with a foreign bank outside the US, the forfeited amount can be taken from a correspondent account held by that bank with an institution within the US. Given that any bank of any size needs to have a correspondent account within the US for dollar clearing purposes, this section potentially has an extremely broad application.

5–48

---

[233] See above at para.5–41.

[234] Set out in an EC communication published in February 2016, available at: *https://eur-lex.europa.eu/resource.html?uri=cellar:e6e0de37-ca7c-11e5-a4b5-01aa75ed71a1.0002.02/DOC_1&format=PDF* [Accessed 2 September 2020].

[235] Identified in EU delegated legislation and listed online at: *https://eur-lex.europa.eu/legal-content/EN/TXT/?uri=CELEX%3A32017L0541* [Accessed 2 September 2020].

[236] Directive (EU) 2017/541 of the European Parliament and of the Council of 15 March 2017 on combating terrorism.

[237] The full title of the Act is "Uniting and Strengthening America by Providing Appropriate Tools Required to Intercept and Obstruct Terrorism (USA PATRIOT ACT) Act of 2001". For discussions of these measures, see generally Pts 1 and 2 of K. Alexander, "United States Financial Sanctions and International Terrorism" (2002) 2 B.J.I.B. & F.L. 80 and (2002) 5 B.J.I.B. & F.L. 213. Parts of the Act have been attacked on constitutional grounds, but the provisions discussed in the text have not thus far been challenged.

[238] It is unnecessary for present purposes to discuss the potential breadth of s.317. Let it be assumed that the legislation is directed primarily towards terrorist funding.

The difficulties which may be posed by this type of extended forfeiture legislation are neatly illustrated by the decision of the Court of Appeal of New South Wales in *European Bank Ltd v Citibank Ltd*.[239]

Briefly, European Bank—an institution incorporated in Vanuatu—held a US dollar account with Citibank Ltd in Sydney. As noted earlier, and as is customary, the deposit was effected or settled by a transfer from European Bank's New York correspondent bank to the head office of Citibank NA, as correspondent bank for Citibank Ltd. However, the deposit was maintained on the books of Citibank Ltd in Sydney and the customer relationship was governed by the law of New South Wales. Consequently, European Bank itself had no deposit account in New York, nor did it have any contractual relationship with the Head Office of Citibank in that city. A warrant was served on Citibank NA in New York to the effect that funds "now held by Citibank, Citigroup or any of their affiliates or subsidiaries, which were credited on or about October 22, 1999 to Account 31625294 on behalf of Citibank NA Sydney in the amount of USD$7,593,532.48 from European Bank Ltd of Vanuatu (Account 316121226) plus all accrued interest since the date of the deposit" were subject to seizure and forfeiture under US law.[240]

The deposit obligation of Citibank Ltd in Sydney was governed by the laws of New South Wales and the debt thereby represented constituted property situate in that State. Under those circumstances, as the court succinctly put it[241]:

> "In the absence of some explicit provision it would be fanciful to think that the debt owed by Citibank to European Bank in Sydney could be discharged by a payment made in New York by someone other than the debtor[242] pursuant to a warrant issued under a foreign penal law which is not enforceable internationally."[243]

This decision perhaps serves to demonstrate that, consistently with the decision in *Foley v Hill*, a foreign currency deposit involves a series of independent debts, each of which may be separately enforced regardless of the fate of the other contracts in the "chain". Thus, European Bank could enforce its contract with Citibank Ltd under New South Wales law. The fact that Citibank Ltd, in its turn, had lost its corresponding claim against Citibank NA in New York was irrelevant. The case also emphasises the broader territorial point that legislative action taken

---

[239] *European Bank Ltd v Citibank Ltd* [2004] NSWCA 76. In view of the *Wells Fargo Asia* litigation referred to earlier, it is significant to note that the respondent in those proceedings was the Australian-incorporated subsidy of Citibank NA, rather than a branch of the parent entity itself.

[240] The US legislation which provided the source and justification is regrettably not discussed in the report. From the, apparently, companion decision in *Evans & Associates v Citibank Ltd* [2003] NSWC 204 (New South Wales Supreme Court), it appears that the US warrants may have been issued under the Federal Trade Commission Act 1914. Nevertheless, the warrant at issue in the *European Bank* case seems to have an effect similar to that described in s.319 of the PATRIOT Act.

[241] *Evans* [2003] NSWC 204 at [51].

[242] And, it may be added, to someone other than the creditor.

[243] It is a generally accepted principle that courts sitting in one country will not lend their process to the enforcement of the penal revenue or public laws of another country, since this would involve the assertion of the sovereignty of the second State within the territory of the first. Among the many authorities for this proposition, see *Huntington v Attrill* [1893] A.C. 150 PC; *India v Taylor* [1955] A.C. 491 HL. The companion litigation in Australia makes the same point, in that the New South Wales Supreme Court declined to give effect to the appointment of a receiver pursuant to the US Federal Trade Commission Act 1914: see *Evans* [2003] NSWSC 204.

in one country cannot affect proprietary rights which are legally situated in another.[244] The warrant was thus not entitled to recognition in Sydney and could not affect the recovery of a debt governed by the law of New South Wales.

As a secondary ground of decision, it may be noted that para.7.1 of the General Account Conditions applicable to the deposit provided that Citibank Ltd would not be liable for failure to repay if it was prevented, hindered or delayed from doing so by a force majeure event (including governmental action) which was beyond its reasonable control. Clause 7.2 likewise exonerated Citibank Ltd if performance would result in a breach of any legal or regulatory requirement binding upon it. As the court remarked,[245] it is reasonable to suppose that these clauses found their way into Citibank's standard terms following the *Wells Fargo Asia* litigation noted above. However, the clause did not protect Citibank Ltd because its contract constituted a simple debt obligation. Performance was not "prevented" by the official action taken in New York. Furthermore, and although the court did not specifically address the point, it would plainly be unreasonable to imply into the contract a term that repayment is conditional on the bank's access to the corresponding funds in New York.[246] Apart from other considerations, the customer has no influence over the choice of correspondent bank.

The decision displays a number of remarkable features. First of all, and even though Citibank had been party to it, the earlier decisions in the *Wells Fargo Asia* litigation seem only to have been discovered after the main hearing, in spite of their obvious relevance. Secondly, it appears that the English decision in the *Libyan Arab* case (above) was not drawn to the court's attention even though the case is well known in banking circles and, again, despite its obvious relevance. Nevertheless, it is submitted that the decision reached by the New South Wales Court of Appeal is plainly correct.

Under these circumstances, it seems fair to conclude that banks established outside the US—including branches and subsidiaries of US banks—will generally have to take the risk that they will have to repay US dollar deposits accepted by them, even though the US Government has taken steps to block the corresponding payments through the New York clearing system or have expropriated an amount equivalent to the deposit concerned.

5–49

---

[244] In the context of garnishee proceedings, the point has been affirmed by the House of Lords in *Société Eram Shipping Co Ltd v Compagnie Internationale de Navigation* [2004] 1 A.C. 260, and see *Taurus Petroleum Ltd v State Oil Marketing Co of the Ministry of Oil, Iraq* [2016] 1 Lloyd's Rep. 42. This decision has received approval elsewhere—see, for example, *Ludgater Holdings Ltd v Gerling Australia Co Pty Ltd* [2010] NZSC 49 (Supreme Court of New Zealand).
[245] *Evans* [2003] NSWC 204 at [80].
[246] Indeed, the New York funds became the property of Citibank NA to deal with as it wished, and it was under no obligation to maintain those particular funds as the source of repayment for its Australian subsidiary. This necessarily follows from the decision in *Foley v Hill*, to which reference has already been made. No such term was implied in *Libyan Arab* [1989] Q.B. 728 QBD (Comm).

The time of payment as between debtor and creditor

5–50   Having discussed both the operation of the funds transfer system and particular cases of difficulty, the present section seeks to draw together some of the threads and to examine the point of time at which payment made through the banking system will be deemed to be tendered or made *as between the debtor and the creditor themselves*. This is, of course, important in terms of the underlying commercial contract,[247] even though it may be obscured by the intricacies of the banking system and the number of correspondent transfers involved. For example, funds may be moved from the transferor bank to the transferee bank without giving rise to payment as between their respective customers, the debtor and the creditor. Conversely, the creditor may receive payment, in a manner effective to discharge the debt, from the transferee bank before the latter itself has been put in funds by the transferor bank. At this point, we are concerned solely with relations between debtor and creditor, not with the question whether, and at what point, there has been a transfer of funds from one bank to the other.[248]

Payment through inter-bank arrangements

5–51   D is to discharge his debt to C by arranging for his bank DB either to transfer funds to C's bank CB for the credit of C's account or to request CB to credit C's account in anticipation of such transfer.[249] At what point is C to be treated in law as having received payment? The essential rule to bear in mind here is that a third party cannot effectively discharge D's debt by a voluntary payment made without the actual or ostensible authority of D[250] or the subsequent ratification by D of a payment expressed to be made by the third party as his agent.[251] Such authorisation or ratification may be made by D directly or through an intermediary who has actual or ostensible authority to give it.[252] But if the third

---

[247] See generally the charterparty cases discussed in Ch.3 above.

[248] It should also be emphasised that the present section is concerned principally with the discharge of the payment obligation by means of inter-bank transfer. The time of payment in credit card and other transactions is both less difficult and—in view of the amounts involved—less likely to be controversial. In those cases, the time of payment has already been considered above in the sections applicable to those particular instruments.

[249] It is here assumed that CB has actual or ostensible authority from C to accept a transfer of funds for his account or to comply with a request to credit his account in advance of the transfer. For the position where CB has no such authority, see the discussion at para.2–29 above.

[250] It is a general principle that the officious payment of another's debt ("officious" in the sense that it is made neither with the authority of the debtor nor under legal compulsion or necessity) is not effective to discharge the debt unless made on behalf of the debtor and ratified by him. See para.2–29 above.

[251] A principal can ratify his agent's act only if the act was expressed to be done on the principal's behalf; *Keighley Maxsted & Co v Durant (t/a Bryan Durant & Co)* [1901] A.C. 240 HL, as referred to in *Secured Residential Funding Plc v Douglas Goldberg Hendeles & Co* (2000) 97(18) L.S.G. 38 CA (Civ Div); *Magellan Spirit ApS v Vital SA* [2016] EWHC 454 (Comm) at [15]; and *Vannin Capital PCC v RBOS Shareholders Action Group Ltd* [2018] EWHC 2821 (Ch) at [28]. The *Keighley Maxsted* principle was recently reiterated by the Supreme Court in *Revenue and Customs Commissioners v Taylor Clark Leisure Plc* [2018] UKSC 35 at [38].

[252] *British Bank of the Middle East v Sun Life Assurance of Canada (UK)* [1983] 2 Lloyd's Rep. 9 HL.

party—in our example, CB—pays or credits C before he has been authorised to do so, then, in the absence of subsequent ratification, this is not a payment of the debt as between D and C, merely an advance by CB to its customer C in anticipation of authority to pay. If authority to pay is not received by the due payment date and CB's credit or payment to C is not ratified, D will be in default of his obligation to C, who will be entitled to exercise any available default remedies. This will, of course, reflect the realities of the situation because CB will reverse the credit entry made on C's account.

DB's authority to CB—whether directly or through an intermediary—to pay or credit C may be given to take effect before DB has remitted funds to CB, or simultaneously with such remittance or after CB has been put in funds. Where CB is to pay C by transferring funds remitted to him for the purpose by DB, a purported transfer is effective only if it complies with DB's payment instructions. So, if DB remits funds which are received by CB on 1 January, with an instruction that the pay date is to be 4 January, any payment or credit by CB to C prior to 4 January must be regarded as an advance by CB from its own funds, not a payment from the funds remitted to CB; and, as between D and C, payment will not be effective until the given pay date, 4 January.[253] This demonstrates the general point that, in view of the number of parties involved in an inter-bank transfer, it is important to identify the relationship under discussion. In this case, there has been a transfer of funds from DB to CB and a transfer by CB to C out of CB's own moneys but—until 4 January arrives—there has not been a payment as between D and C.

Subject to the agency point noted above, payment is deemed to be made when a transfer is made to CB which confers on C immediate and unconditional access to the funds concerned.[254] It is entirely insufficient, therefore, for CB alone to receive unconditional use of the funds; payment must be for C's account. In *K v A*,[255] a fraudster intercepted emails and changed the account details so D made payment to a different fraudulent account with the same bank. Although the funds were recovered from the fraudulent account, there was a shortfall due to fluctuations in foreign exchange rates. D was found to be in breach of its contractual obligation, which was not to make payment to CB but to make payment to CB for C's account. Therefore, the payment needed to be accompanied by the correct account details notified by C.[256]

Finally, where CB does make an authorised payment or credit to C in accordance with DB's instructions, this will still not constitute effective payment as between D and C if the sum paid or credited is not placed freely at C's disposal. Essentially, payment must be an unconditional act.[257] This means not only that C's access to the funds must not be subject to any condition, whether a condition precedent or a condition subsequent (e.g. by reservation of a right of recourse), but must be "unfettered and unrestricted" so C receives "the equivalent to cash, or

5–52

---

[253] *Awilco of Oslo A/S v Fulvia SpA di Navigazione of Cagliari (The Chikuma)* [1981] 1 W.L.R. 314 HL.
[254] *The Brimnes* [1973] 1 W.L.R. 386 QBD (Admlty), affirmed [1975] Q.B. 929 CA (Civ Div).
[255] *K v A* [2019] EWHC 1118 (Comm).
[256] *K v A* [2019] EWHC 1118 (Comm) at [29].
[257] *The Brimnes* [1973] 1 W.L.R. 386 QBD (Admlty), affirmed [1975] Q.B. 929 CA (Civ Div). In strict terms, it may be more accurate to say that *tender* must be an unconditional act.

as good as cash".[258] A payment which is not unconditional in this sense does not discharge D's payment obligation to C even if it is effective to constitute a transfer of funds as between CB and C.

A series of examples will serve to illustrate the above propositions. In each case, DB is acting on the instructions of its customer, D, and the crediting of C's account by C in accordance with D's request or authority is the mode of payment agreed between D and C.

Example 1—CB makes authorised credit before receiving funds
DB requests CB to credit C with the sum of £10,000, for which DB undertakes to reimburse CB in due course. CB expressly or impliedly accepts DB's undertaking and credits C's account accordingly. This constitutes payment as between D and C even though CB has not yet been put in funds by DB.[259] If CB were to go into liquidation before C had withdrawn the £10,000 credited, this would not affect the completion of payment between D and C, since the agreed mode of payment was by the crediting of C's account with CB, and in assenting to this C assumed any risks involved.

Example 2—CB is authorised to pay out of funds remitted by DB
DB requests CB to credit C with the sum of £10,000 from funds which DB is remitting to CB for that purpose. Before CB has received the funds, it credits C's account with the amount in question. This does not constitute payment as between D and C, since it has not been authorised by CB. It is merely an advance by CB to C from C's own moneys. Payment as between D and C would become complete as the result of the credit only upon CB receiving from DB the funds from which payment was to be made or upon ratification of CB's act by DB. Further, if the funds are transferred to CB upon terms which preclude CB from applying them to the credit of C's account until a given date or the fulfilment of some other designated condition, a credit by CB to C's account purportedly from the remitted funds is not effective as payment between D and C until the stipulated date has arrived[260] or the condition has been fulfilled.

Example 3—CB makes an authorised credit but under reserve
In accordance with instructions from DB, CB credits C's account with the sum of £10,000 but tells C that it reserves the right to debit back the payment if it receives instructions from DB to that effect. Such a payment under reserve is not a valid payment as between D and C, for the money credited to C's account is not placed unconditionally at his disposal.[261]

---

[258] *The Chikuma* [1981] 1 W.L.R. 314 HL, at 320 (Lord Bridge). Lord Bridge also used the words "unfettered and unrestricted" in interpreting the meaning of "unconditional".

[259] This is so because CB effectively agrees to advance funds to DB, and the credit to C's account may be regarded as unconditional. This may be contrasted with the discussion at para.5–26 and Example 2 below, where DB does not give a reimbursement undertaking and anticipates that CB will stay its hand until funds arrive from DB.

[260] *The Chikuma* at fn.258 above.

[261] For the meaning of "payment under reserve" see *Banque de l'Indochine et de Suez SA v JH Rayner (Mincing Lane) Ltd* [1983] Q.B. 711 CA (Civ Div).

THE LEGAL IMPLICATIONS OF PAYMENTS THROUGH BANKING AND NON-BANK SYSTEMS

Example 4—Payment instructions received from an intermediary
CB credits C's account in accordance with instructions received not from DB direct but from an intermediary bank, IB. The credit constitutes payment as between D and C if, but only if, IB had actual or ostensible authority from D to give payment instructions.

Receipt and acceptance of funds by CB for C's account

In all the above examples, it has been assumed that CB has reached the point of crediting C's account. However, it is not an essential pre-requisite of payment as between D and C that CB shall actually have carried out the crediting process. It suffices that CB, with actual or ostensible authority from C to do so,[262] accepts a transfer of funds from DB for the account of C. In such a case, payment to CB is payment to C, and the fact that CB has not yet credited C's account, or indeed notified C of the payment, is irrelevant,[263] as is the fact that payment arrives too late to enable to draw out the money on the same day.[264] By stipulating payment to his bank for his account, C prima facie accepts the normal rule that tender is effective if made before midnight at the end of the day fixed for payment.[265] If he wishes to ensure that he has access to the money on the same day, he must fix a time for payment that allows for this. If payment as between D and C is to be complete without CB having paid C or credited his account, it is necessary that CB shall have actually received a transfer of funds from DB for C's account[266] and that the payment by DB to CB shall be, or have become, unconditional, so that the sum transferred is freely at C's disposal. It is, therefore, necessary to distinguish a transfer of funds from a mere commitment by DB to CB, and to distinguish unconditional from conditional transfer.

5–53

(1) Transfer distinguished from commitment

It has been said that payment is to be considered made to C as soon as CB "receives payment in cash, or by means of a banker's cheque, draft, payment

5–54

---

[262] See the discussion at para.2–28 above; and *Law of Bank Payments* (2018), para.3–131 (regarding inter-bank transfers). The situation is different for intra-branch and inter-branch transfers concerning accounts at the same bank (discussed below at paras 5–58 to 5–61).
[263] *Delbrueck & Co v Manufacturers Hanover Trust Co* 609 F.2d 1047 (1979).
[264] This, incidentally, is one of the reasons why the present writer is doubtful that the debtor due to pay a foreign currency debt in England should continue to enjoy the (long accepted) option to pay in sterling at the prevailing rate. Even if the creditor can access the funds on the same day, the exchange rate can move even intraday. The risk of loss is clearly exacerbated if the creditor is compelled to take no action overnight. The rule, therefore, seems inappropriate in the context of modern currency markets. Of course, as noted in *Libyan Arab* [1989] Q.B. 728 QBD (Comm), the debtor may well be obliged to pay in sterling if payment in the foreign currency has become impossible. But that is a different point.
[265] See para.4–03 above.
[266] It is insufficient that CB alone receives the funds, it must receive them for C's account (i.e. the payment must be made to CB with the correct account details for C; *K v A* [2019] EWHC 1118 (Comm). See also *Law of Bank Payments* (2018), para.3–133. Of course, if CB unconditionally credits C's account before receiving funds from DB (for instance, where the banks are correspondent banks), payment will be complete; *Law of Bank Payments* (2018), para.3–132.

[235]

order or transfer which is treated by banks as equivalent to cash".[267] However, this is true only in a loose sense. We have previously seen that a contractual obligation to pay money by a given date may be considered *provisionally* performed by tender of a bill or cheque to the creditor by that date, where this is an acceptable mode of payment, but that acceptance of the instrument is prima facie conditional on its being honoured, and only when this occurs is payment complete.[268] The same is true of tender of an instrument by DB to CB. DB may transfer funds to CB in various ways, e.g. cash, contractual set-off or the crediting of CB's account with a third bank. But a mere commitment to transfer funds, as by giving CB a banker's cheque or payment order, is not the same thing as a transfer of funds itself, and whilst the delivery of the payment instrument by DB to CB and its acceptance by CB constitute a conditional payment as between DB and CB, and thus a conditional payment as between D and C, yet, if the instrument were to be dishonoured by DB on presentation, there would be no receipt of funds by CB and therefore no receipt by C.

(2) Unconditional transfer distinguished from conditional transfer

5–55   Where DB, in transferring funds to CB, imposes conditions that must be satisfied before the funds are made available to C, payment is not effective as between D and C until those conditions have been fulfilled or waived. The typical case is where funds are remitted with a "pay date" (a date when they may be released to C) later than the "value date" (a date when they are placed under the control of CB).[269] In this case, the condition is a condition precedent. What is the position where DB imposes a condition subsequent, as by paying CB under reserve on the footing that if D objects to the payment as not being in conformity with his instructions it is to be repaid by CB to DB? This happens from time to time in documentary credit transactions, where, say, the correspondent bank by whom payment is made is not satisfied that the documents tendered under the credit are in order but agrees to pay under reserve, i.e. on terms that it can recover the payment if its principal refuses to approve it.[270] Payment under a condition subsequent is, of course, an effective transfer of funds as between DB and CB, but unless CB has actual or ostensible authority from C to accept the condition the transfer will not be effective as payment by D to C. C himself is under no obligation to accept a tender upon a condition subsequent,[271] and, prima facie, his bank has no authority to accept such a tender on his behalf. It is, of course, a different matter if—CB having tendered payment to C or credited his account under reserve—C elects to accept the condition. However, unless and until he does so, D's debt to him cannot be considered paid.

---

[267] See materials cited in the first edition (*Goode on Payment Obligations in Commercial and Financial Transactions* (1983)), p.112.
[268] See para.2–23 above.
[269] In *The Chikuma* [1981] 1 W.L.R. 314 HL, the term "value date" was used in the sense of pay date, i.e. the date when the transferred funds became available to the creditor.
[270] For an example of this type of situation, see *Rayner* [1983] Q.B. 711 CA (Civ Div). See para.3–74 above.
[271] See para.2–23 above.

In considering whether a condition subsequent has been imposed entitling DB to reverse a transfer of funds made to CB, regard must be had to negotiable instruments law (where payment is made by negotiable instrument) and to any relevant clearing house rules. In the case of a cheque, for example, the paying bank transfers funds to the collecting bank through the Bank of England in anticipation of the cheque being met when presented, but the customer for whom the cheque is being collected is not obliged to treat the provisional credit of the cheque to his account as payment, and if the cheque is dishonoured then no payment has been made as between the drawer and the customer, even though there has been an anticipatory transfer of funds between the two banks.[272] In the case of a credit transfer, the practice and general understanding of bankers as to the finality of payment may be decisive. The collapse of the German Herstatt Bank in June 1974 gave rise to litigation on both sides of the Atlantic as to the finality of credit transfers, and the courts of both countries reached the same conclusion, namely that initiation of a credit transfer renders the initiating bank's undertaking to pay irrevocable, so that any ensuing transfer of funds must be treated as unconditional.[273]

The American decision, *Delbrueck & Co v Manufacturers Hanover Trust Co*[274] is of particular interest, not only because of the fine calculations of time involved but also because it led to a change in the New York Clearing House rules concerning the finality of CHIPS transfers.

The claimants instructed the defendants by telex to transfer three sums from the claimant's account with the defendants to Chase Manhattan Bank for the account of Herstatt, namely $12.5 million on 26 June and $10 million on 27 June. At 10.30 Eastern Standard Time on 26 June, Herstatt was closed by the German banking authorities. At 11.36 $10 million and at 11.37 £2.5 million was credited to Chase Manhattan's account at the Clearing House.[275] At 12.00 the claimants (who had half an hour earlier sent the defendants instructions to stop the payment due on 27 June) called the defendants, and later telexed them, in an attempt to

---

[272] See para.2–29 above.
[273] *Momm* [1977] Q.B. 790 QBD (Comm), discussed in *Law of Bank Payments* (2018), para.3–127; *Delbrueck* 609 F.2d 1047 (1979). It should be noted that, in this sense, "unconditional" means unconditional as between the immediate parties. In principle, the finality of a payment in this sense would not prejudice the right of a liquidator to challenge the payment as an unfair preference for the purposes of s.239 of the Insolvency Act 1986. Furthermore, the House of Lords has held that the multilateral netting rules of a clearing house cannot prejudice the pari passu distribution of a participant's assets in the event of a liquidation: *British Eagle International Airlines Ltd v Compagnie Nationale Air France* [1975] 1 W.L.R. 758 HL. However, insolvency considerations of this kind can no longer apply to payments through CHAPS by virtue of the Financial Markets and Insolvency (Settlement Finality) Regulations 1999, which implement Directive 98/26/EC of the European Parliament and of the Council of 19 May 1998 on settlement finality in payment and securities settlement systems (the Settlement Finality Directive) in the UK.
[274] See fn.263 above.
[275] This did not constitute payment as between Manufacturers Hanover Trust Co and Chase Manhattan, merely a clearing house settlement followed by an actual transfer of funds the next day through the accounts of the two banks at the Federal Reserve Board. CHIPS now operates on the basis of same-day settlement.

stop or recall the payments already made[276] that day. The claimants unsuccessfully sought to persuade Chase to return the funds; and at about 21.00 on 26 June, Chase formally credited Herstatt's account with the £12.5 million.

The claimants sued the defendants for negligence and breach of contract in failing to revoke the two transfers made on 26 June. The court dismissed the action, holding that the transfer instructions had become irrevocable when processed through CHIPS at 11.36 and 11.37, and the fact that the transfers were not formally credited to Herstatt's account until 21.00 was irrelevant, this being a mere book-keeping entry. In reaching its conclusions, the court commented on the fact that the claimants themselves had initially sought to stop only the payment due on 27 June, indicating that they too must have considered the earlier payment instructions irrevocable; and the court also pointed to a subsequent change in the CHIPS rules allowing time for reversal of transfers.

Payment by inter-bank arrangements—a summary

5–56   It may now be helpful to recapitulate. Where D is to discharge his debt to C through arrangements between DB and CB, whether directly or through an intermediary, IB, payment of the debt will be complete where:

(1) CB pays or credits C with the actual or ostensible authority of DB or IB;
(2) CB, without such authority, pays or credits C purportedly on behalf of DB or IB, who subsequently ratifies such payment; or
(3) CB, having actual or ostensible authority to accept payment on behalf of C, accepts a transfer of funds from DB or IB for C's account;

and, in each case, the payment, credit or transfer is or has become unconditional.

Mere instructions to make transfer to creditor's account is not sufficient

5–57   Payment cannot, however, be considered complete without either a payment or credit by CB to C, authorised (actually or ostensibly) or ratified, or a receipt and acceptance of funds by CB for C's account. A mere request or instruction by DB to CB to credit C's account does not of itself constitute payment.[277] Still less does an instruction by D to his own bank, DB, to transfer funds to CB for C's account.[278] In these cases, there are no funds in C's hands which will enable us to say that CB's receipt and acceptance constitute receipt and acceptance by C, nor is there yet any compliance by CB with the instruction to credit C's account so as to give C a claim against CB. In short, the agreed method of payment, by transfer

---

[276] See fn.263 above.
[277] *Zim Israel Navigation Co Ltd v Effy Shipping Corp* [1972] 1 Lloyd's Rep. 18 QBD (Comm); *The Brimnes* [1975] Q.B. 929 CA (Civ Div).
[278] *Effy* at fn.249 above.

of funds or of a claim,[279] has not yet been carried out. Of course, the parties may agree, either in their contract or subsequently, that a payment instruction, or something else falling short of completed payment, is all that is required to be done by the agreed date of "payment"—in which event, the issue of the instruction or performance of the other designated act by the due date will constitute performance of the contract, so long as payment is duly completed by the carrying out of the instruction or other arrangements for the transfer of funds. The time allowed to convert the instruction to pay into a completed payment is, unless otherwise agreed, such time as is reasonable in the circumstances; and, in determining what is reasonable, the court would have regard to normal banking practice.

In-house transfers

The preceding discussion assumed the existing of two separate banks, DB (the debtor's bank) and CB (the creditor's bank). We must now consider the case of the in-house transfer, where debtor and creditor both bank at the same bank and the payment is to be made by transfer of money from the debtor's account at the bank to the creditor's account at that bank. Obviously, in-house transfers raise different considerations from external payments, in that all the transfer activity takes place under one roof so that no outward communication is necessarily available to establish the fact or time of transfer.

5–58

(1) Cheques

Where D and C bank not only at the same bank but at the same branch and C hands over or sends to the bank for credit to his account a cheque drawn in his favour by B, the presumption is that the bank receives the cheque as D's agent for collection, not as drawee called upon to pay a presented instrument. Accordingly, the bank's retention of the cheque does not itself constitute payment.[280] In its capacity as collecting bank, the bank is entitled to deal with the cheque in the same way as if collecting from another bank in the same place. The position is otherwise where C makes it clear that he is presenting the cheque for payment. In that case, the bank must immediately make up its mind whether or not to pay. If it retains the cheque instead of refusing it, that will constitute payment.[281]

5–59

If D and C bank at different branches and C hands the cheque in at his own branch, the branch will not receive it qua drawee, for the drawer is entitled to have his cheques honoured only at the branch where he maintains his account.[282] C's branch will therefore receive the cheque either as agent for collection,

---

[279] CB credits C's account. CB is now a debtor to CB and D a debtor to DB. So D's claim against DB (in respect of a credit balance, agreed loan or overdraft facility) has become converted into a claim by C against CB.
[280] *Boyd v Emmerson* 111 E.R. 71 KB, followed in *Sutherland v Royal Bank of Scotland plc* 1997 S.L.T. 329.
[281] *Boyd v Emmerson* at fn.252 above.
[282] *Woodland v Fear* 119 E.R. 1339 KB.

presenting this on C's behalf to D's branch for payment or, if D's branch pays against the cheque, as a holder for value who is purchasing the cheque or lending against it.[283]

(2) Credit transfers

5–60 Where D, banking at the same bank as C, instructs the bank to transfer money from his account to C's account, payment is complete when the bank has taken the final decision to treat the instructions for transfer as irrevocable.[284] It is not necessary that the bank shall actually have carried out the transfer process by crediting one account and debiting another. The irrevocable decision to do so suffices. This decision may be established:

i. by notifying the creditor or his agent of the transfer instruction[285];
ii. by the bank's initiating the computer process leading to the debit of D's account and the credit of C's account, notification of this to C being unnecessary[286]; or
iii. by some other internal act of the bank which it regards as the decisive act committing it to complete the transfer, e.g. the passing of the payment authority from one department of the bank to another.[287]

In some cases, a bank making a credit transfer at the request of a particular customer will not know until the following day whether the customer's account is in funds to meet the payment. This is what happened in one of the *Herstatt* cases, *Momm v Barclays Bank International Ltd*.[288] where the defendant bank, having initiated a transfer in favour of the plaintiffs at the request of Herstatt Bank, sought to say that the following morning was to be treated as an extension of the value date because the final balances from the computer showing the state of Herstatt's account with them would not appear until then, so that any initiation of a transfer from Herstatt's account should be treated as provisional and reversible. This argument was rejected by Kerr J, who held that a day was a day, ending at latest at midnight, and that a credit transfer, once initiated, could not be held in suspense for a further period and treated the next morning as never having been made. There was no reason to distinguish an in-house transfer from an external payment in this respect.

(3) Direct debits

5–61 The same principles would seem applicable to an in-house transfer effected by a direct debit instruction. The only difference between this and the credit transfer is

---

[283] See R.M. Goode, "When is a Cheque Paid?" [1993] J.B.L. 164, 165.
[284] *Delbrueck* 609 F.2d 1047 (1979); *Momm* [1977] Q.B. 790 QBD (Comm); *The Brimnes* [1975] Q.B. 929 CA (Civ Div). See discussion of this point in *Law of Bank Payments* (2018), paras 3–125 to 3–129 (intra-branch payments) and para.3–130 (inter-branch payments).
[285] *Delbrueck* 609 F. 2d 1074 (1979).
[286] *Momm* [1977] Q.B. 790 QBD (Comm).
[287] *The Brimnes* [1975] Q.B. 929 CA (Civ Div).
[288] *Momm* [1977] Q.B. 790 QBD (Comm).

that it is C, not D, who gives the instructions to the bank to make the transfer. As before, payment will be complete when the bank has taken the decision that the transfer is to be considered made, so that it would not accept any countermand of payment.

4. NON-BANK PAYMENT SYSTEMS AND SERVICES

One of the most interesting developments in payment services over the past couple of decades has been the growth in non-bank payment systems and services, particularly in the retail payments sector. These are increasingly offering an alternative to the more traditional bank-based payment systems and services. By "non-bank", what is meant here are systems or services which facilitate the transfer of money from debtor to creditor in some way, but where either the service provider is not a deposit-taking institution[289] or the payment system in question operates either wholly or partly outside the existing banking infrastructure. This section will briefly consider various legal issues which may arise in relation to non-bank payments.[290]

5–62

As a preliminary matter, however, it is important to identify the different types of non-bank payment systems and services which exist. To avoid confusion, an initial distinction should be made between, on the one hand, the provision of payment services in conjunction with the existing banking infrastructure by entities other than banks ("payment service providers" or PSPs) and, on the other hand, non-bank payment services and systems which remove the bank from the payment process altogether (referred to as the "shadow payment system"[291]). PSPs, the former category, establish transactions between merchants, consumers and banks and other financial institutions by providing an "interface" between them. The latter category includes "peer-to-peer" (P2P) payment systems and virtual currencies which largely remove the bank from the payment chain (except at the point of the entry of funds into the system).

Non-bank payment services and systems present certain regulatory issues. Although a detailed discussion is beyond the scope of this book,[292] essentially they perform similar functions to banks but have until recently been largely outside the regulatory structures which apply to banks and which are intended to

5–63

---

[289] This broadly corresponds with the definition of "non-bank" given at p.4 of the report by the Bank for International Settlement (BIS), *Non-banks in retail payments* (September 2014), available at: http://www.bis.org/cpmi/publ/d118.pdf [Accessed 6 September 2020], as "any entity involved in the provision of retail payment services whose main business is not related to taking deposits from the public and using these deposits to make loans".

[290] For a more detailed discussion of this topic, see Jakub Górka (ed.), *Transforming Payment Systems in Europe* (Basingstoke: Palgrave MacMillan UK, 2016); Adam Levitin, *Consumer Finance Law: Markets and Regulation* (New York: Wolters Kluwer, 2018), Ch.21 on emerging payment systems.

[291] These have been referred to collectively as the "shadow payment system"; see e.g. Dan Awrey and Kristen van Zwieten, "The Shadow Payment System" (2017) 43 *Journal of Corporate Law* 775.

[292] See e.g. Jonathan Greenacre, "Regulating the Shadow Payment System: Bitcoin, Mobile Money, and Beyond" in Philipp Hacker, Ioannis Lianos, Georgios Dimitropoulus and Stefan Eich (eds), *Regulating Blockchain: Techno-Social and Legal Challenges* (Oxford: Oxford University Press, 2019).

achieve aims including those identified at the beginning of this chapter; consumer protection, the prevention of financial crime and ensuring the stability of financial and payment systems.[293] At the same time, they are capable of providing significant benefits to customers, including improved access to payment services, and promoting competition and innovation in the payments sector, which presents regulators with a dilemma as to how to balance these benefits with the relevant concerns. Given the cross-border nature of many payments through non-bank payment systems, there may also be conflict-of-law issues.[294]

While many of these developments are in their early stages, the use of non-bank PSPs and payment systems has increased in recent years and is likely to increase further. It is interesting therefore to consider the legal effects of using a non-bank PSP or payment system on the respective parties' payment obligations. This section will make some tentative remarks on the following legal aspects of non-bank payments: the time when payment is complete; protection for users of the service or system; and the extent to which the service or system is regulated, including the application of anti-money laundering and counter-terrorism legislation. However, this is an area to which the law has just begun in the past few years to turn its attention and so a large degree of uncertainty remains on some points.

Payment Service Providers

(1) Overview

5–64 The growth of electronic payments and e-money, including internet and mobile payments, has resulted in the rise of non-bank competitors in the payment services industry.[295] Many of these non-bank PSPs remain reliant on banks to process their payments; their role lies in providing an interface or other services to online merchants to initiate customer payments. Most PSPs are internet-based but other methods of providing payment services are growing in popularity, notably mobile payments made using a smart phone or other electronic device.

5–65 The rise of non-bank PSPs was recognised in PSD I, now replaced by PSD II, which sought to regulate PSPs but also promote competition in the payment services industry. The updated regime under PSD II covers two new regulated payment services—"payment initiation services" (PIS) and "account information services" (AIS). PIS are services which "initiate a payment order at the request of the payment service user with respect to a payment account held at another PSP"[296] while AIS are online services which "provide consolidated information on one or more payment accounts held by the payment service user with either another PSP or with more than one PSP".[297] The effect of PSD II, as implemented

---

[293] See paras 5–05 to 5–12.
[294] Discussed in Philip Wood, *International Loans, Bonds, Guarantees and Legal Opinions*, 3rd edn (London: Sweet & Maxwell, 2019), para.46-043.
[295] Well-known examples include Worldpay, TransferWise, Ayden, Stripe, Braintree, SagePay and Amazon Pay.
[296] PSD II art.4(15); 2017 Regulations reg.2(1).
[297] PSD II art.4(16); 2017 Regulations reg.2(1).

through the 2017 Regulations, is to allow these service providers to access the customer account detail held by banks with their customers' consent in order to provide payment services,[298] while also ensuring safeguards for customers using such services.

(2) When is payment complete?

As discussed above, a positive balance in a bank account is essentially a personal claim against the bank. Where payments are processed using non-bank PSP services which interface with banks, this will ultimately involve banks who will make the debits and credits to the bank accounts of the creditor and debtor which represent the "transfer" of funds.[299] Therefore, it seems that, despite the additional intermediaries in the payment process, the payment itself is complete at the same time as if the funds transfer were a simple inter-bank transfer—when funds are transferred to the creditor's bank account and he has immediate and unconditional access to such funds.[300] The position will be different for credit cards, where it was held in *Re Charge Card Services*[301] that "payment" by credit card was not conditional upon receipt of subsequent remittances from the card issuer,[302] and presumably for debit cards, which should also be treated as being akin to cash.[303]

5–66

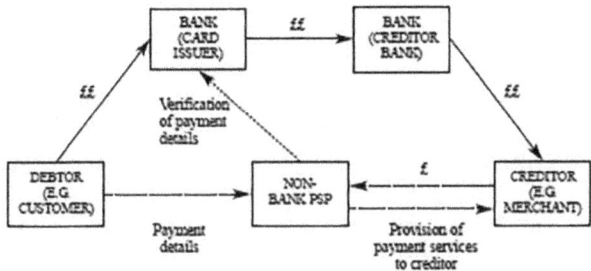

Fig.7: Example of payment structure where non-bank PSP interfaces with bank

(3) Protection for users of PSP services

While facilitating PSP services, the 2017 Regulations also include various protections for customers. These include the requirement for parties providing

5–67

---

[298] 2017 Regulations Pt 8.
[299] The nature of a funds transfer is described in para.5–31 above.
[300] See para.5–47 above
[301] *Re Charge Card Services* [1987] Ch. 150 Ch D (Companies Ct), affirmed [1989] Ch. 497 CA (Civ Div).
[302] See para.5–26 above for a more detailed discussion.
[303] See para.5–27 above.

PIS (PISPs) to implement Strong Customer Authentication (SCA) for transactions above a certain threshold[304] and to keep customers' security credentials secure.[305] In the event of unauthorised transactions, they must refund the unauthorised payments as soon as practicable (and in any event by no later than the end of the following business day).[306] PISPs are also prohibited from retaining customer information for purposes other than completing payments.

There is less protection for customers in the event of a PISP insolvency than if their bank became insolvent. They are not covered by many of the protections which apply to holders of bank accounts, in particular the deposit guarantee scheme. If a non-bank service provider became insolvent while holding customer funds, users would have merely unsecured claims against the PSP. However, both the 2017 Regulations and the Electronic Money Regulations 2011 contain some safeguarding requirements where funds are held by PSPs or e-money issuers. Under the 2017 Regulations, sums received for or from payment service users in relation to the execution of payment transactions must be segregated and, in some circumstances, "backed" by corresponding cash deposits or secured in an equivalent manner.[307] Similarly, the customers of electronic money institutions have a similar degree of protection.[308]

(4) Regulation of PSPs

5–68 Both PSPs and e-money issuers are required to comply with relevant legislation relating to financial crime, including anti-money laundering regulation. They are also subject to the UK's financial sanctions regime. PSPs must provide a description of their internal control mechanisms to comply with anti-money laundering regulations on applying for authorisation under the 2017 Regulations.[309] E-money issuers also have to provide similar information on applying for authorisation under the Electronic Money Regulations 2011.[310]

In terms of ensuring the financial stability of payment systems, it should be noted that s.20 of the Financial Services Act 2010 inserted a new s.206A into the Banking Act 2009. This confers a power on the Treasury to applying the supervisory provisions of Pt 5 of the 2009 Act to "service providers"—defined in s.206A as persons who supply services (such as telecommunication and IT services) that form part of the arrangements of a recognised inter-bank payment system.[311]

---

[304] 2017 Regulations reg.100. The personalised security credentials used for SCA by PISPs appear to be those issued by banks (PSD II Recital 30), on which banks are required to allow PISPs to rely: PSD II art.97(5).
[305] 2017 Regulations reg.100(3).
[306] 2017 Regulations reg.76(2).
[307] 2017 Regulations reg.23.
[308] Electronic Money Regulations 2011 regs 21 and 22.
[309] 2017 Regulations Sch.2 para.11.
[310] Electronic Money Regulations 2011 Sch.1 para.6.
[311] The Banking Act 2009 (Service Providers to Payment Systems) Order 2017 (SI 2017/1167) has subsequently been passed to enable the Bank of England to supervise such service providers to ensure financial stability.

Peer-to-Peer (P2P) Payment Systems

(1) Overview

The rise of e-money has enabled the facilitation of payments by non-bank payment systems—sometimes referred to as "peer-to-peer" or P2P systems—between customers and merchants without recourse to the banking system. The key feature which distinguishes P2P systems from other non-bank PSPs which rely on bank systems to facilitate payments is the existence of "electronic wallets" (or "e-wallets").[312] E-wallets allow holders to store value in the form of electronic data in payment accounts with the service provider, either remotely using a software-based scheme or onto a smart card or electronic device.[313] Since value can be stored in an e-wallet with the P2P payment system, payments are able to be processed without the involvement of a bank.[314]

5–69

PayPal is often regarded as the archetypal example of a non-bank P2P payment system.[315] It is a software-based scheme that allows account holders to send and receive payments online. PayPal removes the need to involve banks in the online payment process since money can been sent instantly and securely to anyone with an email address who sets up a PayPal account. Although customers can link their bank accounts to their PayPal accounts to fund transactions or to transfer funds, they can also retain funds in their PayPal accounts for later use.[316]

Mobile money[317] offers another example of non-bank payment systems, this time made through an electronic device (a mobile phone). A subset of mobile payments (which also includes payments which are simply facilitated by smart phones which allow access to the internet and therefore still involve recourse to a bank), mobile money refers to payments made through mobile network operators (MNOs) where bank accounts are not required. As Awrey and Van Zwieten explain[318]:

> "The term 'mobile money' is used to describe a number of different institutional platforms through which mobile phone companies offer custodial and transactional storage and liquidity".

---

[312] Awrey and Van Zwieten distinguish between *bank-based* P2P systems, which facilitate the direct transfer of funds between deposit accounts (such as Apple Pay) and *proprietary* P2P systems, where funds are held in customer accounts administered by the payment system such as PayPal and Alipay; Dan Awrey and Kristen van Zwieten, "The Shadow Payment System" (2017) 43 *Journal of Corporate Law* 775. The discussion here focuses on the latter category, *proprietary* P2P systems, as the former are still dependent on banks to complete the payment.

[313] See *Law of Bank Payments* (2018), paras 5–049 to 5–059, for more information about e-money or "digital cash" and the legal issues it presents.

[314] E-wallet providers include PayPal, Alipay, Venmo.

[315] Although it moved its headquarters to Luxembourg and became a bank in July 2007. Nevertheless, it is still useful to discuss its structure. Other examples of P2P systems include Amazon Payments, Dwolla and PopMoney.

[316] In *Law of Bank Payments* (2018), para.5–015, it is noted that PayPal "offers a means of making person-to-person payments through a system which only needs to resort to banks at the point of introducing funds into, or removing them from, the PayPal system ... ".

[317] Defined in Ch.1 above.

[318] Dan Awrey and Kristen van Zwieten, "The Shadow Payment System" (2017) 43 *Journal of Corporate Law* 775, 802.

Kenya's M-Pesa system offers an example of this. It is a "mobile money" platform which allows customers to make mobile payments through SMS notifications to each other. Customers can convert cash into e-money and vice versa at retailers including shops and petrol stations. Mobile money has proven particularly popular in developing countries amongst groups with limited internet and banking services access.[319]

(2) When is payment complete?

5–70 For P2P systems where transfers are being made not between the bank accounts of the creditor and debtor but instead their payment accounts with the service provider, the debtor or creditor (or both) will have an account with the service provider (representing a personal claim against the service provider). When a payment is made, the balance of the debtor's account will be reduced and the balance of the creditor's account correspondingly increased (similarly to "in house" transfers for banks).[320] Thus, where payments are made using PayPal, the debtor's balance in its PayPal account will be reduced (or PayPal will draw funds from a connected bank account or credit or debit card if the funds in the PayPal account are insufficient) and the creditor's balance increased by PayPal. PayPal performs the role which a bank would traditionally perform in that it maintains the accounts and debits and credits each account when funds are transferred. It is PayPal's use of e-wallets which allows payments to be made without the involvement of banks. This feature also allows payments to be made in "real time" (i.e. almost instantaneously).[321] If a creditor agrees that a debtor may make a payment using a P2P payment system, it would seem logical to treat the payment as having been completed when the creditor's e-wallet or payment account with the service provider has been credited.

(3) Protection for users of P2P systems

5–71 Most P2P systems in the UK will constitute "electronic money institutions" for the purposes of the Electronic Money Regulations 2011 and the Payment Services Regulations 2017 under Reg.2. Therefore, although not regulated as banks, they will be subject to the regulatory requirements for payment service providers under the 2017 Regulations, including those regarding unauthorised payments. In any case, many P2P systems provide contractual protection for their customers against unauthorised transactions,[322] but there is no equivalent of the

---

[319] Mobile money originated in Kenya in 2007 to allow migrant workers to send money to their families. There are now over 1 billion registered accounts and almost $2 billion in daily transactions: https://www.gsma.com/sotir/wp-content/uploads/2020/03/GSMA-State-of-the-Industry-Report-on-Mobile-Money-2019-Full-Report.pdf [Accessed 28 September 2020]. On the role of mobile money in facilitating access to financial services, see further e.g. Aparna Gosavi, "Can Mobile Money Help Firms Mitigate the Problem of Access to Finance in Eastern sub-Saharan Africa?" (2018) *Journal of African Business* 343.
[320] See para.5–13 above.
[321] *Law of Bank Payments* (2018), para.5–052.
[322] For instance, PayPal, Venmo.

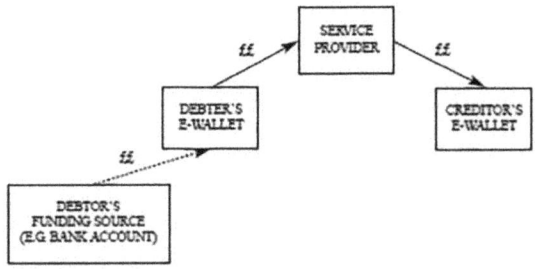

Fig.8: Structure of payment where P2P system and no bank involved in the payment process

protection provided for credit card users in respect of fraudulent transactions.[323] If a service provider becomes insolvent, it is likely that customers for whom P2P systems hold funds in e-wallets would be treated as unsecured creditors.[324] P2P systems are generally unprotected by deposit guarantee schemes.

(4) Regulation of P2P systems

P2P systems which constitute e-money issuers will be subject to the EU anti-money laundering regime.[325] Concerns have been expressed about the potential systemic risks posed to financial systems by widely used P2P systems such as PayPal and M-Pesa and whether a regulatory response is required in relation to these risks.[326]

5–72

Virtual currencies

(1) Overview

Virtual currencies, unlike "cash" in P2P systems, do not have a value which is linked to fiat money. As a result, the recent rise in virtual currencies and their use as "payment" for goods and services[327] is viewed by many as a more radical challenge to traditional banking than the growth of non-bank PSPs, which have now to some extent been integrated into existing regulatory structures.

5–73

---

[323] See the Consumer Credit Act 1974 s.75, which makes credit card providers jointly and severally liable for breaches of contract or misrepresentations by retailers or traders. Although it should be noted that some P2P systems will provide contractual dispute resolution procedures.
[324] As Awrey and Van Zwieten point out in relation to PayPal and mobile money platforms, this is often made clear in the terms and conditions of the payment system: see Dan Awrey and Kristen van Zwieten, "The Shadow Payment System" (2017) 43 *Journal of Corporate Law* 775, 801–802 and 804.
[325] As e-money issuers, the Money Laundering, Terrorist Financing and Transfer of Funds (Information on the Payer) Regulations 2017 (SI 2017/692) will apply to them.
[326] Discussed in Dan Awrey and Kristen van Zwieten, "The Shadow Payment System" (2017) 43 *Journal of Corporate Law* 775.
[327] For example, bitcoins are now accepted as a means of payment by many large organisations including Amazon, Expedia and Microsoft. PayPal accepts bitcoins.

Virtual currencies are not issued and backed by any government or central bank and do not constitute legal tender.[328] Therefore, it is somewhat misleading to talk about the legal implications of virtual currency "payments" since, if one accepts that virtual currencies are not money in the strict legal sense, a "payment obligation" expressed in a virtual currency is actually an obligation to transfer an intangible asset. That said, it is important to recognise that users of virtual currencies are using them to fulfil similar functions to fiat currencies. Therefore, although virtual currencies are not yet widely used, it is possible that some of the issues which arise in relation to conventional funds transfers, for instance, in relation to unauthorised transfers and money laundering or counter-terrorist funding, may also arise for virtual currencies. These issues will be considered here in the context of Bitcoin, perhaps the most well-known virtual currency.[329]

(2) When is "payment" complete?

5–74   Earlier in this book, it was suggested that bitcoins were not strictly "money" but intangible assets instead.[330] If this is the case, a "transfer" of bitcoins does not have the same legal significance as a funds transfer. In addition, bitcoins are arguably not fungible since each bitcoin has its own unique code. Whereas, with a funds transfer, there is no actual "transfer' but instead the bank balance of the debtor is debited and a corresponding credit is made in the bank balance of the creditor, this is not the case with Bitcoin transfers. Instead, it appears that the bitcoin is effectively transferred using the "public key"/"private key" technology which involves a bitcoin being transmitted from debtor to creditor through key pair cryptography, which involves a private key held by the debtor being "paired" with a public key held by the creditor.[331]

Although, arguably, the transfer of a particular bitcoin occurs when the debtor sends a message signed with his private key to the creditor, a distinction needs to be made between "confirmed" and "unconfirmed" transfers. A transfer is only confirmed when it is permanently secured in the blockchain; until then, it might be possible for the debtor to have transferred the bitcoin in question to another party. To permanently secure the transaction, it must be verified by other users of the system—known as "miners"—and sealed with a digital "hash". It is submitted that, if "payment" is intended to take place using bitcoins as the mode of payment, confirmation of transfer is the relevant time of payment since, until the transaction is finalised in this way, it might be possible for "double-spending" to occur.

---

[328] See para.1–13 above.
[329] For a more detailed discussion of legal issues relating to Bitcoin, see Jerry Brito et al, *The Law of Bitcoin* (Bloomington: iUniverse, 2015); Philipp Hacker, Ioannis Lianos, Georgios Dimitropoulus and Stefan Eich (eds), *Regulating Blockchain: Techno-Social and Legal Challenges* (Oxford: Oxford University Press, 2019).
[330] See para.1–13 above.
[331] See para.1–11 above.

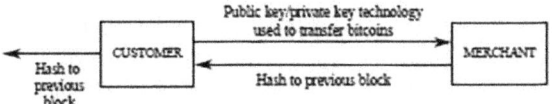

Fig.9: Transfer of a bitcoin

(3) Protection for users of virtual currencies

Unlike for customers of regulated non-bank PSPs, there is very little protection for users of virtual currencies, either in terms of redress in the case of unauthorised transactions or theft or if the issuer of the virtual currency becomes insolvent. This is because virtual currencies fall outside the scope of much of the regulation and legislation which applies to payment services, including that applicable to e-money. The Electronic Money Regulations 2011 define "electronic money" as:

5–75

> "... electronically (including magnetically) stored monetary value as represented by a claim on the electronic money issuer which—
> (a) is issued on receipt of funds for the purpose of making payment transactions;
> (b) is accepted by a person other than the electronic money issuer; and
> (c) is not excluded by regulation 3."[332]

Decentralised virtual currencies such as Bitcoin do not come within this definition because they are not "issued on receipt of funds" and there is no "electronic money issuer" against which users of the currency have a claim; new bitcoins, for instance, are created by a decentralised computer process known as "mining".[333] It is less easy to see why centralised virtual currencies, at least when convertible into real or "fiat" currency, should not come within this definition since they are often issued on receipt of funds by a central administrator against whom they can be redeemed in accordance with the rules of that issuer. Examples of centralised convertible virtual currencies include e-gold and Liberty Dollars (no longer existing) as well as Second Life Linden dollars. The reason why centralised convertible virtual currencies would seem to be different from e-money is because e-money preserves the link to the fiat currency and is expressed in the same unit of account, e.g. sterling, whereas this is not the case in virtual currency schemes where the virtual unit of account is used and the value of the currency is independent to the value of any fiat currency. Therefore, any virtual currency balance is not "monetary value". As a result, virtual currencies as a whole would seem to be outside the reach of the 2011 Regulations and the e-money regime therefore does not apply to them.

Significantly, this presumably means that virtual currencies are also outside the scope of the Payment Services Regulations 2017 and the protection given to users of PSPs in the case of unauthorised transfers. This is because they only apply to "funds transfers" and Bitcoin does not come within the meaning of

---

[332] Electronic Money Regulations 2011 reg.2.
[333] See para.1–11 for more information about the creation of new bitcoins.

"funds" in reg.2, which defines "funds" as banknotes and coins, scriptural money and e-money.[334] While the blockchain technology is designed to make unauthorised transfers of bitcoins impossible, this has not prevented a number of high profile thefts of bitcoins or large numbers of bitcoins going missing.[335] One way in which bitcoins can be stolen is if a third party obtains the private key to the victim's bitcoin address or wallet, in which case all the bitcoins at that location can be transferred. There is no way to reverse such transfers since bitcoin transfers are designed to be irreversible. It is also relatively easy for users to lose bitcoins if the private keys, passwords or digital wallets in which they are stored are lost. It is practically impossible to recover bitcoins once the password has been forgotten or the wallet lost since that would undermine the security of Bitcoin.[336] If issued for fiat currency to consumers (as opposed to business transactions), bitcoins are likely to come within the scope of the recently introduced Consumer Rights Act 2015, which contains rules applying to "digital content"[337] for which the consumer has paid by way of a "facility" for which money was paid.[338] In particular, most contract terms in a consumer contract will be subject to the "fairness" test in the 2015 Act.[339]

The uncertain status of Bitcoin as "money" may have other implications for the consumer who seeks to use it as a means of payment for goods. In particular, in order to attract the benefit of the statutory warranties as to quality, fitness for purpose etc. in the Sale of Good Act 1979, a contract for the sale of goods must involve "a *monetary consideration* called the price...".[340] If the consideration is not a money consideration but is denominated in Bitcoin, the transaction in question may constitute an exchange or barter rather than a sale. On the other

---

[334] As defined by the Electronic Money Regulations 2011.
[335] By far and away most bitcoin thefts result from "hacking" of customers' account details where bitcoins are stored, either privately or at exchanges. Some of the most well-known incidents include the theft of around $100 million worth of bitcoins from customers of Sheep Marketplace, an anonymous online marketplace selling illicit goods; the theft of $350 million from customers of Mt. Gox, now bankrupt, in 2013–2014; the theft of $78 million worth of bitcoins from Bitfinex, a Hong Kong-based exchange, in 2016; the hacking of NiceHash, a Slovenian crypto-currency marketplace, in 2017 and theft of around $63 million worth of bitcoins. An attempt to steal $280,000 worth of bitcoins from Coinbase was blocked in 2020.
[336] See Lauren Orsini, "What Happens To Lost Bitcoins" (13 July 2014), *Readwrite* available at: *http://readwrite.com/2014/01/13/what-happens-to-lost-bitcoins/#awesm=~oBmmgeHW5q8wAJ* [Accessed 12 October 2020].
[337] "Digital content" is defined as "data which are produce and supplied in digital form"—s.2(9) of the 2015 Act.
[338] Interestingly, online banking services are not likely to come within the scope of the 2015 Act. It was noted in a BIS 2012 Consultation Paper (BIS, Department for Business, Innovation & Skills, *Enhancing Consumer Confidence by Clarifying Consumer Law* (July 2012), para.7.17, available at: *https://assets.publishing.service.gov.uk/government/uploads/system/uploads/attachment_data/file/31350/12-937-enhancing-consumer-consultation-supply-of-goods-services-digital.pdf* [Accessed 23 October 2020]), that the "digital content" proposals did not apply to services which are merely online versions of services which could be purchased in stores.
[339] Consumer Rights Act 2015 s.62.
[340] Sale of Goods Act 1979 s.2(1).

hand, if a money price is stipulated which is simply *payable* in Bitcoin (as opposed to the consideration being denominated in Bitcoin), this is likely to be a contract of sale.[341]

Finally, purchasers of virtual currencies should be aware that those currencies fall outside the scope of the deposit guarantee schemes that apply to bank deposits. Consequently, purchasers would be left to bear the entire loss if the system concerned collapsed. An example of this is depositors depositing bitcoins at bitcoin exchanges who would be unsecured creditors if the exchange becomes insolvent. It is possible that purchasers using credit cards to purchase bitcoins from suppliers might be protected under s.75 of the Consumer Credit Act 1974, which makes the credit card issuer jointly liable with the supplier if there is a misrepresentation or breach of contract by the supplier.

These dangers have been substantiated in various Bitcoin thefts and exchange collapses in recent years.[342] By way of example, the collapse in 2014 of Mt Gox, then the world's largest Bitcoin exchange, raised questions of both the security of bitcoin holdings and protection on insolvency of an exchange. In relation to the first point, the trigger for Mt Gox's insolvency was the disappearance of 850,000 bitcoins worth approximately $473 million. Regarding the status of Mt Gox's creditors, the Japanese government treated them as unsecured creditors, although it has since imposed new requirements to protect the users of virtual currency exchanges, including requiring segregation of customer funds and assets.[343]

(4) Regulation of virtual currencies

Virtual currencies raise certain concerns in relation to money laundering and terrorist financing. The Financial Action Task Force originally identified potential risks in 2014 and published guidance in 2015, which it has recently updated.[344] It highlighted the anonymity of users of such systems as being of concern. Consequently, legal systems worldwide have been considering how properly to regulate in this area. The EU has recently responded to these concerns by updating its money laundering regime to include cryptocurrencies.[345]

In the context of financial stability, it is conceivable that a much expanded use of virtual currencies could have wider economic implications. For example, the

5–76

---

[341] On this point see Michael Bridge, Louise Gullifer, Gerard McMeel and Kelvin F.K. Low, *The Law of Personal Property* (London: Sweet & Maxwell, 2019), paras 7-027 and 7-032.

[342] See Peter Susman, "Virtual money in the virtual bank: legal remedies for loss" (2016) 3 J.I.B.F.L. 150 on this issue.

[343] Discussed in Jonathan Greenacre, "Regulating the Shadow Payment System: Bitcoin, Mobile Money and Beyond" in Philipp Hacker, Ioannis Lianos, Georgios Dimitropoulus and Stefan Eich (eds), *Regulating Blockchain: Techno-Social and Legal Challenges* (Oxford: Oxford University Press, 2019).

[344] Available online at: *https://www.fatf-gafi.org/publications/fatfrecommendations/documents/guidance-rba-virtual-assets.html* [Accessed 10 November 2020].

[345] Notably, the Fifth Anti-Money Laundering Directive, implemented in the UK through the Money Laundering and Terrorist Financing (Amendment) Regulations 2019, impose "know-your-customer" and anti-money laundering requirements on electronic wallet providers and crypto-asset exchanges. They do this by by amending the Money Laundering Terrorist Financing and Transfer of Funds (Information on the Payer) Regulations 2017 to include "crypotoasset exchange providers" and "custodian wallet providers": reg.3(1)(b).

ability of a central bank to set a monetary policy rests implicitly on the fact that it issues the currency concerned. If a large part of the payments system consisted of virtual currencies, then the ability of the central bank to maintain an effective monetary policy is plainly eroded. It is also possible to envisage that Bitcoin could impact upon a central bank's responsibility for the stability of the financial system as a whole. If a large number of customers were to borrow money to invest in a virtual currency, then a collapse of that currency could place stresses not only on the borrowers but on the lending institutions themselves. Equally, the central bank's control over payment systems is an essential part of the financial stability function, but this role may also be undermined if virtual currencies became a more common means of payment. At present, it is thought that the use of virtual currencies has not yet reached a point at which these issues are of serious concern and are seen as requiring a regulatory response, but it is clearly a subject that is on the central bank agenda.[346]

5. BREXIT

5–77
On 23 June 2016, the UK voted in a referendum in favour of leaving the EU (Brexit). It formally left the EU on 31 January 2020 and the current transition period is scheduled to end on 31 December 2020. As has been shown in this chapter, the UK owes much of its current payments regulation structure to EU legislation. Therefore, Brexit is likely to signal the start of a period of regulatory uncertainty in this respect. There have been indications that some aspects of the current regime will remain consistent, at least to start with.[347] However, some aspects will change. For example, the scope of application of PSD II after Brexit is likely to be limited[348] and cross-border payments will no longer be covered by the Interchange Fee Regulation.[349] It remains to be seen how far these changes will go.

For instance, it is intended that the PSD II regime will eventually be replaced by the Open Banking initiative, although it is not clear what the practical impact of this will be.

In March 2019, the UK's application to remain in the scope of SEPA was approved.[350] Although it is intended that PSD II will eventually be replaced by Open Banking after Brexit, it is not clear what the practical impact of this will be in the long run.

---

[346] For these and other points, see R. Ali, "The Economics of Digital Currencies" [2014] *Bank of England Quarterly* Q3; Dan Awrey and Kristen van Zwieten, "The Shadow Payment System" (2017) 43 *Journal of Corporate Law* 775.
[347] For example, in March 2019, the UK's application to remain in the scope of SEPA was approved.
[348] Since transactions which would currently be intra-EEA payments will now be "one leg" transactions under PSD II art.2.
[349] Although domestic payments within the UK will still be covered under the Interchange Fee (Amendment) (EU Exit) Regulations 2019 (SI 2019/284).
[350] *https://www.europeanpaymentscouncil.eu/sites/default/files/kb/file/2019-03/EPC065-19%20 EPC%20Board%20Decision%20Paper%20on%20Brexit%20v1.0%20-%207%20March.pdf* [Accessed 10 November 2020]. The UK Government is in the process of publishing transitional legislation to ensure that payments regulation continues to operate effectively after Brexit; see e.g. the Electronic Money, Payment Services and Payment Systems (Amendment and Transitional Provisions) (EU Exit) Regulations 2018 (SI 2018/1201).

CHAPTER 6

FOREIGN MONEY OBLIGATIONS[1]

This final chapter considers the complex problems that arise where the debtor's contractual obligation is expressed in terms of a foreign currency. Even in the—now long distant—days when there were fixed rates of exchange,[2] the measurement of a foreign currency obligation in proceedings brought in England could be a matter of considerable moment. In the present era of floating exchange rates, and sometimes wild fluctuations in exchange rates over a short period of time, the question has become of enormous importance.[3] Currency risk is one of the major hazards of international commerce,[4] and the prudent creditor takes appropriate steps to safeguard himself against diminution in the external purchasing power of the stipulated currency.[5] The present chapter seeks to describe some of the more important legal issues that arise and to discuss the implications of the landmark decision of the House of Lords in *Miliangos v George Frank (Textiles) Ltd*,[6] in which long-established doctrine was finally displaced by the need to do justice to foreign currency creditors. That decision was handed down in 1975 and has won widespread acceptance throughout the common law world. In later years, it also became apparent that foreign currency questions were not limited purely to claims in debt; justice may sometimes demand that an award of damages should likewise be calculated and expressed in a foreign currency. However, before delving into the authorities, we must first briefly consider how these various issues arise.

6–01

---

[1] See further on this topic Law Commission, Private International Law: Foreign Money Liabilities (1981), Working Paper No.80; C. Proctor, Dr C. Kleiner and Dr F. Mohs (eds), *Mann on the Legal Aspect of Money*, 7th edn (Oxford: Oxford University Press, 2012), Chs 4 and 7; *Dicey, Morris & Collins on the Conflict of Laws*, edited by Lord Collins of Mapesbury et al, 15th edn (London: Sweet & Maxwell, 2012), Ch.37; Harvey McGregor et al, *McGregor on Damages*, 20th edn (London: Sweet & Maxwell, 2018), Chs 19 and 20. See also the Council of Europe Convention on Foreign Money Liabilities (1967), the Council of Europe Convention on the Place of Payment of Money Liabilities (1972), and the Law Commission, *Report on the Two Conventions* (1981), Law Com. No.109, Scot. Law Com. No.66.
[2] On the collapse of the Bretton Woods system of fixed exchange rates in the early 1970s, see *Mann* (2012), paras 2.07 onwards.
[3] A particularly acute example occurred on 15 January 2015, when the Swiss National Bank announced that it was abandoning its efforts to cap the value of the Swiss franc vis-à-vis the euro. The Swiss franc appreciated by 30% against the euro in less than an hour, causing massive losses to traders and companies with exposure to the Swiss franc.
[4] Mitigation of currency risk was one of the stated reasons for the introduction of the euro as the single currency of Eurozone Member States.
[5] There are various strategies creditors may use to mitigate this risk; examples include negotiation of payment in advance, diversification of investments and hedging of currency risk using derivatives contracts.
[6] *Miliangos v George Frank (Textiles) Ltd* [1976] A.C. 443 HL.

1. THE PROBLEMS OUTLINED

Discharge of the payment obligation on the due date

6–02   Imagine that a businessman in England contracts a money obligation to a foreigner. What must the Englishman do to discharge his obligation on the due date? This single interrogative raises two entirely distinct questions. The first is how much money the debtor must pay. This is answered by determining the *money of account*, that is to say, the currency by reference to which the debtor's obligation is to be measured. The second concerns the mode of discharging the obligation. This is answered by ascertaining the *money of payment*, that is, the currency in which payment must be tendered. Once again we look to Lord Denning for a vivid illustration of the distinction between the money of account and the money of payment:

> "Suppose an English merchant buys twenty tons of cocoa-beans from a Nigerian supplier for delivery in three months' time at the price of £5 Nigerian a ton payable in pounds sterling in London. Then the *money of account* is Nigerian pounds. But the *money of payment* is sterling. Assume that, at the making of the contract, the exchange rate is £1 Nigerian for £1 sterling—'pound for pound.' Then, so long as the exchange rate remains steady, no one worries. The buyer pays £100 sterling in London. It is transferred to Lagos where the seller receives £100 Nigerian. But suppose that, before the time for payment, sterling is devalued by 14 per cent, whilst the Nigerian pound stands firm. The Nigerian seller is entitled to have the price *measured* in Nigerian pounds. He is entitled to have currency worth £100 Nigerian because the Nigerian pound is the *money of account*. But the *money of payment* is sterling. So the buyer must provide enough sterling to make up £100 Nigerian. To do this, after devaluation, he will have to provide £116.5s. [£116.25] in pounds sterling. So the buyer in England, looking at it as he will in sterling, has to pay much more for his twenty tons of cocoa-beans than he had anticipated. He will have to pay £116.5s. instead of £100. He will have to pass the increase on to his customers. But the seller in Nigeria, looking at it as he will in Nigerian pounds, will receive the same amount as he had anticipated. He will receive £100 Nigerian just the same; and he will be able to pay his growers accordingly. But, now suppose that in the contract for purchase the price had been, not £5 Nigerian, but £5 *sterling* a ton, so that the *money of account* was sterling. After devaluation, the buyer in England would be able to discharge his obligation by paying £100 sterling; but the Nigerian seller would suffer. For, when he transferred the £100 sterling to Nigeria, it would only be worth £86 Nigerian. So, instead of getting £100 Nigerian as he had anticipated, he would only get £86; and he would not have enough to pay his growers. So you see how vital it is to decide, in any contract, what is the *money of account* and what is the *money of payment*."[7]

This distinction was reaffirmed in *Procter and Gamble Co v Svenska Cellulosa Aktiebolaget SCA*,[8] where Lord Denning's dicta were cited. At first instance, Hilyard J referred to the "two-fold function" of money as both a means of measurement and a medium of payment,[9] noting that:

> "... it follows, not so much as a rule of law but as a consequence of this twofold function of money, that an agreement to pay in a currency (the mode or currency of payment) different

---

[7] *Woodhouse AC Israel Cocoa Ltd SA v Nigerian Produce Marketing Co Ltd* [1971] 2 Q.B. 23 CA (Civ Div) at 54.
[8] *Procter and Gamble Co v Svenska Cellulosa Aktiebolaget SCA* [2012] EWHC 498 (Ch), affirmed [2012] EWCA Civ 1413.
[9] Referring to F.A. Mann, *Mann on the Legal Aspect of Money*, 2nd edn (Oxford: Oxford University Press, 1953), p.847.

from the currency of measurement or account does not by inference or implication alter or affect the measurement of the obligation to pay."[10]

The place of payment

In the context of an international or foreign currency payment obligation, the place of payment also carries a certain significance. Where is payment due to be made? Can the debtor validly tender payment in a different place? The general rule in English law is that "the debtor must follow his creditor and must pay wherever his creditor is".[11]

6–03

Frustration of the payment obligation

A further question of some difficulty, which is more likely to arise in the case of international contracts than in relation to domestic transactions, is whether and in what circumstances a payment obligation can be frustrated, and if so, the legal consequences of frustration.[12]

6–04

Default in performance on the due date

The money of account measures the debtor's obligation at the date when payment falls due and, as indicated in the passage from Lord Denning's judgment quoted above, is relevant to the risk of loss arising through changes in exchange rates between the date of contract and the due date of payment. It is by determining the money of account that we ascertain whether that risk falls on the creditor or the debtor. This question is not concerned with remedies for default. We are assuming that payment is to be made on the due date and the only issue is: how much? An entirely separate set of questions arises where the debtor fails to pay the debt due and there is *then* a change in the rate of exchange as between the two currencies considered relevant for this purpose. In this case, the court may be called upon to determine who is to bear the risk of loss resulting from changes in the exchange rate between the due date of performance and the date of judgment (or, perhaps, the date when the judgment is sought to be enforced). It is necessary to

6–05

---

[10] *Procter and Gamble* [2012] EWHC 498 (Ch) at [75], approved by the Court of Appeal in [2012] EWCA Civ 1413 at [13], [21].
[11] *The Eider* [1893] P. 119, 131, 136. The United Nations Convention on Contracts for the International Sale of Goods (CISG) and the Principles of International Commercial Contracts (PICC) follow this approach; arts 57 and 6.1.6(1) respectively.
[12] This may become more pertinent if smart contracts, which are computer programmes or codes which automatically execute legal contracts, grow in popularity since this is likely to involve automated online payments where the place of performance may be unclear, although it has been argued some general categories of "excuses" for non-performance may be identified across legal systems which could be built into smart contracts; see Eric Tjong Tin Tai, "Force Majeure and Excuses in Smart Contracts" (2018) 26 *European Review of Private Law* 787. See Larry A. DiMatteo, Michel Cannarsa and Cristina Poncibò (eds), *The Cambridge Handbook of Smart Contracts, Blockchain Technology and Digital Platforms* (Cambridge: Cambridge University Press, 2009) for further information on the legal issues surrounding smart contracts.

distinguish clearly between pre-breach and post-breach exchange losses, for the rules applicable to the former do not necessarily apply to the latter. This point will be discussed further at a later stage.[13]

Procedural questions

6–06 Issues relating to the money of account, the money and place of payment and liability for exchange losses resulting from default in payment are matters of substantive law. Allied to these are two procedural issues affecting pursuit of the creditor's claim, namely the currency in which the claim must be made and the currency in which judgment is to be given and enforced. To label these questions procedural is perhaps to engender in the creditor's lawyers a false sense of security, for it suggests that we are involved with technical matters of litigation practice involving no more than a laborious examination of the Civil Procedure Rules, rather than questions of substance affecting the financial outcome of the suit. In fact, these procedural issues are of great importance, for they profoundly influence the amount of money the successful claimant will recover at the end of the day. Indeed, it is often overlooked that *Miliangos* laid down not a new rule of substantive law but a new rule of procedure. The significance of this distinction will become apparent a little later.

Conflicts of laws

6–07 The fourth cluster of questions arising in relation to foreign money obligations concerns the conflict of laws. Where a payment obligation is created by a contract involving a foreign element, which law is to govern the substantive rights of the parties, which law controls procedural issues and which courts have jurisdiction? The law which is to be applied depends very much on the nature of the issue before the court. Some questions are governed by the law applicable to the contract[14]; some by the *lex monetae*, i.e. the law of the country in whose currency payment is to be made; some by the law of the due place of payment; some by the law of the place where the proceedings are tried; and some by the law of the currency of judgment. This list by no means exhausts the possibilities, but in

---

[13] See para.6–14 below.
[14] The law applicable to the contract is the system of law which is intended to govern the parties' relationship. The identification of that system of the law is governed by Regulation 593/2008 on the law applicable to contractual obligations (Rome I) [2008] OJ L177/6. On Rome I, see generally, *Dicey, Morris & Collins* (2012), Chs 32 and 33. Under Rome I, the starting point is that a contract is governed by the law selected by the parties (art.3). Specific rules are provided to determine the law which governs particular types of agreements, e.g. contracts for the sale of goods and services, contracts relating to land, and franchise and distribution contracts. Other contracts will be governed by the law of the country in which the party required to perform the obligations which characterise the contract has his habitual residence, but all of these rules give way if it is clear from the circumstances that the contract has a closer connection with another country (art.4). In the present context, it is important to remember that an obligation to pay money does not generally "characterise" a contract for the purpose of applying the provisions just described. It will usually be the obligations of the seller of goods or the provider of services which are characteristic of the agreement between the parties.

most cases the identification of the legal system which is to govern a relevant issue will lead to one or other of the above.

To summarise, we have to establish, first, the measure and mode of performance due from the debtor, a question which involves (inter alia) determining which party bears the risk of pre-breach currency exchange losses; secondly, the creditor's substantive law and procedural rights where the debtor breaks his contract and incurs a liability in debt and/or damages; and thirdly, the state whose law is to be applied to determine a particular issue and whose courts will have jurisdiction to entertain the dispute. Each of these subjects will be considered in turn except for jurisdiction, a subject which falls outside the scope of this work.

2. Performance of the Payment Obligation

(i) The money of account

Establishing the money of account

The money of account is to be determined by construing the contract. Usually, the contract will make express provision for the money of account. Where it does not, the intention of the parties must be inferred from the language of the contract and the surrounding circumstances, and, in construing the contract, it is the law applicable to the contract, not the law of the place of payment, which should normally be applied.[15] Sometimes, the meaning of a currency provision in a contract is ambiguous. For example, a contract providing for payment in dollars may not make it clear whether what is meant is US dollars, Canadian dollars, Australian dollars or the dollar denomination of some other country. In such cases, reference must be made to the law applicable to the debt.[16]

6–08

A contract providing for a specified money of account may, of course, be varied so as to select a different currency as the money of account. It is a question of intention as to whether a variation as to the currency of payment relates to the money of account or merely to the money of payment. A case in point is *Woodhouse AC Israel Cocoa Ltd SA v Nigerian Produce Marketing Co Ltd*,[17] in which Lord Denning gave the expository judgment quoted earlier.

---

[15] Substantive matters concerning the interpretation and performance of a contract are governed by the law applicable to it: see art.12(1) of Rome I, although note that, in assessing matters touching the mode or manner of performance, the court is required to have regard to the law of the place of performance: Rome I art.12(2). See *Bonython v Australia* [1951] A.C. 201 PC and numerous other authorities noted by *Dicey, Morris & Collins* (2012), para.37R–051. The role of the law of the place of performance is discussed below.

[16] *Bonython* [1951] A.C. 201 PC. Where the contract relates to a market which operates in a particular currency (e.g. the oil and gold markets operate in US dollars), it will usually be inferred that the parties intended a reference to that currency. Where a statute is involved, the matter will usually be even clearer; in *Trigg v Revenue and Customs Commissioners* [2016] UKUT 165 (TCC), it was held in the context of the liability of certain corporate bonds to capital gains tax that the word "sterling" in a UK statute referred to the lawful currency of the UK, namely the pound sterling, and could not be interpreted as referring to any other currency.

[17] *Woodhouse* [1971] 2 Q.B. 23 CA (Civ Div) affirmed [1972] A.C. 741.

Nigerian sellers contracted to sell cocoa to English buyers under a contract by which both the money of account and the money of payment were Nigerian pounds. Anticipating the devaluation of sterling, the buyers asked the sellers to agree that payment could be made in sterling. This the sellers did. Soon afterwards, sterling was devalued by 14%, but the Nigerian pound retained its value. The buyers contended that, as the result of the sellers' agreement to allow payment in sterling, the buyers were entitled to tender payment in devalued pounds sterling as if the contract price had been fixed in sterling. This contention was rejected by the Court of Appeal, which held that the money of account had remained Nigerian pounds throughout and that it was by reference to Nigerian pounds that the buyers' payment obligation had to be measured. The sellers' agreement to allow payment in sterling related purely to the money of payment, i.e. the currency in which tender of payment could be made. In consequence, it was the duty of the buyers either to pay the designated price in Nigerian pounds or to pay the sterling equivalent of the Nigerian price as at the date of payment, i.e. at the rate of £116.50s for each NGN £100.

The money of account thus determines the measure or quantum of the obligation. The point is illustrated by the decision in *Procter and Gamble*,[18] where the price of goods was expressed in terms of euros but was payable in sterling. In the absence of a contractually agreed rate, the creditor was thus entitled to receive the sterling equivalent of the specified amount at the rate prevailing on the due date for payment. In other words, the creditor was entitled to receive "euro equivalent value" on that date. If payment was then made after the due date, the creditor would be entitled to damages in respect of exchange rate losses[19] or, if he operated in sterling, to interest in respect of late payment.[20]

Of course, as in the case of any other contractual term, a provision dealing with the money of account may be varied by an express or implied agreement to that effect. This argument was made, although rejected, in *Addax Bank BSC v Wellesley Partners LLP*.[21] The parties had agreed to invest in a joint venture company by subscribing for equity in US dollars. One of the parties remitted his funds in sterling at the GBP/USD exchange rate prevailing on the date of payment. Nevertheless, when part of his subscription monies became repayable at a later date, he sought repayment in dollars. The claim was resisted on the basis that, having contributed sterling, the required repayment should likewise be made in sterling. However, this defence was rejected. The claimant had used sterling as an expedient to meet a US dollar obligation and the company had received the correct amount in terms of the exchange. The original arrangements for a sterling payment thus did not alter the fact that the US dollar provided the contractual currency of account.

---

[18] *Procter and Gamble* [2012] EWCA Civ 1413.
[19] See the discussion at para.6–44.
[20] See *Golden Strait Corp v Nippon Yusen Kubishka Kaisha (The Golden Victory)* [2007] 2 A.C. 353.
[21] *Addax Bank BSC v Wellesley Partners LLP* [2010] EWHC 1904 (QB).

The principle of nominalism

Reference was made earlier to the universally adopted principle of nominalism by which the debtor is required to pay, in the designated money of payment, a sum equal to the nominal value of the money of account, regardless of fluctuations in the internal value of the money of account (through inflation or loss of domestic purchasing power) or in its external value (through an adverse change in exchange rates).[22] In the *Woodhouse* case,[23] it was the debtor who suffered the exchange losses since he had to use his own depreciated currency to purchase a foreign money of account whose value had remained constant. However, if the position had been reversed and the Nigerian pound had been devalued in relation to sterling, the Nigerian sellers would have had to put a brave face on it and accept payment in depreciated currency—Nigerian pounds being the money of account that was what the sellers had to take, for good or ill. Where the unit of account has been changed by the law of the country which issues the currency concerned, the debtor's obligation is to pay in the new currency at the conversion rate furnished by the *lex monetae*.[24] This may sound theoretical but it does happen; the most recent major substitution was effected through the introduction of the euro on 1 January 1999. The respective rates at which individual European currencies were replaced were determined by an EC Regulation[25] which does of course have direct application in the Member States concerned. Since the relevant EU regulations provide the *lex monetae* for the new currency, the conversion rates should be applied internationally, i.e. even in courts sitting outside the EU and even in relation to contracts governed by a non-EU system of law.[26]

6–09

Exceptions to the principle of nominalism

However, whilst the principle of nominalism is strictly applied in England, some exceptions are admitted. Two of these are established, the third is conjectural so far as English law is concerned but is thought to be available in a suitable case.

6–10

(1) Express contract provision: currency clauses

The most common and obvious exception is where the principle is displaced by an express currency clause designed to protect one or both of the parties against a change in exchange rates.[27] A case in point is *Aruna Mills Ltd v Dhanrajmal Gobindram*.[28]

6–11

---

[22] See para.3–02 above.
[23] See fn.17 above.
[24] The conversion rate provides the so-called "recurrent link" between the old currency and its replacement. Debts contracted in the former unit are thus settled in the new currency at the relevant substitution or conversion rate.
[25] Regulation 2866/98 on the conversion rates between the euro and the currencies of the Member States adopting the euro [1998] OJ L359/1. The Regulation has subsequently been amended on a number of occasions to cater for more recent entrants to the Eurozone. See fnn.33 and 34 in Ch.3 above.
[26] See paras 3–09 to 3–10 above for further discussion of the euro.
[27] At least so far as English law is concerned, the application of the principle of nominalism is derived from the *presumed* intention of the contracting parties. It must, therefore, give way to a

The sellers agreed to sell a quantity of cotton to the buyers at a price expressed in Indian rupees. The contract contained a clause by which the buyers agreed to bear and pay the difference, if any, in the exchange rate between the date of the contract and the date on which the full price was paid. The sellers were late in shipping the goods and, between the due date of shipment and the actual shipment date, the Indian rupee was devalued. The buyers paid the appropriately increased price in accordance with the currency clause, but were held entitled (subject to a further finding of fact by the arbitrators) to recover the increase as damages for the sellers' breach of contract in shipping late.

Linking a domestic currency obligation to a foreign currency, as by indexing a sterling obligation by reference to any post-contract increase in the value of the Swiss franc in relation to sterling, has been held to be a legitimate contractual safeguard against a fall in the purchasing power of the amount repayable and consequently not contrary to public policy.[29]

(2) Revalorisation of debt under foreign proper law

6–12 Whilst no English court has yet accepted the argument that, in a contract governed by English law, a debt may be revalorised or devalorised to take account of a fall or increase in the external or internal value of the money of account, there are some jurisdictions where such an argument has succeeded, usually because of a collapse in the value of the currency in question to a degree not experienced in this country.[30] Since currency always retains its nominal value in the country of issue, the impact of a rise or fall in its external or internal purchasing power on the debtor's contractual obligation to pay is a matter not for the *lex monetae* but for the law applicable to the debt.[31] Under English conflict of laws rules, this is the law applicable to the contract creating the debt.[32] If the debt is governed by a foreign law which admits of revalorisation or devalorisation of the debtor's obligation in the events that have occurred, an English court applying the proper law will revalorise or devalorise the debt in the same way as if it were a court of the foreign state concerned.[33] The three leading English cases[34] concerned the German mark, the value of which plummeted to an almost unbelievable extent after the end of the First World War. In 1924, the mark was converted into the reichsmark at the astronomical rate of one billion old marks for one reichsmark. The German legislation made no general provision as to the effect on contractual obligations of the virtual extinction of the old mark, and the German courts eventually established that it was for the court itself to revalorise the debt according to what was just in all the circumstances—having regard to the

---

contrary intention which is explicitly stated. Given the derivation of the rule, there is no principle of English public policy which denies to the parties their right to vary the application of the principle.

[28] *Aruna Mills Ltd v Dhanrajmal Gobindram* [1968] 1 Q.B. 655 QBD (Comm).
[29] *Multiservice Bookbinding Ltd v Marden* [1979] Ch. 84 Ch D. See para.3–06 above.
[30] See *Mann* (2012), paras 13.09 onwards, for a detailed discussion of revalorisation and illustrations.
[31] *Anderson v Equitable Life Assurance Society of the US* (1926) 134 L.T. 557; *Re Schnapper* [1936] 1 All E.R. 322; *Kornatzki v Oppenheimer* [1937] 4 All E.R. 133.
[32] See fn.12 above.
[33] *Re Schnapper*; and *Kornatzki v Oppenheimer* at fn.31 above.
[34] *Anderson*; *Re Schnapper*; and *Kornatzki v Oppenheimer* at fn.15 above.

general requirements of good faith and fair commercial dealing (*Treu und Glauben*) imposed on the debtor by s.242 of the German Civil Code. In two cases, *Re Schnapper*[35] and *Kornatzki v Oppenheimer*,[36] an English court applied German law as the law applicable to the debt and revalorised the debt as if the matter were being heard before a German court.

However, revalorisation of the debt to take account of changes in the value of a designated foreign currency of payment will not be undertaken by an English court merely because the debt would be revalorised under the *lex monetae*. Revalorisation will be allowed only if permitted by the law applicable to the contract at hand since that is the system of the law which governs substantive matters, such as the quantum of the obligation. So where insurance moneys became payable in London in German marks under a policy of insurance governed by English law, the court declined to take account of the fall in the value of the mark between the time the policy was taken out in 1887 and its value when the policy moneys became payable in 1922, and the plaintiff was held entitled to no more than the amount of marks stipulated in the policy or their sterling equivalent in 1922.[37]

It is necessary to emphasise two points concerning the effect of a change in a country's unit of account. The first is that, even where the contract providing for the payment is governed by the law of that country, the mere fact that the legislation fixes a rate for converting old currency into new does not of itself conclude the revalorisation question. The sole effect of such legislation (except so far as it provides otherwise) is that an obligation to pay a given number of units of the old currency is converted into an obligation to pay whatever is the equivalent in the new currency at the given conversion rate. The fact that the *unit of account* has changed is not directly relevant to the question of whether the *debt* should be revalorised. Even the rate of conversion is material only to the extent that it provides evidence of the factual devaluation of the old currency. Hence, unless required to do otherwise by the legislation prescribing the new currency or by other legislation, the courts of the country whose currency is changed will apply the general principles of contract law, or of the law of obligations, to determine the effect on the contracting parties of the factual devaluation that has occurred. The second point is that, even where the law of the country whose currency is altered makes express provision for the effect of the conversion on contract rights, or indeed goes further and provides for revalorisation in order to take account of the factual devaluation in the old currency, a foreign court will regard such law as irrelevant if it does not form part of the law applicable to the contract. So, to return to the example of the depreciated German mark, an English court would ignore any German law providing for the revalorisation of a debt *unless* the contract creating the debt is also governed by German law. German law, as the *lex monetae*, governs the question of what constitutes German currency and the value of the new mark in terms of the old mark, but, so far as an English court is concerned, it has no relevance to the substance or quantum of the debtor's obligation under a contract governed by English law.

---

[35] *Re Schnapper* [1936] 1 All E.R. 322.
[36] *Kornatzki* [1937] 4 All E.R. 133.
[37] *Anderson* (1926) 134 L.T. 557.

(3) Extreme loss of value

6–13 There are few absolutes in English law, and, whilst the reluctance of the English courts to admit the notion of revalorisation reflects a more general unwillingness to regard change of circumstances as affecting a party's duty to perform a contract,[38] one can imagine extreme situations in which the court would be prepared to revalorise a debt—in particular, where a fall in the value of the money of account, whether English or foreign, was so extraordinary as to evidence a virtual extinction of the unit of account. In practice, however, the courts have thus far shown themselves reluctant to invoke the doctrine of frustration in a manner which would detract from the principle of nominalism, perhaps for fear of the uncertainty which this might create in the crucial sphere of monetary obligations; they have instead attempted to assist a disadvantaged creditor by other means. Thus, for example, where the relevant currency depreciates during the course of a long-term contract, the court may afford relief to the creditor by implying the right to terminate on reasonable notice, thereby effectively allowing the creditor to renegotiate the commercial deal.[39] There may also be cases in which the contract contemplates the possibility of price adjustments but does not provide the necessary mechanisms in the event that the parties fail to agree; the court may imply a term requiring the parties to appoint an arbitrator or arrange for an expert determination.[40] These methods provide a measure of justice to a creditor affected by inflation or the loss of value in money without affecting this core monetary law principle. But such solutions are less likely to be adopted in the case of an executory contract, where the court would probably deal with the matter through the more traditional route of frustration.[41]

The effective extinction of a national currency is thankfully a relatively rare event. However, a recent example is offered by Zimbabwe where confidence in the local unit collapsed as hyperinflation asserted its grip over the local economy. This led to a multi-currency regime being introduced in February 2009 and other currencies being used. Ultimately the Zimbabwean dollar was suspended as the national currency in June 2009.[42] In 2015, the country switched to the US dollar as the country's legal tender. Although the Zimbabwean government introduced the renamed "Zimbabwean dollar" in June 2019, this has led to a new period of hyperinflation and it remains to be seen what the result will be. As might be expected, these events caused difficulties where obligations were incurred in the former national unit but the resultant litigation happened after the suspension date of the currency.

---

[38] Thus, it is extremely difficult to persuade an English court that a sharp deterioration in the value of the contract to one of the parties entitles him to treat the contract as frustrated.

[39] See, in particular, *Staffordshire AHA v South Staffordshire Waterworks Co* [1978] 1 W.L.R. 1387 CA (Civ Div).

[40] i.e. it will avoid holding the contract to be void for certainty. For an example of this approach, see the decision of the Privy Council in *Queensland Electricity Generating Board v New Hope Collieries* [1989] 1 Lloyd's Rep. 205 PC. This case has been noted at para.3–08 above.

[41] See *Mann* (2012), para.9.25.

[42] Under the Zimbabwean Presidential Powers (Temporary Measures) (Currency Revaluation and Issue of New Currency) Regulations 2009 (SI 6 of 2009).

The Zimbabwean courts have had to address this issue multiple times. The approach taken appears to depend on the particular context, with courts much more willing to allow conversion in the employment context. In *Madhatter Mining Co Ltd v Tapfuma*,[43] which concerned damages payable in lieu of reinstatement by an employer to an employee, the Supreme Court of Zimbabwe observed that:

> "The principles of equity and social justice ... are all called into question when it comes to determining the basis and formula for computing a debt (e.g., damages) suffered in Zimbabwean currency but claimed in a foreign currency. This is particularly so where such damages, being owed to an employee, can no longer be paid in Zimbabwean currency realistically or in a way that gives due value to the employee ... ."

Nevertheless, the court went on to note that:

> "The undeniable fact is that a debt is not wiped out by the mere fact that there has been a change to the realisable currency. Equity would demand that a formula be found to give effect to the employee's entitlement to payment of, and the employer's obligation to pay, the debt in question ... ."[44]

In this case, the Supreme Court remitted the question of currency conversion to the Labour Court which could apply the relevant principles of equity and social justice, in particular, in deciding whether to apply the prevailing exchange rates as at the date on which the relevant obligation was incurred (i.e. as opposed to the date of the judgment).[45] In another case, it appears to have been specifically argued that an award of damages in US dollars would be inconsistent with the principle of nominalism.[46] The court upheld the conversion on the basis that "the Zimbabwean dollar is no longer in use since the beginning of the multicurrency system ..."[47] and noted an earlier decision[48] to the effect that "this court should declare that in the realm of employment relations, the principle of nominalism has for now, no place until economic normalcy has been restored ...".[49]

Outside the employment context, however, the courts appear more ready to uphold the principle of nominalism. In *Makoni v Sea Harvest*,[50] for example, the plaintiff sought after the introduction of the multi-currency regime in February 2009 to have personal injury damages awarded to him as a result of a motor vehicle accident redenominated in US dollars, rather than Zimbabwean dollars. The High Court refused this, holding that that the principles enunciated in the context of labour disputes, such as social justice and equity, were not applicable in the present context so, in the absence of legislative authority enabling the court

---

[43] *Madhatter Mining Co Ltd v Tapfuma* [2014] ZWSC 51.
[44] *Madhatter Mining* [2014] ZWSC 51 at [16].
[45] As occurred in the earlier Supreme Court case of *Olivine Industries (Pvt) Ltd v Nharara* [2006] ZWSC 77, where damages were awarded at the rates prevailing at that time.
[46] *University of Zimbabwe v Sibanda* [2014] ZWLC 21.
[47] *University of Zimbabwe* [2014] ZWLC 21 at [7]. However, see *Ballantyne Butchery (Pvt) Ltd v Chisvinga & Others (Civil Appeal No. SC 243/12)* [2015] ZWSC 06, where the relevant date was considered to be the suspension of the currency in June 2009 not the start of the multi-currency regime in February 2009 and therefore conversion was denied.
[48] *Gift Bob David Samanyau v Fleximail (Pvt) Ltd* 2011 HH 108–11.
[49] *University of Zimbabwe* [2014] ZWLC 21 at [5].
[50] *Makoni v Sea Harvest (Ref SC 19/08)* [2015] ZWHHC 197.

to look at judgments before dollarization in January 2009, the court must be guided by the usual common law rules. The judge reaffirmed, with reference to earlier cases, that the principle of currency nominalism was part of the law of Zimbabwe.[51]

The principle of nominalism does not affect damages for delay in payment

6–14 It is important to bear in mind that the principle of nominalism is relevant only to the measurement of the debtor's primary contractual obligation. That is to say, the principle features in quantifying the payment obligation *as at the due date of payment*. The award of damages to a creditor for exchange losses suffered because of the debtor's delay in payment is in no way inconsistent with the principle of nominalism. A creditor who makes no provision for exchange losses when specifying sterling as the money of account has no cause for complaint if his debtor tenders payment at the due date in devalued sterling, for that is the bargain the parties have made. But the creditor does not bargain for default in payment, and, upon such default, he is entitled to recover not only the debt but such damages, including loss in exchange, as the applicable law may entitle him to obtain.[52]

Covering exchange risks

6–15 There are various ways in which the prudent creditor can cover himself against exchange risks. These include currency fluctuation clauses in the contract itself; currency matching, by borrowing in the same currency as lending; swaps; and similar instruments.

Covering fluctuations in internal purchasing power

6–16 Similarly, the creditor can protect himself against a fall in the internal purchasing power of the stipulated currency by an indexation clause linking the debtor's repayment obligation to some suitable index.[53] The Supreme Court's decision in *Arnold v Britton*[54] indicates that such protections will most likely be upheld even if they represent an extremely bad bargain for the debtor.

---

[51] *Makoni* [2015] ZWHHC 197, referring to *Shava v Bergus Investments (Pvt) Ltd* 2011 (2)ZLR 430 (HC) and *Mukorera v Ocean Breeze Engine and Cooling Systems* HH 13–-08 (Unreported). Even within the employment context, the Supreme Court recently rejected the contention that the Labour Court has jurisdiction to interfere with already granted awards by converting them into another currency: *First Mutual Life Assurance v Muzivi* [2020] ZWHHC 4.

[52] See para.6–38 below.

[53] See *Multiservice Bookbinding Ltd v Marden* [1979] Ch. 84 Ch D, discussed at para.3–07 above.

[54] *Arnold v Britton* [2015] A.C. 1619, discussed at para.3–08 above. See also *MetLife Seguros De Retiro SA v JP Morgan Chase Bank* [2016] EWCA Civ 1248 applying *Arnold*, where the Court of Appeal rejected the argument that a different method of calculating the redemption amount on structured loan notes should be applied on the basis that the Argentinian government had manipulated the CER inflation index on which the amount was to be based.

(ii) The money of payment

It will be recalled that the money of payment relates not to the substance or measure of the debtor's obligation but simply to the mode of its performance. In what form is the debtor entitled to tender payment of a foreign money obligation? 6–17

Applicable law

It should be said at the outset that the money of account and the money of payment will, in most contractual situations, coincide. Thus, if a lender makes advances in US dollars and the loan agreement provides that "[a]ll payment by the Borrower under this Agreement shall be made . . . in the lawful money of the United States in Federal Reserve Bank Funds . . .", then the US dollar is both the money of account and the money of payment.[55] Issues of the type discussed in this section will normally arise only where the money of account differs from the money of payment. 6–18

The first question is: which law governs the determination of the money of payment? This is not altogether easy to answer, because two conflicting principles of the private international law come into play. It has already been noted that questions touching the substance of a contractual obligation (including its interpretation and legal effect) are governed by the law applicable to the contract.[56] However, in relation to questions touching the mode or manner of performance, the court is required to "have regard" to the law of the place of performance.[57] How do these potentially conflicting principles interact with each other? The starting point should be that, where the contract specifically states that payment is to be made in a particular currency, then that choice should be respected by the court. In other words, the law applicable to the contract should prevail in such a case. It is often said that, otherwise, questions touching the identity of the money of payment should be governed by the law of the place of payment.[58] In practice, it is submitted that it should rarely be necessary to have recourse to the law of the place of performance. In the vast majority of cases, it seems appropriate to assume that the parties intend that the money of account and the money of payment are to be one and the same.

In summary, therefore, the law applicable to the contract will determine the identity of the money of account and, in the absence of some countervailing features, it will also determine the money of the payment. The law of the place of payment may have a role to play in addressing matters not covered by the express or implied terms of the contract, e.g. whether payment is required to be made in cash or whether a cheque may or must be accepted in settlement.

---

[55] This rather obvious point was noted by the Federal Court of Australia in *Robe River Mining Co Pty Ltd v Commissioner of Taxation* [1988] FCA 303.
[56] Regulation 593/2008 on the law applicable to contractual obligations (Rome I) [2008] OJ L117/6.
[57] Rome I art.12(2).
[58] This was the position taken by the first edition of this work: *Goode on Payment Obligations in Commercial and Financial Transactions*, edited by Roy Goode and Charles Proctor, 1st edn (London: Sweet & Maxwell, 1983), p.130. See also *Dicey, Morris & Collins* (2012), para.37R–051.

The money of payment under English law

6–19 Where payment in foreign money is to be made in England, the debtor prima facie has the option of tendering the foreign currency itself or its sterling equivalent.[59] Whilst this rule seems to be well established, it is submitted that the principle would benefit from reconsideration. Whilst the rule is perhaps acceptable and convenient in the context of a fixed exchange rate regime, it may cause loss to the creditor in a modern context. For example, if the debt is due in dollars but the debtor pays in sterling, then the applicable exchange rate may have moved by the time the creditor is able to instruct his bank to convert the proceeds into dollars. It may well be that the debtor should be *obliged* to pay in sterling if it has become unlawful for him to pay in dollars[60] but, in the context of the modern financial markets where foreign currency payments can readily be made, there is no obvious reason why he should have an *option* to do so. The option to pay in sterling can be excluded by the terms of the contract, and it is suggested that the court should be very willing to reach that conclusion where, for example, the contract contemplates a credit to a US dollar account in London.

As noted earlier,[61] the starting presumption is that payment must be made in legal tender under the rules of the *lex monetae* (English, if payment is tendered in sterling; American, if tendered in dollars). It might be thought that this presumption should be readily displaced, especially in high value financial transactions where the delivery of notes will involve the risks of theft or loss. Yet, in *Libyan Arab Foreign Bank v Bankers Trust Co*,[62] Staughton J held that a depositor may be entitled to repayment of US $292,000,000 *in physical cash* if it becomes unlawful to make payment through the New York clearing system. Although the depositor was entitled to judgment in that case, this particular aspect of the decision must be treated with care. Apart from the practical considerations, it should not be difficult to imply a term that payment is to be effected through the banking system or, alternatively, an appropriate meaning may be placed on the express terms of the contract. For example, in *Tenax Steamship Co v Owners of the Motor Vessel Brimnes (The Brimnes)*, a contractual term stipulating for "payment in cash" was construed to mean "any commercially recognised method of transferring the funds the result of which was to give the transferee an unconditional right to the immediate use" of the funds transferred.[63] It is submitted that this approach is plainly right, although it must be carefully

---

[59] *Adelaide Electric Supply Co Ltd v Prudential Assurance Co Ltd* [1934] A.C. 122 HL; *Marrache v Ashton* [1943] A.C. 311 PC; *Barclays Bank International Ltd v Levin Bros (Bradford) Ltd* [1977] Q.B. 270 QBD (Comm). See *Dicey, Morris & Collins* (2012), paras 37–054 to 37–055.

[60] This was one of the solutions discussed in *Libyan Arab Foreign Bank v Bankers Trust Co* [1989] Q.B. 728 QBD (Comm).

[61] See para.2–01 above.

[62] *Libyan Arab* [1989] Q.B. 728.

[63] *Tenax Steamship Co v Owners of the Motor Vessel Brimnes (The Brimnes)* [1973] 1 W.L.R. 386 QBD (Admlty) at 399. This approach to the matter was approved by the Court of Appeal in the same case [1975] Q.B. 929 CA (Civ Div) at 948, 965 and 968, and cited in *PT Berlian Laju Tanker TBK v Nuse Shipping Ltd (The Aktor)* [2008] 2 All E.R. (Comm) 784 at [21]. The approval of the Court of Appeal in *Mardorf Peach & Co Ltd v Attica Sea Carriers Corp of Liberia (The Laconia)* [1976] Q.B. 835 also remains valid even though the actual decision in that case was reversed by the House of Lords [1977] A.C. 850 HL.

noted that the bank transfer will only discharge the payment obligation if the creditor receives immediate and unconditional access to the full amount required.[64]

It may be noted that developments occurring since the decision in the *Libyan Arab* case may also have diluted the creditor's right to demand payment in cash. In particular, modern anti-money laundering legislation is inimical to the receipt of large amounts of physical cash.[65] Considerations of this kind may reinforce the view that the right to payment in physical cash should be readily excluded.

(iii) The place of payment

As noted earlier,[66] it is the duty of the debtor to seek out his creditor, with the result that the place of payment will usually be the country in which the creditor is resident. This may, of course, yield to the express or implied terms of the contract at issue.

6–20

The identification of the place of payment for a foreign money obligation may be important for a variety of purposes. For example, it has already been seen that a court is required to "have regard" to the law of the place of performance in questions concerning the manner or the mode of payment. It will be seen that contracts may not be enforced if payment has become illegal under the laws of the country in which it is required to occur. So where is the place of payment for a foreign money obligation?

This question may occasionally give rise to confusion because, as has been seen,[67] a credit to a US dollar account maintained in London will generally involve a movement across correspondent accounts in New York. In such a case, however, London is the *place of payment* because it is the place in which the bank is required to credit the customer, and it is the place in which his US dollar account is booked. English law therefore supplies the law of the place of performance. New York provides the *place of settlement* but this has very limited relevance for private international law purposes.[68]

As a general rule, the debtor must tender payment in accordance with the terms of the contract, including any requirement as to the place of payment. Where delivery and payment are intended to be concurrent conditions, it may generally be assumed that the place of delivery and the place of payment are to coincide.[69] This point is neatly illustrated by the decision of the Commercial Court in *PT Berlian Laju Tanker TBK v Nuse Shipping Ltd (The Aktor)*.[70] In that case,

6–21

---

[64] For a decision of the House of Lords which emphasises the importance of this point, see *Awilco of Oslo A/S v Fulvia SpA di Navigazione of Cagliari (The Chikuma)* [1981] 1 W.L.R. 314 HL.
[65] See in particular the Proceeds of Crime Act 2002 and the discussion at para.5–41 above.
[66] See para.2–33 above.
[67] See generally Ch.5.
[68] On the distinction between the place of payment and the place of settlement, see *Wells Fargo Asia Ltd v Citibank NA* 936 F.2d 723 C.A.2 (N.Y.) (2nd Cir. 1991), cert. denied 505 U.S. 1204 (1992). See also the decision in *Libyan Arab* [1989] Q.B. 728 QBD (Comm).
[69] This would minimise the difficulties which might otherwise be caused by differing time zones between the places of delivery and the place of payment. It is, however, open to the parties to adopt a different course by the express terms of their contract.
[70] *The Aktor* [2008] 2 All E.R. (Comm) 784.

Indonesian buyers had agreed to purchase a vessel on the Norwegian Sale Form 1993. On signature of the contract, a 10% security deposit was paid into an escrow account with a bank in Singapore. As the time for completion approached, the sellers nominated a bank in Athens to receive the purchase price. The buyers indicated that they would pay the 90% balance to that account, but that the first 10% would be paid by instructing the Singapore bank to release the escrow account to the sellers. In substance, the court held that the 100% of the purchase price was payable at the Athens bank, and that it was the buyers' job to ensure that the 10% also found its way to the nominated bank.[71] The offer of payment in Singapore thus did not constitute a valid tender because the Singapore bank had no authority to accept that tender on behalf of the seller.[72]

The court also rejected the argument that payment in Athens was not a condition of the contract and that refusal to pay there did thus not constitute a repudiatory breach. As the court forcefully observed[73]:

> "The parties cannot have contemplated that the Sellers would be bound to make delivery of a valuable vessel without payment in full of the purchase price in accordance with the terms of the contract. Crediting the Sellers with some or all of the purchase price other than at the place stipulated for payment would be likely to prevent redemption at the time of payment and out of the payment of any mortgage on the vessel, as would ordinarily be expected, and expose the Sellers to risk in transferring the monies from the contractual place where or from which the Buyers purported to make payment, to the place agreed. Monies that pass through the banking system may become unavailable to the payee because of claims to the money, or claims to freeze the money, by banks or others."

In short, a debtor will commit a breach of contract, which may be repudiatory depending on the facts, if he insists on tendering payment in a place other than that stipulated in the contract.

(iv) Can a payment obligation be frustrated?

6–22 Are there any circumstances in which the obligation to pay money may become extinguished through supervening physical impossibility, supervening change of law or executive acts of government? If so, what are the legal consequences of frustration?

Physical impossibility

6–23 Only in very rare situations can physical impossibility arise in relation to the payment of money. This is because a monetary obligation is essentially abstract. The creditor's concern is solely with units of account to a given nominal value,

---

[71] As the court pointed out, the sellers may have had legitimate reasons for this requirement. The ship was mortgaged to the Athens bank and the full proceeds may have been required to redeem that security. In addition, the 10% was an "earnest" deposit and was not of itself part payment for the vessel.

[72] In this respect, the court relied on *Mann* (2012), paras 7.08, 7.12 and 7.19(d), and some of the decisions there noted.

[73] *The Aktor* [2008] 2 All E.R. (Comm) 784 at [68].

not with specific or even quasi-specific[74] coins or notes. A stipulation that a debt of £100 is to be paid only by tender of specific coins or notes, or of unascertained coins or notes from a specific source (e.g. a money box), may be said to make the debtor's obligation one for the delivery of goods, not the payment of money.[75] It follows that, there being no contractual source of supply, the debtor cannot plead the physical destruction of the subject matter of the contract any more than he could in the case of a contract to deliver wholly unascertained goods. For example, the debtor owes £100—he may intend to pay the debt by using the pound notes he has stuffed beneath the mattress in his bedroom, but that is no concern of the creditor. If a thief steals the notes, the debtor must pay with money obtained elsewhere.

The position is no different where the contractual unit of account is replaced, as where legislation is enacted substituting a new national currency for its predecessor. This does not frustrate the payment obligation, for the unit of account is an abstraction, a measure of value, not a tangible object of a delivery obligation. All that happens when the unit of account is changed is that the debtor's obligation to pay a given number of old units becomes converted into an obligation to pay the equivalent value in new units at the conversion rate prescribed by the law creating the new currency.[76] Whether coins or notes of the old currency remain in existence and accessible to the debtor is irrelevant. As they have ceased to be currency, he cannot compel the creditor to accept them.[77]

Supervening illegality

Rather more difficult is the case where, as the result of a change of law or of executive action under the existing law at the place where payment is due, the debtor finds himself legally unable to make payment at that place.[78] The first point to note is that the law of the place of payment, although in some respects relevant to the mode of payment,[79] is not as such relevant in determining the impact on the contract of an obstacle to payment created by or under that law. It is for the law applicable to the contract to declare what effect, if any, the debtor's inability to pay at the due place of performance has on the contract as a whole.[80] So an English court called upon to decide whether a contract governed by French law and providing for payment in Greece is frustrated by the enactment of Greek

6–24

---

[74] i.e. an unascertained part of an identified bulk or source, e.g. a box, a warehouse.
[75] i.e. the obligation refers to designated notes and coins, rather than to money in a fungible sense.
[76] This is the so called "recurrent link" to which reference has already been made: see fn.21 above.
[77] The introduction of the euro offered an interesting demonstration of the fact that a *currency* is abstract, and that physical notes and coins are a *physical* representation of it. Although the euro was introduced as a currency on 1 January 1999, physical notes and coins were only introduced on 1 January 2002. During the interim (or "transitional") period, the national notes and coins constituting the former national currencies "represented" the euro at the prescribed substitution rates. On the whole subject, see *Mann* (2012), paras 29.16–29.21. See paras 3–09 to 3–10 above for more information on the euro.
[78] As has been shown, the place of payment for a Eurodollar deposit is the branch of the bank at which the account is held. New York does not become the place of payment merely because funds may have to move through correspondent accounts in that city.
[79] See para.5–24 above.
[80] Rome I art.12(1)(b) and (d).

legislation prohibiting the payment in or from Greece, will apply French law to determine the issue.[81] Where the contract is governed by English law, the court should, it is submitted, apply the same principles as in the case of prevention of performance by a change in English law. This approach can be seen in the recent case of *Deutsche Bank AG v Unitech Global Ltd*,[82] where, in relation to contracts governed by English law, one argument put forward by the debtor was that the contracts in question should be unenforceable because Indian exchange control regulations meant that it was illegal for it to make repayments and English law will not require a party to do something that is illegal in the place where it must be done. The Court of Appeal impliedly accepted this,[83] but disagreed that India was the place of performance since the contracts required the payment of dollars in New York and it was not illegal for the debtor to make payments of dollars in New York.[84]

There is, in fact, no general principle of English law that a contract is frustrated because of supervening impossibility. Of course, the court cannot order the specific performance of that which has become impossible, but it can and will award damages for non-performance except in circumstances where the event rendering performance impossible is considered such as to justify non-performance. Thus, impossibility does not frustrate the contract where it is self-induced (as where S contracts to sell specific goods to A and instead sells and delivers them to B, or contracts to supply goods for the export of which an export licence is required and neglects to apply for the licence)[85] or where the party disabled from performing had expressly or by implication assumed the risk that performance would be blocked by or under local law.[86] Again, there is no frustration where, under an English statute applicable to the transaction, the prescribed machinery for collecting payment is dispensed with in cases where the use of such machinery becomes impossible.[87]

6–25 However, English law does in general regard a contract as frustrated where, through a change in law or through executive action, it becomes impossible for a

---

[81] *Toprak Mahsulleri Ofisi v Finagrain Compagnie Commerciale Agricole et Financière SA* [1979] 2 Lloyd's Rep. 98 CA (Civ Div); *Power Curber International Ltd v National Bank of Kuwait SAK* [1981] 1 W.L.R. 1233 CA (Civ Div).
[82] *Deutsche Bank AG v Unitech Global Ltd* [2016] EWCA Civ 119, applying *Toprak* at fn.81 above.
[83] See the discussion of this issue, including authorities cited, at *Deutsche Bank* [2016] EWCA Civ 119 at [33]–[38].
[84] See also *Dana Gas PJSC v Dana Gas Sukuk Ltd* [2017] EWHC 2928 (an undertaking by deed forming part of an Islamic finance transaction was not unenforceable as contrary to public policy where the underlying finance transaction was unlawful under United Arab Emirates law since none of the obligations it imposed were intended to be performed in the UAE).
[85] *Agroexport State Enterprise for Foreign Trade v Compagnie Européenne de Céréales* [1974] 1 Lloyd's Rep. 499 QBD (Comm).
[86] *Toprak*, at fn.81 above; *Peter Cassidy Seed Co v Osuustukkukauppa IL* [1957] 1 W.L.R. 273 QBD (Comm). However, the outcome may be different if the party has not assumed the risk, for instance, because there is a pre-condition or a performance condition that a necessary consent or approval will be obtained; see e.g. *Nautica Marine Limited v Trafigura Trading LLC* [2020] EWHC 1986 (Comm) (where a pre-condition was found and therefore there was no obligation to take all reasonable steps to obtain a supplier's approval as there would be with a performance condition).
[87] *Cornelius v Banque Franco-Serbe* [1942] 1 K.B. 29, where failure to present a cheque in Amsterdam by reason of the German invasion of Holland was held to be excused under s.46(2)(a) of the Bills of Exchange Act 1882, as well as under Dutch law.

party lawfully to perform his part of the contract and he has neither been at fault nor contracted to assume the risk of supervening illegality.[88] This rule applies equally where the illegality arises under the law of the place in which the obligations arising under the contract are to be performed. The leading case is *Ralli Bros v Compania Naviera Sota y Aznar*.[89]

A charterparty governed by English law provided for the carriage of jute from Calcutta to Spain. After the contract had been concluded, a decree came into force in Spain fixing the maximum amount of freight that could be paid on imported jute. The freight payable under the charterparty exceeded that maximum, and the court held that, as the freight was payable in Spain, the excess was irrecoverable.

The case is generally regarded as one involving frustration, though, as has been pointed out,[90] the ultimate fate of the contract is not known; indeed, the court carefully refrained from discussing the effect of its ruling on the contract as a whole.[91] Furthermore, Scrutton LJ proceeded on the basis that the refusal to enforce the contract rested on an implied term, rather than the doctrine of frustration.[92] However, in subsequent cases,[93] the general principle has been taken to be that supervening illegality under the law of the place of performance frustrates the contract,[94] at any rate where it would have done if performance had been due in England.[95]

---

[88] As may have occurred recently for various contracts as a result of legislation introduced to address the COVID-19 pandemic in the UK, including the Health Protection (Coronavirus, Restrictions) (England) Regulations 2020, which make many activities illegal.

[89] *Ralli Bros v Compania Naviera Sota y Aznar* [1920] 2 K.B. 287 CA. The *Ralli* principle has been applied in various recent cases including *Colt Technologies Services v SG Global Group SRL* [2020] EWHC 1417 (Ch) (arguable case that payments were illegal under Italian tax law); and *Eurobank Ergasias SA v Kalliroi Navigation Co Ltd* [2015] EWHC 2377 (Comm) (arguable that one tranche of a loan repayment was an illegal commission under Greek law). In *Eurobank*, the argument that *Ralli* had been superseded by Rome I (in particular, art.9(3) which allows courts to apply "mandatory overriding provisions" of domestic law) was rejected and it was held that *Ralli* remains good law (at [36]).

[90] *Mann* (2012), para.16.37. See *Mann* (2012), paras 16.37–16.37 for a discussion of the case.

[91] See the judgment of Warrington LJ in *Ralli* [1920] 2 K.B. 287 CA at 297–298, and of Scrutton LJ at 304.

[92] "Where a contract requires an act to be done in a foreign country, it is in the absence of very special circumstances, an implied term of the continuing validity of such a provision that the act to be done in the foreign country shall not be illegal by the law of that State", in *Ralli* [1920] 2 K.B. 287 CA at 304. It is, however, very difficult to justify such a term on business efficacy grounds. If the carrier has delivered goods in accordance with the contract, the court should not strain to excuse the other party from his duty to pay.

[93] See *AV Pound & Co v MW Hardy & Co Inc* [1956] A.C. 588 HL; *Toprak* [1979] 2 Lloyd's Rep. 98 CA (Civ Div); *Ispahani v Bank Melli Iran* [1998] Lloyd's Rep. Bank. 133 CA (Civ Div); *Beijing Jianlong Heavy Industry Group v Golden Ocean Group Ltd* [2013] 2 All E.R. (Comm) 436.

[94] However, as has been reaffirmed in recent cases, the principle only applies where performance is required to take place in a jurisdiction where it would be illegal, not if performance can take place elsewhere; see e.g. *Cargill International Trading Pte Ltd v Uttam Galva Steels Ltd* [2019] EWHC 476 (Comm) at [123]; *Dana Gas PJSC v Dana Gas Sukuk Ltd* [2017] EWHC 2929 at [59].

[95] It should be noted that the *Ralli* principle only applies where performance would be *illegal*. It does not come into operation merely because the courts of the place of performance would refuse to enforce the contract for some other reason (*Deutsche Bank v Unitech Global Ltd* [2016] EWCA Civ 119), because the creditor has been directed by the central bank of the debtor's place of incorporation not to proceed with the transaction in circumstances where the central bank did not have the power to

Ralli's case and its interpretation in subsequent cases have been criticised on the ground that they ignore the monetary character of a payment obligation and that the place of payment is of relatively minor importance[96] so that an intention should be ascribed to the parties that, where payment at the place fixed for performance becomes impossible under the law of the place of payment, the debtor should pay elsewhere. This argument is not free from difficulty. It is well established that the creditor need not accept a tender of payment which is not made in conformity with the contract.[97] Hence, he may, prima facie, reject a tender made elsewhere than at the place of payment fixed by the contract. In this sense, the place of payment cannot be considered of minor importance in law, however unimportant it might be on the facts. Certainly, the parties are free to provide that, if payment becomes impossible at Place A, it is to be made at Place B, but if the contract is silent, how are we to identify Place B? If, for example, the contract states merely that payment is to be made in Spain, and a change in Spanish law prevents payment in Spain, how are we to determine the substitute place of payment which the parties are supposed to have intended? Also, if we cannot do so, then surely the supposed right to make an alternative tender fails for uncertainty. If this is right, then the monetary character of a payment obligation adds nothing to the argument. The simple fact is that the debtor cannot perform his contractual obligation any more than he could if the contract was to ship goods and shipment was prevented by refusal of an export licence.

6–26 Yet, powerful though these objections are, it is the view of the present writer that they should not prevail. It is true that the creditor is not *obliged* to accept a tender made in a place other than the contractually stipulated place, but should he be denied the right of payment simply because payment has become unlawful in that place? It is submitted that, wherever possible, the creditor should be able to rely on the validity and enforceability of the payment obligation. The court should not disappoint him, even if a little imagination is required to that end. As suggested elsewhere,[98] it should be an implied term of the contract that the creditor is entitled to nominate an alternative place of payment by notice to the debtor to that effect. The due date may have to be deferred pending such nomination, and it may be that any additional cost of making the revised payment should be borne by the creditor. This approach seems to be consistent with Rome I, which tends to downplay the significance of the law of the place of payment,[99] and is surely more commercially appropriate than the outcome in the *Ralli* case itself.

---

deprive the creditor of its accrued right to payment (*Standard Chartered Bank v Ceylon Petroleum Corp* [2011] EWHC 1785 (Comm)) or where, although there are injunctions preventing performance of the main contract, the creditor has the right to recover compensation under cross-undertakings by the company who obtained the injunctions (*Lilly Icos LLC v 8PM Chemists Ltd* [2010] F.S.R. 4).
[96] *Mann* (2012), para.16.36.
[97] See para.2–17 above, and, in the context of a foreign currency obligation, see the decision in *The Aktor* [2008] 2 All E.R. (Comm) 784.
[98] *Mann* (2012), para.16.36.
[99] See art.12(2) of Rome I, which merely requires the court to "have regard" to the law of the place of performance in relation to the method or manner of payment.

It may be that the English courts' approach to this matter in the future should also be influenced by art.9(3) of Rome I, which would apply to any international contract whether governed by an English or a foreign system of law. That article provides that:

> "Effect may be given to the overriding mandatory provisions of the law of the country where the obligations arising out of the contract have to be performed, in so far as those overriding mandatory provisions render the performance of the contract unlawful. In considering whether to give effect to those provisions, regard shall be had to their nature and purpose and to the consequences of their application or non-application."

This provision again suggests that the role of the law of the place of performance is downgraded, because it merely states that effect *may* be given to that law if it renders performance illegal. This again suggests the dilution of the rigid approach to foreign illegality suggested by the *Ralli* decision.

However that may be, what is the current state of the law in this field? In considering whether the prohibition of payment by or under the law of the place of performance frustrates the contract, it is necessary to distinguish cases where this is likely to be purely temporary (in the sense that the delay is unlikely to have a major effect on the contract) and those where it is likely to be either permanent or of such duration as to affect the parties to a degree that they could not reasonably have contemplated. In the former case, the contract is merely suspended.[100] If the frustrating event was reasonably foreseeable, this is likely to prevent frustration as the affected party will be held to have assumed the risk of its occurrence.[101]

The mere fact that payment is *excused* under the law of the place of payment does not frustrate the contract; it is necessary that it should be *unlawful*.[102]

6–27

The principles derived from the decision in *Ralli* operate by virtue of the application of English law as the law applicable to the contract. But, by the same token, where the contract is governed by foreign law, an English court will not order payment where this would be illegal under English law.[103] In this respect, the court is obliged to apply its domestic law, for the English court cannot allow its process to be used in a manner which is manifestly contrary to English public policy.[104]

---

[100] This is the position as regards supervening illegality under English law (see *Chitty on Contracts*, edited by H. Beale and A.S. Burrows, 33rd edn (London: Sweet & Maxwell, 2019), para.23–027) and the same principle would seem to apply in the case of a foreign place of performance. For decisions which confirm this view, see *Arab Bank Ltd v Barclays Bank (Dominion, Colonial and Overseas)* [1954] A.C. 495 HL; *Libyan Arab* [1989] Q.B. 728 QBD (Comm).

[101] *Edwinton Commercial Corp v Tsavliris Russ (Worldwide Salvage & Towage) Ltd (The Sea Angel)* [2007] 2 All E.R. (Comm) 634 at [103]; *Blue Sky One Ltd v Mahan Air* [2009] EWHC 3314 (Comm) at [299] (citing *Edwinton*).

[102] *Jacobs Marcus & Co v Crédit Lyonnais* (1884) 12 Q.B.D. 589 CA. Also, see fn.88 above.

[103] *Boissevain v Weil* [1950] A.C. 327 HL, a case in which the court refused to enforce a foreign law contract which infringed exchange control laws in the UK.

[104] This principle receives recognition at art.21 of Rome I.

Effect of frustration

6–28 Suppose that, in a case where the contract is governed by English law, the court finds that the contract has become frustrated, whether through supervening illegality under the law of the place of payment or on some other ground. Where then do the parties stand? First, each party is discharged from liability for future performance. This is so both at common law[105] and under the Law Reform (Frustrated Contracts) Act 1943.[106] Secondly, where the 1943 Act applies, each party must return money he has received under the contract, less what the court considers it reasonable to allow him for expenses[107] and such sum as the court considers it just to allow for the value of non-monetary benefits received under the contract.[108] Where the 1943 Act does not apply, a party who has paid money can recover it if it was paid on a total failure of consideration,[109] but not otherwise.

These principles apply to loan contracts as well as to contracts involving the supply of goods or services. So, if under a contract governed by English law, A in London lends money to B in Madrid which is to be repaid with interest in Madrid and the loan contract becomes frustrated because of a change in law or executive action in Spain preventing B from repaying the loan, A, though disabled from suing on the contract, is entitled to pursue a restitutionary remedy for recovery of the loan with reasonable interest.[110]

3. FOREIGN CURRENCY CLAIMS AND JUDGMENTS

6–29 Where proceedings are instituted in England in respect of a foreign currency claim, in what currency must the claim be made and judgment entered, and if a claim is required or permitted to be made in sterling, at what date should the conversion into sterling be made?

The old procedural rule

6–30 Until 1975, it was considered settled law in England that, in proceedings in this country in respect of a foreign money obligation, the claim had to be expressed in sterling, judgment had to be given in sterling and the correct date for converting the foreign currency into sterling was not the date of actual payment or of commencement of proceedings or of judgment but the date of the defendant's

---

[105] *Chitty* (2019), para.23–071.
[106] *Chitty* (2019), para.23–074.
[107] Section 1(2) of the Law Reform (Frustrated Contracts) Act 1943. For an example of the application of this section, see *Gamerco SA v ICM/Fair Warning (Agency) Ltd* [1995] 1 W.L.R. 1226 QBD.
[108] Section 1(3) of the 1943 Act.
[109] *Fibrosa Spolka Akcyjna v Fairbairn Lawson Combe Barbour Ltd* [1943] A.C. 32 HL.
[110] This is not enforcement of the contract. In line with the policy of the 1943 Act, it is merely the exercise of a right to require the borrower to return benefits which it would be unjust to allow him to keep.

breach. The rule was of long standing[111] and was reaffirmed by the House of Lords as recently as 1960 in *Re United Railways of Havana and Regla Warehouses Ltd*.[112] Two main reasons were advanced for the rule: foreign currency was to be treated as a commodity,[113] and it was well established that on non-delivery of a commodity, damages were assessed by reference to the market price at the breach date; alternatively, assuming that foreign money was to be treated as money, English procedure precluded a decree of specific performance of a contract to pay foreign money and the remedy was an action for damages, which, to avoid uncertainty, should be calculated as the sterling equivalent of the foreign money as at the date of breach.

The logic of the old rule was far from self-evident, and it was recognised as capable of causing great injustice to the creditor, whose contractual right to a given number of units in a foreign money of account was arbitrarily converted by a rule of procedure into a claim for sterling that might well depreciate between the date of issue of the writ and the date of judgment, and again between the date of judgment and the date it was satisfied voluntarily or that steps were taken to enforce it. As so often in the past, Lord Denning stood out as a lone judicial campaigner against what he regarded as injustice, and in his dissenting judgment in *Owners of Turbo Electric Bulk Carrier Teh Hu v Nippon Salvage Co Ltd (The Teh Hu)*,[114] emphasised the unsatisfactory nature of the rule, urging that it should not be extended to maritime cases of salvage; and once again, it was Lord Denning's heterodoxy that ultimately triumphed.

The modern procedural rule

The breach-date principle reaffirmed by the House of Lords in *Re United Railways of Havana and Regla Warehouses Ltd*[115] came before the House for reconsideration in *Miliangos*,[116] when the House took the rare step of declaring (Lord Simon dissenting) that its earlier decision given a mere 15 years before should no longer be considered a correct statement of the law as regards foreign money *debt* claims.

6–31

By a contract governed by Swiss law, the Swiss claimant agreed to sell to the defendants, an English company, a quantity of polyester yarn. Both the money of account and the money of payment were Swiss francs. The defendants having failed to pay the price, the plaintiff instituted proceedings for the sterling equivalent of the sum due in Swiss francs calculated as at the due date of payment. Thereafter, there was a substantial fall in the value of sterling in relation to the Swiss franc, and, in the light of the decision of the Court of Appeal in

---

[111] In the *United Railways* case (at fn.112 below), Viscount Simonds referred to *Ward v Kidswin* 82 E.R. 283 KB, which itself referred to 34 H.6.12.

[112] *Re United Railways of Havana and Regla Warehouses Ltd* [1961] A.C. 1007 HL. See also *Manners v Pearson & Son* [1898] 1 Ch. 581 CA.

[113] This rather quaint view of foreign currencies has now been largely exploded, at least so far as English law is concerned: see the discussion of this subject at para.1–07.

[114] *Owners of Turbo Electric Bulk Carrier Teh Hu v Nippon Salvage Co Ltd (The Teh Hu)* [1970] P. 106 CA (Civ Div).

[115] *United Railways* [1961] A.C. 1007 HL.

[116] *Miliangos* [1976] A.C. 443 HL.

Schorsch Meier GmbH v Hennin,[117] the plaintiff sought and obtained leave to amend his statement of claim so as to show the amount due in Swiss francs. However, the trial judge, treating *Schorsch Meier* as decided *per incuriam*, gave judgment in sterling as at the breach date. His decision was reversed by the Court of Appeal, which varied the judgment so as to give judgment in Swiss francs or their sterling equivalent at the time of payment. The decision of the Court of Appeal was affirmed by the House of Lords.

The *Miliangos* rule thus lays down that, in foreign currency claims for debt under a contract governed by the law of the currency concerned, the claim may—indeed, must—be made and judgment entered in the foreign currency, and that, where judgment is given in foreign currency, the defendant, if not voluntarily satisfying the judgment in that currency, must pay the sterling equivalent as at the date of payment. For this purpose, "payment" means the actual date of payment where this is made voluntarily or the date when the creditor applies to enforce the judgment, where enforcement becomes necessary.[118]

Extension of the Miliangos rule

6–32   In *Miliangos* itself, the House of Lords was careful to limit its decision to foreign money debt claims governed by the foreign law of the currency concerned, and refrained from deciding whether the rule should be extended to other cases, e.g. claims for unliquidated damages in contract or tort or claims under a contract governed by English law. Since then, the rule has been so extended that it can now fairly be regarded as a rule of general application.[119] It has thus been held to apply to a claim for unliquidated damages for breach of contract,[120] in tort,[121] and to claims under contracts governed by English law where payment is to be made in foreign currency.[122] Recently, it was even held, with reference to *Miliangos*, that courts have jurisdiction to make costs orders in foreign currency.[123] In addition, certain statutory obstacles to the application of the rule[124] have now been removed.[125]

---

[117] *Schorsch Meier GmbH v Hennin* [1975] Q.B. 416 CA (Civ Div).
[118] *Miliangos* [1976] A.C. 443 HL at 468 per Lord Wilberforce.
[119] See *Dicey, Morris and Collins* (2012), para.37–086.
[120] *The Folias* [1979] A.C. 685 HL.
[121] *The Folias* [1979] A.C. 685 HL; *Hoffman v Sofaer* [1982] 1 W.L.R. 1350 QBD.
[122] *Barclays Bank International Ltd v Levin Bros (Bradford) Ltd* [1977] Q.B. 270 QBD (Comm); *Federal Commerce & Navigation Co Ltd v Tradax Export SA (The Maratha Envoy)* [1977] Q.B. 324 CA (Civ Div); *The Folias* [1979] A.C. 685 HL.
[123] *Cathay Pacific Airlines Ltd v Lufthansa Technik AG* [2019] EWHC 715 (Ch). The judge, John Kimbell QC, with reference to *The Folias*, considered that "to the extent that an overarching principle has emerged, it is that a court ought to give judgment in the currency which most truly expresses the claimant's loss" (at [45]).
[124] Bills of Exchange Act 1882 ss.57(2) and 72(4); Foreign Judgments (Reciprocal Enforcement) Act 1933 s.2(3).
[125] All the above provisions were repealed by the Administration of Justice Act 1977 s.4.

Limitations to the Miliangos rule

Although the rule in *Miliangos* rapidly gained acceptance in a number of areas, experience has demonstrated some of its limitations. In particular, the rule does not apply to the claims of creditors upon the insolvency of a company. Here, the policy of insolvency law and the practicalities of administration of the assets of insolvent companies require a different rule, namely that the foreign currency claim be converted into sterling at the date of the winding-up order, in the case of a compulsory winding-up,[126] and the date of the winding-up resolution, in the case of a creditors' voluntary winding-up.[127] It is now specifically provided that foreign currency debts are to be converted into sterling at the mid-market rate on the London foreign exchange market at the close of business on the day the company goes into liquidation or, in the absence of such rate, the rate determined by the court.[128] Accordingly, where there have been mutual dealings between the parties in different currencies, all of the respective amounts would be converted into sterling at that rate, and the creditor would prove for any net balance in sterling.[129] In *Re Elenin's Estate*[130] which concerned the conversion of foreign money claims in released to a deceased bankrupt's estate, the existence of a single date for the ascertainment of liabilities was described as "a fundamental feature of insolvency law".[131]

6–33

This means that creditors with foreign currency claims might suffer a loss due to the conversion happening at the commencement of the winding-up. Do they have a claim for that loss? This question was answered in the negative in *Re Lines Bros (In Liquidation)*,[132] where it was held that, in circumstances where there was a surplus of assets available after paying all the proved debts but insufficient assets to pay all claims to post-liquidation interest in full, foreign currency creditors had no claim to prove for more than the sterling equivalent of their claims at the commencement of winding-up and the right of creditors with contractual claims to interest ranked next. The High Court and Court of Appeal had departed from this position in *Re Lehman Brothers International (Europe) (In*

---

[126] *Re British American Continental Bank Ltd* [1922] 2 Ch. 575 CA; *Re Dynamics Corp of America (In Liquidation) (No.2)* [1976] 1 W.L.R. 757 Ch D; *Re Amalgamated Investment and Property Co Ltd* [1985] Ch. 349 Ch D.

[127] *Re Lines Bros (In Liquidation)* [1983] Ch. 1 CA (Civ Div). The same policy considerations mean that, likewise, the *Miliangos* principle does not apply in the context of a personal insolvency: *Re Debtor (No.51/SD/1991)* [1992] 1 W.L.R. 1294 Ch D; *Re Elenin's Estate* [2016] 1 W.L.R. 2091. The same rule has been applied by the Federal Court of Australia: see *Re Griffiths* [2004] FCAFC 102, where the whole subject is discussed in some detail.

[128] Section 322 of the Insolvency Act 1986 and r.14.21 of the Insolvency (England and Wales) Rules 2016 (previously r.4.90 of the Insolvency Rules 1986) as amended.

[129] i.e. in accordance with r.14.21 of the Insolvency (England and Wales) Rules 2016.

[130] *Re Elenin's Estate* [2016] 1 W.L.R. 2091.

[131] *Re Elenin's Estate* [2016] 1 W.L.R. 2091 at [51]. Although the circumstances of the case were somewhat different in that they involved the administration of a deceased's estate in bankruptcy. The court held debts denominated in foreign currencies were to be converted into sterling for the purpose of proof as at the date of the deceased's death; s.382 of the Insolvency Act 1986, as modified by the Administration of Insolvent Estates of Deceased Persons Order 1986, substituted the date of death for the date of the commencement of the bankruptcy in such circumstances.

[132] *Re Lines Bros* [1983] Ch. 1 CA (Civ Div).

Administration)[133] to hold that claims for currency conversion losses could be brought as non-provable claims against the company once proven claims and statutory interest have been paid in full. However, this decision was reversed by the Supreme Court[134] and therefore the orthodox position that losses due to currency depreciations between the commencement of insolvency proceedings and payment cannot be claimed has been reaffirmed as the current law.

In addition, there may be other types of case in which the *Miliangos* distinction between domestic and foreign currencies will not arise or will not be relevant. For example, *Re Telewest Communications Plc (No.1)*[135] was a case seeking the convening of court meetings of creditors to sanction a scheme of arrangement involving an insolvent company. The company had issued bonds denominated in both sterling and US dollars and, in the light of very significant fluctuations in the applicable exchange rate, the US dollar bondholders wished to be treated as a distinct class of creditors so that they would be entitled to vote separately on the proposed scheme. However, the court held that a fair attempt had been made to deal with the exchange rate distortions and thus decided that all bondholders should be treated as a single class for voting purposes. In its particular context, it is submitted that this decision is right—the challenges of rescuing an insolvent company via a scheme of arrangement should not be exacerbated merely because the company has debt obligations denominated in a number of different currencies.

Finally, the financial crisis created an unusual situation in which foreign currency issues had to be determined in relation to a trust fund. In the period prior to the Group's collapse, a UK member of Iceland's Kaupthing Group had been required to place with the Bank of England sterling deposits equal to certain deposits received by it from customers. All of the deposits placed with the Bank of England under this arrangement were denominated in sterling, but some of the corresponding customer deposits had been paid in a foreign currency. It was found that the funds were held by the Bank of England on trust for the corresponding depositors and, as a result, it became necessary to determine the extent of the interests of the foreign currency beneficiaries. Perhaps with a view to ensuring that the trust fund was not rendered inadequate through exchange rate fluctuations, the court held that the beneficiary's claim was crystallised at the prevailing exchange rate on the date on which the funds were paid to the Bank of England by Kaupthing. They were thus to be paid out by reference to the same exchange rate, regardless of any fluctuations that may have occurred between the two dates.[136]

---

[133] *Re Lehman Brothers International (Europe) (In Administration)* [2015] Ch. 1, affirmed [2016] Ch. 50. An appeal is presently outstanding.
[134] *Re Lehman Brothers International (Europe) (In Administration)* [2017] UKSC 38.
[135] *Re Telewest Communications Plc (No.1)* [2004] B.C.C. 342, affirmed [2005] B.C.C. 29.
[136] *Brazzill v Willoughby* [2010] 2 B.C.L.C. 259.

The Miliangos rule is procedural

It cannot be emphasised too strongly that the *Miliangos* rule is not a rule of substantive law but a rule of procedure. Its sole purpose is to ensure that the creditor gets what he bargained for, namely payment to the full value of the money of account[137] as at the date of payment. Where the money of account is US dollars, the creditor can, in effect, get specific performance of the contract to pay US dollars. It is only if enforcement of a judgment in US dollars becomes necessary that a conversion to sterling has to be made, and this is simply because of practical convenience. The *Miliangos* rule does not in any way affect the substantive law as to the amount recoverable by way of debt or damages. It is thus not designed to give protection to either party against exchange losses occurring after the breach date. If payment is due in US dollars and the dollar increases in value in relation to sterling between the due date of payment and the actual date of payment, then it may be argued that the creditor is better off than he would have been under the old rule,[138] but this result follows not from any concern to protect the creditor against post-breach reduction in the value of sterling but simply from the fact that he is entitled to neither more nor less than what he bargained for, namely payment in US dollars. It follows, of course, that the creditor's rights are governed by the rule for good or ill, so that if the US dollar *declines* in value in relation to the pound he can recover only in dollars or in their reduced sterling equivalent, so far as *Miliangos* is concerned.[139] Whether he is entitled to be compensated for the exchange loss resulting from the debtor's delay in payment is not a question resolved by *Miliangos* but is a matter of substantive law and is governed by the general principles as to remoteness of damages.[140]

6–34

Which foreign currency?

In *Miliangos*, the claim was for payment of a debt and both the money of account and the money of payment were Swiss francs. Accordingly, there was only one possible candidate as the foreign currency of judgment: the Swiss franc. However, the money of payment may be different from the money of account, and, if the claim is for unliquidated damages for breach of contract, then the chances are that the parties will have made no provision for the currency in which they are to be assessed or paid. In the case of a claim for damages in tort where there is no contractual relationship between the parties, the question of agreement on a currency obviously does not arise. In each of these cases, the court may have to consider what the relevant currency is in which claims may be made. This is a

6–35

---

[137] See below at para.6–36.
[138] The argument does, however, presuppose that the creditor has some interest in the relative values of the currencies. If the creditor operates in dollars and draws up its accounts in that currency, then the relative value of sterling will be largely meaningless: see para.6–36.
[139] See the speech of Lord Wilberforce in *Miliangos* [1976] A.C. 443 HL at 466 (where the foreign currency was Swiss francs): "The creditor has no concern with pounds sterling; for him what matters is that a Swiss franc for good or ill should remain a Swiss franc."
[140] In particular, the rule in *Hadley v Baxendale* 156 E.R. 145 Court of Exchequer. The point is considered at para.6–37 below.

matter of procedure and will accordingly be governed by English law regardless of the system of law applicable to the underlying cause of action.

In considering these questions under English law, it is necessary to distinguish three entirely different issues. The first issue is the currency in which the claim should be made; the second, the currency in which judgment should be given; and the third, the currency in which the debtor is entitled to tender payment, whether before or after judgment.

(1) Formulation of the claim

6–36 Both Lord Wilberforce's speech in *Miliangos*[141] and the subsequent Practice Directions[142] state that, if the plaintiff wishes to obtain judgment in a given foreign currency, he should make his claim in that currency. As the Law Commission Working Paper on the subject points out,[143] this implies that the creditor has the choice of suing in sterling or in the relevant foreign currency. Indeed, in the subsequent decision in *Ozalid Group (Export) Ltd v African Continental Bank Ltd*, Donaldson J stated in the following terms that the choice lay with the plaintiff:

> "I have said that under the new rule the plaintiff is *entitled* to make his claim in foreign currency. I use the word advisedly, because I can find no trace in the speeches of any intention to make a claim in this form obligatory. The overriding reason for changing the law was to provide a procedure which would enable the Courts to compensate the claimant in full for the wrong which he had suffered. A change which *required* the plaintiff to claim in foreign currency and to accept sterling at the rate prevailing at the date of judgment could in some circumstances work as great an injustice as the old procedure requiring him to claim in sterling and to adopt the date of breach rate of exchange."[144]

With respect, this is a misunderstanding of the purpose of the *Miliangos* rule, which, as pointed out earlier, was not to provide full compensation to the creditor for delay in payment but simply to give him the benefit of his bargain, i.e. a right to be paid to the value of the designated currency of account without having that currency converted into sterling before he had the benefit of it through payment or initiation of steps to enforce a judgment. If the creditor of a foreign money obligation suffers loss because of a fall in that currency in relation to sterling after the breach date, the correct way of providing him with a remedy is not by allowing him to claim the sterling equivalent at breach date of what was then due in foreign currency (the procedure adopted in *Ozalid* and rightly criticised in the Working Paper as contrary to the *Miliangos* rule)[145] but by awarding him damages for the loss in exchange resulting from the delay in payment.[146] The two routes may well lead to the same result, as in *Ozalid*, but the former is

---

[141] *Miliangos* [1976] A.C. 443 HL at 468; and compare *The Maratha Envoy* [1977] Q.B. 324 CA (Civ Div), reversed in [1978] A.C. 1 HL but not on the currency point.
[142] See Practice Direction 16 para.9.1 which supplements CPR Pt 16.
[143] Law Commission, *Private International Law, Foreign Money Liabilities* (1981), Working Paper No.80, para.2.30.
[144] *Ozalid Group (Export) Ltd v African Continental Bank Ltd* [1979] 2 Lloyd's Rep. 231 QBD (Comm) at 233–234.
[145] See fn.143.
[146] See the discussion at para.6–43 below.

inappropriate because it may enable the creditor to bypass a requirement of a claim to consequential loss, namely that it is of a kind that should have been within the defendant's contemplation at the time of the contract; it may also enable him to avoid the duty to mitigate his loss. Admittedly, Donaldson J allowed the claim in sterling not merely on the basis that the proceedings were brought in England but also because "it is clear that the plaintiffs' loss was incurred in sterling".[147] But the fact that the creditor would have immediately converted the foreign money of account into sterling is not relevant to a claim for a liquidated amount under a contract, where there is an established money of account, and is material only to a claim for consequential loss resulting from the delay in payment.

It is therefore possible to conclude that, where the relevant currency (whatever it may be) is foreign, the creditor must claim in that currency, not in sterling.[148] Of course, if the claim is liquidated, the matter will never be looked at by the court if the defendant fails to take steps to defend the claim, so that judgment is given in default[149] and is not set aside. However, where the case comes before the court, whether at trial of the action or on the assessment of damages, a sterling claim should be ignored where improperly made. What, then, is the appropriate currency in which to make a claim? Four categories must be distinguished: a claim for a debt or liquidated damages; a claim for unliquidated damages in contract; a claim for unliquidated damages in tort; and a restitutionary claim for money.

(a) Debt or liquidated damages. The appropriate currency is the money of account. In many cases, this will be the same as the money of payment, but where they are different, it is the money of account that should be selected.[150] This is because it is the money of account that represents the measure of the creditor's claim and shows the sum into which the money of payment is to be converted where the defendant exercises his option to make payment in the money of payment. That option is in no way interfered with by adopting the money of account as the currency of the claim.

6–37

For example, suppose that S in London sells goods to B in Hamburg at a price of £40,000, payment is to be made to S in London in Swiss francs. If B defaults in payment, S's claim should be for £40,000, not for the equivalent in either sterling or Swiss francs. If judgment is entered for S in the sum of £40,000 then B can satisfy this judgment by paying £40,000 or either the sterling or the Swiss franc equivalent of £40,000 at the time of payment.

(b) Unliquidated damages in contract. Where the contract expressly or by implication provides for the currency in which damages are to be paid (a situation most likely to arise where the claim is for consequential loss for delay in payment

6–38

---

[147] *Ozalid* [1979] 2 Lloyd's Rep. 231 QBD (Comm) at 234.
[148] In other words, whilst the creditor is entitled to the benefit of the bargain he made, the debtor is likewise held only to the bargain which he made, and not to a variation on it as a result of an unnecessary exchange rate operation.
[149] i.e. without judicial consideration.
[150] *George Veflings Rederi A/S v President of India (The Bellami)* [1978] 1 W.L.R. 982 QBD (Comm), affirmed [1979] 1 W.L.R. 59 CA (Civ Div).

of a liquidated claim),[151] the claim should be made in that currency.[152] This may be so even though the money of account is different if payments are made in a particular currency.[153] In other cases, the relevant currency is that in which the creditor's loss is suffered, or more accurately, the currency which the debtor knew or could reasonably have contemplated, at the time of the contract, would be the currency in which the creditor would suffer his loss.[154] This is not necessarily the currency in which the loss is immediately felt. Rather, it is the currency in which he normally conducts his business. So, where a French corporation having its place of business in Paris chartered a vessel from the defendants and, because of the negligence of the latter, had to settle by a payment in Brazilian cruzieros a claim brought by the receivers of the cargo, the French charterers were held entitled to recover by way of damages the amount of French francs they had used to purchase the cruzieros needed to settle the receivers' claim. Since the applicant carried on business in France and was a French company, the defendants could reasonably have contemplated that the applicant would deal in francs and would thus use francs to acquire the requisite Brazilian currency to meet the claim made against it.[155]

The location in which the claimant carries on his business will thus be a pointer to the currency in which an award of damages should be made. But, as the decision in *Société Francaise Bunge SA v Belcan NV (The Federal Huron)*[156] demonstrates, this is not a conclusive factor. In that case, the applicant was again a French corporation carrying on its business in France. It imported a quantity of soya beans which were found to be damaged on arrival. It sold them in the local market at a loss, at a price expressed in French francs. Yet the plaintiffs operated solely in the soya bean market, and that commodity is invariably priced in US dollars. As a result, the plaintiffs traded solely in US dollars and drew up their accounts in that currency. If they ever sold soya beans for a different currency, the claimants immediately converted the proceeds into US dollars, and forward contracts would be hedged against that currency. The defendants argued that the award should be made in francs but, as Bingham J observed,[157] such an award "would mean that the shipowner's breach and the intervention of the court had imposed on the receivers an exchange loss which they would not otherwise have suffered and against which, as a matter of routine conventional practice, they took careful measures to protect themselves". He then noted that:

---

[151] As to which see para.6–43 below.
[152] Referred to as the "currency of the contract" in *The Folias* [1979] A.C. 685 HL.
[153] See e.g. *Harlequin Property (SVG) Ltd v Wilkins Kennedy* [2016] EWHC 3188 (TCC) and [2016] EWHC 3233 where, although the payments were expressed in US dollars, this was simply for accounting purposes and all payments under the contract were made in sterling, hence the court found that the currency in which the loss was felt was sterling and ordered damages to be calculated in sterling.
[154] *The Folias* [1979] A.C. 685 HL; and see J.A. Knott, "Foreign Currency Judgments in Tort: An Illustration of the Wealth-Time Continuum" (1980) 43 M.L.R. 18.
[155] *The Folias* [1979] A.C. 685 HL.
[156] *Societe Francaise Bunge SA v Belcan NV (The Federal Huron)* [1985] 2 Lloyd's Rep. 189 QBD (Comm).
[157] *The Federal Huron* [1985] 2 Lloyd's Rep. 189 QBD (Comm) at 193.

"[A] dollar loss is what the cargo receivers would have forseen as a result of cargo damage. I have no direct evidence of what the shipowners contemplated but I have no reason to doubt that they would have foreseen a loss in dollars if a commodity bought in and shipped from the US were damaged."

This decision is plainly correct and consistent with the principles discussed earlier in this chapter. It does, however, highlight the need for careful factual enquiry in order to identify the currency in which the loss is actually "felt". The judgment of Bingham J quoted above serves to emphasise that the award can only be made in a particular currency if: (i) the applicant does in fact suffer the loss in that currency; *and* (ii) use of the currency was within the contemplation of *both* of the parties.[158]

The importance of the second criterion is emphasised by the decision in *Metaalhandel JA Magnus BV v Ardfields Transport*.[159] In that case, a trading company, based in the Netherlands, purchased a quantity of tungsten rods from a company in Brighton. The buyers engaged Ardfields to collect the rods from Brighton, whence they were taken to the Ardfields warehouse in St Albans. There, the rods were stolen due to inadequate security arrangements put in place by the defendants.

6–39

The claimants ran their business in Dutch guilders, but judgment was awarded in sterling because "the parties to the contract cannot be said to have had in contemplation that damages should be measured in Dutch guilders". In the context of a contract to pick up tungsten rods in Brighton and to store them in St Albans, it is probably fair to say that the defendants would not have contemplated the loss in guilders. Perhaps the mere fact that the claimant is a foreign entity will not of itself be sufficient to bring these principles into play when all other features of the contract are exclusively connected with England.

The second criterion is further emphasised by the decision in *Milan Nigeria Ltd v Angeliki B Maritime Co*,[160] where losses had been incurred in Nigerian naira but it was the invariable practice in the relevant market for local currency receipts to be converted into US dollars. In addition, it was also clear from the pleadings that the claim had been asserted in US dollars without objection by the defendants, and that the parties therefore had that currency in mind as a vehicle for any award of damages.

Perhaps the most difficult and controversial decision in this area is that of the House of Lords in *Attorney General of Ghana v Texaco Overseas Tankships Ltd (The Texaco Melbourne)*.[161] A Texaco group company contracted to transport a cargo across the Ghanaian coast for a government ministry. The oil did not arrive; in which currency should the damages be expressed? The US dollar is, of course, the currency of the oil markets. But the cedi is the local currency in Ghana. The question arose in a particularly acute form in this case. When the breach of contract occurred in 1982, it required just 2.75 cedis to purchase one US dollar. By the time of the first instance judgment, the cedi had collapsed and some 375

---

[158] The latter criterion is necessary to meet the rule in *Hadley* 156 E.R. 145 Court of Exchequer.
[159] *Metaalhandel JA Magnus BV v Ardfields Transport* [1998] 1 Lloyd's Rep. 197 QBD (Comm).
[160] *Milan Nigeria Ltd v Angekliki B Maritime Co* [2011] Arb. L.R. 24.
[161] *Attorney General of Ghana v Texaco Overseas Tankships Ltd (The Texaco Melbourne)* [1994] 1 Lloyd's Rep. 473 HL.

equated to a single US dollar. On the basis that damages were to be assessed with reference to the date of the breach and were to represent the buying price of oil in the nearest available market, an award in dollars would have amounted to US $3,000,000. However, a corresponding award in the (now depreciated) cedi would have been equivalent to approximately US $20,000. The House of Lords held that the loss was "felt" in cedis, partly because Ghana's strict system of exchange control meant that all Ghanaian entities effectively had to operate in the local unit.[162] As a result, the claimants received a mere US $20,000 (equivalent) in respect of the breach. It is submitted that the House of Lords viewed the matter too narrowly. Had the oil been delivered, it is true that it would have been sold to local buyers for cedis, but the proceeds would have been reinvested in further consignments of oil at (or close to) the GHS 2.75:US $1 exchange rate. In other words, the applicant's ordinary trading activities would have provided a hedge against the falling cedi. At all events, and whatever the merits of the analysis, the compensation received by the claimants was plainly inadequate under the circumstances. It is submitted that the court would have reached a more appropriate conclusion via one of the following routes:

i. It is well known that the oil market trades in US dollars. It would thus have been open to the court to hold that the US dollar was the "currency of the contract"[163] and thus award damages in that unit.[164]

ii. The House of Lords circumscribed its own freedom of action by insisting that damages had to be assessed by reference to the circumstances prevailing as at the date of the breach of contract. This overlooks the essential principle that damages are intended to be compensatory, and to place the applicant in the position he would have occupied had the contract been performed. This factor had previously led the House of Lords to allow the court to depart from the breach date rule where it was necessary to do so to achieve justice between the parties.[165] The catastrophic fall in the value of the cedi between the date of the breach and the date of the hearing would surely have provided a valid basis for departing from the breach date rule under the circumstances.

iii. Should a similar case arise today, it appears that damages could now be assessed by reference to the circumstances subsisting as at the date of the hearing itself.[166]

---

[162] It must be said that, where a claimant is based in a country which operates a system of exchange control, the courts tend to find that the loss was felt in the local currency: see *The Transoceanica Francesca and The Nicos V* [1987] 2 Lloyd's Rep. 155 QBD (Admlty).

[163] i.e. as described in *The Folias* [1979] A.C. 685 HL.

[164] Some support for such an approach may be drawn from *Voest Alpine Intertrading GmbH v Burwell & Co SA (Pty) Ltd* [1985] 2 SALR 149.

[165] *Johnson v Agnew* [1980] A.C. 367 HL. See also *Alcoa Minerals of Jamaica Inc v Broderick* [2001] 1 A.C. 371 PC.

[166] See the decision of the House of Lords in *Golden Strait Corp v Nippon Yusen Kubishka Kaisha (The Golden Victory)* [2007] 2 A.C. 353; also *Ageas (UK) Ltd v Kwik-Fit (GB) Ltd* [2014] Bus. L.R. 1338. An interesting recent example of this is found in *Sprint Electric Ltd v Buyer's Dream Ltd* [2020] EWHC 2004 (Ch), where it was accepted at [69] that the outbreak of the Covid-19 pandemic was a matter subsequent to breach which should be considered.

Any of these approaches—or a combination of them—might have helped in the formulation of a more equitable award in *The Texaco Melbourne* itself. But, at all events, it appears that the existence of stringent exchange controls in Ghana influenced the decision in this case. As a result of those controls, the claimant could only fund itself and its operations in cedis, and it therefore had to be taken to have felt its loss in that currency. This point was discussed in *Milan Nigeria Ltd v Angeliki B Maritime Co*,[167] where a different outcome was reached in circumstances where a claim in relation to short delivery of cargo had been submitted to arbitration and it was found to be reasonable to conclude that the parties' shared expectation was that the tribunal's award would be in US dollars. At this point, it may finally be appropriate to note that the Arbitration Act 1996 has been held to allow to arbitrators a relatively broad discretion in determining the currency in which their award should be made, and that they are not necessarily bound by the substantive rules discussed above.[168]

(c) Unliquidated damages in tort. A similar rule applies to claims for unliquidated damages in tort. So, where a claimant incurs expenditure in Japanese yen which he discharges by using US dollars, in which he customarily trades, to purchase the yen, he is entitled to judgment for damages in US dollars where the defendant knew or ought to have known that this would be the currency in which the claimant's loss would be felt.[169] Recent cases have continued to apply the same approach.[170]

6–40

(d) Restitution. Where money is paid, property transferred or services rendered under a contract which becomes ineffective, an applicant with a restitutionary claim is entitled to a money award in the currency in which the benefit was conferred on the respondent and in which that benefit can most fairly be assessed.[171] It will be necessary to take all relevant circumstances into account in determining that currency. Other things being equal, it should be the currency of the money of account under the contract, since this governs the substance of the parties' obligations.[172]

6–41

(2) Entry of judgment

Where the claim is required to be made in foreign currency, judgment should be entered in the same currency. Just as a creditor who has a claim in foreign currency cannot be permitted the option of suing for sterling, so also he ought not to be allowed to take a judgment in sterling, despite the implication to the

6–42

---

[167] *Milan* [2011] Arb. L.R. 24 at [63].
[168] *Lesotho Highlands Development Authority v Impregilo SpA* [2006] 1 A.C. 221. It is submitted that this decision can be criticized on the basis of the reasons given by Lord Phillips in his dissenting judgment in that case.
[169] *The Folias* [1979] A.C. 685 HL, and see Knott, "Foreign Currency Judgments in Tort" (1980) 43 M.L.R. 18.
[170] *Kinetics Technology International SpA v Cross Seas Shipping Corp (The Mosconici)* [2001] 2 Lloyd's Rep. 313 QBD (Comm); *Barings Plc (In Liquidation) v Coopers & Lybrand (No.8)* [2003] EWHC 2371 (Ch).
[171] *BP Exploration Co (Libya) Ltd v Hunt (No.2)* [1982] 1 All E.R. 925 HL.
[172] i.e. opposed to *BP Exploration* [1982] 1 All E.R. 925 HL at 971.

contrary in *Miliangos* itself and the *Ozalid* decision.[173] On the other hand, there can be no objection to allowing a creditor to enter judgment in a form which gives the debtor the option to pay the foreign currency or its sterling equivalent at the date of judgment, for the debtor has the option of paying in sterling anyway.[174]

Yet some difficulties remain. *Miliangos* requires that the foreign currency judgment be converted into sterling as at the date on which the court authorises enforcement, since it is necessary to fix an exchange rate prior to the execution process. As a result, the applicant has an exchange rate exposure between the date of the relevant court order and the actual completion of the execution process. The potential difficulties are illustrated by the decision in *Carnegie v Giessen*.[175] The court had made a charging order against property and had converted the foreign judgment currency into sterling at the time. Unfortunately, the order could not be enforced for an extended period since third parties had an interest in the property. The court refused to refix the relevant exchange rates as of the date of receipt of the sterling proceeds, since *Miliangos* did not permit of such a variation. The applicant thus suffered an exchange loss as a result of the depreciation of sterling. It is submitted that, contrary to *Miliangos*, it should no longer be necessary for the actual exchange rate to be specified in the court order itself. Exchange rates are publicly and regularly available and there is no reason why the sheriff could not simply refer to these rates as at the date on which he receives the proceeds of any enforcement process.

(3) Payment

6–43   Nothing in *Miliangos* or the subsequent cases takes away the option given to the debtor under general law to pay the debt before judgment, or to pay the judgment debt when judgment has been entered, either in sterling or in the money of payment. If the money of account is different from the money of payment and judgment is entered in the currency of account, the debtor has a threefold choice. He can pay in the money of account, for that is what the judgment provides, he can pay the sterling equivalent at the date of payment (as previously defined),[176] or, as a third alternative, the money of payment equivalent at that date.[177]

The recovery of exchange losses as damages

6–44   The difficulties which have confronted the court in dealing with interest by way of damages have already been noted.[178] However, the problems formerly posed by the curiosities of the *London Chatham & Dover Railway Co v South Eastern Railway Co* case[179] have not burdened the recovery of exchange rate losses

---

[173] See para.6–35 above.
[174] On this option, and for criticism of its continued application, see para.6–42 below.
[175] *Carnegie v Giessen* [2004] EWHC 1782 (Ch), affirmed [2005] 1 W.L.R. 2510.
[176] See para.6–32 above.
[177] See the example given at para.6–36 above.
[178] See para.4–55.
[179] *London Chatham & Dover Railway Co v South Eastern Railway Co* [1893] A.C. 429 HL.

flowing from a late payment of moneys due under a contract. As Lord Brandon remarked in *President of India v Lips Maritime Corp (The Lips)*[180]:

> "It appears to me that the claims to recover currency exchange losses as damages for breach of contract, whether the breach relied on is the late payment of a debt or any other breach, are subject to the same rules as apply for breach of contract generally."

In other words, the losses would be recoverable if they arose in the ordinary course of things, or if they were specifically in the contemplation of the parties as at the date of the contract. Subject to that test, there now seems no reason in principle why a creditor who suffers loss through depreciation in the value of the relevant currency between the due date of payment and the actual payment date should not be allowed to recover such loss in exchange where the foreseeability test is satisfied. Indeed, in the New Zealand case of *Isaac Naylor & Sons Ltd v New Zealand Co-operative Wool Marketing Association Ltd*,[181] where the money of account (sterling) fell in relation to the New Zealand dollar between the due date and the payment date, the Court of Appeal of New Zealand had no hesitation in upholding the decision of the trial judge to award the exchange loss as damages to the plaintiff. Similarly, the New Zealand High Court awarded damages for the late payment of a New Zealand dollar debt to a US resident. The recipient would obviously convert the New Zealand sum into US dollars on receipt, and the losses flowing from the depreciation of the New Zealand unit during the period of non-payment were thus "predictably incurred".[182]

The whole subject received attention from the Commercial Court in *Travelers Casualty & Surety Co of Canada v Sun Life Assurance Co of Canada (UK) Ltd*.[183] Sun Life suffered claims made by policyholders in the UK in connection with the sale of its investment products. It sought an indemnity from its insurers but they refused to pay immediately. The payments made by Sun Life to its policyholders were made in sterling, but the professional indemnity policy provided for payment in US dollars. Given that the insurers were found to have delayed reimbursement in breach of the policy, they were found liable to compensate Sun Life for the declining value of the US dollar during the period of non-payment. It was plainly foreseeable that, if Sun Life had to make the necessary sterling payments to its policyholders before the indemnity was provided, then an exchange rate exposure would be created. It is submitted that this decision is commercially sensible but it is not without difficulty in principle.[184]

---

[180] *President of India v Lips Maritime Corp (The Lips)* [1988] A.C. 395 HL.
[181] *Isaac Naylor & Sons Ltd v New Zealand Co-operative Wool Marketing Association Ltd* [1981] 1 NZLR 361. See C.E.F. Rickett, "Contract Damages for Exchange Losses—A New Zealand Development" [1982] L.M.C.L.Q. 566.
[182] *Volk v Hirstlens (NZ) Ltd* [1987] 1 NZLR 385.
[183] *Travelers Casualty & Surety Co of Canada v Sun Life Assurance Co of Canada (UK) Ltd* [2007] Lloyd's Rep. I.R. 619.
[184] In particular, a claim for non-payment under an insurance policy is a claim for *damages*, and it has long been held that one cannot claim damages for late payment of damages. It was for this reason that the claim for foreign exchange rate losses failed in the *The Lips* case; demurrage was paid late but, since demurrage is itself a form of liquidated damages, no additional claim could be made. On the

It hardly needs to be stated that an award can be made in several different currencies if required. In *International Minerals & Chemical Corp v Karl O Helm AG*,[185] the respondent was to pay 12,000,000 Belgian francs (BEF) for the purchase of a company. The assets were situated in the US and it was thus predictable that the seller would convert the proceeds into US dollars on receipt. When payment was not made in accordance with the terms of the contract, the seller was entitled to judgment for: (a) BEF 12,000,000 Belgian francs; and (b) a US dollar payment representing the declining US dollar countervalue of the consideration during the period of default. By the same token, a creditor who receives payment late should be entitled to recover damages for loss in the *internal* purchasing power of the relevant currency where this ought reasonably to have been foreseen by the debtor. Where, for example, the creditor is to be paid in the currency of his own country and inflation in that country is known to be running at a rate of 10% a month at the time of the contract, with little prospect of this being reduced, there seems no reason why the debtor who pays six months later should not be required to compensate the creditor for the diminution in the internal purchasing power of the currency during those six months.[186] In any event, the impact of inflation may to some extent be mitigated if the court assesses damages with reference to the date of the hearing, rather than the date of the breach.[187]

Finally, in a case in New South Wales, a receiver appointed under proceedings in the US sought to attach sums due from Citibank Ltd in Sydney to a bank established in Vanuatu. It was agreed that the funds would be paid into court (rather than direct to the Vanuatu bank) against the receiver providing the usual undertaking in damages. Subsequently, the bank asked the receiver to consent to conversion of these funds into euros, but he refused. The returns earned on the US dollar deposit were lower than those which would have been earned on a euro deposit. The court held that it was foreseeable that the bank would convert the currency since foreign exchange business was a source of profit for the bank. Applying the test in *Hadley*, the court ordered the receiver to meet the losses.[188]

---

whole subject, see Charles Proctor, "Changes in Monetary Values and the Assessment of Damages" in Djakhongir Saidov and Ralph Cunnington (eds), *Contract Damages—Domestic and International Perspectives* (Oxford: Hart Publishing, 2008).

[185] *International Minerals & Chemical Corp v Karl O Helm AG* [1986] 1 Lloyd's Rep. 81 QBD (Comm).

[186] This argument is not, however, entirely free from difficulty. For example, should the court be concerned with rates of inflation generally? In order to satisfy the rule in *Hadley*, it is perhaps more appropriate to consider the rate of inflation affecting the type of asset in which the seller—to the knowledge of the defaulting buyer—was likely to reinvest the proceeds.

[187] On the court's flexibility to set a flexible date of assessment to achieve justice between the parties, see *Johnson v Agnew* [1980] A.C. 367 HL; *The Golden Victory* [2007] 2 A.C. 353; *Ageas* [2014] Bus. L.R. 1338.

[188] *Evans & Associates v Citibank Ltd* [2007] NSWSC 1004.

4. The Applicable Law Under English Conflict of Laws Rules

It may be helpful to conclude with a brief summary of the English conflict of laws rules as to the law to be applied in determining each of the various issues raised.[189]

6–45

Issues assigned to the law applicable to the debt

It is for the applicable law to determine the money of account,[190] the interpretation of the contract as to the money of payment,[191] the extent to which a payment obligation has been duly performed,[192] the right to contractual interest,[193] the rate of exchange for converting the money of account into the money of payment,[194] and the revalorisation (or otherwise) of the debt.[195] Questions concerning the frustration of the contract, or other grounds for its discharge, are also a matter for the applicable law.[196]

6–46

Issues assigned to the *lex monetae*

The *lex monetae* determines the legal currency of a country,[197] the rate at which old currency is to be converted into new currency[198] and the requirements of legal tender.[199]

6–47

Issues assigned to the law of the place of payment

The law of the due place of payment may have an influence on issues as to the manner of payment,[200] including the money of payment where the parties' intention as to the money of payment is not apparent or the effectiveness of their choice is in question.[201]

6–48

---

[189] See generally *Dicey, Morris & Collins* (2012), Chs 32 and 33.
[190] Article 12(1)(a) of Rome I; *Bonython* [1951] A.C. 201 PC. This includes construction of a contract which prescribes an ambiguous currency of payment, e.g. dollars.
[191] See para.6–17 above.
[192] Rome I art.12(1)(b).
[193] *Miliangos v George Frank (Textiles) Ltd* [1977] Q.B. 489 QBD.
[194] *Dicey, Morris & Collins* (2012), para.37R–051.
[195] See cases cited at fn.31 above.
[196] See cases cited at fn.81 above.
[197] *Re Chesterman's Trusts* [1923] 2 Ch. 466 CA.
[198] Rome I art.12(1).
[199] *Re Chesterman's Trusts* at fn.187 above; *Pyrmont Ltd v Schott* [1939] A.C. 145 PC.
[200] Rome I art.12(2); *Mount Albert BC v Australasian Temperance & General Mutual Life Assurance Society Ltd* [1938] A.C. 224 PC.
[201] See para.6–20 above.

Issues assigned to the forum

6–49 The law of the State in which the action is tried is to be applied in deciding the currency in which a claim is to be made and judgment given[202]—these being matters of procedure so far as English law is concerned—and probably the rate at which interest is payable where this is not due under a contract.[203] The selected rate should normally reflect the cost of borrowing in the currency of the main award.[204]

---

[202] *Miliangos* [1976] A.C. 443 HL.
[203] This is the Law Commission's view (Law Commission, *Private Internation Law, Foreign Money Liabilities* (1981), Working Paper No.80, para.2.30); but, in *Helmsing Schiffahrts GmbH v Malta Drydocks Corp* [1977] 2 Lloyd's Rep. 444 QBD (Comm), Kerr J considered that the rate of interest, like the right to interest, was governed by the law applicable to the claim.
[204] *Les Laboratoires Servier v Apotex Inc* (2009) 32(3) I.P.D. 32023.

INDEX

All references are to paragraph number

Abstract payment obligations
  absence of consideration, 3–40—3–41—3–43
  autonomy principle, 3–40
  breach of underlying restriction in the contract, 3–49—3–50
  contract under seal, 3–40
  defences
    fraud of beneficiary, 3–44, 3–45
    illegality, 3–47
    innocent misrepresentation, 3–46
    nullity, 3–51
    set-off, 3–47
    unconscionability, 3–50
    wider range, acceptance of, 3–50—3–51
  demand guarantees, 3–41—3–43
  documentary credits, 3–40
  enforceable by custom, 3–40
  fraud of beneficiary
    allegations of fraud, 3–44, 3–45
    Australian experience, 3–45
    case law, 3–44
    documentary credit system, 3–44
    evidence, 3–44, 3–45
    guarantees, 3–45
    parties to proceedings, 3–45
    performance bonds, 3–45
    unproven fraud, 3–44
    withholding of payment, 3–44
  guarantees, 3–40
  irrevocable letters of credit, 3–40
  performance bonds, 3–41—3–43
  presumption of demand guarantee, 3–41—3–43
  written statement of breach, 3–41—3–43
Acceleration
  see also **Interest**; **Time stipulations**
  time stipulations, 4–02
Acceleration clauses
  automatic acceleration clauses, 3–59, 4–37
  choice of action, 3–59
  damages claims, 3–59
  deferred purchase agreements, 3–59
  enforcement, 3–59
  loan agreements, 3–59
  payment by instalments, 3–59

  reliance on, 3–59
  rule against penalties, 3–59
  specified default, 3–59
  time stipulations, 4–02
  unearned interest, 4–36
Acceleration of liability
  automatic acceleration, 4–36
  express contractual provisions, 3–59
  statutory acceleration, 4–36
Affirmation of contract
  cooperation not necessary, 3–20, 3–22
  employment contracts, 3–22
  legitimate interest, 3–21
Applicable law
  consumer contracts, 5–40
  contractual interest, 6–45
  English law, 6–44—6–48
  exchange rates, 6–45
  foreign money obligations, 6–45
Bank loans
  business efficacy, 4–21
  conflicting provisions, 4–21
  express terms, 4–21
  implied terms, 4–21
  repayable on demand, 4–21
  time of repayment, 4–21
Bank money
  relationship with physical money, 1–08
Bank notes and coins
  bank notes
    good title, 1–08
    negotiable instruments, 1–08
    payment, by, 1–08
    status, 1–02—1–05
    unconditional transfer, 1–08
  discharge of debt, 1–08
  status, 1–02—1–05, 1–08
  transfer, of, 2–23
Banking system
  see also **Non-cash transactions**
  cash transactions, 5–25
  commercial transactions, 5–25
  debtor/creditor relationship, 5–25
  non-cash transactions, 5–25

INDEX

number of transactions, 5–25
value of transactions, 5–25
Bitcoins
see also **Virtual currencies**
blockchain, 1–14
completion of payment, 5–74
Consumer Rights Act 2015, 5–75
creation of bitcoins, 1–14
digital content, 5–75
issues, 5–73
legal nature, 1–21, 1–22
medium of payment, as, 1–23, 5–73
miners, 5–74
money, as, 1–18—1–20
not e-money, 5–75
overview, 1–14
protection for users, 5–75
public key cryptography, 1–14
regulation, 1–21, 5–76
risks, 1–21, 5–75
taxation, 1–19
terrorist financing, 1–20
theft of bitcoins, 5–75
transfer of bitcoins, 1–14, 5–74
user protection, 5–75
value, 1–14
Blockchain
Bitcoin, 1–14
Bribery
anti-bribery legislation, 5–43
Cashless payments
changing landscape, 5–01—5–04
competition in the payments industry, 5–09
consumer protection, 5–10
financial crime, 5–11
innovation in payments industry, 5–09
legal implications, 5–01—5–04
national payments system, 5–14
non-bank payment systems, 5–03
stability of payment systems, 5–12
Cashless payments systems
see also **Virtual currencies**
domestic cheque clearance, 5–19
domestic transactions, 5–16
electronic funds transfers
  Bankers Automated Clearing Services (BACS), 5–21
  Clearing House Automated Payment System (CHAPS), 5–21, 5–22
  EURO1, 5–24
  Faster Payments, 5–21
  STEP1, 5–24
  STEP2, 5–24
  SWIFT, 5–23
  TARGET, 5–24
  TARGET2, 5–24
external transfers, 5–18

foreign currency transfers
  foreign money obligations, 5–23
  settlement process, 5–23
in-house transfers, 5–17
peer-to-peer payment systems, 1–13, 1–14, 5–62, 5–69
settlement mechanism, 5–15
Single European Payments Area (SEPA), 5–06, 5–20
structural issues, 5–15
Charterparties
see also **Frustration of contract**
anti-technicality clause, 4–01, 4–04, 4–31
anti-technicality notice, 4–03
cancellation, 4–03
damages, 4–04
freight rates, 4–01
frustration of contract, 6–25
hire rates, 4–01
notice requirements, 4–03, 4–04
payment delays, 4–01, 4–03
payment mechanisms, 4–01
relief from forfeiture, 4–04
termination, 4–03, 4–04
withdrawal of vessel, 4–01, 4–03, 4–04
Cheque payments
see also **Non-cash transactions**; **Payment under mistake**
agency principles
  actual authority, 5–29
  bank customer's death, 5–29
  breach of mandate, 5–29
  countermand, 5–29
  lack of authority, 5–29
  ostensible authority, 5–29
  revocation of authority, 5–29
cheque cards, 5–30
clearance of cheque, 5–28
contractual payment, 5–28
creditor's acceptance, 5–27, 5–28
date of tender, 5–28
equivalent to cash, 5–27
mistaken payment, 3–82
payment on presentation, 5–28
provisional payment, 5–28
Commodity theory of money
discarded, 1–07
nature of, 1–07
Conflict of laws
see **Applicable law**
Contactless payment
credit/debit cards, 5–33
Contract for services
payment, 4–23
Contractual claims

INDEX

see **International Monetary Fund Agreement;
Payment stipulation; Penalty clauses;
Unconscionable bargains**
  exchange contracts, 3–24
  vitiating factors, 3–23—3–25
Credit cards
  see also **Non-cash transactions**
  acceptance, of, 5–31
  conditional payment, 5–31
  contactless payments, 5–33
  customer's liability, 5–31
  legal implications, 5–31, 5–38
  payment obligation, 5–31
  time of payment, 5–31
  unconditional discharge, 5–31
Credit transfer
  nature of, 2–33
Cross-default clause
  default remedies, 3–64
  international financial agreements, 3–64
Debit cards
  see also **Non-cash transactions**
  acceptance of card, 5–32
  confirmation of payment, 5–32
  contactless payments, 5–33
  Electronic Funds Transfer at Point of Sale (EFTPOS), 5–32
Debit collection
  nature of, 2–34
Default interest
  additional default margin, 4–52
  Admiralty jurisdiction, 4–50, 4–59
  continuation after judgment, 4–52
  contractual provision, 4–51
  credit agreements, 4–51, 4–52
  damages, 4–53, 4–54, 4–56
  enhanced rate/increased risk, 4–51, 4–52
  entitlement, 4–50—4–57
  equitable jurisdiction, 4–50, 4–58
  international loan agreements, 4–51
  judicial discretion, 4–50
  liquidated damages clause, 4–51
  rule against penalties, 4–51
  statutory jurisdiction, 4–50, 4–60
  statutory provision, 4–57
  unfair contract terms, 4–52
Delay in payment
  breach of contract, 4–24
  conceptual difficulties, 4–24
  contract terms, 4–24
  conveyancing transactions, 4–24
  creditor's remedies, 4–24
  damages, 4–24
  implied terms, 4–24
  rescission ab initio, 4–24
Direct debit
  effect, 5–34
  insufficient funds, 5–34

  payment obligation, 5–34
Documentary credit
  as abstract payment undertaking, 3–40
Electronic funds transfers
  Bankers Automated Clearing Services (BACS), 5–21
  Clearing House Automated Payment System (CHAPS), 5–21, 5–22
  Clearing House Interbank Payments System (CHIPS), 5–23
  Electronic Funds Transfer at Point of Sale (EFTPOS), 5–32
  EURO1, 5–24
  Faster Payments, 5–21
  operation of system, 5–20
  STEP1, 5–24
  STEP2, 5–24
  TARGET, 5–24
  TARGET2, 5–24
  time limits for execution of payments, 5–20
Electronic money (e-money, digital cash)
  see also **Virtual currencies**
  definition, 1–11
  regulation, 5–09, 5–10, 5–71, 5–75
Eurocurrencies
  bank money, 1–10
  corresponding credit, 1–10
  "dual account" feature, 1–10
  meaning, 1–10
  means of payment, 1–10
Euros
  continuity of contracts, 3–10
  cross-border payments systems, 5–24
  exchange rate, 3–10
  leaving Eurozone, 3–10
  lex monetae, 3–09, 3–10
  nominalism, 3–09
  payment obligations, 3–09—3–10
  TARGET, 5–24
  TARGET2, 5–24
E-wallets
  non-bank payment systems, 5–69
Exchange
  not payment, 2–18
Exchange contracts
  contractual claims, 3–24
  exchange of currencies, 3–24
  meaning, 3–24
Expropriation of deposits
  see **International expropriation of deposits**
Floating charge
  crystallisation, 3–61, 3–74
Foreign currency claims/judgments
  breach date principle, 6–30, 6–31
  claims in sterling, 6–29, 6–30, 6–35
  company insolvency, 6–32
  date of payment, 6–31, 6–33, 6–41
  determination of appropriate currency, 6–34

INDEX

enforcement of judgment, 6–31
formulation of claim, 6–35
judgment in sterling, 6–30
Miliangos rule, 6–31—6–35, 6–41, 6–42
modern procedural rule, 6–31—6–33
old procedural rule, 6–30
payment, 6–31
restitution, 6–40
sterling conversion, 6–29, 6–30, 6–35
Foreign money obligations
  see also **Foreign currency claims/judgments**
  conflict of laws
    applicable law, 6–08, 6–45
    contractual interest, 6–45
    English law, 6–44
    exchange rates, 6–45
    lex fori, 6–48
    lex monetae, 6–46
    money of account, 6–45
    money of payment, 6–18, 6–45
    payment obligation, 6–07, 6–45
    place of payment, 6–48
    revalorisation of debt, 6–45
  contractual obligation, 6–01
  currency risk, 6–01
  damages awards, 6–01
  exchange losses
    breach of contract, 6–43
    contemplation of parties, 6–43
    damages claims, 6–43
    different currencies, awards in, 6–43
    foreseeability test, 6–43
    inflationary effects, 6–43
    internal purchasing power, 6–43
  exchange risks, 6–15
  floating exchange rates, 6–01
  foreign currency, 6–01
  foreign currency creditors, 6–01
  formulation of claim
    benefit of bargain, 6–35
    choice of currency, 6–35
    consequential loss, 6–35, 6–37
    debt/liquidated damages, 6–36
    delay in payment, 6–35
    duty to mitigate loss, 6–35
    loss in exchange, 6–35
    restitution, 6–40
    unliquidated damages (contract), 6–37, 6–38
    unliquidated damages (tort), 6–39
  frustration
    change in law, 6–25
    charterparties, 6–25
    effect of frustration, 6–28
    executive action, 6–25
    extinguishment of obligation, 6–22
    physical impossibility, 6–23
    place of payment, 6–25—6–27
    place of performance, 6–25, 6–26

    Ralli Bros Case, 6–25—6–27
    supervening illegality, 6–24—6–27
  internal purchasing power, 6–16
  money of account
    ambiguous provisions, 6–08
    applicable law, 6–08, 6–45
    construction of contract, 6–08
    contractual provision, 6–08
    currency of payment, 6–08
    exchange risks, 6–15
    intention of parties, 6–08
    internal purchasing power, 6–15
    nominalism principle, 6–09—6–14
    payment obligation, 6–02, 6–05, 6–06, 6–08—6–16
    relevant foreign currency, 6–36
    specified money of account, 6–08
  money of payment
    applicable law, 6–18
    currency of payment, 6–08
    English law, 6–19
    payment obligation, 6–02, 6–06, 6–17—6–19
  nominalism principle
    contractual safeguards, 6–11
    damages for delay, 6–14
    effect, 6–09
    express currency clauses, 6–11
    extreme loss of value, 6–13
    money of account, 6–09
    revalorisation of debt, 6–12, 6–13
    unit of account, 6–12
  payment obligation
    default on due date, 6–05, 6–14
    discharge on due date, 6–02
    exchange losses, 6–01, 6–06
    frustration, 6–04, 6–22—6–28
    money of account, 6–02, 6–05, 6–06, 6–08—6–16
    money of payment, 6–02, 6–06, 6–17—6–19
    place of payment, 6–03, 6–06, 6–20, 6–21
    place of settlement, 6–20
  place of payment
    case law, 6–21
    contractual terms, 6–21
    country of residence, 6–20
    identification, of, 6–20
    place of delivery, 6–21
  procedural issues, 6–06
  relevant foreign currency
    claimant's business location, 6–37
    contemplation of parties, 6–37, 6–38
    currency in which loss "felt", 6–37
    debt/liquidated damages, 6–36
    entry of judgment, 6–41
    formulation of claim, 6–35—6–37
    governing law, 6–34
    judicial consideration, 6–34
    money of account, 6–36

oil market trades, 6–38
payment, 6–42
restitution, 6–40
unliquidated damages (contract), 6–37
unliquidated damages (tort), 6–39

Forfeiture
relief against, 3–84

Fraud of beneficiary
allegations of fraud, 3–44, 3–45
Australian experience, 3–45
case law, 3–44
documentary credit system, 3–44
evidence, 3–44, 3–45
guarantees, 3–45
parties to proceedings, 3–45
performance bonds, 3–45
unproven fraud, 3–44
withholding of payment, 3–44

Frustration of contract
destruction of subject matter, 3–39
foreign money obligations
  change in law, 6–25
  charterparties, 6–25
  effect of frustration, 6–28
  executive action, 6–25
  extinguishment of obligation, 6–22
  physical impossibility, 6–23
  place of payment, 6–25—6–27
  place of performance, 6–25, 6–26
  Ralli Case, 6–25—6–27
  supervening illegality, 6–24—6–27
pure money obligations, 3–39
supervening illegality, 3–39

Funds transfers
see also **International funds transfers**
agency principles, 5–37
commercial/financial transactions, 5–35
countermands, 5–37
customer's credit balance, 5–36
duties relating to, 5–36
independent instruction, 5–35
legal nature, 5–36, 5–37
payment obligation, 5–36, 5–37
security/trust, creation of, 5–37
specific payment, 5–35
time of payment, 5–37

Gold clauses
bills of lading, 3–04, 3–05
case law, 3–04, 3–05
demonetisation of gold, 3–04
effect, 3–04
guarding against depreciation, 3–04, 3–05
Hague Rules, 3–04, 3–05
standard of value, 3–04
use, 3–04

Illegality
see also **Frustration of contract**
supervening, 6–24

Indexation
appropriate index, 3–06
indexation clauses, 3–06—3–08
inflation rate, 3–06
interest charges, 3–07—3–08
need for, 3–06
public policy, 3–06—3–08
retail/consumer price indices, 3–06
US experience, 3–07—3–08

In-house transfers
cheques, 5–59
credit transfers, 5–60
direct debits, 5–61
payment mechanism, 5–17
transfer activity, 5–58

Inter-bank transfers
see also **National payments system**

Interest
see also **Default interest; Judgment interest; Pre-default interest; Variable rate interest**
calculation of, 4–53
cessation of, 4–49
compound, 4–42
damages, as, 4–53—4–54
debtor's insolvency, 4–38
default interest, 4–38, 4–50—4–57
insolvency proceedings
  contractual interest, 4–62
  entitlement, 4–62
  extortionate credit bargains, 4–62
  post-insolvency interest, 4–62
  rate of interest, 4–62
interest clauses, 4–63
judgment interest, 4–38, 4–61
pre-default interest, 4–38, 4–40—4–49
right to interest
  creditor's entitlement, 4–37
  insolvency proceedings, 4–62
  sources, 4–39
  statutory, 4–60
simple, 4–42
variable rate interest, 4–43—4–48

International expropriation of deposits
see also **US Patriot Act**
anti-terrorist measures, 5–47
deposit obligation, 5–48, 5–49
force majeure, 5–48
foreign currency deposits, 5–48
governing law, 5–48
repayment obligation, 5–48, 5–49
September 11 attacks, 5–47
US Patriot Act, 5–47

International funds transfers
see also **Funds transfers**
blocking legislation, 5–44—5–46
clearing systems, 5–44
currency fluctuations, 5–44

INDEX

currency transactions, 5–44
differing time zones, 5–44
exchange controls, 5–4
governing law, 5–46
Iran hostage crisis, 5–45, 5–46
Libyan sanctions, 5–45, 5–46
payment
   instructions, 5–44
   place of payment, 5–46
   repayment obligation, 5–46
   time of payment, 5–44
Philippines deposits, 5–46
place of performance, 5–46
place of settlement, 5–46
International Monetary Fund Agreement
see also **Exchange contracts**
contravention, of, 3–24
exchange contracts, 3–24
exchange control regulations, 3–24
safeguarding currency resources, 3–24
Internet payments
see also **Non-cash transactions**
consumer protection, 5–10, 5–40
distance selling, 5–40
form of payment
   alternative payment methods, 5–38
   credit card details, 5–38
   security concerns, 5–38
on line shopping, 5–38
performance of contract
   applicable law, 5–39
   choice of law, 5–39, 5–40
   discharge of obligations, 5–39, 5–40
   governing law, 5–38—5–40
   Rome I, 5–39
   UK customer/foreign supplier, 5–38, 5–39
   unfair contract terms, 5–40
ISDA Master Agreement
flawed asset, 2–15
framework, 2–16
generally, 2–13
netting, 2–16
operation, 2–16
single agreement concept, 2–14
Judgment interest
see also **Interest**
arbitrations, 4–61
foreign currency, 4–61
judgment debt, 4–61
judgment for damages, 4–61
rate of interest, 4–61
Krugerrands
not money, 1–04
LIBOR
see **London inter-bank offered rate (LIBOR)**
Liquidated claims
see also **Contractual claims**
defences, 3–23—3–51

Liquidated damages
see also **Default interest; Penalty clauses**
breach of contract, 3–28—3–35
default interest, 4–51
express contractual provisions, 3–63
payment of specified sum, 3–29
payments on insolvency, 3–29
Loans
payment, 2–20
London inter-bank offered rate (LIBOR)
see also **Variable rate interest**
administration, 4–46—4–47
calculation of interest, 4–45—4–47, 4–63
fraudulent misrepresentation, 4–46—4–47
manipulation, 4–45
overview, 4–56, 4–57
reforms, 4–46—4–47
variable rate interest, 4–45
Money
see also **Money transfers; Non-cash transactions**
bank notes and coins, 1–02—1–05, 1–08
commodity theory, 1–07
concept, 1–02—1–03
creation of money
   bank deposits, 1–03
   promissory notes, 1–03
   state monopoly, 1–03, 1–04
currency, 1–02, 1–03, 1–05, 1–08
essential characteristics, 1–03
foreign currency obligations, 1–05
fungible nature, 1–05
institutional framework, 1–06
meaning of expression
   abstract concept, 1–03, 1–08
   economic context, 1–01
   financial obligations, 1–02, 1–05
   introduction, 1–01
   legal context, 1–03
   legal definition, 1–02, 1–03
   physical concept, 1–02
means of payment, 1–03, 1–08
medium of exchange, 1–05
monetary value, 1–05
name/unit of account, 1–04
non-cash transactions, 1–03
physical chattel, 1–03, 1–08
State Theory of Money, 1–03
Money laundering
banking practice
   audit trails, 5–41
   contractual obligations, 5–41, 5–42
   customer identification, 5–41
   reporting procedures, 5–41
   suspicious transactions, 5–41, 5–42
   training processes, 5–41
criminal offences, 5–41, 5–42
legislative provisions, 5–41, 5–42

INDEX

proceeds of crime, 5–41
Serious Organised Crime Agency, 5–42
virtual currencies, 5–41, 5–76
Money of account
    determining, 6–08
    nature, 6–02
Money of payment
    law determining, 6–18
    nature, 6–02
Money transfers
    see also **Interest**
    beneficial ownership, 2–23
    condition precedent, 2–23
    creditor's disposal, 2–23
    debtor's control, 2–23
    interest payable, 2–23
    legal title, 2–23
    money held on trust, 2–23
    payment of debt, 2–23
    specified payment date, 2–23
    unconditional payment, 2–23
National payments system
    automated clearing house, 5–14
    central bank involvement, 5–14
    clearing house, 5–14
    cross-border payments, 5–07, 5–24
    features of, 5–14
    inter-bank communications network, 5–14
    regulatory measures, 5–05—5–12
    self-regulation, move away from, 5–06
Netting
    close-out netting, 2–12
    ISDA Master Agreement, 2–16
    meaning, 2–12
    payment netting, 2–12
    settlement netting, 2–12
    types, 2–12
Nominalism principle
    application, 3–02, 6–10
    euro, 3–09
    foreign money obligations
        contractual safeguards, 6–11
        damages for delay, 6–14
        effect, 6–09
        exceptions, 6–10
        express currency clauses, 6–11
        extreme loss of value, 6–13
        money of account, 6–09
        revalorisation of debt, 6–12, 6–13
        unit of account, 6–12
    foreign proper law, 6–12
    inflation, effects of, 3–02
    intention of parties, 3–02
    lex monetae, 6–12
    meaning, 3–02
Non-bank payment services providers
    see also **Non-bank payment systems**
    bank providers, 5–62

banks, reliance on, 5–65
non-bank providers, 5–63
payment service providers
    completion of payment, 5–66
    non-bank providers, 5–65
    overview, 5–64—5–65
    regulation, 5–68
    user protection, 5–67
peer-to-peer systems
    completion of payment, 5–70
    overview, 5–69
    PayPal, 5–69, 5–70
    regulation, 5–72
    Treasury powers, 5–68
    user protection, 5–71
supervision, 5–72
technical service providers, 5–65
Non-bank payment systems
    see also **Non-bank payment services providers**
    completion of payment, 5–70
    electronic wallets, 5–69
    generally, 5–03
    growth, 5–62
    meaning, 5–62
    payment institutions, 5–65
    payment service providers
        completion of payment, 5–66
        non-bank providers, 5–65
        overview, 5–64—5–65
        regulation, 5–68
        user protection, 5–67
    peer-to-peer systems
        completion of payment, 5–70
        overview, 5–69
        PayPal, 5–69, 5–70
        regulation, 5–72
        Treasury powers, 5–68
        user protection, 5–71
    virtual currencies
        completion of payment, 5–74
        overview, 5–73
        regulation, 5–76
        Treasury powers, 5–72
        user protection, 5–75
Non-cash transactions
    see also **Cheque payments; Credit cards; Debit cards; Direct debit; Internet payments**
    cheque payments, 5–27—5–29
    contactless payments, 5–33
    credit cards, 5–31, 5–38
    debit cards, 5–32
    direct debit, 5–34
    fraud
        cardholder liability, 5–33
        cardholder negligence, 5–33
        "cloning" cards, 5–33

INDEX

EU Payment Services Directive, 5–33
  PIN numbers, 5–33
  theft of cards, 5–33
  unauthorised use, 5–33
manipulation, consequences of, 4–57, 4–59
payment through third parties
  agency principles, 5–26
  discharge of debt, 5–26
  legal effects, 5–26
standing orders
  effect, 5–34
  insufficient funds, 5–34
  payment obligation, 5–34

Non-payment
see **Remedies for non-payment**

Partial performance
bilateral contracts, 3–12
complete performance doctrine, 3–13—3–14
divisible contracts, 3–12
indivisible contracts, 3–12
pro-rata payment, 3–13
substantial performance doctrine, 3–15
voluntary acceptance, 3–16
waiver of right, 3–17

Payment
see also **Payment obligation**; **Payment stipulation**; **Payment under mistake**; **Place of payment**; **Pre-payment**; **Recovery of payment**; **Remedies for non-payment**; **Right to payment**; **Set-off**; **Tender**; **Time of payment**
blocking by legislation, 5–44—5–46
channels of payment
  clearing process, 2–34
  contractual channel, 2–34
  credit transfers, 2–34
  debit collections, 2–34
  direct transfers, 2–34
  inter-bank settlement, 2–34
  non-cash mechanisms, 2–34
  payment mechanism, 2–34
concept of payment
  conditional payment, 2–01, 5–55
  discharge of money obligation, 2–01, 2–23
  dispatch of funds, 2–01
  distinguished from commitment to pay, 2–22, 5–54
  gift, 2–01, 2–23
  legal sense, 2–01
  loan of money, 2–01, 2–23
  offset of items on running account, 2–03
  payment by cheque, 2–01
  purchase of claim, 2–19
  set-off, 2–04—2–11
  transfer of money, 2–01
  transfer reserving an interest, 2–23
  transfer to creditor's account, 2–02
contract for services, 4–23
contractual relationship, 2–05, 2–08
delay in payment
  breach of contract, 4–24
  conceptual difficulties, 4–24
  contract terms, 4–24
  conveyancing transactions, 4–24
  creditor's remedies, 4–24
  damages, 4–24
  implied terms, 4–24
  rescission ab initio, 4–24
distinctions
  advance against projected transfer of funds, 2–21
  commitment to pay, 2–22
  exchange, 2–18
  loans, 2–20
  purchase of claim, 2–19
  tender, 2–17
fact of payment
  cheque payments, 2–35
  credit transfers, 2–35
  currency conversions, 2–35
  interest calculations, 2–35
  money directly tendered, 2–35
  payment instruction, 2–35
  time of payment, 2–35
loans, 2–20
must be earned, 3–11
reform, 4–57, 4–60
set-off, 2–04—2–11
tender/acceptance of goods, 2–05, 2–17
third party payment
  accepted tender, 2–29
  actual authority, 2–29
  mistake, 2–29
  officious payment, 2–29
  ostensible authority, 2–29
transfers
  reserving interest to debtor/debtor's agent, 2–23
  third party, 2–04
  when complete, 2–35
virtual currencies, 1–23

Payment obligation
see also **Funds transfers**; **Right to payment**
abstract obligations, 2–45
bilateral obligations, 2–46
classification, 2–36
consideration, supported by, 2–45
direct debit, 5–34
existing and contingent obligations
  amount provable, 2–38
  contractual set-off, 2–41
  guarantees, 2–37
  legal assignability, 2–38
  nature, of, 2–37
  set-off in bankruptcy, 2–40

INDEX

foreign money obligations
    default on due date, 6–05, 6–14
    discharge on due date, 6–02
    exchange losses, 6–01, 6–06
    frustration, 6–04, 6–22—6–28
    money of account, 6–02, 6–05, 6–06, 6–08—6–16
funds transfers, 5–36, 5–37
legal problems, 3–01
liquidated/unliquidated obligations
    liquidated claims, 2–42
    plea of tender, 2–42
    unliquidated claims, 2–42
    unliquidated damages, 2–42
method of payment, 2–32
money of payment, 6–02, 6–06, 6–17—6–19
payment due, 2–31
place of payment, 2–32, 6–03, 6–06, 6–20, 6–21
place of settlement, 6–20
primary and secondary obligations, 2–44
principal and accessory obligations, 2–44
standing orders, 5–34
unilateral obligations, 2–46
Payment stipulation
see also **Penalty clauses; Unconscionable bargains**
    efficacy, 3–26
    illegality under foreign law, 3–27
    penalty clauses, 3–28—3–35
    unconscionable bargains, 3–36
    unenforceability, 3–26—3–38
Payment under mistake
    cheque payments, 3–82
    forged transfer requests, 3–82
    mistake of fact, 3–82
    mistake of law, 3–82
    mistaken double payment, 3–82
    peer-to-peer payment systems, 5–71
    proprietary claims, 3–82
    recovery of payment, 3–82
    unjust enrichment, 3–82
PayPal
    non-bank payment systems, 5–69
Peer-to-peer payment systems
    cashless payments systems, 1–13, 1–14, 5–62, 5–69
    non-bank payment systems, 5–62, 5–69
    payment under mistake, 5–71
    Paypal, 5–69
    user protection, 5–71
Penalty clauses
    breach of contract, 3–28—3–35
    case law, 3–28—3–35
    challenge in consumer contracts, 3–35
    default interest clauses, 3–30
    genuine pre-estimate of loss, abolition of test, 3–28—3–31
    imposed in terrorem, 3–28

loss of bargain, 3–28—3–35
loss of profit, 3–28—3–35
non-application to contractual rights, 3–32—3–33
non-repudiatory breach, 3–28—3–35
payment of specified sum, 3–29
payment on insolvency, 3–29
repudiatory breach, 3–28—3–35
third party breach, 3–29
whether all out of proportion, 3–31
Performance
    against debtor's wishes, 3–19—3–22
    debtor's obstruction of, 3–18
    entire contracts, 3–13
    partial, 3–12, 3–16
    payment must be earned by, 3–11
    substantial, 3–15
    waiver of, 3–17
Place of payment
    applicable law, 6–18
    general rule, 2–32, 6–20
    relevance of, 2–32, 5–46, 6–03, 6–07, 6–20, 6–24—6–26
    supervening illegality, 6–24
Pre-default interest
see also **Interest**
    accrual of interest, 4–41
    cessation of interest, 4–49
    contractual provision, 4–40
    simple/compound interest, 4–42
    statutory entitlement, 4–40
    variable rate interest, 4–43—4–48
Pre-payment
    accelerate payment, 4–17, 4–18
    contract silent, as to, 4–18
    contractual restriction, on, 4–19
    debtor's election, 4–17
    mortgage redemption, 4–18
    statutory pre-payment, 4–20
    termination fee, 4–17
    voluntary pre-payment, 4–17
Proceeds of crime
    money laundering, 5–41
Public key cryptography
    Bitcoin, 1–14
Recovery of payment
see **Payment under mistake**
    economic duress, 3–83
    failure of consideration, 3–81
    grounds of repayment, 3–79
    irrecoverable payments, 3–79
    payment on condition subsequent, 3–80
    payment under mistake, 3–82
    relief against forfeiture, 3–84
Regulation of payment services
    Deposit Guarantee Schemes Directive, 5–10
    Electronic Commerce Directive, 5–09
    Fifth Anti-Money Laundering Directive, 5–41

INDEX

Financial Collateral Arrangements Directive, 5–12
Financial Conduct Authority, 4–43—4–45, 5–06
Fourth Anti-Money Laundering Directive, 5–11, 5–41, 5–47
General Data Protection Regulation, 5–10
Payment Account Directive, 5–06
Payment Services Directive, 5–06
Payment Systems Regulator
  cheque payment systems, 5–19
  role, 5–06, 5–30
Payments Council, 5–19, 5–30
Second Electronic Money Directive, 5–10
Second Payment Services Directive, 5–06, 5–08, 5–09, 5–20
Settlement Finality Directive, 5–12
Single European Payments Area (SEPA), 5–06, 5–20
Sixth Anti-Money Laundering Directive, 5–41
strong customer authentication, 5–10

Remedies for non-payment
see also **Acceleration clauses; Time of the essence**
creditor's remedies, 3–52
crystallisation of floating charge, 3–61, 3–74
damages, 4–34
default remedies
  damages resulting from termination, 3–76
  damages without termination, 3–72
  defaulting debtor, against, 3–69
  enforcement of security, 3–73
  interest on overdue payments, 3–71
  repudiatory breach, 3–75, 3–76, 4–35
  termination of agreement, 3–75
  withholding of performance, 3–70
express contractual provisions
  acceleration of liability, 3–59
  consolidation of liabilities, 3–65, 3–66
  cross-default clause, 3–64
  enforcement of security, 3–60
  enforcement under separate agreement, 3–64
  flawed asset provisions, 3–56
  indemnity against costs, 3–68
  interest on overdue payments, 3–58
  liquidated damages, 3–63
  material adverse change clause, 3–64
  remedies on default, 3–53
  termination/repossession, 3–62
  withholding of performance, 3–54—3–57
material breach, 4–34
repudiatory breach, 4–35
right of repurchase, 3–67
right of termination, 4–34
Sale of Goods Act, 3–78
secured creditors, 4–34
set-off, 3–66, 3–77

Repudiatory breach
circumstances, 4–39

penalty clauses, 3–28—3–35
remedies for non-payment, 3–75, 3–76, 4–35
time of the essence, 4–31, 4–33

Rescission
duress, 4–24
improper inducement, 4–24
misrepresentation, 4–24
undue influence, 4–24

Restitution
see also **Foreign money obligations**
foreign money obligations, 6–40

Retention of title
passing of property, 4–22
time stipulations, 4–22

Right to payment
see **Nominalism principle**
complete performance doctrine
  effect, 3–13
  entire contracts, 3–13
entitlement
  conditions of payment, 3–11
  conditions precedent, 3–11
  contractual commitments, 3–11
  contractual duties, 3–11
  creditor's rights, 3–11
  division of performance, 3–11
  partial performance, 3–11
  payment in advance, 3–11
  payment to be earned, 3–11
  sale of goods, 3–11
  stage payments, 3–11, 3–13
obstruction of performance, 3–18
partial performance
  bilateral contracts, 3–12
  complete performance doctrine, 3–13
  divisible contracts, 3–12
  indivisible contracts, 3–12
  pro-rata payment, 3–13
  substantial performance doctrine, 3–15
  voluntary acceptance, 3–16
  waiver of right, 3–17
performance against debtor's wishes, 3–19—3–22
revalorisation devices
  gold clauses, 3–04, 3–05
  indexation, 3–06—3–08
  introduction, 3–03
substantial performance doctrine, 3–15

Sale of goods
see also **Time of the essence**
delivery, 3–11, 4–22
passing of property, 3–11, 4–22
payment, 3–11, 4–22
payment on day certain, 4–22
price, 4–22
time of the essence, 4–26

Set-off
analogous rights, 2–09

INDEX

claims/cross claims, 2–04, 3–48, 3–77
contractual set-off, 2–04, 2–41
deemed payment, 2–10
discharge of debt, 2–04
documentary credits, 3–48
guarantees, 3–48
guarantors, 3–48
independent set-off, 2–05, 2–06
insolvency set-off, 2–04, 2–40, 3–71
meaning, 2–04
need to assert, 2–04
right to set-off, 2–04, 3–48
time of set-off, 2–11
transaction set-off, 2–05, 2–07
Single European Payments Area (SEPA)
cross-border payments, 5–06
Standing orders
effect, 5–34
insufficient funds, 5–34
payment obligation, 5–34
Tender
acceptance
conditional acceptance, 2–25
conformity with contract, 2–17
mere receipt, 2–25
non-acceptance, 2–17
receipt by creditor's agent, 1–21—1–23
simultaneous payment/acceptance, 2–25
third party, 2–29
legal effects, 2–17
passing of property, 2–17
payment
actual authority, 2–29
duty to pay, 2–29
ostensible authority, 2–29
receipt by creditor's agent
authorised receipt, 2–28
unauthorised receipt, 2–27
right to return, 2–17
sale of goods, 2–17
sale of property, 2–17
Termination of contract
see also **Time of the essence**
delay in payment
breach of contract, 4–24
conceptual difficulties, 4–24
contract terms, 4–24
conveyancing transactions, 4–24
creditor's remedies, 4–24
damages, 4–24
implied terms, 4–24
rescission ab initio, 4–24
Time of payment
see also **Time of the essence**
acceptance/receipt of funds
breach of contract, 5–55
commitment/transfer distinguished, 5–54
condition subsequent, 5–55

conditional transfer, 5–55
crediting process, 5–53
effective lender, 5–53
negligence, 5–55
transfer of funds, 5–53—5–55
unconditional transfer, 5–55
breach of condition, 4–40
debtor/creditor relations, 5–50
in-house transfers
cheques, 5–59
credit transfers, 5–60
direct debits, 5–61
transfer activity, 5–58
innominate terms, 4–41
inter-bank arrangements
actual authority, 5–51
agency principles, 5–51
authorisation, 5–51, 5–52
effective payment, 5–52
ostensible authority, 5–51
payment subject to condition, 5–52
ratification, 5–51
receipt of payment, 5–51
third parties, 5–51
unconditional payment, 5–52
voluntary payments, 5–51
mere instructions to transfer, 5–57
payment of debt, 5–56
stipulations as to time, 4–02—4–16
Time of the essence
commercial contracts, 4–27
common law position, 4–26
condition of contract, 4–26
construction of contract, 4–36
equitable rules, 4–26
exercise of options, 4–30
express stipulation, 4–28
intention of parties, 4–26
nature of contract, 4–29
presumption against, 4–27
provision/requirement
case law, 4–31
conveyancing cases, 4–31
improper conduct, 4–31
post-default, 4–31
prior to default, 4–31
reasonable notice, 4–31
repudiation, 4–31, 4–33
sale/purchase of shares, 4–31
two stage process, 4–31
relief against forfeiture, 4–26
sale of goods, 4–26
significance, 4–25
stipulated performance, 4–26
waiver, 4–32
Time stipulations
see also **Charterparties**; **Pre-payment**
delays in payment, 4–01

[301]

INDEX

effect, 4–01
express stipulations
  acceleration clauses, 4–02
  charterparties, 4–03, 4–04
  corresponding date rule, 4–06
  "day", meaning of, 4–07
  "from" time stated, 4–09
  loan agreements, 4–02
  midnight deadline ("witching hour"), 4–03
  "month", meaning of, 4–08
  "not later than...days" before stated date, 4–10
  "on demand", 4–11
  "on or about" given date, 4–12
  payment due on non-business day, 4–05
  "punctual"/"punctually", 4–13
  "till", 4–16
  "until", 4–16
  "within a reasonable time", 4–15
  "within...days after" stated date, 4–14
implied terms
  bank loans, 4–21
  sale of goods, 4–22
  supply of services, 4–23
interpretation, 4–01
lawful termination, 4–01
litigation, 4–01
retention of title clauses, 4–22

Unconscionable bargains
cost of transaction, 3–38
credit agreements, 3–36
equitable jurisdiction, 3–36
extortionate credit bargains, 3–38
oppressive terms, 3–36
unfair terms, 3–36, 3–38

Unfair credit relationships
payment stipulation unenforceable as such, 3–37

Unit of account
see **Money**

Unjust enrichment
see **Payment under mistake**
mistaken payment, 3–82

US Patriot Act
see also **International expropriation of deposits**
arrest warrants, 5–47
extra-territorial jurisdiction, 5–47
forfeiture of funds, 5–47
inter-bank accounts, 5–47
restraining orders, 5–47
seizure warrants, 5–47, 5–48

Variable rate interest
certificates of deposit, 4–48—4–49
consumer contracts, 4–43—4–44
discretion, as to, 4–43
floating rate interest charges, 4–48
floating rate notes, 4–48
index clauses, 4–46
LIBOR rates, 4–45
loan agreements, 4–45
market conditions, 4–46
meaning, 4–43
"screen" rates, 4–46—4–47
unfair credit relationships, 4–43

Virtual currencies
Bitcoin, 1–13, 1–14
centralised currencies, 1–13
completion of payment, 5–74
convertible currency, 1–13
creation, 1–14
definition, 1–12
designation as monetary unit, 1–13
determination of value, 1–14
digital content, 5–75
examples, 1–13
financial stability, 5–75
increased use, 1–13
intermediaries, 1–14
issue, 1–14
medium of payment, 1–23, 5–73
miners, 5–74
money, as, 1–16—1–22, 5–73
money laundering, 5–41, 5–76
non-bank payment systems, 5–73—5–76
non-centralised currencies, 1–13, 1–14
non-convertible currency, 1–13
not e-money, 5–75
overview, 5–73
payment, 1–23
protection for users, 5–75
public key cryptography, 1–14
Q Coins, 1–13
regulation, 1–13, 5–75, 5–76
renunciation, 4–42
terrorist financing, 5–76
theft, 5–75
transfer, 5–74
use, 5–73
user protection, 5–75
valuation, 1–14
World of Warcraft Gold, 1–13

Also available:

1 The Modern Contract of Guarantee 4th Edition

Authors: Professor John Phillips, Professor James O'Donovan and Professor Wayne Courtney

ISBN: 9780414067479

Publication date: November 2020

Formats: Hardback/ ProView eBook

The Modern Contract of Guarantee provides readers with a detailed reference work on the law of guarantees. It provides practical insights into areas such as the validity and construction of guarantees, how to avoid a guarantee being discharged and common difficulties with enforcement. It also contains drafting guidance and a useful comparative discussion of developments in England and Commonwealth countries.

2 Salinger on Factoring 6th edition

Authors: Simon Mills and Noel Ruddy

ISBN: 9780414067592

Publication date: February 2020

Formats: Hardback/ProView eBook/Westlaw UK

Salinger on Factoring is renowned for its highly practical approach to the law and practice relating to factoring and invoice finance. It combines a clear understanding of the law with clear and concise guidance on its implementation. This title has been the trusted guide to this complex area of law for nearly 30 years providing a detailed examination of, and guide to, the legal issues that arise from domestic and international factoring.

Also available as a Standing order

Contact us on: Tel: +44 (0)345 600 9355

Order online: sweetandmaxwell.co.uk